Lionel Corley.
Sheepscombe
10. IV. 2001

256
260
263
267
268
391
→ 424

THE BRITISH UNION CATALOGUE OF MUSIC PERIODICALS

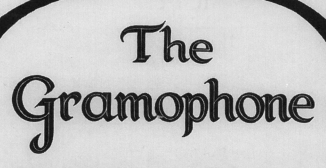

The Gramophone

Edited by COMPTON MACKENZIE

Contents

Vol. I. No. 1   APRIL (for May) 1923   Monthly 6d.

Cover page of the first issue of *The Gramophone*, Britain's
longest-lived magazine covering records and recording.

Reproduced by kind permission of the British Library

The British Union Catalogue of Music Periodicals

Second Edition
Including the Holdings of Six Libraries from the
Republic of Ireland

Edited by John Wagstaff

Compiled by the Editor and by Members of the
Documentation Committee of the
International Association of Music Libraries,
Archives and Documentation Centres (UK Branch)

I
A
M
L(UK)

Ashgate

Aldershot • Brookfield USA • Singapore • Sydney

Published by
Ashgate Publishing Limited
Gower House
Croft Road
Aldershot
Hants GU11 3HR
England

Ashgate Publishing Company
Old Post Road
Brookfield
Vermont 05036–9704
USA

British Library Cataloguing-in-Publication data

The British Union catalogue of music periodicals. – 2nd ed.
   1.Music – Periodicals – Bibliography
   I. Wagstaff, John
   016.7'85

Library of Congress Cataloging-in-Publication data

Wagstaff, John.
   The British Union catalogue of music periodicals. – 2nd ed., including the holdings of six libraries from the Republic of Ireland/edited by John Wagstaff; compiled by the editor and members of the Documentation Committee of the International Association of Music Libraries, Archives and Documentation Centres (UK Branch)

   1. Music – History and criticism – Periodicals – Bibliography – Union Lists. 2. Music – Serials–Lists. I. Wagstaff, John. British union catalogue of music periodicals. II. International Association of Music Libraries, Archives, and Documentation Centres. United Kingdom Branch. Documentation Committee. III. Title.

ML128.P24H6 1988
016.78'05–dc21   97–32581
             CIP
             MN

ISBN 1 85928 133 8

Printed on acid-free paper

Typeset in Times by Pat FitzGerald

Printed and bound in Great Britain by
MPG Books Ltd, Bodmin, Cornwall

Contents

Preface

The publication in 1985 of the first edition of the *British Union Catalogue of Music Periodicals* was a landmark of musico-bibliographic literature. It had been eagerly awaited and immediately became a standard reference tool for music libraries in the United Kingdom and worldwide. The music library profession, and indeed all concerned for the effective identification and location of music periodical literature, will greet publication of this much expanded and thoroughly revised second edition – BUCOMP2 – with renewed acclamation.

IAML(UK) has been privileged to offer support for BUCOMP2. Its editor, John Wagstaff, is characteristically generous in his acknowledgements, yet all concerned would in turn readily acknowledge that the greatest burden of work has undoubtedly been borne by the editor himself. To his perseverance, meticulousness and dedication, exercised with customary patience, courtesy and good humour, we are all vastly indebted. John Wagstaff can be assured that a generation of music librarians and users of music periodical literature will have good cause to acclaim his major achievement.

Roger Taylor
President, IAML(UK)

Acknowledgments

This project could not have been completed without the aid and support of a large number of people. First among these must be those library staff who took such pains to supply accurate and comprehensive information on their periodical holdings. Several contributions indicated many hours of work by respondents, and the Project Committee is grateful to everyone who contributed. In cases where respondents gave their names, these are noted alongside the address of their library in the alphabetical listings below.

Second, considerable support has been given to the project both by IAML(UK) and by our publisher, Ashgate Publishing. Sue MacNaughton and, more recently, Rachel Lynch of Ashgate have shown remarkable patience in awaiting the results of this large and unwieldy project. Their vision, and that of two Presidents of IAML(UK), Malcolm Lewis and Roger Taylor, has been invaluable.

Lucinda Field spent many hours inputting material to the database of what has, inevitably, come to be known as 'BUCOMP2'. Hers was a hugely useful contribution, without which the project would have foundered at a very early stage. John Webb, formerly of the Royal Academy of Music, went far beyond the reasonable call of duty in interpreting some of the more obscure written replies to our questionnaires received from libraries, and in bringing them to a stage where editing, and entry of information onto the database, became possible. Debra Godrich, formerly of the BBC Music Library in London, painstakingly provided data on the holdings of the English Folk Dance and Song Society's Library; and Christina Bashford provided thoughtful advice and practical support at every stage.

History of the Project

The first edition of the *British Union Catalogue of Music Periodicals* (henceforth *BUCOMP1*) was compiled by Anthony Hodges, edited by Raymond McGill, and published by IAML(UK) and the United Kingdom Library Association in 1985. It was the first really comprehensive listing, with locations, of music periodicals held in libraries in the United Kingdom, and was rendered more useful by the fact that it also included details of the holdings of various libraries in the Republic of Ireland, a principle which has been carried over into this new edition. Before *BUCOMP1*, librarians and researchers in the United Kingdom had been obliged to rely on (a) the *British Union Catalogue of Periodicals* (London: British Museum, 1955-62), which of necessity could not be as comprehensive as required; (b) locally-produced efforts by particular libraries or by a group of libraries, of which the longest survivor has been Anthea Baird's *Union List of Periodicals in Music in the Libraries of the University of London and Some Other London Libraries* (London, 1969); and (c) Imogen Fellinger's *Verzeichnis der Musikzeitschriften des 19. Jahrhunderts* (Regensburg: Gustav Bosse, 1968), which Dr Fellinger supplemented by data published between 1970 and 1976 in *Fontes artis musicae*, the journal of the International Association of Music Libraries, Archives and Documentation Centres. Much information on the bibliographic and publication histories of titles that appeared in *BUCOMP1* was drawn directly from Fellinger's catalogue. The 1968 *Verzeichnis* had, however, at least one drawback, which was its being confined to the period from 1798 (year of the foundation of the *Allgemeine musikalische Zeitung* in Leipzig) to 1918. Fortunately for the compilers of both editions of *BUCOMP*, Dr Fellinger developed her path-breaking work in two subsequent publications: first, her article 'Periodicals' in *The New Grove Dictionary of Music and Musicians* (London: Macmillan, 1980), which amended and supplemented the data in the 1968 *Verzeichnis*, and added details of items published since the end of World War I; and second, her *Periodica Musicalia (1789–1830)* (Regensburg: Gustav Bosse, 1986), which was an inventory of musical scores published in periodical form. Although both editions of *BUCOMP* are primarily concerned with periodicals composed of prose text, the 1986 catalogue has nonetheless been very useful in supplying data on a number of titles for this new edition of *BUCOMP*. Data from the 1968 *Verzeichnis* is given in *BUCOMP2* as a date followed by an entry number (for example, Fellinger 1968/220), while information from the 1986 catalogue is given with page numbers (Fellinger 1986, pp. 156–58). Additional bibliographic information has been gleaned from, or checked in, the following sources:

Deutsches Bibliotheksinstitut, *Staatsbibliothek zu Berlin, Preussischer Kulturbesitz: Zeitschriften Datenbank (ZDB): Teilausgabe Musik/Theater* (Berlin: Deutsches Bibliotheksinstitut, 1995) [Microfiche index, with notes]

Eva-Brit Fanger, *Katalog over Musiktidsskrifter i Danske Forskningsbiblioteker* (Copenhagen: Det Kongelige Bibliotek, 1997)

Wilhelm Freystätter, *Die musikalischen Zeitschriften seit ihrer Entstehung bis zur Gegenwart: chronologisches Verzeichniss der periodischen Schriften über Musik*. Reprint ed. (Amsterdam: Frits Knuf, 1971)

Leanne Langley, *The English Musical Journal in the Early Nineteenth Century* (Thesis (PhD) – University of North Carolina at Chapel Hill, 1983). Langley covers several later titles in her article "Music" in J. Don Vann and Rosemary T. Van Arsdel, eds, *Victorian Periodicals and Victorian Society* (Aldershot: Scolar Press, 1994) pp. 99–126. This is referred to in the catalogue as Langley 1994.

Larry C. Lewis, ed., *Union List of Periodicals in Canadian Libraries*. 2nd ed. (Ottawa: Canadian Association of Music Libraries, 1981)

Mary O'Mara, ed., *Union Catalogue of Music Serials in Australian Libraries* (Brisbane: International Association of Music Libraries, Archives and Documentation Centres (Australian Branch), 1992)

[Music Library Association of Japan], *Union List of Periodicals in Music*. Revised and enlarged edition (Tokyo: Music Library Association of Japan, 1993)

[Société Suisse des Auteurs et Editeurs], *Schweizer Musik-Handbuch = Guide musicale suisse = Guida musicale svizzera 1995/96* (Zurich: Atlantis, 1995). A list of 'Periodische Schriften' appears on p. 270–82 of this publication.

Jean-Adrien Thoumin, *Bibliographie rétrospective des périodiques français de littérature musicale, 1870–1954* (Paris: Editions Documentaires Industrielles et Techniques, 1957)

William J. Weichlein, *A Checklist of American Music Periodicals, 1850–1900* (Detroit: Information Coordinators, 1970)

Data from the above sources has been supplemented by material from online catalogues in Australia, Finland, France, Norway, Sweden, Switzerland, the United Kingdom and the United States; by the electronic bibliographic databases offered by OCLC and RLIN; and by other standard reference sources such as the serials directories produced by Ulrich.

Methodology

Although data for both the first and second editions of *BUCOMP* was gathered by questionnaire, the methodologies used were different. The compilers of the first edition drew up a list of several hundred music periodical titles which was then circulated to those libraries that they wished to include in their survey. Libraries willing to add further titles to the original list were invited to do so. In the case of *BUCOMP2* no such list was circulated, and libraries surveyed were asked simply to provide details of all their periodical holdings, on pre-printed forms. This method, which had the advantage of eliciting information on a much larger number of periodical titles, turned out also to have a number of disadvantages, not least of which was that a considerable amount of extra checking of bibliographic detail was required. Furthermore, some libraries supplied data on titles which were not, strictly, musical – journals on dance, theatre, and folk life and customs being the principal categories – while others confined themselves more closely to musical titles. Choosing whether to omit or include certain titles in *BUCOMP2* was difficult, and in the end it was necessary to be pragmatic, as the compilers of *BUCOMP1* seem likewise to have been, and to assume that, in the majority of cases, libraries supplied details of particular titles because they themselves regarded them as suitable candidates for *BUCOMP2*. This pragmatic approach has resulted in the inclusion of many titles which may be regarded as ephemeral or of dubious relevance to a catalogue like this, such as fanzines, material produced for local consumption by concert societies, and titles covering radio, electronics, and broadcasting: but we did not regard it as our prerogative to take decisions on behalf of the UK and Irish music library communities concerning what to leave out, and what to include. It should be borne in mind, however, that information on titles which are concerned more with theatre, dance, folk life and customs, and so on, is, in effect, a 'value added' extra which probably reflects a trend, in public libraries at least, to place all performing arts resources under one roof; in other libraries that maintain a distinction between locations of stock solely concerned with music, and material covering other performing arts, one would not expect a returned questionnaire to cover anything more than the specifically musical material in those libraries. Therefore it should not be assumed that, in the case of general performing arts titles, they are not also held by other libraries: it simply means that such libraries did not consider it within the brief they were given to return information on them. The same principle may be applied to titles which have begun to be published only recently, such as Cambridge University Press's *Organised Sound*: some libraries were very diligent in keeping us up-to-date with new holdings, while others did not have the same opportunities to do so. Where possible, however, details of new titles appearing since the issue of the original *BUCOMP2* questionnaires in 1994 have been added to the catalogue: and, in fact, our publisher has been very accommodating in allowing additions, deletions and corrections to be added at a late stage, towards the end of 1998.

In attempting to cope with these and other issues we were helped enormously by the expansion in electronic communications which has come about since the publication of *BUCOMP1*. The ability to access the catalogues of academic libraries through services provided by the UK's Joint Academic Network [JANET] made the resolution of many small queries much easier, with electronic mail being used to contact librarians themselves when catalogue details were too vague or ambiguous to permit resolution by other means. On a more mundane level, the availability of word-processing software to shape the catalogue into an acceptable form for publication has been indispensable.

Presentation of Information

Information for each title is presented in a standard format, as follows:

i   Filing title and subtitle(s), in **bold** type. This is usually the earliest title borne by a periodical, which explains, for example, why the title *Journal of Renaissance and Baroque Music* is used in preference to the perhaps better-known *Musica Disciplina*; and why *Proceedings of the Musical Association* is used in place of the item's current title of *Journal of the Royal Musical Association*. Changes of title are noted where known, and cross-referenced. The presence of a subtitle in an entry does not necessarily mean that the periodical carried that subtitle throughout its existence.

     Titles are filed using the 'word by word', rather than 'letter by letter' system. Thus titles beginning with 'Music' appear before those beginning 'Musica', which in turn precede titles beginning 'Musical', 'Musicalia', 'Musicology', and so on. Where more than one periodical bears exactly the same title as another, entries are numbered and filed according to the start date of publication, with the oldest first. Where main titles are identical, but with some also bearing subtitles, those without subtitles will appear first, with subtitled items following, as for example:

> Musica [1]
> Musica [2]
> Musica [3]
> Musica: Boletin
> Musica: Rassegna della Vita Musicale Italiana
> Musica: Revista Trimestral
> Musica Antiqua
> Musica Antiqua: Actuele Informatie over Oude Muziek
> Musica Asiatica

     Note also that title and subtitle are always separated by a colon, irrespective or whether or not this is a faithful reproduction of the actual title page of an item. Similarly, the character '&', which occasionally appears in titles, has been spelled out in all cases (and, et, und, och) to help the user locate a title in the correct place in the sequence.

ii   International Standard Serial Number (ISSN) or other identifier. Where ISSNs are known to exist, they have been used, and are presented in the standard form of two sets of four digits separated by a dash, e.g. 0007–0173. In the case of older titles, which do not bear ISSNs, other identifying data has been used where available. In particular, the running numbers given to periodicals in Fellinger's 1968 and 1986 catalogues, and in her 'Periodicals' article in *The New Grove*, have been cited where possible, not only because they help to identify a title unambiguously, but also because Fellinger's lists provide more data than *BUCOMP2* could ever hope to do concerning frequency of publication, editors, variants in subtitles, and so on. The lists are cited as 'Fellinger 1968', 'Fellinger 1986' and 'TNG' (for *The New Grove*) as required. Finally, in the case of 19th-century British titles, data from Leanne Langley's doctoral thesis on *The English Musical Journal in the Early Nineteenth Century* (University of North Carolina at Chapel Hill, 1983), an indispensable source for any researcher in this field, is cited where appropriate. Such entries are designated as 'Langley' plus a page number or numbers, e.g. 'Langley, p. 499–505'.

iii Publication Information. This is cited as place of publication: publisher, and date of publication. An open date (e.g. 1971–) indicates that, as far as can be ascertained, the periodical is still being published. The same information followed by a question mark (1971–?) means that, while the title *may* still be published, attempts to ascertain this beyond all doubt have not been successful.

iv Miscellaneous Notes. One of the most prominent of these is the phrase 'Not in *BUCOMP1*', to indicate a title added since the previous edition. It is recognised that some users may wish to retain copies of the first edition of *BUCOMP* even after appearance of *BUCOMP2*, and that they may, on occasion, wish to compare data between the two editions. The compilers of *BUCOMP1* surveyed more libraries than we did for this second edition, and there may therefore, very occasionally indeed, be extra information on holdings of a particular title in the first edition. While in numerical terms we surveyed fewer libraries, it should be noted, firstly, that several of the libraries covered by BUCOMP1 have now been subsumed into larger institutions, with their holdings consequently returned as part of a larger unit's questionnaire response; and that, secondly, we re-surveyed any institution which was listed in *BUCOMP1* as the unique location for an item. Where 'Not in BUCOMP1' does not appear, it may be assumed that in most cases the title appears in *BUCOMP1* in an identical place in the alphabetical sequence.

Other notes record changes in the title or subtitle of a periodical, absorption of/by other titles, and any other information which it was felt might be useful, often supplied by contributing libraries.

v Locations. These are presented in the form of the library's siglum (that is, its unique identifying symbol, as listed in the sigla list below) in **bold** type, followed by holdings information. Further information on the construction and filing of sigla may be found at the opening of the sigla list below. An entry ending with a hash sign (#) indicates that the library concerned has a current subscription to the title in question. It seemed useful to use this symbol, rather than to leave an entry open as in *BUCOMP1*, firstly because it eliminates ambiguity, and secondly because it enables the eye quickly to locate entries for libraries which have a current subscription.

Holdings information may be displayed in a number of ways:

(a) for titles in which a particular volume number applies to a particular year, or span of years:

25 (1972)–27 (1974)
12 (1950/51)–24 (1962/63)
1 (1909/13)–11 (1976/81)

(b) for titles issued in separate numbers, rather than volumes, irrespective of whether a regular number of issues appears in a year or not:

21–34, 1960–63
19, 21, 22, 1947–48; 32–34, 1958

(c) yearbooks. The *BUCOMP2* entry provides the year borne by the item, irrespective of its date of publication. Where a yearbook also carries a volume number, this is usually omitted. Thus:

1970; 1972–75; 1977; 1979–81

Note that in the above example the library holds all the issues from 1972 to 1975 inclusive, and likewise for 1979 to 1981. If the volume for 1975 had borne the cover title '1972–75', it would be indicated in *BUCOMP2* as 1972/75, not 1972–75.

Finally, it should be noted that dates move from the largest to the smallest unit – year, month, day; or year, season. Thus:

27 (1985), Nov–29 (1987), May
1985, Dec–1987, May
1946, Mar 26–1963, June 19
3 (1876), Sum–57 (1903), Spr

Abbreviations

Countries of the world

Each entry contains publication data, including a 1–4 letter code designating the country of origin of the title referred to in that entry. The abbreviations used generally follow those used on international vehicle registration plates – GB for Great Britain, E for Spain, and so on. The following have been used in this catalogue:

A	Austria
ARG	Argentina
AUS	Australia
B	Belgium
BG	Bulgaria
BR	Brazil
C	Canada
CH	Switzerland
CHL	Chile
CHN	China
CO	Colombia
CU	Cuba
CZ	Czech Republic
D	Germany
DK	Denmark
E	Spain
ECU	Ecuador
EG	Egypt
EIRE	Ireland
ETH	Ethiopia
EW	Estonia
F	France
FIN	Finland
GAB	Gabon
GB	Great Britain
GR	Greece
GRG	Georgia
H	Hungary
HK	Hong Kong
HR	Croatia
I	Italy
IL	Israel

IN	India
IND	Indonesia
IS	Iceland
J	Japan
KEN	Kenya
L	Luxembourg
LT	Lithuania
MA	Macedonia [formerly part of Yugoslavia]
MC	Monte Carlo
ME	Mexico
N	Norway
NGR	Nigeria
NL	The Netherlands
NZ	New Zealand
P	Portugal
PA	Pakistan
PL	Poland
RF	Russia
RO	Romania
S	Sweden
SA	South Africa
SGP	Singapore
SI	Slovenia
SQ	Slovakia
SRB	Serbia
TR	Turkey
UKR	Ukraine
URG	Uruguay
US	United States of America
VNZ	Venezuela

[*]

The asterisk indicates that holdings of a title are not complete. For example:

1 (1963)–5 (1968)*

In some cases libraries supplied very detailed information about which parts of their holdings were complete, and which not. While such detail was not originally requested, given its usefulness it has been produced in the catalogue where available. Thus the user might discover the following:

1 (1946)–6 (1951)*; 7 (1952)–9 (1955); 10 (1956)–15 (1960)*

This indicates that volumes 7–9 are complete, but that there are some gaps in coverage of volumes 1–6 and 10–15; while

1 (1946)–15 (1961)*

indicates that all or part of the holdings are incomplete.

One of the idiosyncrasies of *BUCOMP1* was that, in the case of some larger libraries such as the British Library in London and at Boston Spa, and the Bodleian Library in Oxford, because it was at that time impractical to discover exact details of those libraries' vast holdings, the * symbol was used *irrespective of whether the library listed had an incomplete run or not*. The advent of electronic access to library catalogues has meant that it has in many cases been possible in *BUCOMP2* to provide more complete information on holdings for those libraries: but, even so, the symbols **Lbl*** and **Ob*** remain in some cases, and can mean either that there are gaps in that library's holdings of a title, or that the title is, in fact, held complete.

[w]

The symbol [w], meaning 'without', has much the same function as the [*] symbol, in that it indicates gaps in holdings. It is used in cases where only a few, known, parts are missing. Thus:

1–25, 1946–71 [w 23, 1969]

is a shorthand for 1–22, 1946–68; 24, 25, 1970–71

[c]

Symbol [c], when it appears alone, signifies that only the latest (current) issue of a title is retained by the library concerned. This applies most frequently to periodicals which contain information that quickly goes out of date. As in the case of [w], some libraries gave more information than was requested on this point, and this data has been incorporated into the database when supplied. Thus [c (2 years)] indicates that the library retains the past two years' issues of a title; while [c (4 issues)] signifies that only the four most recent issues are held.

[m] [part m]

[m] indicates that the title cited is held in microform (i.e. on microfilm or microfiche). The symbol [part m] has been employed in *BUCOMP2*, in preference to the [m+] used in the previous edition, to indicate that only part of a title is in microform.

Miscellaneous

n.s.   New Series (for example, 1–4, 1909–14; n.s. 1 (1915))

n.F.   Neue Folge (the German equivalent of n.s. above)

q.v.   Quod vide (i.e. refer to that entry)

[Reprint ed.]   The copy held by the library is a reprint (perhaps in separately-published facsimile) of the original.

[CD-ROM] version   The title is held in CD-ROM format. '[+ CD-ROM version]' would signify that the title is held both in paper and in CD-ROM formats.

Months of the year

Jan   Feb   Mar   Apr   May   June   July   Aug   Sep   Oct   Nov   Dec

Seasons

Spr   Spring
Sum   Summer
Aut   Autumn
Win   Winter

John Wagstaff

Statistics

BUCOMP2 contains the details of 3678 of which 1630 did not appear in *BUCOMP1*. There are a further 1377 cross references from variant forms of the titles. The breakdown of titles per country is as follows:

Argentina	12	Israel	9
Australia	33	Italy	118
Austria	61	Japan	4
Belgium	31	Kenya	1
Brazil	5	Lithuania	2
Bulgaria	7	Macedonia [formerly part of Yugoslavia]	1
Canada	37	Mexico	8
Chile	1	Monte Carlo	1
China	11	The Netherlands	53
Colombia	1	New Zealand	7
Croatia	5	Nigeria	1
Cuba	6	Norway	12
Czech Republic	34	Pakistan	1
Denmark	25	Poland	24
Ecuador	1	Portugal	6
Egypt	1	Romania	7
Estonia	1	Russia	31
Ethiopia	1	Serbia	3
Finland	3	Singapore	1
France	156	Slovakia	10
Gabon	1	Slovenia	1
Georgia	1	South Africa	9
Germany	309	Spain	28
Great Britain	1923	Sweden	29
Greece	2	Switzerland	35
Hong Kong	3	Turkey	2
Hungary	21	Ukraine	3
Iceland	1	United States of America	500
India	16	Uruguay	2
Indonesia	1	Venezuela	4
Ireland	56		

The Project Group

Members of the IAML(UK) Documentation Committee, 1994–7:

Paul Andrews
Chris Banks
Peter Baxter
Almut Boehme
Christopher Bornet
Julie Crawley
Rosalind Cyphus
Katharine Hogg
Richard Turbet
John Wagstaff

List of Libraries Participating in *BUCOMP2*, Arranged by Town/City

ABERDARE. Aberdare Central Library, Green Street, Aberdare, Mid Glamorgan CF44 7AG (Alice Percival; tel. 01685–885318; fax 01685–881181) **ABDp**

ABERDEEN. City of Aberdeen Central Library, Rosemount Viaduct, Aberdeen AB9 1GU (Alan R. Fulton; tel. 01224–634622, ext. 225/226) **Ap**

ABERDEEN. Aberdeen University Library, Queen Mother Library, Meston Walk, Aberdeen AB9 2UE (Richard Turbet; tel. 01224–272592) **Au**

ABERYSTWYTH. College of Librarianship Wales *see* **ABERYSTWYTH. Hugh Owen Library**

ABERYSTWYTH. Hugh Owen Library, University of Wales Aberystwyth, Penglais, Aberystwyth SY23 3DZ (Bob Prichard; tel. 01970–622391; fax 01970–622404) **ABc**. Holdings of the library of the College of Librarianship Wales are now held in the Information and Library Studies Library on the same premises; these are indicated by the siglum **ABc (ILS)**.

ABERYSTWYTH. Llyfrgell Genedlaethol Cymru/National Library of Wales, Aberystwyth, Dyfed SY23 3BU (Tudor Henson; tel. 01970–623816; fax 01970–615709) **AB**

ABERYSTWYTH. National Library of Wales *see* **ABERYSTWYTH. Llyfrgell Genedlaethol Cymru/National Library of Wales**

ALDEBURGH. The Britten-Pears Library, The Red House, Aldeburgh, Suffolk IP15 5PZ (Dr Paul Banks; tel. 01728–452615; fax 01728–453076; e-mail bpl@uea.ac.uk) **ALb**

ALDERSHOT *see* **WINCHESTER. Hampshire County Library Service**

ALSAGER. Manchester Metropolitan University, Alsager Site Library, Hassall Road, Alsager, Stoke-on-Trent ST7 2HL (tel. 0161–247 5356) **Mmu (a)**

ALTON *see* **WINCHESTER. Hampshire County Library Service**

AMERSHAM *see* **AYLESBURY. Buckinghamshire County Library**

ANDOVER *see* **WINCHESTER. Hampshire County Library Service**

AYLESBURY. Buckinghamshire County Library, County Library Headquarters, Walton Street, Aylesbury, Buckinghamshire HP20 1UU (Margaret Roll; tel. 01296–383206; fax 01296–382405) **Bu-AYp**
Buckinghamshire County Libraries also operates the following branch library sites:

Amersham Library, Chiltern Avenue, Amersham, Buckinghamshire HP6 5AG (tel. 01494–724691) **Bu-AME**

Bletchley Library, Westfield Road, Bletchley, Buckinghamshire MK2 2RA (tel. 01908–372797) **Bu-BLE**

Buckingham Library, Verney Close, Buckingham, Buckinghamshire MK18 1JP (tel. 01280–813229) **Bu-BUC**

Chesham Library, Elgiva Lane, Chesham, Buckinghamshire HP5 2JB (tel. 01494–772322) **Bu-CHE**

High Wycombe Library, Queen Victoria Road, High Wycombe, Buckinghamshire HP11 1BD (tel. 01494–464004) **Bu-HW**

Milton Keynes Library, 555 Silbury Boulevard, Saxon Gate East, Milton Keynes MK9 3HL (tel. 01908–835010) **Bu-MK**

Princes Risborough Library, Bell Street, Princes Risborough, Buckinghamshire HP17 9AA (tel. 01844–343559) **Bu-PR**

AYR. Carnegie Library, 12 Main Street, Ayr, KA8 8ED, Scotland (Charles Deas; tel. 01292–286385; fax 01292–611593) **AR**

BANGOR. University College of North Wales Bangor, Bangor, Gwynedd LL57 2DG (Elizabeth Bird; tel. 01248–382187; e-mail ISS063@uk.ac.bangor) **BG**. The response also includes holdings of the Bangor Coleg Normal, which became part of Bangor University in 1996: at the university library's request these holdings have not been assigned a separate siglum.

BARNSLEY. Barnsley Central Library, Shambles Street, Barnsley, South Yorkshire S70 2JF (Wendy Mann; tel. 01226–733241; fax 01226–285458) **BAR**

BASINGSTOKE *see* **WINCHESTER. Hampshire County Library Service**

BATH. Bath Spa University College, Newton Park, Newton St Looe, Bath BA2 9BN (Marilyn Floyd; tel. 01225–875875; fax 01225–875505) **BAc**

BBC *see* **LONDON. British Broadcasting Corporation**

BEDFORD. Bedford Central Library, Harpur Street, Bedford MK40 1PG (Paul Andrews; tel. 01234–350931; fax 01234–342163) **BEp**

BELFAST. Belfast Music Library, Belfast Central Library, Royal Avenue, Belfast BT1 1EA, Northern Ireland (Felicity Jones; tel. 01232–243233; fax 01232–332819) **BLp**

BELFAST. British Broadcasting Corporation Music Library, BBC Broadcasting House, Ormeau Avenue, Belfast BT2 8HQ, Northern Ircland (Ruth Gregory; tel. 01232–338295; fax 01232–338807) **BLBBC**

BELFAST. Queen's University of Belfast, University Square, Belfast BT7 1LS, Northern Ireland (Stuart Rawson; tel. 01232–245133; fax 01232–323340) **BLu**

BIRMINGHAM. Music Services, Birmingham Central Library, Chamberlain Square, Birmingham B3 3HQ (Joy Stapleton/Jean Weston; tel. 0121–235–2448/2482; fax 0121–233–4458) **Bp**

BIRMINGHAM. Birmingham Conservatoire Library, University of Central England, Paradise Place, Birmingham B3 3HG (tel. 0121–331 5914; e-mail music.library@uk.ac.university-central-england) **Bs**

BIRMINGHAM. Barber Music and Fine Art Library, The University of Birmingham, Edgbaston, Birmingham B15 2TT (Ian Ledsham; tel. 0121–414–5851; fax 0121–414 5853) **Bu**

BLETCHLEY *see* **AYLESBURY. Buckinghamshire County Library**

BOLTON. Bolton Central Library, Civic Centre, Le Mans Crescent, Bolton, Lancashire BL1 1SE (Ms Val Byrne; tel. 01204–22311, ext. 2177) **BOL**

BOSTON SPA. Music Section, The British Library Document Supply Centre, Boston Spa, Wetherby, West Yorkshire LS23 7BQ (Frank Wray; tel. 01937–546168) **BSdsc**

BOURNEMOUTH. Bournemouth Music Library, Meyrick Road, Lansdowne, Bournemouth, Dorset BH1 3DJ (C. Butterworth; tel. 01202–553781; fax 01202–291781) **DS**

BRADFORD. Music Library, Bradford City Council Central Library, Prince's Way, Bradford BD1 1NN (tel. 01274–753564) **BDp**

BRIDGEND. Mid Glamorgan County Libraries, Coed Parc, Park Street, Bridgend, Mid Glamorgan CF31 4BA (Elizabeth Roberts; tel. 01656–767451; fax 01656–645719) **BRDp** Mid-Glamorgan Libraries also operate the following branch library sites:

Pencoed Library, Penybont Road, Pencoed CF35 5RA (tel. 01656–860358) **BRDp (pen)**

Pontypridd Central Library, Library Road, Pontypridd CF37 2DY (tel. 01443–486850) **BRDp (pon)**

Porthcawl Library, Porthcawl CF36 3AG (tel. 01656–782059) **BRDp (por)**

BRIGHTON. Brighton Music Library, East Sussex County Library Service, 115 Church Street, Brighton, East Sussex BN1 1UD (Jane M. Cox; tel. 01273–674841) **BTp**

BRIGHTON. University of Sussex Library, Falmer, Brighton, East Sussex BN1 9QL (Cherry Horwill; tel. 01273–606755; fax 01273–678441; e-mail library@uk.ac.sussex.central) **BTu**

BRISTOL. Bristol Music Library, Central [Public] Library, College Green, Bristol BS1 5TL (Christine Stephens; tel. 0117–922–6121, ext. 219; fax 0117–922 6775) **BRp**

BRISTOL. Music Library, University of Bristol, Tyndall Avenue, Bristol BS8 1TJ (Peter King; tel. 0117–930–3030; fax 0117–925–5334) **BRu**

BRITISH BROADCASTING CORPORATION *see* **LONDON. British Broadcasting Corporation**

BRITISH INSTITUTE OF JAZZ STUDIES *see* **CROWTHORNE. British Institute of Jazz Studies**

BRITISH LIBRARY *see* **LONDON. British Library**

BRITISH LIBRARY DOCUMENT SUPPLY CENTRE *see* **BOSTON SPA**

BRITISH MUSIC INFORMATION CENTRE *see* **LONDON**

BUCKINGHAM *see* **AYLESBURY. Buckinghamshire County Library**

BURY. Reference Library, Central Library, Manchester Road, Bury, Lancashire BL9 0DG (Ms Pat Banks; tel. 0161–705–5871; fax 0161–705–5915) **BYp**

CAMBRIDGE. Anglia Polytechnic University Library, East Road, Cambridge CB1 7PT (Sian Davies/Christine Moore; tel. 01223–63271, ext. 2372; fax 01223–352973) **Cat** The University also has a site at Brentford **Cat (b)**

CAMBRIDGE. Libraries and Information Service, Cambridgeshire County Council, 7 Lion Yard, Cambridge CB2 3QD (James Yardley; tel. 01223–65252, ext. 210; fax 01223–62786) **Cap**

CAMBRIDGE. Pendlebury Library, University Music School, University of Cambridge, West Road, Cambridge CB3 9DP (Andrew Bennett; tel. 01223–335183; fax 01223–335067; e-mail ab164@cus.cam.ac.uk) **Cpl**

CAMBRIDGE. Cambridge University Library, West Road, Cambridge CB3 9DR (Richard Andrewes; tel. 01223–333072; fax 01223–333160; e-mail rma@ula.cam.ac.uk) **Cu**

CANTERBURY. The Templeman Library, University of Kent at Canterbury, Canterbury, Kent CT2 7NU (Brian Hogben; tel. 01227–764000; fax 01227–475495) **CAu**

CARDIFF. Cardiff Central Music Library, St David's Link, Frederick Street, Cardiff CF1 4DT (Sheila Basford; tel. 01222–382116, ext. 1625; fax 01222–238642) **CDCp**

CARDIFF. University of Wales, Cardiff, P.O. Box 78, Cardiff CF1 1XL (Gillian Jones; tel. 01222–874000) **CDu**

CARMARTHEN. Dyfed County Library, St Peters Street, Carmarthen SA31 1LN (Dewi Thomas; tel. 01267–233333) **CAR**

CHANDLER'S FORD *see* **WINCHESTER. Hampshire County Library Service**

CHELTENHAM *see* **GLOUCESTER. Gloucestershire County Library**

CHESHAM *see* **AYLESBURY. Buckingham County Library**

CHESTER. Cheshire County Council Libraries, Arts and Archives, 91 Hoole Road, Chester, Cheshire CH2 3NG (tel. 01244–320055; fax 01244–313079) **CHEp**

CHESTERFIELD. Chesterfield Central Library, New Beetwell Street, Chesterfield , Derbyshire S40 1QN (D. Bennell; tel. 01246–209292; fax 01246–209304) **CH**

COLCHESTER. Colchester Institute Library, Sheepen Road, Colchester, Essex CO3 3LL (Mary Pelowski; tel. 01206–718642) **CCtc**

COLCHESTER. Essex County Council County Music Collection, Colchester Library, Trinity Square, Colchester CO1 1JB (Viv Kuphal; tel. 01206–562243; fax 01206–562413) **CFp**

COVENTRY. City Library, City of Coventry Leisure Services, Smithford Way, Coventry CV1 1FY (Jane Black; tel. 01203–832331) **COp**

CROWTHORNE. British Institute of Jazz Studies, 17 The Chase, Crowthorne, Berkshire RG11 6HT (Graham Langley; tel. 01344–775669) **Cbijs**

CWMBRAN. Gwent Libraries, County Library Headquarters, County Hall, Cwmbran, Gwent NP44 2XL (Sue Johnson; tel. 01633–832171; fax 01633–832129) **CW**

DARTINGTON COLLEGE OF ARTS *see* **TOTNES**

DORKING. The Colles Library, The Royal School of Church Music, Cleveland Lodge, Dorking, Surrey CR9 5AD (John Parkinson; tel. 01306–877676; fax 01306–887240). The Royal School of Church Music moved from its former premises in Addington Palace, Croydon, to Dorking in 1997/98, very late in the preparation of this catalogue. Its holdings are therefore still shown at siglum **Lrscm** in *BUCOMP2*, pending the assignment of a new siglum which is likely to be **CRsc. Lrscm**

DORKING. Surrey Performing Arts Library, Vaughan Williams House, West Street, Dorking, Surrey RH4 1BY (Andrew Woods; tel. 01306–887509/744743; fax 01306–875074) **DOR**

DUBLIN. The Contemporary Music Centre, 92 Lower Baggot Street, Dublin 2, Ireland (Eve O'Kelly; tel. +353–1–661–2105; fax +353–1–676–2639) **EIR:Dcmc**

DUBLIN. Dublin Public Libraries, Music Library, ILAC Centre, Henry Street, Dublin 2, Ireland (V. Kilboy; tel. +353–1–873–4333) **EIR:Dp**

DUBLIN. The Royal Irish Academy of Music, 36–38 Westland Row, Dublin 2, Ireland (Philip Shields; tel. +353–1–676 4412) **EIR:DRiam**

DUBLIN. Music Section, The Main Library, University College Dublin, Belfield, Dublin 4, Ireland (Claire Moran; tel. +353–1–706–7777; fax +353–1–283–7667; e-mail library@irlearn.ucd.ie) **EIR:Duc**

DUBLIN. Music Section, Trinity College Library, College Street, Dublin 2, Ireland (Roy Stanley; tel. +353–1–677–2941; fax +353–1–671–9003) **EIR:Dtc**

DUDLEY. Dudley Library, St James Road, Dudley, West Midlands DY1 1HR (Stuart Wilson; tel. 01384–453556) **DDp**

DUNDEE. Dundee District Libraries, Central Library, The Wellgate, Dundee DD1 6TB (tel. 01382–434326; fax 01382–434036) **DU**

DURHAM. Durham County Council Arts, Libraries and Museums Department, County Hall, Durham DG1 5TY (Alan Hood; tel. 0191–386–4411; fax 0191–384 1336) **DRp**

DURHAM. Durham University Library, Palace Green, Durham DH1 3RN (Roger Norris; tel. 0191–374 3003) **DRu**

EASTBOURNE. Eastbourne Music Library, Grove Road, Eastbourne, East Sussex BN21 4TL (Pauline Kennard; tel. 01323–739119) **Ea**

EAST KILBRIDE. The Central Library, The Olympia, East Kilbride G74 1PG, Scotland (Christopher Lorimer; tel. 013552–20046; fax 013552–29365) **EK**

EASTLEIGH *see* **WINCHESTER. Hampshire County Library Service**

EDINBURGH. The Music Library, Edinburgh City Libraries, George IV Bridge, Edinburgh EH1 1EG (Peter Baxter; tel. 0131–225 5584; fax 0131–225 8783) **Ep**

EDINBURGH. The Music Library, The National Library of Scotland, George IV Bridge, Edinburgh EH1 1EW (Roger Duce; tel. 0131–226 4531; fax 0131–220 6662) **En**

EDINBURGH. The Reid Music Library, Edinburgh University, Alison House, 12 Nicolson Square, Edinburgh EH8 9DF (Jeremy Upton; tel. 0131–650–2436; fax 0131–650–2425; e-mail j.upton@ed.ac.uk) **Er**

ELGIN. Elgin Library, Cooper Park, Elgin, Moray, I30 1HS, Scotland (Graham McDermid; tel. 01343–542746; fax 01343–549050) **EG**

ENGLISH FOLK DANCE AND SONG SOCIETY *see* **LONDON**

EXETER. University of Exeter Library, Stocker Road, Exeter, Devon EX4 4PT (Julie Crawley; tel. 01392–263860; fax 01392 263871; e-mail j.a.crawley@exeter.ac.uk) **EXu**

FAREHAM *see* **WINCHESTER. Hampshire County Library Service**

FARNBOROUGH *see* **WINCHESTER. Hampshire County Library Service**

FLEET *see* **WINCHESTER. Hampshire County Library Service**

GLASGOW. Glasgow University Library, Hillhead Street, Glasgow GL2 8QE (tel. 0141–330 6797; fax 0141–330 4592) **Gul**. Holdings from the university's Euing Collection are indicated by the siglum **Gul (e)**.

GLASGOW. The Mitchell Library, Arts Department, North Street, Glasgow G3 7DN (Karen Cunningham/Jennifer Larmour; tel. 0141–305 2934; fax 0141–305 2815) **Gm**

GLASGOW. The Royal Scottish Academy of Music and Drama, 100 Renfrew Street, Glasgow G2 3DB (Kenneth Wilkins; tel. 0141–332 4101; fax 0141–332 8901) **Gam**

GLASGOW. Scottish Music Information Centre, 1 Bowmont Gardens, Glasgow GL2 9LR (Sheila Craik; tel. 0141–334 6393; fax 0141–337 1161) **Gsmic**

GLOUCESTER. Gloucestershire County Library, Music and Drama Library, Quayside Wing, Gloucester GL1 2HY (Linda Marsden; tel. 01452–426983; fax 01452–426982) **GLp** Gloucestershire County Libraries also operate the following branch library site:

Cheltenham Library, Clarence Street, Cheltenham, Gloucestershire GL50 3JT (tel. 01242–522476; fax 01242–510373) **CHL**

GOSPORT *see* **WINCHESTER. Hampshire County Library Service**

HARTLEPOOL *see* **MIDDLESBROUGH. Cleveland County Libraries**

HASTINGS. The Music Library, Hastings Library, 13 Claremont, Hastings, East Sussex TN34 1HE (Jane Campbell; tel. 01424–420501; fax 01424–430261) **HA**

HATFIELD. Hertfordshire Libraries, Arts and Information Central Resources Library, New Barnfield, Travellers Lane, Hatfield, Hertfordshire AL10 8XG (Philip Robinson; tel. 01707–281530; fax 01707–281514) **HE**

HAYLING ISLAND *see* **WINCHESTER. Hampshire County Library Service**

HIGH WYCOMBE *see* **AYLESBURY. Buckinghamshire County Library**

HORSHAM. Horsham Library, Lower Tanbridge Way, Horsham, West Sussex RH12 1RJ (Jackie Usher; tel. 01403–217013; fax 01403–211972) **HOp**

HULL. Brynmor Jones Library, University of Hull, Cottingham Road, Hull, North Humberside HU6 7RX (tel. 01482–466311; fax 01482–466205) **HUu**

HYTHE *see* **WINCHESTER. Hampshire County Library Service**

IPSWICH. County Reference Library, Northgate Street, Ipswich, Suffolk IP1 3DE (tel. 01473–264556; fax 01473–225491) **IP**

KEELE. Keele University Library, Keele, Staffordshire ST5 5BG (Margaret Greive; tel. 01782–583232; fax 01782–711553; e-mail library@keele.ac.uk) **KE**

KINGSTON-UPON-THAMES. Kingston University Library, Kingston Hill, Kingston-upon-Thames, Surrey KT2 7LB (tel. 0181–547 2000; fax 0181–547 7312) **Lki**

KIRKCALDY. Kirkcaldy District Libraries, East Fergus Place, Kirkcaldy, Fife KY1 1XF, Scotland (J. Klak; tel. 01592–268386; fax 01592–643399) **KC**

LANCASTER. Lancaster University Library, Bailrigg, Lancaster LA1 4YH (tel. 01524–65201; fax 01524–63806) **LAu**

LEEDS. The Brotherton Library, University of Leeds, Woodhouse Lane, Leeds LS2 9JT (Kate Alderson-Smith; tel. 0113–233 5510; fax 0113–233 5561) **LEbc**

LEEDS. The Central Library, Town Hall, The Headrow, Leeds LS1 3AB (Helen O'Neill; tel. 0113–247 8330; fax 0113–247 7747) **LEc**

LEICESTER. The Library, De Montfort University, Scraptoft, Leicester LE7 9SU (Sally Luxton; tel. 01162–551551; fax 01162–577866) **LCdM**

LEIGH PARK *see* **WINCHESTER. Hampshire County Library Service**

LEWES. The Music Library, Lewes Library, 47 St Anne's Crescent, Lewes, East Sussex BN7 1SD (Sara Sage; tel. 01273–481537) **LT**

LINCOLN. The Music and Drama Library, Lincolnshire County Council Recreational Services Department, Brayford House, Lucy Tower Street, Lincoln LN1 1XN (A. Helen Mason; tel. 01522–552866; fax 01522–552858) **LIp**

LIVERPOOL. The Music Library, Liverpool City Libraries, Central Library, William Brown Street, Liverpool L3 8EW (Kit Siddons-Smith; tel. 0151–225 5463; fax 0151–207 1342) **LVp**

LIVERPOOL. The University Library, University of Liverpool, P.O. Box 123, Liverpool L69 3DA (D. Cartmill; tel. 0151–794 2682; fax 0151–794 2681; e-mail qlis17@uk.ac.liverpool) **LVu**

LONDON. BALHAM *see* **LONDON. Wandsworth**

LONDON. Barbican. The Barbican Library, Barbican Centre, London EC2Y 8DS (Robert Tucker; tel. 0171–638 0672; fax 0171–638 2249) **Lbar**

LONDON. Barking. Barking Central Library, Axe Street, Barking, Essex IG11 7NB (C. J. Clare; tel. 0181–517 8666) **Lbk**

LONDON. Barnet. Hendon Library, Barnet Libraries, Arts and Museums, The Burroughs, London NW4 4BQ (Liz Hart; tel. 0181–202 5625; fax 0181–203 4782) **Lba**

LONDON. Battersea *see* **LONDON. Wandsworth**

LONDON. Bexleyheath. Central Reference Library, London Borough of Bexley, Townley Road, Bexleyheath, Kent DA6 7HJ (Pamela Rew; tel. 0181–301–5151; fax 0181–303–7872) **Lbx**

LONDON. British Broadcasting Corporation. British Broadcasting Corporation Music Library, Broadcasting House, Portland Place, London W1A 1AA (Rachel Ladyman; tel. 0171–765 3724; fax 0171–765 5304) **Lbbc**. The BBC response includes holdings of the former BBC West London Music Library.

LONDON. British Library. The British Library Music Library, 96 Euston Road, London NW1 2DB (Malcolm Turner; tel. 0171–412 7529; fax 0171–412 7751). **Lbl**

LONDON. British Library. The British Library National Sound Archive, 29 Exhibition Road, London SW7 2AS (Jane Harvell; tel. 0171–412 7430; fax 0171–412 7416). In late 1997 the collection was moved to the new British Library building at St Pancras (see **Lbl** above). **Lsa**

LONDON. British Library. The British Library Oriental and India Office, Orbit House, 197 Blackfriars Road, London SE1 8NG (Hedley Sutton; tel. 0171–412 7873; fax 0171–412 7858) **Lio**

LONDON. British Music Information Centre. The British Music Information Centre, 10 Stratford Place, London W1N 9AE (Tom Morgan; tel. 0171–499 8567; fax 0171–499 4795) **Lmic**

LONDON. Bromley. Music and Audio Library, London Borough of Bromley, High Street, Bromley, Kent BR1 1EX (David Cook; tel. 0181–460–9955, ext. 266; fax 0181–313–0475) **Lbo**

LONDON. Brompton *see* **LONDON. Kensington and Chelsea**

LONDON. Charing Cross *see* **LONDON. Westminster**

LONDON. Chelsea *see* **LONDON. Kensington and Chelsea**

LONDON. Church Street Library *see* **LONDON. Westminster**

LONDON. Churchill Gardens Library *see* **LONDON. Westminster**

LONDON. City University. The City University Library, Northampton Square, London EC1V 0HB (Pamela Lighthill; tel. 0171–477 8000, ext. 4007; fax 0171–490 4419) **Lcu**

LONDON COLLEGE OF FURNITURE LIBRARY *see* **LONDON. Guildhall University**

LONDON. Enfield. Audio Visual Services, London Borough of Enfield, Town Hall, Green Lanes, London N13 4XD (Ruth Hellen; tel. 0181–967 9370; fax 0181–982 7378) **Len**

LONDON. English Folk Dance and Song Society. The English Folk Dance and Song Society Library (Vaughan Williams Memorial Library), Cecil Sharp House, 2 Regent's Park Road, London NW1 7AY (Debra Godrich/Malcolm Taylor; tel. 0171–485 2206; fax 0171–284 0523) **Lcs**

LONDON. Fulham *see* **LONDON. Hammersmith and Fulham**

LONDON. Goldsmiths College *see* **LONDON. University. Goldsmiths College**

LONDON. Great Smith Street Library *see* **LONDON. Westminster**

LONDON. Greenwich. London Borough of Greenwich Support Services, Plumstead Library, Plumstead High Street, London SE18 1JL (Martin Stone; tel. 0181–317 4466; fax 0181–317 4868) **Lgr**

LONDON. Guildhall School. Guildhall School of Music and Drama, The Barbican, London EC2Y 8DT (Adrian Yardley; tel. 0171–628–2571; fax 0171–256–9438) **Lgsm**

LONDON. Guildhall University. London Guildhall University, 41 Commercial Road, London E1 1LA (tel. 0171–320 1867; fax 0171–320 1830) **Lgu**. Part of this collection was formerly located in the London College of Furniture Library, listed in BUCOMP1 as **Lcf**.

LONDON. Hackney. London Borough of Hackney, Hackney Central Library, Mare Street, London E8 1HG (Don Badenoch; tel. 0181–985 8262; fax 0181–533 3712) **Lh**

LONDON. Hammersmith and Fulham. Hammersmith and Fulham Central Library, Shepherd's Bush Road, London W6 7AT (E. Stephens; tel. 0181–576 5055; fax 0181–576 5022) **Lha**
Hammersmith and Fulham Library Service also operates the following branch library:

Fulham Library, 598 Fulham Road, London SW6 5NX (tel. 0181–576 5253) **Lha (f)**

LONDON. Haringey. Haringey Central Library, High Road, Wood Green, London N22 6XD (Robert Missen; tel. 0181–888 1292) **Lhg**

LONDON. Harrow. Harrow Music Library, Gayton Library, Gayton Road, Harrow, Middlesex HA1 2HL (J. Roche; tel. 0181–427 8986/6012) **Lhr**

LONDON. Hendon *see* **LONDON. Barnet**

LONDON. Heythrop College. Heythrop College Library, Kensington Square, London W8 5HQ (Sr. Rowley; tel. 0171–795 4250; fax 0171–795 4253) **Lhey**

LONDON. Islington. Islington Central Library, 2 Fieldway Crescent, London N5 1PF (Chris Millington; tel. 0171–609 3051; fax 0171–607 6409) **Lis**

LONDON. Kensington and Chelsea. Central Library, The Royal Borough of Kensington and Chelsea, Phillimore Walk, London W8 7RX (tel. 0171–937 2542; fax 0171–937 0515) **Lk**
Kensington and Chelsea Library Service also operates the following branch libraries:

Brompton Library, 210 Old Brompton Road, London SW5 0BS (tel. 0171–373 3111) **Lk (b)**

Chelsea Library, King's Road, London SW3 5EZ (tel. 0171–352 6056) **Lk (c)**

North Kensington Library, 108 Ladbroke Grove, London W11 1PZ (tel. 0171–727 6583) **Lk (nk)**

LONDON. King's College *see* **LONDON. University. King's College**

LONDON. Lambeth. London Borough of Lambeth Public Library and Archives Service, Directorate of Environmental Services, 8th Floor, International House, Canterbury Crescent, London SW9 7QE (David Strong; tel. 0171–926 9324; fax 0171–926 9333/0171–926 9467) **Ll**

LONDON. Maida Vale Library *see* **LONDON. Westminster**

LONDON. Marylebone Library Music Library *see* **LONDON. Westminster**

LONDON. Middlesex University. Middlesex University Library, Trent Park, Bramley Road, London N14 4XS (John Collis; tel. 0181–362 5000; fax 0181–441 4672) **Lmi**

LONDON. North Kensington *see* **LONDON. Kensington and Chelsea**

LONDON. Paddington Library Music Library *see* **LONDON. Westminster**

LONDON. Pimlico *see* **LONDON. Westminster**

LONDON. Polish Library. The Polish Library, 238–246 King Street, London W6 0RF (Dr Z. Jagodzinski; tel. 0171–741–0474) **Lp**

LONDON. Putney *see* **LONDON. Wandsworth**

LONDON. Queen's Park Library *see* **LONDON. Westminster**

LONDON. Richmond-upon-Thames. London Borough of Richmond-upon-Thames, Bibliographical and Computer Services, The Cottage, Little Green, Richmond, Surrey TW9 1QL (tel. 0181–940 0031; fax 0181–940 7568) **Lri**

LONDON. Roehampton Institute. Roehampton Institute of Higher Education, Southlands College Library, Wimbledon Parkside, London SW19 5NN (Lisa Bryden; tel. 0181–392 3454; fax 0181–392 3459) **Lro**

LONDON. Royal Academy of Music. The Library, The Royal Academy of Music, Marylebone Road, London NW1 5HT (John Webb/Katharine Hogg; tel. 0171–935 5461; fax 0171–873 7374) **Lam**
The Royal Academy Library also holds the collection of the Organ Club, listed here at **Lam (o)**

LONDON. Royal College of Music. The Library, The Royal College of Music, Prince Consort Road, London SW7 2BS (Christopher Bornet; tel. 0171–589 3643; fax 0171–589 7740) **Lcm**
The Royal College of Music Library also holds music periodicals in its Museum of Instruments, listed here at **Lcm (m)**, and compiled by Richard Gowman; and in its Department of Portraits, listed here at **Lcm (p)**, and compiled by Paul Collen.

LONDON. Royal College of Organists. The Royal College of Organists, 7 St Andrew Street, Holborn, London EC4A 3LQ (Robin Langley; tel. 0171–936 3606; fax 0171–353 8244) **Lrco**

LONDON. Royal Holloway and Bedford New College *see* **LONDON. University. Royal Holloway and Bedford New College**

LONDON. Royal School of Church Music. The Royal School of Church Music, formerly at Addington Palace, Croydon, Surrey CR9 5AD, moved to Dorking in 1997/98. See entry at **DORKING**

LONDON. St John's Wood Library *see* **LONDON. Westminster**

LONDON. Sutton. Music and Arts Department, Sutton Library, The London Borough of Sutton, St Nicholas Way, Sutton, Surrey SM1 1EA (Patrick Ford; tel. 0181–770 4765; fax 0181–770 4777) **Lsut**

LONDON. Thames Valley University. Thames Valley University Learning Resource Centre, Walpole House, 18–22 Bond Street, London W5 5AA (Colin Steele; tel. 0181–231 2648; fax 0181–231 2631; e-mail steele-c@uk.ac.tvu.s) **Ltv**

LONDON. Tower Hamlets. London Borough of Tower Hamlets, Whitechapel Music and Art Library, 77 Whitechapel High Street, London E1 7QX (Angela Haynes; tel. 0181–247 5272) **Lth**

LONDON. Trinity College of Music. Academic Studies Centre, 10–11 Bulstrode Place, London W1M 5FW (Kate Sloss; tel. 0171–935 5773; fax 0171–486 6018) **Ltc**

LONDON. University. Music Library, University of London Library, Senate House, Malet Street, London WC1E 7HU (Ruth Darton; tel. 0171–636 8000, ext. 5038; fax 0171–436 1494) **Lu**
London University Library also holds the library of the Royal Musical Association, listed here at **Lu (RMA)**

LONDON. University. Goldsmiths College. Goldsmiths College, University of London, Lewisham Way, London SE14 6NW (Peter Morris; tel. 0181–692 7171, ext. 2261; fax 0181–692 9190; e-mail library@uk.ac.goldsmiths.scorpio) **Lgo**

LONDON. University. Institute of Education. Institute of Education, University of London, 20 Bedford Way, London WC1H 0AL (Judy Allsopp; tel. 0171–580 1122; fax 0171–612 6126) **Lie**

LONDON. University. King's College. King's College, University of London, The Strand, London WC2R 2LS (Evelyn Cornell; tel. 0171–873 2139; fax 0171–872 0207) **Lkc**

LONDON. University. Royal Holloway and Bedford New College. Royal Holloway and Bedford New College, University of London, Egham Hill, Egham, Surrey TW20 0EX (tel. 01784–434455; fax 01784–437520) **LRHBNC**

LONDON. University. School of Oriental and African Studies. School of Oriental and African Studies, University of London, Serials Office, Thornhaugh Street, Russell Square, London WC1H 0XG (Michael Williams; tel. 0171–637 2388, ext. 2302; fax 0171–426 3844) **Lso**

LONDON. University. School of Slavonic and East European Studies. School of Slavonic and East European Studies Library, University of London, Senate House, Malet Street, London WC1E 7HU (J. E. Screen; tel. 0171–637 4934, ext. 4094; fax 0171–436 8916; e-mail ssees-library@uk.ac.ukcc.clus1) **Ls**

LONDON. Waltham Forest. London Borough of Waltham Forest, Central Library, High Street, Walthamstow, London E17 7JN (Barbara Humm; tel. 0181–520 4733) **Lwf**

LONDON. Walthamstow *see* **LONDON. Waltham Forest**

LONDON. Wandsworth. Wandsworth Public Libraries, Balham Music Library, Ramsden Road, London SW12 8QY (Frank Daniels; tel. 0181–871 7195; fax 0181–675 4015) **Lww** Wandsworth Libraries also operate the following branch libraries:

Balham Public Library, Ramsden Road, London SW12 8QY (tel. 0181–871 7195) **Lwwb**

Battersea Public Library, Lavender Hill, London SW11 1JB (tel. 0181–871 7466) **Lwwbat**

Putney Public Library, Disraeli Road, London SW15 2DR (tel. 0181–871 7090) **Lwwput**

LONDON. Westminster. City of Westminster Music Library, 160 Buckingham Palace Road, London SW1W 9UD (tel. 0171–798 2192) **Lcml** Westminster City Council also operates the following branch libraries:

Charing Cross Library, 4 Charing Cross Road, London WC2H 0HG (tel. 0171–798 2056) **Lcml (c)**

Church Street Library, Church Street, London NW8 8EU (tel. 0171–798 1480) **Lcml (ch)**

Churchill Gardens Library, 131 Lupus Street, London SW1V 3NE (tel. 0171–798 2196) **Lcml (cg)**

Great Smith Street Library, 30 Great Smith Street, London SW1P 3DG (tel. 0171–798 2989) **Lcml (g)**

Maida Vale Library, Sutherland Avenue, London W9 2QT (tel. 0171–798 3659) **Lcml (mv)**

Marylebone Library Music Library, Marylebone Road, London NW1 5PS (tel. 0171–798 1038) **Lcml (m)**

Paddington Library Music Library, Porchester Road, London W2 5DU (tel. 0171–798 3696) **Lcml (p)**

Pimlico Library, Rampayne Street, London SW1V 2PU (tel. 0171–798 2983) **Lcml (pim)**

Queen's Park Library, 666 Harrow Road, London W10 4NE (tel. 0171–798 3575) **Lcml (q)**

St John's Wood Library, 20 Circus Road,London NW8 6PD (tel. 0171–798 1487) **Lcml (sjw)**

Westminster Reference Library, 35 St Martin's Street, London WC2H 7HP (tel. 0171–798 2036) **Lcml (r)**

LONDON. Westminster Reference Library *see* **LONDON. Westminster**

LOUGHTON. The National Jazz Foundation Archive, Loughton Library, Loughton, Essex IG10 1HD (Ken Jones; tel. 0181–502 0181; fax 0181–508 5041) **LOnjfa**

LUTON. Luton Central Library, St George's Square, Luton, Bedfordshire LU1 2NG (Malcolm Thatcher; tel. 01582–30161; fax 01582–24638) **LXp**

LYMINGTON *see* **WINCHESTER. Hampshire County Library Service**

MANCHESTER. The Henry Watson Music Library, Central Library, St Peter's Square, Manchester M2 5PD (M. Keeley; tel. 0161–234 1976; fax 0161–234 1963) **Mpl**

MANCHESTER. The John Rylands University Library of Manchester, Oxford Road, Manchester M13 9PP (A. D. Walker/J. P. Tuck/Dr Rosemary Williamson; tel. 0161–275 3738; fax 0161–273 7488) **Mu**

MANCHESTER. Manchester Metropolitan University, All Saints Library, Oxford Road, Manchester M15 6BH (tel. 0161–247 6104) **Mmu**
Manchester Metropolitan University also operates sites at Alsager (**MMu (a)** (q.v.)), and at Didsbury: Didsbury Site Library, 799 Wilmslow Road, Manchester M20 2RR (tel. 0161–247 6121) **Mmu (d)**

MANCHESTER. The Royal Northern College of Music, 124 Oxford Road, Manchester M13 9RD (Anthony Hodges; tel. 0161–273 6283; fax 0161–273 7611) **Mcm**

MAYNOOTH. The Library, St Patrick's College, Maynooth, County Kildare, Ireland (Regina Whelan Richardson; tel. +353–1–708–3882) **EIR:Metc**

MIDDLESBROUGH. Cleveland County Libraries, Victoria Square, Central Reference Library, Middlesbrough, Cleveland TS1 2AY (L. Bruce; tel. 01642–263364; fax 01642–230690) **MI**
Cleveland County Libraries also operates the following branch library site:

Hartlepool Group Library, 124 York Road, Hartlepool TS26 9DE (tel. 01429–272905) **MI (h)**

MILTON KEYNES. The Open University Library, Walton Hall, Milton Keynes, Buckinghamshire MK7 6AA (Anthony J. Coulson; tel. 01908–274066; fax 01908–653744; e-mail OULibrary@open.ac.uk) **MK**

MILTON KEYNES see also **AYLESBURY. Buckinghamshire County Library**

MOLD. Clwyd Library and Information Service, Civic Centre, Mold, Clwyd CH7 6NW (Miss E. Jones; tel. 01352–702379; fax 01352–704744) **MO**

MORPETH. Northumberland County Council Amenities Division, The Willows, Morpeth, Northumberland NE61 1TA (L. C. Kelly; tel. 01670–512385; fax 01670–518012) **MP**

NATIONAL JAZZ FOUNDATION ARCHIVE see **LOUGHTON**

NEWCASTLE-UPON-TYNE. Newcastle-upon-Tyne City Libraries and Arts, Central Library, Princess Square, Newcastle-upon-Tyne NE99 1DX (Eileen Burt; tel. 0191–261 0691; fax. 0191–261 1435) **NTp**

NEWTOWNABBEY. University of Ulster at Jordanstown, Shore Road, Newtownabbey, County Antrim BT37 0QB, Northern Ireland (Anne-Marie Black; tel. 01232–365131; fax 01232–362819; e-mail adbj@uk.ac.ulster.upvax) **Uu**

NORTHAMPTON. Northamptonshire Libraries and Information Service, P. O. Box 259, 27 Guildhall Road, Northampton NN1 1BA (Jonathan Willmott; tel. 01604–20262; fax 01604–26789) **NHp**

NORWICH. University of East Anglia, University Plain, Norwich NR4 7TJ (tel. 01603–56161; fax 01603–259490) **NWu**

NOTTINGHAM. Central Library, Nottinghamshire County Libraries, Angel Row, Nottingham NG1 6HP (Christine Hallam; tel. 0115–947 3591; fax 0115–950 4207) **NOp**

NOTTINGHAM. The Music Library, University of Nottingham Arts Centre, University Park, Nottingham NG7 2RD (Andrew Russell; tel. 0115–951–5151, ext. 2089; fax 0115–951–4558; e-mail uazawr@uk.ac.nott.vme) **NO**

NOTTINGHAM. Library and Information Services, Nottingham Trent University, Dryden Street Library, Nottingham NG1 4FZ (Caroline Williams; tel. 01602–418418; fax 01602–484266) **NOTu**

OLDHAM. Oldham Central Library, Union Street, Oldham, Lancashire OL1 1DN (Richard Lambert; tel. 0161–678 4632) **OL**

OXFORD. The Bodleian Library Music Library, Broad Street, Oxford OX1 3BG (Peter Ward Jones; tel. 01865–277063) **Ob.** The Bodleian Library also holds several Chinese musical titles in its Institute for Chinese Studies Library, Walton Street, Oxford OX1 2HG (Tony Hyder; tel. 01865–280430; fax 01865–280431). Items held by the Institute are indicated by the siglum **Ob (ICS)**

OXFORD. Oxford Brookes University Library, Gipsy Lane Campus, Headington, Oxford OX3 0BP (Ann Edmunds; tel. 01865–483133; fax 01865–483998) **Oub**
The university also has a campus at Wheatley, listed here at **Oub (w)**

OXFORD. Oxford Central Music Library, The Westgate, Oxford OX1 1DJ (Patricia Tipler; tel. 01865–815388) **Op**

OXFORD. Oxford University Music Faculty Library, St Aldate's, Oxford OX1 1DB (John Wagstaff; tel. 01865–276146; fax 01865–286260; e-mail john.wagstaff@music.ox.ac.uk) **Ouf**. Materials in the library's Frank Howes Collection of folk music materials are indicated by the siglum **Ouf (Howes)**

PENCOED *see* **BRIDGEND. Mid-Glamorgan County Libraries**

PERTH. A.K. Bell Library (formerly Sandeman Public Library), 2–8 York Place, Perth PH2 8EP, Scotland (E. Durkin; tel. 01738–444949) **P**

PETERSFIELD *see* **WINCHESTER. Hampshire County Library Service**

PONTYPRIDD *see* **BRIDGEND. Mid Glamorgan County Libraries**

PORTHCAWL *see* **BRIDGEND. Mid Glamorgan County Libraries**

PORTSMOUTH *see* **WINCHESTER. Hampshire County Library Service**

PRESTON. Lancashire County Library, County Library Headquarters, Corporation Street, Preston PR1 2UQ (Alison Thies; tel. 01772–264051; fax 01772–555919) **PRp**

PRINCES RISBOROUGH *see* **AYLESBURY. Buckinghamshire County Library**

READING. Berkshire County Music and Drama Library, Reading Central Library, Abbey Square, Reading, Berkshire RG1 3BQ (Mrs Chris Muncy; tel. 0118–950 9244; fax 0118–958 9039) **Rp**

READING. Bulmershe Library, University of Reading, Woodlands Avenue, Earley, Reading, Berkshire RG6 1HY (Barbara Morris; tel. 0118–931 8651; fax 0118–935 2080; e-mail vlsmorba@reading.ac.uk) **Re**

READING. The Music Library, University of Reading, 35 Upper Redlands Road, Reading, Berkshire RG1 5JE (Dr Margaret Laurie; tel. 0118–931 8413; fax 0118–931 4404) **R**

ROEHAMPTON INSTITUTE *see* **LONDON**

ROMSEY *see* **WINCHESTER. Hampshire County Library Service**

ROYAL SCHOOL OF CHURCH MUSIC *see* **LONDON. Royal School of Church Music**

SAINT ANDREWS. Saint Andrews University Library, North Street, Saint Andrews, Fife KY16 9TR, Scotland (Margot Gunn Munro; tel. 01334–462304) **SA**

ST AUSTELL. County Music and Drama Library, 2 Carlyon Road, St Austell, Cornwall PL25 4LD (Jonathan Lloyd Roberts; tel. 01726–61702) **SAu**

ST HELIER. Jersey Library, Halkett Place, St Helier, Jersey JE2 4WH, Channel Islands (Maureen Corrigan; tel. 01534–59991; fax 01534–69444) **Je**

ST PETER PORT. Guille-Allès Library, Market Street, St Peter Port, Guernsey GY1 1HB, Channel Islands (Sarah Fletcher; tel. 01481–720392; fax 01481–712425) **GU**

SALFORD. The Adelphi Library, University College Salford, Peru Street, Salford, Lancashire M3 6EQ (Alex Maclean; tel. 0161–834 6633, ext. 492; fax 0161–834 3327) **Msuc**

SALFORD. University of Salford Academic Information Services, Clifford Whitworth Building, Salford, Lancashire M5 4WJ (Lorna Cotman; tel. 0161–745 5000, ext. 3784; fax 0161–745 5888) **Msu**

SHEFFIELD. Central Music and Video Library, Sheffield Libraries and Information Services, Surrey Street, Sheffield S1 1XZ (Sarah Hogan; tel. 01142–734733; fax 01142–735009) **SFp**

SHEFFIELD. Music Library, University of Sheffield, 38 Taptonville Road, Sheffield S10 5BR (Tom McCanna; tel. 01142–667234; fax 01142–668053) **SFu**

SHREWSBURY. Shropshire Performing Arts Library, Column House, 7 London Road, Shrewsbury, Shropshire SY2 6NW (Mrs K. Woodward; tel. 01743–352602; fax 01743–253678) **SHRp**

SOLIHULL. Music Library, Central Library, Homer Road, Solihull, West Midlands B91 3RG (Anyon Nazir; tel. 0121–704–6983) SOL

SOUTHAMPTON. Southampton University Library, Hartley Library, Highfield, Southampton SO17 1BJ (tel. 01703–592180; fax 01703–593007) **SOu**

SOUTHAMPTON *see also* **WINCHESTER. Hampshire County Library Service**

STAFFORD. Stafford Library, Staffordshire Libraries, Arts and Archives Headquarters, The Green, Stafford ST17 4BJ (Andrew Baker; tel. 01785–278300) **STAp**

STIRLING. University of Stirling Information Services, Stirling FK9 4LA, Scotland (Karen King; tel. 01786–467218; fax 01786–466866) **SLGu**

STOCKPORT. Stockport Central Library, Wellington Road South, Stockport SK1 3RS (Lynne Ranson; tel. 0161–474 4540; fax 0161–474 7750) **SK**

TOTNES. Dartington College of Arts, Totnes, Devon TQ9 6EJ (Rosemary Burn; tel. 01803–862224; fax 01803–863569) **TOd**

TOTTON *see* **WINCHESTER. Hampshire County Library Service**

TREORCHY. Treorchy Library, Station Road, Treorchy, Rhondda, Mid Glamorgan CF42 6NN (Denise Price; tel. 01443–773204/773592; fax 01443–777047) **RH**

VENTNOR. Ventnor Library, High Street, Ventnor, Isle of Wight (Mike Lister; tel. 01983–852039) **IOW**

WAKEFIELD. Yorkshire Libraries Joint Music and Drama Collection, Wakefield Library Headquarters, Balne Lane, Wakefield WF2 0DQ (Stuart Waumsley; tel. 01924–302229; fax 01924–302245) **WF**

WARWICK. Warwickshire County Library Service, Barrack Street, Warwick CV34 4TH (Kathleen Collins; tel. 01926–412168; fax 01926–412471) **WW**

WATERLOOVILLE *see* **WINCHESTER. Hampshire County Library Service**

WINCHESTER. Hampshire County Library Service, County Music Library, County Library Headquarters, 81 North Walls, Winchester, Hampshire SO23 8BY (Mrs A. J. McGrave; tel. 01962–846097; fax 01962–856615) **WCp**
Hampshire County Library Service also operates the following branch library sites:

Aldershot Library, 109 High Street, Aldershot, Hampshire GU11 1DQ (tel. 01252–322456) **WCp (ald)**

Alton Library, Vicarage Hall, Alton, Hampshire GU34 1HT (tel. 01420–83147) **WCp (alt)**

Andover Library, Chantry Centre, Andover, Hampshire SP10 1LT (tel. 01264–352807; fax 01264–365939) **WCp (a)**

Basingstoke Library, 19/20 Westminster House, Potters Walk, Basingstoke, Hampshire RG21 7LS (tel. 01256–63793; fax 01256–470666) **WCp (b)**

Chandler's Ford Library, Oakmount Road, Chandler's Ford, Eastleigh, Hampshire SO53 2LH (tel. 01703–267398; fax 01703–251327) **WCp (cf)**

Eastleigh Library, Swan Centre, Eastleigh, Hampshire SO50 8SF (tel. 01703–612513) **WCp (e)**

Farnborough Library, Pinehurst Avenue, Farnborough, Surrey GU14 7JZ (tel. 01252–513838) **WCp (f)**

Fareham Library, County Library, Osborn Road, Fareham PO16 7EN (tel. 01329–221424; fax 01329–221551) **WCp (far)**

Fleet Library, 236 Fleet Road, Fleet GU13 8BX (tel. 01252–614213; fax 01252–627242) **WCp (fle)**

Gosport Library, High Street, Gosport, Hampshire PO12 1BT (tel. 01705–523431/2; fax 01705–501911) **WCp (g)**

Hythe Library, The Car Park, New Road, Hythe, Southampton SO45 6SP (tel. 01703–843574) **WCp (h)**

Hayling Island Library, Elm Grove, Hayling Island, Hampshire PO11 9EE (tel. 01705–463921)**WCp (hi)**

Lymington Library, County Library, The Old School, Cannon Street, Lymington, Hampshire SO41 9BR (tel. 01590–675767) **WCp (l)**

Leigh Park Library, 16 Greywell Road, Leigh Park, Hampshire PO9 5AL (tel. 01705–484519) **WCp (lp)**

Portsmouth Library, Central Library, Guildhall Square, Portsmouth, Hampshire PO1 2DX (tel. 01705–819311; fax 01705–839855) **WCp (p)**

Petersfield Library, 27 The Square, Petersfield, Hampshire GU32 3HH; tel. 01730–263451; fax 01730–264425) **WCp (pet)**

Romsey Library, Station Road, Romsey, Hampshire SO51 5DN (tel. 01794–513299) **WCp (r)**

Winchester Reference Library, 81 North Walls, Winchester, Hampshire SO23 8BY (tel. 01962–846059) **WCp (ref)**

Southampton Central Library, Civic Centre, Southampton SO14 7LW (tel. 01703–832460; fax 01703–336305) **WCp (s)**

Southampton East Library, Bitterne Road East, Southampton SO18 5EG (tel. 01703–449909)**WCp (se)**

Southampton (Lords Hill) Library, Lords Hill District Centre, Southampton SO16 8HY (tel. 01703–732845) **WCp (sl)**

Totton Library, Library Road, Totton, Hampshire SO40 3RS (tel. 01703–862203) **WCp (t)**

Waterlooville Library, County Library, The Precinct, Waterlooville, Hampshire PO7 7DT (tel. 01705–254626/7; fax 01705–232957) **WCp (w)**

Yateley Library, School Lane, Yateley, Hampshire GU17 7NL (tel. 01252–873883) **WCp (y)**

WINCHESTER REFERENCE LIBRARY *see* **WINCHESTER. Hampshire County Library Service**

WOLVERHAMPTON. Audio Visual Department, Wolverhampton Central Library, Snow Hill, Wolverhampton WV1 3AX (Anthony Stamp; tel. 01902–312025; fax 01902–714579) **WH**

WORCESTER. Hereford and Worcester County Library, City Library, Foregate Street, Worcester WV1 1DT (Richard Davies; tel. 01905–765310; fax 01905–726664) **WOp**

YATELEY *see* **WINCHESTER. Hampshire County Library Service**

YEOVIL. County Music and Drama Library, King George Street, Yeovil, Somerset BA20 1PY (Roger Taylor; tel. 01935–472020; fax 01935–431847) **Y**

YORK. The Music Section, The J. B. Morrell Library, University of York, Heslington, York YO1 5DD (Dr David Griffiths; tel. 01904–433867; fax 01904–433866; e-mail dg7@uk.ac.york.vaxa) **Yu**

List of Libraries Participating in *BUCOMP2*, Arranged by Sigla

The following list of library codes ("Sigla") is based on those used in the first edition of *BUCOMP*, which itself used the principles laid down by *RISM* – the *Répertoire International des Sources Musicales*. In addition, *BUCOMP1* used the suffixes **p** and **u**, in some cases, to distinguish Public and University libraries, while libraries in London were distinguished by an upper-case L, followed by lower-case letters. Unfortunately the sigla did not, in all cases, reflect the alphabetical ordering of the names of the towns and cities to which they belonged: **LV** designated Liverpool, for example, which by the rules of alphabetical logic should *follow*, not precede, London locations such as *Lbbc*. In order to make use of the *BUCOMP2* catalogue as straightforward as possible, entries, both in the following list and in the catalogue itself, are filed in alphabetical order, regardless of the use of upper- and lower-case letters within a particular siglum.

AB Llyfrgell Genedlaethol Cymru/National Library of Wales, Aberystwyth, Dyfed SY23 3BU (Tudor Henson; tel. 01970–623816; fax 01970–615709)

ABc Hugh Owen Library, University of Wales Aberystwyth, Penglais, Aberystwyth SY23 3DZ (Bob Prichard; tel. 01970–622391; fax 01970–622404). Holdings of the library of the College of Librarianship Wales are now held in the Information and Library Studies Library on the same premises; these are indicated by the siglum **ABc (ILS)**.

ABc (ILS) *see* **ABc**

ABDp Aberdare Central Library, Green Street, Aberdare, Mid Glamorgan CF44 7AG (Miss Alice Percival; tel. 01685–885318; fax 01685–881181)

ALb The Britten-Pears Library, The Red House, Aldeburgh, Suffolk IP15 5PZ (Dr Paul Banks; tel. 01728–452615; fax 01728–453076; e-mail bpl@uea.ac.uk)

Ap City of Aberdeen Central Library, Rosemount Viaduct, Aberdeen AB9 1GU (Alan R. Fulton; tel. 01224–634622, ext. 225/226)

AR Carnegie Library, 12 Main Street, Ayr, KA8 8ED, Scotland (Charles Deas; tel. 01292–286385; fax 01292–611593)

Au Aberdeen University Library, Queen Mother Library, Meston Walk, Aberdeen AB9 2UE (Richard Turbet; tel. 01224–272592)

BAc Bath Spa University College, Newton Park, Newton St Looe, Bath BA2 9BN (Marilyn Floyd; tel. 01225–875875; fax 01225–875505)

BAR Barnsley Central Library, Shambles Street, Barnsley, South Yorkshire S70 2JF (Wendy Mann; tel. 01226–733241; fax 01226–285458)

BDp Music Library, Bradford City Council Central Library, Prince's Way, Bradford BD1 1NN (tel. 01274–753654)

BEp Bedford Central Library, Harpur Street, Bedford MK40 1PG (Paul Andrews; tel. 01234–350931; fax 01234–342163)

BG University College of North Wales Bangor, Bangor, Gwynedd LL57 2DG (Elizabeth Bird; tel. 01248–382187; e-mail ISS063@uk.ac.bangor). Data includes the holdings of the Bangor Coleg Normal, which became part of the University College of North Wales in 1996: at the university library's request they have not been assigned a separate siglum.

BLBBC British Broadcasting Corporation Music Library, BBC Broadcasting House, Ormeau Avenue, Belfast BT2 8HQ, Northern Ireland (Ruth Gregory; tel. 01232–338295; fax 01232–338807)

BLp Belfast Music Library, Belfast Central Library, Royal Avenue, Belfast BT1 1EA, Northern Ireland (Felicity Jones; tel. 01232–243233; fax 01232–332819)

BLu Queen's University of Belfast, University Square, Belfast BT7 1LS, Northern Ireland (Stuart Rawson; tel. 01232–245133; fax 01232–323340)

BOL Bolton Central Library, Civic Centre, Le Mans Crescent, Bolton, Lancashire BL1 1SE (Ms Val Byrne; tel. 01204–22311, ext. 2177)

Bp Music Services, Birmingham Central Library, Chamberlain Square, Birmingham B3 3HQ (Joy Stapleton/Jean Weston; tel. 0121–235–2448/2482; fax 0121–233–4458)

BRDp Mid Glamorgan County Libraries, Coed Parc, Park Street, Bridgend, Mid Glamorgan CF31 4BA (Elizabeth Roberts; tel. 01656–767451; fax 01656–645719)
Mid-Glamorgan Libraries also operate the following branch library sites:

Pencoed Library, Penybont Road, Pencoed CF35 5RA (tel. 01656–860358) **BRDp (pen)**

Pontypridd Central Library, Library Road, Pontypridd CF37 2DY (tel. 01443–486850) **BRDp (pon)**

Porthcawl Library, Porthcawl CF36 3AG (tel. 01656–782059) **BRDp (por)**

BRDp (pen) *see* **BRDp**

BRDp (pon) *see* **BRDp**

BRDp (por) *see* **BRDp**

BRp Bristol Music Library, Central [Public] Library, College Green, Bristol BS1 5TL (Christine Stephens; tel. 0117–922 6121, ext. 219; fax 0117–922 6775)

BRu Music Library, University of Bristol, Tyndall Avenue, Bristol BS8 1TJ (Peter King; tel. 0117–930 3030; fax 0117–925 5334)

Bs Birmingham Conservatoire Library, University of Central England, Paradise Place, Birmingham B3 3HG (tel. 0121–331 5914; e-mail music.library@uk.ac.university-central-england)

BSdsc Music Section, The British Library Document Supply Centre, Boston Spa, Wetherby, West Yorkshire LS23 7BQ (Frank Wray; tel. 01937–546168)

BTp Brighton Music Library, East Sussex County Library Service, 115 Church Street, Brighton, East Sussex BN1 1UD (Jane M. Cox; tel. 01273–674841)

BTu University of Sussex Library, Falmer, Brighton, East Sussex BN1 9QL (Cherry Horwill; tel. 01273–606755; fax 01273–678441; e-mail library@uk.ac.sussex.central)

Bu Barber Music and Fine Art Library, The University of Birmingham, Edgbaston, Birmingham B15 2TT (Ian Ledsham; tel. 0121–414–5851; fax 0121–414 5853)

Bu-AME *see* **BU-AYp**

Bu-AYp Buckinghamshire County Library, County Library Headquarters, Walton Street, Aylesbury, Buckinghamshire HP20 1UU (Margaret Roll; tel. 01296–383206; fax 01296–382405)
Buckinghamshire County Libraries also operates the following branch library sites:

Amersham Library, Chiltern Avenue, Amersham, Buckinghamshire HP6 5AG (tel. 01494–724691) **Bu-AME**

Bletchley Library, Westfield Road, Bletchley, Buckinghamshire MK2 2RA (tel. 01908–372797) **Bu-BLE**

Buckingham Library, Verney Close, Buckingham, Buckinghamshire MK18 1JP (tel. 01280–813229) **Bu-BUC**

Chesham Library, Elgiva Lane, Chesham, Buckinghamshire HP5 2JB (tel. 01494–772322) **Bu-CHE**

High Wycombe Library, Queen Victoria Road, High Wycombe, Buckinghamshire HP11 1BD (tel. 01494–464004) **Bu-HW**

Milton Keynes Library, 555 Silbury Boulevard, Saxon Gate East, Milton Keynes MK9 3HL (tel. 01908–835010) **Bu-MK**

Princes Risborough Library, Bell Street, Princes Risborough, Buckinghamshire HP17 9AA (tel. 01844–343559) **Bu-PR**

Bu-BLE *see* **BU-AYp**

Bu-BUC *see* **Bu-AYp**

Bu-CHE *see* **Bu-AYp**

Bu-HW *see* **Bu-AYp**

Bu-MK *see* **Bu-AYp**

Bu-PR *see* **Bu-AYp**

BYp Reference Library, Central Library, Manchester Road, Bury, Lancashire BL9 0DG (Ms Pat Banks; tcl. 0161–705–5871; fax 0161–705–5915)

Cap Libraries and Information Service, Cambridgeshire County Council, 7 Lion Yard, Cambridge CB2 3QD (James Yardley; tel. 01223–65252, ext. 210; fax 01223–62786)

CAR Dyfed County Library, St Peters Street, Carmarthen SA31 1LN (Dewi Thomas; tel. 01267–233333)

Cat Anglia Polytechnic University Library, East Road, Cambridge CB1 7PT (Sian Davies/ Christine Moore; tel. 01223–63271, ext. 2372; fax 01223–352973) **Cat**
The University also has a site at Brentford **Cat (b)**

Cat (b) *see* **Cat**

CAu The Templeman Library, University of Kent at Canterbury, Canterbury, Kent CT2 7NU (Brian Hogben; tel. 01227–764000; fax 01227–475495)

Cbijs British Institute of Jazz Studies, 17 The Chase, Crowthorne, Berkshire RG11 6HT (Graham Langley; tel. 01344–775669)

CCtc Colchester Institute Library, Sheepen Road, Colchester, Essex CO3 3LL (Mary Pelowski; tel. 01206–718642)

CDCp Cardiff Central Music Library, St David's Link, Frederick Street, Cardiff CF1 4DT (Sheila Basford; tel. 01222–382116, ext. 1625; fax 01222–238642)

CDu University of Wales, Cardiff, P.O. Box 78, Cardiff CF1 1XL (Gillian Jones; tel. 01222–874000)

CFp Essex County Council County Music Collection, Colchester Library, Trinity Square, Colchester CO1 1JB (Viv Kuphal; tel. 01206–562243; fax 01206–562413)

CH Chesterfield Central Library, New Beetwell Street, Chesterfield , Derbyshire S40 1QN (D. Bennell; tel. 01246–209292; fax 01246–209304)

CHEp Cheshire County Council Libraries, Arts and Archives, 91 Hoole Road, Chester, Cheshire CH2 3NG (tel. 01244–320055; fax 01244–313079)

CHL *see* **GLp**

COp City Library, City of Coventry Leisure Services, Smithford Way, Coventry CV1 1FY (Jane Black; tel. 01203–832331)

Cpl Pendlebury Library, University Music School, University of Cambridge, West Road, Cambridge CB3 9DP (Andrew Bennett; tel. 01223–335183; fax 01223–335067; e-mail ab164@cus.cam.ac.uk)

Cu Cambridge University Library, West Road, Cambridge CB3 9DR (Richard Andrewes; tel. 01223–333072; fax 01223–333160; e-mail rma@ula.cam.ac.uk)

CW Gwent Libraries, County Library Headquarters, County Hall, Cwmbran, Gwent NP44 2XL (Sue Johnson; tel. 01633–832171; fax 01633–832129)

DDp Dudley Library, St James Road, Dudley, West Midlands DY1 1HR (Stuart Wilson; tel. 01384–453556)

DOR Surrey Performing Arts Library, Vaughan Williams House, West Street, Dorking, Surrey RH4 1BY (Andrew Woods; tel. 01306–887509/744743; fax 01306–875074)

DRp Durham County Council Arts, Libraries and Museums Department, County Hall, Durham DG1 5TY (Alan Hood; tel. 0191–386 4411; fax 0191–384 1336)

DRu Durham University Library, Palace Green, Durham DH1 3RN (Roger Norris; tel. 0191–374 3003)

DS Bournemouth Music Library, Meyrick Road, Lansdowne, Bournemouth, Dorset BH1 3DJ (C. Butterworth; tel. 01202–553781; fax 01202–291781)

DU Dundee District Libraries, Central Library, The Wellgate, Dundee DD1 6TB (tel. 01382–434326; fax 01382–434036)

Ea Eastbourne Music Library, Grove Road, Eastbourne, East Sussex BN21 4TL (Pauline Kennard; tel. 01323–739119)

EG Elgin Library, Cooper Park, Elgin, Moray, I30 1HS, Scotland (Graham McDermid; tel. 01343–542746; fax 01343–549050)

EIR:Dcmc The Contemporary Music Centre, 92 Lower Baggot Street, Dublin 2, Ireland (Eve O'Kelly; tel. +353–1–661–2105; fax +353–1–676–2639)

EIR:Dp Dublin Public Libraries, Music Library, ILAC Centre, Henry Street, Dublin 2, Ireland (V. Kilboy; tel. +353–1–873–4333)

EIR:DRiam The Royal Irish Academy of Music, 36 38 Westland Row, Dublin 2, Ireland (Philip Shields; tel. +353–1–676 4412)

EIR:Dtc Music Section, Trinity College Library, College Street, Dublin 2, Ireland (Roy Stanley; tel. +353–1–677–2941; fax +353–1–671–9003)

EIR:Duc Music Section, The Main Library, University College Dublin, Belfield, Dublin 4, Ireland (Claire Moran; tel. +353–1–706–7777; fax +353–1–283–7667; e-mail library@irlearn.ucd.ie)

EIR:Metc The Library, St Patrick's College, Maynooth, County Kildare, Ireland (Regina Whelan Richardson; tel. +353–1–708–3882)

EK The Central Library, The Olympia, East Kilbride G74 1PG, Scotland (Christopher Lorimer; tel. 013552–20046; fax 013552–29365)

En The Music Library, The National Library of Scotland, George IV Bridge, Edinburgh EH1 1EW (Roger Duce; tel. 0131–226 4531; fax 0131–220 6662)

Ep The Music Library, Edinburgh City Libraries, George IV Bridge, Edinburgh EH1 1EG (Peter Baxter; tel. 0131–225 5584; fax 0131–225 8783)

Er The Reid Music Library, Edinburgh University, Alison House, 12 Nicolson Square, Edinburgh EH8 9DF (Jeremy Upton; tel. 0131–650–2436; fax 0131–650–2425; e-mail j.upton@ed.ac.uk)

EXu University of Exeter Library, Stocker Road, Exeter, Devon EX4 4PT (Julie Crawley; tel. 01392–263860; fax 01392–263871; e-mail j.a.crawley@exeter.ac.uk)

Gam The Royal Scottish Academy of Music and Drama, 100 Renfrew Street, Glasgow G2 3DB (Kenneth Wilkins; tel. 0141–332 4101; fax 0141–332 8901)

GLp Gloucestershire County Library, Music and Drama Library, Quayside Wing, Gloucester GL1 2HY (Linda Marsden; tel. 01452–426983; fax 01452–426982)
Gloucestershire County Libraries also operate the following branch library site:

Cheltenham Library, Clarence Street, Cheltenham, Gloucestershire GL50 3JT (tel. 01242–522476; fax 01242–510373) **CHL**

Gm The Mitchell Library, Arts Department, North Street, Glasgow G3 7DN (Karen Cunningham/Jennifer Larmour; tel. 0141–305 2934; fax 0141–305 2815)

Gsmic Scottish Music Information Centre, 1 Bowmont Gardens, Glasgow GL2 9LR (Sheila Craik; tel. 0141–334 6393; fax 0141–337 1161)

GU Guille–Allès Library, Market Street, St Peter Port, Guernsey GY1 1HB, Channel Islands (Sarah Fletcher; tel. 01481–720392; fax 01481–712425)

Gul Glasgow University Library, Hillhead Street, Glasgow G12 8QE (Stella Money; tel. 0141–339 8855; fax 0141–330 4592). Material in the library's Euing Collection is listed under the siglum **Gul (e)**

HA The Music Library, Hastings Library, 13 Claremont, Hastings, East Sussex TN34 1HE (Jane Campbell; tel. 01424–420501; fax 01424–430261)

HE Hertfordshire Libraries, Arts and Information Central Resources Library, New Barnfield, Travellers Lane, Hatfield, Hertfordshire AL10 8XG (Philip Robinson; tel. 01707–281530; fax 01707–281514)

HOp Horsham Library, Lower Tanbridge Way, Horsham, West Sussex RH12 1RJ (Jackie Usher; tel. 01403–217013; fax 01403–211972)

HUu Brynmor Jones Library, University of Hull, Cottingham Road, Hull, North Humberside HU6 7RX (tel. 01482–466311; fax 01482–466205)

IOW Ventnor Library, High Street, Ventnor, Isle of Wight (Mike Lister; tel. 01983–852039)

IP County Reference Library, Northgate Street, Ipswich, Suffolk IP1 3DE (tel. 01473–264556; fax 01473–225491)

Je Jersey Library, Halkett Place, St Helier, Jersey JE2 4WH, Channel Islands (Maureen Corrigan; tel. 01534–59991; fax 01534–69444)

KC Kirkcaldy District Libraries, East Fergus Place, Kirkcaldy, Fife KY1 1XF, Scotland (J. Klak; tel. 01592–268386; fax 01592–643399)

KE Keele University Library, Keele, Staffordshire ST5 5BG (Margaret Greive; tel. 01782–583232; fax 01782–711553; e-mail library@keele.ac.uk)

Lam The Library, The Royal Academy of Music, Marylebone Road, London NW1 5HT (John Webb/Katharine Hogg; tel. 0171–935 5461; fax 0171–873 7374). The Royal Academy Library also holds the collection of the Organ Club, listed here at **Lam (o)**

Lam (o) *see* **Lam**

LAu Lancaster University Library, Bailrigg, Lancaster LA1 4YH (tel. 01524–65201; fax 01524–63806)

Lba Hendon Library, Barnet Libraries, Arts and Museums, The Burroughs, London NW4 4BQ (Liz Hart; tel. 0181–202 5625; fax 0181–203 4782)

Lbar The Barbican Library, Barbican Centre, London EC2Y 8DS (Robert Tucker; tel. 0171–638 0672; fax 0171–638 2249)

Lbbc British Broadcasting Corporation. British Broadcasting Corporation Music Library, Broadcasting House, Portland Place, London W1A 1AA (Rachel Ladyman; tel. 0171–765 3724; fax 0171–765 5304). The BBC response includes holdings of the former BBC West London Music Library.

Lbk Barking Central Library, Axe Street, Barking, Essex IG11 7NB (C. J. Clare; tel. 0181–517 8666)

Lbl The British Library Music Library, 96 Euston Road, London NW1 2DB (Malcolm Turner; tel. 0171–412 7529; fax 0171–412 7751).

Lbo Music and Audio Library, London Borough of Bromley, High Street, Bromley, Kent BR1 1EX (David Cook; tel. 0181–460–9955, ext. 266; fax 0181–313–0475)

Lbx Central Reference Library, London Borough of Bexley, Townley Road, Bexleyheath, Kent DA6 7HJ (Pamela Rew; tel. 0181–301 5151; fax 0181–303 7872)

LCdM The Library, De Montfort University, Scraptoft, Leicester LE7 9SU (Sally Luxton; tel. 01162–551551; fax 01162–577866)

Lcf *see* **Lgu**

Lcm The Library, The Royal College of Music, Prince Consort Road, London SW7 2BS (Christopher Bornet; tel. 0171–589 3643; fax 0171–589 7740). The Royal College of Music Library also holds music periodicals in its Museum of Instruments, listed here at **Lcm (m)**, and compiled by Richard Gowman; and in its Department of Portraits, listed here at **Lcm (p)**, and compiled by Paul Collen.

Lcm (m) *see* **Lcm**

Lcm (p) *see* **Lcm**

Lcml City of Westminster Music Library, 160 Buckingham Palace Road, London SW1W 9UD (tel. 0171–798 2192)
Westminster City Council also operates the following branch libraries:

Charing Cross Library, 4 Charing Cross Road, London WC2H 0HG (tel. 0171–798 2056) **Lcml (c)**

Church Street Library, Church Street, London NW8 8EU (tel. 0171–798 1480) **Lcml (ch)**

Churchill Gardens Library, 131 Lupus Street, London SW1V 3NE (tel. 0171–798 2196) **Lcml (cg)**

Great Smith Street Library, 30 Great Smith Street, London SW1P 3DG (tel. 0171–798 2989) **Lcml (g)**

Maida Vale Library, Sutherland Avenue, London W9 2QT (tel. 0171–798 3659) **Lcml (mv)**

Marylebone Library Music Library, Marylebone Road, London NW1 5PS (tel. 0171–798 1038) **Lcml (m)**

Paddington Library Music Library, Porchester Road, London W2 5DU (tel. 0171–798 3696) **Lcml (p)**

Pimlico Library, Rampayne Street, London SW1V 2PU (tel. 0171–798 2983) **Lcml (pim)**

Queen's Park Library, 666 Harrow Road, London W10 4NE (tel. 0171–798 3575) **Lcml (q)**

St John's Wood Library, 20 Circus Road, London NW8 6PD (tel. 0171–798 1487) **Lcml (sjw)**

 Westminster Reference Library, 35 St Martin's Street, London WC2H 7HP (tel. 0171–798 2036) **Lcml (r)**

Lcml (c) *see* **Lcml**

Lcml (cg) *see* **Lcml**

Lcml (g) *see* **Lcml**

Lcml (m) *see* **Lcml**

Lcml (mv) *see* **Lcml**

Lcml (p) *see* **Lcml**

Lcml (pim) *see* **Lcml**

Lcml (q) *see* **Lcml**

Lcml (r) *see* **Lcml**

Lcml (sjw) *see* **Lcml**

Lcs The English Folk Dance and Song Society Library (Vaughan Williams Memorial Library), Cecil Sharp House, 2 Regent's Park Road, London NW1 7AY (Debra Godrich/Malcolm Taylor; tel. 0171–485 2206; fax 0171–284 0523)

Lcu The City University Library, Northampton Square, London EC1V 0HB (Pamela Lighthill; tel. 0171–477 8000, ext. 4007; fax 0171–490 4419)

LEbc The Brotherton Library, University of Leeds, Woodhouse Lane, Leeds LS2 9JT (Kate Alderson-Smith; tel. 0113–233 5510; fax 0113–233 5561)

LEc The Central Library, Town Hall, The Headrow, Leeds LS1 3AB (Helen O'Neill; tel. 0113–247 8330; fax 0113–247 7747)

Len Audio Visual Services, London Borough of Enfield, Town Hall, Green Lanes, London N13 4XD (Ruth Hellen; tel. 0181–967 9370; fax 0181–982 7378)

Lgo Goldsmiths College, University of London, Lewisham Way, London SE14 6NW (Peter Morris; tel. 0181–692 7171, ext. 2261; fax 0181–692 9190; e-mail library@uk.ac. goldsmiths.scorpio)

Lgr London Borough of Greenwich Support Services, Plumstead Library, Plumstead High Street, London SE18 1JL (Martin Stone; tel. 0181–317 4466; fax 0181–317 4868)

Lgsm Guildhall School of Music and Drama, The Barbican, London EC2Y 8DT (Adrian Yardley; tel. 0171–628–2571; fax 0171–256–9438)

Lgu London Guildhall University, 41 Commercial Road, London E1 1LA (tel. 0171–320 1867; fax 0171–320 1830). Part of this collection was formerly located in the London College of Furniture Library, listed in BUCOMP1 as **Lcf**.

Lh London Borough of Hackney, Hackney Central Library, Mare Street, London E8 1HG (Don Badenoch; tel. 0181–985 8262; fax 0181–533 3712)

Lha Hammersmith and Fulham Central Library, Shepherd's Bush Road, London W6 7AT (E. Stephens; tel. 0181–576 5055; fax 0181–576 5022)
Hammersmith and Fulham Library Service also operates the following branch library:

Fulham Library, 598 Fulham Road, London SW6 5NX (tel. 0181–576 5253) **Lha (f)**

Lha (f) *see* **Lha**

Lhey Heythrop College Library, Kensington Square, London W8 5HQ (Sr. Rowley; tel. 0171–795 4250; fax 0171–795 4253)

Lhg Haringey Central Library, High Road, Wood Green, London N22 6XD (Robert Missen; tel. 0181–888 1292)

Lhr Harrow Music Library, Gayton Library, Gayton Road, Harrow, Middlesex HA1 2HL (J. Roche; tel. 0181–427 8986/6012)

Lie Institute of Education, University of London, 20 Bedford Way, London WC1H 0AL (Judy Allsopp; tel. 0171–580 1122; fax 0171–612 6126)

Lio The British Library Oriental and India Office, Orbit House, 197 Blackfriars Road, London SE1 8NG (Hedley Sutton; tel. 0171–412 7873; fax 0171–412 7858)

LIp The Music and Drama Library, Lincolnshire County Council Recreational Services Department, Brayford House, Lucy Tower Street, Lincoln LN1 1XN (A. Helen Mason; tel. 01522–552866; fax 01522–552858)

Lis Islington Central Library, 2 Fieldway Crescent, London N5 1PF (Chris Millington; tel. 0171–609 3051; fax 0171–607 6409)

Lk Central Library, The Royal Borough of Kensington and Chelsea, Phillimore Walk, London W8 7RX (tel. 0171–937 2542; fax 0171–937 0515)
Kensington and Chelsea Library Service also operates the following branch libraries:

Brompton Library, 210 Old Brompton Road, London SW5 0BS (tel. 0171–373 3111) **Lk (b)**

Chelsea Library, King's Road, London SW3 5EZ (tel. 0171–352 6056) **Lk (c)**

North Kensington Library, 108 Ladbroke Grove, London W11 1PZ (tel. 0171–727 6583) **Lk (nk)**

Lk (b) *see* **Lk**

Lk (c) *see* **Lk**

Lk (nk) *see* **Lk**

Lkc King's College, University of London, The Strand, London WC2R 2LS (Evelyn Cornell; tel. 0171–873 2139; fax 0171–872 0207)

Lki Kingston University Library, Kingston Hill, Kingston-upon-Thames, Surrey KT2 7LB (tel. 0181–547 2000; fax 0181–547 7312)

Ll London Borough of Lambeth Public Library and Archives Service, Directorate of Environmental Services, 8th Floor, International House, Canterbury Crescent, London SW9 7QE (David Strong; tel. 0171–926 9324; fax 0171–926 9333/0171–926 9467)

Lmi Middlesex University Library, Trent Park, Bramley Road, London N14 4XS (John Collis; tel. 0181–362 5000; fax 0181–441 4672)

Lmic The British Music Information Centre, 10 Stratford Place, London W1N 9AE (Tom Morgan; tel. 0171–499 8567; fax 0171–499 4795)

LOnjfa The National Jazz Foundation Archive, Loughton Library, Loughton, Essex IG10 1HD (Ken Jones; tel. 0181–502 0181; fax 0181–508 5041)

Lp The Polish Library, 238–246 King Street, London W6 0RF (Dr Z. Jagodzinski; tel. 0171–741–0474)

Lrco The Royal College of Organists, 7 St Andrew Street, Holborn, London EC4A 3LQ (Robin Langley; tel. 0171–936 3606; fax 0171–353 8244)

LRHBNC Royal Holloway and Bedford New College, University of London, Egham Hill, Egham, Surrey TW20 0EX (tel. 01784–434455; fax 01784–437520)

Lri London Borough of Richmond-upon-Thames, Bibliographical and Computer Services, The Cottage, Little Green, Richmond, Surrey TW9 1QL (tel. 0181–940 0031; fax 0181–940 7568)

Lro Roehampton Institute of Higher Education, Southlands College Library, Wimbledon Parkside, London SW19 5NN (Lisa Bryden; tel. 0181–392 3454; fax 0181–392 3459)

Lrscm The Royal School of Church Music, formerly at Addington Palace, Croydon, Surrey CR9 5AD; moved to Dorking in 1997/98. See entry under DORKING in town/city list above.

Ls School of Slavonic and East European Studies Library, University of London, Senate House, Malet Street, London WC1E 7HU (J. E. Screen; tel. 0171–637 4934, ext. 4094; fax 0171–436 8916; e-mail ssees-library@uk.ac.ukcc.clus1)

Lsa The British Library National Sound Archive, 29 Exhibition Road, London SW7 2AS (Jane Harvell; tel. 0171–412 7430; fax 0171–412 7416) (to November 1997; after this date the collection is housed at the new British Library building at St Pancras; see **Lbl** above).

Lso School of Oriental and African Studies, University of London, Serials Office, Thornhaugh Street, Russell Square, London WC1H 0XG (Michael Williams; tel. 0171–637 2388, ext. 2302; fax 0171–426 3844)

Lsut Music and Arts Department, Sutton Library, The London Borough of Sutton, St Nicholas Way, Sutton, Surrey SM1 1EA (Patrick Ford; tel. 0181–770 4765; fax 0181–770 4777)

LT The Music Library, Lewes Library, 47 St Anne's Crescent, Lewes, East Sussex BN7 1SD (Sara Sage; tel. 01273–481537)

Ltc Trinity College of Music, Academic Studies Centre, 10–11 Bulstrode Place, London W1M 5FW (Kate Sloss; tel. 0171–935 5773; fax 0171–486 6018)

Lth London Borough of Tower Hamlets, Whitechapel Music and Art Library, 77 Whitechapel High Street, London E1 7QX (Angela Haynes; tel. 0181–247 5272)

Ltv Thames Valley University Learning Resource Centre, Walpole House, 18–22 Bond Street, London W5 5AA (Colin Steele; tel. 0181–231 2648; fax 0181–231 2631; e-mail steele-c@uk.ac.tvu.s)

Lu Music Library, University of London Library, Senate House, Malet Street, London WC1E 7HU (Ruth Darton; tel. 0171–636 8000, ext. 5038; fax 0171–436 1494). London University Library also holds the library of the Royal Musical Association, listed here at **Lu (RMA)**

Lu (RMA) *see* **Lu**

LVp The Music Library, Liverpool City Libraries, Central Library, William Brown Street, Liverpool L3 8EW (Kit Siddons-Smith; tel. 0151–225 5463; fax 0151–207 1342)

LVu The University Library, University of Liverpool, P.O. Box 123, Liverpool L69 3DA (D. Cartmill; tel. 0151–794 2682; fax 0151–794 2681; e-mail qlis17@uk.ac.liverpool)

Lwf London Borough of Waltham Forest, Central Library, High Street, Walthamstow, London E17 7JN (Barbara Humm; tel. 0181–520 4733)

Lww Wandsworth Public Libraries, Balham Music Library, Ramsden Road, London SW12 8QY (Frank Daniels; tel. 0181–871 7195; fax 0181–675 4015)
Wandsworth Libraries also operate the following branch libraries:

Balham Public Library, Ramsden Road, London SW12 8QY (tel. 0181–871 7195) **Lwwb**

Battersea Public Library, Lavender Hill, London SW11 1JB (tel. 0181–871 7466) **Lwwbat**

Putney Public Library, Disraeli Road, London SW15 2DR (tel. 0181–871 7090) **Lwwput**

Lwwb *see* **Lww**

Lwwbat *see* **Lww**

Lwwput *see* **Lww**

LXp Luton Central Library, St George's Square, Luton, Bedfordshire LU1 2NG (Malcolm Thatcher; tel. 01582–30161; fax 01582–24638)

Mcm The Royal Northern College of Music, 124 Oxford Road, Manchester M13 9RD (Anthony Hodges; tel. 0161–273 6283; fax 0161–273 7611)

MI Cleveland County Libraries, Victoria Square, Central Reference Library, Middlesbrough, Cleveland TS1 2AY (L. Bruce; tel. 01642–263364; fax 01642–230690)
Cleveland County Libraries also operates the following branch library site:

Hartlepool Group Library, 124 York Road, Hartlepool TS26 9DE (tel. 01429–272905) **MI (h)**

MI (h) *see* **MI**

MK The Open University Library, Walton Hall, Milton Keynes, Buckinghamshire MK7 6AA (Anthony J. Coulson; tel. 01908–274066; fax 01908–653744; e-mail OULibrary@open.ac.uk)

Mmu Manchester Metropolitan University, All Saints Library, Oxford Road, Manchester M15 6BH (tel. 0161–247 6104)

Mmu (a) Manchester Metropolitan University, Alsager Site Library, Hassall Road, Alsager, Stoke-on-Trent ST7 2H (tel. 0161–247–5356)

Mmu (d) Manchester Metropolitan University, Didsbury Site Library, 799 Wilmslow Road, Manchester M20 2RR (tel. 0161–247–6121)

MO Clwyd Library and Information Service, Civic Centre, Mold, Clwyd CH7 6NW (Miss E. Jones; tel. 01352–702379; fax 01352–704744)

MP Northumberland County Council Amenities Division, The Willows, Morpeth, Northumberland NE61 1TA (L. C. Kelly; tel. 01670–512385; fax 01670–518012)

Mpl The Henry Watson Music Library, Central Library, St Peter's Square, Manchester M2 5PD (M. Keeley; tel. 0161–234 1976; fax 0161–234 1963)

Msu University of Salford Academic Information Services, Clifford Whitworth Building, Salford, Lancashire M5 4WJ (Lorna Cotman; tel. 0161–745 5000, ext. 3784; fax 0161–745 5888)

Msuc The Adelphi Library, University College Salford, Peru Street, Salford, Lancashire M3 6EQ (Alex Maclean; tel. 0161–834 6633, ext. 492; fax 0161–834 3327)

Mu The John Rylands University Library of Manchester, Oxford Road, Manchester M13 9PP (A. D. Walker/J. P. Tuck/Dr Rosemary Williamson; tel. 0161–275 3738; fax 0161–273 7488)

NHp Northamptonshire Libraries and Information Service, P. O. Box 259, 27 Guildhall Road, Northampton NN1 1BA (Jonathan Willmott; tel. 01604–20262; fax 01604–26789)

NO The Music Library, University of Nottingham, University Park, Nottingham NG7 2RD (Andrew Russell; tel. 0115–951–5151, ext. 2089; fax 0115–951–4558; e-mail uazawr@uk.ac.nott.vme)

NOp Central Library, Nottinghamshire County Libraries, Angel Row, Nottingham NG1 6HP (Christine Hallam; tel. 0115–947 3591; fax 0115–950 4207)

NOTu Library and Information Services, Nottingham Trent University, Dryden Street Library, Nottingham NG1 4FZ (Caroline Williams; tel. 01602–418418; fax 01602–484266)

NTp Newcastle-upon-Tyne City Libraries and Arts, Central Library, Princess Square, Newcastle-upon-Tyne NE99 1DX (Eileen Burt; tel. 0191–261 0691; fax. 0191–261 1435)

NWu University of East Anglia, University Plain, Norwich NR4 7TJ (tel. 01603–56161; fax 01603–259490)

Ob The Bodleian Library Music Library, Broad Street, Oxford OX1 3BG (Peter Ward Jones; tel. 01865–277063). The Bodleian Library also holds several Chinese musical titles in its Institute for Chinese Studies Library, Walton Street, Oxford OX1 2HG (Tony Hyder; tel. 01865–280430; fax 01865–280431). Items held by the Institute are indicated by the siglum **Ob (ICS)**

OL Oldham Central Library, Union Street, Oldham, Lancashire OL1 1DN (Richard Lambert; tel. 0161–678–4632)

Op Oxford Central Music Library, The Westgate, Oxford OX1 1DJ (Patricia Tipler; tel. 01865–815388)

Oub Oxford Brookes University Library, Gipsy Lane Campus, Headington, Oxford OX3 0BP (Ann Edmunds; tel. 01865–483133; fax 01865–483998)
The university also has a campus at Wheatley, listed here at **Oub (w)**

Oub (w) *see* **Oub**

Ouf Oxford University Music Faculty Library, St Aldate's, Oxford OX1 1DB (John Wagstaff; tel. 01865–276146; fax 01865–286260; e-mail john.wagstaff@music.ox.ac.uk). In addition to its main collection, the library also holds the Frank Howes Collection of folk song material, here indicated by **Ouf (Howes)**

P A.K. Bell Library (formerly Sandeman Public Library), 2–8 York Place, Perth PH2 8EP, Scotland (E. Durkin; tel. 01738–444949)

PRp Lancashire County Library, County Library Headquarters, Corporation Street, Preston PR1 2UQ (Alison Thies; tel. 01772–264051; fax 01772–555919)

R The Music Library, University of Reading, 35 Upper Redlands Road, Reading, Berkshire RG1 5JE (Dr Margaret Laurie; tel. 0118–931 8413; fax 0118–931 4404)

Re Bulmershe Library, University of Reading, Woodlands Avenue, Earley, Reading, Berkshire RG6 1HY (Barbara Morris; tel. 0118–931 8651; fax 0118–935 2080; e-mail vlsmorba@reading.ac.uk)

RH Treorchy Library, Station Road, Treorchy, Rhondda, Mid Glamorgan CF42 6NN (Denise Price; tel. 01443–773204/773592; fax 01443–777047)

Rp Berkshire County Music and Drama Library, Reading Central Library, Abbey Square, Reading, Berkshire RG1 3BQ (Mrs Chris Muncy; tel. 0118–950 9244; fax 0118–958 9039)

SA Saint Andrews University Library, North Street, Saint Andrews, Fife KY16 9TR, Scotland (Margot Gunn Munro; tel. 01334–462304)

SAu County Music and Drama Library, 2 Carlyon Road, St Austell, Cornwall PL25 4LD (Jonathan Lloyd Roberts; tel. 01726–61702)

SFp Central Music and Video Library, Sheffield Libraries and Information Services, Surrey Street, Sheffield S1 1XZ (Sarah Hogan; tel. 01142–734733; fax 01142–735009)

SFu Music Library, University of Sheffield, 38 Taptonville Road, Sheffield S10 5BR (Tom McCanna; tel. 01142–667234; fax 01142–668053)

SHRp Shropshire Performing Arts Library, Column House, 7 London Road, Shrewsbury, Shropshire SY2 6NW (Mrs K. Woodward; tel. 01743–352602; fax 01743–253678)

SK Stockport Central Library, Wellington Road South, Stockport SK1 3RS (Lynne Ranson; tel. 0161–474 4540; fax 0161–474 7750)

SLGu University of Stirling Information Services, Stirling FK9 4LA, Scotland (Karen King; tel. 01786–467218; fax 01786–466866)

SOL Music Library, Central Library, Homer Road, Solihull, West Midlands B91 3RG (Anyon Nazir; tel. 0121–704–6983)

SOu Southampton University Library, Hartley Library, Highfield, Southampton SO17 1BJ (tel. 01703–592180; fax 01703–593007)

STAp Stafford Library, Staffordshire Libraries, Arts and Archives Headquarters, The Green, Stafford ST17 4BJ (Andrew Baker; tel. 01785–278300)

TOd Dartington College of Arts, Totnes, Devon TQ9 6EJ (Rosemary Burn; tel. 01803–862224; fax 01803–863569)

Uu University of Ulster at Jordanstown, Shore Road, Newtownabbey, County Antrim BT37 0QB, Northern Ireland (Anne-Marie Black; tel. 01232–365131; fax 01232–362819; e-mail adbj@uk.ac.ulster.upvax)

WCp Hampshire County Library Service, County Music Library, County Library Headquarters, 81 North Walls, Winchester, Hampshire SO23 8BY (Mrs A. J. McGrave; tel. 01962–846097; fax 01962–856615)
Hampshire County Library Service also operates the following branch library sites:

Aldershot Library, 109 High Street, Aldershot, Hampshire GU11 1DQ (tel. 01252–322456) **WCp (ald)**

Alton Library, Vicarage Hall, Alton, Hampshire GU34 1HT (tel. 01420–83147; fax 01420–544109) **WCp (alt)**

Andover Library, Chantry Centre, Andover, Hampshire SP10 1LT (tel. 01264–352807; fax 01264–365939) **WCp (a)**

Basingstoke Library, 19/20 Westminster House, Potters Walk, Basingstoke, Hampshire RG21 7LS (tel. 01256–63793; fax 01256–470666) **WCp (b)**

Chandler's Ford Library, Oakmount Road, Chandler's Ford, Eastleigh, Hampshire SO53 2LH (tel. 01703–267398; fax 01703–251327) **WCp (cf)**

Eastleigh Library, Swan Centre, Eastleigh, Hampshire SO50 8SF (tel. 01703–612513) **WCp (e)**

Fareham Library, County Library, Osborn Road, Fareham PO16 7EN (tel. 01329–221424; fax 01329–221551) **WCp (far)**

Farnborough Library, Pinehurst Avenue, Farnborough, Surrey GU14 7JZ (tel. 01252–513838) **WCp (f)**

Fleet Library, 236 Fleet Road, Fleet GU13 8BX (tel. 01252–614213; fax 01252–627242) **WCp (fle)**

Gosport Library, High Street, Gosport, Hampshire PO12 1BT (tel. 01705–523431/2; fax 01705–501911) **WCp (g)**

Hayling Island Library, Elm Grove, Hayling Island, Hampshire PO11 9EE (tel. 01705–463921)**WCp (hi)**

Hythe Library, The Car Park, New Road, Hythe, Southampton SO45 6SP (tel. 01703–843574) **WCp (h)**

Leigh Park Library, 16 Greywell Road, Leigh Park, Hampshire PO9 5AL (tel. 01705–484519) **WCp (lp)**

Lymington Library, County Library, The Old School, Cannon Street, Lymington, Hampshire SO41 9BR (tel. 01590–675767) **WCp (l)**

Petersfield Library, 27 The Square, Petersfield, Hampshire GU32 3HH; tel. 01730–263451; fax 01730–264425) **WCp (pet)**

Portsmouth Library, Central Library, Guildhall Square, Portsmouth, Hampshire PO1 2DX (tel. 01705–819311; fax 01705–839855) **WCp (p)**

Romsey Library, Station Road, Romsey, Hampshire SO51 5DN (tel. 01794–513299) **WCp (r)**

Southampton Central Library, Civic Centre, Southampton SO14 7LW (tel. 01703–832460; fax 01703–336305) **WCp (s)**

Southampton East Library, Bitterne Road East, Southampton SO18 5EG (tel. 01703–449909)**WCp (se)**

Southampton (Lords Hill) Library, Lords Hill District Centre, Southampton SO16 8HY (tel. 01703–732845) **WCp (sl)**

Totton Library, Library Road, Totton, Hampshire SO40 3RS (tel. 01703–862203) **WCp (t)**

Waterlooville Library, County Library, The Precinct, Waterlooville, Hampshire PO7 7DT (tel. 01705–254626/7; fax 01705–232957) **WCp (w)**

Winchester Reference Library, 81 North Walls, Winchester, Hampshire SO23 8BY (tel. 01962–846059) **WCp (ref)**

Yateley Library, School Lane, Yateley, Hampshire GU17 7NL (tel. 01252–873883) **WCp (y)**

WCp (a) *see* **WCp**

WCp (ald) *see* **WCp**

WCp (alt) *see* **WCp**

WCp (b) *see* **WCp**

WCp (cf) *see* **WCp**

WCp (e) *see* **WCp**

WCp (f) *see* **WCp**

WCp (far) *see* **WCp**

WCp (fle) *see* **WCp**

WCp (g) *see* **WCp**

WCp (h) *see* **WCp**

WCp (hi) *see* **WCp**

WCp (l) *see* **WCp**

WCp (lp) *see* **WCp**

WCp (p) *see* **WCp**

WCp (pet) *see* **WCp**

WCp (r) *see* **WCp**

WCp (ref) *see* **WCp**

WCp (s) *see* **WCp**

WCp (se) *see* **WCp**

WCp (sl) *see* **WCp**

WCp (t) *see* **WCp**

WCp (w) *see* **WCp**

WCp (y) *see* **WCp**

WF Yorkshire Libraries Joint Music and Drama Collection, Wakefield Library Headquarters, Balne Lane, Wakefield WF2 0DQ (Stuart Waumsley; tel. 01924–302229; fax 01924–302245)

WH Audio Visual Department, Wolverhampton Central Library, Snow Hill, Wolverhampton WV1 3AX (Anthony Stamp; tel. 01902–312025; fax 01902–714579)

WOp Hereford and Worcester County Library, City Library, Foregate Street, Worcester WV1 1DT (Richard Davies; tel. 01905–765310; fax 01905–726664)

WW Warwickshire County Library Service, Barrack Street, Warwick CV34 4TH (Kathleen Collins; tel. 01926–412168; fax 01926–412471)

Y County Music and Drama Library, King George Street, Yeovil, Somerset BA20 1PY (Roger Taylor; tel. 01935–472020; fax 01935–431847)

Yu The Music Section, The J. B. Morrell Library, University of York, Heslington, York YO1 5DD (Dr David Griffiths; tel. 01904–433867; fax 01904–433866; e-mail dg7@uk.ac.york.vaxa)

3: The Radio Three Magazine
GB–London: IPC Magazines, 1982–84
[Succeeded by *Radio 3 Magazine*]

> **ALb** 2 (1983), 6
> **Bp** 1 (1982)–3 (1984)
> **CFp** 1 (1982)–3 (1984)
> **Cpl** 2 (1983), 2–3 (1984), 3
> **Ep** 1 (1982)–3 (1984)
> **Lam** 2 (1983), 9, 11; 3 (1984), 2–4
> **Lbar** 1 (1982)–3 (1984)
> **Lbbc** 1 (1982)–3 (1984), 4
> **Lbl** 1 (1982)–2 (1983), 9
> **Lsa** 1 (1982)–3 (1984), 4
> **Lu** 2 (1983), 6
> **Mcm** 1 (1982)–3 (1984)
> **Ob***

The 10 Years Flexi-Disc
GB–London: Palach Press, 1987–
[NOT IN BUCOMP1]

> **Ob** 1 (1987)–

19th Century Music
TNG US878; 0148–2076
US–Berkeley, CA: University of California,
1977–

> **Au** 1 (1977/78)–13 (1990/91)
> **BAc** 4 (1980/81)–#
> **BDp** 1 (1977/78)–5 (1981/82)
> **BG** 1 (1977/78)–#
> **BLp** 1 (1977/78)–#
> **BLu** 1 (1977/78)–#
> **Bs** 1 (1977/78)–#*
> **BSdsc** 1 (1977/78)–#
> **BTu** 1 (1977/78)–#
> **Bu** 1 (1977/78)–#
> **CAu** 1 (1977/78)–7 (1983/84), 2;
>   8 (1984/85)–9 (1985/86), 2
> **CCtc** 1 (1977/78)–#
> **CDu** 1 (1977/78)–#
> **Cu** 1 (1977/78)–#
> **DRu** 1 (1977/78)–#
> **EIR:Dp** 6 (1982/83), 3–#*
> **EIR:Dtc** 1 (1977/78)–#
> **EIR:Duc** 1 (1977/78)–#
> **En** 1 (1977/78)–#
> **Er** 1 (1977/78)–#
> **EXu** 1 (1977/78)–#
> **Gam** 1 (1977/78)–# [w 13 (1989), 3]
> **Gul** 1 (1977/78)–#
> **HUu** 2 (1978/79)–#
> **KE** 1 (1977/78)–#
> **Lam** 16 (1992/93), 3; 17 (1993/94)–#

> **LAu** 1 (1977/78)–#
> **Lbbc** 1 (1977/78)–9 (1985/86)
> **Lbl** 1 (1977/78)–#
> **Lcm** 1 (1977/78)–#
> **Lcml** 1 (1977/78)–#
> **Lcu** 16 (1992/93)–#
> **LEbc** 1 (1977/78)–#
> **LEc** 1 (1977/78)–#
> **Lgo** 1 (1977/78)–#
> **Lgsm** 4 (1980/81), 2–#
> **Lkc** 1 (1977/78)–#*
> **LRHBNC** 1 (1977/78)–#
> **Lro** 1 (1977/78)–#
> **Ltv** 1 (1977/78)–12 (1988/89);
>   14 (1990/91)–#
> **Lu** 1 (1977/78)–#
> **LVu** 1 (1977/78)–#
> **Mcm** 1 (1977/78)–#
> **MK** 3 (1979/80)–#
> **Mmu(a)** 4 (1980/81)–#
> **Mpl** 1 (1977/78)–#
> **Mu** 1 (1977/78)–# [w 7 (1983/84)]
> **NO** 1 (1977/78)–#
> **NWu** 1 (1977/78)–#
> **Ob** 1 (1977/78)–#
> **Oub** 18 (1994/95)–#
> **Ouf** 1 (1977/78)–#
> **R** 1 (1977/78)–#
> **SA** 1 (1977/78)–#
> **Sfu** 1 (1977/78)–#
> **SLGu** 7 (1983/84), 3; 8 (1984/85)–#
> **SOu** 1 (1977/78)–#
> **TOd** 3 (1979/80)–#
> **Uu** 1 (1977/78)–#
> **Yu** 5 (1981/82)–#

20th Century Music *see* **Twentieth Century Music**

23: ein Wiener Musikzeitschrift *see* **Drei-und-Zwanzig: eine Wiener Musikzeitschrift**

24-7
0969–9589
GB–Ely: Music Maker, 1993–
[NOT IN BUCOMP1]

> **Lbl***

25 Years the King, 1956–81
GB–Leicester: Official Elvis Presley Fan Club
Worldwide, 1981– 82
[NOT IN BUCOMP1]

> **Cu** 1–10, 1981–82
> **Lbl** 2–10, 1981–82

33 1/3
ME–Mexico: Mexico City, 1952–59
[Succeeded by *Audiomusica* (q.v.)]

> **Lsa** 1953, Jan, Mar, Dec; 1955, June/July; 5 (1957)–7 (1959)

78 RPM
GB–London, 1968–69

> **Lsa** 1–8, 1968–69

A

A Arte musical: Revista de Doutrina, Noticiário e Crítica
TNG P16
P–Lisbon: Juventuda Musical Portuguesa, 1931–60; n.s. 1961–

> **BSdsc***
> **Lcml** 16 (1947), 1
> **Lu** n.s. 2 (1963), Mar

A Little Angry in a Very Nice Place
0955–5536
GB–Bristol: Rest Home Enterprises, 1988–
[NOT IN BUCOMP1]

> **Lbl***
> **Ob** 1, 1988–#

Aarbog for Musik [= Music Yearbook]
TNG DK40
DK–Copenhagen: Gyldendalske Boghandel/Nordisk Forlag, 1923–26
[Succeeded by *Musikhistorisk Arkiv* (q.v.)]

> **AB** 1923–26
> **Cu** 1923–26
> **Lu** 1923

ABBA Magazine
0141–8394
GB–Knutsford: Poster Plus; London: Seymour Press, 1977–
[NOT IN BUCOMP1]

> **Lbl***

Abe's Folke Musicke Almanacke
GB–Leeds: University of Leeds Students' Union, Ballad and Blues Society, 1962–
[NOT IN BUCOMP1]

> **Lbl***
> **Lcs** 3 (1964/65), 1–5; 4 (1966), 2; 6 (1968), 2

Ability Development: Journal of the British Suzuki Institute
1353–3169
GB–Welwyn: British Suzuki Institute, 1985–
[NOT IN BUCOMP1]

> **Bp** 1 (1985/89)–#
> **Ep** 1 (1985/89), 7, 9, 10; 2 (1990/91)–#*
> **Lam** 1 (1985/89), 4
> **Lcm** 1 (1985/89)–#*
> **Lu** 1 (1985/89), 4
> **Mcm** 1 (1985/89), 4, 5, 7, 8

About the House
TNG GB497; 0001–3242
GB–London: Friends of Covent Garden, 1962–92
[Each volume covers several years, and contains 12 numbers. Continued by *Opera House: the Magazine of the Royal Ballet, the Royal Opera and the Birmingham Royal Ballet* from 1993]

> **AB** 1 (1962/65)–8 (1988/92)
> **Bp** 3 (1968/72), 11–8 (1988/92)
> **Cu** 1 (1962/65)–8 (1988/92), 11
> **EIR:Dtc** 1 (1962/65)–8 (1988/92)
> **En***
> **Er** 5 (1976/80), 8–12; 6 (1980/84)–8 (1988/92), 4
> **Lam** 3 (, 8,1969/72), 3; 5 (1976/80), 12; 6 (1980/84), 1– 4; 7 (1984/88), 5–8 (1988/92), 1
> **Lbar** 1 (1962/65)–8 (1988/92)
> **Lbl***
> **Lcm(p)** 1 (1962/65), 2–12; 2 (1965/68)– 3 (1968/72), 1–5, 7–12; 4 (1972/76)– 8 (1988/92), 10
> **Lcml** 1 (1962/65)–8 (1988/92)
> **Lcml (m)** 1 (1962/65)–2 (1965/68)*; 3 (1969/72)–8 (1988/92)
> **Lgsm** 1 (1962/65)–8 (1988/92)
> **Lmi** 1 (1962/65)–8 (1988/92)
> **Lu** 1 (1962/65)–8 (1988/92)*
> **Mcm** 1 (1962/65); 2 (1965/68), 2–3 (1969/72), 9, 11
> **Mpl** 1 (1962/65)–6 (1980/84)
> **Ob***
> **R** 1 (1962/65), 9–2 (1965/68), 1, 3, 4
> **SFu** 6 (1980/84), 6; 7 (1984/88), 5–7

Abstracts of Papers Read at the Annual Meeting of the American Musicological Society
TNG US792; 0893–1305
US–St Louis, MO: American Musicological Society, ?1935–
[NOT IN BUCOMP1]

> **Cu** 61 (1995)–#
> **Lkc** 35 (1969)–38 (1972)
> **Lu** 35 (1969)–38 (1972)
> **NO** 37 (1971)–38 (1972)
> **Ob***
> **Ouf** 37 (1971)
> **SA** 37 (1971)

ACA Bulletin *see* **American Composers' Alliance Bulletin**

Academic Gazette of Trinity College
TNG GB111
GB–London: Trinity College of Music, 1884–1916
[Formerly entitled *The Journal of Trinity College* (q.v.)]

> **AB** 16 (1914), 3–6; 17 (1916), 1
> **Gm** 11 (1898)–17 (1916), 2
> **Lbl***
> **Ob***

Academic Yearbook [of the Royal Academy of Music] *see* **Royal Academy of Music Academic Yearbook**

The Academite
TNG GB269
GB–London: Royal Academy of Music, 1917–23
[NOT IN BUCOMP1]

> **Lam** 1–18, 1917–23 [w 3, 1918]
> **SFu** 1–18, 1917–23 [w 3, 1918]

ACBM Nouvelles *see* **Canadian Association of Music Libraries (CAML) Newsletter**

Access All Areas
0960–6416
GB–London: Force 10, ?1991–
[NOT IN BUCOMP1]

> **Lbl** 2 (1992)–#

Accordion Digest: a Text-Book of Accordion Knowledge
TNG GB368
GB–London: National Accordion Association, 1939; 1952–56
[Entitled *N.A.O. Review, incorporating Accordion Digest*, 1952–56]

> **Lam** 3 (1954), 1
> **Lbl** 1939; 1 (1952)–5 (1956)

Accordion Times and Harmonica News
TNG GB346; 0001–4656
GB–London, 1935–39; 1950–
[From 1950 entitled *Accordion Times and Modern Musician*]

> **Lam** 9 (1954), 10
> **Lbl***
> **Mpl** 9 (1954)*; 19 (1963)–21 (1965)

Accordion Times and Modern Musician *see* **Accordion Times and Harmonica News**

Acoustic Music: Successor to Folk News *see* **Folk News [2]**

Acoustic Music, and Folk Song and Dance News *see* **Folk News [2]**

Acoustics Abstracts
0001–4974
GB–London: Multi-Science Publishing Company, 1967–

> **EIR:Dtc** 1 (1967/68)–#
> **En** 1 (1967/68)–#
> **Ob***

Acta Acustica
0371–0025
CHN–Beijing: Chung–Kuo Sheng Hsueh Hsueh Hui, 1978–
[Chinese title is *Sheng Hsueh Hsueh Pao*; succeeded by the *Chinese Journal of Acoustics* (ISSN 0217–9776)]

> **Lsa** 1980–90*

Acta Ethnomusicologica Danica
TNG DK94; 0587–2413
DK–Copenhagen: Akademisk Forlag [for the Dansk Folkemindesamling], 1969–

> **Lbl***
> **Ob***
> **SA** 1 (1969)

Acta Janáčkiana
0567–7629
CZ–Brno: Moravske Museum, 1968–
[Vol. 2 published 1985]

Lam 1 (1968)
Ob 1 (1968)–#

Acta Mozartiana
TNG D943; 0001–6233
D–Augsburg: Deutsche Mozart-Gesellschaft,
1954–

CDu 23 (1976)–#
Cu 1 (1954)–#
LAu 1 (1954)–5 (1958), 3; 6 (1959)–8 (1961),
3; 9 (1962), 3, 4; 10 (1963), 1, 3;
11 (1964)–15 (1968), 3
Lbl*
Lcml 1 (1954), 1
Ob*

Acta Musica: Källscrifter och Studier utgivna av Musikvetenskapliga Seminariet vid Åbo Akademi [= Essays and Studies Published by the Musicological Department of the Åbo Academy]
S–Åbo: Åbo Academy, 1937–78

Lbl*
Ob*

Acta Musicologica *see* **Mitteilungen der Internationalen Gesellschaft für Musikwissenschaft**

Acta Organologica
TNG D1056; 0567–7874
D–Berlin: Merseburger [for the Gesellschaft der Orgelfreunde], 1967–
[NOT IN BUCOMP1]

Lam (o) 1 (1967)–16 (1982); 19 (1987)–21
(1989)
Lbbc 15 (1981)
Lrco 5 (1971)–22 (1991)*
Ob*
Yu 1 (1967)–22 (1991)

Acta Sagittariana: Mitteilungen der Internationalen Heinrich- Schütz-Gesellschaft
TNG INTL20; 0001–6942
D–Kassel: Heinrich-Schütz Gesellschaft, 1963–

LAu 1964, 2–5; 1965, 1, 3; 1966, 1–4;
1967/68
Lbl 1963, 1–#*

The Acting Manager and Musical Director: the Official Organ of the Society of Entertainment Managers and Musical Directors
GB–London, ?1927–31

Lbl 2 (1928), 3–3 (1931), 8

Actuel *see* **Actuel: Jazz, Musique Contemporaine, Théâtre, Poésie**

Actuel: Jazz, Musique Contemporaine, Théâtre, Poésie
TNG F699
F–Paris, 1968–
[From 1970 entitled *Actuel*]

Cbijs 1968, Nov; 1969, Jan–Mar

Adam International Review
0001–8015
RO/GB–Bucharest, 1929–39; London, 1941–

EIR:Dtc 13 (1941), 152–28 (1961), 298;
33 (1966), 301–#
En*
Lbl*
Lu 13 (1941), 153–# [w 349–50; 355–60;
367–69]
Mcm 34 (1967), 316–318

AES
US–New York: Audio Engineering Society,
?1953–
[NOT IN BUCOMP1]

Lsa 27 (1979)–#*

Africa Music: the International Entertainment Magazine
GB–London: Tony Amadi International, 1981–

Lsa 6–23, 1981–84

African Music
TNG SA6; 0065–4019
SA–Roodeport: African Music Society, 1954–
[Formerly *African Music Society Newsletter* (q.v.)]

BLu 1 (1954/56)–#
BTu 1 (1954/56), 1–3
Cu 1 (1954/56)–#
En 1 (1954/56)–#
Er 1 (1954/56), 2, 3; 3 (1964/65), 3, 4;
4 (1966/70), 1, 4; 5 (1971/76), 1, 3, 4;
6 (1980/87)
LAu 1 (1954/56), 3

Lbl*
Lcml 1 (1954/56)–5 (1971/76)
Lgo 1 (1954/56)–#
Lsa 1 (1954/56)–3 (1964/65), 1, 2;
    4 (1966/70)–5 (1971/76), 2–4; 6 (1980/87),
    1, 2, 4; 7 (1991), 1, 2
Lso 1 (1954/56)–#
Lu 1 (1954/56), 1
Mu 1 (1954/56)–5 (1971/76), 1
TOd 3 (1964/65), 3; 4 (1966/70), 3, 4;
    5 (1971/76), 1, 2

African Music Society Newsletter
TNG SA4
SA–Roodeport: African Music Society, 1948–53
[Previously entitled the *Newsletter of the
African Music Society*; succeeded by *African
Music* (q.v.)]

Cu 1 (1948/53), 1–6
Lbl*
Lso 1 (1948/53), 1–6
Mu 1 (1948/53), 1–6

African Musicology
KEN–Nairobi: Eleza Services Ltd [for the
Institute of African Studies, University of
Nairobi], 1983–
[NOT IN BUCOMP1]

Lsa 1 (1983), 1
Lso 1 (1983), 1

Agenda *see* Agenda: Information on Electro-Acoustic Music

Agenda: Information on Electro-Acoustic Music
GB–?London, 1986–
[NOT IN BUCOMP1; entitled *Agenda* from no.
11, 1990]

Lgu 1–46, 1988–96

AGO Quarterly *see* The American Guild of Organists Quarterly

A.I.M.S. Bulletin
TNG EIRE9
EIRE–Dublin: Association of Irish Music
Societies, 1965– [BUCOMP1]
[Became *Show Times* from 1993]

EIR:Dp 21 (1986)–#
EIR:Dtc 9 (1974), 6–27 (1993); 1993–#
EIR:MEtc 9 (1974)–12 (1977)

Airwaves
GB–London, 1985–
[NOT IN BUCOMP1]

Lsa*

Aisling
0790–7591
EIRE–Ballyheigue: Comhaltas Ceoltoiri
Eireann, 1985–
[NOT IN BUCOMP1]

EIR:Duc 1 (1985)–3 (1991)
Ob*

A.I.V.S. Newsletter
TNG US862; 0148–0383
US–New York: American Institute for Verdi
Studies, 1976–
[Entitled *Verdi Newsletter* from no. 3, 1977]

Cu 1, 1976–#
En*
Ob*

The Alan Rawsthorne Society Newsletter
GB–?Manchester [etc.]: Alan Rawsthorne
Society, ?1987–
[NOT IN BUCOMP1]

Lam 2, 1987
Lu 1, 2, 1987

Albert Roussel *see* Cahiers Albert Roussel

Aldeburgh Soundings: the Newsletter of the Friends of the Aldeburgh Foundation
0952–5815
GB–Aldeburgh: Aldeburgh Foundation, 1984–
[NOT IN BUCOMP1; entitled *Soundings* from
no. 22, 1992]

ALb 1, 1984–#
Cu 1, 1984–#
EIR:Dtc 1, 1984–# [w 22]
En 1, 1984–#
Lbl*
Ob 8, 1987–#

Alkan Society Bulletin
GB–London: The Alkan Society, 1982–

Lbar 1982, Oct–1992, June
Ob*

All-American Band Leaders *see* Band Leaders

All Music
GB–Milton Keynes, 197?–
[NOT IN BUCOMP1]

    Cbijs 1971–73

Allahabad University Journal of Music
IN–Allahabad, ?1947–

    Cpl 2 (1948)
    Lam 2 (1948)

Allegro: House Magazine of Boosey and Hawkes
GB–London: Boosey and Hawkes Musical Instrument Division, 1988–
[NOT IN BUCOMP1]

    Lbl 1, 1988–#
    TOd 4, 1990

Allen's Poop Sheet
US–Highland Park, NJ: W. C. Allen, 1958–74

    Cbijs 1–14, 1958–74

Alley Music
AUS–Victoria: Bob Eagle, 1968
[Only one volume was published]

    Cbijs 2, 3, 1968

Allgemeine Deutsche Musik-Zeitung: Wochenschrift für die Reform des Musiklebens der Gegenwart
Fellinger 1968/672; TNG D203
D–Berlin [etc.]: Luckhardt'sche Verlagshandlung, 1874–1943
[From 1883 entitled *Allgemeine Musik-Zeitung*; from 1925: *Allgemeine Musikzeitung*; ceased publication with vol. 70 (1943), when it was absorbed into *Musik im Kriege* (q.v.)]

    Bu 32 (1905)–41 (1914)
    Ep 62 (1935)–63 (1936)
    Lbl 39 (1912), 43 [Special Richard Strauss
      number]

Allgemeine Kunst-Chronik *see* **Österreichische Kunst-Chronik**

Allgemeine musikalische Zeitung [1]
Fellinger 1968/1; TNG D32
D–Leipzig: Breitkopf und Härtel/Rieter-Biedermann, 1798–1848
[Succeeded by a Neue Folge 1 (1863)–3 (1865) (see next entry); and a 3rd series, 1866–82, under title *Leipziger allgemeine musikalische Zeitung* (q.v.)]

    Bu 9 (1806)
    CDu 1 (1798)–50 (1848) [m]
    Cu 1 (1798)–50 (1848)
    DRu 1 (1798)–50 (1848)
    Er 1 (1798)–50 (1848)
    EXu 1 (1798)–50 (1848) [m]
    Gul(e) 1 (1798)–21 (1819); another copy 12
      (1810), 56; 16 (1814), 37, 42–45, 48
    Lbl 1 (1798)–50 (1848)
    Lu 1 (1798)–50 (1848) [Reprint ed.]
    Mpl 1 (1798)–50 (1848)
    NO 1 (1798)–50 (1848) [m]
    Ob 1 (1798)–50 (1848)

Allgemeine musikalische Zeitung [2]
Fellinger 1968/467; TNG D154
D–Leipzig: Breitkopf und Härtel, 1863–65
[Regarded as a Neue Folge to the *Allgemeine musikalische Zeitung* [1] (q.v.); preceded by the *Deutsche Musik-Zeitung* (q.v.); succeeded from 1866–1882 by the *Leipziger allgemeine musikalische Zeitung* (q.v.)]

    Er 1 (1863)–3 (1865)
    Lbl 1 (1863)–3 (1865)
    Lu 1 (1863)–3 (1865)
    NO 1 (1863)–3 (1865) [m]
    Ob 1 (1863)–3 (1865)
    Ouf 2 (1864)–3 (1865) [Reprint ed.]

Allgemeine musikalische Zeitung mit besonderer Rücksicht auf den Österreichischen Kaiserstaat
Fellinger 1968/36; TNG A14
A–Vienna: Steiner, 1817–24
[Also bore title *Wiener allgemeine musikalische Zeitung* from 8 (1824)]

    Bu 1 (1817)–4 (1820)
    EXu 1 (1817)–8 (1824) [m]

Allgemeine Musik-Zeitung [Musikzeitung]
see **Allgemeine Deutsche Musik-Zeitung**

Allgemeine Theaterzeitung *see* **Wiener Theater-Zeitung**

Allgemeine Theaterzeitung und Originalblatt für Kunst, Literatur, Musik, Mode und geselliges Leben *see* **Wiener Theater-Zeitung**

Allgemeine Theaterzeitung und Unterhaltungsblatt für Freunde der Kunst, Literatur, und des geselligen Lebens *see* **Wiener Theater-Zeitung**

Allgemeine Wiener Musik-Zeitung
A–Vienna: Breitkopf und Härtel, 1841–48
Fellinger 1968/176; TNG A22
[79 nos in total; from 1845 entitled *Wiener allgemeine Musik-Zeitung*]

Cu 1 (1841)–8 (1848) [Reprint ed.]
EXu 1 (1841)–8 (1848) [m]
Lu 1 (1841)–6 (1846) [Reprint ed.];
  7 (1847)–8 (1848)
Ob 1 (1841)–8 (1848) [m]

Allgemeiner Cäcilien-Verein für Deutschland, Österreich und die Schweiz:
Cäcilienvereinsorgan *see* Fliegende Blätter für katholische Kirchenmusik

Allgemeiner Cäcilienverein für die Diozesan Deutschlands, Österreich-Ungarns und der Schweiz *see* Fliegende Blätter für katholische Kirchenmusik

Allgemeiner Cäcilienverein zur Förderung der katholischen Kirchenmusik:
Cäcilienvereinsorgan *see* Fliegende Blätter für katholische Kirchenmusik

Allgemeiner musikalischer Anzeiger
Fellinger 1968/85; TNG A17
A–Vienna: Tobias Haslinger, 1829–40

Lbl 1 (1829)–5 (1833)

Allwedd y Tannau: Cylchgrawn Cymdeithas Cerdd Dant [= The Key of the Strings: the Journal of the Society for Instrumental Music]
TNG GB357
GB–Liverpool: Cymdeithas Cerdd Dant Cymru, 1936–

AB 1 (1936)–#
ABc 1 (1936)–3 (1938); 40 (1981)–42 (1983)
Lbl*
MO 1 (1936)–#
Ob*

Almanac of the Janáček Academy of Musical Art [translated title] *see* Sborník Janáčkovy Akademie Múzikých Umění

Almanach de la Musique
TNG F617; 0401–4855
F–Paris: Editions de Flore, 1950–51
[NOT IN BUCOMP1]

Cu 1950–51
Lbl*
Lu 1950–51

Almanach der Deutschen Musikbücherei
TNG D583
D–Regensburg: Gustav Bosse, 1921–27
[NOT IN BUCOMP1]

Cu 1921–27
Lu 1924–27

Almanach des allgemeinen deutschen Musikvereins
Fellinger 1968/573; TNG D175
D–Leipzig: C. F. Kahnt, 1868–70

Lbl 1 (1868)–3 (1870)

Almanach du Disque
TNG F625
F–Paris: Editions de Flore, 1951–58

Lbl*
Lsa 1952–55
Lu 1952–58

Almanach für die musikalische Welt
Fellinger 1968/2106
D–Berlin: L. Schmidt, 1912–13
[NOT IN BUCOMP1]

Er 1912/13

Almanach Illustré Chronologique, Historique, Critique et Anecdotique de la Musique
Fellinger 1968/492; TNG F105
F–Paris, 1866–68

Er 2 (1867)
Gul(e) 1 (1866)–3 (1868)*
Lbl 1 (1866)
Ob 2 (1867)

Almanach Musical [1]
TNG F4; 1146–9978
F–Paris, 1775–83; 1788–89
[Continued as *Calendrier Musical Universel* (vols 9 (1788)–10 (1789)]

Au 1/2 (1775/76)–9/10 (1788/89) [Reprint ed.]
Cu 1/2 (1775/76)–9/10 (1788/89) [Reprint ed.]
HUu 1/2 (1775/76)–9/10 (1789/90) [Reprint ed.]
Lbl 1/2 (1775/76)–9/10 (1788/89) [Reprint ed.]
Ob 1/2 (1775/76)–9/10 (1788/89) [Reprint ed.]

Almanach Musical [2]
Fellinger 1968/331; TNG F67
F–Paris: A. Ikelmer, 1854–70

> **Er** 1 (1854)–2 (1855); 4 (1857)–17 (1870)
> **Lbl** 9 (1862)
> **Ob** 3 (1856)–17 (1870)

The Alternative One Magazine
0265–3249
GB–London: Alternative One, 1983–
[NOT IN BUCOMP1]

> **Lbl***

Alternative Sounds
GB–Coventry, ?1979–
[NOT IN BUCOMP1]

> **Lsa** 1–17, 1979–80

Alvorada
?I–Porto, 1973–?79

> **Lsa** 1973–79*

Amateur Dancer *see* **The Dancing Times**

The Amateur Musician
TNG GB344
GB–London, 1934–39

> **Ep** 2 (1935/38), 7, 8; 3 (1938/39), 1–4
> **Lbl***
> **Lcm** 1 (1934), 1–7; 2 (1935/38), 1, 5, 6, 8;
> 3 (1938/39), 1, 2, 4
> **Lcml** 3 (1938/39), 1, 2

The Amateur Musician: a Fortnightly High-Class Magazine Addressed to All Lovers of Music
Fellinger 1968/1091; TNG GB129
GB–London, 1889

> **Gm** 1 (1889), 1–9
> **Lbl** 1 (1889), 1–3
> **Mpl** 1 (1889)
> **Ob***

The Amateur Orchestra [1]
Fellinger 1968/1463; TNG GB181
GB–London, 1899
[Only six numbers were published]

> **Lbl** 1–6, 1899

The Amateur Orchestra [2]
Fellinger 1968/1950; TNG GB238
GB–London, 1909
[Only six numbers were published]

> **Lbl***

Amateur Stage
GB: London, 1926–
[NOT IN BUCOMP1]

> **CH** 1974–#*

Amateur Tape Recording: the Magazine of the British Tape Recording Club
GB–London: Lane and Potton, 1959–67
[NOT IN BUCOMP1; later incorporated into *Hi-Fi Sound* (q.v.)]

> **EIR:Dtc** 1 (1959)–9 (1967), 3
> **Lbl***

The Amazing Pudding: the Original Pink Floyd and Roger Waters Magazine
0951–8304
GB–Birmingham: ?A. Mabbett, 1983–
[NOT IN BUCOMP1]

> **Lbl***
> **Lsa** 1–10, 1983–85; 40–60, 1989–93

Ambrosius: Rivista Liturgico-Pastorale
I–Milan: Centro Ambrosiano di Documentazione e Studi Religiosi, 1925–

> **Lbl***
> **Lu** 31 (1955), 1–6; 32 (1956), 1, 2
> **Ob***

AMC News *see* **Australian Music Centre: Quarterly Newsletter**

American Brahms Society Newsletter
8756–8357
US–Seattle: The American Brahms Society, 1983–
[NOT IN BUCOMP1]

> **Cu** 1 (1983)–#
> **Lam** 2 (1984), 2
> **Lcm** 2 (1984), 2
> **LEbc** 8 (1990)–#
> **Ouf** 2 (1984)–#

American Choral Foundation: Research Memorandum
0002–788X
US–New York: American Choral Foundation/Association of Choral Conductors, 1959–

Lbl*
Mcm 20 (1978), 2, 3; 22 (1980), 1; 23 (1981), 3

American Choral Review
TNG US690; 0002–7898
US–New York: American Choral Foundation, 1958–
[NOT IN BUCOMP1; vol. 1 nos 1 and 2 entitled *Bulletin of the American Concert Choir and Choral Foundation*]

Cpl 6 (1964), 1, 2

American Composers' Alliance Bulletin
TNG US546
US–New York: American Composers' Alliance, 1938; 1952–65
[Ceased with vol. 13 (1965); former title (from 1938) was *ACA Bulletin*]

Cpl 9 (1960), 3

The American Guild of Organists Quarterly
TNG US674; 0569–4957
US–New York: The American Guild of Organists, 1956–67
[NOT IN BUCOMP1; ceased publication with vol. 12 (1967); entitled *AGO Quarterly* (ISSN 0027–4208), 1956–57; succeeded by *Music: the AGO Magazine* (q.v.)]

Lrco 5 (1960), 3, 4; 8 (1963)–9 (1964), 1, 3, 4; 10 (1965)–12 (1967), 3

American Harp Journal
TNG US766; 0002–869X
US–New York [etc.]: American Harp Society, 1967–
[Preceded 1950–66 by *Harp News [of the West]* (TNG US650; ISSN 0440–3215)]

BG 15 (1995)–#
Lam 14 (1993), 2–#
Lbl 7 (1979/80), 1–4; 8 (1981/82), 2–4
Ltc 18 (1997)–#
Lu 13 (1992), 3–#
Mcm 13 (1992)–#

American Institute for Verdi Studies *see* A.I.V.S. Newsletter

American Jazz Review
US–Flushing, NY: American Jazz Club, 1945–

Cbijs 3 (1947), 4

American Journal of Music and Musical Visitor *see* The Musical Visitor

American Liszt Society Newsletter
0749–341X
US–Washington, DC: American Liszt Society, 1984–
[NOT IN BUCOMP1]

Lsa 9 (1992), 2; 10 (1993)–#

American Morris Newsletter
1074–2689
US–Brattleboro, VT [etc.]: F. Breunig, 1977–
[NOT IN BUCOMP1]

Lcs 1 (1977)–#

American Music
GB–London, 1953–

Lam 6 (1958), 11–8 (1960), 1; 9 (1961), Jan–Apr, June
Lbl*
Lcml 7 (1959)–9 (1961)
LVp 8 (1960)

American Music: a Quarterly Journal Devoted to All Aspects of American Music and Music in America
0734–4392
US–Champaign, IL: The Sonneck Society/Illinois University Press, 1983–

Bu 1 (1983)–#
Cu 1 (1983)–#
EXu 1 (1983)–#
KE 1 (1983)–
Lbl 1 (1983)–#
Lgo 10 (1992)–#
Lu 10 (1992)–#
Mmu(a) 1 (1983)–#
Ob 1 (1983)–#
Uu 1 (1983)–#

American Music Lover
TNG US538; 0003–0716 (as *American Record Guide*)
US–Pelham, NY, 1935–72; 1976–
[Succeeded *The Music Lover's Guide* (q.v.); issue for Sep. 1944 was entitled *Listener's Record Guide*; from October 1994 the title was *American Record Guide: the Record Connoisseur's Magazine*]

Bp 34 (1967)–42 (1979), 8
BSdsc 40 (1976)–52 (1989)
Lsa 1 (1935)–6 (1940), 4; 9 (1943)–37 (1973); 40 (1976)– 46 (1983) [w 2, 5]; 47 (1984)–49 (1986) [w 49, 1]; 50 (1987)–51 (1988); 52 (1989), 5–#
LVp 18 (1951)–19 (1953)

American Music Research Center Journal
1058–3572
US–Boulder, CO: American Music Research Center, 1991–
[NOT IN BUCOMP1]

Bu 1 (1991)–2 (1992)

American Music Teacher
TNG US653; 0003–0112
US–Baldwin, NY: Music Teachers' National Association, 1951–
[Preceded by the *Bulletin of the Music Teachers' National Association* (TNG US541), 1935–50]

Lam 43 (1994), 4–#
Lcm 9 (1959/60), 3–5; 10 (1960/61), 1–6; 11 (1961/62), 1, 2
LVp 7 (1957/58)–23 (1973/74) [w 19 (1969/70), Jan]
Mcm 5 (1956), 4; 23 (1973/74), 2–6; 24 (1974/75); 25 (1975/76), 3, 5, 6; 26 (1976/77), 2–6; 27 (1977/78)– 33 (1983/84), 1

American Musical Digest
TNG US793; 0003–0120
US–New York: American Musical Digest Inc., 1969–70
[Ceased publication Mar. 1970]

En 1969–70
Lam 1969, Apr
Lu 1969 [pre-publication issue]

American Musical Instrument Society: Bulletin
0362–3300
US–Wellesley, MA [etc.]: American Musical Instrument Society, 1975–

[From 1978 entitled *Journal of the American Musical Instrument Society*]

BG 21 (1995)–#
COLC 1 (1975)–#
Cu 1 (1975)–#
Er 1 (1975)–#
Lcm (m) 1 (1975)–#
Lgu 1 (1975)–#
Lu 1 (1975)–#
Ob 1 (1975)–#

American Musical Instrument Society Newsletter *see* Newsletter of the Historical Musical Society

American Musical Journal
TNG US5
US–New York, 1834–35

Cu [m]
Mu [m]

American Musical Magazine
US–New Haven, CT: Doolittle and Read, 1786/87

Lbl*
Mu 1786/87 [m]
Ob 1786/87

American Musical Magazine, or, Repository of Sacred Music
Fellinger 1986, pp. 130–131
US–Northampton, MA, 1800–01
[NOT IN BUCOMP1]

Mu 1 (1800)–2 (1801) [m]

American Musicological Society Abstracts *see* Abstracts of Papers Read at the Annual Meeting of the American Musicological Society

American Musicological Society Directory
US–Philadelphia, PA: The American Musicological Society, 197?–
[NOT IN BUCOMP1]

CDu 1987–#
Gul [c]
Ltc [c]
SA 1972–#
SOu [c]

American Musicological Society Newsletter
TNG US809; 0402–012X
US–New York [etc.]: American Musicological
Society, 1971–
[The official issue 1 (1971) was preceded by
three, unnumbered, issues, dated 1969, 1970,
Feb. and 1970, Sep.; later entitled *AMS
Newsletter*]

   Au 22 (1992)–#
   BG 23 (1993), 2–#
   BLp [c]
   Bs 12 (1982), 2–22 (1992), 2
   Bu 13 (1983)–#
   CDu 1 (1971)–#
   Cpl 6 (1976)–#
   Cu 1 (1971)–#
   EIR:Dtc 13 (1983)–#
   EIR:Duc 10 (1980), 2–14 (1984)
   EIR:MEtc 5 (1975), 2–#
   En 1 (1971)–#
   Gam 4 (1974), 2–#
   KE 10 (1980)–#
   Lam 6 (1976), 2–8 (1978), 1; 9 (1979),
     1–22 (1992), 2; 24 (1994)–#
   LAu 10 (1980)–#
   Lbl 1 (1971)–#
   Lcml 14 (1984), 1; 18 (1988), 2–#
   Lmi 8 (1978)–#
   LRHBNC 8 (1978), 1; 9 (1979)–14 (1984), 1;
     15 (1985), 1; 17 (1987), 2–19 (1989), 1;
     20 (1990)–#
   Ltc 27 (1997)–#
   LVu 1 (1971)–#
   Mcm 8 (1978), 2–14 (1984), 2; 15 (1985), 2;
     17 (1987), 1; 18 (1988)–19 (1989)
   NO 1 (1971)–#
   Ob*
   Ouf 1 (1971)–4 (1974); 8 (1978), 2;
     11 (1981)–14 (1984); 16 (1986)–#
   R*
   SA 1 (1971)–#
   TOd 13 (1983)–#
   Uu [c (2 years)]

American Organ Monthly
TNG US466
US–Boston, MA: Boston Music Company,
1920–34
[Entitled *American Organ Quarterly* (ISSN
0748–9382) from vol. 3 (1922), and published
New York: H. W. Gray; ceased publication with
vol. 15 (1934), no. 48]

   Lbl*

American Organ Quarterly *see* **American
Organ Monthly**

The American Organist
Fellinger 1968/2303; TNG US459; ISSN 0003–
0260
US–New York: American Guild of Organists,
1918–70

   Cpl 21 (1938), 2–24 (1941), 2; 47 (1964), 4
   Lam (o) 1 (1918)–3 (1920); 14 (1931)*;
     16 (1933)–18 (1935)*; 20 (1937)–
     23 (1940), 11; 32 (1949)–53 (1970), 6
   Lrco 9 (1926)–10 (1927), 3; 26 (1943), 4–9,
     12; 27(1944), 1–7, 9–12; 30 (1947), 7–8,
     12; 31 (1948), 1– 8; 46 (1963), 7;
     51 (1968), 2, 3
   LVp 39 (1956)–43 (1960); 46 (1963)–
     53 (1970)

**American Organist: the Official Journal of the
American Guild of Organists and the Royal
Canadian College of Organists** *see* **Music: the
A.G.O. Magazine**

**American Record Guide: the Record
Connoisseur's Magazine** *see* **American Music
Lover**

American Record Letter
US–Washington, 1950–59

   Lsa 1–5, 1950–55*

American Recorder
TNG US710; 0003–0724
US–New York: American Recorder Society,
1960–

   BLp 1 (1960)–18 (1978) [m]; 19 (1979)–#
   Ob 5 (1964)–#

American Society of University Composers
see **A.S.U.C. Journal of Music Scores**

American String Teacher
TNG US654; 0003–1313
US–Lawrenceville, NJ [etc.]: American String
Teachers' Association, 1951–

   Cpl 2 (1952)–17 (1967), 4*
   Lbl*
   Lcml 14 (1964), 4–16 (1966), 1*
   Ltc [c]
   Mpl 1 (1951)–#
   Uu [c (2 years)]

American Suzuki Journal
0193–5372
US–Muscatine, Iowa: Suzuki Association of the Americas, 1973–
[NOT IN BUCOMP1]

> EIR:Dp 14 (1986)–17 (1989), 6

AMIS see **American Musical Instrument Society**

AMS Newsletter see **American Musicological Society Newsletter**

Anacreontic Magazine, or, Songster's Musical Companion
GB–London: Printed for W. Locke, 1792–?93
[NOT IN BUCOMP1]

> EIR:Dtc 2 (1793)

Analecta Gregoriana
0066–1376
I–Rome: Gregorian University Press, 1930–

> Ob 1 (1930)–?

Analecta Musicologica: Studien zur italienischen Musikgeschichte
0569–9827 [Vols also have individual ISBNs]
A/D: Graz/Cologne: Böhlau Verlag; Laaber: Laaber-Verlag, 1963–

> Bu 1 (1963)–#
> DRu 12 (1973)–28 (1988)
> Er 1 (1963)–#
> LAu 1 (1963)–25 (1987)
> Lbbc 1 (1963)–#
> Lbl*
> Lu 1 (1963)–#
> NO 1 (1963)–#
> Ob 1 (1963)–#
> Ouf 1 (1963)–#

Analyse Musicale: la Musique et Nous
0295–3722
F–Paris: Société Française d'Analyse Musicale, 1985–93
[NOT IN BUCOMP1; ceased publication with no. 32, 1993]

> Cu 1–32, 1985–93
> Lbl 1–32, 1985–93
> Lcml 22–32, 1991–93
> Lcu 26–32, 1992–93
> Lkc 1–32, 1985–93
> Ob 1–32, 1985–93
> SOu 1–32, 1985–93

The Analyst: a Monthly Journal of Science, Literature, and the Fine Arts
GB–London, 1834–
[Later entitled *The Analyst: a Quarterly Journal of Science* (Langley, pp. 560–2)]

> Lbl*

The Analyst: a Quarterly Journal of Science
see **The Analyst: a Monthly Journal of Science, Literature, and the Fine Arts**

Anbruch: Monatsschrift für moderne Musik
see **Musikblätter des Anbruch**

Ancilla Musicae
I–Lucca: Società Italiana di Musicologia, 1990–
[NOT IN BUCOMP1]

> Cu 1 (1990)–#

The André Previn Appreciation Society [Newsletter]
GB–London, 1982–?

> Lbar 1982–86, Sep

The Angel: the Magazine of St Mary-of-the-Angels Song School
TNG GB281
GB–Offington, Sussex, 1920–

> Lbl*

Annales Chopin see **Rocznik Chopinowski**

Annales de la Musique, ou Almanach Musical, par Un Amateur
Fellinger 1968/45; TNG F11
F–Paris, 1819–20

> Lu 1819–20 [Reprint ed.]
> Ob 1819–20 [Reprint ed.]

Les Annales du Théâtre et de la Musique
Fellinger 1968/693; TNG F156
F–Paris: P. Ollendorff, 1875–1916
[Ceased publication with vol. 41 (1916)]

> Cu 1 (1875)–40 (1914/15)
> Lbl 1 (1875)–40 (1914/15)
> Lu 1 (1875)–11 (1885); 13 (1887)–15 (1889);
> 21 (1895)–23 (1897); 26 (1900);
> 31 (1905)–32 (1906)

Annales Hindemith see **Hindemith-Jahrbuch**

Annales Musicologiques: Moyen-Age et Renaissance
TNG F638; 0583–8363
F–Paris: Société de Musique d'Autrefois, 1953–77

> Bp 1 (1953)–7 (1964/77)
> BRu 1 (1953)–7 (1964/77)
> Bu 1 (1953)–7 (1964/77)
> CDu 1 (1953)–6 (1958/63)
> Cpl 1 (1953)–7 (1964/77)
> Cu 1 (1953)–7 (1964/77)
> DRu 1 (1953)–6 (1963)
> Er 1 (1953)–7 (1964/77)
> Gul 1 (1953)–7 (1964/77)
> HUu 1 (1953)–7 (1964/77)
> Lbbc 1 (1953)–7 (1964/77)
> Lbl*
> Lcml 1 (1953)–7 (1964/77)
> Lkc 1 (1953)–7 (1964/77)
> Lu 1 (1953)–7 (1964/77)
> LVp 1 (1953)–3 (1955)
> LVu 1 (1953)–7 (1964/77)
> Mpl 1 (1953)–7 (1964/77)
> Mu 1 (1953)–7 (1964/77)
> NO 1 (1953)–7 (1964/77)
> Ob 1 (1953)–7 (1964/77)
> Ouf 1 (1953)–7 (1964/77)
> R 1 (1953)–6 (1963)

Annales Paderewski
CH–Morges: Société Paderewski, 1979–
[NOT IN BUCOMP1]

> Lp 1–4, 6, 1979–#

L'Année de l'Opéra et de la Danse
0184–0878
F–Paris: Calmann-Levy, 1977–?79
[NOT IN BUCOMP1]

> Ob†

L'Année Musicale [1]
Fellinger 1968/1010; TNG F203
F–Paris: Delagrave, 1886–94
[From 1892 entitled *L'Année Musicale et Dramatique*]

> Lbl 1 (1886)–7 (1893)

L'Année Musicale [2]
Fellinger 1968/2060; TNG F417; ISSN 1149–4751
F–Paris: Félix Alcan, 1912–14

> HUu 1 (1911)–3 (1913) [Reprint ed.]

Lbl*
Lu 1 (1911); 3 (1913)
Ob*

L'Année Musicale et Dramatique *see* L'Année Musicale [1]

L'Année Musicale, ou Revue Annuelle des Théâtres Lyriques et des Concerts, des Publications Littéraires relatives à la Musique et des Evènements Remarquables appartenant à l'Histoire de l'Art Musical
Fellinger 1968/405; TNG F87
F–Paris: Hachette, 1860–62
[Succeeded by *La Musique en l'Année 1862, ou Revue Annuelle des Théâtres Lyriques et des Concerts* […] (q.v.)]

> Bu 1860
> Lbl 1860–62
> Lcm (p) 1860–62

Annuaire de la Nouvelle Société Suisse de Musique *see* Schweizerisches Jahrbuch für Musikwissenschaft

Annuaire du Conservatoire Royal de Musique de Bruxelles
TNG B26
B–Brussels, 1876–

> BLu 1946–49
> Lbl*
> Ob*

Annuaire du Disque
F–Paris, ?1960–?
[NOT IN BUCOMP1]

> Lsa 1960–61

Annuaire du Monde Musical *see* Jahrbuch der Musikwelt

Annuaire Musical
Fellinger 1968/376; TNG F80
F–Paris, 1857

> Ob*

Annuaire Musical et Orphéonique de France
Fellinger 1968/694; TNG F154
F–Paris: Administration de l'Annuaire Musical et Orphéonique de France, 1875–78

> Lbl 1 (1875)–3/4 (1877/78)

Annuaire Spécial des Artistes Musiciens
Fellinger 1968/469; TNG F102
F–Paris, 1863

Lbl 1863

Annual Bibliography of European Ethnomusicology *see* Musikethnologische Jahresbibliographie Europas

Annual Byrd Supplement *see* Early Music Review

Annual Guide to Recorded Music
GB–London: The Sir Thomas Beecham Trust, 1981–
[Consists of cumulated issues, in book form, of *The Monthly Guide to Recorded Music* (q.v.)]

CHEp [c (1 year)]
Cu 1 (1981)–6 (1985)
Ep 1 (1981)–6 (1985), 6
EXu 5 (1984)–6 (1985), 6
Lcml (m) 1 (1981)–6 (1985), 6
Lsa 5 (1984)–6 (1985)
Mcm 1 (1981)–#
Ob*

Annual Index to Popular Music Record Reviews
0092–3486
US–Metuchen, NJ: Scarecrow Press, 1972–77

Cpl 1972–76
KE 1972–77
Ob*

Annual Record of Musical Winter Evenings
GB–London: Musical Union, 1852

Lbl 1852

Annual Record of the Musical Union *see* The Record of the Musical Union

Annual Review of Jazz Studies
0731–0641
US/GB–New Brunswick, NJ; London: Rutgers Institute of Jazz Studies/Transaction Books, 1982–
[Preceded 1973–79 by *Journal of Jazz Studies: Incorporating Studies in Jazz Discography* (q.v.)]

CDu 1 (1982)–4 (1988)
Cu 1 (1982)–#
EXu 1 (1982)–3 (1985)
KE 1 (1982)–2 (1983); 5 (1991)–#

Lbl 2 (1983)–#
Lcml 1 (1982)–#
Lgo 1 (1982)–# [w 2 (1983)]
Lsa 1 (1982)–4 (1988)
Mpl 1 (1982)–2 (1983)
Ob*
SLGu 1 (1982)–3 (1985)

Annuario *see also* Anuario

Annuario del Conservatorio Gioacchino Rossini Pesaro
I–Pesaro: Conservatorio Gioacchino Rossini, ?1990–
[NOT IN BUCOMP1]

Bu 1990/91–1991/92
Lu 1990/91–1991/92

Annuario Musicale Italiano
I–Rome: CIDIM [Centro Italiano di Initiativa Musicale], 1981–
[NOT IN BUCOMP1]

Lbl 1981–#
Ob 1981–#

Anregungen für Kunst, Leben und Wissenschaft
Fellinger 1968/36; TNG D133
D–Leipzig, 1856–61

Lbl 1 (1856)–6 (1861)
Ob 1 (1856)–6 (1861)

Anstalt zur Wahrung dem Aufführungsrechte auf der Gebiete der Musik *see* A.W.A. Kontakte

Anthos
EIRE–Dublin: Whitehall Musical and Dramatic Society, 1972–

EIR:Dtc 1–3, 1972–73
Ob*

Anti-Climax
GB–Ipswich: Anti-Climax, ?1972–
[NOT IN BUCOMP1]

Lbl 9, 1981/82–#*

Antique Phonograph Monthly
TNG US834
US–New York, ?1973–
[NOT IN BUCOMP1]

Lsa 1 (1973)–4 (1976)

Antique Phonograph News *see* Canadian
Antique Phonograph Society Newsletter

Antique Records
GB–Thames Ditton: J. Hall, 1972–75

Cu 1972, Oct–1974, Oct
EIR:Dtc 1972, Oct–1974, Oct
En 1972, Oct; 1973, May, Nov; 1974, May,
Sep, Oct
Lam 1972, Oct
Lsa 1972–75*
Ob*

Anuario *see also* Annuario

Anuario Musical
TNG E91; 0211–3538
E–Barcelona: Instituto Español de Musicologia,
1946–

AB 1 (1946)–23 (1968)
CDu 25 (1970)–30 (1975)
Cu 1 (1946)–#
En 1 (1946)–#
Er 1 (1946)–2 (1947); 4 (1949)–11 (1956);
14 (1959)–18 (1963); 20 (1965); 26
(1971)–#
EXu 2 (1947); 9 (1954); 23 (1968)–40 (1985)
HUu 1 (1946)–21 (1966)
Lbbc 1 (1946)–#
Lcml 1 (1946)–3 (1948); 6 (1951)–
33/35 (1978/80)
Lkc 30 (1975)–45 (1990); 47 (1992)–#
Lu 1 (1946)–#
LVu 1 (1946)–27 (1972)
Mcm 27 (1972)–28/29 (1973/74)
Ob 1 (1946)–#

Anuario [of the] Sociedad Folklorica de
Mexico *see* Sociedad Folklorica de Mexico:
Anuario

Anuario/Yearbook
US–Austin, TX: Tulane University, Inter-
American Institute for Musical Research/
Instituto Interamericano de Investigacíon
Musical, 1965–75
[Also known as the *Yearbook for Inter-
American Musical Research*]

BSdsc*
Lam 10 (1974)
Lu 1 (1965)–11 (1975) [w 9 (1973)]
Mcm 8 (1972)–11 (1975)
Ob*
SOu 1 (1965)–10 (1974)

Anzeiger für Schallplatten historischer,
klassischer und moderner Musik
TNG D1029
D–Freiburg im Breisgau, 1962–?
[NOT IN BUCOMP1]

Lsa 1–4, 1962–65

Apollon: eine Zeitschrift
Fellinger 1968/7; TNG D36
D–Penig, 1803

Cu 1 (1803)

Apollon: Illyustrirovanniy Ezhemesyatsnik
[= Apollo: Illustrated Monthly]
Fellinger 1968/1951; TNG USSR31
RF–St Petersburg: S.K. Mahovskii [et al.],
1909–17

Lbl*

Apollo's Gift
GB–London, 1829–30

Lbl 1829–30

Applause: the International Live Music
Business Monthly
0960–6254
GB–London: Applause Publications, 1989–
[NOT IN BUCOMP1]

Cu 1, 1989–#
Lbl 11, 1990–#
Ob 1, 1989–#

L'Approdo Musicale: Rivista Trimestrale di
Musica
TNG I248
I–Turin: ERI, 1958–67
[Ceased publication with no. 24, 1967. Preceded
by the *Rivista Musicale Italiana* (q.v.) and
succeeded by the *Nuova Rivista Musicale
Italiana* (q.v.)]

Cpl 3, 1958
Lam 1, 1958
LAu 3, 5, 7–9, 1958–60
Lcml 5, 1959
Lu 1–24, 1958–67
Ob 1–24, 1958–67

A.P.R.A.: Magazine of the Australasian
Performing Right Association *see* A.P.R.A.
Journal

15

A.P.R.A. Journal
TNG AUS22; 0001–2246
AUS–Sydney: Australian Performing Rights
Association, 1969–81; 1982–
[The official issue no. 1 was preceded by 12
unnumbered issues, covering the period 1969–
75. Entitled *A.P.R.A.: Magazine of the
Australasian Performing Rights Association*
from 2 (1982), 10. Also sometime entitled
*Journal of the Australasian Performing Rights
Association*]

  Lam 1 (1974/75), 11, 12; 2 (1976/79), 1, 3–6

Ar Soner: la Revue du Folklore Vivant de Bretagne
F–[s.l.]: Bodadeg ar Sonerion, 1949–
[NOT IN BUCOMP1]

  AB 1, 1949–#*
  Lcs 284–288, 1985

Arbeitsberichte – Mitteilungen [Institut für Musikethnologie, Graz]
A–Graz: Pannonische Forschungsstelle des
Instituts für Musikethnologie an der Hochschule
für Musik und Darstellende Kunst, 1990–
[NOT IN BUCOMP1]

  Ob 2, 1990–

A.R.C.E. Newsletter
IN–New Delhi: Archives and Research Centre
for Ethnomusicology, 1985–
[NOT IN BUCOMP1]

  Lsa 1985–#

Archiv für Musikforschung
TNG D776
D–Leipzig: Breitkopf und Härtel, 1936–43
[Preceded 1918–35 by the *Zeitschrift für
Musikwissenschaft* (q.v.); continued as *Die
Musikforschung* (q.v.)]

  AB 1 (1936)–6 (1941)*
  Cpl 1 (1936)–4 (1939), 2
  Cu 1 (1936)–8 (1943)
  Lbl*
  Lcm 1 (1936)–3 (1938); 8 (1943), 2–4
  Lcml 1 (1936)–4 (1939)
  Lu 1 (1936), 1, 3, 4; 2 (1937), 1, 2, 4;
    4 (1939), 1, 2; 8 (1943), 2–4
  LVu 1 (1936)–3 (1938); 5 (1940)
  Mpl 1 (1936)–8 (1943)
  Ob 1 (1936)–7 (1942)
  Ouf 1 (1936)–8 (1943)

Archiv für Musikorganologie
TNG D1090; 0171–4104
D–Munich [etc.]: Institut für Musikorganologie,
1976–
[NOT IN BUCOMP1]

  Cu 1 (1976)–3/4 (1978/79)
  Lbl 1 (1976), 1; 2 (1977), 1; 3/4 (1978/79), 3

Archiv für Musikwissenschaft
TNG D552; 0003–9292
D–Wiesbaden: F. Steiner, 1918–26; 1952–
[*See also Beihefte zum Archiv für
Musikwissenschaft*]

  AB 1 (1918)–30 (1973)
  BLu 32 (1975)–#
  CDu 21 (1964); 28 (1971)–#
  Cpl 1 (1918)–28 (1971)*
  Cu 1 (1918)–#
  DRu 26 (1969)–35 (1978)
  EIR:MEtc 2 (1919)–4 (1921)
  Er 1 (1918)–8 (1926); 19 (1962)–20 (1963),
    3, 4; 25 (1968), 2
  EXu 29 (1972)–51 (1994), 1
  Gul 37 (1980)–#
  HUu 9 (1952)–49 (1992)
  LAu 9 (1952), 1; 10 (1953), 3, 4; 11 (1954)–
    14 (1957); 19 (1962)–20 (1963)
  Lbbc 3 (1921)–8 (1926)*; 9 (1952)–
    11 (1954)*; 17 (1960)
  Lbl*
  Lcm 1 (1918)–41 (1984), 1
  Lcml 1 (1918)–6 (1924); 9 (1952)*;
    12 (1955)*; 19 (1962)– #
  LEbc 9 (1952)–#
  Lkc 1 (1918)–6 (1924); 8 (1926)–#
  LRHBNC 34 (1977)–#
  Lu 1 (1918)–# [1 (1918)–8 (1926) in reprint
    ed.]
  LVp 1 (1918)–7 (1925)
  LVu 9 (1952)–#
  Mcm 30 (1973)–#
  Mpl 1 (1918)–8 (1926)
  Mu 25 (1968)–#
  NO 13 (1956)–42 (1985); 45 (1988)–#
  NWu 1 (1918)–8 (1926) [m]; 26 (1969)–
    43 (1986)
  Ob 1 (1918)–#
  Ouf 1 (1918)–49 (1992)
  R 19 (1962)–31 (1974)
  SA 1 (1918)–44 (1987)
  SFu 1 (1918)–8 (1926)
  SOu 48 (1991)–#

Archivio Musicale: Pubblicazione Periodica di Estetica, Acustica, Storia, Didattica e Critica Musicale, Contrappunto, Armonia, Canto, Istrumentazione, Biografie, Arte Contemporanea, Controversie
Fellinger 1968/877; TNG I67
I–Naples: Istituto Casanova, 1882–84
[NOT IN BUCOMP1]

Er 1 (1882)–2 (1883/84), 18

Archivio per l'Informazione sulla Musica Antica see Bollettino dell'AIMA

Archivos Venezolanos de Folklore
VNZ–Caracas: Universidad Central de Venezuela, 1952–

Ouf (Howes) 1 (1952), 1, 2; 3 (1955/56), 4; 5 (1959/60), 6

Arla
GB–Liverpool: Liverpool Repertory Opera, 1928–?

Lcml 1 (1928), 10; 2 (1929), 1; 3 (1929), 2; 4 (1929), 3; 5 (1929), 4

Aria: the Magazine of Scottish Opera and its Friends
GB–Glasgow: Scottish Opera, 1990–
[NOT IN BUCOMP1]

Ep 1 (1990/91)–2 (1991/92)

Ars et Labor, Musica e Musicisti see Gazzetta Musicale di Milano

Ars Media: Publiaçaõ Semanal da Fundaçaõ Palácio das Artes
BR–Belo Horizonte: Fundaçaõ Palácio das Artes, 1973–
[NOT IN BUCOMP1]

Lbl 3 (1975), 114–#*

Ars Nova: UNISA Musica: Tydskrif van die Departement Muziekwetenskap, Universiteit van Suid-Afrika/Journal of the Department of Musicology, University of South Africa
0379–6485
SA–Pretoria: Department of Music, University of South Africa, 1969–
[NOT IN BUCOMP1]

Ob 6 (1980)–#

Ars Organi: Zeitschrift für das Orgelwesen
TNG D898; 0004–2919
D–Berlin: Merseburger, 1953–
[NOT IN BUCOMP1]

BSdsc*
Lam(o) 31 (1983), 4; 32 (1984), 4; 33 (1985), 1, 4
Yu 9 (1961), 18–40 (1992), 2*

ARSC Journal see Association for Recorded Sound Collections: Journal; and Association for Recorded Sound Collections: Bulletin

Art and Artists see Seven Arts

Art and Music [translated title] see Lidová Tvořivost

L'Art Musical: Journal de Musique
Fellinger 1968/416; TNG F88
F–Paris, 1860–70; 1872–94
[From 1894 incorporated into Le Guide Musical: Revue International de la Musique et des Théâtres (q.v.)]

Er 21 (1882), 47; 24 (1885)–27 (1888)*
Lbl 1 (1860)–33 (1894)

Art of Music see Yin Yueh Yi Shu

The Art of Record Buying: a List of Recommended Microgroove Recordings
GB–London: EMG Hand-Made Gramophones Ltd., 1938–80
[Annual cumulation of E. M. G. Hand-Made Gramophones Ltd.: the Monthly Letter: a Review of Recent Recordings (q.v.)]

AB 1957–60; 1962; 1964–80
Bp 1960–61; 1963; 1965–70; 1972–80
Cu 1951–71; 1973, 3–1980
En*
Ep 1956–58; 1960–77; 1979–80
Gm 1955; 1962; 1965; 1967; 1970; 1973–79
Lbl*
Lsa 1936; 1938; 1942; 1955–60; 1963; 1965–67; 1971–80
Ob*

Art Psychotherapy
0197–4556
US–Fayetteville, NY: Ankho International,
1973–
[NOT IN BUCOMP1; later entitled *Arts in
Psychotherapy*]

Lgsm 15 (1988)–#

**Arti Musices: Musikoloski Zbornik
[= Musicological Journal]**
TNG YU38; 0587–5455
HR–Zagreb: Muzikoloski Zavod, Muzicke
Akademije u Zagrebu, 1969–

BSdsc*
Cu 2 (1971)–#
Lam 1 (1970); 4 (1973); 1979
Lbbc 1 (1970)–8 (1977) [w 2 (1971)]
Lbl*
Lu 2 (1971)–# [+ 2 special issues, 1970,
1979]
Mcm 4 (1973)
Ob*

**Articulations: the Arena for Cultural Debate
in Music**
0957–1582
GB–Neilston: Articulations, 1989–
[NOT IN BUCOMP1]

Lbl*

**Articulos sobre Musica en Revistas Españolas
de Humanidades**
E–Madrid: Instituto de Bibliografia Musical,
1982–
[?Only one published]

Cu 1 (1982)
Ob*
Ouf 1 (1982)

**Artist: Teatral'niy, Muzykal'niy i
Chudozhestvenniy Zhurnal [= Theatre, Music
and Art Journal]**
Fellinger 1968/1093; TNG USSR16
RF–Moscow, 1889–95

Lbl*

Artist: Theatre, Music and Art Journal
[translated title] *see* **Artist: Teatral'niy,
Muzykal'niy i Chudozhestvenniy Zhurnal**

The Arts Business *see* **Southern Arts: Diary
and Review**

Arts in Psychotherapy *see* **Art Psychotherapy**

Arts Management Weekly
0961–9313
GB–London: Rhinegold, 1989–
[NOT IN BUCOMP1]

Gam 84–96, 1990; 187, 1992–#

Artswork
0267–8020
GB–London: Greater London Arts, 1985–
[NOT IN BUCOMP1]

Lcm 1–3, 1985; 7–10, 1986; 11, 12, 15, 1987
Ob*

Asbri [= Vivacity]
GB–Carmarthen, 1969–

AB 1969–78; 2 (1989), 1, 2

**Asian Music: Journal of the Society for Asian
Music**
TNG US781; 0044–9202
US–New York: Society for Asian Music, 1969–

BLu 1 (1969), 2–#
BSdsc 1 (1969), 2–#
Cu 1 (1969)–#
Er 8 (1976)–10 (1978), 1; 11 (1979)
Lbl*
Lcml 1 (1969), 2–#
Lcu 23 (1991)–#
Lgo 23 (1991)–#
Lki 1 (1969)–#
Lsa 1 (1969)–11 (1979); 15 (1983);
19 (1987/88)–#
Lso 1 (1969), 2; 2 (1970)–#
Lu 1 (1969), 1
Ob*
TOd 2 (1970)–6 (1974); 7 (1975),
2–12 (1980); 15 (1983), 1; 19 (1987/88);
20 (1989), 2–25 (1994)–#
Yu 1 (1968)–#

**Associacaõ Portuguesa de Educaçaõ Musical:
Boletin**
P–?: ?1963–?
[NOT IN BUCOMP1]

Lu 42, 43, 1984; 48, 1986

Association for Recorded Sound Collections: Bulletin
TNG US782; 0587–1956
US–Washington, DC [etc.]: Association for Recorded Sound Collections, 1968–
[Later incorporated into *ARSC Journal*]

> **Lsa** 2 (1969); 6 (1973)–7 (1974); 9 (1976)–
> 10 (1977); 14 (1981)–17 (1984);
> 22 (1989)–#

Association for Recorded Sound Collections: Journal
TNG US769; 0004–5438
US–Washington, DC [etc.]: Association for Recorded Sound Collections, 1967–
[Entitled *ARSC Journal* from vol. 17 (1985); formerly the *Journal of the Association for Recorded Sound Collections*]

> **Lsa** 1 (1967)–10 (1978), 1; 11 (1979)–
> 15 (1983), 1; 16 (1984)–17 (1985);
> 19 (1987), 2, 3; 21 (1990)–#

Association for Recorded Sound Collections: Newsletter
US–Albuquerque [etc.]: Association for Recorded Sound Collections, 1977–

> **Lsa** 1977–#

Association Nationale Hector Berlioz: Bulletin de Liaison
TNG F686
F–Côte-Saint-André: Association Nationale Hector Berlioz, 1964–

> **En** 1, 1964–#
> **Lbl***
> **Lcm** 1–15, 1964–81 [w 5, 11, 12]
> **Ob***

Association of Irish Choirs: Annual Report
see **Cumann Naisiunta Na gCor/Association of Irish Choirs: Annual Report**

Associazione Italiana Biblioteche: Bollettino d'Informazione
0004–5934
I–Rome: Associazione Italiana Biblioteche, 1961–91

[NOT IN BUCOMP1; preceded 1955–59 by *Notizie A.I.B.* (Rome; ISSN 0519–2064); entitled *Bollettino AIB* (ISSN 1121–1490) from vol. 32 (1992)]

> **Lam** 24 (1984), 2, 3

A.S.U.C. Journal of Music Scores
0196–1438
US–New York: American Society of University Composers, 1973–
[NOT IN BUCOMP1; from vol. 16 (1989) entitled *S.C.I. Journal of Music Scores* (ISSN 1059–7921)]

> **Cu** 1 (1973)–15 (1986)
> **Mu** 1 (1973)–11 (1980)

Atari ST Review *see* **Atari ST User**

Atari ST User
0952–3006
GB–Macclesfield: Database Publications, 1987–
[NOT IN BUCOMP1; from 1994 continued as *Atari ST Review*]

> **Lbl***
> **Msuc** 1991, June–1993, July

Athenaion-Blätter
D–Potsdam, 1931–

> **Gul** 1 (1931)
> **Lcm** 2 (1932), 1, 2; 3 (1934), 1

Yr Athraw Cerddorol [= **Music Teacher**]
GB–Llanidloes, 1854

> **AB** 1 (1854), 1–4

Audio
0004–752X
US–Philadelphia, PA, 1916–
[Variant titles included *Pacific Radio News*; and *Audio Engineering*]

> **Bp** 34 (1950)–#
> **Lbl***
> **Lu** 39 (1955)–43 (1959), 1–7, 9–12

Audio: the Hi-Fi and Record Magazine *see* **Audio: the Hi-Fi Magazine for Leisure Listening**

Audio: the Hi-Fi Magazine for Leisure Listening
TNG GB560
GB–London, 1972–
[Entitled *Audio: the Hi-Fi and Record Magazine* (ISSN 0142–016X) from 1974, Nov; *Practical Hi-Fi and Audio* (ISSN 0306–6495) from 1975, July; *Practical Hi-Fi* from 6 (1978), also incorporating the *Hi-Fi Buyer's Guide* (q.v.); from 11 (1983), 127 entitled *Hi-Fi Today*]

AB 8 (1980)–16 (1988)
Bp 1 (1972), 1–10; 7 (1979), 3–13 (1985), 2
CFp 5 (1977)–12 (1984)
Cu 1 (1972), Nov–12 (1984), 142
EIR:Dtc 1 (1972), Nov–13 (1985), 2
En*
Lbar 11 (1983)–13 (1985), 2
Lsa 8 (1980)–11 (1983); 12 (1984), 9
MI 6 (1978)–13 (1985), 2
Ob*

Audio and Record Review *see* Record Review

Audio Annual
0067–0545
GB–Croydon, 1966–71
[Succeeded by *Hi-Fi News and Record Review Annual*]

Cu 1966–71
Lbl*
Ob*

Audio Engineering *see* Audio

Audio Media
0960–7471
GB–St Ives, Cambridgeshire: SOS Publications, 1990–
[NOT IN BUCOMP1]

BG 14,1991–#
CDCp [c (2 years)]
CDu 25, 1992; 31, 1993–#
EIR:Dtc 1, 1990–#
En 1, 1990–#
Lsa 1, 1990–# [w 2–4; 10–12; 15; 18; 20; 41]
Mu 40, 1994–#
NO 5, 1990–#
Ob*
TOd 23, 1992–#

Audio Record Review *see* Record Review

Audio Visual
0305–2249
GB–Croydon: Current Affairs Ltd, 1972–

BLp [c]
BSdsc*
En*
Lcml [c (1 year)]
Lcml (r) [c (5 years)]
Lis 1972–1982
Lsa 1–46, 1972–75; 49–71, 1976–77; 73–166, 1978–85; 168–206, 1985–89; 208, 1989–#
Ob*
Oub [c (5 years)]
Tod*

Audio Visual Instruction
0004–7635
US–Washington, DC: Association for Educational Communications Technology, 1956–78
[NOT IN BUCOMP1]

Lis 1967–74

Audio Visual Librarian *see* Audiovisual Librarian

Audiomusica
ME–Mexico City, 1959–68
[Succeeded *33 1/3* (q.v.)]

Lsa 1 (1959)–9 (1968) [w 4 (1962), 73–96; 7 (1965), 165; 8 (1967), 172]

Audion: the New-Music Magazine
0958–0972
GB–Leicester: Ultima Thule/Audion–Auricle, 1986–
[NOT IN BUCOMP1]

Cu 21, 1992–#
Lbl*
Ob 22, 1992–#

Audiophile with Hi-Fi Answers
0959–7697
GB–Teddington: Haymarket Magazines, 1990–94
[NOT IN BUCOMP1; later entitled *What Hi-Fi?*]

Bp 1990, May–1994
HOp 1990, May–1993, Oct
Lsa 1990, May–1994, June [w 1992, Dec]

Audiovisual Group Bulletin *see* **Sound Recordings Group Newsletter**

Audiovisual Librarian
0302-3451
GB–London [etc.]: Audiovisual Group of the [UK] Library Association, 1973–
[NOT IN BUCOMP1; from vol. 20 (1994) entitled *AVL: the Multimedia Information Journal*; from vol. 22 (1996) entitled *AVL: Multimedia Information*. Succeeded the Library Association Audiovisual Group *Sound Recordings Group Newsletter* (q.v.). From 1998, Sum entitled *Multimedia Information and Technology*]

> **EIR:Dtc** 1 (1973)–#
> **En** 1 (1973)–5 (1979), 3; 6 (1980), 1–3; 7 (1981)–#
> **Lam** 5 (1979)–7 (1981), 3; 8 (1982)–11 (1985), 4; 12 (1986), 2–14 (1988), 4, 15 (1989), 2–18 (1992), 4
> **Lbbc** [c]
> **Lbx** 14 (1988)–#
> **Len** 1 (1973)–#
> **Lis** [c (5 years)]
> **Lsa** 1 (1973), 5–#*
> **Mcm** 1 (1973)–#
> **Ouf** 17 (1991), 2–#
> **SFp** 13 (1987), 1, 2, 4; 15 (1989)–#
> **TOd** 1 (1973), 4–6 (1980), 1; 11 (1985), 2–#
> **WCp** 1 (1973)–#

Das audiovisuelle Archiv *see* **Das Schallarchiv: Informationsblatt der Arbeitsgemeinschaft Österreichischer Schallarchive**

Aufsätze über musikalische Tagesfragen
Fellinger 1968/814; TNG D240
D–Eichstatt; Munich, 1880–95; 1903–06
[Entitled *Musikalische Tagesfragen: Zeitschrift für Musik und Musikfreunde* from 4 (1887)–6 (1889); entitled *Tagesfragen: Kissinger Blätter: Organ für Musiker, Musikfreunde und Freunde der Wahrheit* from 7 (1890)–12 (1895); from 1895 had head title *Kissinger Blätter: Tagesfragen*; entitled *Tagesfragen* from 1903–1906]

> **Lbl** 1 (1880) [w 2, 7]; 2 (?1881)–12 (1895), 5

Der Aufstieg
TNG D733
D–Berlin, 1930–34; 1937–44
[Entitled *Wir teilen mit: Hausmitteilungen des Musikverlages* (Berlin: Bote and Bock), from 1938, 1–6; later relaunched (1954) as *Aus unserem Tagebuch* (q.v.)]

> **LAu** 1933, 7; 1934, 9

Der Auftakt: Musikblätter für die Tschechoslowakische Republik
TNG CS103
CZ–Prague: Deutscher Musikpädagogischer Verband, 1920–38
[Superseded by *Blätter der Sudetendeutschen*, 1936–38 (Brno)]

> **Cpl** 1 (1920)–18 (1938)*
> **Lcml** 2 (1922)–16 (1936)*

Augsburger Jahrbuch für Musikwissenschaft
D–Tutzing: Schneider, 1984–91; 1992–
[NOT IN BUCOMP1; succeeded by the *Neues musikwissenschaftliches Jahrbuch* from 1992]

> **Cu** 1 (1984)–#
> **Lbl** 1 (1984)–8 (1991)

Aus unserem Tagebuch
D–Berlin; Wiesbaden: Bote und Bock, 1954–72
[Entitled *Tagebuch* (Berlin; Wiesbaden: Bote and Bock), 1971– 72; succeeded *Der Aufstieg* (q.v.)]

> **LAu** 23, 1964
> **Lcm** 1–30, 1954–71 [w 3, 5, 6, 8]

The Australasian Sound Archive *see* **International Association of Sound Archives (Australia) Newsletter**

Australia Music Centre: Quarterly Newsletter
0811-3149
AUS–Sydney: Australian Music Centre, 1983–
[NOT IN BUCOMP1. Issues 5–14, 1984–87 entitled *AMC News*; from 15, 1987 entitled *Sounds Australian: Journal of Australian Music* (ISSN 1030–4908)]

> **ALb** 33, 1992
> **Gsmic** [c]

Australian Disc and Tape Review
0310-5989
AUS–St Ives, New South Wales: David Frith Publications, 1972– 75

> **Lsa** 1972, Feb–Sep, Dec; 1973, Feb–Oct; 1974, Jan–Mar; 1975, Jan, Apr, July

Australian Jazz Quarterly
AUS–Clayton: W. Haesler et al., 1946–57
[Ceased publication with no. 31, 1957]

    Cbijs 1–10, 1946–50; 28–31, 1956–57

The Australian Journal of Music Education
TNG AUS21; 0004–9484
AUS–Nedlands, Western Australia: Australian
Society for Music Education, 1967–82
[Superseded by the *International Journal of
Music Education* (q.v.)]

    BSdsc*
    Lam 1–31, 1967–82
    Lcm 8, 1971
    Lie 2–29, 1968–81 [w 25]
    Mcm 12–17, 1973–75; 19–31, 1976–82
    Re 1–31, 1967–82; 35, 1986–#
    TOd 25, 1979

Australian Music and Dramatic News *see*
Australian Musical News

Australian Musical News
TNG AUS8
AUS–Melbourne, 1911–63
[From 1913 entitled *Australian Music and
Dramatic News*; from 1914 reverted to
Australian Musical News; from 31 (1940), 3
entitled *Australian Musical News and Musical
Digest*; from 50 (1959) entitled *Music and
Dance*]

    Lcm 50 (1959), 4–54 (1963), 3
    Lcml 40 (1949)–41 (1951)*

Australian Musical News and Musical Digest
see **Australian Musical News**

**Australian Performing Rights Association
Journal** *see* **A.P.R.A. Journal**

Australian Tradition
0005–0377
AUS–Port Melbourne, Victoria: Folk Lore
Society of Victoria and the Victorian Folk Music
Club, 1964–75
[Ceased publication with no. 37, 1975]

    BSdsc*

Autonomy 1
GB–Southwell: Autonomy 1, 197?–
[NOT IN BUCOMP1]

    Lbl*

L'Avant-Scène Opéra
0764–2873
F–Paris: L'Avant–Scène/Éditions Premières
Loges, 1976–

    ALb 31, 1981; 146, 1992; 158, 1994
    Mcm 158, 1993
    Ob*
    Ouf*

AVL: Multimedia Information *see*
Audiovisual Librarian

AVL: the Multimedia Information Journal *see*
Audiovisual Librarian

AVSCOT Update
GB–Glasgow: Library Association Audiovisual
Group, Scottish Branch, 1985–
[NOT IN BUCOMP1]

    En 1, 1985–#

A.W.A. Kontakte
D–Berlin: Anstalt zur Wahrung der
Aufführungsrechte auf dem Gebiete der Musik,
1985–
[NOT IN BUCOMP1]

    Lam 1986, 1; 1987, 2; 1988, 1; 1990, 1
    Lcml 1989–#
    Ob*

B

**Bach: Journal of the Riemenschneider
Institute**
0005–3600; TNG US799
US–Berea, OH: Bach–Riemenschneider
Institute, Baldwin–Wallace College, 1970–

    Bu 1 (1970), 3, 4; 20 (1989), 1, 2
    CDu 3 (1973)–#
    Cu 1 (1970)–#*
    En 1 (1970)–#
    Er 1 (1970)–2 (1971); 15 (1984)
    HUu 1 (1970)–24 (1993)
    Lbl*
    Lcm 9 (1978), 4; 13 (1982), 3
    Lcml 1 (1970)*; 2 (1971)–#
    Lu 1 (1970)–2 (1971); 3 (1972), 4; 4 (1973),
       1, 2, 4; 5 (1974)–7 (1976)
    Ob*
    Ouf 1 (1970), 2, 4; 21 (1990)–#
    SFu 1 (1970)–13 (1982)

Bach-Jahrbuch
Fellinger 1968/1704; TNG D434; 0084–7682
D–Leipzig [etc.]: Breitkopf und Härtel, 1904–

Bp*
BRu 1 (1904)–38 (1950) [m]; 65 (1979)–79 (1993)
Bs 71 (1985)–74 (1988)
BSdsc*
Bu 1 (1904)–29 (1932); 62 (1976); 64 (1978)–75 (1989)
CDu 1 (1904)–39 (1952); 41 (1954); 43 (1956); 45 (1958)–#
Cu 1 (1904)–#*
Er 1 (1904)–#
Gul 10 (1913)–37 (1940/48)
HUu 50 (1963)–78 (1992)
Lam 1 (1904); 3 (1906)–10 (1913); 12 (1915)–18 (1921); 20 (1923); 22 (1925); 24 (1927)–28 (1931); 30 (1933)
LAu 14 (1917); 39 (1952)
Lbbc 1 (1904)–#
Lbl*
Lcm 1 (1904)–32 (1935); 46 (1959)
Lkc 41 (1954); 44 (1957); 54 (1967)–#·
Lu 1 (1904)–41 (1954); 43 (1956)–45 (1958); 48 (1961)–#
Mcm 63 (1977)–#
Mpl 48 (1961)–#*
Mu 1 (1904)–39 (1952); 67 (1981)–70 (1984); 72 (1986)–#
NO 1 (1904)–39 (1952)
Ob 1 (1904)–#
Ouf 1 (1904)–49 (1962); 52 (1965)–#
R 39 (1952)–#
SA 22 (1925)–38 (1950); 48 (1961); 50 (1963); 66 (1980)–73 (1987)
SFu 38 (1950)–# [w 40 (1953)]

Bach Society Bulletin
GB–Granborough, 1977–

EIR:Dtc 1 (1977), 1
Lbbc 1 (1977), 1
Lbl*
Lsa*
Ob*

Ballade: Tidsskrift for Ny Musikk [= Journal for New Music]
TNG N48; 0332–5148
N–Oslo: Ny Musikk, 1977–
[NOT IN BUCOMP1; superseded from 1995 by *Musikkmagasinet Ballade*]

Lbl 7, 1983–#

Ballet [1]
TNG GB369
GB–London: Ballet Publications, 1939; 1946–52
[From 1948 entitled *Ballet and Opera*; from 1953 absorbed into *Opera* (q.v.)]

BRp 7, 8, 1949
EIR:Dtc 2–12, 1946–52
Lba 2–6, 1946–48
Lbl*
Ob*

Ballet [2]
F/GB–Paris; London, 1950–

BSdsc 4 (1954); 9 (1959)

Ballet: the Russian Ballet League Periodical
GB–Tunbridge Wells: The Russian Ballet League, 1945–47
[From 1948 entitled *Ballet World* (q.v.)]

Lbl*

Ballet Album
GB–Edinburgh: Albyn Press, 1947–?

Lbl*
Ob*

Ballet and Opera *see* **Ballet [1]**

The Ballet Annual: a Record and Yearbook of the Ballet
TNG GB406
GB–London: A. and C. Black, 1947–64

BSdsc*
Lba 1 (1947)–18 (1963)
Lbl*
Lu 1 (1947)–18 (1963)
Ob*

Ballet Annual and Year Book *see* **The Dancing Times**

Ballet Carnaval
GB–London: Pendulum Publications, 1946–47
[Ceased publication with no. 6, July 1947]

Lbl*

Ballet-Hoo *see* **Ballethoo**

Ballet Review [1]
GB–Edinburgh: The Albyn Press, 1947
[Only one was published]

Lbl 1 (1947)
Ob 1 (1947)

Ballet Review [2]
0522–0653
US–New York: Dance Research Foundation,
1965–
[NOT IN BUCOMP1]

BSdsc 7 (1978/79)–#
Lbl*

Ballet Today
GB–London: Newman Wolsey Ltd, 1946–70
[Ceased publication with vol. 18 (1970), no. 10]

EIR:Dtc 1 (1946/48), 12–18 (1970), 10
Lba 15 (1967)–18 (1970), 10
Lbl*
Ob*

Ballet World
GB–London, 1948–?49
[Succeeded *Ballet: the Russian Ballet League
Periodical* (q.v.)]

Lbl*

Ballethoo
0045–1347
C–Winnipeg: Friends of the Royal Winnipeg
Ballet, 1969–
[NOT IN BUCOMP1]

BSdsc*

Ballett International
0722–6268
D–Cologne: Ballet-Bühnen-Verlag, 1978–93;
1994–
[NOT IN BUCOMP1; combined with *Tanz
aktuell* in 1993 to become *Ballett International,
Tanz aktuell* (1 (1994)–; published Seelze: E.
Friedrich, 1994–; ISSN 0947–0484)]

BSdsc 6 (1983)–#

Ballett International, Tanz aktuell *see* **Ballett
International**

Ballett Journal
0720–3896
D–Kielsberg: Ulrich Steiner Verlag für
Tanzliteratur, ?1952–
[NOT IN BUCOMP1]

BSdsc*

Balletto Oggi: Attualità e Cultura di Danza
I–Milan: Editrice Dansmedia, 1980–
[NOT IN BUCOMP1; also entitled *Ballettoggi*]

BSdsc*

Ballettoggi *see* **Balletto Oggi: Attualità e
Cultura di Danza**

**Ballroom and Band: the Journal of Better
Dancing to Better Music**
GB–London: Rolls House Publishing, 1934–?

Lbl*
Ob*

Ballroom Dancing Annual
0011–605X
GB–London: Dancing Times, 1946–?

Lbl*
Ob 1947–55

Ballroom Dancing Times
0005–4380
GB–London: Dancing Times, 1956–?
[NOT IN BUCOMP1]

EIR:Dtc 1 (1956), 1–7
Lbl*

**Balungan: a Publication of the American
Gamelan Institute**
0885–7113
US–Oakland, CA: American Gamelan Institute,
1984–
[NOT IN BUCOMP1]

Cu 1 (1984)–#
Yu 1 (1984)–#

B.A.M. *see* **Buenos Aires Musical**

Bam Balam
SA–Durban, 1975–
[NOT IN BUCOMP1]

Lsa 1, 2, 1975; 4–14, 1976–85

Band International: the Journal of the International Military Music Society
0263–5240
GB–London: International Military Music Society, 1978–
[NOT IN BUCOMP1]

   AB*
   Cu 4 (1982)–#
   En 4 (1982)–10 (1988), 1, 3; 11 (1989)–#
   EIR:Dtc 4 (1982), 1, 2
   Lbl 4 (1982)–#*

Band Leaders
US–Mount Morris, IL: Comic Corporation of America, 1943–46
[NOT IN BUCOMP1; entitled *Band Leaders and Record Review* from 3 (1946), 6; also related to earlier title of *All-American Band Leaders*]

   LOnjfa*

Band Leaders and Record Review *see* **Band Leaders**

The Bandmaster
TNG GB308
GB–London, 1925

   Lbl*
   Ob*

The Bandmaster's Help: a Register of Musicians Open to Engagements, and Entertainers' Advertiser
GB–London, 1901–04 [8 numbers in total]

   Lbl*

The Bandsman and Songster
TNG GD228
GB–London, 1907–37
[From 1909, Jan, entitled *The Bandsman, Songster and Local Officer of the Salvation Army*; from 1938 entitled *The Musician of the Salvation Army* (q.v.)]

   Lbl*

The Bandsman, Songster and Local Officer of the Salvation Army *see* **The Bandsman and Songster**

The Bandsman's World
TNG GB332
GB–London, 1929–30

   Lbl*
   Ob*

Bandstand: South Africa's Music Magazine
SA–Johannesburg, 1951–?

   Lbl*

Bandwagon
GB–London: Norman Kark, 1942–
[NOT IN BUCOMP1]

   EIR:Dtc 4 (1946)–14 (1953), 2

Banff Letters
0713–9179
C–Banff, Alberta: Banff Centre School of Fine Arts, 1982–
[NOT IN BUCOMP1]

   Lam 1984, Win, Spr

The Banjo World: a Journal devoted to the Banjo, Mandoline and Guitar
Fellinger 1968/1202; TNG GB153
GB–London, 1893–1917
[Ceased publication with no. 267, 1917]

   En 1 (1893), 4
   Lcs 1 (1893)–4 (1897), 35; 6 (1898/99), 48–59
   Ob 1–267, 1893–1917

The Bantock Society Journal
1365–7143
GB–Bristol: Bantock Society, n.s. 1996–
[NOT IN BUCOMP1]

   Lbar 1, 1996–#
   Ltc 1996, Oct–#

The Bantock Society Newsletter
GB–London: The Bantock Society, 1984–?

   Lam 1984, Spr
   Lbar 1984–87, Aut
   Mcm 1984, Spr–Aut; 1985, Win; 1987, Aut; 1988, Aut

Der Bär: Jahrbuch von Breitkopf und Härtel
TNG D618
D–Leipzig: Breitkopf und Härtel, 1924–30

Cu 1 (1924)–6 (1930)
Lbl 1 (1924)–6 (1930) [2 copies]
Lcm 1 (1924)–6 (1930)
Lu 1 (1924)–2 (1925); 4 (1927)
Ob 3 (1926)

Barbican
GB–London: Barbican Centre, 198?–
[NOT IN BUCOMP1]

Lcm 1986, Dec/1987, Jan
Lcm (p) 1986, Dec/1987, Jan; 1987,
Mar/Apr, May/July; 1988, June/July–
Oct/Nov

Barbirolli Society Newsletter
GB–Retford [etc.]: Barbirolli Society, 1972–
[NOT IN BUCOMP1]

Cu 17, 1978–#
EIR:Dtc 17–35, 1978–90
En 17, 1978–# [w 20]
Mcm 1, 1972–#
Mpl 1, 1972–#

Das Bärenreiter-Jahrbuch
TNG D615
D–Kassel: Bärenreiter, 1925–30

Lu 1925–30

B.A.S.B.W.E. Journal *see* **Journal of the British Association of Symphonic Bands and Wind Ensembles**

B.A.S.B.W.E. London and Home Counties News
GB–Harrow: British Association of Symphonic Bands and Wind Ensembles, 1989–
[NOT IN BUCOMP1]

Lbl*

B.A.S.B.W.E. Newsletter
GB–?: British Association of Symphonic Bands and Wind Ensembles, ?–?
[NOT IN BUCOMP1]

Lam 1985, June; 1990, 4

B.A.S.C. News
0953–7538
GB–London: British Association of Sound Collections, 1987–
[NOT IN BUCOMP1; preceded 1980–86 by the *International Association of Sound Archives, UK Branch: Newsletter* (q.v.)]

Cu 1 (1987)–#
EIR:Dtc 1 (1987)–#
Lsa 1 (1987)–# [w 3]

B.A.S.C.A. News: Incorporating Songwriters' Guild News
0144–9621
GB–London: British Academy of Songwriters, Composers and Authors, 19?–

Cu 116, 1980–#
EIR:Dtc 154, 1990–#
Lbl*
Ob*

Basler Jahrbuch für historische Musikpraxis
TNG CH180
CH–Winterthur: Amadeus, 1977–

Bu 1981
Cu 1977–#
Gul 1977–#
Lbbc 1977–82
Lu 1977–#
Ob*
Ouf 1977–#

The Bass Drum
Fellinger 1968/1660; TNG GB200
GB–London, 1903
[6 nos only]

Lbl*

The Bass Drum: the Official Gazette of the N.F.P.M.
Fellinger 1968/2109; TNG GB255
GB–London: National Federation of Professional Musicians, 1912–13
[17 nos published]

Lbl*

Bassist and Bass Techniques
GB–Bath, 1996–
[NOT IN BUCOMP1]

Cu 1996–#

Bat Kol: Israel's Music Journal
TNG IL6
IL–Tel Aviv: The Israel Composers' League,
1956; 1960–61
[NOT IN BUCOMP1]

    Lcml 1961, 1

The Baton: a Newsletter for Readers of the
Great Musicians
GB–?London, 1983
[NOT IN BUCOMP1]

    ALb 47, 1983
    Lcm 1–47, 1983

The Baton: Magazine of the Philatelic Music
Circle
TNG GB543: 0951–9555
GB–Harrow: Philatelic Music Circle, 1969–
[NOT IN BUCOMP1]

    Cu 14–18, 1973–74
    EIR:Dtc 4 (1973), 2–6 (1974), 2

The Bawbee Bagpipe: Being a Choice
Selection of Amusing and Instructive Tales,
Scotch Songs, Dreams, etc.
GB–Edinburgh, 1833
[12 numbers in all]

    Lbl*

Bax Society Bulletin
TNG GB536
GB–London: Bax Society, 1968–73
[Ceased publication with vol. 2 no. 11 (1973)]

    AB 1 (1968)–2 (1973), 11
    Cu 1 (1968), 2–2 (1973), 4
    EIR:Dtc 1 (1968)–2 (1973), 11
    En 1 (1968)–2 (1973), 11
    Lam 1 (1968), 2
    Lbl*
    Lcml 1 (1968)–2 (1973), 4
    Lsa 1 (1968)–2 (1973), 11 [w 8]
    Lu 1 (1968), 2
    Ob*

Bayreuth-Album 1889 [–1896]
Fellinger 1968/1094; TNG D301
D–Berlin; Elberfeld, 1889–96

    Lbl 1889, 1891, 1892, 1896

Bayreuther Blätter: Monatschrift des
Bayreuther Patronatvereines [...]
Fellinger 1968/755; TNG D225
D–Bayreuth: E. Schmeitzner, 1878–1938
[Ceased publication with vol. 61 (1938)]

    EIR:Dtc 1 (1878)–2 (1879)
    Lbl 1 (1878)–61 (1938)
    Lu 19 (1896)–21 (1898)

Bazaar: South Asian Arts Magazine
GB–London: South Asian Arts Forum, 1987–
[NOT IN BUCOMP1]

    Lbl*
    Lsa 1–5, 1987–88
    Ob*
    TOd 1–23, 1987–93

B.B. Review: the Official Journal of the
British Blues Network
0953–8739
GB–London: BB Review, 1988–
[NOT IN BUCOMP1]

    Lbl*

B.B.C. Folk Club Magazine
GB–London: BBC, ?1965–
[NOT IN BUCOMP1; later entitled Shindig]

    Lcs 10–21, 1967–68

B.B.C. Music Club Magazine see Music Club
Magazine

B.B.C. Music Magazine
0966–7180
GB–London: BBC, 1992–
[NOT IN BUCOMP1]

    AB 1 (1992/93), 5–#
    ALb 1 (1992/93), 7–
    BLBBC 1 (1992/93)–#
    BRp [c (2 years)]
    Bs 1 (1992/93)–#
    BTp [c (1 year)]
    CDu 1 (1992/93), 3–#
    Cu 1 (1992/93)–#
    DDp [c (1 year)]
    EIR:Dtc 1 (1992/93)–#
    En 1 (1992/93)–#
    Ep 1 (1992/93)–#
    GU 1 (1992/93), 6, 8–#
    HE 1 (1992/93),4–#
    IOW 1 (1992/93), 3–#
    IP [c (2 years)]

Lam 1 (1992/93), 7; 3 (1994/95)–#
Lbbc 1 (1992/93)–#
Lbk 1 (1992/93), 12–#
Lbl*
Lbo 2 (1993/94), 7, 10–#
Lcu 1 (1992/93), 2–#
Lsa 1 (1992/93)–#
Lsut [c (1 year)]
Ltc 3 (1994/95)–#
LVp 1 (1992/93)–#
Mcm 1 (1992/93)–#
Mmu (a) 1 (1992/93), 10–#
Mu 1 (1992/93)–#
NOp [c (2 years)]
Ob*
Op 1 (1992/93), 7–#
Oub 2 (1993/94)–#
Ouf 5 (1996/97), 10–#
PRp [c (1 year)]
SHRp 1 (1992/93)–#

B.B.C. Philharmonic Club Magazine
GB–London: BBC, ?1982–?
[NOT IN BUCOMP1]

Mcm 4–7, 1983–84

B.B.C. Popular Music Almanac
GB–London: BBC, 1987–?
[NOT IN BUCOMP1]

Lbbc 1 (1987)–#

B.B.C. Radio Orchestra Radio Big Band Fan Club [Newsletter]
GB–London: BBC, ?1983–?
[NOT IN BUCOMP1]

Lam 4, 1986

B.B.C. Symphony Club Newsletter
GB–London: BBC, ?1982–?
[NOT IN BUCOMP1]

Lcm 4, 1984

B.C.M.A. Bulletin
GB–Newton Abbot: British Country Music Association, 1976–

AB 1980, June–1983, Apr*
BDp 1979–80; 1982–87
Cu 1976–#
EIR:Dtc 1976–83
Ob*

Bealoideas: the Journal of the Folklore of Ireland Society
0332–270X
EIRE–Dublin: Folklore of Ireland Society, 1927–

AB 1 (1927)–#
EIR:Dtc 1 (1927)–#
Lbl*
Lcs 1 (1927)–58 (1990)*
Ob*

The Beat
GB–London, ?1984–
[NOT IN BUCOMP1]

Ob 26, 1987–#

The Beat: Official Magazine of the Ted Heath Club
TNG GB407
GB–London: Ted Heath Club, 1947–49
[From 1949–50 continued as *The New Beat: the World's Brightest Modern Music Magazine (incorporating Zest)* (TNG GB426)]

Lbl*

The Beat: Reggae, African, Caribbean, World Music
1063–5319
US–Los Angeles, CA: Bongo Productions, 1982–
[NOT IN BUCOMP1]

Lbl*
Msuc 12 (1993), July–#

Beat: the Heart of the Music Scene
TNG GB463
GB–Liverpool, 1957–

Cbijs 1 (1957), 1; 2 (1958), 5
Lbl*

Beat Box *see* Beatbox

Beat Instrumental Monthly *see* Beat Monthly

Beat Instrumental, Songwriting and Recording *see* Sound International

Beat Monthly
TNG GB501
GB–London, 1963–80
[From 18, 1964, entitled *Beat Instrumental Monthly*]

AB 2–12, 1963/64 [w 6, 7, 11]
Cu 1–139, 1963–74; 140–64, 1975–80*
EIR:Dtc 112–160, 1972–80
En 3, 1963/64
En 1–160, 1963–80*
Lbl*
Lsa 1975*; 1978*
Ob*

Beat of the Street
0958–0417
GB–London: Beat of the Street, 1989–
[NOT IN BUCOMP1]

Lbl 2, 1989–#

Beatbox
0962–7200
GB–London: Dennis Oneshots, 1991–
[NOT IN BUCOMP1]

Lbl*

The Beatles Book
0261–1600
GB–London: Beat Publications, 1963–69;
reissued 1976–82
[Also known as *Beatles Book Monthly*]

AB 2–9, 1963–64
Cu 1–77, 1963–69; 1976–82
EIR:Dtc 1976–82
En 1976–82
Lbl*
Ob*

Beatles Book Monthly *see* **The Beatles Book**

Beethoven-Forschung
Fellinger 1968/2062; TNG A167
A–Vienna, 1911–25

Cu 1 (1911)–10 (1925)
Lbl*

Beethoven Forum
1059–5031
US–Lincoln, NA: University of Nebraska Press,
1992–
[NOT IN BUCOMP1]

BRu 1 (1992)–2 (1993)
BSdsc*
Cu 1 (1992)–#
Lbbc 1 (1992)–#
Mu 1 (1992)–#
Ob 1 (1992)–#

Beethoven-Jahrbuch *see* **Beethovenjahrbuch**

Beethoven Journal *see* **The Beethoven Newsletter**

The Beethoven Newsletter
0898–6185
US–San Jose, CA: San Jose University, Ira F.
Brilliant Center for Beethoven Studies/
American Beethoven Society, 1986–
[NOT IN BUCOMP1; entitled *Beethoven Journal* from 10 (1995)]

Bu 1 (1986), 1; 3 (1988)–#
Cu 1 (1986)–#
Lam 1 (1986), 1
Lcml 1 (1986)–2 (1987); 3 (1988)*;
4 (1989)–#
Lu 1 (1986), 1
SOu 1 (1986)–#

Beethovenjahrbuch
Fellinger 1968/1907; TNG D473; 0522–5949
D–Munich, 1908–09; Bonn: Beethovenhaus,
1953–
[From 1942 entitled *Neues Beethoven-Jahrbuch*
(q.v.); from 1953 entitled *Beethoven-Jahrbuch*
(TNG D925), with new numbering sequence]

Au n.s. 6 (1965/68); 8 (1971/72)–10
(1978/81)
BSdsc*
Bu n.s. 1 (1953/54)–5 (1961/62)
CDu n.s. 1 (1953/54)–#
Cu 1 (1908)–2 (1909); n.s. 1 (1953/54)–#
Er 1 (1908)–2 (1909)
HUu n.s. 9 (1973/77)–10 (1978/81)
Lbbc 1 (1908)–6 (1935); n.s. 1 (1953/54)–
2 (1956)
Lbl*
Lcm 7 (1969)
Lu 1 (1953/54)–#
Mcm 10 (1978/81)–#
Mu 6 (1965/68)–10 (1978/81)
NO 1 (1953/54)–10 (1978/81)
Ob*
SFu 1 (1908)–2 (1909); n.s. 1 (1953/54)–#
SOu 1 (1908); 1 (1953/54)–10 (1978/81)

Beihefte zu den Denkmälern Deutscher Tonkunst
D–Wiesbaden: Breitkopf und Härtel, 1960–
[NOT IN BUCOMP1]

Ouf 1, 2, 1960

Beihefte zum Archiv für Musikwissenschaft
TNG D552; 0570–6769
D–Wiesbaden, 1966–

BSdsc*
Lbl*
Ob*
Ouf 1 (1966)–#
SA 1 (1966)–18 (1979)

Beiträge [der] Österreichische Gesellschaft für Musik
TNG D1057; 0078–3471
D–Kassel: Bärenreiter, 1967–
[NOT IN BUCOMP1]

Cu 1967–#
Lu 1968
Mu 1972/73; 1976/78
Ob*

Beiträge zur Bachforschung
0233–0105
D–Leipzig: Nationale Forschungs– und
Gedenkstatten J.S. Bach der DDR, 1982–91
[NOT IN BUCOMP1]

Cu 1 (1982)–9/10 (1991)
Ob 3 (1984)–9/10 (1991)

Beiträge zur Gregorianik
D–Regensburg: Gustav Bosse, 1985–
[NOT IN BUCOMP1]

Bu 3 (1986)–#
Cu 1 (1985)–#
Ob 1 (1985)–#

Beiträge zur Jazzforschung/Studies in Jazz Research
A–Graz: Akademische Druck– und
Verlagsanstalt, 1969–

Lbl*
Ob*

Beiträge zur Musikforschung
D–Halle; Berlin, 1935–43

BSdsc*
Lbl*
Ob*

Beiträge zur Musikreflexion
D–Steinfeld: Salvator Verlag, 1975–
[NOT IN BUCOMP1]

BSdsc*

Beiträge zur Musikwissenschaft
TNG D1013; 0005–8106
D–Berlin: Verlag Neue Musik, 1959–

Bs 26 (1984)–34 (1992)
BSdsc*
CDu 8 (1966)–34 (1992); Beiheft 1 (1993)
Cu 1 (1959)–34 (1992); Beiheft 1 (1993)–#
LAu 5 (1963)–6 (1964), 1; 9 (1967), 2–4
Lbl*
Lcm 23 (1981), 3
Lgo 1 (1959)–4 (1962)
Lu 5 (1963)–13 (1971); 30 (1988)–#
Ob*

Beiträge zur musikwissenschaftlichen Forschung in der DDR
D–Leipzig: VEB Deutscher Verlag für Musik,
1971–
[NOT IN BUCOMP1]

BSdsc*

Beiträge zur Volksmusikforschung
D–Berlin: Humboldt-Universität, 1939–

Lbl*
Ob*

Het Belgisch Muziekleven [= Belgian Musical Life]
B–Brussels, ?1962–
[NOT IN BUCOMP1; also known as *Het Muziekleven in Belgie*]

HUu 12 (1973), 3–18 (1979), 2

Belgisch Tijdschrift voor Muziekwetenschap
see Revue Belge de Musicologie

The Bell
GB–London: Stainer and Bell, ?–
[NOT IN BUCOMP1]

ALb 1991, Spr

Bell News and Ringers' Record
GB–London, 1881–1915

Bp 4 (1884)–34 (1915)
Cu 1 (1881)–34 (1915)
Lbl*
Mpl 6 (1886)–12 (1892)
Ob*

Bellringer
GB–Manchester, 1907

Ob*

Bells and Bellringing
GB–Tunbridge Wells, 1966–

BSdsc*
Ob*

Benjamin Carr Musical Journal *see* **The Musical Journal for the Piano-Forte in two Sections, one of Vocal, and one of Instrumental Music: Selected, and, Arranged by Benjamin Carr**

Benslow Bulletin
GB–?Hitchin: Benslow Music Trust, ?1968–
[NOT IN BUCOMP1]

Re 20 (1987) #

BeQuadro: Bollettino Trimestrale del Centro di Ricerca e di Sperimentazione per la Didattica Musicale
I–San Domenico di Fiesole: CRSDM, 1981–
[NOT IN BUCOMP1]

Lbl 4 (1984), 14; 5 (1985), 18/19–8 (1988), 32; 9 (1989), 34–10 (1990), 37/38

Berlin Komische Oper Jahrbuch *see* **Jahrbuch der Komischen Oper Berlin**

Berliner Allgemeine musikalische Zeitung
Fellinger 1968/64; TNG D53
D–Berlin: Schlesinger, 1824–30
[NOT IN BUCOMP1]

Mpl 1824–29*

Berliner Beiträge zur Musikwissenschaft
D–Leipzig, 1925

Lbl*

Berliner Musik-Zeitung Echo
Fellinger 1968/290; TNG D119
D–Berlin: Schlesinger, 1851–79
[Entitled *Echo: Berliner Musik-Zeitung* from vol. 26 (1876)–29 (1879)]

Lbl 19 (1869), 20–22, 26, 33, 34

Berlinische musikalische Zeitung
Fellinger 1968/13; TNG D38
D–Berlin: Frölichschen Buch- und Musikhandlung, 1805–06

Cu 1 (1805)–2 (1806), 52
EXu 1 (1805)–2 (1806)
Lbl*
Lu 1 (1805)–2 (1806) [Reprint ed.]

Berlinische musikalische Zeitung: historischen und kritischen Inhalts
TNG D28
D–Berlin, 1793–94

Er 1–52, 1793–94
Lbl*

Berlinisches litterarisches Wochenblatt *see* **Literatur- und Theater-Zeitung**

Berlioz Society Bulletin
TNG GB443
GB–London: Berlioz Society, 1952–

Cu 56, 1967–#
DS 101, 1978–#
EIR:Dtc 57, 1967–#
En 20, 1957–# [w 37]
Lam 68, 1970–#
Lba [c]
Lbl*
Lcm 68, 69, 1970
Lcml 38–66, 1962–70*; 68, 1970–#
Lsa 1, 1952–# [w 2, 5, 7–10, 12–15, 134]
Lu 57, 1967
Ob*

Berühmte Musiker
D–Berlin: Harmonie-Verlagsgesellschaft, 1898–1917

Lbl*
Ob*

Besson's Brass Band Budget
GB–London, 1901–11

Lbl*

Betrachtungen der Mannheimer Tonschule
TNG D15
D–Mannheim, 1778–81

Cu 1 (1778)–3 (1781) [Reprint ed.]
Ob* [Reprint ed.]

Bibliografia Republicii Socialiste Romania:
Note Muzicale, Discuri, Casete
RO–Bucharest, ?1968–
[NOT IN BUCOMP1]

   Cu 20 (1987)–#

Bibliografický Katalog [= Bibliographic
Catalogue]
CZ–Prague, 1922–
[Entitled *Bibliograficky Katalog Ceskoslovenské
Republiky: Čast B: Hudebniny* from 5 (1937)–7
(1939), and 13 (1945)–14 (1946); entitled
*Bibliograficky Katalog Československé
Republiky: C: Hudebniny* from 15 (1947)–18
(1950); entitled *Bibliograficky Katalog ČSR:
České a Slovenské Hudebniny*, 1951–54, and
1955–60. From 1955 included sound recordings
data, as *Bibliograficky Katalog CSR: Slovenské
Knihy/Slovenské Hudebniny* (1955–59);
*Bibliograficky Katalog CSSR: Ceské Hudebniny
a Gramofonove Desky*, 1960–88 (ISSN 0323–
1569); *Bibliograficky Katalog CSFR: Ceské
Hudebiny, Gramofonové Desky a Kompaktni
Disky*, 1989–# (ISSN 0862–8580)]

   Cu 1989–#
   Lbl*
   Lsa 1949–83; 1989–92
   Ob*

Bibliograficky Katalog Československé
Republiky: C: Hudebniny *see* Bibliografický
Katalog

Bibliograficky Katalog Ceskoslovenské
Republiky: Čast B: Hudebniny *see*
Bibliografický Katalog

Bibliograficky Katalog CSFR: Ceské
Hudebiny, Gramofonové Desky a Kompaktni
Disky *see* Bibliografický Katalog

Bibliograficky Katalog ČSR: České a
Slovenské Hudebniny *see* Bibliografický
Katalog

Bibliograficky Katalog CSR: Slovenské
Knihy/Slovenské Hudebniny *see*
Bibliografický Katalog

Bibliograficky Katalog CSSR: Ceské
Hudebniny a Gramofonove Desky *see*
Bibliografický Katalog

Bibliografija Jugoslavije: Knjige, Brosure i
Muzikalije [= Books, Pamphlets and Scores]
SRB–Belgrade, 1950–
[NOT IN BUCOMP1]

   Cu 1950–#

Le Bibliographe Musicale
Fellinger 1968/647; TNG F142
F–Paris, 1872–76
[NOT IN BUCOMP1]

   Cu 1–29, 1872–76 [Reprint ed.]
   Ob 1–29, 1872–76 [Reprint ed.]

Bibliographia Musicologica
0084–7844
NL–Utrecht: Joachimsthal, 1968–76
[Ceased publication with vol. 9 (1976)]

   Bp 1 (1968)–9 (1976)
   Cu 1 (1968)–9 (1976)
   EIR:Duc 1 (1968)–9 (1976)
   Ob*
   Ouf 1 (1968)–9 (1976)

Bibliographic Guide to Music 1975 [–1996
etc.]
0360–2753
US–Boston, MA: G. K. Hall, 1975–
[NOT IN BUCOMP1]

   BRp 1975–#
   EIR:Duc 1975–#
   EIR:MEtc 1976–#
   Lbbc 1975–#
   Lgo 1978–80
   Mpl 1977
   Yu 1975–80

Bibliographie des Musikschrifttums
TNG D777; 0340–2169
D/GB–Mainz; London: Schott [for the
Staatliches Institut für Musikforschung
Preussischer Kulturbesitz], 1936–41; 1950–

   BTu 1961–77
   Bu 1936–39; 1952; 1956–68
   Cu 1936–37; 1950–#
   EIR:MEtc 1972–78
   Lbbc*
   Lbl*
   LEbc 1950–#
   Lu*
   Ob 1936–#
   Ouf 1950–81
   R 1950–1967
   SFu 1954–71
   Yu 1950–80

Bibliographie Musicale [Française] *see*
Catalogue des Nouvelles Oeuvres Musicales
Françaises

Bibliographie Nationale Française:
Supplément 3, Musique
F–Paris: Bibliothèque Nationale, 1990–
[NOT IN BUCOMP1]

　　Ob 1990–#

Bibliography of Jazz Literature in Periodicals
see Jazz Index: Bibliographie unselbständiger
Jazzliteratur/Bibliography of Jazz Literature
in Periodicals

Bibliomusica: Revista de Documentacion
Musical
ME–Mexico: Consejo Nacional para la Cultura
y las Artes, Instituto Nacional de Bellas Artes,
1991–
[NOT IN BUCOMP1]

　　Lu 2, 1992

Biblioteca Illustrata della Gazzetta Musicale
di Milano *see* Gazzetta Musicale di Milano

Biblioteka Muzyczna [= Music Library]
PL–Szczecin: Stowarzyszenie Bibliotekarzy
Polskich, Sekcja Bibliotek Muzycznych, and
International Association of Music Libraries,
Archives and Documentation Centres, Polish
Section, 1979–
[NOT IN BUCOMP1]

　　Ob 1983/84–#

Bielefelder Jazz
D–Bielefeld, ?1960–
[NOT IN BUCOMP1]

　　Lsa 16 (1975/76); 19 (1981); 21 (1983)–22
　　(1984); 24 (1986); 27 (1989)–#

Bielefelder Katalog: K *see* Bielefelder
Katalog: Katalog der Schallplatten
klassischer Musik

Bielefelder Katalog: Katalog der
Schallplatten klassischer Musik
0006–2103
D–Bielefeld, ?1953–
[NOT IN BUCOMP1; succeeded by *Bielefelder
Katalog: K* 22 (1974)– 28 (1980) (ISSN 0171–
9483); later succeeded by *Bielefelder Katalog:
Klassik* 28 (1980), 2–# (ISSN 0721–7153)]

LAu 20 (1972)–30 (1982)
Lsa 8 (1960)–# [w 14 (1966), 1; 18 (1970), 1,
　　2; 20 (1972), 2; 22 (1974)–24 (1976), 1]

Bielefelder Katalog: Klassik *see* Bielefelder
Katalog: Katalog der Schallplatten
klassischer Musik

Big Bands Unlimited
GB–Blackburn, ?–1974

　　Cbijs 23, 24, 1973
　　LOnjfa*

Big Beat
GB–London, 1963–?

　　Lbl*
　　Ob*

Bijdragen tot een Repertorium der
Nederlandsche Muzik-Literatur
[= Contributions to a Repertory of Dutch
Music Literature]
NL–Amsterdam, 1908–?
[NOT IN BUCOMP1]

　　Cu 1 (1908)

The Billboard *see* Billboard Advertising

Billboard: the International Music-Record-
[Tape] Newsweekly *see* Billboard Advertising

Billboard Advertising
TNG US260; 0006–2510
US–Cincinnati, OH: Billboard Advertising
Company, 1894–
[From 1 Nov. 1896 entitled *The Billboard*;
entitled *Billboard International Buyer's Guide of
the Music-Record Industry* from 1958; from
1960 entitled *Billboard International Buyer's
Guide of the Music Record Tape Industry* (ISSN
0067–8600); from 9 Jan. 1961 entitled *Billboard
Music Week*; from 5 Jan. 1963 entitled *Billboard:
the International Music-Record Newsweekly*;
from 7 June 1969 entitled *Billboard: the
International Music-Record-Tape Newsweekly*]

　　BLp [c]
　　Lam 105 (1993), 10–34, 36–52; 106 (1994),
　　　3–5, 6, 7, 10, 12–16, 18–21, 23–108
　　　(1996), 5
　　Lbbc [c]
　　Lcml 100 (1988)–#
　　Lsa 1962, Sep–#*
　　Msuc 105 (1993), May 29–#

Billboard Country Music Sourcebook *see*
Country Music Source Book

Billboard International Buyer's Guide of the
Music-Record Industry *see* Billboard
Advertising

Billboard International Buyer's Guide of the
Music Record Tape Industry *see* Billboard
Advertising

Billboard Music Week *see* Billboard
Advertising

Bilten, SOKOJ [=Bulletin]
HR–Belgrade: Union of Yugoslav Composers'
Organisations, 1972–93
[NOT IN BUCOMP1; English title is *Union of
Yugoslav Composers Organisations Bulletin.*
Succeeded from 1998 by the *SOKOJ Letter*]

   Cpl 45–66, 1978–80*

Bim Bam Boom
US–Bronx, NY: Bim Bam Boom Publications,
1971–74
[NOT IN BUCOMP1]

   Lsa 1–13, 1971–74

Bing: the Magazine of the Crosby Circle
GB–Cwmbran [etc.]: International Crosby
Circle, 1950–?65; n.s. 1966–
[NOT IN BUCOMP1]

   LOnjfa*

Bingo
0523–6207
F–Paris: Bingo, 1953–
[NOT IN BUCOMP1]

   Lsa 452–460, 1990–91

B.I.O.S. Journal
0141–4992
GB–Oxford: British Institute of Organ Studies,
1977–

   Bu 6 (1982); 12 (1988)
   Cu 1 (1977)–13 (1989)
   EIR:Dtc 2 (1978)–13 (1989)
   EIR:Duc 1 (1977)–7 (1983)
   EIR:MEtc 8 (1984)–#
   En 1 (1977)–6 (1982); 8 (1984); 10 (1986)–#
   Gul 1 (1977)–#
   Lam 1 (1977)–15 (1991)

Lam (o) 1 (1977); 4 (1980)–8 (1984);
   10 (1986); 13 (1989)
Lbar 1 (1977)–#
Lcm 1 (1977)–#
Lcml 1 (1977)–#
Lgsm 1 (1977)–#
LRHBNC 1 (1977)–10 (1986)
Lrco 1 (1977)–#
Lu 4 (1980)
Mcm 5 (1981)–#
Mpl 1 (1977)–#
NO 1 (1977)–6 (1982)
Ob 1 (1977)–#
R 1 (1977)–#
Yu 1 (1977)–6 (1982); 9 (1985)

B.I.O.S. Reporter
0309–8052
GB–Mansfield: British Institute of Organ
Studies, 1977–

   Cu 1 (1977)–#
   EIR:Dtc 1 (1977)–#
   En 1 (1977)–9 (1985), 3; 10 (1986), 1–3;
     11 (1987)–13 (1989), 4; 14 (1990)–#
   Lbl*
   Lcm 1 (1977)–3 (1979), 3; 4 (1980)–
     9 (1985), 3; 10 (1986)– 12 (1988), 1, 3;
     13 (1989)–#
   Lrco 1 (1977)–#
   Mcm 1 (1977)–#
   Ob*

The Birmingham and Midlands Musical
Journal and Dramatic News
Fellinger 1968/945; TNG GB112
GB–Birmingham: James Handley, 1884–85

   Lbl 1884, 1–8, 14

Birmingham Musical Examiner and
Dramatic Review
Fellinger 1968/229; TNG GB35
GB–Birmingham: Thomas Harrison, 1845–46
[19 numbers published, between 1845, Sep and
1846, Jan]

   Bu 1–19, 1845–46
   Lbl 1–10, 1845

B.I.R.S. Bulletin *see* British Institute of
Recorded Sound: Bulletin

A Bit of Culture
GB–York, 1980–
[NOT IN BUCOMP1]

   Lbl*

Biuletyn Fonograficzny/Bulletin Phonographique
0067–8996
PL–Poznan: Nakl. Poznanskiego Towarzystwa Przyjaciol Nauk, 1953–75
[Ceased publication with vol. 16 (1975)]

BSdsc 4 (1961)–16 (1975)

B.J.M.E. see **British Journal of Music Education**

Black Dwarf
0142–2804
GB–Bristol, 1978–
[NOT IN BUCOMP1]

Lbl*

Black Echoes
GB–London, 198?–
[NOT IN BUCOMP1; later called Echoes]

Lbbc [c]
Lcml (q) [c (3 months)]
LEc [c (1 year)]
Lgr (p) [c]
Lgr (w) [c (6 months)]
Lgr (wg) [c (1 year)]
Lh [c (1 year)]
Lha [c (6 months)]
Lhg 1993–#
Lis [c (1 year)]
Lk(nk) [c (1 month)]
Ll [c]
Lsa 1986–#
Ob*
TOd 1982, May 22

Black Music
TNG GB565
GB–London: IPC Magazines, 1973–78
[Absorbed in 1978 into Black Music and Jazz Review (q.v.)]

Cbijs 1 (1973/74), 1–12
Cu 2 (1975), 20–5 (1978), 52
EIR:Dtc 2 (1975)–5 (1978), 52
En 2 (1975)–5 (1978), 52
Lgo 1 (1973/74), 10–5 (1978), 49, 51, 52 [w 2 (1974/75), 17; 3 (1976), 26; 4 (1977), 39–43]
Lsa 1 (1973/74)–5 (1978), 51
Lu 1 (1973/74)
MK 3 (1976)–5 (1978)
Ob*

Black Music and Jazz Review
0307–2169
GB–London: IPC Magazines, 1978–84
[Preceded by Black Music (q.v.); incorporated into Blues and Soul and Disco Music Review (q.v.) in Aug 1984. Also known as BM]

AB 2 (1979/80), 9–7 (1984), 1
Cu 1 (1978)–7 (1984), 1
EIR:Dtc 1 (1978)–7 (1984), 1
En 1 (1978)–7 (1984)
Lbl*
Lcml 1 (1978)–7 (1984), 1
Lgo 1 (1978)–7 (1984) [w 4 (1981), 9; 5 (1982), 4–7, 9, 10, 2; 6 (1983), 8, 9, 11]
LOnjfa*
Lsa 1 (1978), Apr–7 (1984)*
Mmu 1 (1978)–2 (1979/80)
Ob*

Black Music Research Bulletin
0898–8536
US–Chicago, IL: Center for Black Music Research, 1978–?
[NOT IN BUCOMP1. Formerly entitled Black Music Research Newsletter]

TOd 10 (1988)–12 (1990), 2

Black Music Research Journal
0276–3605
US–Nashville, TN: Institute for Research in Black American Music, 1980–
[NOT IN BUCOMP1]

EXu 1 (1980)–#
Lmi 10 (1990)–13 (1993), 2
Lu 12 (1992)–#
TOd 8 (1988)–#

Black Music Research Newsletter see **Black Music Research Bulletin**

The Black Perspective in Music
TNG US835; 0090–7790
US–New York: Foundation for Research in the Afro-American Creative Arts, 1973–

BSdsc 1 (1973)–18 (1990)
Cu 1 (1973)–#
Exu 1 (1973)–18 (1990)
Lcml 1 (1973)–#
Lsa 1 (1973), 1; 2 (1974)–13 (1985); 15 (1987)–18 (1990)
Lu 3 (1975), 3
MK 1 (1973)–5 (1977)

Black Rose: the Thin Lizzy Magazine
0963–8881
GB–Belfast: C. Winstanley, 1989–
[NOT IN BUCOMP1]

Lbl 6, 1991–#

Black Wax Magazine
GB–London, 1973–?

Cbijs 1, 3–5, 1973

Blam!
GB–Chelmsford, ?1981–83
[NOT IN BUCOMP1]

Lbl*

Blätter aus dem Clementi-Archiv, Wenum
TNG NL107
NL–Wenum: Clementi Archiv, 1961–64
[12 nos published in total]

Gul 1 (1961/62)–2 (1962/63), 7
Lbl*
Lcml 1 (1961/62), 1, 2
Lu 1 (1961/62), 3

Blätter der Bayerischen Staatsoper
TNG D828
D–Munich: Bayerische Staatsoper, 1948–
[NOT IN BUCOMP1; continued as *Journal der Bayerischen Staatsoper*]

Lbl*
Lcm(p) 1979–80*

Blätter der Staatsoper
TNG D569
D–Berlin: Deutsche Staatsoper, 1920–43
[Ceased publication with vol. 23 (1943)]

Lbl*
Lcm 4 (1924), 6

Blätter der Sudetendeutschen *see* Der Auftakt

Blätter für Hymnologie
Fellinger 1968/914; TNG D261
D–Gotha: F. A. Perthes, 1883–89; 1894

Ob 1 (1883)–8 (1894)

Blätter für Kirchenmusik und Männergesang
Fellinger 1968/597; TNG A62
A–Vienna: A. Pickler's Witwe und Sohn, 1869–70

Lbl 1 (1869)–2 (1870)

Blodau Cerdd [= Flowers of Music]
GB–Aberystwyth; Llanidloes, 1852–54

AB 1–7, 1852–53

Blood and Honour: the Independent Voice of Rock Against Communism
GB–London: BM Skrewdriver [*sic*], 199?–
[NOT IN BUCOMP1]

Lbl 9, 199?

Blue Band Magazine: Journal of the Royal Marines Band Service and Royal Marines School of Music, Deal
GB–Deal, ?1950–

Cu 31 (1980), 3–#
EIR:Dtc 31 (1980)–#
Ob 31 (1980), 3–#

Bluegrass and Old Time Mandolin
GB–Crawley, ?1980–#

Cu 3 (1983), 6–4 (1984), 2
Ob*

Bluegrass Unlimited
0006–5137
US–Broad Run, VA: Bluegrass Unlimited, Inc., 1966–

Lsa 1975–# [w 1982, Mar–Dec; 1983–84, Feb; 1988, Feb–May; 1989, May]

Blues
B–Brussels, 1969

Cbijs 1 (1969), 2

Blues: Magazine of the New Rhythms
US–Columbus, Mississippi, 1929–30
[NOT IN BUCOMP1]

BRu 1929–30 [Reprint ed.]

Blues and Rhythm: the Gospel Truth
GB–Cheadle; London, 1984–
[NOT IN BUCOMP1; formerly *Sailor's Delight*]

EIR:Dp 33–73, 1987–92
EXu 1, 1984–#
Lbl*
LOnjfa*
Lsa 8, 9, 11, 1985; 83, 1993; 88, 1994–#

Blues and Soul and Disco Music Review
TNG GB526; 0045–2297
GB–London: Napfield, 1966–
[Incorporated *Black Music and Jazz Review*
(q.v.) from 1984, Aug.]

    AB 454, 1986
    BDp 1978–#
    BLp [c]
    BRp [c (2 years)]
    Cbijs 10, 11, 13, 1966; 60, 1971; 95, 1972;
      108, 117, 1973
    CH [c (1 year)]
    Cu 151–411, 1975–84
    EIR:Dp 474, 1987–#
    EIR:Dtc 167, 1975–#
    En 151, 1975–#*
    Lba [c (6 months)]
    Lbl*
    Lcml 412, 1984–#
    Lcml(q) [c (1 year)]
    Lgo 412, 1984
    Lgr(w) [c (1 year)]
    Lhg 1992–#
    Lha(f) [c (1 year)]
    Lh [c (1 year)]
    Lk [c (1 year)]
    Ll [c]
    LOnjfa 1972–84*; 1985–#
    Lsa 320–456, 1981–86*
    Lsut [c (1 year)]
    Lwf [c (6 months)]
    Lwwb [c]
    MK 1984–#
    Ob*
    SFp [c]
    WH [c (1 year)]

Blues-Link
0307–2241
GB–Barnet: Blues–Link, 1973–75
[Incorporated *Blues World* (q.v.) from 1974]

    Cbijs 1–6, 1973–75
    Cu 1–6, 1973–75
    EIR:Dtc 1–6, 1973–75
    Lsa 1–5, 1973–75
    Ob 1–6, 1973–75

Blues News
NZ–?, ?1969–?

    Cbijs 3, 1969

Blues Notes
A–Linz, 1969–

    Cbijs 21, 1974

Blues Research
US–Brooklyn, NY: Record Research, 1959–?

    Cbijs 8, 1962; 12, 1964
    Lsa 1–16, 1959–67 [w 2, 5, 6, 9]

Blues Revue *see* **Blues Revue Quarterly**

Blues Revue Quarterly
US–West Union, WV, 1991–
[NOT IN BUCOMP1; continued as *Blues Revue*
(ISSN 1076–6162)]

    Lsa 1, 1991; 10, 1993; 12, 1994–#

Blues Unlimited: the Journal of the Blues
Appreciation Society
TNG GB502; 0006–5153
GB–Bexhill-on-Sea: Blues Unlimited, 1963–

    Bp 60–148/49, 1969–87 [w 68–71; 113; 115;
      120; 131, 132]
    Cbijs 7, 1963; 10, 13–38, 1964–66; 50, 1968;
      63, 68, 1969; 71–114, 1970–75
    Cu 29–149, 1966–87
    EXu 1, 1963–#
    Lbl*
    LOnjfa*
    Lsa 6, 7, 1963; 13–17, 1964; 19, 23, 1965;
      41–55, 1967– 68; 57–69, 1969; 71–141,
      1970–81*
    MK 1979–87
    Ob*

Blues Unlimited Collectors Classics *see*
Collectors Classics

Blues World
TNG GB516
GB–Bristol, 1965–74
[Superseded by *Blues-Link* (q.v.)]

    Cbijs 7, 1966; 24–50, 1969–74
    Lsa 25–50, 1969–74

B.M. *see* **Black Music and Jazz Review**

B.M.G. *see* **B.M.G.: a Journal Devoted to the
Banjo, Mandoline and Guitar**

B.M.G.: a Journal Devoted to the Banjo,
Mandoline and Guitar
TNG GB197
GB–London, 1903–?83
[From 1973, Nov entitled *B.M.G.*; continued as
Guitarist (q.v.) from 1984]

AB 73 (1976), 850–852
BLp [c]
Bp*
Cu 56 (1959), 649–70 (1973), 818
EIR:Dtc 56 (1959), 649–70 (1973), 818
En 56 (1959), 649–70 (1973), 819
Lbl*
Lcm 43 (1946), 490; 52 (1955), 595; 69
 (1972), 801
Len [c (1 year)]
LOnjfa*
Lsa 60 (1963)–68 (1971)
Mpl 40 (1943)–42 (1945)
Ob*

BMI Canada: Newsletter
0380–5158
C–Ontario: Performing Right Organization of
Canada, 1965–90
[NOT IN BUCOMP1. Entitled *Music Scene*
from 237, 1967; absorbed into *Canadian
Composer* (q.v.) from 1990; 371 numbers in all]

Cu 305–371, 1979–90
Er 311–71, 1980–90
Gam 301–303, 1978; 306, 308–315,
 1979–80; 317–332, 1981–83; 334–339,
 1983–84; 341–344, 1985; 347, 350– 353,
 1986–87; 355, 356, 1987; 361, 363, 1988
Lbbc*
Mcm 262–263, 1971–72; 272–276, 1973–74
Yu 269–281, 284, 285, 287, 293, 294,
 1973–77

B.M.I. Music World
1042–6736
US–New York: BMI Corporate Relations
Department, 1987–
[NOT IN BUCOMP1; continuation of *B.M.I.:
the Many Worlds of Music*]

Lcml 1–4, 1987–88

B.M.I.: the Many Worlds of Music *see* B.M.I.
Music World

B.M.S. *see* British Music Society Bulletin

B.M.S. Live Performances Bulletin
GB–London: British Music Society, 1994–
[NOT IN BUCOMP1]

ALb 1, 1994–#

Le Boléro: Journal des Bals, Fêtes et Concerts
F–Paris, 1850

Lbl*

Boletim do Conservatorio Nacional
P–Lisbon: Conservatorio Nacional, 1947–?
[NOT IN BUCOMP1]

Lam 1 (1946/49), 1–3

Boletín de la Fundacion Archivo Manuel de
Falla
E–Granada: Fundacion Archivo Manuel de
Falla, 1991–
[NOT IN BUCOMP1]

ALb 1 (1991), 1

Boletín de las Juventudes Musicales de Cuba
CU–Vedado: Juventudes Musicales de Cuba,
1957–?
[NOT IN BUCOMP1]

ALb 1 (1957), 3

Boletín de Musica y Artes Visuales
TNG US649; 0553–0458
US–Washington, DC: Departamento de Asuntos
Culturales, Union Panamericana, 1950–56
[Ceased publication with no. 76, 1956]

Lbl*
Mpl 1952–56

Boletin del Consejo Interamericano de
Musica
US–Washington, DC: Consejo Interamericano
de Musica, 1974–
[NOT IN BUCOMP1]

Cpl 1, 1974

Boletín del Hot Club de Buenos Aires
ARG–Buenos Aires, 1959–

Cbijs 2 (1960), 1, 2

Boletín del Instituto de Folklore
0505–1398
VNZ–Caracas: Instituto Nacional de Cultura y
Bellas Artes, Departamento de Folklore, 1953–
65
[Ceased publication with vol. 4 (1965)]

> **Lbl***
> **Lsa** 2 (1955)–4 (1965)
> **Ouf (Howes)** 2 (1956/57), 5–8; 3 (1958/59),
> 1–4, 6, 7; 4 (1961/65), 1–8

**Boletin Informativo de la Orquesta Sinfonica
de Euskadi** *see* **Euskor: Euskadiko Orkestra
Sinfonikoaren Boletin Albistaria**

Boletín Interamericano de Musica
TNG US679; 0006–6400
US–Washington, DC: Organizacion de las
Estudos Americanos, 1957–73
[Ceased publication with no. 87, 1973]

> **BSdsc***
> **Cpl** 1–87, 1957–73*
> **Lbl***
> **Lcml** 1–87, 1957–73
> **Ob***

Boletín Latino-Americano de Música
TNG UR3; 0797–5376
URG/BR–Montevideo: Instituto de Estudios
Superiores del Uruguay; Rio de Janeiro:
Editorial Cooperation Interamericana de
Compositores, 1935–38; 1941; 1946
[Ceased publication with vol. 6 (1946)]

> **Cu** 1 (1935)–6 (1946), 1
> **Lbl***
> **Lcm** 6 (1946)
> **Lcml** 1 (1935)–3 (1937); 5 (1941)–6 (1946)
> **Lu** 3 (1937)–6 (1946), 1 [+ musical
> supplements to 5 (1941) and 6 (1946)]
> **Ob***
> **Ouf (Howes)** 5 (1941)

Bollettino AIB *see* **Associazione Italiana
Biblioteche: Bollettino d'Informazione**

Bollettino Bibliografico Musicale
TNG I232
I–Milan, 1926–33; n.s. 1952–

Cpl n.s. 1 (1952), 1–6
Lbl 1 (1926)–6 (1931); n.s. 1 (1952), 1–8
Lcml 2 (1927), 10–12; n.s. 1 (1952), 1–4
Ouf 1 (1926)–8 (1933) [m]

**Bollettino degli Amici del Pontificio Istituto
de Musica Sacra**
TNG I226
I–Rome: Pontificio Istituto di Musica Sacra,
1949–62
[Ceased publication with vol. 14 (1962)]

> **Lcml** 1 (1949)–2 (1950)

Bollettino dei Musicisti
TNG I208
I–Rome: Sindicato Nazionale Fascista Musicisti,
1933–43
[Entitled *Il Musicista* from 1937]

> **Lbl** 2 (1934/35), 1/2, 9/10; 3 (1935/36), 5,
> 8/9; 4 (1936/37), 2, 6, 8; 5 (1937/38), 6, 8

Bollettino del Centro Rossiniano di Studi
TNG I239; 0411–5384
I–Pesaro: Fondazione Rossini, 1955–

> **Cu** 1956–#
> **Lbl***
> **Lu** 1972; 1981–#
> **Ob***
> **Ouf** 1972–92

Bollettino dell'Accademia Musicale Chigiana
TNG I222
I–Siena: Accademia Musicale Chigiana,
1948–62

> **ALb** 14 (1961), 3
> **Lcml** 1 (1948)*; 2 (1949)–4 (1951);
> 5 (1952)–8 (1955)*

**Bollettino dell'AIMA, Archivio per
l'Informazione sulla Musica Antica**
I–Florence: Archivio per l'Informazione sulla
Musica Antica, 1981–
[NOT IN BUCOMP1]

> **Lbl** 1–8, 1981–83

**Bollettino dell'Associazione Italiana Amici
del Disco** *see* **Microsolco: Rassegna di Musica
Incisa**

Pescadores chimus   José Sabogal. 1929

LA MUSICA EN LA AMERICA LATINA
Y SU NACIONALIZACION

Guillermo Salinas Cossío   **Lima**

A sistimos todavía, en la América latina, al conmovedor espectáculo de un hombre nuevo ante un mundo nuevo. Del choque fecundo del Hombre y de la Naturaleza, de una raza inquieta — en la que las costumbres adquiridas y el refinamiento ancestral de viejas razas entrechocan, a la impetuosidad caótica y contradictoria de la raza nueva — y de una naturaleza exhuberante que no sabe producirse sino por mani-

British and Irish music library collections are by no means confined to English-language journals: this evocative illustration is from the *Boletín Latino-Americano de Música* (URG-Montevideo, 1935–46)

Reproduced by kind permission of the British Library

Bollettino dell'Istituto di Studi Verdiani
TNG I247; 0042–3734
I–Parma: Istituto di Studi Verdiani, 1960–89
[Also known as *Verdi: Bollettino Quadrimestrale dell'Istituto di Studi Verdiani*]

> Cpl 1, 2, 8, 10, 1960–89
> Cu 1, 1960–#
> EIR:Metc 1–8, 1960–73
> Er 1–8, 1960–73
> HUu 1–10, 1960–89
> Lbl*
> Lcm 1–10, 1960–89
> Lcml 1–3, 1960–65
> Lkc 1–8, 1960–73
> Lu 1, 1960–#
> Ob*
> SFu 1, 1960
> SOu 1–8, 1960–73

Bollettino Mensile
TNG I194
I–Milan, 1927–37

> Lcml 4 (1930), 1

Bomp! *see* **Who Put the Bomp?**

Boogie Woogie and Blues Collector
NL–Amsterdam, 1971–

> Cbijs 42, 43, 1974

Books and Bookmen *see* **Seven Arts**

Boosey and Hawkes GmbH: Verlagsnachrichten
D–Bonn: Boosey and Hawkes, ?1971–
[NOT IN BUCOMP1; from 1985, June, entitled *Nota Bene*]

> ALb 36, 37, 1980; 40, 1981; 42–46, 1982–83; 48–50, 1984; n.s. 1 (1985)–#*

Boosey and Hawkes Music Bulletin
GB–London: Boosey and Hawkes, 1966–
[NOT IN BUCOMP1]

> ALb 1966, Spr; 1967, Aut; 1975, Spr; 2–6, 1976–78; 8, 1979; 10, 1980; 13, 1981
> Lbl*

Boosey and Hawkes News-Letter
GB–London: Boosey and Hawkes, ?1960–69
[Succeeded by *Music: Boosey and Hawkes* (q.v.)]

> Lbl 2 (1961), 2–10 (1969), 1 [w 7 (1966), 1]

Boosey's Musical and Dramatic Review
Fellinger 1968/493; TNG GB64
GB–London, 1864
[From 1864, 10 entitled *Musical and Dramatic Review*; 14 nos in total]

> Lbl*

Bop City
0959–678X
GB–Manchester: Bop City, 1989–
[NOT IN BUCOMP1]

> Lbl*

Boston Musical Gazette
TNG US6
US–Boston, MA, 1838–39

> Cu 1838–39 [m]
> Mu 1838–39 [m]

Boston Musical Review
TNG US16
US–Boston, MA, 1845

> Cu [m]
> Mu [m]

Boston Musical Visitor *see* **The Musical Visitor**

The Boston Musical Year-Book
Fellinger 1968/915; TNG US178
US–Boston, MA: G. H. Ellis, 1883–?93
[From vol. 3 (1885/86) entitled *The Boston Musical Year-Book, and Musical Year in the United States*; also sometime entitled *The Musical Year-Book of the United States*]

> EIR:Dtc 1 (1883/84)
> Lbl 1 (1883/84)–10 (1892/93)

The Boston Musical Year-Book, and Musical Year in the United States *see* **The Boston Musical Year-Book**

Bouwsteenen [= Stones]: Jaarboek der Vereeniging voor Noord-Nederlandsche Muziekgeschiedenis
Fellinger 1968/599; TNG NL20
NL–Amsterdam: 1869–81
[Continued as *Tijdschrift der Vereniging voor Noord-Nederlands Muziekgeschiedenis* (q.v.)]

> Cu 1 (1869/72)–3 (1874/81)
> Lbl*
> Lu 1 (1869/72)–3 (1874/81)

Bouwsteenen voor een Geschiedenis der Toonkunst in de Nederlanden [= Materials for a History of Music in the Netherlands]
TNG NL116
NL–Amsterdam, 1965, 1971, 1979–
[NOT IN BUCOMP1]

Ob 1965–#

The Box
0968–2457
GB–?Bath: Real World Trading Ltd, 1992–
[NOT IN BUCOMP1]

Lbl*

Box and Fiddle
0140–6329
GB–Stranraer: National Association of Accordion and Fiddle Clubs, 1977–
[NOT IN BUCOMP1]

Lbl*

Boz *see* **Jazz at the Pizza Express**

BPI Review
0143–3172
GB–London: British Phonographic Industry, 1979–
[NOT IN BUCOMP1]

Lbl*

BPI Statistical Handbook *see* **BPI Yearbook**

BPI Yearbook: a Statistical Description of the British Record Industry
GB–London: British Phonographic Industry, 1979?–
[NOT IN BUCOMP1; from 1992 entitled *BPI Statistical Handbook* (ISSN 0142–7636)]

Lcml (r) 1986; 1988/89–#
NTp 1979–#

Brahms-Studien
0341–941X
D–Hamburg: K. D. Wagner, 1974–

Cu 1 (1974)–#
Lbl*
Lu 1 (1974)–#
Ob*

Braille Musical Magazine
TNG GB243; 0006–8837
GB–London: National Institute for the Blind, 1910–

AB 28–45, 1921–64 [w 29]
EIR:Dp 1988–93, Nov

Brass and Woodwind Quarterly
TNG US756; 0006–9221
US–Durham, NH: Appleyard Publications, 1967–69
[Succeeded *Brass Quarterly* (q.v.)]

AB 1 (1967)–2 (1969)
BSdsc*
Lbl*
Lcml 1 (1967)–2 (1969)
Lu 1 (1967)–2 (1969)
LVp 1 (1967)–2 (1969)
Mpl 1 (1967)–2 (1969)
Ob*

The Brass Band Annual
Fellinger 1968/1251; TNG GB161
GB–Sibsey, 1894–1910

Lbl 1894
Ob 1894

Brass Band News
TNG GB100
GB–Gloucester, 1970–

AB 1 (1970), 2–16 (1985), 8*
BDp 2 (1971)–7 (1976)
Cu 2 (1971)–16 (1985)
En 2 (1971)–16 (1985)
Lbl 14 (1983), 10–#
LVp 4 (1973)–7 (1976)
Ob*

Brass Band Review
GB–Harrow: Romsail, 1974–
[NOT IN BUCOMP1]

AB 13, 1975
Lbl 1–16, 1974–75 [w 12, 14, 15]

Brass Band World: an Independent Monthly Magazine for Bands
0961–6373
GB–Chapel-en-le-Frith: Caron Publications, 1991–
[NOT IN BUCOMP1]

AB 1, 1991
Bs 16, 1992–# [w 30]

Lbl 1, 1991–#
Mcm 33, 1994–#
Msuc 16, 1992–#
Ob*
RH [c]

Brass Bulletin: International Brass Chronicle/Chroniques Internationales du Cuivre
TNG INTL33; 0303–3848
CH–Moudon; Bulle: BIM, 1971–

Bs 33–65, 1981–89; 69, 1990–#
CCtc 21, 1978–#
Gam 61, 1988–#
Lam 29, 1980–#
Lbar 22, 25, 28, 1978–79; 41–55, 1983–86
Lcm 77, 1992–#
Lgsm 45, 1984–#
Mcm 3–52, 1972–85
Mpl 41, 1983–#
Msuc 21, 1978–#
TOd 45, 1984–#
Uu [c (2 years)]

Brass International see Sounding Brass and the Conductor

Brass Players' Guide
0197–8845
US–North Easton, MA: R. King Music Company
[NOT IN BUCOMP1; also known as *Brass Players' Guide to the Literature*]

BSdsc*

Brass Players' Guide to the Literature see Brass Players' Guide

Brass Quarterly
TNG US680; 0524–2142
US–Durham, NC: Brass Quarterly, 1957–64
[Ceased publication with vol. 7 (1964); succeeded by *Brass and Woodwind Quarterly* (q.v.)]

AB 1 (1957)–7 (1964)
Cpl 4 (1960), 2; 5 (1961), 1
Lbl*
Lcml 1 (1957)–7 (1964)
Lu 1 (1957)–7 (1964)
LVp 1 (1957)–7 (1964)
Ob*

Brighton and Hove Musical News
TNG GB292
GB–London, 1922–23

AB 1–8, 1922–23
Lbl*
Ob*

Brio
TNG GB508; 0007–0173
GB–London [etc.]: International Association of Music Libraries, Archives and Documentation Centres (UK Branch), 1964–

AB 1 (1964)–#
ABc(ILS) 1 (1964)–#
ALb 15 (1978)–# [w 18 (1981), 1]
Au 1 (1964)–#
BAc 1 (1964)–#
BDp 1 (1964)–22 (1985)
BLp 1 (1964)–#
Bp 1 (1964)–#
BRp 1 (1964)–#
Bs 5 (1968)–#*
BSdsc*
Bu 1 (1964)–#
CCtc 17 (1980)–#
CDCp 16 (1979)–#
CDu 1 (1964)–#
CFp 11 (1974)–#
CH 1 (1964)–27 (1990)
Cpl 1 (1964)–#
Cu 1 (1964)–#
DOR 15 (1978)–#
DS 13 (1976)–#
En 1 (1964)–#
Ep 1 (1964)–#
Er 1 (1964)–#
EIR:Dp 23 (1986)–#
EIR:Dtc 1 (1964)–#
EIR:Duc 1 (1964)–28 (1991)
EIR:MEtc 25 (1988)–#
EXu 10 (1973)–#
Gam 1 (1964)–#
Gm 1 (1964)–26 (1989)
Gsmic 24 (1987)–#*
Gul 1 (1964)–#
HE 9 (1972)–27 (1990)
KE 19 (1982), 2; 21 (1984)–#
Lam 1 (1964)–# [w 30 (1993), 1]
LAu 9 (1972)–#
Lba 1 (1964)–#
Lbar 1 (1964)–# [w 19 (1982), 1]
Lbbc 1 (1964)–#
Lbl*
Lbo 24 (1987), 2–#

Lcm 1 (1964)–#
Lcml 1 (1964)–#
Lcs 25 (1988)–#
LEc 1 (1964)–#
Len 1 (1964), 2–#
Lgo 11 (1974)–# [w 18 (1981), 2]
Lgsm 18 (1981)–#
Lha (f) 23 (1986); 24 (1987), 2; 25 (1988)–27 (1990)
LIp 1 (1964)–#
Lis [c]
Lk 1 (1964)–#
Lkc 13 (1976)–#
Lki 14 (1977)–#
LRHBNC 1 (1964)–9 (1972); 18 (1981)–#
Lro 21 (1984)–#
Lsa 1 (1964)–#
Lsut [c]
Ltc 19 (1982)–#
Lu 1 (1964)–#
LVp 1 (1964)–#
LVu 1 (1964)–#
LXp 9 (1972), 1; 10 (1973), 2; 11 (1974)–19 (1982), 1; 20 (1983)–#
Mcm 1 (1964)–#
MK 9 (1972)–#
Mmu 7 (1970)–#
Mpl 1 (1964)–#
Msuc 28 (1991)–#
Mu 1 (1964)–#
NO 16 (1979)–#
NOp 22 (1985)–#
NTp 1 (1964)–#
NWu 4 (1967)–5 (1968); 6 (1969)*; 7 (1970)–20 (1983)
Ob*
Ouf 1 (1964)–#
R 1 (1964)–#
RH 20 (1983), 1; 22 (1985)–25 (1988), 1; 26 (1989)–#
Rp 26 (1989)–#
SAu 7 (1970)–#
SFp 12 (1975), 2–27 (1990), 2
SFu 1 (1964)–#
SHRp 26 (1989); 28 (1991)–#
SOu 1 (1964)–30 (1993)
STAp 5 (1968)–16 (1979), 1
WF 1 (1964)–#
WOp [c]
WW [c]
Y 1 (1964)–#
Yu 6 (1969)–#

Bristol Folk News
GB–Bristol: English Folk Dance and Song
Society (Bristol District), 1970–?
[NOT IN BUCOMP1; also known as *Folk News*]

> BRp 9–19, 1972–77

British Academy of Songwriters, Composers and Authors *see* B.A.S.C.A.

British and Colonial Piano Journal *see* The Pianoforte Dealers' Guide

British Association of Sound Collections *see* B.A.S.C.

British Association of Symphonic Bands and Wind Ensembles *see* B.A.S.W.B.E.

The British Bandsman: a Monthly Magazine for Bandmasters and Members of Military and Brass Bands
Fellinger 1968/1039; TNG GB124; 0007–0319
GB–London, 1887–
[From 1891 entitled *The Orchestral Times and Bandsman*; from 1893, *The British Musician*; from 1899, *The British Bandsman [and Contest Field]*. Incorporated *British Mouthpiece: Brass and Military Band Journal* (q.v.) from 1990]

> AB 1965–#
> Bp 3642, 1972–#
> Bs 4695, 1992–#
> BSdsc*
> Bu 4 (1891)–8 (1895)
> CDCp [c (2 years)]
> Cu 3831, 1975–#
> EIR:Dtc 3831, 1975–#
> En*
> Lam 2747, 1954
> Lbl*
> Mpl 5 (1892)–9 (1896); 1990–#
> Msuc 1957, Nov–1958, Jan; 1963–#
> Ob 136–1502, 1899–1930; 3836, 1975–#
> RH [c]
> Rp [c]

The British Bandsman [and Contest Field] *see* The British Bandsman: a Monthly Magazine for Bandmasters and Members of Military and Brass Bands

British Bluegrass News
GB–Chelmsford, ?1977–

> Cu 7 (1983/84), 1–4
> Ob*

British Broadcasting Corporation *see* B.B.C.

British Catalogue of Music
TNG GB470; 0068–1407
GB–London: British Library Bibliographic
Services Division, 1957–91; London: Bowker-
Saur [for the British Library], 1992–
[NOT IN BUCOMP1]

> **BRp** 1988–#
> **BRu** 1957–# [w 1962]
> **BTu** 1957–# [w 1962]
> **Bu** 1957–#
> **BuAyp** 1957–#
> **BuHW** 1957–#
> **BuMK** 1957–#
> **CCtc** 1957–90
> **CDu** 1957–#
> **CFp** 1957–#
> **COp** 1957–#
> **Cpl** 1957–#
> **Cu** 1957–#
> **DU** 1976–#
> **EIR:Dp** 1988, July–#
> **EIR:Duc** 1957–#
> **EIR:MEtc** 1975–#
> **En** 1957–#
> **Ep** 1957–#
> **Er** 1957–#
> **Gm** 1957–#
> **HOp** 1957–#
> **HUu** 1957–#
> **KE** 1957–#
> **Lam** 1957–#
> **LAu** 1957–88
> **Lba** 1957–#
> **Lbbc** 1958–#
> **Lbx** 1957–#
> **Lcml** 1957–#
> **Lcu** 1967–69; 1974–#
> **Lgo** 1957–#
> **Lha (f)** 1957–92
> **Lk** 1957–#
> **Lkc** 1974–#
> **Lki** 1975–#
> **Ll** 1957–#
> **Lro** 1957–#
> **Lsa** 1957; 1959; 1975–85
> **Lu** 1957–#
> **LVp** 1957–# [w 1970, 1972, 1974, 1977]
> **Lwwb** 1957–#
> **MK** 1957–#
> **Mmu (a)** 1992–#
> **Mpl** 1957–#
> **Mu** 1957–83
> **NO** 1957–#

> **Ob** 1957–#
> **Oub** 1980–#
> **Ouf** 1957–#
> **R** 1957–82
> **SOu** 1957–#
> **WCp** 1957–#
> **WCp(f)** 1960–83
> **WCp(far)** 1957–#
> **WCp(p)** 1957–#
> **WCp(s)** 1957–#
> **Yu** 1960–#

**The British, Colonial and Allied Countries
Music Trade Directory** *see* **The British,
Colonial and Foreign Trade Directory**

**The British, Colonial and Foreign Trade
Directory**
Fellinger 1968/1122; TNG GB133
GB–London, 1890–1939
[From 1915 entitled *The British, Colonial and
Allied Countries Music Trade Directory*; from
1925, *The Music Trade Directory*]

> **Cu** 1916; 1918–23; 1925–39
> **En** 1916; 1918; 1920–23; 1925–39
> **Lbl***

British Country Music Association Bulletin
see **B.C.M.A. Bulletin**

British Country Music Association Yearbook
0308–4698
GB–Newton Abbot: British Country Music
Association, ?1978–

> **NTp** [c (5 years)]
> **Ob***

British Country Music Roots
0960–7617
GB–Hopton-on-Sea: Pebble View, 1990–
[NOT IN BUCOMP1]

> **Lbl** 1 (1990), 8–#

**The British Federation of Brass Bands:
Directory**
GB–Rochdale: British Federation of Brass
Bands, 197?–
[NOT IN BUCOMP1]

> **Mpl** 1975–#

**British Federation of Festivals for Music,
Dance and Speech: Yearbook** *see* **British
Federation of Music Festivals: Yearbook**

The British Federation of Music Festivals: Yearbook
TNG GB301
GB–London, 1921–
[Later entitled the *British Federation of Festivals for Music, Dance and Speech: Yearbook* (Macclesfield: The British Federation of Music Festivals; ISSN 0309–8044)]

> **Lbl***
> **Lcm** 1939; 1960–63
> **Lu** 1950–#
> **NTp** [c (2 years)]
> **Ob***
> **Uu** 1973–76; 1978; 1981; 1984; 1988–

British Forum for Ethnomusicology: Newsletter
GB–Twickenham [etc.], 198?–
[NOT IN BUCOMP1]

> **Cu** 10, 1995–#
> **Msuc** 10, 1995–#

British Institute of Jazz Studies Newsletter
GB–Crowthorne: British Institute of Jazz Studies, 1966–

> **Cbijs** 1966–#

British Institute of Organ Studies Journal *see* B.I.O.S. Journal

British Institute of Recorded Sound: Bulletin
TNG GB464; 0524–6253
GB–London: British Institute of Recorded Sound, 1956–60
[Succeeded by *Recorded Sound: Journal of the British Institute of Recorded Sound* (q.v.)]

> **AB** 1–18, 1956–60
> **ALb** 17–18, 1960
> **BTu** 1–18, 1956–60
> **Cpl** 4, 6, 9–12, 1957–59
> **En** 1–18, 1956–60
> **Gm** 1–18, 1956–60
> **Lam** 1–3, 1956
> **Lbl***
> **Lcm** 1–18, 1956–60
> **Lcml** 1–18, 1956–60
> **Lcs** 1, 1956; 6, 1957; 14, 1959
> **Lk** 1–18, 1956–60
> **Lkc** 1–18, 1956–60
> **Lsa** 1–18, 1956–60
> **Ob***
> **Ouf** 1–18, 1956–60 [w 13, 1959]
> **R** 17, 18, 1960
> **TOd** 1–18, 1956–60

British Journal of Aesthetics
0007–0904
GB–London: Oxford University Press, 1960–
[NOT IN BUCOMP1]

> **Lcm** 2 (1962), 3, 4; 5 (1965), 4; 6 (1966), 1, 2; 7 (1967), 3; 8 (1968), 3
> **Ob***

British Journal of Ethno-Musicology
0968–1221
GB–London: London University, School of Oriental and African Studies [for the International Council for Traditional Music (UK Chapter)], 1992–
[NOT IN BUCOMP1]

> **BLu** 1 (1992)
> **CCtc** 1 (1992)–#
> **Cpl** 1 (1992)–#
> **Cu** 1 (1992)–#
> **En** 1 (1992)–#
> **Er** 1 (1992)–#
> **Lbl***
> **Lgo** 1 (1992)–#
> **Lsa** 1 (1992)–#
> **Lso** 1 (1992)–#
> **Msuc** 1 (1992)–#
> **Ob***

British Journal of Music Education
0265–0517
GB–Cambridge: Cambridge University Press, 1984–

> **AB** 1 (1984)–#
> **BAc** 1 (1984)–# [w 5 (1988), 1]
> **BLp** 1 (1984)–#
> **Bs** 7 (1990), 2, 3; 8 (1991), 3; 9 (1992), 1–3; 10 (1993), 1–3
> **BSdsc** 1 (1984)–#
> **Cat** 3 (1986)–#
> **CCtc** 1 (1984)–#
> **Cu** 1 (1984)–#
> **EIR:Dp** 5 (1988)–#
> **EIR:Dtc** 1 (1984)–#
> **En** 1 (1984)–#
> **Ep** 1 (1984)–#
> **Lam** 1 (1984)–7 (1990), 3; 9 (1992)–#
> **Lbl***
> **Lcm** 1 (1984)–#
> **Lcml** 1 (1984)–#
> **Lgo** 1 (1984)–#
> **Lgsm** 4 (1987)–#
> **Lie** 1 (1984)–#
> **Lki** 1 (1984)–#

Lmi 1 (1984)–#
LRHBNC 1 (1984)–#
Lro 1 (1984)–#
Ltc 1 (1984); 3 (1986), 2, 3; 4 (1987),
2–6 (1989), 2; 7 (1990), 2, 3; 8 (1991), 3;
14 (1997)–#
Ltv 1 (1984)–4 (1987), 1, 3; 5 (1988), 2, 3;
6 (1989)–#
Mcm 1 (1984)–#
MK 7 (1990)–#
Mmu (d) 4 (1987)–#
Msuc 1 (1984)–#
Ob*
Oub (w) 6 (1989)–#
Mpl 2 (1985)–#
Re 1 (1984)–#
SFu 1 (1984)–#
SOu 8 (1991)–#
TOd 1 (1984)–#
Uu 1 (1984)–#
Yu 1 (1984)–#

British Journal of Music Therapy
0308–244X
GB–London: British Society for Music Therapy,
1968–87
[Ceased publication with vol. 18 (1987);
succeeded by the *Journal of British Music
Therapy* (q.v.), and by the *British Society for
Music Therapy Bulletin* (q.v.)]

BSdsc*
Bu 1 (1968)–18 (1987)
EIR:Dtc 1 (1968), 2, 3
En 1 (1968)–18 (1987), 2
Lie 1 (1968), 2; 2 (1970)–11 (1979), 1, 4;
12 (1980)–18 (1987)
Lki 1 (1968)–18 (1987)
Mmu(a) 5 (1974)–16 (1985)
Mmu(d) 1 (1969)–17 (1986)
Mu 1 (1969), 4, 5–18 (1987), 2
Ob*
Re 1 (1968)–15 (1984)
SFu 2 (1970)–4 (1972)*
TOd 9 (1977)–17 (1986)

The British Minstrel, and Musical and Literary Miscellany [1]
Fellinger 1968/208; TNG GB31
GB–Glasgow: William Hamilton and John
McLeod; Edinburgh: J. Menzies and N.
Bowack; Dublin: S. J. Machen; London:
William Hamilton, 1843–45
[Ceased publication with vol. 3 no. 120 (1845,
June); reissued in 1867]

Gm 1 (1843)–3 (1845)
Gul (e) 1 (1843)–3 (1845)
Lbl 1 (1843)–3 (1845)
LEu 1 (1843); 1867
Mpl 1 (1843)–3 (1845)
Ob*

The British Minstrel and Musical and Literary Miscellany [2]
GB–Glasgow, 1854–59

Gm 1854–55; 1857; 1859
Lcm 2 (1854)

British Mouthpiece: Brass and Military Band Journal
TNG GB473
GB–Ramsbottom: Council of Brass Band
Associations, 1959–90
[Incorporated into *British Bandsman: a Monthly
Magazine for Bandmasters and Members of
Military and Brass Bands* (q.v.) from 1990]

AB 7 (1965), 27–18 (1976), 7*
BDp 21 (1979)–27 (1985)*
Cu 21 (1979)–32 (1990), 9
EIR:Dtc 21 (1979)–32 (1990), 9
Lbl*
Mpl 1 (1959)–32 (1990)
Msuc 22 (1980)–32 (1990)
Ob*

British Music: Journal of the British Music Society
0958–5664
GB–Upminster: British Music Society, 1979–
[NOT IN BUCOMP1; formerly *Journal of the
British Music Society* (ISSN 0143–7402); also
known as *British Music Society Journal*]

AB 6 (1984)–10 (1988); 12 (1990);
14 (1992)–#
ALb 1 (1979)–11 (1989); 13 (1991)–#
Au 1 (1979)–#
BG 14 (1994)–#
BLp [c]
Bu 9 (1987)–12 (1990)
CCtc 1 (1979)–#
CDu 1 (1979)–10 (1988)
Cpl 1 (1979)–#
Cu 1 (1979)–#
DOR 3 (1981)–#
EIR:Dtc 1 (1979)–#
En 1 (1979)–#
KE 11 (1989)
Lam 12 (1990)

Lbar 1 (1979); 3 (1981)–#
Lbbc 1 (1979)–#
Lbl*
LCdM 1 (1979); 3 (1981)–#
Lcm 2 (1980)–18 (1996)
Lcml 1 (1979); 3 (1981)–#
Lmic 3 (1981)–#
LRHBNC 13 (1991)
Mcm 1 (1979)–#
NOp 14 (1994)–#
NWu 1 (1979)–4 (1982)
Ob*
Y 1 (1979)–#
Yu 9 (1987)–#

British Music Bulletin *see* The British Music Society Bulletin

British Music Education Yearbook
0266–2329
GB–London: Rhinegold, 1984–
[NOT IN BUCOMP1; from 1993 called *Music Education Yearbook* (ISSN 1353–8896); also known sometimes as *Music Teachers' Yearbook*]

BAc [c]
BRp 1984–#
Cat [c]
CDu [c]
Ep 1984–#
Er 1984; 1988/89
Gul 1988–91
Lbl*
Lbo [c]
LCdM [c]
Lcu 1992/93–#
Lgo 1986/87–#
Lgu [c]
Lwwb [c]
Lwwbat [c]
Lwwput [c]
Mpl 1984–#
Msuc [c]
NTp [c (2 years)]
Ob*
Ouf [c (2 years)]
SFp [c]
WW [c]
Yu 1984–92; [c]

British Music Society Annual
TNG GB278
GB–London, 1920; 1922–?
[From 1922 entitled *British Music Society Catalogue of Composers*]

Lam 1920
Lbl*
Lcm 1920, 1922
Ob*

The British Music Society Bulletin
TNG GB273
GB–London: The British Music Society, 1919–29; 1931–33
[From 1920 entitled *The British Music Bulletin*; from 1923 entitled *The Music Bulletin*; from 1929 combined with *Incorporated Society of Musicians: Monthly Report* to form *A Music Journal: Comprising the Report of the Incorporated Society of Musicians, and the Bulletin of the British Music Society* (q.v.); from 1930 carried subtitle *The Official Journal of the Incorporated Society of Musicians*. Also known as *BMS*]

AB 1 (1919), 3–11; 3 (1921), 1, 3–12; 4 (1922)–11 (1929); 13 (1931)–15 (1933), 3
Bu 1 (1919)–4 (1922)
Cpl 1 (1919)–4 (1922)*; 5 (1923)–11 (1929), 7
Cu 1 (1919)–11 (1929), 7
Gm 1 (1919)–10 (1928); 12 (1930), 2–13 (1931)
Lam 2 (1920), 5, 11; 3 (1921), 7–12; 4 (1923), 2, 7
Lbl*
Lcm 1 (1919), 1, 2; 4 (1922); 5 (1923), 4
Lcml 15 (1933), 3
LEc 1 (1919)–11 (1929)
Lu 1 (1919), 2; 2 (1920)–4 (1922)*; 6 (1924)–11 (1929)*
Mpl 1 (1919)–11 (1929)
Ob*
Yu 5 (1923)–11 (1929)

British Music Society Catalogue of Composers *see* British Music Society Annual

British Music Society Journal *see* British Music: Journal of the British Music Society

British Music Society Live Performances Bulletin *see* B.M.S. Live Performances Bulletin

The British Music Society Newsletter
GB–Stourbridge: British Music Society, 1978–

ALb 7–14, 1980–82; 17, 1983–#
Au 9, 1981–#
BLp [c]
CDu 5, 1980–#
Cu 1–10, 1978–81 [w 7, 8]
DOR 15, 1982–#
EIR:Dtc 1–10, 1978–81
Lbar 17, 1983; 33, 1987–# [w 49, 1991]
LCdM 18, 1983–#
Lcm 66–72, 1993–95
Lcml 8, 1981–#
Mcm 5, 1980–# [w 7, 8, 11, 14–17, 23–27, 31]
Ob*

British Music Worldwide
0954–1802
GB–London: Rhinegold, 1985–
[NOT IN BUCOMP1]

AB 1988/89–#
Cu 1988/89–#
EIR:Dtc 1985/86; 1992/93–#
Lbl*
NTp 1991/92–#
Ob 1988/89–#

British Music Yearbook see The Music
Yearbook

British Musician see The Midland Musician

British Musician: a Monthly Journal for
Instrumentalists
GB–London, 1891
[NOT IN BUCOMP1]

Lbl 1 (1891), 1–5
Ob 1 (1891), 1–5

The British Musician see also The British
Bandsman: a Monthly Magazine for
Bandmasters and Members of Military and
Brass Bands

British Musician and Musical News see The
Midland Musician

British Performing Arts Yearbook
0951–5208
GB–London: Rhinegold, 1988–
[NOT IN BUCOMP1]

BRp 1992–#
Er 1988
Lbo [c]
Ob*

British Phonographic Industry Review see
BPI Review

British Phonographic Industry Yearbook see
BPI Yearbook

British Society for Music Therapy Bulletin
0953–7511
GB–London: British Society for Music Therapy,
1987–
[Also known as B.S.M.T. Bulletin. Succeeded
the British Journal of Music Therapy (q.v.)]

Cu 20/21, 1994–#
EIR:Dp 2–16, 1988–92
En 1–2, 1987–88
EXu 22, 1995–#
Lam 15, 1992; 17–19, 1993
Lbl 1, 1987–#
Lcml (m) 1, 1987–#
Lcu 1, 1987–#
Mmu (d) 1, 1987–#
TOd*
Yu 10, 1990–#

British Songwriter and Dance Band
TNG GB397
GB–London, 1947–48
[Formerly British Songwriter and Poet (q.v.)]

Lbl*

British Songwriter and Poet
TNG GB373
GB–London, 1940–46
[Succeeded by British Songwriter and Dance
Band (q.v.)]

Lbl*

Broadbeat see The Broadsheet

Broadcast Sound
0263–5682
GB–Croydon: Link House, 1982–

EIR:Dtc 1 (1982)–4 (1985), 1
Lsa 1 (1982), Sep–3 (1984)

Broadcast Systems Engineering
0267–565X
GB–Croydon: Link House, ?1975–
[NOT IN BUCOMP1; entitled *Broadcast Systems International* from 1985]

    EIR:Dtc 11 (1985), 5–17 (1991), 8
    Lsa 11 (1985)–#*

Broadcast Systems International *see*
Broadcast Systems Engineering

The Broadsheet
GB–?London [etc.]: National Early Music Association, 198?–?91
[NOT IN BUCOMP1; from April 1988 entitled *Broadbeat*]

    EIR:Dp 1986, Nov–1991, July*
    Gm 1981, June–1988, Mar*; 1991, May
    Lam 1985–87*

Broken Arrow
1353–307X
GB–Bridgend: Neil Young Appreciation Society, 198?–
[NOT IN BUCOMP1]

    Lbl 53, 1993–#

Brolga: National Arts Magazine
AUS–Sydney, 1951–

    Lbl*

Brolga Review
0521–2006
AUS–Sydney: Recording Society of Australia, 1957–68
[Ceased publication with no. 87, 1968]

    Lsa 34–87, 1962–68*

Bros Official Annual
GB–Manchester: World International, 1989–
[NOT IN BUCOMP1]

    Cu 1989–#
    Lbl*

Brother Beyond Official Annual
GB–Manchester: World International, 1990–
[NOT IN BUCOMP1]

    Cu 1990–#
    Lbl*

Bruce Broughton Society Journal
0966–4807
GB–Bridport: Bruce Broughton Society, 1992–
[NOT IN BUCOMP1]

    Lbl*

Bruckner-Blätter: Mitteilungen der Internationalen Brucknergesellschaft
TNG INTL6
A–Vienna: Internationale Brucknergesellschaft, 1929–42

    Lbl*

Bruckner Jahrbuch
1013–8897
A–Linz: Anton Bruckner Institut, 1980–

    Cu 1980–#
    Lbl*
    Ob*

The Brussels Museum of Musical Instruments Bulletin
TNG B160
B–Brussels: Brussels Museum of Musical Instruments, 1971–87
[Ceased publication with no. 17, 1987]

    BSdsc 6 (1976)–17 (1987)
    Lcml 1 (1971)–2 (1972); 4 (1974)–17 (1987)
    Lu 1 (1971)–17 (1987)
    Ob*

Bryan Ferry Magazine
NL–Nijmegen: IBF Magazines, 1985–
[NOT IN BUCOMP1]

    Lbl 1 (1985)–#

B.S.M.T. Bulletin *see* **British Society for Music Therapy Bulletin**

A Bucketful of Brains
GB–London: Bucketful of Brains, 1979–
[NOT IN BUCOMP1]

    Cu 1–10, 1979–84
    Lbl*
    Lsa 1, 2, 1979–80

Buddy Holly Weekly
GB–London, 1979–

    EIR:Dtc 1 (1979), 4

Budget Price Records: a Complete and
Classified Catalogue of Every Long-Playing
Record under £1
GB–St Austell: Francis Anthony Ltd, 1966–77

> EIR:Dtc 7–26, 1969–77
> Lsa 2–4, 6, 1966–68; 12, 13, 1971–72;
> 16–20, 1973–75; 22–26, 1976–77
> Ob*

Budkavlen: Organ för Brages Sektion för
Folklivsforskning och Institutet för Nordisk
Etnologi vid Åbo Akademi
0302–2447
S–Åbo: Åbo Akademi, 1922–
[NOT IN BUCOMP1]

> Ep 1952

Buenos Aires Musical
TNG AR25; 0007–3113; 0327 2575
ARG–Buenos Aires, 1946–
[Also known as B.A.M.]

> BSdsc*
> Lbl*
> Lcml 4 (1949/50)*; 5/6 (1951); 7 (1952)*;
> 14 (1959), 12

The Bugle Call Rag
GB–London: Harry Roy Appreciation Society,
1972–

> Cbijs 1974, Spr
> LOnjfa*
> Lsa 1989–#

Die Bühne: Zeitschrift für die Gestaltung des
deutschen Theaters
D–Berlin, 1935–44

> Lbl 1942, 21; 1943, 4–6, 9/10, 17/18, 21/22,
> 23/24; 1944, 1/2–7/8, 15/16, 17/18

Bulgarska Muzyka [= Bulgarian Music]
0323–9314
BG–Sofia: Bulgarian Society of
Composers/Bulgarian Ministry of Culture,
1953–

> Ob*

Bulgarsko Muzykoznanie [= Bulgarian
Musicology]
0204–823X
BG–Sofia: Bulgarskata Akademiia na Naukite,
1971–

[NOT IN BUCOMP1; ? absorbed Muzykoznanie
(q.v.) in 1980]

> Lbl 3 (1979)–#
> Lcs 10 (1986)–#
> Ob 1 (1971)–#

Bulletin: Musikrat der DDR
TNG D1042
D–Berlin: Musikrat der DDR, 1964–90
[Included a supplement, Kurzinformation,
1975–90]

> Bs 14 (1977)–15 (1978)
> Cpl 1 (1964)–#*
> En 14 (1977)–18 (1981); 19 (1982), 2, 3; 20
> (1983)–24 (1987), 2; 25 (1988), 1, 3; 26
> (1989)–27 (1990), 1
> Gam 12 (1975), 1; 13 (1976), 3; 14 (1977), 2;
> 15 (1978)– 16 (1979), 1; 17 (1980)–19
> (1982), 3; 20 (1983), 1; 21 (1984), 3; 23
> (1986), 1; 25 (1988), 2; 26 (1989), 1
> Lam 6 (1969), 1, 2; 8 (1971), 2–11 (1974), 1,
> 2; 11 (1974), 4; 12 (1975), 2, 3; 13 (1976),
> 3–16 (1979), 3; 17 (1980), 2, 3; 18 (1981),
> 2, 3; 19 (1982), 1, 3; 20 (1983)–22 (1985),
> 3; 23 (1986), 2; 24 (1987), 1, 2; 25 (1988),
> 1, 2; 26 (1989), 1, 2; 27 (1990), 1
> Lbbc 7 (1970)–27 (1990)*
> Lbl*
> Lcm 6 (1969)–9 (1972)*; 11 (1974), 1, 2, 4;
> 13 (1976), 3–22 (1985), 3*; 24 (1987)–26
> (1989), 2*
> Lcml 1 (1964)–2 (1965)*; 3 (1966)–5 (1968);
> 6 (1969)–8 (1971)*; 9 (1972)–27 (1990)
> Mcm 8 (1971), 2; 11 (1974), 4; 12 (1975),
> 1–3; 13 (1976), 1–3; 14 (1977), 1–3; 16
> (1979), 2–18 (1981), 3; 19 (1982), 3;
> 20 (1983)–22 (1985)
> Ob*

The Bulletin: the Official Magazine of the
National Association of Teachers of Singing
TNG US583
US–Chicago [etc.]: National Association of
Teachers of Singing, 1944–
[NOT IN BUCOMP1; entitled The NATS
Bulletin (ISSN 0027–6073) from 1962–85;
entitled National Association of Teachers of
Singing: Journal (ISSN 0884–8106) from 1985–
95, June; entitled Journal of Singing from 52
(1995), Sep]

> ALb 32 (1976), 4
> Lgsm 38 (1982), 3–#
> Lu 48 (1991), 2–49 (1992), 2

Bulletin de l'Association des Organistes et
Maîtres de Chapelle Protestants Romands *see*
La Tribune de l'Orgue: Revue Suisse
Romande

Bulletin de la Revue Ancienne et Moderne *see*
Revue de Musique Ancienne et Moderne

Bulletin de la Société des Compositeurs de
Musique
F–Paris, 1863–69
[NOT IN BUCOMP1]

   Gul (e) 1 (1863)–2 (1869)

Bulletin de la Société Française de
Musicologie
Fellinger 1968/2285; TNG F462; 0991–9228;
0035–1601
F–Paris: Fischbacher, 1917–
[Entitled *Revue de Musicologie*, 1922–39; from
1942–43, nos 1– 5, entitled *Société Française de
Musicologie: Rapports et Communications*;
from 1945 entitled *Revue de Musicologie*]

   AB*
   BG 27 (1948)–75 (1989)
   Bu 36 (1954)–50 (1964); 61 (1975)–#
   Cpl 1 (1917/19); 2 (1920), 7; 3 (1922), 4; 4
      (1923), 5, 6; 11 (1930), 33–12 (1931), 40
   Cu 1 (1917)–#
   EIR:Duc 50 (1964)–#
   En 24 (1945)–#
   Er 1 (1917/19)–61 (1975)
   Gul 43 (1959)–#
   HUu 1 (1917/19)–#
   Lam 31 (1952), 101, 102; 32 (1953) 107, 108
   LAu 64 (1978)–74 (1988)
   Lbl*
   Lcm 1 (1917/19)–11 (1930), 33; 20 (1939),
      70
   Lcml 1 (1917/19), 2, 3; 2 (1920/21), 5–#
   Lkc 3 (1922)–20 (1938); 28 (1949)–
      49 (1963); 51 (1965)–53 (1967); 55 (1969);
      57 (1971)–#*
   LRHBNC 58 (1972)–#
   Lu 1 (1917/19), 3, 3; 2 (1920/21), 8–10
   LVu 69 (1983)–#
   Mcm 59 (1973)–69 (1983), 2
   NWu 53 (1967)–#
   Ob*
   Ouf 1 (1917/19)–18 (1837) [Reprint ed.];
      24 (1945)–29 (1950); 33 [i.e. 31] (1951)–
      #*
   SOu 77 (1991)–#

Bulletin de la Société Internationale de
Musicologie *see* Mitteilungen der
Internationalen Gesellschaft für
Musikwissenschaft

Bulletin de la Société Suisse de Musicologie
see Mitteilungen der Schweiz[erischen]
Musikforschenden Gesellschaft

Bulletin de la Société "Union Musicologique"
TNG INTL4
NL–The Hague: Martin Nijhoff, 1921–26

   Cu 1 (1921)–6 (1926)
   Lbl*
   Lcm 1 (1921)–6 (1926)
   Ob 1 (1921)–2 (1922)
   Ouf 1 (1921)–6 (1926) [m]

Bulletin de l'Atelier d'Études sur la Musique
Française des 17. et 18. Siècles
0997–7872
F–Versailles: Centre de Musique Baroque de
Versailles, 1989–
[NOT IN BUCOMP1]

   Mu 1 (1990)–3 (1992); 5 (1994)–#
   Ouf 2 (1991)–#

Bulletin de l'Institut de Musique *see* Izvestiya
na Instituta za Muzika

Bulletin d'Information de la Vie Musicale
Belge
TNG B152
B–Brussels: Conseil National de la Musique,
1962–75; 1977–
[Cover title *La Vie Musicale Belge*; vols 15/16
published in a single vol. in 1977]

   BSdsc*
   Cpl 17 (1978), 1; 18 (1979), 1
   Lam 15/16 (1977/78)
   Lbbc 11 (1972)–15/16 (1977)*
   Lcm 8 (1969)–10 (1971) [w 10 (1971), 3];
      12 (1975), 1, 2; 19 (1980),1
   Lcml 8 (1969); 9 (1970)*; 10 (1971)–11
      (1972); 12 (1973)–14 (1975)*
   Lsa 1 (1962)–14 (1975), 3 [w 10 (1971), 3;
      12 (1973), 2]
   Lu 6 (1967), 2, 4; 7 (1968), 1–4; 8 (1969),
      1–6; 9 (1970), 1
   Mcm 12 (1973), 1, 2, 4–6; 13 (1974), 1, 2;
      15/16 (1977/78); 17 (1978), 1, 2; 18 (1979),
      1, 2; 19 (1980), 1; 20 (1981), 1, 2
   Ob*

Bulletin du Centre de Documentation de Musique Internationale
TNG INTL13
F–Paris: Centre de Documentation de Musique Internationale, 1951–54
[From 1952–54 entitled *Cahiers d'Information Musicale* (ISSN 0526–7773)]

> **Lcml** 1951, May
> **Lu** 1951, May
> **Mpl** 1951–54

Bulletin du Conservatoire National: Musique, Art, Dramatique *see* **Bulletin du Conservatoire National de Musique**

Bulletin du Conservatoire National de Musique
TNG F602
F–Paris: Conservatoire National de Musique, 1947–55
[From July 1949 entitled *Bulletin du Conservatoire National: Musique, Art Dramatique*; from 1950 entitled *Le Conservatoire*]

> **Lam** 2, 1948; 8–10, 1949–50; 17, 1951; 18, 1952; 23, 24, 1953; 44, 1955

Bulletin du Hot Club de France *see* **Jazz-Hot: Revue Internationale de la Musique de Jazz**; and **La Revue du Jazz**

Bulletin Français de la S.I.M. *see* **Le Mercure Musical**

Bulletin/Mitteilungen
NL–Utrecht: Institute of Musicology, 1961–67
[NOT IN BUCOMP1; ceased with no. 16, 1967]

> **Yu** 1, 2, 9–14, 16, 1961–67

Bulletin, Moravian Music Foundation *see* **News Bulletin of the Moravian Music Foundation**

Bulletin Musical
TNG PL48
PL–Warsaw, 1927–30
[NOT IN BUCOMP1; supplement to *Muzyka* [2] (q.v.)]

> **Cpl** 1 (1927), 1

Bulletin of Historical Research in Music Education
0739-5639
US–Lawrence, KS: Department of Art and Music Education and Music Therapy, University of Kansas, 1980–
[NOT IN BUCOMP1]

> **Re** 1 (1980)–13 (1992)

Bulletin of Musashino Academia Musicae/Musashino Ongaku Daigaku Kenkyu Kiyo
J–Tokyo: Musashino Ongaku Daigaku, 1962–
[NOT IN BUCOMP1]

> **Cpl** 5 (1971)–#*
> **En** 3 (1969)–5 (1971); 8 (1974)–#

Bulletin of the American Composers' Alliance *see* **American Composers' Alliance: Bulletin**

Bulletin of the American Concert Choir and Choral Foundation *see* **American Choral Review**

Bulletin of the American Musicological Society *see* **Bulletin of the New York Musicological Society**

Bulletin of the Bach Society *see* **Bach Society Bulletin**

Bulletin of the Council for Research in Music Education
TNG US 729 0010–9894; 0574–2722
US–Urbana, IL: Council for Research in Music Education, School of Music, University of Illinois, 1963–

> **BRu** 19–48, 1970–76
> **Lie** 1, 1963–# [w 53, 86]
> **Lki** 64, 1980–#
> **Lu** 19, 1970–#
> **Re** 1, 1963–#
> **SFu** 87–127, 1986–95
> **SOu** 3–31, 1964–72 [w 6, 8–10, 12–15]
> **Yu** 19, 1970–#

Bulletin of the Dolmetsch Foundation
TNG GB498; 0419–618X
GB–Haslemere: Dolmetsch Foundation, 1962–

> **AB** 1–14, 1962–68; 21–44, 1974–85; 46, 1986
> **Au** 26, 1976–#
> **BDp** 22–38, 1975–82

BLu 7, 1965–#
BRp [c (2 years)]
BSdsc*
Cpl 8–37, 1965–82*
EIR:Duc 6–41, 1964–84
Er 8–54, 1965–89
Gul 8–66, 1965–93
HUu 7–64, 1965–92
Lam 8–48, 1965–87; 52–60, 1988–91; 62–65, 1991–92
Lbbc 20–54, 1973–89 [w 21, 31, 33, 46, 48, 50]
Lcm 35–39, 1981–83; 41, 42, 44, 45, 47–49, 1984–87; 51– 60, 1988–91
Lcml 3, 1963–#
Lcu 23, 1975–#
LIp 2–59, 1962–90
LRHBNC 34–60, 1980–91; 62, 63, 1991–92; 65, 1992–#
Lu 7, 1965–#
LVp 14–15, 1968–69; 18, 1971–#
LVu 9, 1965–#
Mcm 22–46, 1974–86; 49–55, 1987–89
Mpl 7, 1965–#*
Mu 7–10, 1965–66; 13–15, 1968–69; 17–27, 1970–77; 30–33, 1978–80; 35, 36, 1981; 39–45, 1983–86
NO 7–44, 1965–85
Ob*
SA 12–34, 1967–80
SOu 1, 1962–# [w 16, 1969]
Uu 42 (1984)–#*

Bulletin of the Folk-Song Society of the North-East
TNG US511
US–Cambridge, MA, 1930–37

Lcs 1, 1930; 3–6, 1931–33
Ob*

Bulletin of the Guild of Carillonneurs in North America
0827–5955
C–Ottawa: The Guild of Carillonneurs in North America, 1940–
[NOT IN BUCOMP1]

Cpl 1 (1940)–15 (1963), 1

Bulletin of the International Council for Traditional Music see **International Folk Music Council: Bulletin**

Bulletin of the International Folk Music Council see **International Folk Music Council: Bulletin**

Bulletin of the London Association of Organists
GB–London, ?1950–73

Lam (o) 1–70, 1950–73
Lcm 65–70, 1972–73 [w 68]

Bulletin of the Music Teachers' National Association see **American Music Teacher**

Bulletin of the National Federation of Gramophone Societies
GB–Orpington [etc.]: National Federation of Gramophone Societies, 1948–?

BSdsc*
EIR:Dtc 106–112, 1987–90
En 106–112, 1987–90
Lbl*
Lsa 36, 1959–# [w 38, 41–43, 51, 52, 69, 80]
Mcm 71–100, 1969–84
NTp 1, 1948–#
Ob*
SFp 1954–74*

Bulletin of the New York Musicological Society
US–Boston, MA, 1931–34; 1936–48
[Entitled *Bulletin of the American Musicological Society* from 1936; continued as the *Journal of the American Musicological Society* (q.v.) from 1948]

BRu 3, 1939; 11–13, 1948
CDu 1–6, 1936–42
Cpl 1–13, 1936–48
Cu 1–4, 1936–40
Lbl*
Lkc 2–5, 1937–41; 9–13, 1947–48
Lu 1–5, 1936–41; 9/10, 1947; 11/13, 1948
Mpl 1–13, 1936–48
Ouf 6–7, 1942–43

Bulletin of the Society for Publishing Danish Music [translated title] see **Samfundet til Udgivelse af Dansk Musik: Bulletin**

Bulletin of the Union of Czechoslovak Choral Societies [translated title] see **Vestník Jednoty Zpěvákých Spolků Ceskoslovanských**

Bulletin Phonographique *see* Biuletyn
Fonograficzny/Bulletin Phonographique

Bulletin Trimestriel des Amis de l'Orgue
TNG F533; 0398–8082
F–Paris, 1929–40; 1947–
[From 1947 entitled *L'Orgue: Bulletin
Trimestriel* (ISSN 0030–5170); with supplement
entitled *Cahiers et Mémoires de l'Orgue* (q.v.)]

    Cu 83–190, 1957–84*; 201, 1987–#
    Lbl*
    Lcm 133–139b, 1970–71; 140–142b, 1971–
      72; 143–146, 1972– 73; 225, 1993–#
    Lcml 70–73, 1954/55; 75–94, 1956–60 [w 83,
      86, 88]
    Ob*
    Yu 71, 1954; 109–175, 1964–80

Das Bundesblatt: Mitteilungen des
Sudwestdeutschen Brucknerbundes
D–Weinheim, 1933–

    LAu 3 (1935), 1; 10 (1953), 3

Bunk Johnson Appreciation Society
Newsletter
GB–Westcliff-on-Sea, 1954–60

    Cbijs 1955, May–1956, May; 1959, Feb–
    1960, Mar

Buzz: Folk Topics and News from Greater
Manchester and Cheshire
TNG GB517
GB–English Folk Dance and Song Society,
Greater Manchester and Cheshire Districts,
1982–
[NOT IN BUCOMP1; also known as *Folk Buzz*]

    Lbl*
    Lcs 1–3, 1982; 5–38, 1983–92; 40, 41, 1993;
      43, 1994–#
    Ob 1, 1982–#

Buzzbox
1354–3083
GB–Nottingham: G. Coates, 1994–
[NOT IN BUCOMP1]

    Lbl*

Bwletin Cymdeithas Emynau Cymru
[= Welsh Hymn Society Bulletin]
GB–Caernarfon, 1968–

    AB 1 (1968)–#

C

The C.A.A. Magazine
TNG GB366
GB–London: Concert Artistes' Association,
1938–?41
[Continued from *The Concert World: the
Official Organ of the Concert Artistes'
Benevolent Association* (q.v.)]

    Lbl*

Cäcilia: Organ für katholische Kirchenmusik
Fellinger 1968/448; TNG L1
L–Luxembourg, 1862–78

    Lbl 1 (1862)

Cäcilia: eine Zeitschrift für die musikalische
Welt
Fellinger 1968/66; TNG D54
D–Mainz: B. Schott's Söhne, 1824–39; 1842–48
[108 numbers in all, in 27 vols; included a
supplement, *Intelligenzblatt zur Cäcilia*]

    Cpl 1–20, 1824–39*
    Er 1–4, 1824–26; 7–13, 1828–31
    EXu 1–27, 1824–48 [m]
    Gul (e) 1–20, 1824–39 [+ supplements 1–76
      (1824–37)]
    Lbl*
    Lgo 1–27, 1824–48 [m]
    Mpl 1–27, 1824–48
    Ob 1–27, 1824–48

Cäcilienvereinsorgan *see* Fliegende Blätter
für katholische Kirchenmusik

Cäcilienvereinsorgan/Musica Sacra *see*
Fliegende Blätter für katholische
Kirchenmusik

Cadence: the American Review of Jazz and
Blues
0162–6973
US–Redwood, NY: Cadence Jazz and Blues
Magazine; B. Rusch, 1976–

    EXu 4 (1978), 7–#
    LOnjfa 9 (1983)–21 (1995)*
    Lsa 5 (1979), 1–8; 9 (1983), 12; 10 (1984), 1,
      2, 7–9; 11 (1985), 2; 14 (1988), 12

Caecilia: Algemeen Muzikaal Tijdschrift van Nederland

Fellinger 1968/221; TNG NL12
NL–Utrecht: Kemink & Zn, 1844–
[NOT IN BUCOMP1; from vol. 91 (1933/34)
merged with *De Muziek: Officieel Orgaan van
de Federatie van Nederlandsche
Toonkunstenaars-Vereenigingen* to form
Caecilia en de Muziek (Fellinger 1968/221)]

Lbl 33 (1876)–?*

Caecilia: Zeitschrift für katholische Kirchenmusik

Fellinger 1968/1205; TNG D324
D–Breslau, 1893–1918

Lbl 1 (1893)–9 (1901)

Caecilia en de Muziek *see* [De] Muziek: Officieel Orgaan van de Federatie van Nederlandsche Toonkunstenaars-Vereenigingen

Caecilien-Kalender

Fellinger 1968/710; TNG D215
D–Regensburg, 1876–85
[Superseded by *Kirchenmusikalisches Jahrbuch* (q.v.)]

Cpl 1 (1876)–10 (1885)
Ep 1 (1876)–10 (1885)
Er 1 (1876)–10 (1885)
Lbl 1 (1876)–10 (1885)
Ob 1 (1876)–10 (1885)

Cahiers Albert Roussel

B–Brussels: Amis Belges d'Albert Roussel, 1978–81

Cu 1 (1978)–4 (1981)
Lcml 1 (1978)–4 (1981)
Lu 1 (1978)–2 (1979)
Mcm 1 (1978)–4 (1981)

Cahiers Canadiens de Musique/Canada Music Book

0007–9634; TNG C46
C–Montreal: Canadian Music Council, 1970–76
[NOT IN BUCOMP1]

Er 1–12, 1970–76
Lbbc 1–12, 1970–76
Lu 1, 1970
Ob*

Cahiers de la Guitare

0294–6939
F–Kremlin-Bicetre: D. Ribouillault, 1982–
[NOT IN BUCOMP1]

Lu 2, 1982

Cahiers de la Musique

TNG B103
B–Brussels, 1936–39
[NOT IN BUCOMP1]

Lu 1–22, 1936–39

Cahiers de Musiques Traditionelles

CH–Geneva: Ateliers d'Ethnomusicologie, 1988–
[NOT IN BUCOMP1]

Cu 1 (1988)–#
DRu 1 (1988)–#
Lbl 1 (1988)–#
Lso 3 (1990)–#

Cahiers Debussy

TNG F717; 0395–1200
F–Saint-Germain-en-Laye: Centre de Documentation Claude Debussy, 1974–

BG 1 (1974)–3 (1976); n.s. 1 (1977)–9 (1985)
Bu 1 (1974)–3 (1976); n.s. 1 (1977)–8 (1984)
CDu 1 (1974)–3 (1976); n.s. 1 (1977)–#
Cu 1 (1974)–3 (1976); n.s. 1 (1977)–#
Lbbc n.s. 1 (1977)–#
Lcml n.s. 1 (1977)–#
Lkc n.s. 1 (1977)–#
Ob*
SFu n.s. 1 (1977)–7 (1983)
SOu 1 (1974)–3 (1976); n.s. 1 (1977)

Cahiers d'Information Musicale *see* Bulletin du Centre de Documentation de Musique Internationale

Les Cahiers du Disque

TNG F614
F–Chambray-les-Tous, 1952–

Lsa 4, 6–11, 1953–55; 78, 79, 1964; 107, 108, 112, 1967; 184–190, 196, 1974–75

Cahiers et Mémoires de l'Orgue
TNG F533
F–Paris, 1971–
[Entitled *L'Orgue* from no. 21, 1979;
supplement to the *Bulletin Trimestriel des Amis
de l'Orgue* (q.v.)]

    Lcm 49–50, 1993
    Yu*

Cahiers Maurice Ravel
0769–7945
F–Paris: Fondation Maurice Ravel, 1985–
[NOT IN BUCOMP1]

    Cu 1 (1985)–#

Cajun Times
GB–Reading, 1995–

    EXu 1, 3, 1995–#

Calendar for **1931–32**, including Report of the
Proceedings for the Year, a History of the
College [etc.] *see* The College of Organists:
Prospectus and [1st-] Annual Report

Calendar for 1**932–33**, including the
Proceedings of the Year, Report and the
Lectures, a Short History of the Choral
Foundations in English Cathedrals [etc.] *see*
The College of Organists: Prospectus and
[1st-] Annual Report

Calendar for **1941/42 [etc.]]**, including the
Proceedings of the Year *see* The College of
Organists: Prospectus and [1st-] Annual
Report

Calendar of the Royal College of Organists
see The College of Organists: Prospectus and
[1st-] Annual Report

Calendrier Musical Universel *see* Almanach
Musical [1]

California Traditional Music Society Journal
1053–3664
US–Tarzana, CA: The California Traditional
Music Society, 1984/85–
[NOT IN BUCOMP1]

    Lcs 1 (1985)–# [w 6 (1989/90), 1]

Call Boy
GB–British Music Hall Society, 1964–
[NOT IN BUCOMP1]

    Lcml (r) 1 (1964)–2 (1965)*; 3 (1966)–#
    Ob*

Cambridge Opera Journal
0954–5867
GB–Cambridge: Cambridge University Press,
1989–
[NOT IN BUCOMP1]

    ALb 1 (1989)–#
    BAc 1 (1989)–#
    BG 6 (1994)–#
    Bu 5 (1993)–#
    Cat 1 (1989)–#
    CCtc 1 (1989)–#
    CDu 1 (1989)–#
    Cpl 4 (1992)–#
    EIR:Dtc 1 (1989)–#
    En 1 (1989)–#
    Er 1 (1989), 1; 2 (1990), 1, 2; 3 (1991), 1, 3;
      4 (1992)–#
    EXu 1 (1989)–#
    Gul 5 (1993)–#
    KE 2 (1990)–#
    LAu 1 (1989)–#
    Lbl 1 (1989)–# [w 1 (1989), 2]
    Lcml 1 (1989)–#
    Lcu 5 (1993)–#
    LEbc 1 (1989)–#
    Lgo 1 (1989)–# [w 1 (1989), 3]
    Lkc 1 (1989)–#
    LRHBNC 1 (1989)–#
    Lro 1 (1989)–#
    Ltc 1 (1989)–#
    Lu 1 (1989)–#
    Mmu (a) 5 (1993)–#
    Mu 1 (1989)–#
    NO 1 (1989)–#
    NWu 1 (1989)–#
    Ob 1 (1989)–#
    Oub 1 (1989)–#
    Ouf 1 (1989)–#
    SFu 1 (1989)–#
    SOu 1 (1989)–# [w 1 (1989), 3]
    Uu 3 (1991)–#

Canada Folk Bulletin *see* Come All Ye

Canada Music Book *see* Cahiers Canadiens
de Musique

Canadian Antique Phonograph Society Newsletter
0845–8731
C–Toronto: Canadian Antique Phonograph Society, ?1966–
[NOT IN BUCOMP1; from issue 24 no. 3 entitled *Antique Phonograph News* (ISSN 1192–0211)]

> Cu 21 (1986)–24 (1991), 2; 1992–#

Canadian Association of Music Libraries (CAML) Newsletter
0825–3730; 0383–1299
C–Ottawa: Canadian Association of Music Libraries, 1972–77, 1978–
[NOT IN BUCOMP1; preceded by the *Canadian Music Library Association Newsletter* (ISSN 0068–9343), 1957–71; French title is *ACBM Nouvelles*]

> ABc (ILS) 3 (1977/78)–19 (1990), 2

Canadian Composer/Le Compositeur Canadien
0008–3259
C–Toronto: Society of Composers, Authors and Music Publishers of Canada, 1965–89; 1990–93
[NOT IN BUCOMP1; relaunched as *Words and Music* [3] (q.v.) from 1994. *See also BMI Canada: Newsletter*]

> Cu 1 (1990)–4 (1993)
> Er 1 (1990)–#
> Lu 1 (1990), 2; 2 (1991), 1, 2

Canadian Folk Music Bulletin
0829–5344; 0068–8746
C–Calgary: Canadian Folk Music Society, 1965–
[NOT IN BUCOMP1]

> Lcs 16 (1982)–#*

Canadian Folk Music Journal
TNG C51; 0318–2568
C–Calgary: Canadian Society for Musical Traditions/Société Canadienne pour les Traditions Musicales, 1973–
[NOT IN BUCOMP1]

> Lcs 1 (1973)–#

Canadian Music Centre Newsletter *see* Musicanada

Canadian Music Educator/Le Musicien Educateur au Canada
TNG C33
C–Etobikoke, Ontario: Canadian Music Educators' Association, 1959–
[NOT IN BUCOMP1]

> Mcm 14 (1972/73), 3, 4; 15 (1973/74), 1, 2, 4; 16 (1974/75), 1–3
> Re 9 (1967)–10 (1969), 1, 3; 12 (1971), 1, 2, 4; 13 (1972), 1, 4#
> TOd 30 (1989), 2 [suppl.]; 33 (1991)

Canadian Music Educators' Association Newsletter
0045–5172
C–St Catherine's, Ontario: Canadian Music Educators' Association, 1968–88
[NOT IN BUCOMP1; ceased publication with no. 72, 1988]

> Mcm 18–21, 1973; 24, 25, 1974

Canadian Music Journal
TNG C30; 0576–5773;
C–Toronto: Canadian Music Council, 1956–62
[NOT IN BUCOMP1]

> Cpl 5 (1961), 2–6 (1962), 1
> Lcml 1 (1956)–2 (1957)*; 3 (1958)–6 (1962)
> Lu 1 (1956), 3; 2 (1957), 1

Canadian Music Library Association Newsletter *see* Canadian Association of Music Libraries (CAML) Newsletter

Canadian University Music Review
0710–0353
C–Ottawa: Canadian University Music Society, 1980–

> Cu 1 (1980)–#
> Lbl 1 (1980)–#

Y Caniedydd Milwrol
[= The Military Songster]
GB–Caernarfon, 1888

> AB 1888, Aug

The Canon: Australian Journal of Music
TNG AUS16
AUS–Hunter's Hill, NSW, 1947–66
[Ceased publication with vol. 17 no. 7 (1966)]

> Lam 8 (1954), 5; 12 (1958/59), 2
> LAu 16 (1962/63)
> Lbl*

Lcm 1 (1947/48)–2 (1948/49) [w 6, 8, 9]; 16
(1962/63), 5, 6, 10, 11
Lcml 1 (1948/49), 3–6; 10 (1956/57)–11
(1957/58)
Lu 10 (1956/57), 4, 6; 12 (1958/59), 2
Ob*

**Canor: Pismo Poświęcone Interpretacjom
Muzyki Dawnej [= Bulletin for the Study of
Old Music]**
PL–Toruń: Fundacja Sztuki Współczesnej
TUMULT, 1991–
[NOT IN BUCOMP1]

Ob 2 (1992), 2–#

Cantonese Music [translated title] *see* **Ling
Nan Yin-Yueh**

Canu Gwerin *see* **Cylchgrawn Cymdeithas
Alawon Gwerin Cymru**

Canzona
NZ–Wellington: Composers' Association of
New Zealand, 1979–
[NOT IN BUCOMP1; formerly entitled
*Composers' Association of New Zealand:
Newsletter* (q.v.)]

Cpl 1 (1979), 1–4
Lcml 2 (1980), 5–#

Capella Novocastriensis
GB–Newcastle: ?Newcastle Cathedral, ?–?
[NOT IN BUCOMP1]

NTp 1960–65

Capital M: Music in the Capital
0952–7044
GB–London: Capital M, 1985–88
[NOT IN BUCOMP1; later entitled *Highly
Strung* (ISSN 0955–0151)]

Cu 1987, Dec–1988, Aug
Lbl*
Ob*

The Capitol News
?US–?, 1943–?

Cbijs 3 (1945), July–4 (1946), Jan, July–Sep,
Nov; 5 (1947), Jan, July, Nov; 6 (1948),
Apr, Sep, Nov; 8 (1950), Sep

Car Hi-Fi
0953–0924
GB–South Ruislip: Quest Magazines, 1986–
[NOT IN BUCOMP1]

AB 1 (1986), Spr–4 (1989), 3

Les Carnets Critiques *see* **La Revue Musicale**
[3]

CAS Journal *see* **The Catgut Acoustical
Society Newsletter**

Cash Box
0008–7289
US–New York: Cash Box, 1939–

Lsa 24 (1962/63), 47, 51; 25 (1963/64), 1, 7,
24, 35, 45; 26 (1964/65), 7, 28

C.A.S.S. News
0308–9053
GB–Norwich: A. Milne, 1976–80; Wilmington:
CASS [Clarinet and Saxophone Society of Great
Britain], ?1980–
[Entitled *Clarinet and Saxophone* (ISSN 0260–
390X) from vol. 5 no. 3 (1980)]

CCtc 6 (1981)–#
Cu 1 (1976)–#
EIR:Dtc 1 (1976)–#
En 5 (1980), 3, 4; 6 (1981)–#
Gam 13 (1988)–#
Lam 8 (1983), 1; 9 (1984), 3–12 (1987), 4; 13
(1988), 2–#
Lbl*
Lcml 1 (1976)–#
Lgsm 14 (1989), 4–#
Ltc 15 (1990)–19 (1994)*; 20 (1995)–21
(1996)
Mcm 3 (1978)–#
Msuc 14 (1989)–#
Ob*

Cassette Scrutiny
0260–521X
GB–London: Ealing College, School of Library
and Information Studies, 1981–
[Entitled *Sound Scrutiny* (ISSN 0264–0996)
from 1983]

CFp 1981–82
EIR:Dtc 1981–83
Lcml 1983–#
NTp [c (1 year)]
Ob*

Cassettes and Cartridges
GB–London: General Gramophone
Publications, 1973–77
[NOT IN BUCOMP1; included in *The
Gramophone* after 1977]

> CAu 24–54, 1975–77
> CFp 3–54, 1973–77
> Cu 1–54, 1973–77
> EIR:Dtc 1–54, 1973–77
> Ep 4–54, 1973–77
> Gam 20, 1974; 1975–77, Sep
> Lcml (m) 1–54, 1973–77
> Lcml (p) 1–23, 1973–75
> LVp 1–54, 1973–77
> WF 20–54, 1974–77

Cat Talk
GB–Feltham: Technimedia, ?1975–
[NOT IN BUCOMP1]

> Cu 4 (1979)–8 (1982)
> Lbl*

Catalogue des Nouvelles Oeuvres Musicales Françaises
Fellinger 1968/698; TNG F155
F–Paris, 1875–1920
[From 1876 entitled *Bibliographie Musicale*;
from 1879, *Bibliographie Musicale Française*;
ceased publication with vol. 47 (1920), no. 192]

> Lbl*
> Ob [Reprint ed.]

Catalunya Musica *see* Revista Musical Catalana: Butlletí del "Orfeó Català"

The Catgut Acoustical Society Newsletter
0576–9280
US–Montclair, NJ: Catgut Acoustical Society,
1964–90
[NOT IN BUCOMP1; entitled *Journal of the
Catgut Acoustical Society* (ISSN 0882–2212)
from no 42, 1984; entitled the *CAS Journal*
(ISSN 1053–7694) from n.s. 1(1990)]

> Lu 42, 1984

The Cathedral Quarterly
Fellinger 1968/2160; TNG GB260
GB–Leighton Buzzard, 1913–16

> Lbl*
> Mpl 1 (1913)–2 (1914)
> Ob 2 (1914), 6–3 (1916), 12

Catholic Music Educators' Bulletin *see* Pastoral Music

C.B.D.N.A. Journal
0742–8480
US–Columbus, OH: College Band Directors
National Association, 1984–

> Mcm 1 (1984),1; 2 (1985/86), 1–2

C.B.M.R. Digest
1043–1241
US–Chicago, IL: Centre for Black Music
Research, 1988–
[NOT IN BUCOMP1]

> LOnjfa*
> Lu 5 (1992), 1, 2; 6 (1993), 1, 2; 7 (1994), 1
> TOd 1 (1988)–6 (1993), 2

CBS News
GB–London: CBS Records, ?1979–
[NOT IN BUCOMP1]

> Cu 1979, Apr 20–1983, Nov 18

CD Classics
0967–4411
GB–London: Northern and Shell, 1992–
[NOT IN BUCOMP1]

> ALb 1 (1992), 4
> Lbl 1 (1992), 3–#

C.D.M.C. *see* Ostinato: Lettre d'Information Trimestrielle du CDMC

CD Review
0269–9737
GB–Berkhamsted: CES Publishing, 1985–
[NOT IN BUCOMP1; not published 1993, July–
Nov]

> BLp [c]
> CDCp [c (2 years)]
> Cu 1, 1985; 15–17, 1987; 49, 1991–#
> EIR:Dtc 15, 16, 1987
> Ep 49, 1991–#
> Lbl*
> LEc [c (5 years)]
> Lsa 45, 1990–#
> Ob*
> WCp (e) [c (1 year)]

CD Review Digest: Classical
US–Vooheesville, NY, ?1987–

Lsa 6 (1992), 1

CD Review Digest: Jazz, Popular, etc
US–Vooheesville, NY, ?1987–

Lsa 1989, Sum/Aut; 6 (1992), 1

C.D.S.S. Directory
US–New York: Country Dance and Song
Society, ?–
[NOT IN BUCOMP1]

Lcs 1987; 1991/92; 1992/93; 1994/95–#

CD Video Magazine see **What Video**

**Central Council of Church Bell Ringers:
Education Committee Publications**
GB–London, 1974–
[NOT IN BUCOMP1]

Cu 1, 1974–#

Central Opera Service Bulletin
TNG US701; 0008–9508
US–New York: Central Opera Service, 1959–90
[Ceased publication with vol. 30 no. 4 (1990)]

Lsa 15 (1973), 3, 4; 16 (1973/74), 1, 3, 4; 17
(1974), 1

**Centre de Documentation de la Musique
Contemporaine** see **Ostinato: Lettre
d'Information Trimestrielle du CDMC**

Centre for Black Music: Research Digest see
C.B.M.R. Digest

Century 22
0956–4101
GB–Iver Heath: Pinewood Studios/Century 22,
1989–
[NOT IN BUCOMP1]

Lbl*

Ceol: a Journal of Irish Music
TNG EIRE8; 0009–0174
EIRE–Dublin, 1963–?86

AB 1 (1963/64), 1, 3, 4; 2 (1965)–8 (1986)
ABc 1 (1963/64)–5 (1981/82), 1
BG 4 (1972/1981)–5 (1981/82), 1, 2; 6
(1983/84), 1/2; 7 (1984), 1, 2; 8 (1986), 1, 2
Cu 2 (1965)–8 (1986), 2

EIR:Dtc 1 (1963/64)–7 (1984)
EIR:Dub 1 (1963/64)–8 (1986)
EIR:MEtc 1 (1963/64)–2 (1965); 5
(1981/82)–8 (1986), 1,
En 1 (1963/64), 1; 2 (1965/66), 1, 3, 4; 3
(1967/70)–4 (1972/81), 2
Gm 1 (1963)–8 (1986)
Lcs 1 (1963/64), 1, 4; 2 (1965)–3 (1968/70),
1, 2, 4; 4 (1972/81), 1–4; 7 (1984), 1, 2
Lgo*
Ob*

Ceol na hEireann [= Music in Ireland]
EIRE–?, 1993–
[NOT IN BUCOMP1]

EIR:Dtc 1 (1993)–#

Y Cerbyd Cerddorol [= The Musical Vehicle]
GB–Lixum Clwyd, 1860

AB 1860

**Le Cercle Musical: Organe du Club National
du Disque**
TNG F657
F–Paris, 1955–61

Lsa 10–29, 1957–60*

Y Cerddor [= The Musician]
Fellinger 1968/1096; TNG GB132, GB336
GB–Wrexham: Hughes and Son, 1889–1921;
continued as *Y Cerddor Newydd: the Welsh
Musical Magazine* (TNG GB297), with new
numbering system, 1922–29; from 1931–39
reverted to *Y Cerddor*]

AB 1 (1889)–33 (1921); n.s. 1 (1922)–8
(1929); n.s. 1 (1930)–9 (1939)*
ABc n.s. 1 (1922)–8 (1929), n.s. 1 (1930)–9
(1939)
CDCp 1 (1889)–25 (1914), 311; 26 (1915),
313–33 (1921); n.s. 1 (1922)–8 (1929); n.s.
1 (1930)–9 (1939)
Cu n.s. 1 (1930)–9 (1939), 10
En n.s. 1 (1922)–8 (1929)
Lbl 1 (1889)–33 (1921)
LVp 11 (1899)–18 (1906); 21 (1909)–32
(1920); n.s. 1 (1922)–8 (1929); n.s. 1
(1930)–9 (1939)
MO 1 (1889)–33 (1921); n.s. 1 (1922)–8
(1929)
Ob*

Y Cerddor Cymreig [= The Welsh Musician]
Fellinger 1968/13; TNG GB58
GB–Merthyr Tydfil: J. Roberts, 1861–73
[From vol. 3 published Wrexham: Hughes and
Son]

> **AB** 1 (1861)–11 (1873)
> **ABc** 1 (1861)–11 (1873)
> **CDCp** 1 (1861)–11 (1873)
> **Lbl** 47–141, 1865–70*
> **MO** 1 (1861)–9 (1870)

**Y Cerddor Newydd: the Welsh Musical
Magazine** *see* Y Cerddor

Cerddor Sol-Ffa *see* Cerddor y Tonic Sol-Ffa

**Cerddor y Cymry [= The Musician of the
Welsh]**
Fellinger 1968/916 and 1968/1097; TNG
GB104, GB128
GB–Llanelli: D. Williams and Son, 1883–94
[?From 1886–88 amalgamated with *Cyfaill yr
Aelwyd* (q.v.)]

> **AB** 1 (1883)–12 (1894) [w 10 (1892), 7;
> 11 (1893), 11; 12 (1894), 2, 4]
> **CDCp** 1 (1883)–12 (1894)
> **Lbl** 1 (1883)–12 (1894)

**Cerddor y Tonic Sol-Ffa [= Tonic Sol-Fa
Musician]**
GB–Wrexham, 1869–86
[From 1881 entitled *Cerddor Sol-Ffa*]

> **AB** 1869–86
> **CDCp** 1869–72

Cerddoriaeth Cymru *see* Welsh
Music/Cerddoriaeth Cymru

**C. F. Whistling's Handbuch der
musikalischen Literatur, oder Allgemeines
systematisch-geordnetes Verzeichniss der in
Deutschland und in den angrenzenden
Ländern gedruckten Musikalien, auch
musikalischen Schriften und Abbildungen mit
Anzeige der Verleger und Preise**
Fellinger 1968/222; TNG D101
D–Leipzig, 1844–1943
[Entitled *Hofmeister's Handbuch der
Musikliteratur* from 1924; preceded by the
*Handbuch der musikalischen Literatur, oder
Allgemeines systematisch-geordnetes
Verzeichniss der bis zum Ende des Jahres 1815
gedruckten Musikalien, auch musikalischen
Schriften und Abbildungen mit Anzeige der
Verleger und Preise* (q.v.)]

> **Lbl***
> **Ob***

Chainsaw
GB–London, ?1976–?

> **Cu** 3–6, 1977–78
> **Lsa** 5, 1978; 8, 1979; 10, 1980

Chamber Music
GB–London, 1913–16
[A supplement to *The Music Student: the
Magazine of the Home Study Union and of the
Music Teachers' Association* (q.v.), appearing
alternate months under the direction of Walter
Willson Cobbett; ceased publication with no.
22a (1916)]

> **Cpl** 1–22a, 1913–16
> **Cu** 1–22a, 1913–16
> **Ep** 5–11, 1914
> **Gm** 9–22a, 1914–16
> **Lbl***
> **Lcml** 1–19, 1913–16
> **Mcm** 1–22a, 1913–16
> **Mpl** 1–19, 1913–16

Change
0590–6180
US–Detroit: Artists Workshop Press, 1965–?

> **Cbijs** 1, 2, 1965–66
> **LOnjfa***

Chapbook
GB–Aberdeen: Chapbook Publications, ?1965–
69

> **Cu** 3 (1967)–5 (1969), 3*
> **Gm** 2 (1966), 3–6; 3 (1967), 1–6; 4 (1968),
> 1–6; 5 (1969), 1–3
> **Lbl***
> **Lcs** 2 (1966)–3 (1967), 1–4, 6; 4 (1968); 5
> (1969), 2
> **Ob** 3 (1967)–5 (1969), 3

**Chapter and Verse: the A-Z of Hi-fi and
Home Entertainment Systems**
0959–2938
GB–Kingston-upon-Thames: Magazines
International, 1990–
[NOT IN BUCOMP1]

> **EIR:Dtc** 1 (1990)–#

The Chart Book
0968–512X
GB–London: Spotlight, 1991–
[NOT IN BUCOMP1]

  Cu 1993–#
  Lbl 1991–#

Chart Club
0956–4446
GB–Iver Heath: Century, 1983–?88; n.s. 1989–
[NOT IN BUCOMP1]

  Cu 1–7, 1983; n.s. 1 (1989)–4 (1991), 3*
  EIR:Dtc n.s. 1 (1989)–4 (1991), 3
  Lbl*

Chart Hits
0962–1768
GB–London: Dennis Oneshots, 1990–
[NOT IN BUCOMP1]

  Lbl*

Chart Now
0962–7219
GB–London: Goodies, 1991–
[NOT IN BUCOMP1]

  Lbl 2, 1991–#

Chart Smash
0961–6187
GB–London: Dennis Oneshots, 1991–
[NOT IN BUCOMP1]

  Lbl*

Chart Songwords
GB–Hastings: Dormbourne Ltd, 1979–?84

  Cu 1–50, 1979–84
  EIR:Dtc 1–50, 1979–84
  Lbl*
  Ob 1–50, 1979–84

Chart Watch: Britain's Densest Music
Quarterly
0262–9577
GB–Ilminster: Chartwatch, 1981–
[NOT IN BUCOMP1]

  Cu*
  Lbl*

Chartbusters
0960–183X
GB–London: Dennis Oneshots, 1990–
[NOT IN BUCOMP1]

  Lbl 1990–#

The Charts
GB–London, 1971–?

  Lsa 1971, Mar 29–Aug 30

Chelys: a Journal for the Plucked String *see*
Chelys: Monthly Journal of the New England
Society for the Plucked String

Chelys: Monthly Journal of the New England
Society for the Plucked String
US–?, 1976–?
[NOT IN BUCOMP1; vol.2, nos 1–2 bore
subtitle *A Journal for the Plucked String*; from
vol. 2, nos 3–4 the title and subtitle changed to
*The Electric Chelys: an Iconoclastic Journal for
the Plucked String*]

  AB 1 (1976)–2 (1979)

Chelys: the Journal of the Viola da Gamba
Society
TNG GB537; 0952–8407
GB–Hedley [etc.]: Viola da Gamba Society,
1969–
[Preceded by the *Viola da Gamba Society:
Bulletin* (q.v.) from 1948–68]

  AB 11 (1982)–17 (1988)
  Bp 1 (1969)–#
  BSdsc*
  Bu 2 (1970); 6 (1975/76)–#
  CCtc 1 (1969)–#
  Cpl 1 (1969)–#
  Cu 1 (1969)–#
  EIR:Dtc 1 (1969)–#
  En 1 (1969)–#
  Er 1 (1969)–#
  Lam 1 (1969)
  Lbbc 1 (1969)–#
  Lbl*
  Lcm 1 (1969)–#
  Lcml 1 (1969)–4 (1972)
  Lgu 2 (1970); 6 (1975/76)–#
  Lkc 1 (1969)–15 (1986)
  LRHBNC 1 (1969)–3 (1971); 6 (1975/76)–11
  (1982)
  Lu 1 (1969); 11 (1982)
  NO 9 (1980)–#
  Ob 1 (1969)–#
  Ouf 1 (1969)–#
  SA 3 (1971)
  Uu 1 (1969)–#

The Chesterian
Fellinger 1968/2238; TNG GB268, GB274
GB–London: J. and W. Chester, 1915–19 (20
nos); n.s. 1919–40; 1947–61 (208 numbers)]

AB 1–20, 1915–19; n.s. 1–150, 1919–40
Bp 1–18, 1919–21; n.s. 25, 1923; 72, 1928;
74–77, 1928–29; 80, 81, 1929; 95, 97, 99,
1931; 124, 1935
BRu 28, 31, 32, 1923; 50, 1925; 53, 1926; 62,
1927; 86, 1930
Cpl n.s. 3–27, 1919–22; 50, 1925; 68, 69,
1927; 85, 1930; 90, 95, 1931; 134, 1937;
152, 1947
Cu n.s. 1–208, 1919–61
EIR:Dtc 1–20, 1915–19; n.s. 1–208, 1919–61
En n.s. 1–208, 1919–61
Ep n.s. 118–122, 1934–35; 123– 127, 129,
1935–36; 131–134, 1936–37; 1937–40,
147, 148; 156, 1948
Gm 1–20, 1915–19; n.s. 1–150, 1919–40;
182–208, 1955–61
Lam n.s. 153, 155, 1948; 174, 1953; 190,
1957
Lbl*
Lcm 1–20, 1915–19; n.s. 9–16, 1920–21; 23,
1922; 42, 1924; 49–80, 1925–29; 84, 1930;
95, 1931; 103, 1932; 138, 1938
Lcml n.s. 1–208, 1919–61
Lu n.s. 1–208, 1919–61*
LVp n.s. 1, 1919; 18, 1921; 27, 1922; 31, 33,
1923; 39–41, 1924; 46, 1925; 54, 57, 1926;
60, 63, 65–67, 1927; 72, 1928; 77, 1929
Mcm n.s. 47, 1925; 56, 1926; 65–71,
1927–28; 81–88, 1929–30
Mpl n.s. 1–208, 1915–61
NO n.s. 1–207, 1919–61*
Ob n.s. 1–208, 1919–61
Ouf n.s. 123–146, 1935–39
SFp n.s. 1–148, 1919–39
SFu n.s. 14–205, 1921–61*

The Chesterian Musical Record
TNG GB274
GB–London, 1930–41; 1947–61
[Later entitled *The Musical Record*]

Cu 35–44, 1940–53 [w 37, 41]
Ep 13, 1933; 20–30, 1935–37; 35–40, 42, 43,
1947–53
Lbl*

Chetham's News
GB–Manchester: Chetham's School of Music,
?–?
[NOT IN BUCOMP1]

Mpl 1973–75

Chethams' Today
GB–Manchester: Chetham's School of Music,
?–?
[NOT IN BUCOMP1]

Mpl 1973–79

Chigiana
TNG I266; 0069–3391
I–Florence: Olschki, 1939–63; 1964–
[NOT IN BUCOMP1; entitled *Chigiana:
Rassegna Annuale di Studi Musicologici* from
1964]

Cu 21 (1964)–#
DRu 26/27 (1969)–38 (1982)
Lbl*
LRHBNC 37 (1980)–#
Lu 21 (1964)–#
NO 26/27 (1969)–36 (1979)
Ob*
Ouf 1 (1939)–3 (1941); 5 (1948)–7 (1950);
9 (1952); 14 (1957); 20 (1963)–42 (1990)
SFu 21 (1964)–31 (1974)

**Chigiana: Rassegna Annuale di Studi
Musicologici** *see* **Chigiana**

The Children's Harp [translated title] *see*
Telyn-y-Plant

**Chime: Newsletter of the European
Foundation for Chinese Music Research**
0926–7263
B–Leiden: European Foundation for Chinese
Music Research, 1990–
[NOT IN BUCOMP1; also known as *Ching*]

Cu 1, 1990–#
Lbl 2, 1990–#
Lio 1, 1990–#
Lsa 4, 1991–#
Lso 1, 1990; 3, 1991–#

Chimes *see* **The Croydon Folksong Club
Newsletter**

Chinese Journal of Acoustics *see* **Acta
Acustica**

Chinese Music [translated title] *see* Zhong Guo Yin Yue

Chinese Music: Official Publication of the Chinese Music Society of North America *see* Chinese Music General Newsletter

Chinese Music General Newsletter
0192-3749
US–Woodbridge, IL: The Chinese Music Society of North America, 1978–
[From 2 (1979), 2 entitled *Chinese Music: Official Publication of the Chinese Music Society of North America*]

> Cu 1 (1978)–#
> Lbl 3 (1980)–#
> Lgo 2 (1979)–#*
> Lso 17 (1994)–#

Chinese National Folk Music [translated title] *see* Min Zu Mian Jian Yin Yue

Ching *see* Chime: Newsletter of the European Foundation for Chinese Music Research

The Choir
Fellinger 1968/786; TNG GB94
GB–London, 1879
[11 nos in total. Succeeded *The Choir and Musical Record: a Journal Chiefly Devoted to the Interests and Advancement of Church Music* (q.v.); and was absorbed by the *Saturday Musical Review* to become *Saturday Musical Review: a Record of Music and the Drama, with which is incorporated "The Choir"* (q.v.)]

> Bp 1 (1879/80), 1–11

The Choir: a Magazine Devoted Chiefly to Church Music and Hymnology
Fellinger 1968/2008; TNG GB247
GB–London: Novello, 1910– 64
[Ceased publication with vol. 55 (1964); entitled *The Choir and Musical Journal* from 1911, following merger with *The Musical Journal* (formerly *The Nonconformist Musical Journal* (q.v.))]

> AB 1 (1910)–25 (1934)
> EIR:Dtc 20 (1929), 235–21 (1930), 241
> En 19 (1928)–26 (1935)
> Lbl*
> Lcml 48 (1957), 5
> Lrco 9 (1918), 99
> LVp 48 (1957)
> Mpl 1 (1910)–55 (1964)
> Ob*

The Choir: a Monthly Journal of Church Music
TNG US308
US–Cincinnati, OH: Fillmore Music House, 1899–1922
[NOT IN BUCOMP1]

> AB 3 (1903), 1
> Lbl*

The Choir and Musical Journal *see* The Choir: a Magazine Devoted Chiefly to Church Music and Hymnology

The Choir and Musical Record: a Journal Chiefly Devoted to the Interests and Advancement of Church Music
Fellinger 1968/474; TNG GB61
GB–London: J. Wright, 1863– 78
[Continued from 1879 by the *Saturday Musical Review* (q.v.); and from 1879/80 as *The Choir* (q.v.); 630 numbers in total]

> AB 1 (1863)–2 (1864), 48; 3 (1865)–20 (1875)*
> Bp 1 (1863)–23 (1878), 630
> Cu 1 (1863)–23 (1878) [w 16 (1872), 19–20]
> Er 5 (1866/67)–7 (1868/69); 9 (1870)–15 (1873)
> Gul (e) 1 (1863)–19 (1875), 440
> Lbl 1 (1863)–23 (1878), 630
> Lrco 1 (1863); 4 (1866)*; 5 (1866/67); 7 (1868/69)–8 (1869); 11 (1871)–19 (1875); 21 (1876)–23 (1878)
> Mpl 1 (1863)–16 (1873)
> Ob 1 (1863)

The Choir and Musical Record Almanack
Fellinger 1968/534; TNG GB69
GB London: Metzler, 1866
[Only one vol. published]

> Lbl 1866

Choir and Organ
0968-7262
GB–London: Orpheus Publications, 1993–
[NOT IN BUCOMP1; originally supplied free of charge with *The Musical Times*; later became separate, priced publication. Six issues per year]

> ALb 1 (1993)–#
> Au 1 (1993)–#
> BEp 2 (1994), 2–#
> BG 1 (1993)–#
> BLu 1 (1993), 2–#
> BRu 1 (1993)–#

Bs 1 (1993)–#
Bu 1 (1993)–#
Cat 1 (1993)–#
DOR 1 (1993)–#
EIR:Dp 1 (1993), 2–#
EIR:Driam 1 (1993)–
EIR:Dtc 1 (1993)–#
EIR:Dub 1 (1993)–#
EIR:MEtc 1 (1993)–#
En 1 (1993)–#
Er 1 (1993)–#
EXu 1 (1993)–#
Gul 1 (1993)–#
HE 1 (1993)–#
HUu 1 (1993)–#
Lam 1 (1993)–#
LAu 1 (1993)–#
Lbar 1 (1993)–#
Lbl*
Lbo 1 (1993)–#
Lcm 1 (1993)–# [w 1 (1993), 2]
Lcu 1 (1993)–#
LEbc 1 (1993)–#
Lgsm 1 (1993)–#
Lkc 1 (1993)–#
Lsa 1 (1993)–#
Lsut [c (1 year)]
Ltc 1 (1993), 1; 3 (1995), 6–#
Lu 1 (1993)–#
LVp 1 (1993)–#
Mcm 1 (1993)–#
MK 1 (1993)–#
Mmu (a) 1 (1993), 2–4 (1996)
Mpl 1 (1993)–#
Msuc 1 (1993)–#
Mu 1 (1993)–2 (1994)
NOp [c (2 years)]
NOTu 1 (1993)–#
NWu 1 (1993)–#
Ob*
Op [c (3 years)]
Oub 1 (1993)–#
Ouf 1 (1993)
R 1 (1993)–#
SA 1 (1993)
SFu 1 (1993)–#
SLGu 1 (1993), 2–#
SOu 1 (1993)–#
TOd 1 (1993)–#
Yu 1 (1993)

The Choir Journal
TNG US317
US–Boston, MA: B. F. Wood Music, 1899–1908

AB 65, 72, 1901
Lbl*

The Choir Musician: a Journal for Choirs and Sunday Schools
Fellinger 1968/1523; TNG GB188
GB–Leeds, 1900–27; Boston Spa, 1928–29
[From no. 177, 1928 entitled *Sunday School and Choir Music*]

Lbl 123–176, 1911–27, July; 1928–29*

Choir Schools Directory
GB–London: English Choir Schools' Association, 1965–

Lbl*

Choir Schools Review
GB–Peterborough: Choir Schools Association, 1982–85
[NOT IN BUCOMP1; in 1986 became *Choir Schools Today: the Annual Journal of the Choir Schools' Association* (q.v.)]

Cu 1982–85
En 1982–84
Ob*
Re 1982–84

Choir Schools Today: the Annual Journal of the Choir Schools' Association
GB–Market Weston: Choir Schools' Association, 1986–
[NOT IN BUCOMP1; succeeded *Choir Schools Review* (q.v.)]

ALb 1 (1986)
CCtc 2 (1988)–#
Cu 1 (1986)–#
EIR:Dtc 1 (1986)–#
En 1 (1986)–#
Ob*

The Choirmaster *see* **The Church Choirmaster and Organist**

The Choirmaster's Journal
Fellinger 1968/1565; TNG GB191
GB–Bradford: Bradshaw and Company, 1901

Lbl*

Chopin-Jahrbuch
TNG INTL17; 0577–9715
A–Vienna [etc.]: International Chopin-
Gesellschaft, 1956–70

 Cu 1 (1956)–3 (1970)
 Lbl*
 Ob*

Chopin Studies
0239–8567; vols also carry separate ISBNs
PL–Warsaw: The Frederick Chopin Society,
1985–
[NOT IN BUCOMP1]

 Bu 1 (1985)
 Lu 2 (1987)
 Ob*
 Ouf 1 (1985)–5 (1995)

The Choral Advocate and Singing-Class
Journal
Fellinger 1968/273; TNG US25
US–New York; Boston: Tappan, Whittemore and
Mason, 1850– 73
[Entitled the *Musical Review and Choral
Advocate,* 1852–53; the *New York Musical
Review and Choral Advocate*, 1854–55; and the
New York Musical Review and Gazette, 1855–
59; combined with *The Musical World* in 1860,
to become *The Musical Review and Musical
World*, 1860–64; *The New York Weekly Review of
Music, Literature, Fine Arts and Society*, 1865–
66; and *The New York Weekly Review*, 1867–73]

 AB 9 (1858)–15 (1864)
 Lbl*

The Choral Guild [translated title] *see* Greal y
Corau

Choral Journal
TNG US705; 0009–5028
US–Tampa, FL: American Choral Directors'
Association, 1959–

 BSdsc*

Choral Review
0958–9104
GB–Bungay, Suffolk: Choral Review, 1990–91
[NOT IN BUCOMP1; ceased publication July
1991]

 Lbl*
 Mcm 1990–91
 TOd 1, 1990

Chorale
0261–362X
GB–Cookham: Chorale Publications, 1980–83

 Cu 1 (1980)–3 (1983), 4
 EIR:Dtc 1 (1980)–3 (1983), 4
 Lbl*
 Lcml 1 (1980)–2 (1982); 3 (1983), 1–3
 Lgo 1 (1980), 3–3 (1983), 4
 Ob*

Chord
GB–London: South London Philharmonic
Society, 1923–24

 Cpl 1 (1923), 1, 2
 Lbl*
 Lcm 1 (1923)
 Lgo*

The Chord: a Quarterly devoted to Music
Fellinger 1968/1472; TNG GB182
GB–London: At the Sign of the Unicorn, 1899–
1900

 AB 1–5, 1899–1900 [w 3]
 Au 1–5, 1899–1900
 BDp 1–5, 1899–1900
 BLu 1, 3, 5, 1899–1900
 Bu 1–4, 1899–1900
 Cu 1–5, 1899–1900
 EIR:Dtc 1–5, 1899–1900
 EIR:Dub 1–5, 1899–1900 [w 2]
 En 1–5, 1899–1900
 Ep 1–5, 1899–1900
 Gm 1–4, 1899–1900
 Gul 1–5, 1899–1900
 Lam 1–4, 1899–1900
 Lbl 1–5, 1899–1900
 Lcm 1–5, 1899–1900
 Lcml 1–5, 1899–1900
 Lu 1–5, 1899–1900 [w 4, 1900]
 LVp 1–5, 1899–1900
 Mcm 1, 1899
 Mpl 1–5, 1899–1900
 NO 1–5, 1899–1900
 Ob*
 R 1–5, 1899–1900
 SA 1, 1899

Chord and Discord: a Journal of Modern Musical Progress
TNG US520; 0069–3758
US–New York: Bruckner Society of America, 1932–

ALb 3 (1969), 1
BTu 1 (1932/39)–3 (1969), 1
Cu 1 (1932/39)–3 (1969), 1
LAu 2 (1940/63)
Lbl*
Lcm 1 (1932/39), 9
Lcml 1 (1932/39)*; 2 (1940/63), 1–8
Mcm*
Mpl*
SFu 2 (1940/63)*

Choreography and Dance
0891–6381
CH–Chur: Harwood Academic Publishers, 1988–
[NOT IN BUCOMP1]

EIR:Dtc 1 (1988)–#

The Chorister: a Magazine for Choirboys
TNG GB353
GB–London: School of English Church Music, 1935–40

Lbl*

Christian Music
0958–2630
GB–Worthing: Christian Music, 1988–93
[NOT IN BUCOMP1; succeeded *Music in Worship* (q.v.); entitled *Deo: Today's Music and Worship* from Sum 1993]

CCtc 1988–93
CFp 1990–93
CH 1989, 1; 1990, 4; 1992, 1–3; 1993, 1
Cu 1988–93
En 1988–93
Lbl*
Ob*

La Chronique Musicale: Revue Bi-Mensuelle de l'Art Ancien et Moderne
Fellinger 1968/662; TNG F146
F–Paris, 1873–76
[Ceased publication with vol. 11 (1876), no. 66]

Cu 1 (1873)–11 (1876)
Gul (e) 1 (1873)–11 (1876)* [+ musical supplements 1–15, 17–22]
Lbl 1 (1873)–11 (1876)
Lu 1 (1873)–11 (1876), 60, 62, 63
Ob*

Chronique Musicale de Paris
Fellinger 1968/142; TNG F28
F–Paris: Joseph Mainzer, 1838 [no more published]
[NOT IN BUCOMP1]

Ob 1838

Chroniques Internationales du Cuivre *see* **Brass Bulletin: International Brass Chronicle**

The Church Choir
US–Chicago, IL: George F. Rosche, ?1898–1920
[NOT IN BUCOMP1; ceased publication with vol. 23 (1920)]

AB 22 (1919), 4, 11; 23 (1919), 1

The Church Choirmaster and Organist
GB–?London, ?1867–69
[NOT IN BUCOMP1; entitled *The Choirmaster*, Jan–Apr 1869; *The Musician, Organist and Choirmaster*, May–Dec 1869. Succeeded *The Organist: a Monthly Musical Journal and Review* (q.v.)]

Bp 1 (1867)–3 (1869)
Lrco 1 (1867)–3 (1869)

Church Music [1]
TNG GB482; 0009–644X
GB–London: Church Music Association, 1959–74
[Combined with *Life and Worship* and *Music and Liturgy* (TNG GB573)]

AB 1 (1959/63)–3 (1970/74)
ALb 2 (1964/69), 28
Bp 3 (1970/74), 3, 12–24, 26–28
BSdsc*
CCtc 3 (1970/74)*
Cu 1 (1959/63)–3 (1970/74)
EIR:Dtc 1 (1959/63)–3 (1970/74), 28
En 1 (1959/63)–3 (1970/74)
Lam 2 (1964/69), 27
Lbl*
Lcm 2 (1964/69), 2–3 (1970/74), 28*
Lcml 2 (1967/69)*; 3 (1970/74), 1–28
Lsa*
Mpl*
Ob*

Church Music [2]
TNG US757; 0009–6458
US–St Louis, MO: Concordia Publishing, 1966–80

  ALb 2 (1968), 28
  BSdsc*
  Lsa 6 (1974)–8 (1976)
  Lu 2 (1968), 23, 24
  Ob*
  R 2 (1968), 17, 21, 23, 24; 3 (1971), 7–9

Church Music: a Magazine for the Clergy, Choirmasters and Organists
Fellinger 1968/1767; TNG US358
US–Philadelphia, PA: Dolphin Press, 1905–09

  EIR:Dtc 1 (1905)–3 (1908), 2
  Lbl*
  LVp 1 (1905)–4 (1909)
  Ob*

Church Music of Today *see* **The Church Music Review**

Church Music Quarterly *see* **Promoting Church Music**

The Church Music Review
TNG GB339
GB–London, 1931–33
[From 1932 entitled *Church Music of Today*]

  AB 1931–32
  Cu*
  En 1931–32
  Lbl*
  Ob*

Church Music Review and Official Bulletin of the American Guild of Organists
Fellinger 1968/1566; TNG US339
US–New York: Novello, Ewer and Co., 1901–35
[Entitled *New Music Review and Church Music Review* from 1904/05, Nov; ceased publication 1935, Sep]

  Bp 9 (1909)–34 (1935), Sep

Church Music Society Annual Report
TNG GB217
GB–London, 1906–
[NOT IN BUCOMP1]

  AB 1984/85–1989/90
  Lbl*

Lcm 1960; 1965–89
Lu 1949–#*
Ob 1959–#

Church Music Society: Occasional Papers
TNG GB244
GB–London, 1910–
[NOT IN BUCOMP1]

  Lu 1 (1910)–#*
  Ob 1 (1910)–#

Church Music Society: Shorter Papers
TNG GB270
GB–London: Oxford University Press and the Society for the Promotion of Christian Knowledge, 1917–
[NOT IN BUCOMP1]

  Lu 1 (1917)–#*

The Church Musician
0009–6466
US–Nashville, TN: Southern Baptist Convention, Sunday School Board, 1950–

  BSdsc*

The Church Musician: a Monthly Journal of the Church Choir Guild
Fellinger 1968/1156; TNG GB142
GB–London: Church Choir Guild, 1891–95
[Ceased publication with no. 60, Dec 1895; combined with *The Musical Observer* (q.v.) in 1896 to become *The Musical Observer and Church Musician* (TNG GB145)]

  BSdsc*
  En 1891–95
  Lbl 1891–95
  Mpl 1891–95
  Ob*

The Church Musician: Official Journal of the Incorporated Guild of Church Musicians
TNG GB333
GB–London: Incorporated Guild of Church Musicians, 1929–31; 1935–39

  Bp 1929 [Preliminary issue]; 1–4, 1929–31; n.s. 1–4, 1935–36; 1937, Sep/Oct, Nov/Dec; 1938, Apr/June; 1939, Apr/June
  Cpl 1939, Apr/June
  Cu 1929 [Preliminary issue]; 1–4, 1929–31; n.s. 1–4
  Lbl*
  Ob*

The Church's Musical Visitor
TNG US86
US–Cincinnati, 1871–97
[Later entitled simply *The Musical Visitor*]

Cu 1 (1871)–12 (1893)* [m] [w 4–9]
Mu 1 (1871)–26 (1897) [m]

The Cine-Musician
TNG GB309
GB–London, 1925

Lbl*

Cinema Organ: Journal of the Cinema Organ Society
0958–255X
GB–London: Cinema Organ Society, 1952–
[From 1966, 74 entitled simply *Cinema Organ*]
[NOT IN BUCOMP1]

Cu 3 (1954)–#
En 32 (1984)–#*
EIR:Dtc 32 (1984)–#
Gm 16 (1968)–#
Lam 181, 182, 1994
Lam (o) 2 (1953)–4 (1955), 5
Lbl*
Ob*

The Cinema Organ Herald
GB–London, 1933–

Lbl*

The Clarinet
TNG US836; 0361–5553
US–Pocatello, ID [etc.]: Idaho State University, 1973–

CCtc 14 (1986)–19 (1992)
Lam 6 (1978), 1; 11 (1983)–17 (1990), 3; 18 (1991)–#
Ltc 20 (1993)–22 (1995)*

Clarinet and Saxophone *see* C.A.S.S. News

Clarinet and Saxophone Society of Great Britain Year Book
0260–1702
GB–Wilmington: Clarinet and Saxophone Society of Great Britain, ?–

Ob*

Classic CD
0959–7204
GB–Bath: Future Publishing, 1990–
[NOT IN BUCOMP1]

AB 1, 1990–#
ALb 37, 1993
BLp 1, 1990–#
CCtc 1, 1990–#
Cu 1, 1990–#
EIR:Dtc 5, 1990–#
Ep 1991, Jan–#
IOW 1992, Dec–#
Lbl*
Lbo 47, 1994–#
LEc [c (5 years)]
Lha (f) [c (5 years)]
Lis [c (2 years)]
Lsa 6, 1990–# [w 37, 1993]
Msuc [c (3 years)]
NTp 1991, Apr–#
Ob*
PRp [c (2 years)]
SAu 37, 1993–#
SHRp 21, 1992–#
STAp 4, 1990–#

Classic FM
GB–London, 1995–
[NOT IN BUCOMP1]

Cu 1, 1995–#
Ltc 1, 1995–#

The Classical Catalogue *see* The Gramophone Long Playing Classical Record Catalogue

Classical Collection
GB–London: Orbis Publishing, ?1992–
[NOT IN BUCOMP1]

AB 1992–#
EIR:Dtc 1992–#
Msuc 1992–#

Classical Collectors Review
GB–Richmond, 1980–82
[NOT IN BUCOMP1]

Ob 1 (1980)–3 (1982), 3, 7, 9

Classical Guitar
0950–429X
GB–Gateshead: Ashley Mark, 1982–
[Incorporated *Guitar International* from 1991, Dec.]

CCtc 1 (1982/83)–#
Cu 1 (1982/83)–#
EIR:Dp 6 (1987/88), 5–#
EIR:Dtc 1 (1982/83)–#
EK [c (2 years)]
En 1 (1982/83)–#
Gam 12 (1994), 10–#
Gm 11 (1992/93)–#
KE 6 (1987/88)–11 (1992/93)
Lam 1 (1982/83), 1, 3, 6; 2 (1982/83)–#
Lbl*
Lcm 8 (1989/90)–#*
Lcml 1 (1982/83)–#
Lgsm 8 (1989/90), 5–#
Lgu 1 (1982/83)–#
Lsut [c (1 year)]
Ltc 13 (1995), 10–#
Lu 10 (1991/92), 3–#
Mcm 1 (1982/83)–#*
NOp [c (2 years)]
Ob*

Classical Music and Album Reviews *see*
Classical Music [Weekly]

Classical Music Fortnightly *see* **Classical
Music [Weekly]**

Classical Music [Weekly]
TNG GB575; 0308–9762
GB–London: Rhinegold, 1976–
[From 1978–79, June entitled *Classical Music
and Album Reviews*; from 1979, June, entitled
Classical Music. Subtitled *The Magazine of the
Classical Music Profession* from 1996, Sep.
Also known as *Classical Music Fortnightly*.
Classical Piano (q.v.); *Early Music Today* (q.v.);
and *The Singer* (q.v.) are issued as supplements]

AB 1986–#
ABc 1985–89*
ALb 1977–#*
BAc [c (3 years)]
BDp 1976–#
BEp [c (1 year)]
BLBBC 1988, Nov*; 1990, Oct–Dec;
    1991–#*
BLp [c]
BRp [c (2 years)]
Bs 1989, July–#
BTp 1987–#*
Bu 1993–#
CAR [c (1 year)]
Cat 1980–#*
CCtc 1978–82; 1984–#

CDCp 1986, Aug–#
CDu 1990, Oct–#
CFp 1980–#
CH [c (1 year)]
CHEp [c (1 year)]
Cpl 1978–79*; 1979, June 16–1981, Sep 5
Cu 1978–#
DDp [c (2 years)]
DOR 1981, July–1986, July; 1993, Dec–#
DS 1976–#
Ea [c (3 years)]
EIR:Dcmc 1990–#
EIR:Dp 1986, Jan 11–#
EIR:Driam 1993–#
EIR:Dtc 1978, May 29–Sep 16; 1978, Sep
    30–1979, June 2;1979, June 16–#
EIR:Dub 1980–89
En 1978–#
Ep 1981–#*
Er 1979–#
Gam [c]
GLp [c]
Gm 1977–#
Gsmic 1982–#*
GU [c (3 years)]
HA 1991, June–#
HE 1991–#
HUu 1979, Jan 13–1987, Apr 11
IOW 1993–#
IP [c (3 years)]
Je [c (2 years)]
KE 1978, Apr 29–Sep 16; 1978, Sep 30–*#
Lam 1981–#*
Lba [c (1 year)]
Lbar 1976–#*
Lbbc 1991–#; second copy [c]
Lbk [c (2 years)]
Lbo 1984, Jan–#
Lbx 1981–# [m]
Lcm 1976–85*; 1986–#
Lcml 1976, Feb–#
Lcml (c) [c (1 year)]
Lcml (p) [c (6 months)]
Lcml (m) [c (6 months)]
LEc [c (5 years)]
Len [c (2 years)]
Lgo 1976–#*
Lgr (b) [c (6 months)]
Lgsm 1990–#
Lgu [c (3 years)]
Lha (f) [c (2 years)]
Lhr [c]
LIp 1981, June–#
Lk [c (3 months)]
Lk (c) [c (3 months)]

Lkc 1976–87
Lki 1977, July–1991, Oct
Lmi 1980, Jan –#
LRHBNC [c]
Lri [c (2 years)]
Lro 216, 1983–#
Lsa 1976–# [w 1986, 292, 294; 1988, 352]
Lsut [c (6 months)]
LT [c (1 year)]
Ltc [c]
Ltv 1978, Apr–#
Lu 1976–#
LVp 1977–#
Lwwb [c (1 year)]
Lwwput [c (1 year)]
LXp [c (1 year)]
Mcm 1976–#*
Mmu 1980*; 1981–#
Mpl 1978–#
Msu 1987, Mar–#
Msuc 1992–#
Mu 1980–#*
NOp [c (2 years)]
NOTu 1982–#
Ob*
Op [c (2 years)]
Oub 1982–#
PRp [c (3 years)]
R [c]
Re 1980–89*
Rp 1990, Sep–#
SA 1980, Mar 1–1987, Apr 11*
SFp 1982, 188–#
SHRp 1993–#
SK [c (1 year)]
STAp 1985–#
TOd 1979–#
Uu 1992–#
WF 1981, June 27–#
WH [c (6 months)]
Y 1989, Jan 14–#
Yu 1990–#

Classical Music Worldwide
GB–London: Rhinegold, ?1992–
[NOT IN BUCOMP1]

Ep 1993, 3–5

Classical Piano
0969–5818
GB–London: Rhinegold, 1993–
[NOT IN BUCOMP1; supplied with *Classical Music [Weekly]* (q.v.)]

AB 1 (1993)–#

ALb 1 (1993)–#
Bs 1 (1993)–#
Bu 1 (1993)–#
Cat 1 (1993)–#*
CDCp 1 (1993)–#
Cu 1 (1993)–#
DOR 2 (1994)–#
EIR:Dp (1993)–#
EIR:Driam 1 (1993)–
EIR:Dtc 1 (1993)–#
En 1 (1993)–#
Ep 1 (1993)–#
Gsmic 1 (1993)–#
HE 1 (1993)–#
Lam 1 (1993)
Lbar 1 (1993)–#
Lbbc 1 (1993)–#; second copy [c]
Lbo 2 (1994)–#
Lcm 1 (1993)–#
Lgsm 1 (1993)–#
Lgu 2 (1994), 4–#
Lsa 1 (1993)–#
Ltc 3 (1995)–#
Lu 1 (1993)–#
Mcm 1 (1993)–#
Msu 1 (1993)–#
Mu 1 (1993)–#*
Ob*
TOd 1 (1993)

Classical Sounds
0262–8961
GB–Stamford: Key Publications, 1982–

EIR:Dtc 1–3, 1982
Lbl*
Ob*

Classics: the Best Buys in Classical Recordings
0965–2701
GB–Harrow: General Gramophone Publications, 1992–
[NOT IN BUCOMP1]

AB 1992–#
ALb 1992, Feb
Cu 1992–93
Lbl*
SOL 1992–93

Classics Magazine: the Record and Tape Collector's Journal
GB–London: Polydor, ?–?
[NOT IN BUCOMP1]

AB 1980

Clave: Revista Cubana de Musica
CU–Havana: Ediciones Cubanas, 1986–
[NOT IN BUCOMP1]

Lbl 7, 1987–#
Lsa 1–6, 1986–87; 8, 9, 11, 1988

Clavier: a Magazine for Pianists and
Organists
TNG US718; 0009–854X
US–Evanston, IL: Instrumentalist Company,
1962–

Lam 6 (1967), 7; 32 (1993), 2, 3, 5, 7, 8
Lcml 7 (1968)

The Clavier: the Quarterly Journal of the
VPC Society
Fellinger 1968/1391; TNG GB173
GB–London: Virgil Practice Clavier Society,
1897–1905; superseded by *The Clavier and the
Musical Profession: a Magazine for Teachers
and Students of Music* (q.v.)]

Lbl 1 (1897)–9 (1905)
LEbc 1 (1897)–9 (1905)

The Clavier and the Musical Profession: a
Magazine for Teachers and Students of Music
Fellinger 1968/1815; TNG GB221
GB–London: Virgil Practice Clavier Society,
1906–17
[Preceded by *The Clavier: the Quarterly
Journal of the VPC Society* (q.v.)]

Lbl 1 (1906)–11 (1917)
LEbc 1 (1906)–5 (1911)

Clef
US–Santa Monica, CA: Otto–Marble
Publications, 1946
[Only seven numbers published]

Cbijs 1 (1946), 5

Clés *see* Clés pour la Musique: Mensuel
d'Actualité Musicale

Clés pour la Musique: Mensuel d'Actualité
Musicale
TNG B158; 0776–8389
B–Brussels: Association pour l'Information
Culturelle, 1969–
[Entitled *Clés* (ISSN 0776–8397) from 7 (1975)
–8 (1976), 3; continued as *Clés pour les Arts*]

Cu 1 (1969)–6 (1974), 72*
Lu 1 (1969), 3–4 (1972), 47 [w 2 (1970), 20]
Ob*

Clés pour les Arts *see* Clés pour la Musique:
Mensuel d'Actualité Musicale

Close Harmony: a Magazine of Music and
Associated Arts
TNG GB444
GB–Worthing, 1953

Lbl*

Club Beethoven
BR–Rio de Janeiro, 1882–83

Lbl*

Club Folk
GB–London: British Federation of Folk Clubs,
1967–
[NOT IN BUCOMP1]

AB 1969, 2
Bp 1967–70

Club Sandwich
0262–9054
GB–Westcliff, Essex: Paul McCartney Fan
Club, 1977–
[NOT IN BUCOMP1; later published by Wings
Fan Club]

AB 23, 1981–#
Cu 14, 1979–#
Lbl*

C.M.N. Education Bulletin
0960–9466
GB–London: Arts Council/Contemporary Music
Network, 1990–
[NOT IN BUCOMP1]

Lbl 1990, Aut–#

CMS *see* Country Music Source Book

Cocks's Musical Almanack
Fellinger 1968/263; TNG GB40
GB–London, 1849–51

Ap 1849
BTu 1849–51
Cu 1850–51
Lbl*
Ob 1849–51

Cocks's Musical Miscellany
Fellinger 1968/275; TNG GB43, 36
GB–London, 1850–53; n.s. 1 (1852)– 2 (1853),
18, under title *Cocks's Musical Miscellany:
Enlarged Series* (Fellinger 1968/299)]

Lbl 1850–53
Ob 1850–53

Cocks's Musical Miscellany: Enlarged Series
see Cocks's Musical Miscellany

Coda
GB–Corby: Fentone Music, 1989–
[NOT IN BUCOMP1]

Cu 1 (1989), 1–9
Lbl*

Coda: Canada's Jazz Magazine
TNG C31; 0010–017X
C–Toronto: Coda Publications, 1958–
[From issue 151 entitled *Coda: the Jazz
Magazine*; from 177 became *Coda Magazine:
the Jazz Magazine* (ISSN 0820–926X); from
197 became *Coda Magazine: the Journal of
Jazz and Improvised Music*]

Cbijs 4 (1961/62), 5, 12; 5 (1962/63), 6, 7, 9,
12; 6 (1963/65), 1–4, 7, 12; 7 (1965/67), 2–
11; 8 (1967/69), 1–3, 6–12; 9 (1969/71); 10
(1971/73), 4–6, 9–12; 11 (1973/74)–12
(1974/75), 9; 142, 143, 1975; 144–146,
1976
LOnjfa 1970–#*
Lsa 1973–85*
Lu 10 (1971/73), 5–11; 11 (1973/74), 1–7, 9–
12; 12 (1974/75), 1–3, 5– 7; 140–222,
1975–88*

Coda: the Jazz Magazine *see* Coda: Canada's
Jazz Magazine

Coda Magazine: the Jazz Magazine *see* Coda:
Canada's Jazz Magazine

**Coda Magazine: the Journal of Jazz and
Improvised Music** *see* Coda: Canada's Jazz
Magazine

Cogar
EIRE–Dublin: Comhaltas Ceoltoiri Eireann,
1974

BLu 1 (1974)
EIR:Dtc 1 (1974)
EIR:Duc 1 (1974)

**Coliseum: Magazine of Friends of English
National Opera**
GB–London: English National Opera, 1989–
[NOT IN BUCOMP1]

SFu 1, 1989; 1990, Spr; 32, 1993

**The Collaborator: a Monthly Magazine
Devoted to the Interests of the Composer and
the Lyricist**
TNG US518
US–New York, 1931

Lbl*

Collecta
GB–Watford, 1968–

Cbijs 2, 1968; 12, 1970; 18, 1972; 19, 1973
LOnjfa*
Lsa 23–25, 1975–76

Collectable 45s
GB–London: Vintage Record Centre, 1981–

Lbl*

Collectable Kids
0960–1821
GB–London: Dennis Oneshots [for New Kids
on the Block Fan Club], 1990–
[NOT IN BUCOMP1]

Lbl*

Collectanea Historiae Musicae
0069–5270
I–Florence: Olschki, 1953–66
[Ceased publication with no. 4 (1966)]

Bu 1 (1953)–4 (1966)
Cpl 1 (1953)–4 (1966)
Lbl*
NO 1 (1953)–4 (1966)
Ob 1 (1953)–4 (1966)
Ouf 1 (1953)–4 (1966)

Collection of Information [translated title] *see*
Informatsionniy Sbornik

Collector's Classics
GB–Bexhill–on–Sea: Blues Unlimited, 1964–68

Cbijs 2,4, 1964; 7–9, 1965; 11, 13, 14, 1966

Collector's Items
0261–2550
GB–Walton–on–Thames: J. Holley, 1980–
[NOT IN BUCOMP1; a jazz and blues journal]

Cu 1–8, 1980–81
Lbl*
LOnjfa*

College Band Directors National Association
Journal *see* C.B.D.N.A. Journal

College Music Symposium: Journal of the
College Music Society
TNG US712; 0069–5696
US–Binghampton, NY [etc.]: College Music
Society, 1961–

BSdsc 21 (1981)–#
Cpl 5 (1965)
EXu 30 (1990)–#
KE 15 (1975)
Lcm 1 (1961); 3 (1963)–11 (1971); 16
(1976)–23 (1983)
Lgo 16 (1976)–24 (1984)
Lkc 1 (1961)–#
Ob*
Ouf 4 (1964); 6 (1966)–14 (1974); 32
(1992)–#
SOu 31 (1991)–#

The College of Organists: Prospectus and
[1st-] Annual Report
Fellinger 1968/1948; TNG GB65
GB–London: Royal College of Organists, 1864–
1963
[NOT IN BUCOMP1; later entitled *The Royal
College of Organists: [29th (etc.)] Annual
Report*; from 1904 entitled *The Royal College of
Organists: Calendar and Annual Report* (TNG
GB210); 1931/32 edition entitled *Calendar for
1931–32, including Report of the Proceedings
for the Year, a History of the College* [etc.];
1932/33 edition entitled *Calendar for 1932–33,
including the Proceedings of the Year, Report
and the Lectures, a Short History of the Choral
Foundations in English Cathedrals* [etc.]; from
1941/42 until 1963/64 entitled *Calendar for
[1941/42 (etc.)], including the Proceedings of
the Year.* Succeeded by the *Royal College of
Organists: Year Book* (q.v.)]

BRp 1947–63
BRu 1924/25–1959/60*
Lam 1909/10; 1912/13; 1917/18; 1933/34;
1935–63

Lam (o) 1899/1900; 1904/05–1908/09;
1910/11–1911/12; 1913/14–1916/17;
1918/19–1934/35
Lcm 1905/06–1962/63
Lu 1939/40; 1941/42; 1946/47–1947/48;
1949/50; 1951/52; 1953/54–1962/63
Mpl 1878–84
Ob*

Collegium Musicum
NL–Utrecht, 1946–?

Lbl*

Collegium Musicum: Blätter zur Pflege der
Haus- und Kammermusik
TNG D751
D–Kassel: Bärenreiter, 1932–43; 1946–?62
[From vol. 2 (1933), 5–12 (1943), 2 entitled
Zeitschrift für Hausmusik; ceased publication
with vol. 12 (1943); restarted, under title
Mitteilungen, in 1946; entitled *Hausmusik* from
1949–?62; incorporated into *Musica:
Zweimonatsschrift* (q.v.) in 1962]

Lcml 1 (1932)
Lu 3 (1934)–8 (1939)

Collusion
0262–7078
GB–London: Music Context, 1981–
[NOT IN BUCOMP1]

Lbl*
Ob*
TOd 1–5, 1981–83 [w 3]

Coloquio: Artes
0870–3841
P–Lisbon: Fundacaõ Calouste Gulbenkian,
1971–
[NOT IN BUCOMP1]

SOu 3, 1971–# [w 8, 1972; 11, 14, 1973; 98,
1993]

Colorado Journal of Research in Music
Education
TNG US739; 0588–5000
US–Fort Collins, CO: Colorado Educators'
Association [et al.], 1964–73
[5 vols published in total]

BSdsc*

Columbia Record Club Magazine
US–New York, 195?–?
[NOT IN BUCOMP1]

   Lsa 7 (1962), 12–13 (1966)*

Columbia Stereo Tape Club Magazine
US–New York, 1962–?
[NOT IN BUCOMP1]

   Lsa 1 (1962)–6 (1966), 4*

Come All Ye
0316–0378
C–Vancouver, BC: Vancouver Folk–Song
Society, 1972–77; 1978–
[Superseded in 1978 by Canada Folk Bulletin]

   Lcs 2 (1973), 10, 12; 3 (1977), 1–6, 12;
   n.s. 11 (1990), 2, 4; 13 (1992), 4; 14
   (1993), 1–3; 15 (1994)–#

Come For to Sing
0270–4609
US–Chicago: Old Town School of Folk Music,
1975–
[NOT IN BUCOMP1]

   Lcs 3 (1977)–11 (1985), 4

Comment: a Review of New Music Industry
Ideas
GB–London: Boosey and Hawkes, 197?–?
[NOT IN BUCOMP1]

   AB 3, 1972; 6–12, 1974–78

Commodore: for the Enthusiast of Light
Music on 78s
GB–Purley: Commodore Society, 1971–74
[Ceased publication with no. 15, 1974;
succeeded by Vintage Light Music: for the
Enthusiast of Light Music on 78 r.p.m. Records
(q.v.)]

   Cbijs 1–8, 1971–72
   Lsa 1–15, 1971–74

Common Stock
GB–Edinburgh, Portobello: Lowland and
Border Pipers' Society, 1984–
[NOT IN BUCOMP1]

   Cu 1 (1984)–3 (1987), 2; 8 (1993), 2–#

Compact Disc and Video Insight
GB–London, 1988–
[NOT IN BUCOMP1]

   Cu 2, 3, 5, 6, 1988

Comparative Drama
0010–4078
US–Kalamazoo, MI: Comparative Drama,
1967–
[NOT IN BUCOMP1]

   Lgsm 1994–#

The Composer
TNG GB480; 0010– 4337
GB–London: British Music Information Centre,
1958–87
[From 1962 entitled Composer; 92 numbers
published in total. Preceded 1947–58 by
Composers' Guild of Great Britain: Bulletin
(q.v.)]

   AB 20–92, 1966–87
   ALb 5, 1960; 9–42, 1962–71; 44–92,
      1972–87
   Au 11–21, 23, 1963–67
   BAc 12, 13, 1963; 16–21, 1965–66; 23–51,
      1966–74; 54, 57, 59–92, 1976–87
   BDp 11–86, 1963–85
   BEp 75–92, 1982–87 [w 76, 77]
   BG 1, 1958; 3–12, 1959–63; 22, 1966/67;
      28, 1968; 35, 1970; 38–45, 1970–72;
      47–53, 1973–1974; 59–64, 1976–78;
      66, 68, 70, 1979/80; 91, 1987
   Bp 42–92, 1971–87
   BRp 23–92, 1967–87
   BRu 8–92, 1961–87 [w 9–11, 14, 51–53]
   Bs 2–57, 1958–76*
   BSdsc 18–92, 1966–87
   CCtc 54–91, 1975–87
   CDu 19, 21, 1966; 23–50, 1967–73 [w 48]
   Cpl 32–45, 1962–72
   Cu 1–92, 1958–87 [w 7]
   EIR:Dtc 6–92, 1961–87
   EIR:Duc 14–92, 1964–87
   En 6, 8–92, 1961–87*
   Er 8–92, 1961–87
   EXu 30–92, 1968–87
   Gam 11–92, 1963–87 [w 76, 77]
   Gm 74–92, 1981–87*
   Gsmic 54–92, 1975–87*
   HUu 11–68, 1962–79
   KE 42, 1971; 51–92, 1974–87
   Lam 10–12, 1962–63; 14, 1964; 19, 1966;
      22–92, 1967–87

LAu 33–92, 1969–87
Lbar 12–92, 1963–87 [w 14, 15, 22]
Lbbc 41–90, 1971–87*
Lbl*
Lcm 10–92, 1962–87 [w 91]
Lcml 1, 1958; 3, 1959; 9–22, 1962–67;
  24–92, 1967–87
LEbc 68–77, 1979–82
Lgo 19–92, 1966–87
Lgsm 1–92, 1958–87 [w 71]
LIp 7–92, 1961–87
Lkc 13–80, 1964–83 [w 71]
Lki 52–92, 1974–87
Lmi 42–92, 1971–87
Lmic 1–92, 1958–87
LRHBNC 28–92, 1968–87
Lsa 5, 1960; 10–79, 1962–83; 84, 1985;
  90–92, 1987
Lu 1–92, 1958–87
LVp 10–92, 1962–87
LVu 17–92, 1965–87
Mcm 1–92, 1958–87
Mpl 12–92, 1963–87
NO 18–92, 1966–87
NTp 18–89, 1966–86
NWu 19–42, 1966–71
Ob*
Ouf 11–92, 1963–87 [w 36, 48, 66, 78, 90]
R 17–92, 1965–87
SA 15–67, 1965–79
SFu 16–92, 1 965–87
SLGu 63–92, 1978–87
TOd 13–17, 1964–65; 20–22, 1966–67
Yu 15–92, 1965–87

Composer News: the Journal of the Composers' Guild of Great Britain
1350–8067
GB–London: Composers' Guild of Great
Britain, ?1989–
[NOT IN BUCOMP1]

Gsmic [c]
Lbl 12, 1993–#

Composers' Association of New Zealand: Newsletter
NZ–Wellington: Composers' Association of
New Zealand, ?–1979
[NOT IN BUCOMP1; succeeded by *Canzona*
(q.v.)]

Lcml 1976–79*

Composers' Guild of Great Britain: Bulletin
TNG GB398
GB–London, 1947–58
[Continued as *The Composer* (q.v.)]

Lu 1–20, 1947–58 [w 17, 18]

Le Compositeur Canadien *see* Canadian Composer/Le Compositeur Canadien

Computer Music Association Newsletter
US–San Francisco, CA: Computer Music
Association, 1980–
[NOT IN BUCOMP1]

Gul 1980–82

Computer Music Journal
TNG US871; 0148–9267
US–Cambridge, MA [etc.]: MIT Press, 1977

BAc 8 (1984)–#
BG 19 (1995)–#
BLu 17 (1993)–#
BSdsc 1 (1977)–#
Bu 5 (1981)–#
Cat 16 (1992)–#
CCtc 2 (1978)–16 (1992)
Cu 9 (1985)– #
EIR:Dp 11 (1987), 4
EIR:Dtc 15 (1991), 4–#
EIR:Duc 6 (1982)–#
En 8 (1984), 2, 3; 9 (1985)–#
Er 2 (1978), 3, 4; 3 (1979), 1; 4 (1980);
  5 (1981), 1, 2; 6 (1982), 1; 7 (1983), 2–4;
  8 (1984), 2–4; 9 (1985)–#
Gul 1 (1977)–#
KE 12 (1988)–#
LAu 9 (1985), 4–#
Lcm 17 (1993)–#
Lcml 2 (1978), 2–4; 3 (1979), 1, 2; 4
  (1980)–#
Lcu 1 (1977)–#
LEbc 13 (1989)–#
Lgo 7 (1983)–#
Lgu 5 (1981)–#
Lmi 17 (1993), 4 –#
Lro 1 (1977)–#
Lsa 8 (1984), 1–3; 9 (1985)–11 (1987), 1;
  12 (1988)–14 (1990), 1–3; 15 (1991), 1, 2,
  4; 16 (1992), 1–3; 17 (1993)–#
Ltc 19 (1995), 4–#
Lu 2 (1978), 1; 4 (1980), 1
MK 11 (1987)–#
Mpl 2 (1978)–#
Msuc 14 (1990)–#
Mu 11 (1987)–#

NO 1 (1977)–#
NOTu 16 (1992)–#
NWu 2 (1978)–#
Oub 18 (1994)–#
Ouf 1 (1977)–# [w 17 (1993), 1]
Re 11 (1987)–#
SFu 13 (1989)–#
SOu 1 (1977), 2–# [w 2 (1978), 2]
TOd 5 (1981)–#
Uu 2 (1978); 4 (1980)–#*
Yu 3 (1979)–#

Computer Musician *see* **Electronics and Music Maker**

Computers and the Humanities
0010–4817
US/NL–New York: Pergamon; Dordrecht, Netherlands: Kluwer Academic Publishers, 1966–
[NOT IN BUCOMP1]

Lkc 1 (1966)–15 (1981)

Computers in Teaching Initiative *see* **CTI Music News**

Computing in Music Research
US–Wisconsin Center for Music Technology, University of Wisconsin School of Music, 198?–
[NOT IN BUCOMP1]

SOu 2 (1990)–#

Computing in Musicology: an International Directory of Applications *see* **Directory of Computer-Assisted Research in Musicology**

Con Brio [1]
TNG AUS29
AUS–Sydney: New South Wales Conservatorium of Music, 1973
[Only one issue published]

Lu 1, 1973

Con Brio [2]
0140–8771
GB–London: Philharmonia Orchestra/Philharmonia Club, 1976–
[From 1982 entitled the *Philharmonia Club Magazine*]

Cu 7–10, 1978–81
EIR:Dtc 7–10, 1978–1981; 1982
En 7–10, 1978–1981
Lbl*

Con Brio: a Scots Music Magazine for the Modern Music Lover
TNG GB385
GB–Glasgow, 1946–51
[The 1949 issue was entitled *Scottish Music and Drama*; that of 1950, *Music and Drama 1950*. Published annually during the Edinburgh International Festival]

En 1946–51
Er 1949–51
Gm 1949–50*
Lbl*
Ob 1946, 1–3

Concert Artistes' Journal: with which is incorporated The Concert Artistes' Benevolent Association Gazette
Fellinger 1968/1816; TNG GB218
GB–London, 1906–08

Lbl*

Concert Club News
GB–Aberdeen, 198?–
[NOT IN BUCOMP1]

En 1989, 1–4; 1991, Oct–#

The Concert Companion *see* **The Theatrical and Concert Companion**

The Concert Companion and Musical Journal *see* **The Theatrical and Concert Companion**

The Concert Companion, and Record of Music and the Drama *see* **The Theatrical and Concert Companion**

Concert and Theatrical Companion and Record of Music and the Drama *see* **The Theatrical and Concert Companion**

The Concert Goer's Annual
TNG GB471
GB/US–London: John Calder; New York: Doubleday, 1957–58

Ap 1 (1957)
Bp 1 (1957)–2 (1958)
Cu 1 (1957)–2 (1958)
Ep 1 (1957)–2 (1958)
Lbl*
Lu 1 (1957)–2 (1958)
LVp 1 (1957)
Ob*

Concert Magazine
0263-3841
GB–London: Ernest Read Music Association,
1981–
[NOT IN BUCOMP1]

  Cu 1 (1981)–2 (1982), 3; 8 (1988)–#
  Lbl 1 (1981), 5–#
  Ob 1 (1981)–2 (1982), 3; 13 (1993)–#

**The Concert World: the Official Organ of the
Concert Artistes' Benevolent Association**
TNG GB282
GB–London: Concert Artistes' Benevolent
Association, 1920–23
[Succeeded by *C.A.A. Magazine* (q.v.)]

  Lbl 1 (1920)–4 (1923)
  Ob*

Concertina Magazine
AUS–Bell, NSW: Concertina Magazine, 1982–
[NOT IN BUCOMP1]

  Lcs 1–15, 1982–86

**The Concertina Newsletter: the Specialist
Magazine for Concertina and Free-Reed
Enthusiasts** *see* **The Concertina Newsletter
for Players and Collectors of the Concertina
and Related Metal Reed Instruments**

**The Concertina Newsletter for Players and
Collectors of the Concertina and Related
Metal Reed Instruments**
TNG GB559; 0308- 2148
GB–Nottingham, 1971–77
[From 11, 1973 entitled *The Concertina
Newsletter: the Specialist Magazine for
Concertina and Free-Reed Enthusiasts*; from 12,
1973 entitled *Free Reed: the Concertina
Newsletter*]

  EIR:Dtc 22–24, 1975–76
  Lcs 1–24, 1971–76 [w 3, 6, 8]
  Ob*

Concerto: das Magazin für alte Musik
D–Cologne: Gitarre und Laute, 1983–
[NOT IN BUCOMP1]

  Bu 1 (1983/84)–4 (1987)
  Lcm 1 (1983/84)*

Concert-Programm-Austausch
Fellinger 1968/1206; TNG D320
D–Leipzig: Breitkopf und Härtel, 1893–1923
[NOT IN BUCOMP1. Also known as *Konzert-
Programm-Austausch*]

  Lbl 16 (1901)–21 (1906)*

**Concordia: a [Weekly] Journal of Music and
the Sister Arts**
Fellinger 1968/699; TNG GB82
GB–London: Novello, Ewer and Co., 1875–76
[Ceased publication with vol. 2 no. 52 (1876)]

  Bu 1 (1875)– 2 (1876)
  En 1 (1875)–2 (1876)
  Lbl 1 (1875)–2 (1876), 52
  Lcm 1 (1875)–2 (1876), 52
  Mpl 1 (1875)–2 (1876)
  Ob*

**The Conductor: the Quarterly Journal of the
National Association of Brass Band Conductors**
TNG GB462; 0010-5430
GB–London: National Association of Brass
Band Conductors, 1955–70
[NOT IN BUCOMP1; continued as *Sounding
Brass and the Conductor* (q.v.)]

  Lam 5 (1961), 11
  SFu 5 (1961), 11

Connaissance de l'Orgue *see* **Renaissance de
l'Orgue**

**The Connoisseur: a Journal of Music and the
Fine Arts**
Fellinger 1968/230; TNG GB36; Langley, pp.
632–5
GB–London: E. Mackenzie, 1845–46
[Later subtitled *A Monthly Record of the Fine
Arts, Music and the Drama*; ceased publication
with vol. 2, no. 17 (1846)]

  Cu 1 (1845)–2 (1846)
  EIR:Dtc 1 (1845)–2 (1846)
  Lbl*
  Ob*

**The Connoisseur: a Monthly Record of the
Fine Arts, Music and the Drama** *see* **The
Connoisseur: a Journal of Music and the Fine
Arts**

Consensus and Review [of the Latest Issues of Recorded and Classical Music]
GB–London: Henry Stave, 1960–?73
[Entitled *New Consensus and Review* from issue 1971, 9]

Cu 6 (1965)–14 (1973), 9
EIR:Dtc 3 (1962)–14 (1973), 9
Lcml (m) 5 (1964)–11 (1970)
Lsa 1 (1960)–14 (1973)*
Ob*

Le Conservatoire *see* Bulletin du Conservatoire National de Musique

Conservatorio
TNG CU7
CU–Havana: Conservatorio Municipal, 1943–

Lcml 8 (1950), 2–4

Conservatorio Gioacchino Rossini: Annuario
see Annuario del Conservatorio Gioacchino Rossini Pesaro

The Conservatory *see* The Conservatory Bi-Monthly: a Musical Magazine

The Conservatory Bi-Monthly: a Musical Magazine
Fellinger 1968/1618; TNG C10
C–Toronto, 1902–13
[Entitled *The Conservatory* from 1912]

Lbl 1 (1902), 3

Console: Quarterly Bulletin of the Edinburgh Society of Organists
GB–Edinburgh: Edinburgh Society of Organists, ?–
[NOT IN BUCOMP1]

Ep 1967–#

The Consort [1]
TNG GB334; 0268–9111
GB–Godalming: Dolmetsch Foundation, 1929–
[Subtitled *European Journal of Early Music* from 1994]

AB 1 (1929)–40 (1984)
Au 5 (1948)–6 (1949); 20 (1963)–#
BDp 25 (1969)–38 (1982) BG 18 (1961)–35 (1979); 37 (1981)–49 (1993)
BLu 17 (1960)–#
Bp 5 (1948)–#
BRp 24 (1967)–47 (1991)

BSdsc*
Bu 3 (1934)–11 (1954)
Cpl 5 (1948)–16 (1959); 19 (1962); 21 (1964)–37 (1981)
Cu 1 (1929)–#; 2nd copy 22 (1965)–#
EIR:Dtc 1 (1929)–42 (1986)
EIR:Duc 21 (1964)–40 (1984)
En 1 (1929)–42 (1986)
Er 5 (1948)–43 (1987)
Gm 3 (1934)–44 (1988)
Gul 3 (1934)–#
HUu 22 (1965)–48 (1992)
Lam 5 (1948)–6 (1949); 8 (1951); 22 (1965)–24 (1967); 26 (1971)–48 (1992)
LAu 21 (1964); 23 (1966)–24 (1967)
Lbl*
Lbbc 5 (1948)–43 (1987) [w 9 (1952), 11 (1954), 14 (1957, 18 (1961)–19 (1962), 27 (1971), 29 (1973)]
Lcm 22 (1965)–47 (1991); 50 (1994)–#
Lcml 3 (1934)–#
Lcs 1 (1929)–22 (1965) [w 6 (1949); 8 (1951)]
Lgsm 21 (1964)–#
LIp 20 (1963)–45 (1989)
Lkc 1 (1929)–31 (1975); 33 (1977)–37 (1981)
LRHBNC 5 (1948)–6 (1949); 8 (1951)–16 (1959); 19 (1962); 27 (1971)–#
Lsa 18 (1961)–22 (1965)
Lu 1 (1929)–#
LVp 19 (1962)–#
LVu 1 (1929)–3 (1934); 23 (1966)–#
Mcm 18 (1961)–20 (1963); 29 (1973)–#
Mpl 3 (1934)–#*
Mu 20 (1963); 22 (1965)–41 (1985)
NO 3 (1934)–4 (1937); 6 (1949); 13 (1956)–14 (1957); 16 (1959); 19 (1962)–29 (1973); 31 (1975)–41 (1985)
Ob*
Ouf 5 (1958)–46 (1990); 50 (1994), 2 [w 18 (1961); 22 (1965); 25 (1969)]
SA 2 (1934); 24 (1967)–37 (1981)
SFu 25 (1969)–47 (1991)
SOu 6 (1949)–12 (1955); 15 (1958)–31 (1975); 33 (1977)
TOd 29 (1973); 46 (1990)
Uu 40 (1984)–#

The Consort [2]
GB–London, 1969–
[NOT IN BUCOMP1; the periodical was issued for sale to London Promenade concertgoers to raise funds for the Malcolm Sargent Cancer Fund for Children]

AB 1 (1969), 1–5
Cu 1 (1969)–2 (1970)
En 1 (1969)–2 (1970)
Lam 4 (1973), 4
Ob 1 (1969), 1–5; 2 (1970), 1–4

The Consort: European Journal of Early
Music *see* The Consort [1]

Contact: Contemporary Music Magazine *see*
Contact: Today's Music

Contact: Today's Music
TNG GB553; 0308–5066
GB–York; London: Contact Magazine, 1971–89
[From 1972 subtitled *Contemporary Music
Magazine*; ceased publication with no. 34, 1989]

BAc 25–34, 1982–89
BG 11–34, 1975–89
BRp 32–34, 1988–89
Bs 1, 1971; 9, 1974; 11–31, 1975–87; 33, 34,
1988–89
BSdsc*
BTu 12–34, 1975–89
Bu 1–34, 1971–89
CCtc 2–34, 1971–89
CDu 20–34, 1979–89
Cpl 11–34, 1975–89
Cu 1–34, 1971–89
EIR:Dtc 7–34, 1973–89 [w 24, 1981]
EIR:Duc 18–34, 1977–89
EIR:MEtc 19–34, 1978–89
En 1–34, 1971–89*
Er 1–34, 1971–89
EXu 10–34, 1974–89
Gam 7–34, 1973–89
Gm 4–34, 1972–89
Gul 11–34, 1975–89
HUu 19–34, 1978–89
KE 11–34, 1975–89 [w 27, 1983]
Lam 1–34, 1971–89
LAu 14–34, 1976–89 [w 15]
Lbbc 5, 8, 10–34, 1972–89
Lbl 8–34, 1974–89
LCdM 11–34, 1975–89
Lcm 11–34, 1975–89 [w 20]
Lcml 3–34, 1971–89
Lgo 1–34, 1971–89
Lgsm 18–33, 1977–88
Lki 16–30, 1977–87
Lmi 12–34, 1975–89
LRHBNC 5–9, 1972–74; 12–34, 1975–89
Lro 20–34, 1979–89
Lsa 11–34, 1975–89

Ltc 12–20, 1975–79; 24–34, 1982–89
Lu 1–34, 1971–89
LVu 24–34, 1982–89
Mcm 14–34, 1976–89
Mmu 12–14, 1975–76
Mmu (a) 12–34, 1975–89
Mu 8, 1974; 10, 11, 1974–75; 13–34, 1976–
89
NO 14–34, 1976–89
NWu 12–34, 1975–89
Ob*
Ouf 11–34, 1975–89
R 21, 1980; 22, 1981; 26–34, 1983–89
TOd 11–34, 1975–89
Uu 13–34, 1976–89*
Yu 1–34, 1971–89

Contemporary Arts in Pakistan
PA–Karachi: Pakistan Publications, 1960–64

Gam 1 (1960), 3–7; 3 (1962), 3; 4 (1963)–5
(1964), 2
Lbl*
Ob*

Contemporary Jazz
GB–London, 1965–

Cbijs 2, 1965

Contemporary Keyboard
TNG US853; 0361–5820
US–Saratoga, CA [etc.]: Keyboard Players
International, 1975–
[NOT IN BUCOMP1; from vol. 7 no. 7 (July
1981) entitled *Keyboard: Keyboard Magazine*
(ISSN 0730–0158)]

KE 11 (1985), 6–12 (1986) [w 12 (1986), 1]
Lam 19 (1993), 4, 6–#
Lgo 7 (1981), 7–#
Msuc [c (5 years)]

Contemporary Music [translated title] *see*
Muzyka Współczesna

Contemporary Music [translated title] *see also*
Muzykal'niy Sovremennik; and
Sovremennaya Muzyka

Contemporary Music Almanac
0196–6200
US/GB–New York: Schirmer; London: Collier
Macmillan, 1980–

Lbl*
Ob*

Contemporary Music Network Education
Bulletin *see* C.M.N. Education Bulletin

Contemporary Music News
1354–3954
GB–London: Peters, 1994–
[NOT IN BUCOMP1]

    Cu 1, 1994–#
    Lbl*

Contemporary Music Newsletter *see*
Newsletter of the Group for Contemporary
Music at Columbia University

Contemporary Music Review
0749–4467
CH/GB–Chur; London [etc.]: Harwood, 1984–
[NOT IN BUCOMP1]

    BTu 1 (1984)–#
    Bu 1 (1984)–#
    CDu 1 (1984)–#
    Cu 1 (1984)–#
    DRu 1 (1984)–#
    EIR:Dtc 1 (1984)–#
    En 1 (1984)–#
    Er 1 (1984)–#
    EXu 6 (1991)–#
    Gul 1 (1984)–#
    KE 1 (1984)–#
    LAu 6 (1991)–#
    Lbbc 1 (1984)–#
    Lbl*
    Lcm 6 (1991)–8 (1993), 2; 12 (1994)–#
    Lcml 1 (1984)–#
    Lcu 7 (1992)–#
    Lgo 1 (1984)–#
    Lmi 2 (1987)–#
    Lsa 2 (1987); 6 (1991)–#
    Ltc 14 (1996), 3–#
    Lu 5 (1989)–#
    LVu 1 (1984)–#
    MK 1 (1984)–#
    Mmu (a) 12 (1995)–#
    Mpl 1 (1984)–#
    Msuc 12 (1995)–13 (1996)
    Mu 1 (1984)–#
    NO 3 (1989)–#
    NOTu 8 (1993)–#
    Ob*
    Ouf 1 (1984)–#*
    R 1 (1984)–2 (1987); 5 (1989)–7 (1992), 1
    SOu 3 (1989)–#
    TOd 1 (1984)–#
    Yu 1 (1984)–#

Continuo: the Magazine of Old Music
0706–6656
C–Toronto, Ont., 1977–
[NOT IN BUCOMP1]

    Lu 2 (1978), 10, 11; 3 (1979), 1, 2; 6 (1983),
    8

Contrechamps: Revue Semestrielle
CH–Lausanne: L'Age d'Homme, 1983–
[NOT IN BUCOMP1]

    Bu 2–12/13, 1984–90

Contrepoints: une Revue de Musique
TNG F598
F–Paris: Editions de Minuit, 1946; 1949–52
[Nos 1–5 subtitled *Une Revue de Musique
paraissant chaque mois*; no. 6 subtitled *Revue
Musicale Trimestrielle*; no. 7 subtitled *Une
Revue de Musique paraissant chaque trimestre*]

    Cu 1–8, 1946–52
    Lbl*
    Lcm 6, 1949
    Lcml 1–8, 1946–52
    Mcm 7, 1951
    Ob*
    Ouf 1–8, 1946–52

Contributions to the History of Czech Music
[translated title] *see* **Príspěvky k Dejinám
Ceské Hudby**

Controversy: Prince Magazine
GB–London: Controversy, 1986–
[NOT IN BUCOMP1]

    Lbl*

Cornett and Sackbutt
TNG D1100
D–Essen, 1979–

    Mcm 1979, 1

Correspondance des Amateurs Musiciens
Fellinger 1968/6; TNG F6
F–Paris, 1802–5
[Entitled *Correspondance des Professeurs et
Amateurs de Musique* from 1804, Jan–1805,
Apr]

    Cu 1802–05
    Ob 1802–05 [Reprint ed.]

Correspondance des Professeurs et Amateurs de Musique *see* Correspondance des Amateurs Musiciens

Corvina: Rassegna Italo-Ungharese
H–Budapest: Società Corvino, 1921–55

 Lcml 6 (1949)

Council for Music in Hospitals: Newsletter
GB–?, 199?–
[NOT IN BUCOMP1]

 En 6, 1994–#

Council for Music in Hospitals: Report
GB–Horsham, 1995–
[NOT IN BUCOMP1]

 Cu 1995–#

Council for Research in Music Education: Bulletin *see* Bulletin of the Council for Research in Music Education

Counterpoint *see* M.A.I. Monthly Bulletin

Counterpointe
GB–Edinburgh, 1972–?

 Ob 1 (1972)

Counterpoints: Newsletter of the Friends of the British Music Information Centre
GB–London: British Music Information Centre, 1994–
[NOT IN BUCOMP1]

 ALb 1, 1994–#
 Gsmic [c]

Country Dance and Song
0070–1262
US–New York: Country Dance and Song Society of America, 1968–
[NOT IN BUCOMP1; succeeded *Country Dancer* (q.v.)]

 Lcs 1 (1968)–#

Country Dance and Song Society News
1070–8251
US–New York: Country Dance and Song Society, 197?–
[NOT IN BUCOMP1]

 Lcs 26, 1979; 32, 33, 1980; 55, 1983; 57, 1984–# [w 114]

Country Dance and Song Society *see also* C.D.S.S. Directory

Country Dancer
0574–3265
US–New York: Country Dance Society of America, 1948–68
[NOT IN BUCOMP1; in 1968 became *Country Dance and Song* (q.v.)]

 Lcs 1948–59, Spr; 1960, Spr; 1960/61, Win; 1961, Sum–1966

Country Dancer in Wartime
US–New York: Country Dance Society of America, 1943–46 ·
[NOT IN BUCOMP1]

 Lcs 1–9, 1943–46 [w 2, 5, 6]

Country Music
0090–4007
US–New York: KBO Publishers, 1972–
[NOT IN BUCOMP1]

 NHp [c (12 months)]
 SOL 23 (1994), 8–12; 24 (1995)–#

Country Music Foundation Newsletter *see* Journal of Country Music

Country Music People
TNG GB548; 0591–2237
GB–Sidcup: Country Music Press, 1970–

 BLp 1 (1970)–#
 CDCp 24 (1993)–#
 Cu 6 (1975)–#
 EIR:Dp 25 (1994)–#
 EIR:Dtc 6 (1975)–18 (1987), 7
 En 6 (1975), 1–10; 7 (1976)–#
 Gm 9 (1978)–#
 Lbo 25 (1994)–#
 Lha (f) [c (2 years)]
 Lsa 20 (1989), 1–9; 21 (1990), 5–7; 22 (1991), 1
 NOp [c (2 years)]
 Ob*
 SFp [c]

Country Music Review
TNG GB554
GB–London, 1972–77

Cu 1 (1972)–6 (1977), 10
EIR:Dtc 1 (1972)–6 (1977), 10
En 1 (1972), 1, 10–12; 2 (1973)–6 (1977)
Lsa 3 (1974), 2–6, 8; 4 (1975), 1–6, 8–11; 5
(1976), 5
Ob*

Country Music Round Up
0140–5721
GB–North Hykeham: AMD Magazine
Distributors, 1977–

COp [c (4 months)]
En 1 (1977), 2–12; 2 (1978)–13 (1989), 9, 11,
12; 14 (1990)–#
Lbl*
Ob*

Country Music Source Book
0889–4949
US–New York: Billboard, 1983–
[NOT IN BUCOMP1. Also known as *Billboard
Country Music Sourcebook* (ISSN 0273–1428);
and *CMS*]

BSdsc*

Country News and Views
GB–Great Yarmouth, 1962–

Cu 5 (1967), 3–6 (1968), 4
Lbl*
Ob*

Country People
GB–London: IPC Magazines, 1979–
[NOT IN BUCOMP1]

Lbl*

County Music News
GB–?Chester, ?–
[NOT IN BUCOMP1]

CHEp [c (1 year)]

The Courier
GB–Manchester: Manchester Opera House,
1932–34

AB 1–6, 1932–34
Cu 1–6, 1932–34
EIR:Dtc 1–6, 1932–34
Lbl*

Le Courrier du Disque Microsillon
F–Paris, 1950–60

Lsa 44, 45, 66–73, 76, 77, 80–97, 1958–60

**Le Courrier Musical, Artistique et Littéraire
du Littoral**
Fellinger 1968/1430; TNG F289
F–Menton, 1898–99; Paris, 1899–1914; 1916–
35
[From 1899 entitled *Le Courrier Musical,
Hebdomadaire, Artistique et Littéraire*; from
1914, *La Revue Musicale S.I.M. [et Courrier
Musical Réunis]*; from 1922, *Le Courrier
Musical et Théâtral*; from 1933, *Le Courrier
Musical, Théâtral, Cinématographique*]

Mpl 25 (1923)–27 (1925); 29 (1927)–34
(1932)

Le Courrier Musical de France
TNG F685; 0011–0620
F–Paris: L'Association pour la Diffusion de la
Pensée Française, 1963–80

Bs 1974; 1976–77
BSdsc*
EIR:Driam 1967–76*
Er 41–72, 1973–80
Lam 31, 1970; 38, 1972; 44, 1973; 53, 56,
1976; 58, 59, 1977; 67, 1979
Lcm 7–10, 1964/65; 12–36, 1965–71; 45–47,
1974; 51, 52, 1975; 55, 1976; 61, 63, 64,
1978; 68, 1979; 70, 1980
Mcm 51, 1975; 1976–80

Le Courrier Musical et Théâtral *see* Le
Courrier Musical, Artistique et Littéraire du
Littoral

**Le Courrier Musical, Hebdomadaire,
Artistique et Littéraire** *see* Le Courrier
Musical, Artistique et Littéraire du Littoral

**Le Courrier Musical, Théâtral,
Cinématographique** *see* Le Courrier Musical,
Artistique et Littéraire du Littoral

The Covent Garden Journal [1]
Fellinger 1968/429; TNG GB56
GB–London, 1861
[From 1861, July 6, entitled *The Westminster
and Covent Garden Journal*]

Lbl*

The Covent Garden Journal [2]
GB–Newhaven, 1915

    EIR:Dtc 1915
    Lbl*

The Covent Garden Theatrical Gazette
Fellinger 1968/35; TNG GB5
GB–London, 1816–17
[140 nos in total]

    Lbl 1–140, 1816–17

Cowethas Ylow Kernewek Newsletter
GB–?: The Cornish Music Guild, ?–
[NOT IN BUCOMP1]

    Cu 6, 1991–#
    Gsmic [c]

Cramer's Music Library Bulletin
GB– London: Cramer Music, ?–
[NOT IN BUCOMP1]

    EIR:Dtc 81, 1976; 89, 1978
    HE 111, 1985–#

Crawdaddy
US–Encinitas, CA, 1967–
[NOT IN BUCOMP1]

    Cu 14, 1996–#

Crazy Rhythm: the Newsletter of the Crazy
Cavan 'n' The Rhythm Rockers Fan Club
GB–London: The Crazy Cavan 'n' Rhythm
Rockers Fan Club, 1977–
[NOT IN BUCOMP1]

    Lbl 1977–#*

CRC Jazz Journal *see* CRC Newsletter

CRC Newsletter
US–Decatur, GA: Collector's Record Club,
1975–87
[NOT IN BUCOMP1; continued from 1987 as
CRC Jazz Journal; formerly *Jazzology*]

    LOnjfa*

The Creel: Journal of the Alan Rawsthorne
Society and the Rawsthorne Trust
0963–0244
GB–Rotherham: Alan Rawsthorne Society,
1989–
[NOT IN BUCOMP1]

    ALb 1 (1989)–#

    Cu 1 (1989), 5–#
    Lbl 1 (1989), 4–#
    Ltc 1996–#
    Mcm 1 (1989)–#
    Ob 1 (1989), 5–#

The Cremona: with which is incorporated
"The Violinist", a Record of the String World
Fellinger 1968/1817; TNG GB222
GB–London: Sanctuary Press, 1906–11
[Ceased publication with vol. 5, no. 61 (1911)]

    Lbl*
    Ob*

Crescendo [1]
US–Abilene, TX: Hardin–Simmons University,
195?–
[NOT IN BUCOMP1]

    Lam 4 (1954/56), 2

Crescendo [2]
0962–7472
GB–London: Crescendo Publishing, 1962–
[Entitled *Crescendo International* (ISSN 0011–
118X) from 1967, May–1990, Dec; *Crescendo
and Jazz Music* from vol. 28 (1991)]

    AB 1 (1962)–#
    BSdsc*
    Cbijs 1 (1962)–8 (1969); 9 (1970) [w Sep]; 10
       (1971), Feb–June, Oct; 11 (1972), Jan, Sep–
       Dec; 12 (1973), July–Dec; 13 (1974/75),
       Feb–#
    CCtc 20 (1981)–#
    Cu 1 (1962)–#
    EIR:Dtc 1 (1962)–#
    En 1 (1962)–#
    Er 14 (1975/76)–30 (1993)
    EXu 1 (1962)–22 (1985); 24 (1987); 28 (1991)
    Lam 24 (1987), 1, 4–#
    Lbl 1 (1962)–#
    Lcm 1 (1962)–#*
    Lcml 22 (1985), 3, 5, 6
    LEc 13 (1974)–#
    Lgo 6 (1967)–7 (1968)*; 11 (1972)–13
       (1974/75)*; 14 (1975/76)–27 (1990)
    Lgsm 24 (1987)–#
    Lki 16 (1979)–25 (1988)
    Lmi 19 (1982)–#
    LOnjfa*
    Lsa 2 (1963)–26 (1989), Feb*; 31 (1994), 4–#
    LVp 28 (1991)–#
    Mcm 12 (1973), 9–12; 13 (1974/75), 11
    Msuc 33 (1996)–#
    Ob*

Crescendo [3]
GB–Scottish Chamber Orchestra, 1978–
[NOT IN BUCOMP1]

   Cu 1–4, 1978–79
   Ob*

Crescendo[4]
0111–8994
NZ–Auckland: International Association of
Music Libraries, Archives and Documentation
Centres (New Zealand), 1982–
[NOT IN BUCOMP1]

   BSdsc 28, 1991–#
   Lcm 1, 1982–# [w 32, 38]

Crescendo: a Magazine Devoted to Young
Concert-Goers
GB–London: Robert Mayer Concerts, 1946–

   Lbl*
   Lcml 23–117, 1949–61*

Crescendo and Jazz Music *see* Crescendo [2]

Crescendo International *see* Crescendo [2]

Crest Musical Bulletin
US–New York, 1907–10
[From 1908 entitled *Entertaining*]

   Lbl*

The Critic
GB–London, 1968–?

   Gam 1 (1968), 1, 2, 4, 6–12
   Lam 1 (1968), 1, 3, 4
   Lbl*
   Lcm (p) 1 (1968), 1–12

The Critic: a Fortnightly Review of
Literature, the Fine Arts, Music and the
Drama
US–New York, 1881–83
[NOT IN BUCOMP1]

   Lbl*

Critic: Review of the Arts
GB–Oxford: Oxford University, ?1988–
[NOT IN BUCOMP1]

   Cu 3, 4, 1989
   EIR:Dtc 3, 4, 1989

Critica Dramatica y Musical: Anales del
Teatro y de la Musica
Fellinger 1968/949; TNG E33
E–Madrid, 1884
[Only one vol. published]

   Lbl 1884

Critica Musica, d.i. Grundrichtige Untersuch-
und Beurtheilung vieler theils vorgefassten,
theils einfältigen Meinungen, Argumenten
und Einwürfe, so in alten und neuen,
gedruckten und ungedruckten musicalischen
Schrifften zu finden …
TNG D1
D–Hamburg, 1722–25

   Lbl*
   Ob 1722–25 [Reprint ed.]

La Critica Musicale
TNG I167
I–Florence, 1918–23

   Lcml 5 (1922), 12

Critical Musicology Newsletter
GB–Oxford: Oxford Brookes University, 1993–
[NOT IN BUCOMP1. Issues post-1994
produced in electronic form only, at URL http://
www.leeds.ac.uk/music/Info/CMJ/cmj.html]

   Bu 1993–#
   Ouf 1994–#

Critique: a Monthly Review of Gramophone
Records
TNG GB418
GB–London, 1949–55

   Lsa 1 (1949)–6 (1955)*
   Lu 3 (1952), 8–6 (1955), 11

Der critische Musicus an der Spree
TNG D8
D–Leipzig, 1749–50
[NOT IN BUCOMP1]

   Cu 1749–50 [Reprint ed.]

Critischer Musicus
TNG D4
D–Leipzig: Johann Adolf Scheibe, 1737; 1740;
Neue Auflage 1745

   Cu 1737–40 [Reprint ed.]
   Lbl*
   Ob*
   Ouf [m]

Cronaca Wagneriana
Fellinger 1968/1207; TNG I79
I–Bologna, 1893–95

> **Lbl** 1 (1893), 1–4; 2 (1895), 1–6; 3 (1896), 7, 8

Cronicl y Cerddor [= The Musician's Chronicle]
GB–Treherbert, 1880–83

> **AB** 1880–83

The Crosby Collector
GB–London: R. S. Harding, 1966–

> **Cbijs** 6 (1972), 5
> **LOnjfa***

Cross Rhythms
0967–540X
GB–Plymouth: Cornerstone House, 1990–
[NOT IN BUCOMP1]

> **Lbl** 11, 1992–#

The Croydon Folksong Club Newsletter
GB–Croydon: Croydon Folksong Club, 1981;
n.s. 1986–?91
[NOT IN BUCOMP1; previously entitled
Chimes]

> **Lbl***
> **Lcs** 1 (1981); n.s. 1–27, 1986–91 [w 13]

Crystal Palace Matters: Magazine of the Crystal Palace Foundation
GB–Crystal Palace Foundation, 198?–
[NOT IN BUCOMP1]

> **Lam** 14–17, 1983–84

CTI Music News
1350–6935
GB–Lancaster: CTI [Computers in Teaching Initiative] Music, 1993–
[NOT IN BUCOMP1]

> **BRu** 1 (1993)–#
> **Cu** 1 (1993)–#
> **EIR:Dtc** 1 (1993)–#
> **Gul** 1 (1993)–#
> **LAu** 1 (1993)–#
> **Lbl***
> **NWu** 1 (1993)–#
> **Ob***
> **Ouf** [c]

CTMS Journal *see* California Traditional Music Society Journal

Cuadernos de Musica Iberoamericana
E–Madrid, 1996–
[NOT IN BUCOMP1]

> **Cu** 1 (1996)–#

Cue
0144–6088
GB–Faringdon: Twynam, 1979–
[NOT IN BUCOMP1; later entitled *Cue International*]

> **Lgsm** 1987–90*

Cue International *see* Cue

La Cultura Musicale
TNG I175
I–Bologna, 1922–23
[Ceased publication with vol. 2 no. 3 (1923)]

> **Lcml** 1 (1922), 1–3, 5, 6

Cultural Trends
0954–8963
GB–London: Policy Studies Institute, 1989–
[NOT IN BUCOMP1]

> **Lcm** 7–16, 1990–92 [w 8]
> **Lgsm** 1, 1989–#
> **Mcm***
> **Ob***

Cum Notis Variorum
0161–1186
US–Berkeley, CA: Music Library, University of California at Berkeley, 1976–89
[NOT IN BUCOMP1; ceased publication with no. 136, 1989]

> **Au** 126–36, 1988–89
> **Cpl** 78–136, 1983–89
> **Cu** 124–136, 1988–89
> **Lu** 101, 105, 110–15, 119–34, 136, 1986–89
> **Ouf** 105–136, 1986–89

Cumann Naisiunta Na gCor/Association of Irish Choirs: Annual Report
EIRE–Association of Irish Choirs, ?–
[NOT IN BUCOMP1]

> **EIR:MEtc** 1989–#

Curfew: Oxford's Music Magazine
GB–Oxford: Curfew Newspaper, 1991–
[NOT IN BUCOMP1]

Ob 31, 1993–#

Current Contents in Folklore
0955–7725
GB–London: Folklore Society, 1989–91
[NOT IN BUCOMP1; ceased publication with
no. 5, 1991; succeeded by *Current Folklore*
(ISSN 0966–1603), 1992–#]

Lcs 1–4, 1989–90

Current Folklore *see* **Current Contents in
Folklore**

Current Musicology
TNG US747; 0011–3735
US–New York: Columbia University, 1965–

AB 1–18, 1965–74
Au 28–44, 1979–90
BG 3, 1966–#
CDu 11, 1971–#
Cpl 1–30, 1965–80
Cu 1, 1965–#
EIR:Duc 5, 1967–#
Er 1, 1965–#
EXu 7, 1969–#
Gul 29, 1980–#
HUu 7, 1969–#
Lbbc 1, 1965–#
Lbl*
Lcm 1, 1965; 3, 4, 1966
Lcml 1–3, 1965–66; 6, 1968–#
Lcu 1–10, 1965–70; 15, 1973–#
Lgo 21, 1976–#
Lkc 1, 1965–#
Lki 21–40, 1976–85
LRHBNC 1, 2 1965–66; 6–8, 1968–69;
  10, 1970–#
Lu 1, 1965–#
LVu 33, 1982–#
Mcm 1, 1965–#
Mu 7, 1968; 9–25, 1969–78; 27, 1979–#
NO 3–38, 1966–84
NWu 1, 1965–#
Ob*
Ouf 1, 1965–#
R 1, 1965–#
SFu 1, 1965–#
SOu 6, 1968–# [w 9, 26, 42, 53]
Uu 33–42, 1982–86 [w 35, 36, 1984]
Yu 19, 1975–#

Current Studies in Baroque Music
0269–6940
GB–London: Graham Dixon and Judith
Roles/The Royal Musical Association, 1986–
[NOT IN BUCOMP1]

Cu 1 (1986)–2 (1990)
EIR:Dtc 1 (1986)–2 (1990)
En 1 (1986)–#
Lbl*
Lu 1 (1986)
Ouf 1 (1986)–#

Curwen Bulletin
GB–London, 19?–
[NOT IN BUCOMP1]

Cu 1934, Apr–1942, May

Cut
GB–Edinburgh: Independent Design and
Editorial Associates, 1986–
[NOT IN BUCOMP1]

Gm 1 (1986), Oct–4 (1989), Sep
Ob 2 (1987), 2– #*

Cybernoise
0966–7636
GB–Penarth: Essential, 1992–
[NOT IN BUCOMP1]

Lbl*

Cyfaill yr Aelwyd [= Friend of the Hearth]
GB–Llanelli, 1880–94
[See also *Cerddor y Cymry*]

AB 1880–94, 3
Lbl*
Ob*

**Cylchgrawn Cymdeithas Alawon Gwerin
Cymru [= Journal of the Welsh Folk-Song
Society]**
Fellinger 1968/1962; TNG GB235; 0967–0599
[latest series]
GB–Bangor: Welsh Folk–Song Society, 1909–
77; 1978–
[Previously entitled *Cymdeithas Caneuon
Gwerin Cymru*; from 1978 entitled *Canu
gwerin*]

AB 1 (1909)–5 (1977); n.s. 1, 1978–#
ABc 1 (1909)–4 (1948/54); n.s. 1–10, 1978–
  87
BG n.s. 1, 1978–# [w 4]
Bp 1 (1909)–5 (1955/77), 3

Cpl 1 (1909)–2 (1925)
Cu 1 (1909)–5 (1955/77); n.s. 1, 1978–#
EIR:Dtc 1 (1909); 2 (1925), 4; 3 (1930/41)–4
(1948/54)
EIR:Duc 1 (1909)–3 (1930/41)
Lbl*
Lcml 4 (1948/54), 3; 5 (1955/77), 1
Lcs 1 (1909); 4 (1948/54), 2; 5 (1955/77), 2,
3; n.s. 1–3, 1978– 80; 5, 1982–#
LVp*
MO*
Mpl 1 (1909)*
Ob*
Ouf (Howes) 4 (1948/54), 1, 4

**Cylchlythyr Cyfeillion Cerddorion Ifanc
Ceredigion** see The Friends of the Ceredigion
Young Musicians: Newsletter

Cymdeithas Caneuon Gwerin Cymru see
Cylchgrawn Cymdeithas Alawon Gwerin
Cymru

**Cymdeithas Ddawns Werin Cymru:
Cylchlythyr [= Welsh Folk Dance Society
Newsletter]**
GB–Welsh Folk Dance Society, 1953–
[NOT IN BUCOMP1]

AB 1 (1953)–7 (1960); 1985, Christmas;
1986, Easter
EIR:Dtc 1986, Aug
Ob 1986, Aug–#

Cywair [= Key]
GB–Wrexham, 1976–79

AB 1976–79

Czech Miscellany of Musicological Works
[translated title] see Miscellanea Musicologica:
Cesky Sborník Hudebně Vědeckých Praci

Czech Music 95 [96, etc.]
CZ–Prague: Český Hudební Fund of the Czech
Music Information Centre, 1995–
[Succeeded Music News from Prague (q.v.)]

BLp [c]
BRu [c (1 year)]
BSdsc*
Bu*
Cpl*
En*
Gsmic [c]
Lbbc*
Lbl*

Lcml*
Lki*
Mcm*
NO*
Ob*

**Czech Music: the Journal of the Dvořák
Society [of Great Britain]** see Czech Music:
the Newsletter of the Dvořák Society [of
Great Britain]

**Czech Music: the Journal of the Dvořák
Society for Czech and Slovak Music** see
Czech Music: the Newsletter of the Dvořák
Society [of Great Britain]

**Czech Music: the Journal of the Dvořák
Society for Czech Music** see Czech Music: the
Newsletter of the Dvořák Society [of Great
Britain]

**Czech Music: the Journal of the Dvořák
Society for the Music of Czechoslovakia** see
Czech Music: the Newsletter of the Dvořák
Society [of Great Britain]

**Czech Music: the Newsletter of the Dvořák
Society [of Great Britain]**
0261–2801
GB–London: Dvořák Society, 1974–
[Vol. 1 (1974), 2–5 entitled The Journal of the
Dvořák Society of Great Britain: Newsletter;
vols 2 (1975)–4 (1978), 1 entitled Zprava:
Journal of the Dvořák Society of Great Britain.
From 4 (1978), 2–5 (1979), 1 entitled Czech
Music: the Journal of the Dvořák Society of
Great Britain; from 5 (1979), 2–10 (?1984)
entitled Czech Music: the Journal of the Dvořák
Society; from 11 (1985)–15 (1989), 1 entitled
Czech Music: the Journal of the Dvořák Society
for Czech Music; from 15 (1989), 2–17 (1992), 2
entitled Czech Music: the Journal of the Dvořák
Society for the Music of Czechoslovakia; from 18
(1993) entitled Czech Music: the Journal of the
Dvořák Society for Czech and Slovak Music]

Cu 4 (1978), 2–#
EIR:Dtc 1 (1974), 1–5; 2 (1975)–#
En*
Lbar 6 (1980), 2–7 (1981), 3; 8 (1982), 1, 3,
4; 9 (1983)–14 (1988); 15 (1989), 2; 16
(1990), 2; 17 (1991)–#
Lbl 6 (1980)–#
Lcm 15 (1989)–#
Mcm*
Ob*

Czechoslovak Music
TNG CS167
CZ–Prague, 1945–49

Lbl*

D

Da Capo: the Voice of Music Education at Reading University
GB–Reading: Reading University, 1993–
[NOT IN BUCOMP1]

Re 1 (1993)–#

The Dalcroze College Journal
GB–London, 1913

Lbl* [Special English number of 1913]

Dallas Musical Monthly and Advertiser
US–Dallas, TX, 1908–16

Lbl*
Ob*

Dance
GB–London: Imperial Society of Teachers of Dancing, 1986–
[NOT IN BUCOMP1]

Lcs 1, 1986; 3, 1987; 6, 1988

Dance [translated title] *see* **Dawns: the National Magazine of Welsh Traditional Dancing**

Dance and Dancers
0011–5983
GB–London: Hansom Books, 1950–

BRp 33 (1982), 385–#
BSdsc 26 (1975), 11–#
Bu 2 (1951)–34 (1983)
EIR:Dtc 2 (1951)–31 (1980), 5; 32 (1981), 382–41 (1990), 486; 44 (1993), 513–#
Ep 25 (1974)–#*
Lba 6 (1955)–31 (1980), June; 32 (1981)–#*
Lbl*
Lu*
Ob*

Dance and Dancers *see also* **Seven Arts**

The Dance Band and Jazz Musician
GB–London, 1961–

Cbijs 3 (1963), 6

Dance Chronicle
0147–2526
US–New York: Marcel Dekker, 1977–
[Preceded by *Dance Perspectives* (ISSN 0011–6033; New York, 1959–77)]

BSdsc 1 (1977)–#

Dance Current Awareness Bulletin
0265–6523
GB–Guildford: National Resource Centre for Dance, 1983–
[NOT IN BUCOMP1]

Bu 4, 1985; 31, 1993–#
EIR:Dtc 1, 1983–#
Lcs 1, 1983
Ob*
SOu 1, 1983– #

Dance Gazette: the Journal of the Royal Academy of Dancing
0306–0128
GB–London: Royal Academy of Dancing, 1930–
[NOT IN BUCOMP1]

Ep 218, 1995–#

Dance Index
US–New York: Arno Press, 1942–48

Lbl*

The Dance Journal: Official Organ of the Imperial Society of Dance Teachers
GB–London: Imperial Society of Dance Teachers, 1907–18; n.s. 1987–

Lbl*
Ob*

Dance Lovers' Magazine
US–New York, 1923–31
[Entitled *The Dance Magazine* from vol. 5, no. 2 (1925)]

Lbl*

Dance Magazine
0011–6009
US–New York: Dance Magazine, 1926–

Bu 22 (1948)–24 (1950)*
Lu 22 (1948), 3–53 (1979), 11*

The Dance Magazine *see also* **Dance Lovers' Magazine**

Dance Music Annual
GB–London: Dance Music Annual, 1951
[NOT IN BUCOMP1; only one vol. published]

Lbl 1951
Ob 1951

Dance News
0011–6017
US–New York: Dance News, 1942–83
[NOT IN BUCOMP1; ceased publication with
vol. 68 no. 6 (1983)]

Lu 26–62, 1955–77*

Dance News *see also* Danceland [2]

Dance News Ireland
0790–5203
EIRE–Dublin: Dance Council of Ireland, 1985–
[NOT IN BUCOMP1; also known as
Dancenews Ireland]

EIR:Dtc 1 (1985)–#

Dance Now
0966–6346
GB–London: Dance Books, 1992–
[NOT IN BUCOMP1]

Bu 2 (1993)–#

Dance Perspectives *see* Dance Chronicle

Dance Research: the Journal of the Society
for Dance Research
0264–2875
GB–London: Society for Dance Research;
Oxford: Oxford University Press, 1983–
[NOT IN BUCOMP1]

Bu 1 (1983)–#
EIR:Dtc 1 (1983)–#
Lcs 1 (1983)–5 (1987), 2 [w 3 (1985), 1]
Ob*
SOu 13 (1995)–#

The Dance Review
GB–Liverpool, 1925–?

Lbl*

The Dance Review: a News Magazine
GB–London, 1939–?

Lbl*

Dance Scope
0011–6041
US–New York: American Dance Guild, 1964–
81
[Ceased publication with vol. 15 no. 3 (1981)]

BSdsc 3 (1966)–15 (1981), 3

Dance Studies
GB–St Peter, Jersey: Centre for Dance Studies,
1976–
[NOT IN BUCOMP1]

Lbl 1 (1976)–#
Lcs 8 (1984); 10 (1986)
Ob 1 (1976)–#

Dance Theatre Journal
0264–9160
GB–London: Friends of the Laban Centre,
1983–
[NOT IN BUCOMP1]

EIR:Dtc 1 (1983)–#
Gam 9 (1991), 1, 3, 4; 10 (1992)–#

Dance Tone
GB–London, 1935–?

Lbl*

Dance World
0070–2692
US–New York: Crown Publishers, 1966–72

BSdsc*

Danceland [1]
GB–London, 1922

Lbl*

Danceland [2]
GB–London, 1937–?
[From 1941–42 entitled *Dance News*; from 1943
reverted to *Danceland*]

Lbl*

Dancenews Ireland *see* Dance News Ireland

The Dancer
GB–London, 1928–?

Lbl*

The Dancer and Cabaret
GB–London, 1931–?

Lbl*

Dancing
C–Toronto [etc.]: Press of Terpsichore, 1891–93

Bu 1 (1891)–2 (1893)
Lbl*

Dancing: an Annual and Year-Book for Dancers
GB–London, 1924–25

Lbl*

Dancing and the Ballroom see The Dancing Times

Dancing Forth: Bulletin of the Edinburgh Branch of the Royal Scottish Country Dance Society
GB–Edinburgh: Royal Scottish Country Dance Society (Edinburgh Branch), ?–
[NOT IN BUCOMP1]

Ep 1985–#

Dancing News
EIRE–Longford: Dancing News, 1976–
[NOT IN BUCOMP1]

EIR:Dtc 1 (1976)–2 (1978), 26

Dancing On
GB–Melton Mowbray: Open Morris, 198?–
[NOT IN BUCOMP1]

Lcs 10–13, 1984; 35, 1994–#

Dancing Record and London Amusements
GB–London, 1924–25

Lbl*

The Dancing Times
0011–605X
GB–London: Dancing Times, 1894–
[Numbering recommenced with a new series in 1910. Absorbed various titles, such as Ballet Annual and Year Book; Amateur Dancer; and Dancing and the Ballroom]

BSdsc*
EIR:Dtc 24 (1933/34), 273–#
Ep 27 (1936/37)–30 (1940/41); 34 (1943/44), 4–#*
Lba 30 (1940/41)–36 (1945/46); 38 (1947/48)–#*
Lbl*
Lcs 34 (1943/44)–58 (1968); 72 (1982)–73 (1983); 77 (1987)–#*

Lha (f) [c (3 years)]
Lu 14 (1923)–68 (1978)*
Ob*

The Dancing World see The Palais Dancing News

Danish Music Bibliography [translated title] see Dansk Musikfortegnelse

Dansk Aarbog for Musikforskning
[= Danish Yearbook for Musicology]
TNG DK88; 0416–6884
DK–Copenhagen: Dansk Selskab for Musikforskning, 1961–

Cpl 1961–#
Cu 1961–#
Lbl*
Lu 1972–#
Mpl 1977
Ob 1961–#

Dansk Musik Tidsskrift [= Danish Music Journal]
TNG DK41; 0011–6386
DK–Copenhagen: Gads Forlag, 1925–
[From 1930 entitled Dansk Musiktidsskrift; in 1959 merged with Nordisk Musikkultur (q.v.); also incorporated Levende Musik (TNG DK65); entitled dmt from 47 (1972/73)]

ALb 24 (1949), 8
Cu*
Lcml 23 (1948)–24 (1949)*; 25 (1950); 26 (1951)–29 (1954)*
Lu 36 (1961), 1; 39 (1964), 6–8; 40 (1965)– 42 (1967)
Ob*

Dansk Musikfortegnelse [= Danish Music Bibliography]
0105–8045
DK–Copenhagen: Dansk Bibliotekscenter, 1922–71; 1972–
[NOT IN BUCOMP1; entitled Dansk Musikhandler-Forenings Musikfortegnelse, 1922–71]

Cu 1981/83–#
Ob*

Dansk Musikhandler-Forenings Musikfortegnelse see Dansk Musikfortegnelse

Dansk Musiktidsskrift see Dansk Musik Tidsskrift

Dantzariat
E–Bilbao: Euskal Dantzarien Biltzarra, 1978–
[NOT IN BUCOMP1]

  Lcs 1, 1978; 9–10, 1979; 13, 15, 1980; 16, 18,
  1981; 20–27, 1982–83

Dark Star
GB–Northolt, 1975–
[NOT IN BUCOMP1]

  Lsa 1–26, 1975–81 [w 19, 1979]

Dark Times
GB–Birmingham, 1995–
[NOT IN BUCOMP1]

  Cu 1, 1995–#

Darmstädter Beiträge zur neuen Musik
0418–3878
D– Mainz: B. Schott's Söhne, 1958–
[NOT IN BUCOMP1]

  Cpl 1–5, 9, 10, 12, 1958–70

David Cassidy Magazine *see* Superstars'
Official David Cassidy Magazine

Dawns [= Dance]: the National Magazine of
Welsh Traditional Dancing
GB–Bangor: Welsh Folk Dance
Society/Cylchgrawn Cymdeithas Ddawns Werin
Cymru, 1960–

  AB 1960–62; 1965–67; 1969/70–1976/77;
  1978/79; 1980/81; 1983/84–#
  EIR:Dtc 1985/86–#
  Lbl*
  Lcs 1960/61–1962/63; 1965/66; 1970/71–#
  [w 1989/90]
  Ob*
  RH 1976/77–1979/80

db: the Sound Engineering Magazine
0011–7145
US–Commack, NY, 1967–
[NOT IN BUCOMP1]

  Lsa 1984–*

DC: the Magazine of the Friends of D'Oyly
Carte *see* D'Oyly Carte News: the Journal of
the Friends of D'Oyly Carte

Dee Jay and Radio Monthly
GB–Hitchin, 1972–73

  Cu 1–12, 1972–73
  Lsa 1–9, 1972–73
  Ob*

Deeper and Deeper Soul Magazine
0140–4350
GB–Birkenhead: K. Murray, 1977–79

  Cu 1–8, 1977–79*
  Lbl*
  Ob*

Deletion Times; Complete Catalogue of
Deleted Albums, Cassettes, Singles, 8 Tracks
GB–London: SP&S Records (London) Ltd.,
?1981–
[NOT IN BUCOMP1]

  Ep 4 (1984), 11

The Delius Society Journal *see* Delius Society
Newsletter

Delius Society Newsletter
0306–0373
GB–Maidstone [etc.]: Delius Society, 1962–
[Entitled *DSJ* [Delius Society Journal] from no.
43, 1974]

  BDp 43, 1974–#
  Bs 40–112, 1973–93*
  BSdsc 47–112, 1975–93
  Cu 16, 1967–#
  DOR*
  EIR:Dtc 16, 1967–#
  En 16, 1967–#
  Gam 48–103, 1975–90
  Lam 52, 1976–#
  Lbar 32, 1971; 39, 1973; 50, 1976–# [w 51,
  55, 57, 58]
  Lbl*
  Lcm 46–103, 1975–90
  Lcml 45–48, 1974–75; 50, 1976–#
  Lgsm 59–61, 1978; 66, 1980–#
  Lmic 56, 1977–#
  Lsa 89, 1986; 106, 1991; 113, 1994–#
  Ltc 198187*; 1988–92
  Mcm 43, 1974–#
  Ob*
  Yu 55–103, 1977–90

Y Delyn [= The Harp]: the Welsh Musical
Review
TNG GB409
GB–Llangollen, 1947

    AB 1947
    En 1947, 1–3
    Lbl*
    Ob*

Demo: the UK's Alternative "Top 20"
Magazine
0961–6489
GB–Epsom: Demo Chart, 1990–
[NOT IN BUCOMP1]

    Lbl 12, 1990–#

Deo: Today's Music and Worship
1350–9519
GB–Worthing: Herald House, 1993–
[NOT IN BUCOMP1; succeeded *Christian
Music* (q.v.); entitled *Worship Together* from 17,
1996]

    CCtc 1993–#
    CFp 1993–#
    Cu 1993–#
    Lbl*
    Ob*

Derbyshire Arts and Music
0264–133X
GB–Ilkeston: M. White, 1982–
[NOT IN BUCOMP1]

    Lbl*

Destination Jarre
0968–1825
GB–Penarth: G. Needham/Jean–Michel Jarre
Appreciation Society, ?1990–
[NOT IN BUCOMP1]

    Lbl*

Deutsche Bibliographie:
Musiktonträgerverzeichnis *see* Deutsche
Bibliographie: Schallplatten-Verzeichnis

Deutsche Bibliographie: Reihe M: Musikalien
und Musikschriften *see* Deutsche
Musikbibliographie

Deutsche Bibliographie: Schallplatten-
Verzeichnis
D–Frankfurt–am–Main: Deutsche Bibliothek,
Abteilung Deutsches Musikarchiv, ?–
[Later entitled *Deutsche Bibliographie:
Musiktonträgerverzeichnis* (ISSN 0170–1029);
from 1974 entitled *Deutsche
Nationalbibliographie: Reihe T,
Musiktonträger*]

    Mpl 1985–#
    Ob 1974–#

Deutsche Musikbibliographie
0939–0596; 0170–124X
D–Frankfurt, 1943–
[Entitled *Deutsche Bibliographie: Reihe M:
Musikalien und Musikschriften* from 1991.
Succeeded the *Musikalisch-literarischer
Monatsbericht neuer Musikalien, musikalischer
Schriften und Abbildungen* (q.v.)]

    Lbl*
    Lu 1944–#
    Mu 1977–95
    Ob 1976–#

Deutsche Musikbücherei
D–Regensburg: Gustav Bosse, 1912–38

    Lbl*

Deutsche Musikkultur: Zweimonatshefte für
Musikleben und Musikforschung
TNG D778
D–Kassel: Bärenreiter/Staatliches Institut für
Deutsche Musikforschung zu Berlin, 1936–44
[Ceased publication with vol. 9 (1944)]

    Lbl*
    Lu 1 (1936), 3

Deutsche Musik-Zeitung
Fellinger 1968/419; TNG A44
A–Vienna: Wessely und Büsing, 1860–62
[Continued as *Allgemeine musikalische Zeitung
[2]* (q.v.)]

    Lbl 1 (1860), 2–3 (1862)

Deutsche Nationalbibliographie: Reihe T,
Musiktonträger *see* Deutsche Bibliographie:
Schallplatten-Verzeichnis

Deutsche Tonkünstler-Zeitung: Fachblatt für
Musiker und Musikerzieher
Fellinger 1968/1667
D–Berlin, 1903–43; 1949–68
[From 1938 entitled *Der Musikerzieher*; from
1949 entitled *Musik im Unterricht*; superseded
in 1969 by *Musik und Bildung: Zeitschrift für
Theorie und Praxis der Musikerziehung* (q.v.)]

    LAu 1949, 3, 4; 1953, 4

Deutscher Musikrat: Musikforum *see*
Deutscher Musikrat: Referate und
Informationen

Deutscher Musikrat: Referate und
Informationen
TNG D1047
D–Hamburg/Bonn [etc.]: Präsidium des
Deutschen Musikrats/Schott, 1965–
[Entitled *Musikforum: Referate und
Informationen des Deutschen Musikrates* (ISSN
0935–2562) from vol. 24 (1988)]

    BSdsc*
    Cu*
    Gsmic [c]
    Gul 1–8, 1965–68
    Lam 1, 1965; 5, 7–16, 1967–70; 18–22,
        1971/72; 24–26, 1973/74; 28–30, 1975;
        32–41, 1976–79; 43–67, 1979–87
    Lbbc 18, 1971–#
    Lbl*
    Lcm 1–3, 1965–66; 5–8, 1967–68; 10,
        1968/69; 14–19, 1970/71; 22, 23, 1972/73;
        27, 1974; 32, 1976; 35, 1977; 37–41,
        1977–79; 43–56, 1979–84; 61, 1985–#
    Lcml 3, 1966–#
    Lu 1, 1965–#
    Mcm 39–50, 1978–82 [w 41]

Deutsches Bach-Fest
Fellinger 1968/1570; TNG D408
D–Leipzig: Breitkopf und Härtel, 1901–39;
1950–

    Ob*

Deutsches Jahrbuch der Musikwissenschaft
TNG D980; 0070–4504
D–Leipzig: Peters, 1956–77; 1978–
[Succeeded the *Jahrbuch der Musikbibliothek
Peters* (q.v.); succeeded 1978–87 by *Jahrbuch
Peters*]

    Cu 1956–77; 1978–#
    Lam 1963–66
    LAu 1958; 1961
    Lbl*
    Lcm 1965–66
    Lu 1956–81
    Mu 1961; 1965–66; 1968
    Ob 1956–77; 1978–#
    Ouf 1977; 1981

Deutsches Mozartfest der Deutschen Mozart
Gesellschaft
0418–8896
D–Augsburg ; Mannheim [etc.]: Deutsche
Mozart–Gesellschaft, 1954–92

    Ob*

Deutsches Musikgeschichtliches Archiv
Kassel: Mitteilungen und Katalog der
Filmsammlung
D–Kassel: Deutsches Musikgeschichtliches
Archiv, 1955–

    Lbl*
    Lu 1 (1955)–#
    Ob*
    Ouf 1 (1955)–3 (1984); 19–23, 1985–91

Deutsches Musikleben *see* There's Music in
Germany

Development News: the Newsletter of the
Royal Opera House Development Office
GB–London: Royal Opera House, 1992–
[NOT IN BUCOMP1]

    Lbl 1992, Mar–#

The Devil's Box
0092–0789
US–Madison, Alabama [etc.]: Tennessee Valley
Old–time Fiddlers' Association, ?1967–
[NOT IN BUCOMP1]

    Lcs 13 (1979), 4–14 (1980), 1, 3, 4; 16
        (1982), 2, 3

The Diapason: Devoted to the Organ, the
Harpsichord, the Carillon and Church Music
Fellinger 1968/1965; TNG US395; 0012–2378
US–Chicago, IL [etc.]: Scranton Gilette [for the
National Union of Organists], 1909–

    BSdsc*
    Lam (o) 23 (1932)–24 (1933); 39 (1947), 2–
        74 (1983)

Lcml 81 (1990)–#
Lrco 1957–58*; 1962–68*; 1972–#*
LVp 54 (1963)–#
Mcm 40 (1948), 8–12; 41 (1949), 2–4, 6–8;
72 (1981)–73 (1982), 3, 12; 74 (1983)–75
(1984), 2
Ob 75 (1984)–#

**Diapason: le Magazine de la Musique, du
Disque et du Son** *see* Diapason: la Revue
du Disque Microsillon

Diapason: la Revue du Disque Microsillon
TNG F661
F–Paris, 1956–
[From 1976 subtitled *Le Magazine de la
Musique, du Disque et du Son*]

Lsa 1, 1956–# [w 7, 9, 10, 1956; 16, 1957;
207, 1976; 301, 302, 1985]
Mcm 1978–83*

Diapason Catalogue
F–Paris, 1964–
[NOT IN BUCOMP1]

Lsa 1964–# [w 1974, 1976, 1983, 1987]

Didactics of Music Education
CZ–Prague: Charles University, 1982–
[NOT IN BUCOMP1]

Cu 1981/82–85; 1987–88
Lbl*
Lu 1984–85;1987–88

**Different Drummer: the Magazine for Jazz
Listeners**
0731–1621
US–Rochester, NY: BOAPW, 1973–75
[Ceased publication with vol. 1 no. 15, 1975]

Cbijs 1 (1973), 4
LOnjfa*

Digital Music Magazine *see* DMM: Digital
Music Magazine

Directory of British Brass Bands
GB–Rochdale: British Federation of Brass
Bands, 1975–
[NOT IN BUCOMP1]

ABDp 1992/93–#
Lbl*
Ob 1975–#

**Directory of Computer-Assisted Research in
Musicology**
1057–9478
US–Menlo Park, CA: Center for Computer
Assisted Research in the Humanities, 1985–
[NOT IN BUCOMP1; continued as *Computing
in Musicology: an International Directory of
Applications*]

Cu 10 (1995/96)–#
KE 3 (1987)–#
Lgo 2 (1986)–#
Lkc 5 (1989)–#
NO 1 (1985)–#
Ob*
Ouf 2 (1986)–#
Yu 2 (1986)–#

Directory of Northern Music
GB: Ashington: Mid–Northumberland Arts
Group, 1978, 1981
[NOT IN BUCOMP1]

Lbl 1978, 1981
Ob 1978, 1981

Directory of the British Music Industries
GB–?London, 19?–
[NOT IN BUCOMP1]

Ob 1951, 1955

**Directory of the Provincial Music Trades
Association**
GB–Windsor: T. E. Luff, 1889–?
[NOT IN BUCOMP1]

Lbl*
Ob*

Directory of Traditional Music
0893–3065
US–New York: Columbia University/
International Council for Traditional Music,
1987–
[NOT IN BUCOMP1; previously entitled the
ICTM Directory of Interests and Projects (New
York: Columbia University/ICTM, 1985)]

BRp 1987–#
Gul [c]
Lcs 1987; 1989; 1991; 1993–#
Lsa 1987–#

Disc
TNG GB386
GB–Bristol: Bristol Gramophone Society, 1947–
53

BRp 1 (1947)–6 (1953)
Lam 2 (1948), 5
Lbl*
Lcml 1 (1947)–6 (1953)*
Lsa 1 (1947)–6 (1953), 22
Ob*

Disc and Music Echo
TNG GB474; 0012–3501
GB–Haywards Heath, 1958–75

Lbl*
Ob*

Disc Debates [translated title] see Disco
Discussies

Disc News [translated title] see Platenieuws

Disc Parade [translated title] see Plade Parade

Disc World [translated title] see Platenwereld

Disco: Musik- och Grammofontidskrift
[= Music and Gramophone Journal]
TNG S87
S–Stockholm, 1944–45

Lsa 1–5, 1944–45

Disco 45
GB–Rye [etc.]: T. Bolton, 1969–

Cu 15–159, 1972–84
Lsa 80–89, 1977–78
Ob 15–22, 1972

Disco and Club News International see Disco
and Club Trade International

Disco and Club Trade International
GB–London: Mountain Lion Productions, 197?–
[NOT IN BUCOMP1; preceded by Disco and
Club News International; succeeded by Disco
Club and Leisure International (1990–95)]

Lbl*
Ob 110, 1985–#

Disco Club and Leisure International see
Disco and Club Trade International

Disco Discussies [= Disc Debates]
NL–Amsterdam, 19?–
[NOT IN BUCOMP1]

Lsa 1962, July–Dec; 1963, Mar, Apr,
July–Sep, Nov, Dec; 1964; 1965, Feb

Discofilia
E–Madrid, 1956–

Lsa 1–49, 1956–60 [w 8, 9, 12, 14, 15,
18–26, 28–38, 40–43, 46–48]

Discografia Internazionale
I–Milan: Discografia Italiana, 1966–?67

Lsa 2 (1967), 1–9

Discographical Forum
TNG GB491; 0012–3544
GB–London: M. Walker, 1960; 1968–
[Not published between 1961 and 1967]

Cbijs 2, 1960; 5, 1968; 15–19, 21–37,
1969–77
LOnjfa*
Lsa 32–44, 1973–79
Ob*

La Discographie de la France see La
Discographie Française

La Discographie Française
F–Paris, 1956–63; 1966–
[Succeeded by La Discographie de la France,
1966–]

Lsa 2, 1956; 5, 12, 14–17, 19–21, 1957; 42,
1958; 57, 66, 1959; 73, 74, 78, 81–85, 87,
1960; 88–93, 96, 97, 99, 100–101, 1961;
112–140, 1962–63; 1–73, 1966–69; 76,
1969; 88, 1970

Discography: for the Jazz Student
GB–London: Clifford James, 1942–44

Cbijs 1942–44
LOnjfa*

The Discophile: the Magazine for Record
Information
TNG GB425
GB–Barking [etc.]: D. Coller, 1948–58
[Ceased publication with no. 61, 1958;
incorporated into Matrix: Jazz Record Research
Magazine (q.v.) in 1959]

Cbijs 1–61, 1949–58
Lbl*
Lsa 26–61, 1952–58

Discoteca: Rivista Mensile di Dischi, Musica e Alta Fedeltà *see* Discoteca alta Fedeltà: Rivista Mensile di Dischi e Musica

Discoteca alta Fedeltà: Rivista Mensile di Dischi e Musica
TNG I255; 0012–3560
I–Milan: Casa Editrice L'Esperto, 1960–?81
[? Entitled *Discoteca: Rivista Mensile di Dischi, Musica e Alta Fedeltà*, 1969–70; entitled *Discoteca Alta Fedeltà*, 1971–78; entitled *Discoteca Hi–Fi*, 1979–81]

   Lsa 2, 3, 1960; 5, 6, 8–15, 1961; 1962–68; 1970; 1972; 1974–77

Discoteca di Stato: Bollettino
I–Rome, ?1969–

   Lsa 12/14 (1980)–#

Discoteca Hi-Fi *see* Discoteca alta Fedeltà: Rivista Mensile di Dischi e Musica

Discothèque and Dance
GB–London, 1970–

   Lbl*

Disc'ribe: a Journal of Discographical Information
US–Ann Arbor, MI [etc.]: Wildmusic, 1980–82

   EXu 1 (1980*)*–2 (1981)

Disk: kritisch Maandblad voor Discofielen [= Critical Monthly for Discophiles]
TNG NL119; 0012–3722
NL–Amersfoort: J. de Kruijff, 1967–

   Lsa 1–59, 1967–71; 84–155, 1974–79; n.s. = 1–12, 1980

Diskothek
D–Darmstadt, 1960–

   Lsa 1961–70

Disques
TNG US512
US–Philadelphia, PA: H. Royer Smith Company, 1930–33
[From 1933 entitled *The New Records* [1] (q.v.)]

   Lcml 3 (1932), 3, 4
   Lsa 1 (1930), 5; 2 (1931), 3–7, 9, 11, 12; 3 (1932), 1–6

Disques: Revue Mensuelle [Classiques-Danse-Chansons-Jazz]
TNG F558
F–Paris, 1934–62
[from 1947 entitled *Disques: Revue Mensuelle (Classiques–Danse–Chansons–Jazz)*

   Lsa 25–53, 1937–39; n.s. 1 (1947)–13 (1961)

Disques du Longue Durée
F–Paris, ?–?
[NOT IN BUCOMP1]

   Lsa 1953–63

Dissonance *see* Dissonnanz/Dissonance

Dissonanz/Dissonance: die neue schweizerische Musikzeitschrift
CH–Gumlingen: Zytglogge [for the Schweizerischer Tonkünstlerverein], 1984–
[NOT IN BUCOMP1. Succeeded the *Schweizerische Musikzeitung und Sängerblatt* (q.v.)]

   Lbl 1 (1984)–#*

Ditson and Co's Musical Record
Fellinger 1968/764; TNG US127
US–Boston, MA: O. Ditson and Company, 1878–1903
[Entitled *The Musical Record* (ISSN 0737–1519) from vol. 1 no. 2 (1878); entitled *The Musical Record and Review*, 1901–03 (nos 468–502)]

   AB 472, 477, 1901; 482, 487, 488, 1902
   Lbl*

DJ: Disc Jockey *see* Jocks

DJ Yearbook
GB–London: Orpheus, 1992–
[NOT IN BUCOMP1]

   Lbl*
   Ob 1992–#

DMM: Digital Music Magazine
GB–Edgware: Warner, 1987–
[NOT IN BUCOMP1]

   Lbl*

dmt *see* Dansk Musik Tidsshrift

Dobells News
GB–London, 1958–?

Cbijs 1 (1958), 4, 7

Doblingers Verlagsnachrichten
0070–6795
A–Vienna: Doblinger, ?1959–78
[NOT IN BUCOMP1]

Lcm 10 (1968)–12 (1970)

Doctor Jazz [Magazine]
0166–2309
NL–Amsterdam [etc.], 1963–
[Entitled *Doctor Jazz Magazine* from no. 42, ?1970]

Cbijs 1, 1963
LOnjfa*
Lsa 33, 1968; 37–45, 1969–71

Doctoral Dissertations in Musicology
US–Philadelphia, PA: American Musicological Society, 1952–
[NOT IN BUCOMP1; new material post-1996, plus some earlier items, available in electronic form via *DMM Online* at http://www.music.indiana.edu/ddm/]

BRu 1971; 1984/85–#
Lam 1979; 1983/84; 1984/85; 1990/91
Lbl*
Ob*
Ouf*
R 1983/84–#
TOd 1983/84, 1986/87
Uu 1983/84–#

Documenta Bartókiana
0419–5094
D–Mainz: B. Schott's Söhne, 1964–1970; n. F. 1977–

Cpl 1 (1964)–4 (1970)
Lam 1 (1964)
Lu 1 (1964)–5 (1977)
Ob 1 (1964)–6 (1981)

Dokumenty k Dejinám Slovenskej Hudby
[= Documents For a History of Slovak Music]
CZ–Prague, 1964–

Ob*

Dolmetsch Historical Dance Society: Journal
0261–0965
GB–Southampton [etc.]: Dolmetsch Historical Dance Society, 1971–79; 1979–
[NOT IN BUCOMP1; from 2 (1980) entitled *Historical Dance: the Journal of the Dolmetsch Historical Dance Society* (ISSN 0261–0965)]

Bu 2 (1980), 4
EIR:Dtc 3 (1973)–9 (1979); n.s. 2 (1980), 1; 3 (1992)–#
Lbl*
Lcs 1 (1971)–9 (1979) [w 2, 4, 6]; n.s. 2 (1980), 1–5

The Dome: an Illustrated Magazine and Review of Literature, Music, Architecture and the Graphic Arts
GB–London, 1897–1900
[NOT IN BUCOMP1]

Cpl 1–5; n.s. 1 (1897), 2, 3; 3 (1899), 7, 8
Cu 1–5; n.s. 1 (1897)–3 (1899), 7

The Dominant
TNG GB317
GB–London: Oxford University Press, 1927–29
[Ceased with vol. 2 no. 5 (Nov 1929)]

AB*
Bp 1 (1927)–2 (1929), 5
Bu 1 (1927)–2 (1929), 5
CDu 1 (1927)–2 (1929)
Cpl 1 (1927), 2 –2 (1929), 3
Cu 1 (1927)–2 (1929), 5
EIR:Dtc 1 (1927)–2 (1929), 5
En 1 (1927)–2 (1929)
Ep 1 (1927), 1
Gam 1 (1927)–2 (1929), 5
Gm 1 (1927), 1, 6, 10, 11; 2 (1929), 1, 3
Lam 1 (1927)–2 (1929), 2
Lbl*
Lcm 1 (1927), 1–4, 7; 2 (1929), 1–4
Lcml 1 (1927)–2 (1929), 5
Lu 1 (1927)–2 (1929), 5
Mcm 2 (1929), 5
Mp 1 (1927)–2 (1929), 5
Ob*
Ouf 1 (1927)–2 (1929), 5
SFu 1 (1927)–2 (1929)*

Donizetti Society Journal
TNG GB572; 0307–1448
GB–London: Donizetti Society, 1974–

AB 1 (1974)–5 (1984)
Bp 1 (1974); 3 (1977)–6 (1988)
Cu 1 (1974)–6 (1988)
EIR:Dtc 1 (1974)–6 (1988)
En 1 (1974)–#
Lam 1 (1974)–5 (1984)
Lbar 1 (1974)–5 (1984)
Lbbc 1 (1974)–5 (1984)
Lbl*
Lcm (p) 1 (1974)–2 (1975); 4 (1980)–
  5 (1984)
Lu 1 (1974)–#
LVp 1 (1974)
Mpl 3 (1977)–6 (1988)
Ob 1 (1974)–#
Ouf 1 (1974)–6 (1988)

Donizetti Society Newsletter
TNG GB566
GB–London: Donizetti Society, 1973–
[NOT IN BUCOMP1]

Lbar 49, 1990–#
Lbbc 47, 1989–# [w 55]
Lu 50, 1990–#

Doodlin'
GB–Liverpool, 1970

Cbijs 1970

A Dose of the Heavies
GB–Cambridge: A DOTH Publications, 198?–
[NOT IN BUCOMP1]

Lbl*

Double Bassist
1362–0835
GB–London: Rhinegold, 1996–
[NOT IN BUCOMP1]

Lam 1, 1996–#
Lcm 3, 1997–#
Ltc 1, 1996–#
Mcm*

The Double Reed
TNG US883; 0741–7659
US–East Lansing, MI [etc]: International
Double Reed Society, 1978–

Gam 1 (1978), 3–2 (1979), 5; 6 (1983), 4–14
  (1991), 1, 3; 15 (1992)–#

Lam 5 (1982)–# [w 6 (1983), 2]
Lcm 6 (1983), 1, 3, 4–# [w 8 (1985), 3, 4; 9
  (1986), 1, 3, 4; 12 (1989), 1, 4; 15 (1992),
  2–4]
Lgsm 5 (1982), 2–15 (1992), 1*
Ltc 16 (1993), 3–18 (1995), 2, 4; 19 (1996),
  1–3
Mcm 1 (1978)–#
Mpl 5 (1982)–6 (1983)
Ob*

Double Reed News
GB–London [etc.]: British Double Reed Society,
1987–
[NOT IN BUCOMP1]

Bs 2, 1988–# [w 15, 1991]
CCtc 11, 1990–#
Lam 6–21, 1989–92 [w 15, 1991]
Lgsm 1, 1987–#*

Down Beat *see* **Downbeat: Jazz, Blues, and
Beyond**

Downbeat: the Contemporary Music Magazine
see **Downbeat: Jazz, Blues, and Beyond**

Downbeat: Jazz, Blues, and Beyond
TNG US526; 0012–5768
US–Chicago, IL [etc.]: Maher Publications, Inc.,
1934–
[Sometime subtitled *The Contemporary Music
Magazine*]

BDp 42 (1975)–#
Cat 53 (1986), 4–#
Cbijs 26 (1959), 18; 27 (1960), 9, 13, 14, 16,
  19, 21, 23, 24, 26; 28 (1961) [w 3, 10, 11,
  13]; 29 (1962) [w 4, 7]; 30 (1963)–37
  (1970), 3, 5, 7, 9, 15, 16, 19–22; 39 (1972),
  8–12, 14, 15, 17; 40 (1973), 2–4, 6, 7, 12;
  41 (1974), 2, 4, 17, 19
Er 47 (1980), 12–48 (1981), 11
KE 52 (1985), 10–53 (1986), 6
Lcml 55 (1988), 2–#
LOnjfa 4 (1937); 6 (1939)–26 (1959) [m]; 27
  (1960)–#*
Lsa 14 (1947)–24 (1957)*; 28 (1961)–29
  (1962)*; 31 (1964), June 18; 32 (1965)–36
  (1971)*; 40 (1973)–45 (1978)*; 48 (1981)–
  #*
Lu 33 (1966), 6–46 (1979), 18*
Mpl 52 (1985)–#
Msuc 58 (1991)–#
Oub 63 (1996)–#
Yu 29 (1962)*; 30 (1963), 1, 2, 7

Downbeat Music Handbook *see* Down Beat's
Music Handbook

Downbeat Yearbooks *see* Down Beat's Music
Handbook

Down Beat's Music Handbook
0077–2372
US–Elmhurst, IL: Maher Publications, 1956–?
[NOT IN BUCOMP1; also entitled *Downbeat
Yearbooks* and *Downbeat Music Handbook*]

   LOnjfa*

D'Oyly Carte News: the Journal of the
Friends of D'Oyly Carte
GB–London: Friends of D'Oyly Carte, 1990–
[NOT IN BUCOMP1; preceded by *New
Savoyard* (q.v.); continued as *DC: the Magazine
of the Friends of D'Oyly Carte*]

   Lam 2, 1990
   Ob 1, 1990–#

Dramatic Almanack *see* The General
Dramatic, Equestrian and Musical Agency
and Sick Fund Association Almanack

Dramatic and Musical Almanack *see* The
General Dramatic, Equestrian and Musical
Agency and Sick Fund Association Almanack

The Dramatic and Musical Circular: an
Epitome of Dramatic, Operatic, and Music
Hall Requirements
Fellinger 1968/788; TNG GB95
GB–London: A. Andrews, 1879
[Entitled *The London Mirror, in which is
incorporated the Dramatic and Musical Mirror*
from no. 30, 1879; ceased publication with no.
31]

   Lbl 1879, 1–29*; 30, 31, 1879

The Dramatic and Musical Directory of the
United Kingdom
Fellinger 1968/919; TNG GB105
GB–London: C. H. Fox, 1883–98
[NOT IN BUCOMP1]

   En 1883–84; 1887–93

The Dramatic and Musical Review: a Record
of Public Amusements
Fellinger 1968/190; TNG GB28; Langley, pp.
607–10
GB–London: Joseph Onwhyn, 1842–52

[Vols 1 (1842)–6 (1847) published weekly in
300 numbers; n.s. 1 (1848)–5 (1852) either
monthly or semi-monthly as nos 301–77]

   Bu 1 (1842)–6 (1847); n.s. 1 (1848)–4 (1851)
   Cu 8 (1849)–10 (1851)
   En n.s. 1 (1848)–5 (1852)
   Gul (e) 1 (1842)–6 (1847) [w 41–48, 50, 52–
      63, 65–174, 177, 236, 248, 265]
   Lbl 1–144, 1842–44; 197–300, 1846–47
   Lcm 3 (1843), 55
   Lu 1 (1842)–6 (1847)
   Ob*

Dramatic Art Circular and Monthly Record
of the British Musical and Dramatic Institute
Fellinger 1968/702; TNG GB83
GB–London, 1875
[Only one volume published]

   Lbl 1875, 1, 3, 4

Dramatic, Equestrian and Musical Agency
and Sick Fund Association Almanack *see* The
General Dramatic, Equestrian and Musical
Agency and Sick Fund Association Almanack

Dramatic, Equestrian and Musical Sick Fund
Almanack *see* The General Dramatic,
Equestrian and Musical Agency and Sick
Fund Association Almanack

Dramatic Mirror and Review of Music and
the Fine Arts
Fellinger 1968/245; TNG GB38
GB–London, 1847–48
[37 numbers in total]

   Lbl 1–37, 1847–48

The Dramatic Review: a Journal of
Theatrical, Musical and General Criticism
Fellinger 1968/988; TNG GB117
GB–London, 1885–94
[512 nos in total]

   Lbl*
   Ob*

Dreams
0961–6357
GB–London: City Rock Magazines, 1991–
[NOT IN BUCOMP1]

   Lbl*

Dreams: Take That
0968–3895
GB–London: Dreams Machine/Take That Fan
Club, ?1993–
[NOT IN BUCOMP1]

   Lbl*

Der Dreiklang: Monatsschrift für Musik
TNG A225
A–Vienna: Krystall–Verlag, 1937–38

   Cu 1–9, 1937–38 [Reprint ed.]
   Lu 1–9, 1937–38 [Reprint ed.]
   SOu 1–9, 1937–38

**Drei-und-Zwanzig: eine Wiener
Musikzeitschrift**
TNG A217
A–Vienna: O. Kerry, 1932–37

   Cpl 1–33, 1932–37
   Cu 1–33, 1932–37 [Reprint ed.]
   LAu 1–33, 1932–37 [Reprint ed.]
   Lbl*
   Lcml 11–14, 1933–34; 24, 25, 1936
   Lu 1–33, 1933–37 [Reprint ed.]
   Mu 1–33, 1932–37 [Reprint ed.]
   Ob 1–33, 1932–37

Drum Study
GB–Brighton, 1991–
[NOT IN BUCOMP1]

   Cu 1, 1991–#

**The Drummer: the Exclusive Drummer's
Magazine**
TNG GB323
GB–London, 1928–39

   Lbl*

Drums and Percussion
GB–London: Musical News Services, 1974–76

   Cbijs 1, 1974
   Lam 1, 1974
   Lcml 1–12, 1974–76

D.S.C.H. Journal
F–St Didier au Mont d'Or: DSCH, 1994–
[NOT IN BUCOMP1; formerly *D.S.C.H.: the
Newsletter of the Shostakovich Society* (q.v.)]

   ALb 1, 1994–#
   Lbar 1, 1994–#

**D.S.C.H.: the Newsletter of the Shostakovich
Society**
GB–London: Shostakovich Society, 1987–92
[NOT IN BUCOMP1; later entitled *D.S.C.H.
Journal* (q.v.)]

   ALb 4–21, 1987–92
   Cu 1–21, 1987–92
   En 1–20, 1987–92
   Lbar 1–20, 1987–92
   Ob*

DSJ *see* **Delius Society Journal**

The Dulcimer Player's News
TNG US854; 0098–3527
US–Winchester, VA [etc.]: M. MacNeil, 1975–
[NOT IN BUCOMP1]

   Lcs 8 (1982), 3, 4; 9 (1983), 2–10 (1984), 3;
     14 (1988), 3; 15 (1989), 1, 2, 4; 16 (1990)–#

The Dunedin Magazine
Fellinger 1968/2113; TNG GB256
GB–Edinburgh: The Dunedin Association,
1912–15
[Ceased publication with vol. 3 no. 3 (1915)]

   Au 1 (1912), 2–3 (1915)
   En 1 (1912)–3 (1915)
   Ep 1 (1912)–3 (1915), 3
   Gm 1 (1912)–3 (1915)
   Lbl*

Dutch Arts
NL–The Hague: Department of International
Relations, Ministry of Cultural Affairs, 1985–
[NOT IN BUCOMP1]

   Lbl*
   Lcm 2 (1985)

Dutch Popular Music
TNG NL100
NL–Amsterdam, 1952–?
[English edition of *Onze Lichte Muziek*]

   Lcml 1952, June

Dvořák Society: Czech Music Newsletter
GB–London [etc]: Dvořák Society of Great
Britain, 1988–
[NOT IN BUCOMP1; from 7, 1990, entitled
*Dvořák Society for the Music of
Czechoslovakia: Newsletter*]

   EIR:Dtc 1, 1988–#
   En 9, 1990; 25, 1993–#

Lbar 1–3, 1988–89; 7, 1990; 10, 14, 1991; 17, 1992; 23, 1993–#
Lbl*
Ob*

Dvořák Society for the Music of Czechoslovakia: Newsletter *see* Dvořák Society: Czech Music Newsletter

Dvořák Society of Great Britain: Newsletter *see* Dvořák Society: Czech Music Newsletter

Dwight's Journal of Music: a Paper of Art and Literature
Fellinger 1968/300; TNG US28
US–Boston, MA; O. Ditson, 1852–81

    Cu 1–41, 1852–81 [Reprint ed.]
    Gul (e) 1–7, 1852–58 [w 5, 1856, 4]
    Lbl 1–41, 1852–81 [Reprint ed.]; second, original copy *
    Ob 1–41, 1852–81 [Reprint ed.]

E

E and MM: Electronics and Music Maker: the Music Technology Magazine *see* Electronics and Music Maker

Ear
0734–2128
US–New York: New Wilderness Foundation, 1973–92
[NOT IN BUCOMP1; from 1976 entitled *Ear: Magazine of New Music* (ISSN 0893–9500); ceased publication with vol. 16 no. 2 (1992)]

    LCdM 4 (1978)–12 (1987), 3; 13 (1988), 1–8
    Lsa 1 (1975)–16 (1991) [w 12 (1987), 2–9]

Ear: Magazine of New Music *see* Ear

Early Dance News
GB–London, 1987–
[NOT IN BUCOMP1]

    EIR:Dtc 1 (1987)–2 (1989), 2
    Ob 1 (1987)–#

The Early English Musical Magazine
Fellinger 1968/1159; TNG GB143
GB–London: Sampson Low, Marston and Co., 1891
[8 nos in total]

    Cu 1 (1891), 1–6
    En 1 (1891)

Lbl 1 (1891)–2 (1891), 8
LEu 1 (1891), 1–6
Mpl 1 (1891)
Ob*

Early Keyboard Journal
US–Charlotte, NC [etc.]: Southeastern Historical Keyboard Society, 1982–
[NOT IN BUCOMP1]

    Cu 1 (1982)–#

Early Music
TNG GB567; 0306–1078
GB–London: Oxford University Press, 1973–
[*See also Early Music Gazette*]

    AB 1 (1973)–#
    ALb 1 (1973), 2–2 (1974), 3; 3 (1975)–8 (1980), 1, 3, 4; 9 (1981)–13 (1985), 2; 16 (1988), 4
    Au 1 (1973)–#
    BAc 1 (1973)–#
    BDp 1 (1973)–13 (1985)
    BEp [c (5 years)]
    BG 1 (1973)–#
    BLBBC 6 (1978)–8 (1980), 3; 9 (1981)–#
    BLp 1 (1973)–#
    BLu 1 (1973)–#
    Bp 1 (1973)–#
    BRp 1 (1973)–#
    BRu 1 (1973)–#
    Bs 1 (1973)–#*
    BSdsc 1 (1973)–#
    BTu 1 (1973)–10 (1982)
    Bu 1 (1973)–#
    Cat 2 (1974), 2–#
    CAu 1 (1973)–#
    CCtc 1 (1973)–#
    CDCp 17 (1989)–#
    CDu 1 (1973)–#
    CFp 1 (1973)–#
    Cpl 1 (1973)–#
    Cu 1 (1973)–#
    DRu 1 (1973)–#
    DS 1 (1973)–#
    EIR:Dp 16 (1988)–#*
    EIR:Dtc 1 (1973)–#
    EIR:Duc 1 (1973)–#
    EIR:MEtc 3 (1975)–#
    En 1 (1973)–#
    Ep 1 (1973)–#
    Er 1 (1973)–#
    EXu 1 (1973)–# [w 6 (1978), 3, 4]

Gam 1 (1973)–3 (1975), 2–4; 4 (1976), 2, 3; 5
  (1977), 1, 3, 4; 6 (1978)–10 (1982), 1, 2, 4;
  11 (1983)–12 (1984), 1, 4; 13 (1985)–#
Gm 8 (1980)–#
Gul 1 (1973)–#
HE 15 (1987), 2–#
HUu 1 (1973)–#
KE 1 (1973)–#
Lam 1 (1973), 1, 2, 4; 2 (1974)–5 (1977), 2–#
  [w 8 (1980), 2; 17 (1989), 2]
LAu 1 (1973)–#
Lbar 1 (1973)–#
Lbbc 1 (1973)–#
Lbl*
LCdM 12 (1984)–15 (1987); 19 (1991)–#
Lcm 1 (1973)–#
Lcm (m) 1 (1973)–#
Lcm (p) 1 (1973)–3 (1975)
Lcml 1 (1973)–#
Lcu 1 (1973)–#*
LEbc 1 (1973)–#
LEc 1 (1973)–#
Lgo 1 (1973)–#
Lgsm 1 (1973)–# [w 2 (1974), 2; 4 (1976),1]
Lgu 1 (1973)–#
LIp 1 (1973)– #
Lk 1 (1973)–#
Lkc 1 (1973)–6 (1978); 7 (1979)*; 8 (1980)–
  12 (1984); 13 (1985)*; 14 (1986)–#
Lki 1 (1973)–#
Lmi 1 (1973)–#
LRHBNC 1 (1973)–#
Lro 1 (1973)–#
Lsa 1 (1973)–#
Ltc 1 (1973), 4; 3 (1975), 3–12 (1984), 2, 4;
  13 (1985)–14 (1986); 15 (1987), 1, 3–17
  (1989), 1, 3, 4; 18 (1990), 1, 2, 4– 19
  (1991), 1, 3, 4; 20 (1992), 1, 2; 21 (1993);
  22 (1994), 2–24 (1996), 1, 3, 4; 25 (1997)–#
Ltv 1 (1973)–18 (1990), 2, 4; 19 (1991)–#
  [w 21 (1993), 4]
Lu 1 (1973)–#
LVp 1 (1973)–#
LVu 1 (1973)–#
Lwwput [c]
Mcm 1 (1973)–#
MK 1 (1973)–#
Mmu (a) 5 (1977)–#
Mpl 1 (1973)–#
Msu 2 (1974), 1, 2, 4–3 (1975); 4 (1976), 2, 4;
  5 (1977), 1, 3–7 (1979), 3; 8 (1980), 1
Mu 1 (1973)–#
NO 1 (1973)–#
NOp 19 (1991)–#
NWu 1 (1973)–#

Ob 1 (1973)–#
Op 16 (1988)–#
Oub 16 (1988)–#
Ouf 1 (1973)–#
R 1 (1973)–#
SA 1 (1973)–#
SFu 1 (1973)–#
SLGu 12 (1984)–#
SOu 1 (1973)–#
TOd 1 (1973)–#
Uu 1 (1973)–12 (1984); 13 (1985)*; 14
  (1986)–#
Y 1 (1973)–20 (1992)
Yu 1 (1973)–#

**Early Music America: the Magazine of
Historical Performance** *see* **Historical
Performance: the Journal of Early Music
America**

Early Music Association of Ireland Newsletter
0791–010X
EIRE–Dublin: Early Music Association of
Ireland, 1987–
[NOT IN BUCOMP1]

  EIR:Dtc 3–8, 1987–88
  EIR:Duc 1–8, 1987–88

**The Early Music Forum of Scotland
Newsletter**
GB–Castle Douglas, Galloway: Early Music
Forum of Scotland, ?1990–
[NOT IN BUCOMP1]

  Au 5, 1993–#
  Ep 5, 1993–#
  Gsmic [c]

Early Music Gazette
TNG GB567
GB–London: Oxford University Press, 1978–
[NOT IN BUCOMP1; published as a
supplement to *Early Music* (q.v.)]

  Cu 1978, Oct
  EIR:Dtc 1978, Jan–July
  Lcml 1978, Jan–July

**Early Music History: Studies in Medieval and
Early Modern Music**
0261–1279
GB–Cambridge: Cambridge University Press,
1981–

  AB 1 (1981)–#
  Au 1 (1981)–#

BAc 1 (1981)–#
BG 1 (1981)–#
BLu 1 (1981)–11 (1992)
BRu 1 (1981)–#
BSdsc 1 (1981)–#
Bu 1 (1981)–#
CCtc 1 (1981)–#
Cpl 1 (1981)–#
Cu 1 (1981)–#
DRu 1 (1981)–#
EIR:Dtc 1 (1981)–#
EIR:Duc 11 (1992)–#
En 1 (1981)–#
Er 1 (1981)–#
EXu 1 (1981)–#
Gul 1 (1981)–#
KE 1 (1981)–3 (1983); 9 (1990)–#
Lbbc 1 (1981)–#
Lbl 1 (1981)–#
Lcm 1 (1981)–#
Lcml 1 (1981)–#
LEbc 1 (1981)–#
Lgo 1 (1981)–#
Lkc 1 (1981)–#
LRHBNC 1 (1981)–#
Lu 1 (1981)–#
MK 8 (1988)–#
Mu 1 (1981)–#
NO 1 (1981)–#
Ob 1 (1981)–#
Oub 1 (1981)–#
Ouf 1 (1981)–#
SA 1 (1981)–#
SFu 1 (1981)–#
SLGu 1 (1981)–#
SOu 1 (1981)–11 (1992)
Yu 1 (1981)

Early Music New Zealand
0112–5532
NZ–Auckland: Early Music New Zealand,
1985–87
[NOT IN BUCOMP1; ceased publication with
vol. 3 no. 4 (1987)]

BSdsc 2 (1986)–3 (1987), 4
Lu 1 (1985), 3

Early Music News
0140–1696
GB–London, 1977–
[Relaunched 1996 as unpriced periodical]

Au 40, 1981–#
BAc [c (2 years)]
BDp 1–99,1977–86

Bu 35, 1980–#
Cpl 1–46, 1977–81
Cu 1, 1977–#
EIR:Dp 116, 1988–#
EIR:Dtc 1, 1977–#
En 1, 1977–#
Er 27, 1980–#
EXu 20–147, 1979–90
Gam 1, 1977–# [w 88, 1985]
HUu 7–20, 1978–79
Lam 166, 1992–#
Lbar 166, 1992; 174, 1993–#
Lbbc 21, 1979–# [w 86, 106, 111]
Lbl*
Lcm 77–80, 1984; 82–86, 89, 1985–#
Lcml 1, 1977–#
Lcml (p) [c (6 months)]
Lcs 192, 1995–#
Lcu 117, 1988–#*
Lgsm 137, 1990–#
Lgu 82, 1985–#
Lmi 23–179, 1979–93
LRHBNC 21–99, 1979–86*
Lsa 1984–85*; 1987–#*
Ltc 192, 1995–#
Lu 13, 1978; 24, 1979; 72–83, 1984–95
    [w 75, 79, 81, 82]
Mcm 1, 1977–# [w 8, 20]
MK 1, 1977–#
Mu 214, 1997–#
Ob 1, 1977–#
Ouf 77, 1984–#
TOd 21–99, 1979–86

Early Music Records: Monthly Review
GB–Saffron Walden: Early Music Record
Services, 1980–
[NOT IN BUCOMP1]

Cu 3–11, 1980–81
EIR:Dtc 5–11, 1980–81
Lbl*

Early Music Review
1355–3437
GB–Wyton: King's Music, 1994–
[NOT IN BUCOMP1; includes an *Annual Byrd
Supplement* each June from 1994]

Au 1, 1994–#
Cu 8, 1995–#
Er 1, 1994–#
Lam 1, 1994–#
Lbar 1, 1994–#
Lbl 2, 1994–#
Lcm 1, 1994–#
Lcs 5, 1994–#

Lgu 1, 1994–#
Lsa 1, 1994–#
Mcm*
Ob*
Ouf 1, 1994–#
TOd 1, 1994–#

Early Music Today
1352–0059
GB–London: Rhinegold Publishing, 1993–
[NOT IN BUCOMP1; supplied with *Classical Music [Weekly]* (q.v.)]

ALb 1 (1993), Sep–#
Au 1 (1993)–#
Bs 1 (1993)–#
Bu 1 (1993), Nov–#
Cat 2 (1994)–#
CDCp 1 (1993)–#
Cu 1 (1993)–#
DOR 2 (1994)–#
EIR:Dp 2 (1994)–#
EIR:Driam 1 (1993), Sep–#
EIR:Dtc 1 (1993), Sep–#
En 1 (1993)–#
Ep 1 (1993)–#
Gsmic 1 (1993), Nov–#
HE 1 (1993), Sep–#
Lam 1 (1993)–#
Lbar 1 (1993)–#
Lbbc 1 (1993)–#; second copy [c]
Lbl*
Lbo 1 (1993)–#
Lcm 1 (1993)–2 (1994), 3
Lgsm 1 (1993)–#
Lgu 2 (1994), 5–#
Lsa 2 (1994)–#
Ltc 1 (1993)*; 2 (1994)–#
Lu 1 (1993)–#
Mcm*
Msu 1 (1993), Sep–#
Mu 1 (1993)–#
Ob*
TOd 1 (1993), Nov–#
Uu 1 (1993), Sep–#

The Early Music Yearbook
0967–6619
GB–Cambridge: National Early Music Association, 1992–
[NOT IN BUCOMP1; formerly the *NEMA Register of Early Music* (q.v.)]

Cu 1993–#

Ep 1993
Er 1993
KE 1993
Lbl*
Lbo [c]
Lgu [c]
Ob*
WW [c]

Easy Listening and Living with Stereo
GB–London: Cardfont Publishers/Billboard, 1972–73
[10 nos in all; incorporated *Good Listening and Record Collector* from June 1973]

Cbijs 10, 1973
Cu 1972, Sep–10, 1973
EIR:Dtc*
Ob 1–10, 1972/73

Echo: Berliner Musik-Zeitung *see* **Berliner Musik-Zeitung Echo**

L'Echo Musical [1]
Fellinger 1968/602; TNG B20
B–Brussels, 1869–97

Ob 16 (1884)–26 (1896)

L'Echo Musical [2]
Fellinger 1968/2114; TNG F433
F–Paris, 1912–14; 1919–20
[NOT IN BUCOMP1]

Lcm 2 (1913), 2

Echoes *see* **Black Echoes**

Eddie Thompson Appreciation Society Newsletter
GB–Hornchurch, 1973–

Cbijs 1973–

Edgar Hunt's Recorder Newsletter
TNG GB374
GB–London, 1940–41

Lbl*

The Edinburgh Theatrical and Musical Review
Langley, pp. 567–69
GB–Edinburgh, 1835

Ep*
Lbl 5–34, 1835

The Edinburgh Theatrical Observer, and
Music Review
GB–Edinburgh, 1823

 Ep*
 Lbl*

Edison Phonograph Monthly
US–New York: Wendell Moore, 1903–?14
[NOT IN BUCOMP1]

 Lsa 1 (1903)–12 (1914) [Reprint ed.]

Editio Musica Budapest *see* E.M.B. News

L'Édition Sonore
F–Paris, 1977–
[NOT IN BUCOMP1]

 Lsa 1–7, 1977–79 [w 5]

L'Editore di Musica
TNG I224
I–Como, 1948–52

 Lcml 1 (1948), 1; 2 (1949), 1–3, 6

Edizioni Suvini Zerboni *see* ESZ News:
Notizario delle Edizioni Suvini Zerboni

Educacion Musical
ECU–?, 1982–
[NOT IN BUCOMP1]

 Lsa 1–3, 1982–84

Education
EIRE–Dublin: Tara Publishing, ?–
[NOT IN BUCOMP1]

 EIR:Driam 1991–#

Education *see also* The Journal of Trinity
College

L'Education Musicale: Journal Mensuel
TNG F591; 0013–1415
F–Paris: EGP, 1945–
[At some time subtitled *Revue Mensuelle*]

 Lam 21 (1965), 121, 123

L'Education Musicale: Revue Mensuelle *see*
L'Education Musicale: Journal Mensuel

Educazione Musicale: Rassegna Trimestrale
degli Insegnanti di Musica
TNG I267
I–Milan: Angelicum, 1964–75

 BSdsc*

E.F.D.S. News
TNG GB285
GB–London: English Folk Dance and Song
Society, 1921–36
[Continued as *English Dance and Song* (q.v.);
47 nos. in 4 vols.]

 AB 3 (1932)–4 (1936)
 Cpl 3 (1932), 7–4 (1936), 13
 EIR:Dtc 1, 2, 1921; 36–47, 1934–36
 En 4 (1934–36), 2–13
 Gm 30–47, 1932–36
 Gul*
 Lbl*
 Lcm 4, 1922; 6, 1923; 8–47, 1924–36 [w 18]
 Lcs 1–47, 1921–36
 Mpl 1–47, 1921–36
 NTp 3 (1932)–4 (1936)
 Ob 1–12, 1921–26; 17–20, 1928–29; 22–47,
 1930–35

E.F.D.S.S. Members' Newsletter
GB–?: English Folk Dance and Song Society,
1962–64
[NOT IN BUCOMP1]

 Gul 1–?4, 1962–63
 Lcs 1–5, 1962–64

E.F.D.S.S. News
GB–London: English Folk Dance and Song
Society, 1965–78
[NOT IN BUCOMP1; supplement to *English
Dance and Song* (TNG GB358)]

 EIR:Dtc 1965–78
 Lcs 1965–78

E.F.D.S.S. Newsletter
GB–London: English Folk Dance and Song
Society, 198?–
[NOT IN BUCOMP1]

 Lcs 1986, Dec; 1987, Feb, Aug

Éigse Cheol Tíre *see* Irish Folk Music Studies

The Electric Chelys: an Iconoclastic Journal for the Plucked String *see* Chelys: Monthly Journal of the New England Society for the Plucked String

Electric Shock Treatment *see* EST: Electric Shock Treatment

Electro-Acoustic Music: Journal of the Electro-Acoustic Music Association of Great Britain
0269–0748
GB–York [etc.]: Electro–Acoustic Music Association, 1984–
[NOT IN BUCOMP1; *see also Electro-Acoustic Music Association of Great Britain: Newsletter*]

> **EIR:Dtc** 1 (1984)–3 (1987), 5
> **Lbl***
> **Lgu** 3 (1987)–4 (1989), 2
> **NO** 1 (1984)–#
> **Ob** 1 (1984)–#
> **TOd** 6 (1992/93), 6, 7

Electro-Acoustic Music Association of Great Britain: Bulletin *see* Electro-Acoustic Music Association of Great Britain: Newsletter

Electro-Acoustic Music Association of Great Britain: Newsletter
GB–York [etc.]: Electro–Acoustic Music Association, 1979–?84
[NOT IN BUCOMP1; ? superseded by *Electro-Acoustic Music: Journal of the Electro-Acoustic Music Association of Great Britain*; sometime known also as *Electro-Acoustic Music Association of Great Britain: Bulletin*]

> **Lbbc** 4 (1982)–5 (1983/84)*
> **Lu** 4 (1982), 1/2, 4; 5 (1983/84), 1, 2
> **NO** 1 (1979)–5 (1983/84)
> **Ob** 1 (1979)–5 (1983/84), 4*

Electronic Music and Musical Acoustics: Annual Report
TNG DK97; 0105–2942
DK–Aarhus: University of Aarhus Institute of Musicology, Department of Musical Acoustics, 1975–77
[Ceased publication with no. 3, 1977]

> **Cu** 1–3, 1975–77
> **Er** 1–3, 1975–77
> **Lbl***
> **Lu** 1–3, 1975–77

Electronic Music Educator
1044–3150
US–Northfield, IL: Instrumentalist Company, 1988–
[NOT IN BUCOMP1]

> **Lcml** 1 (1988)–#

Electronic Music Reports
TNG NL121
NL–Utrecht: Instituut voor Sonologie, 1969–71
[Succeeded by *Interface: Journal of New Music Research* (q.v.)]

> **Lam** 1–4, 1969–71
> **Lbl***
> **NWu** 1–4, 1969–71
> **Ouf** 1–4, 1969–71

Electronic Music Review
TNG US772; 0424–8260
US–Trumansburg, NY: Independent Electronic Music Center, 1967– 68
[Ceased publication with no. 7, 1968]

> **CDu** 1–7, 1967–68
> **Cpl** 1–7, 1967–68
> **Lam** 1–3, 1967; 6, 7, 1968
> **LAu** 1, 1967
> **Lbl***
> **Lcml** 1–5, 1967–68
> **Lkc** 1–7, 1967–68
> **Lsa** 1–7, 1967–68
> **Lu** 1–7, 1967–68
> **Mcm** 1, 1967
> **Mu** 1–7, 1967–68
> **Ob***

Electronic Musician
0884–4720
US–Berkeley, CA: Electronic Musician, 1985–
[NOT IN BUCOMP1; preceded 1976–85 by *Polyphony* (Emeryville, CA; ISSN 0163–4534)]

> **Gul** 8 (1992)–#
> **TOd** 8 (1992), 9–#

Electronic Organ Review
0141–0466
GB–Heathfield: Electronic Organ Review, 1976–80

> **BSdsc***
> **Lbl***

Electronic Organs
US–Indianapolis, IN, 1973–

> BSdsc*

Electronic Soundmaker and Computer Music
0268–5264
GB– London: Cover Publications, 1983–
[NOT IN BUCOMP1; entitled *Soundmaker*
from vol. 2 (1984), 6]

> Cu 1 (1983)–3 (1985), 8
> EIR:Dtc 2 (1984)–3 (1985), 8
> Lbl 3 (1985), 3–#

Electronics and Music Maker
0957–6606
GB–London: Glidecastle Publishing;
Cambridge: Music Technology Ltd, 1981–86
[Subtitled *The No. 1 Monthly for the Modern
Musician* from 3 (1983), 5; subtitled
Incorporating Computer Musician from 3
(1983), 6. Vol. 5 (1986), 6 entitled *E and MM:
Electronics and Music Maker: the Music
Technology Magazine*. Ceased publication with
5 (1986), 8. Entitled *Music Technology:*
formerly *E and MM* (q.v.) from 1986 with new
numbering system]

> AB 3 (1983/84), 12 –5 (1986), 8
> BAc 2 (1982/83)–5 (1986), 8
> EIR:Dtc 1 (1981/82)–5 (1985/86), 5
> Er 4 (1984/85), 2–4, 6–9; 5 (1986), 2–8
> Gam 5 (1986), 6–8
> Lbl*
> Lbx 3 (1983)–5 (1986), 8
> Lgo 1 (1982), 11– 5 (1986), 8*
> Lgu 1 (1981)–5 (1986), 8
> Lsa 4 (1984/85), Apr, July, Aug
> Ltv 1 (1981)–5 (1986), 8
> Mmu (a) 1 (1981)–5 (1986)
> Ob 1 (1982), Sep–5 (1986), 7
> Oub 1 (1982)–5 (1986), 8

Elgar Society Journal *see* **Elgar Society
Newsletter**

Elgar Society Newsletter
0309–4405
GB–New Barnet: Elgar Society 1973–76; n.s.
1977–78; 1979–
[10 issues in first series, 6 in second. From 1979
entitled *Elgar Society Journal*]

> AB 6 (1984)–#
> BRp [c (2 years)]
> Cu n.s. 1, 1977–78; 1 (1979)–#

DOR 4 (1982), 2–#
DS 12 (1990)–#
EIR:Dtc n.s. 1–6, 1977–78; 1 (1979)–#
En n.s. 2–6, 1977–78; 1 (1979)–#
LAu n.s. 1–6, 1977–78; 1 (1979)–#
Lbar n.s. 1–6, 1977–78; 1 (1979)–#
Lbl 1–10, 1973–76; n.s. 1–6, 1977–78;
    1 (1979)–#
Lcm 1 (1979), 1–3, 6; 2 (1981), 1, 3, 4, 6;
    3 (1983), 1–3, 5, 6
Lcml n.s. 1–6, 1977–78; 1 (1979)–#
Lsa 5–8, 10, 1975–76; n.s. 1–6, 1977–78;
    1 (1979), 1–4, 6
Lu n.s. 1, 1977; 1 (1979), 3–#
Mcm 1–10, 1973–76 [w 2, 3, 6]; n.s. 1–6,
    1977–78; 1 (1979)–#
Ob*
WOp n.s. 1–6, 1977–78; 1 (1979)–#

Elvis: the Legend
GB–Heanor [etc]: Official Elvis Presley Fan
Club Worldwide, 1980–
[NOT IN BUCOMP1]

> Cu 3, 1980–#
> Ob 3, 1980–#

Elvis Extra
GB–Leicester, 1987–90
[NOT IN BUCOMP1]

> Cu 1987–90

Elvis Monthly
GB–Nottingham, 1959–

> Cu 108, 1969–#
> En 328, 1987–#
> Lbl*

Elvis Monthly Collectors' Special
GB–Heanor, 1983–

> Cu 1, 1983–#

Elvis Special
GB–Manchester: World International, 1962–
[NOT IN BUCOMP1]

> Ob 1979–#

Ely Music Rag
GB–Ely: Ely Diocesan Synod, 1996–
[NOT IN BUCOMP1]

> Cu 1, 1996–#

EM: Annuario degli Archivi di Etnomusicologia dell'Accademia Nazionale di Santa Cecilia
I–?Rome: Accademia Nazionale di Santa Cecilia, 1993–
[NOT IN BUCOMP1]

Lsa 1993–#

EMAS Journal *see* Electro Acoustic Music: Journal of the Electro-Acoustic Music Association of Great Britain

EMAS Newsletter *see* Electro-Acoustic Music Association of Great Britain: Newsletter

E.M.B. News
H–Budapest: Editio Musica Budapest, ?–
[NOT IN BUCOMP1]

Lcm 1981, 1, 2; 1982, 2; 1984, 1, 2; 1985, 2; 1986, 1

E.M.G. Hand-Made Gramophones Limited: the Monthly Letter: a Review of Recent Recordings
TNG GB360
GB–London: EMG, 1930–80
[Cumulated as *The Art of Record Buying: a List of Recommended Microgroove Recordings* (q.v.)]

CFp 39 (1969)–50 (1980)
Cpl 17 (1947)–31 (1961)*
Cu 21 (1951), 10–50 (1980)*
DOR 43 (1973)–49 (1979), May
Ep 27 (1957)–50 (1980)
KE 20 (1950)–24 (1954), 5
Lbl*
Lcml (m) 22 (1952)–50 (1980)
Lsa 6 (1936)–50 (1980)
LVp 41 (1971)–43 (1973); 46 (1976)–50 (1980)
Mcm 44 (1974)–50 (1980)
Mpl 32 (1962)–49 (1979)
NTp 8 (1958)–50 (1980)
Ob*
SA 18 (1948), 10–40 (1970), 3 [w 20 (1950), 4; 22 (1952), 4; 35 (1965), 3; 37 (1967), 3]
STAp 32 (1962)–49 (1979)

EMI News
GB–London: EMI, ?–?

Lsa 72–155, 1970–79

E-Mix: New Age, Synthesizer and Experimental Music
0960–3425
GB–London: E–Mix, 1992–
[NOT IN BUCOMP1]

Lbl*

The Encore
GB–London, 1956–?65

EIR:Dtc 1956–65
Lba 1956–65
Lbl*

The Encore: a Music Hall and Theatrical Review
Fellinger 1968/1180; TNG GB147
GB–London, 1892–1930

Lbl*

Encore: the Journal of Birmingham Philharmonic Orchestra
0956–0254
GB–Edgbaston, Birmingham: Robert Blunsom, 1988–
[NOT IN BUCOMP1]

Lbl 2, 1988–#

Énekszó [= Song]
TNG H71
H–Budapest, 1933–49

Lbl*
Lu 10 (1943), 4–14 (1946), 75

English Church Music: a Quarterly Record of the Art
TNG GB337; 0265–4563
GB–Croydon: Royal School of Church Music, 1931–80 ; 1981–86
[Published in annual volumes from 1964. Succeeded from 1981–86 by *The World of Church Music*]

AB 1 (1931)–26 (1956)
Bp 33 (1963); 37 (1967)–50 (1980);. 1982–86
BTu 37 (1967); 39 (1969); 41 (1971)–43 (1973)
Cu 1, 1963–#
EIR:Dtc 1 (1931)–32 (1962), 3
En 1 (1931)– 32 (1962)
Ep 34 (1964); 37 (1967)–42 (1972); 45 (1975)–50 (1980); 1982; 1984–85
Er 15 (1945), 3; 16 (1946), 1, 3, 4; 17 (1947)–20 (1950), 1, 3, 4; 21 (1951)–22

(1952), 3; 23 (1953), 1, 4; 24(1954)–26
(1956), 1, 3; 27 (1957)–29 (1959), 2; 30
(1960), 1, 3; 31(1961)–32 (1962)
Lam 24 (1954), 4; 28 (1958), 1; 29 (1959)–32
(1962), 3
LAu 36 (1966)–37 (1967); 39 (1969)–40
(1970); 42 (1972); 45 (1975)–50 (1980);
1981–82; 1984–86
Lcm 28 (1958)–33 (1963); 35 (1965)–47
(1977); 49 (1979)–50 (1980); 1983–86
Lcml 22 (1952)–50 (1980); 1981– 86
Lrscm 1 (1931)–50 (1980); 1981–86
Lu 33 (1963)–34 (1964); 36 (1966)–50
(1980); 1981–86
LVp 28 (1956)–33 (1963); 35 (1965)–37
(1967); 39 (1969)–41 (1971)
Mcm 43 (1973)–50 (1980); 1981–86
Mu 33 (1963); 35 (1965)–39 (1969)
Ob*
Ouf 18 (1948), 2–4; 19 (1949), 1, 2; 20
(1950)–21 (1951), 2, 4; 22 (1952)–24
(1954), 3; 25 (1955)–26 (1956), 3; 27
(1957)–31 (1961), 2; 32 (1962), 2; 1964;
1976, 1977; 1979–82; 1986
SFu 36 (1966)–50 (1980); 1981–82
TOd 41 (1971)–42 (1972); 44 (1974)–48
(1978)
Yu 40 (1970)–50 (1980); 1981–86

**English Dance and Song: the Magazine of the
English Folk Dance and Song Society**
TNG GB358; 0013–8231
GB–London: English Folk Dance and Song
Society, 1936–
[Formerly *E.F.D.S. News* (q.v.). Sometime
subtitled *England's Foremost Folk Music
Magazine*; *see also E.F.D.S.S. News*]

AB*
ALb 25 (1962), 2, 3, 5, 6, 26 (1963), 1, 2, 4–
33 (1971), 1; 40 (1978), 2, 3
Au 46 (1984)–48 (1986)
BAc 46 (1984)–49 (1987), 3; 50 (1988)–53
(1991), 1
BDp 36 (1974)–54 (1992)
BG 1 (1936)–8 (1943), 4, 6; 9 (1944), 1–5; 10
(1945)–14 (1949), 1–3; 15 (1950)–16
(1951), 1, 3–6; 17 (1952)–19 (1954), 1–5;
20 (1955), 1, 4–6; 21 (1956)–22 (1957), 1,
4–6; 23 (1959), 1–5; 24 (1960), 2, 3, 5; 25
(1961), 1, 2, 6; 26 (1963)–33 (1971), 3; 34
(1972)–37 (1975), 3; 38 (1976)–40 (1978),
1, 3; 41 (1979)–#
BLp 1 (1936)–#
BRp 29 (1967)–#
BSdsc 10 (1945), 4–#

Cat 33 (1971)–41 (1979), 1; 42 (1980)–#
CCtc 37 (1975)–#
CH 51 (1989)–#
Cpl 1 (1936)–12 (1948), 1
EIR:Dp 50 (1988)–53 (1991), 1
EIR:Dtc 1 (1936)–#
En 1 (1936)–#
EXu 29 (1967)–56 (1994), 1
Gm 1 (1936)– #
Gul 1 (1936)–50 (1988)
HE 47 (1985)–#
Lam 32 (1970), 3
LAu 32 (1970)–38 (1976)*
Lbar 12 (1948), 4–36 (1974) [w 16 (1951), 2;
25 (1961), 2]; 38 (1976)–40 (1978); 44
(1982)–45 (1983)
Lbl*
Lcm 1 (1934)–9 (1944), 5; 10 (1945)–11
(1946), 5; 13 (1948)–14 (1949), 3; 15
(1950); 16 (1951), 2, 4 –23 (1959), 5; 24
(1960), 1, 3–5; 25 (1961), 1, 3, 4, 6; 26
(1963), 2; 27 (1965), 5; 28 (1966), 1, 2, 4,
5; 29 (1967)–31 (1969), 3; 32 (1970)–49
(1987), 1, 3–#
Lcml 12 (1947)*; 14 (1949)–16 (1951); 17
(1952)*; 18 (1953)–#
Lcml (m) [c (1 year)]
Lcs 1 (1936)–49 (1987), 3; 50 (1988)–#
Lgo 35 (1973), 2– 52 (1990)
Llp 22 (1957)–#
Lkc 28 (1966)–39 (1977); 40 (1978)*; 41
(1979)–46 (1984); 47 (1985)–48 (1986)*
Lsa 19 (1954)–#
Lu 6 (1941)–#
LVp 1 (1936)–53 (1991)
Mmu (a) 41 (1979)–#
Mpl 1 (1936)–#
NO 45 (1983), 2–53 (1991), 1
NOp 35 (1973)–#
NTp 1 (1936)–#
Ob*
Op 3 (1938)–50 (1988)
Oub 44 (1982)–49 (1987)
Ouf (Howes) 5 (1940/41), 1–6; 6 (1941/42),
1–6; 7 (1942/43), 1, 3, 4, 6; 8 (1943/44), 1;
25 (1962/63), 1; 26 (1963/64), 1, 4, 5; 27
(1964/65), 1–5; 28 (1966), 1–5; 29 (1967),
1–4; 30 (1968), 1–4; 31 (1969), 1–4; 33
(1971), 2; 36 (1974), 1
R 47 (1985), 3; 48 (1986)–49 (1987), 2
SFp 1 (1936)–14 (1949); 16 (1951)–25
(1961); 28 (1966)–53 (1991)
TOd 27 (1965), 4–#
WF 28 (1966), 4, 5; 29 (1967)–#
Yu 30 (1968)–52 (1990)

English Folk Dance and Song Society Bulletin
TNG GB410
GB–London, 1948–50

> **AB** 3–13, 1948–50 [w 8]
> **CCtc** 8 (1956)–9 (1964)
> **En** 1948–50
> **Lbl***
> **Lu** 1, 3–13, 1948–50
> **Ob***

English Folk Dance and Song Society Reports
GB–London: English Folk Dance and Song
Society, ?1914–89
[NOT IN BUCOMP1]

> **Gm** 1931–71
> **Gul** 1922–36*
> **LAu** 1970–73
> **Lu** 1942
> **Ob***

English Folk Dance and Song Society *see also*
E.F.D.S.S.

English Folk Dance Society *see also* E.F.D.S.

The English Folk Dance Society's Journal
TNG GB265 (1st ser.)
GB–London: English Folk Dance Society,
1914–15
[Succeeded by the *Journal of the English Folk
Dance Society* (q.v.)]

> **AB***
> **Au** 1 (1914/15), 1, 2
> **BDp** 1 (1914/15)
> **EIR:Dtc** 1 (1914–15), 2
> **HUu** 1 (1914/15), 1, 2 [Reprint ed.]
> **Lbl***
> **Lcm** 1 (1914/15)
> **Lcml** 1 (1914/15)*
> **Lcs** 1 (1914/15), 1, 2
> **Mpl** 1 (1914/15)
> **Ob***

English Folklore in Dance and Song
NZ–?: English Folk Dance and Song Society
New Zealand, 1938–44
[NOT IN BUCOMP1]

> **Lcs** 1–15, 1938–44

**English Harpsichord Magazine and Early
Keyboard Instrument Review** *see* **The
Harpsichord Magazine and Early Keyboard
Instrument Review**

**The English Musical Gazette, or, Monthly
Intelligencer**
Fellinger 1968/46; TNG GB8
GB–London: Sherwood, Neely and Jones, 1819
[Only seven numbers issued]

> **Bu** 1819, Jan–July
> **Cu** 1819, Jan–July
> **Gul (e)** 1819, Jan–July; another copy, 1819,
> Jan 1
> **Lbl** 1819, Jan–July

**English Song: Bulletin of the English Song
Award**
GB–Blandford Forum: English Song Award,
1984–
[NOT IN BUCOMP1]

> **Lbar** 1–7, 1984–88

ENO and Friends
GB–London: English National Opera, ?–
[NOT IN BUCOMP1; from 1980–82 entitled
*Friends: Magazine of Friends of English
National Opera*]

> **Lcml** 35–46, 197?–?

Ensemble [1]
TNG GB306
GB–Leicester, 1925–26

> **Lbl***

Ensemble [2]
GB–London, 1966–?

> **Cbijs** 5, 7, 8, 10, 11, 1967–68

The Entertainer
Fellinger 1968/1530; TNG GB189
GB–Birmingham: Langford's Entertainment
Agency, 1900–02

> **Ob***

Entertaining *see* **Crest Musical Bulletin**

Entertainment News
EIRE–Castleblayney, 1978–
[NOT IN BUCOMP1]

> **Cu** 1 (1978), 18–4 (1981), 4*
> **Ob** 1 (1978), 17–#

Entretemps
F–Paris: Entretemps, 1986–92
[NOT IN BUCOMP1; ceased publication with no. 10, 1992]

   Cu 3–9, 1987–90
   Lkc 3–10, 1987–92
   Ouf 1–3, 1986–87

Eolian Review
TNG US470
US–New York: National Association of Harpists, 1921–32
[From vol. 4 (1925) entitled *Eolus*]

   Lcml 8 (1929), 1

Eolus *see* **Eolian Review**

Eonta
0960–3417
GB–London: Eonta, 1991–
[NOT IN BUCOMP1]

   EXu 1 (1991)–3 (1993)
   Ob*

Ephemeriden der Litteratur und des Theaters
see **Literatur- und Theater-Zeitung**

E.P.T.A. UK Bulletin
GB–London: European Piano Teachers' Association [EPTA] (UK Branch), 198?–
[NOT IN BUCOMP1]

   Lbl 27, 1987–#

The Era Annual *see* **The Era Dramatic and Musical Almanack**

The Era Dramatic and Musical Almanack
GB–London, 1868–1919
[Entitled *The Era Annual* from 1893–1919]

   Lbl*
   Ob*

The Erich Wolfgang Korngold Society Newsletter
GB–Paisley: Erich Wolfgang Korngold Society, 1982–87

   Cu*
   Lbar 1–17, 1982–86
   Lbl*
   Lcml 1–17, 1982–86
   Mpl*
   Ob*

The Ernest Bloch Society Bulletin
0071–1195
US–Gualala, CA [etc.]: The Ernest Bloch Society, 1967–

   AB 14 (1982)
   Cpl 3 (1970)–10 (1977)
   En 17 (1985)–20 (1988); 23 (1991)–#
   Gam 8 (1975)–10 (1977); 15 (1983)–23 (1991)
   Lam 7 (1974)–8 (1975); 10 (1977); 12 (1980); 23 (1991)
   Lbbc 7 (1974)–10 (1977); 14 (1982); 16 (1984)–#
   Lcm 12 (1980)–23 (1981)
   Lcml 3 (1970)–15 (1983)
   Lu 18 (1986)–19 (1987); 20 (1988)–23 (1991)
   Ob*
   Ouf 7 (1974)–#
   R 17 (1985)–19 (1987)

ESCOM Newsletter
B–Liege: European Society for the Cognitive Sciences of Music, 1992–
[NOT IN BUCOMP1]

   Cu 1, 1992–#

ESEM
F–Toulouse: European Seminar in Ethnomusicology, 19?–
[NOT IN BUCOMP1]

   Lsa 25, 1995–#

Esercizi: Arte, Musica, Spettacolo
I–Perugia: Università degli Studi di Perugia [etc.], 1978–91
[NOT IN BUCOMP1; last number issued was no. 10 (1991), which bore concurrent numbering of n. s. 1, and title *Esercizi: Musica e Spettacolo* (q.v.)]

   Cu*

Esercizi: Musica e Spettacolo
I–Perugia: Cattedra di Storia della Musica/Università degli Studi, 1991–
[NOT IN BUCOMP1; succeeded *Esercizi: Arte, Musica, Spettacolo* (q.v.)]

   Bu 10 (1991)–11 (1992) [= n.s. 1, 2]
   Lbl 10 (1991)–# [= n.s. 1]
   Lu 11 (1992) [= n.s. 2]
   Ouf 12 (1993)–# [= n.s. 3]

Essercizi: the Nottingham Concert
Supplement
0964–2048
GB–Nottingham, 1991
[NOT IN BUCOMP1]

Lbl*

Essex Folk News
GB–South Benfleet: English Folk Dance and
Song Society, Essex District, 1973–
[NOT IN BUCOMP1]

Cu 38, 1983–#
Lbl*

EST: Electric Shock Treatment
0965– 6170
GB–Winchester, 1991–
[NOT IN BUCOMP1]

Lbl*

E.S.T.A. News and Views
GB–Penrith [etc.]: European String Teachers'
Association, 1977–
[NOT IN BUCOMP1; a selection of items from
this journal is published occasionally in E.S.T.A.
Review (2 vols published to date, in 1980 and
1994)]

ALb 2 (1977), 2; 3 (1978), 1
BLp [c]
Cu 6 (1981)–#
Gam 16 (1991), 3–#
Lam 1 (1976/77); 5 (1980), 2; 7 (1982), 3; 8
   (1983), 3; 11 (1986), 2–18 (1993), 4; 19
   (1994), 2–#
Lcm 11 (1986), 1; 12 (1987), 2; 16 (1991), 3;
   17 (1992), 3; 18 (1993)–19 (1994), 3
Lgsm 16 (1991), 3; 17 (1992)–#
Ltc 16 (1991), 1, 3; 18 (1993)–19 (1994), 2;
   20 (1995), Spr; 21 (1996), Sum; 22 (1997)–
   #
Mcm 5 (1980), 2; 10 (1985), 3; 11 (1986), 1;
   12 (1987)–#
NTp [c (2 years)]

E.S.T.A. Review see E.S.T.A. News and Views

ESZ News: Notizario delle Edizioni Suvini
Zerboni
I–Milan: Edizioni Suvini Zerboni, ?–
[NOT IN BUCOMP1]

ALb 1993, Feb, Apr

État Actuel de la Musique de la Chambre du
Roi et des Trois Spectacles de Paris
F–Paris, 1759–60; 1767–78
[From 1767 entitled État Actuel de la Musique
du Roi et des Trois Spectacles de Paris]

Lbl*

État Actuel de la Musique du Roi et des Trois
Spectacles de Paris see État Actuel de la
Musique de la Chambre du Roi et des Trois
Spectacles de Paris

Eternity: the Magazine for the Scene
1350–8504
GB–Wakefield: Eternity Magazine, ?1992–
[NOT IN BUCOMP1]

Lbl*

Ethnic: a Quarterly Survey of English Folk
Music, Dance and Drama
0423–5355
GB–London, 1959
[Ceased publication with vol. 1 no. 4 (1959)]

EIR:Dtc 1 (1959), 1–4
Lbl*
Ob 1 (1959), 1–4

Ethnomusicologie
0299–3201
F–Paris: SELAF, 1985–
[NOT IN BUCOMP1]

BSdsc*

Ethnomusicology see Ethno-Musicology
Newsletter

Ethnomusicology and Systematic Musicology
at UCLA: Newsletter
US–Los Angeles, CA: University of California,
Department of Ethnomusicology and Systematic
Musicology, 1983–

Cu 1 (1983)–#
Lsa 1 (1983), 2–# [w 3 (1985), 2, 3; 5 (1987),
   2, 3]
Lu 8 (1993), 1

Ethno-Musicology Newsletter
TNG US664; 0014–1836; 0046–2624
US–Bloomington, IN: Society for Ethno-
Musicology, Indiana University, 1953–
[From 1957 entitled Ethnomusicology
Newsletter; from 1957, 9, Ethnomusicology]

ALb n.s. 3 (1959), 2
BAc n.s. 27 (1983)–#
BLu 1–11, 1953–57; n.s. 1 (1957)–#*
Bp n.s. 8 (1964)–12 (1968); 16 (1972)–#
Bs n.s. 34 (1990), 3–#
BSdsc*
Bu n.s. 16 (1972)–33 (1989)
Cat n.s. 19 (1975)–24 (1980), 2; 25 (1981)–
    27 (1983), 2, 3 [w 1]; 28 (1984), 2, 3;
    29 (1985)–31 (1987), 1; 32 (1988)–#
Cpl n.s. 30 (1986)–#Cu 1–11 1953–57; n.s.
    1 (1957)=#
DRu n.s. 2 (1958)–#
EIR:Dtc n.s. 2 (1958)–#
En n.s. 2 (1958)–#
EXu n.s. 27 (1983)–28 (1984), 2, 3; 29
    (1985)–#
Gam n.s. 33 (1989)–#Gul n.s. 36 (1992)–#
KE n.s. 31 (1987)–#
Lbl*
Lcml 4, 1955; 7, 1956; n.s. 12 (1968)–#
Lcs*
Lcu 1–11, 1953–57; n.s. 2 (1958), 1, 2; 3
    (1959)–8 (1964), 2; 9 (1965), 1, 2; 10
    (1966); 11 (1967), 2; 12 (1968)–#
Lgo 1–11, 1953–57
Lkc n.s. 11 (1967)–31 (1987); 33 (1989)–#
Lki n.s. 21 (1977)–#
LRHBNC n.s. 21 (1977)–#
Lro n.s. 20 (1976)–#
Lsa 1–5, 1953–55; n.s. 2 (1958)–#
Lso 1–11, 1953–57; n.s. 2 (1958)–#
Lu 1–11, 1953–57; n.s. 1 (1957)–#
Mu n.s. 24 (1980)–#
NO n.s. 2 (1958), 3; 5 (1961)–7 (1963);
    19 (1975)–34 (1990)
Ob*
Ouf 1–11, 1953–57; n.s. 1 (1957)–36 (1992),
    3
SLGu n.s. 24 (1980) 28 (1984), 3; 29
    (1985)–#
SOu n.s. 35 (1991)–#
TOd n.s. 16 (1972), 3; 21 (1977)–22 (1978);
    24 (1980)–34 (1990), 2; 35 (1991)–38
    (1994),1
Uu n.s. 24 (1980)–29 (1985)
Yu 1–11, 1953–57; n.s. 2 (1958)–#

The Etude: a Monthly Journal for Musicians
Fellinger 1968/922; TNG US181
US–Philadelphia, PA: Theodore Presser, 1883–
1957
[From vol. 14 (1896) entitled The Etude and

Musical World; from vol. 40 (1922), 2–66
(1948), 11 entitled The Etude Music Magazine;
from vol. 66 (1948), 12 entitled Etude: the
Music Magazine; ceased publication with vol.
75 (1957), 5]

Ep 36 (1918)–37 (1919); 39 (1921)–41
    (1923); 43 (1925)–46 (1928)
Er 42 (1924), 11; 43 (1925), 1–11; 44 (1926),
    1–9, 12; 45 (1927)–51 (1933), 1
Lam 29 (1911), 2; 71 (1953), 10–73 (1955),
    8, 10, 11; 74 (1956), 2–75 (1957), 5
Lbl 38 (1920), 4–42 (1924), 12
Lcm (p) 46 (1928), 2; 49 (1931), 3; 56
    (1938), 9, 11; 58 (1940), 3, 5; 70 (1952), 4
LEbc 53 (1935), 12; 54 (1936), 2–6, 8, 9, 11;
    55 (1937), 1, 5–7
LVp 72 (1954); 75 (1957)
Mcm 65 (1947), 1

Etude: Music...Ballet...Opera
GB–London: Rossimer Musical Enterprises, ?–
[NOT IN BUCOMP1]

AB 1963, July–Sep

Etude: the Music Magazine see The Etude: a
Monthly Journal for Musicians

The Etude and Musical World see The Etude:
a Monthly Journal for Musicians

The Etude Music Magazine see The Etude: a
Monthly Journal for Musicians

Etudes Grégoriennes
TNG F647; 0071-2086
F–Solesmes: Editions Abbaye S. Pierre de
Solesmes, 1954–

Lu 1 (1954)–#
Ob*
Ouf 1 (1954)–23 (1989)

Eureka
GB–London, 1897–1903
[From 1898 entitled The Favourite Magazine]

Lbl*

Eureka: the Bi-Monthly Magazine of New
Orleans Jazz
GB–London: New Orleans Jazz Society, 1960–

Cbijs 1 (1960), 4, 6; 2 (1961), 1
LOnjfa*

Eurojazz Review
GB–Sussex, 1994–
[NOT IN BUCOMP1]

   Lsa 1, 1994–#

Europe Etc.: Music Week's European Trade
Commentary
GB–London, 1992–
[NOT IN BUCOMP1]

   AB 1992, Jan–Nov
   Lsa 1992, Mar, May–Oct; 1993–#

European Piano Teachers' Association: U.K.
Bulletin see E.P.T.A UK Bulletin

European Seminar in Ethnomusicology see
ESEM

European Society for the Cognitive Sciences
of Music see ESCOM Newsletter

European String Teachers' Association see
E.S.T.A. News and Views

European String Teachers' Association see
also E.S.T.A. Review

Eurovision Network News
0962–0281
GB–London: Eurovision Network, 1989–
[NOT IN BUCOMP1]

   Lbl 11, 1990–#

Euskor: Euskadiko Orkestra Sinfonikoaren
Boletin Albistaria/Boletin Informativo de la
Orquesta Sinfonica de Euskadi
E–Donostia: Euskadiko Orkestra Sinfonika,
198?–
[NOT IN BUCOMP1]

   Lbl 12, 1985–#

Euterpe, or the Musical Quarterly
Fellinger 1968/1969; TNG GB236
GB–London, 1909–10

   EIR:Dtc 1–4, 1909–10
   Lbl*
   Ob 1–4, 1909–10

The Euterpean: a Critical Review of Music
and the Drama, and Record of Public
Entertainment

Fellinger 1968/264; TNG GB41
GB–London, 1849
[14 nos in total]

   Bu 1–14, 1849
   Lbl*

The Euterpeiad: an Album of Music, Poetry
and Prose
TNG US4
US–New York, 1830–31

   Cu [m]
   Mu [m]

The Euterpeiad, or Musical Intelligencer and
Ladies Gazette
Fellinger 1968/51; TNG US1
US–Boston, MA: T. Badger [et al.], 1820–23;
n.s. 1823, 1, 2

   Au 1 (1820)–3 (1823) [Reprint ed.]
   Cu 1 (1820)–3 (1823); n.s. 1, 2 (1823)
      [Reprint ed.]
   KE 1 (1820)–3 (1823); n.s. 1, 2 (1823)
      [Reprint ed.]
   Mu 1 (1820)–3 (1823); n.s. 1, 2 (1823) [all
      m]
   Ob 1 (1820)–3 (1823) [Reprint ed.]

The Ewe Lamb [translated title] see Oenig

Excelsior
GB–Treorchy: Treorchy and District Male
Choir, 1948–

   AB 1985; 1988–#

Explosive Hits
0961–7817
GB–London: Dennis Oneshots, 1991–
[NOT IN BUCOMP1]

   Lbl*

Extra Kerrang!
GB–London, 198?–
[NOT IN BUCOMP1]

   Cu 3–8, 1984–85

F

Faber Music News see Fortissimo!: Faber
Music News

Fabulous
GB–London, 1964–?
[From 1966 entitled *Fabulous 208* (TNG
GB509); from 1968 cumulated in *Fabulous 208
Annual*]

  Lbl*
  Ob*

Fabulous 208 [Annual] *see* Fabulous

The Face
0263–1210
GB–London: Wagadon, 1980–
[NOT IN BUCOMP1]

  AB*
  Lbl*
  Lsa 7–47, 1980–84
  NTp ?40, 1983–#
  Ob 10, 1981–#

Face Out
0141–6987
GB–Wendover: Face Out, 1978–81

  Cu 1–8, 1978–81
  EIR:Dtc 1–8, 1978–81
  Lbl*
  Ob*

Family Minstrel: a Musical and Literary
Journal
US–New York: J. Devoe, 1835–36
[NOT IN BUCOMP1]

  Mu 1 (1835/36), 1–24 [m]

Fan Library
GB–London, 1982–83

  Cu 1–12, 1982–83

Fanfare: a Monthly Magazine Published…in
the Interest of the Professional Musician, the
Amateur and All those People interested in
Jazz and the Modern Music
TNG GB380
GB–London, 1943–?46; 1946–47
[Continued as *Music of Today* (London: Fanfare,
1946–47); issue for 1946, Dec entitled *Musical
Fare*; for 1947, Jan, *Musical Review and
Pictorial*; for 1947, Mar–Sep, *Musical Accent*]

  Lbl*
  LOnjfa*

Fanfare: a Musical Causerie
TNG GB286
GB–London: Goodwin and Tabb, 1921–22
[Incorporated into *The Musical Mirror and
Fanfare* from Feb. 1922]

  AB*
  Bu 1 (1921/22), 1–7
  Cu 1 (1921/22), 1–7
  EIR:Dtc 1 (1921/22), 1–7
  En 1 (1921/22)
  Lam 1 (1921/22), 1–7
  Lbbc 1 (1921/22), 1–4
  Lbl*
  Lu 1 (1921/22)
  Ob*

Fanfare: Journal of the Royal Military School
of Music, Kneller Hall
TNG GB533; 0967–9081
GB–Twickenham: Royal Military School of
Music, 1968–

  AB*
  Cu 1 (1968/77)–#
  EIR:Dtc 1 (1968/77)–#
  En 1 (1968/77)–#
  Lam 1 (1968/77); 2 (1979/87), 3, 4, 6, 8–10;
    3 (1989/90), 2, 3
  Lcm 1 (1968–77)–2 (1979/87), 1, 6, 9; 3
    (1989/90), 2
  Lgsm 1 (1968/77)

Fanfare: the Bulletin of the Birmingham
School of Music
TNG GB387
GB–Birmingham: Birmingham School of
Music, 1946–?

  Bu 1 (1946), 9–2 (1952), 9

Fanfare: the Magazine for Serious Record
Collectors
TNG US872; 0148–9364
US–Tenafly, NJ: Fanfare, Inc., 1977–
[NOT IN BUCOMP1]

  Ea [c (3 years)]
  Lsa 1, 1977, Sep–#
  Ob*

Fanfare: the Newsletter of the Folk Arts
Network
GB–Newcastle-upon-Tyne: Folk Arts Network,
?–
[NOT IN BUCOMP1]

  Lcs 1993, Sum–#

Fanfare from the Royal Philharmonic Society
GB–London: Royal Philharmonic Society,
1993–
[NOT IN BUCOMP1]

    Cu 1, 1993–#
    Lam 1, 1993–#

Fanz
0957–5480
GB–Huntingdon: Diphold, 1988–
[NOT IN BUCOMP1]

    Lbl 1988–#*

Farben
0969–5044
GB–Brighton: Orchid Publishing, 1991–
[NOT IN BUCOMP1]

    Cu 1 (1991)–#
    KE 1 (1991)–#
    Lbl*
    Ob*

Fast Forward
GB–London: BBC Magazines, 1989–
[NOT IN BUCOMP1; incorporating *Number One*]

    Cu 57, 1990–#
    Ob 57, 1990–#

The Favourite Magazine *see* **Eureka**

Federation of British Music Industries: Convention Journal *see* **The Federation of British Music Industries Journal**

The Federation of British Music Industries Journal
TNG GB288
GB–London, 1921–29
[From 1927 entitled *Federation of British Music Industries: Convention Journal* (TNG GB315)]

    Lbl*
    Ob*

Federation of Recorded Music Societies Bulletin *see* **FRMS Bulletin**

Fellowship of Makers and Restorers of Historic Instruments: Bulletin
TNG GB574
GB–Oxford, 1975–
[From 2, 1976, entitled *Fellowship of Makers and Restorers of Historic Instruments: Bulletin and Communications*; from 12, 1978, entitled *FOMRHI Quarterly*]

    Cpl 10, 1978–#
    Cu 34, 1984–#
    EIR:Dtc 34, 1984–#
    Er 71, 1993–#
    Lcm (m) 1, 1975–#
    Lkc 1–10, 1975–78; 12– 15, 1978–79
    Mcm 1, 1975–#
    Ob*

Fender Musician
0261–8222
GB–Enfield: CBS Arbiter, 1981–

    Lbl*

Fenton's Letter: a Monthly Review of New Records
TNG GB419
GB–London, 1949–50
[From 1950, Sep. entitled *The Record Review*]

    Lsa 1–13, 1949–50
    Lu 1–13, 1949–50

Festival Times
GB–Edinburgh, 1974–

    En*

Feuilles Musicales: Revue Musicale Romande et Courrier Suisse du Disque
TNG CH137; 0035–3744
CH–Lausanne, 1948–
[From 1963 entitled *Revue Musicale du Suisse Romande: Feuilles Musicales, Courrier Suisse du Disque et Revue Romande de Musique réunis*]

    Lbl*
    Lcm 36 (1983), 3, 4; 37 (1984), 1–4; 38 (1985), 2–4; 39 (1986), 1, 2, 4; 41 (1988), 2, 3; 42 (1989), 1; 44 (1991), 2–6; 45 (1992), 4; 46 (1993), 1–3; 47 (1994)–#
    Mcm 26 (1973), 3, 4; 27 (1974), 1–4; 28 (1975), 1, 2; 29 (1976), 1–4; 30 (1977)–#
    Ob*

Feuillets Suisses de Pédagogie Musicale *see* **Schweizer Muzikpädagogische Blätter/ Feuillets Suisses de Pédagogie Musicale**

The Fiddler: a Quarterly Journal Devoted to All Stringed Instruments Played with the Bow
Fellinger 1968/953; TNG GB113
GB–London, 1884–87

   Lbl 1 (1884)–2 (1885); 3 (1887), 24, 25
   Ob 1 (1884)–3 (1887), 27

The Fifth Stave Accordionist
GB–London, 1937–38

   Lbl*

Figaro: Journal for Literatur, Kunst og Musik
Fellinger 1968/178; TNG DK5
DK–Copenhagen. G. Carstensen, 1841–42
[6 nos in total]

   Lbl*

The Figaro: News from the Welsh National Opera
GB–Bristol: Welsh National Opera, 1984
[NOT IN BUCOMP1]

   AB 1, 1984
   Ob 1, 1984

Film and Filming *see* Seven Arts

Film Music
US–New York, 1989–
[NOT IN BUCOMP1]

   Cu 1, 1989–#

Film Score Monthly
1077–4289
US–Los Angeles, CA: Lukas Kendall, ?1996
[NOT IN BUCOMP1]

   Lam 2 (1997)–#

Financial Times Music and Copyright
0968–0322
GB–London: Financial Times Business Enterprises, 1992–
[NOT IN BUCOMP1]

   EIR:Dtc 1, 1992–#
   Lam 2–16, 1992–93 [w 6]; 19–25, 1993 [w 23]; 30, 1993–# [w 34, 42]
   Lsa 1, 1992–#
   Ob*

Finnish Music Quarterly
0782–1069
FIN–Helsinki: Performing Music Promotion Centre, 1985–
[NOT IN BUCOMP1]

   BLBBC 1985, 1, 2; 1986, 3; 1987, 2–4; 1988, 1, 2, 4; 1989, 2; 1990, 1, 2; 1991, 1; 1992, 1–3; 1993, 2; 1994, 1–#
   Bu 1985, 1–#
   CDu 1993, 3–#
   Cu 1985–87; 1993–#*
   EIR:Driam 1992, 4–#
   En*
   Gsmic [c]
   Lam 1985, 3, 4–1990, 3, 4; 1991, 2–#
   Lbbc 1989, 1–#*
   Lbl 1987, 1–#
   Lcm 1985, 3, 4; 1986–94
   Ouf 1985, 1–# [w 1992, 1]

The Finzi Trust Friends Newsletter
GB–?: The Finzi Trust, ?1983–

   Lbar 5 (1987), 2–#
   Mcm 1 (1983)–#

Il Flauto Dolce: Rivista per lo Studio e la Pratica della Musica Antica
TNG I286
I–Roma: Società Italiana del Flauto Dolce, 1971–88
[NOT IN BUCOMP1; succeeded from 1989 by *Recercare: Rivista per lo Studio e la Pratica della Musica Antica* (q.v.)]

   Mpl 3 (1973)
   Ob 1 (1971)–19 (1988)

Flexipop
GB–London: Colourgold Ltd, 1980–

   Cu 26–32, 1982–83
   Lbl 2, 1980–#*
   Lsa 11–22, 1981–82
   Ob*

Fliegende Blätter für katholische
Kirchenmusik
Fellinger 1968/536; TNG D168; ISSN 0179–
356X
XD–Regensburg: Allgemeiner Cäcilienvereins,
1866–
[Subtitled *Allgemeiner Cäcilienverein für die
Diozesan Deutschlands, Österreich-Ungarns
und der Schweiz*; entitled *Cäcilienvereinsorgan*
from 35 (1900)–36 (1901), 8; *Allgemeiner
Cäcilienverein zur Förderung der katholischen
Kirchenmusik: Cäcilienvereinsorgan* (36 (1901),
9–59 (1927/28); *Allgemeiner Cäcilien-Verein für
Deutschland, Österreich und die Schweiz:
Cäcilienvereinsorgan/Musica Sacra* 60 (1929)–
68 (1937), following merger in 1929 with
*Musica Sacra: Beiträge zur Reform und
Förderung der katholischen Kirchen-Musik*
(q.v.). Succeeded by *Die Kirchenmusik:
Zeitschrift des Allgemeinen Cäcilien-Vereins für
Deutschland, Österreich und die Schweiz* (q.v.),
1 (1938)–7 (1944), 2 [q.v.]; resumed as
*Zeitschrift für Kirchenmusik: CVO: Cäcilien-
Vereins-Organ* (Cologne: Bachem) from vol. 69
(1949)–75 (1955) (ISSN 0179–3578); then
continued as *Musica Sacra: Zeitschrift der
Allgemeinen Cäcilienverbandes für den Landern
der deutschen Sprache* from vol. 76 (1956)
(ISSN 0179–356X)]

> **EIR:MEtc** 9 (1874)–15 (1880); 18 (1883)–23
> (1888); 30 (1897)–54 (1921)*
> **Lbl***

Flourish!
GB–London: Trinity College of Music, 1994–
[NOT IN BUCOMP1]

> **Ep** 1, 1994

Flower Scene and the Love Generation
GB–Nottingham, 1967–

> **AB** 1968–69, 1–4
> **Ob***

Flowers of Music [translated title] *see* Blodau
Cerdd

Flute Talk
0744–6918
US–Evanston, IL: The Instrumentalist
Company, 1981–
[NOT IN BUCOMP1]

> **BLp** [c]
> **EIR:Dp** 13 (1994), Feb–Dec

The Flutist
TNG US467
US–Asheville, NC: E. Medicus, 1920–29
[Ceased publication with vol. 10 no. 2 (1929)]

> **Mcm** 5 (1924), Nov; 6 (1925), Feb; 9 (1928),
> Sep/Oct; 10 (1929), Jan

**The Flutist's Magazine and Musical
Miscellany**
Fellinger 1968/77; TNG GB14; Langley, p. 534
GB–London: Boosey and Co.; Simpkin and
Marshall, 1827–ca. 1830

> **Lbl** 1 (1827)

**Flypost: Free Info on the Best of the Capital's
Music Scene**
0957–4301
GB–London: 19?–
[NOT IN BUCOMP1]

> **Lbl** 22, 1990–

FMQ *see* Finnish Music Quarterly

The Fo'c'sle News
GB–Southampton: Fo'c'sle Folk Music Club, ?–
[NOT IN BUCOMP1]

> **Lbl***
> **SOu** 1972–82

Folk
GB–London: English Folk Dance Society
Publications, 1962–63

> **Cu** 1–3, 1962–63
> **Lbl***
> **Lsa** 1–3, 1962–63

Folk 88 [–90]
GB–Nottingham: Singabout, 1988–90
[NOT IN BUCOMP1]

> **Lcs** 1988–90*

Folk and Country [1]
GB–London; Nantwich, 1971–
[From 1971, 5, entitled *Folk Review*]

> **Cu** 1 (1971/72), 5–8 (1979), 7
> **En** 1 (1971/72), 4–11; 2 (1972/73), 2–12; 3
> (1973)–8 (1979), 7
> **Lcs** 1 (1971/72), 1–4
> **Lsa** 4 (1975), 5–9, 11; 5 (1976), 1–9, 11, 12;
> 6 (1977), 1–8, 10, 12; 7 (1978), 1, 4–12;
> 8 (1979), 1–10, 12
> **Ob***

Folk and Country [2]
FIN–Helsinki: Finnish Folk and Country Music
Society, 198?–
[NOT IN BUCOMP1]

 Lcs 3 (1986), 84

Folk and Country Magazine
GB–Salisbury: Folk and Country, 1974–
[NOT IN BUCOMP1]

 EIR:Dtc 1 (1974), 1

Folk Bulletin
1–?, 1989–
[NOT IN BUCOMP1]

 Lcs 1 (1989)–4 (1992), 1*

Folk Buzz see **Buzz: Folk Topics and News
from Greater Manchester and Cheshire**

The Folk Dancer
GB–Manchester [etc.]: Colonel Henry R.
Baldrey, 1954–64
[Entitled *Folklorist* from 1957; from vol. 8
(1963/64) entitled *Folk Musician and Singer*]

 EIR:Dtc 1 (1954)–8 (1963/64)
 En 1 (1954)–8 (1963/64)
 Lbl*
 Lcml (w) 1 (1954)–7 (1963), 1; 8 (1963/64),
 1–6
 Lcs 1 (1954), 1, 4–2 (1955/56), 2, 6; 3 (1956),
 1–5; 4 (1957)–8 (1963/64), 6
 Mpl 1 (1954)–8 (1963/64)
 Ob*

Folk Directory
TNG GB523; 0430–876X
GB–London: English Folk Dance and Song
Society, 1965–
[NOT IN BUCOMP1]

 AB 1984; 1987–91
 BTu 1986
 Ep 1980–#
 Lk 1965–1966, 1968–#
 Lwwput [c]
 NTp [c (2 years)]
 Ob*
 SA 1986

Folk Harp Journal
TNG US828; 0094–8934
US–Mount Leguna, CA, 1973–

 BG 87, 1995–#
 En 10, 1975–#

**Folk in Kent: the Magazine of the English
Folk Dance and Song Society in Kent, East
and West District**
GB–Tonbridge: The Society, 1960–
[NOT IN BUCOMP1]

 Lbl*

Folk in School
GB–?London, 1971–?

 Mcm 1–6, 1971–73

Folk Life
0430–8778
GB–Cardiff: Folk Life Society, 1963–

 BSdsc*
 EIR:Dtc 1 (1963)–#
 Lbl*
 Lsa 1 (1963)
 Ob*

Folk London
GB–London: English Folk Dance and Song
Society, ?–
[NOT IN BUCOMP1]

 Lbl*
 Lsa 1984, Feb, Mar

**Folk-Lore: a Quarterly Review of Myth,
Tradition, Institution and Custom** see
Folklore: the Journal of the Folklore Society

Folk Music
GB–London, 1965

 AB 1 (1965), 2, 7–11
 Lcs 1 (1965), 1–11

Folk Music, Ballads and Songs
GB–Cheshire: K. F. Dallas, 1966–?67
[NOT IN BUCOMP1]

 LAu 1–5, 1966–67 [w 4]
 Lcs 1–5, 1966–67
 Mpl*

Folk Music Journal
TNG GB518; 0531–9684
GB–London: English Folk Dance and Song
Society, 1965–
[Preceded by the *Journal of the English Folk
Dance and Song Society* (TNG GB341). Five
numbers, published annually, comprise one
volume]

AB 1 (1965/69)–#
ALb 1 (1965/69), 2–2 (1970/74), 1; 3
(1975/79)–4 (1980/84), 1, 3; 5 (1985/89), 1
Au 1 (1965/69)–#
BDp 1 (1965/69)–6 (1990/94)
BG 1 (1965/69), 2, 4, 5; 2 (1970/74), 1, 4, 5;
3 (1975/79), 1, 3–#
BLp 1 (1965/69)–#
BRp 1 (1965/69)–#
BRu 1 (1965/69)–4 (1980/84), 2
BSdsc 1 (1965/69)–#
BTu 4 (1980/84)–#
Cat 2 (1970/74), 2–4 (1980/84), 1, 3, 4;
5 (1985/89)–#
CCtc 3 (1975/79)–#
CFp 1 (1965/69)–#
CH 5 (1985/89)–#*
EIR:Dp 5 (1985)–6 (1990/94), 1
EIR:Dtc 1 (1965/69)–#
En 1 (1965/69)–#
Ep 1 (1965/69)–#
EXu 1 (1965/69)–6 (1990/94), 4
Gm 1 (1965/69)
Gul 1 (1965/69)–5 (1985/89), 4
HE 6 (1990/94), 1–4
LAu 1 (1965/69), 1, 2, 5; 2 (1970/74)–3
(1975/79), 4
Lbar 1 (1965/69)–2 (1970/74), 1, 3, 4
LCdM 3 (1975/79), 2–#
Lcm 1 (1965/69)–#
Lcml 1 (1965/69)–#
Lcml (m) [c (1 year)]
Lcs 5 (1985/89), 2–6 (1990/94), 4
Lcu 6 (1990/94), 3–#
Len 1 (1965/69)
Lgo 1 (1965/69)–6 (1990/94), 1
LIp 1 (1965/69)–#
Lkc 1 (1965/69)–5 (1985/89)*
Lki 2 (1970/74), 4–4 (1980/84), 5
Lmi 2 (1970/74)–6 (1990/94), 2
Lro 5 (1985/89), 1–6 (1990/94), 3
Lsa 1 (1965/69)–# [w 5 (1985/89), 2]
Lu 1 (1965/69)–#
LVp 1 (1965/69)–6 (1990/94), 2
Mmu (a) 1 (1965/69)–#
Mpl 1 (1965/69)–#

NO 4 (1980/84), 4–5 (1985/89), 1, 4, 5;
6 (1990/94), 1
NOp 5 (1985/89), 3–#
NTp 1 (1965/69)–4 (1980/84), 3
Ob*
Oub 4 (1980/84), 3–5 (1985/89), 3
Ouf 1 (1965/69)–3 (1975/79), 5 [w 1
(1965/69), 2]
PRp 3 (1975/79)–4 (1980/84), 3; 5
(1985/89)–6 (1990/94), 2
R 1 (1965/69)–5 (1985/89), 3
SFp 1 (1965/69), 2; 5 (1985/89)*; 6
(1990/94), 1
TOd 2 (1970/74), 5; 3 (1975/79), 1, 2, 4;
4 (1980/84)–#
WF 1 (1965/69), 2–#
Yu 1 (1965/69), 3–6 (1990/94), 2

Folk Music News
GB–London: Goldcity, 1982–?
[NOT IN BUCOMP1]

Lcs F1–F4, 1982

Folk Musician
GB–Kegworth: English Folk Dance and Song
Society, 1993–
[NOT IN BUCOMP1]

Lcs 1, 1993–#

Folk Musician [translated title] *see also*
Spelmannen

Folk Musician and Singer *see* **The Folk
Dancer**

Folk News [1]
GB–London: British Federation of Folk Clubs,
1971–?
[NOT IN BUCOMP1]

Lcs 3 (1971), July

Folk News [2]
0140–0851
GB–London: Folk News Publications, 1977–81
[From 1980 entitled *Acoustic Music: Successor
to Folk News* (ISSN 0143–568X; London: Gold
City); issue 25 entitled *Acoustic Music, and
Folk Song and Dance News*]

Cu 24–32, 1979–81
EIR:Dtc 1–23, 1977–79; 26–32, 1980–81
En*
Lbl*

Lcs 1, 2, 1977–78; 16–23, 1978–79; 25–32, 1979–81
Lsa 1, 2, 1977–78; 16–23, 1978–79; 24–32, 1979–81
Ob*

Folk News [3]
GB–Oxford: English Folk Dance and Song Society (Oxfordshire District), 19?–
[NOT IN BUCOMP1]

Lbl*
Ob 1979, Dec–#

Folk News *see also* **Bristol Folk News**

Folk News Kernow
GB–St Colomb: English Folk Dance and Song Society, Cornwall District, ?1972–
[NOT IN BUCOMP1]

Lbl*
Ob 4 (1975)–#

Folk North West *see* **North West Federation of Folk Clubs News**

Folk Notes *see* **Scottish Folk Notes**

Folk on Tap: Magazine for the Southern Counties Folk Federation
GB–?Southampton: Southern Counties Folk Federation, ?1977–
[NOT IN BUCOMP1]

Ob*
SOu 2–3, 1978–79; 5, 1979; 9, 1981
WCp (p) 1982–85, 1987–#
WCp (s) 1991–#

Folk Penny Bit: a Magazine of Local Folk News [for East Anglia]
GB–Ipswich, 1980–
[NOT IN BUCOMP1]

Ob 1, 1980–#

Folk Review
TNG GB538
GB–London: Hanover Books, 1969–79
[Ceased publication with vol. 8 no. 7 (1979)]

EIR:Dtc 2 (1971), 6–8 (1979), 7
Lbl 3 (1972), 5–8 (1979), 7
Lcs 3 (1972)–8 (1979)
Lsa 4 (1975)–8 (1979)*
Ob*

Folk Review *see also* **Folk and Country [1]**

Folk Roots *see* **Southern Rag**

Folk Scene
GB–Woodham Walter, 1964–66

Cu 1–18, 1964–66
Lbl*
Ob*

Folk Song Research
GB–Andover, 1982–

AB 1 (1982)–2 (1984); 6 (1988), 2, 3
Cu 1 (1982)–2 (1984); 6 (1988), 2–#
En*
Lcs 4 (1986), 3–6 (1988), 3
Ob*

Folk Write from Gloucestershire
0967–9189
GB–Cheltenham: English Folk Dance and Song Society (Gloucestershire District), 1977–
[NOT IN BUCOMP1; from vol. 3 (1979) entitled *Folkwrite: the Folk Magazine for Gloucestershire with Hereford and Worcester Dates*]

Lbl*
Lcs 1, 1977–#
Lsa 45–47, 1992–93; 52, 1994–#
Ob 11, 1982–#

Folklore
GB–English Folk Dance and Song Society, Dorset District, 198?–
[NOT IN BUCOMP1]

Lbl*

Folklore: the Journal of the Folklore Society
0015–587X
GB–London: Folklore Society, 1878–
[NOT IN BUCOMP1; previously entitled *Folk-Lore: a Quarterly Review of Myth, Tradition, Institution and Custom*]

TOd 76 (1965), 3–88 (1975)*

Folklore and Folk Music Archivist
TNG US698; 0430–8840
US–Bloomington, IN: Indiana University, 1958–68

Lbl*
Lsa 1 (1958)–10 (1967/68)
Ob*
Yu 10 (1967/68), 1–3

Folklore Macdonien *see* Makedonski Folklor

Folklorist *see* The Folk Dancer

Folk's On!: a Folk Music Journal for South-East Scotland
0267–3665
GB–Edinburgh: Edinburgh Folk Club, 1983–
[NOT IN BUCOMP1]

  Ep 1 (1983/84)–3 (1985/86), 3
  Lbl*
  Ob*

Folksong in the Classroom: a Network of Teachers of History, Literature, Music and the Humanities
US–Northampton, MA [etc.]: L. Seidman, 1980–
[NOT IN BUCOMP1]

  Lcs 1 (1980)–#*

Folksouthern
GB–Templecombe: Slades Hill Nurseries, 1968–?73
[NOT IN BUCOMP1]

  SOu 1–58, 1968–73, July [w 29, 30, 1971; 44, 1972; 56, 1973]

Folkwrite: the Folk Magazine for Gloucestershire with Hereford and Worcester Dates *see* Folk Write from Gloucestershire

FOMRHI Quarterly *see* Fellowship of Makers and Restorers of Historic Instruments: Bulletin

Fondation Eugène Ysaye: Bulletin d'Information
TNG B151; 0015–6051
B–Brussels: Fondation Eugène Ysaye, 1961–
[Also entitled *Information: Fondation Eugène Ysaye*]

  Lsa 2, 3, 1962; 20, 21, 1969; 25, 1970; 42, 44–46, 48, 1974–75

Fonn
EIRE–Newry: Cómhaltas Ceoltóirí Éireann, 1963–65

  Cu 1–13, 1963–65
  EIR:Dtc 1–12, 1963–65
  Lbl*
  Ob*

Fono-Forum: Magazin für gute Musik und Hi-Fi
TNG D985
D–Bielefeld: Bielefelder Verlagsanstalt, 1979–
[NOT IN BUCOMP1]

  ALb 1980, June

Fono-Forum: Zeitschrift für die Freunde guter Musik *see* Fono-Forum: Zeitschrift für Schallplatte, Musik und Hi-Fi Technik

Fono-Forum: Zeitschrift für Schallplatte, Musik und Hi-Fi Technik
0015– 6140
D–Hamburg, 1956–
[? Sometime subtitled *Zeitschrift für die Freunde guter Musik*]

  Lam 2, 3, 1956
  Lsa 4–27, 1959–82; 1983–85

Fonografiek [= Phonographic]
NL–Amersfoort, 1967–

  Lsa 1–22, 1967; 33–67, 1968–69

Fontes Artis Musicae: Review of the International Association of Music Libraries
TNG INTL16; 0015–6191
D/US–Kassel: Bärenreiter, 1954–92; Madison, WI: A–R Editions [for the International Association of Music Libraries, Archives and Documentation Centres], 1993–
[Preceded 1952–53 by the *International Association of Music Libraries: Bulletin d'Information* (q.v.); subtitled *Journal of the International Association of Music Libraries, Archives and Documentation Centres (IAML)* from 40 (1993)]

  AB*
  ABc (ILS) 2 (1955)–3 (1956); 7 (1960); 9 (1962)–#
  ALb 25 (1978), 4–# [w 27 (1980), 3, 4; 37 (1990), 2–4; 38 (1991), 1]
  Au 13 (1966)–#
  BAc 13 (1966)–14 (1967); 17 (1970)–18 (1971), 3; 20 (1973)–33 (1986)
  BDp 11 (1964)–32 (1985)
  BLp 6 (1959)–#
  BLu 1 (1954)–#
  Bp 1 (1954)–#
  BRp 1 (1954); 3 (1956)–#
  BRu 1 (1954)–27 (1980)
  Bs 12 (1965)–#*
  BSdsc*

BTu 18 (1971)–#
Bu 1 (1954)–#
CAu 11 (1964)–#
CCtc 27 (1980)–#
CDCp 1 (1954)–29 (1982)
CDu 13 (1966)–#
CFp 18 (1971)–#
CH [c (5 years)]
Cpl 1 (1954)–#
Cu 1 (1954)–#
DOR 25 (1978)–#
DRu 19 (1972)–#
EIR:Dp 34 (1987), 4–#
EIR:Dtc 1 (1954)–#
EIR:Duc 6 (1959)–#
EIR:MEtc 38 (1991)–#
En 1 (1954)–16 (1969); 17 (1970)*; 18
    (1971)–#
Ep 1 (1954)–#
Er 1 (1954)–#
EXu 20 (1973)–#
Gam 4 (1957), 1; 5 (1958)–13 (1966), 1, 2, 4;
    14 (1967)–30 (1983), 1, 2, 4; 31 (1984), 1,
    2–37 (1990), 1, 3, 4; 38 (1991)–#
Gm 1 (1954)–#
Gsmic 35 (1988)–#
Gul 1 (1954)–#
HUu 1 (1954)–39 (1992)
KE 31 (1984)–35 (1988)
Lam 1 (1954)–#
LAu 13 (1966), 1; 19 (1972)–#
Lba 1 (1954)–34 (1987), 1
Lbar 12 (1965)–21 (1974); 29 (1982)–#
    [w 35 (1988), 2–4]
Lbbc 1 (1954)–# [w 24 (1977), 3]
Lbl*
Lbo 34 (1987), 1; 35 (1988), 1; 40 (1993)–#
Lcm 1 (1954)–# [w 31 (1984), 3; 33 (1986),
    1]
Lcml 1 (1954)–#
Len 1 (1954)–#
Lgo 21 (1974)–# [w 35 (1988), 2–37 (1990)]
Lgsm 37 (1990)–#
LIp 11 (1964)–35 (1988), 1
Lk 1 (1954)–#
Lkc 13 (1966)–15 (1968); 16 (1969)*; 17
    (1970)–#
Lki 1 (1954)–8 (1961); 24 (1977)–#
LRHBNC 1 (1954)–#
Lro 31 (1984)–#
Lsa 1 (1954)–16 (1969); 21 (1974)–30
    (1983); 31 (1984), 2, 4; 32 (1985)–35
    (1988); 36 (1989), 1, 2, 4–37 (1990);
    38 (1991), 2–#

Lsut [c]
Ltc 29 (1982), 1, 2; 30 (1983), 3–35 (1988),
    1; 40 (1993), 1, 4–41 (1994), 2; 43 (1996)–
    #
Lu 1 (1954)–#
LVp 2 (1955)–19 (1972); 21 (1974)–#
LVu 1 (1954)–#
Mcm 11 (1964)–#
MK 19 (1972)–#
Mmu 17 (1970)–#
Mpl 1 (1954)–#
Msuc [c (5 years)]
Mu 11 (1964)–#
NO 1 (1954)–#
NOp 24 (1977), 3–#
NTp 1 (1954)–35 (1988) ; 38 (1991)–#
NWu 5 (1958)–30 (1983)
Ob 1 (1954)–#
Ouf 1 (1954)–#
R 1 (1954)–#
SFp 13 (1966)–37 (1990)
SOu 1 (1954)–40 (1993) [w 21 (1974), 3]
STAp 11 (1964)–29 (1982)
WF 31 (1984)–#
WOp [c]
Y 11 (1964)–#
Yu 16 (1969)–#

Fonti Musicali in Italia: Studi e Ricerche
1120–8260
I–Rome: CIDIM/Società Italiana di Musica,
1987–93; 1996–
[NOT IN BUCOMP1. Entitled *Fonti Musicali
Italiani* from ?1996]

Ouf 1 (1987)–#

Fonti Musicali Italiani *see* **Fonti Musicali in
Italia: Studi e Ricerche**

Footnote: the Magazine for New Orleans Jazz
0308–1990
GB–Cambridge: Footnote, 1969–89
[Ceased publication with vol. 20 no. 6 (1989).
Succeeded by *New Orleans Music* (q.v.)]

Cbijs 1 (1969)–20 (1989), 6
EIR:Dtc 12 (1980/81)–20 (1989), 6
En*
Lbl*
LOnjfa*
Lsa 2 (1970)–8 (1976)*
Ob*

For the Record
GB–London: Mechanical Copyright Protection
Society, 1986–
[NOT IN BUCOMP1]

> Lsa 1–22, 1986–92 [w 4–6]
> Ob 1, 1986–#

Fortissimo! Faber Music News
GB–London: Faber Music, 196?–
[NOT IN BUCOMP1]

> AB 1965, Sum; 1966, Aut
> ALb 1991, Aut; 1994, Spr
> EIR:Dtc 1965, Sum

The Forty Fiver
US–New York, 195?–?

> Lsa 5–7, 1956–57*

Forum Musicologicum
TNG CH177
CH–Bern: Francke, 1975–79; Winterthur:
Amadeus, 1980–
[NOT IN BUCOMP1]

> Lu 1 (1975)–#
> Ouf 1 (1975)–4 (1984)

**Forum Musikbibliothek: Beiträge und
Informationen aus der musik
bibliothekarischen Praxis**
0173–5187
D–Berlin: Deutsches Bibliotheksinstitut, 1980–
[NOT IN BUCOMP1]

> Lbl*
> Ouf 1990–#

Foster Hall Bulletin *see* Lilly-Foster Bulletin

Foyer: a Quarterly of Music, Opera and Ballet
see Foyer: a Survey of Music, Opera and
Ballet Past, Present and Future

**Foyer: a Survey of Music, Opera and Ballet
Past, Present and Future**
TNG GB435
GB–London: Staples Press, 1951–52
[Variant subtitle *A Quarterly of Music, Opera
and Ballet*]

> AB 1 (1951)–2 (1952)
> Bp 1 (1951)–2 (1952)
> EIR:Dtc 1 (1951)–2 (1952)
> Lam 1 (1951)
> Lbl*

> Lcml 1 (1951)–2 (1952)
> Lu 1 (1951)–2 (1952)
> Mpl 1 (1951)–2 (1952)
> Ob 1 (1951)–2 (1952)

La France Musicale
Fellinger 1968/135; TNG F26
F–Paris: La France Musicale, 1837–70
[Vols. 1 (1837)–11 (1848) and 15 (1851)–34
(1870), 31 entitled *La France Musicale*; vols.
for 1849–50 entitled *La Musique: Gazette
Universelle des Artistes et Amateurs*]

> Gul (e) 2 (1839)–11 (1848)*; 22 (1858)–23
> (1859)*
> Lbl*
> Lu 7 (1844)–8 (1845)
> Ob*

Frank Comments
GB–Liverpool, 1959–?

> Cbijs 1, 2, 1959

Frankfurter Musik- und Theaterzeitung
TNG D455
D–Frankfurt, 1906–08

> Lbl*

Fraser's Musical Reformer
GB–Edinburgh, 1843–45
[NOT IN BUCOMP1]

> En 1–9, 1843–45

Free Reed: the Concertina Newsletter *see* The
Concertina Newsletter for Players and
Collectors of the Concertina and Related
Metal Reed Instruments

Freeze Frame
GB–London, 1984–?
[NOT IN BUCOMP1]

> Cu 1 (1984/85), 1

**Freie Bühne für den Entwickelungskampf der
Zeit** *see* Freie Bühne für modernes Leben

Freie Bühne für modernes Leben
D–Berlin: S. Fischer, 1890–
[Entitled *Freie Bühne für den
Entwickelungskampf der Zeit*, 1892–93; *Neue
Deutsche Rundschau*, 1894–1903; *Die neue
Rundschau* (ISSN 0028–3347) from 1904]

EIR:Dtc 1 (1890)–14 (1903); 31 (1920)–35
(1924); 38 (1927)–44 (1933); 56 (1945)–#
LAu 41 (1930), 4
Lbl*
Ob*

Fretwire
GB–Macclesfield: Fretwire Enterprises, 1977–
[NOT IN BUCOMP1]

BDp*
Cu 5 (1981), 3–6 (1981), 1–6
EIR:Dtc 6 (1981), 1–3/4
Lam 6 (1981), 1
Ob*

Freund's Musical Weekly *see* **Freund's Weekly**

Freund's Weekly
Fellinger 1968/1211; TNG US252
US–New York, 1893–1914
[Entitled *Freund's Musical Weekly* from vol. 4
(1893), Dec–1896; entitled *The Musical Age*
from vol. 12 (1896), 10]

Lcm (p) 34 (1901), July 25

Friend of the Hearth [translated title] *see*
Cyfaill yr Aelwyd

**Friends: Magazine of Friends of English
National Opera**
GB– London, 1980?–
[NOT IN BUCOMP1; formerly entitled *ENO
and Friends* (q.v.)]

Lcml 1, 1980–#
SFu 19–26, 1989–91

Friends of Cecil Sharp House Newsletter *see*
**News and Views: Friends of Cecil Sharp
House Newsletter**

The Friends of D'Oyly Carte Newsletter
GB–London: D'Oyly Carte Opera, ?1980–
[NOT IN BUCOMP1]

Ob 4, 1983–#

Friends of English National Opera *see* **ENO
and Friends**

**The Friends of the Ceredigion Young
Musicians: Newsletter/Cylchlythyr Cyfeillion
Cerddorion Ifanc Ceredigion**
GB–?Ceredigion, 1979–?

[NOT IN BUCOMP1]

AB 2, 1980; 5, 1982; 1987, Aut; 1989; 1990,
Win; 1991–#

**Friends of the Musical Museum: Members'
Newsletter**
GB–Brentford, 1987–
[NOT IN BUCOMP1; succeeded *The Musical
Museum and Friends*]

AB 6, 1989–#
Cu 3, 1988–#
EIR:Dtc 3, 1988–#
En 3, 1988–#
Lbl*
Ob*

**Friends of the Royal Academy of Music:
Newsletter**
GB–London: Royal Academy of Music, 1988–
[NOT IN BUCOMP1]

Lam 1, 1988–# [w 3, 4, 10, 12, 14]

**Friends of the Welsh National Opera:
Newsletter**
GB–Cardiff: Friends of the Welsh National
Opera, 1985–
[NOT IN BUCOMP1]

AB 1–17, 1985–90; 19, 1991–#
Cu 1, 1985–#
Lbl*
Ob 1, 1985–#*

FRMS Bulletin
0962–8150
GB–Macclesfield: Federation of Recorded
Music Societies, ?–
[NOT IN BUCOMP1]

Cu 115, 1991–#
En 115, 1991–#
Lbl 113, 1990–#
Ob 114, 1991–#

**Il "Fronimo": Rivista Trimestrale di Chitarra
e Liuto**
TNG I287
I–Milan: Edizioni Suvini Zerboni, 1972–

Lam 1 (1972), 1
Lbl 1 (1972)–17 (1989), Apr
Lcml 13 (1985), 50–#
Lu 1 (1972), 1
Lu (RMA) 1 (1972), 1–5
Mcm 1 (1972), 4; 8 (1980), 30

Full Orchestra
GB–Edinburgh: National Association of Youth
Orchestras, 19?–
[NOT IN BUCOMP1]

Ep 1995–#

Full Quota: the Status Quo Fanzine
1354–5817
GB–Oxford: Full Quota, 1992–
[NOT IN BUCOMP1]

Lbl 9, 1994–#

Full Score
GB–London: Music Sales, ?–
[NOT IN BUCOMP1]

Cu 1994–#
Lam 1986, Spr, Sum
Lsa 1994–#

**Future Music: Making Music with Modern
Technology**
0967–0378
GB–Bath: Future Publishing, 1992–
[NOT IN BUCOMP1]

Cu 1 (1992)–#
EIR:Dtc 1 (1992)–#
En 1 (1992)–#
Lbl*
Msuc 1996–#

G

Gaceta Musical
TNG F527
F–Paris: Gaceta Musical, 1928–29
[NOT IN BUCOMP1; ceased publication with
vol. 2 no. 1 (1929)]

Cpl 1 (1928)–2 (1929), 1

The Galpin Society Bulletin
TNG GB399
GB–London [etc.]: Galpin Society, 1947–
[NOT IN BUCOMP1]

BLp [c]
Lam 32, 1966; 35–65, 1968–85 [w 42, 46, 47,
55, 57, 58]; 81, 1991; 84, 1992; 87, 1993–#
LCdM 64, 1984–#

The Galpin Society Journal
TNG GB415; 0072–0127
GB–London [etc.]: Galpin Society, 1948–

AB 1 (1948)–#
ALb 6 (1953)
Au 1 (1948)–#
BDp 1 (1948)–39 (1986)
BG 48 (1995)–#
BLp 13 (1960)–35 (1982); 37 (1984)–#
BLu 1 (1948)–#
Bp 1 (1948)–#
BRp 1 (1948)–#
BRu 1 (1948)–# [w 39 (1986); 43 (1990)]
Bu 1 (1948)–#
CCtc 37 (1984)–#
CDu 20 (1967)–#
Cpl 1 (1948)–#
Cu 1 (1948)– #
DRu 5 (1952)–#
EIR:Dtc 1 (1948)–#
EIR:MEtc 28 (1975)–35 (1982)
En 1 (1948)–35 (1982); 37 (1984)–#
Er 1 (1948)–#
EXu 25 (1972)–#
Gm 14 (1961); 16 (1963)–31 (1978)
Gul 1 (1948)–#
HE 35 (1982)–37 (1984)
HUu 1 (1948)–#
Lam 1 (1948)–38 (1985); 44 (1991)–#
LAu 26 (1973)
Lbar 1 (1948)–28 (1975); 38 (1985)–#
Lbl*
LCdM 33 (1980)–#
Lcm 1 (1948)–#
Lcm (m) 1 (1948)–#
Lcml 1 (1948)–# [w 21 (1968)]
LEbc 1 (1948)–5 (1952); 27 (1974)–#
Lgo 1 (1948)–42 (1989)
Lgsm 1 (1948)–10 (1957); 12 (1959)–39
(1986); 41 (1988)–42 (1989)
Lkc 1 (1948)–#
Lki 1 (1948)–15 (1962)
Lmi 27 (1974)–44 (1991)
LRHBNC 1 (1948)–#
Lro 1 (1948)–#
Lsa 1 (1948)–38 (1985)
Lu 1 (1948)–#
LVp 1 (1948)–9 (1956); 13 (1960)–27 (1974);
29 (1976)–36 (1983)
Mcm 28 (1975)–#
Mpl 1 (1948)–#
Mu 19 (1966)–43 (1990)
NO 1 (1948)–39 (1986)
NWu 1 (1948)–20 (1967); 22 (1969)–25
(1972); 27 (1974)–44 (1991)
Ob 1 (1948)–#
Ouf 1 (1948)–45 (1992)
R 1 (1948)–43 (1990)

SA 1 (1948)–39 (1986)
SFp 1 (1948)–42 (1989)
SFu 1 (1948)–#
SOu 1 (1948)–37 (1984)
TOd 14 (1961); 17 (1964)–24 (1971); 26 (1973)–37 (1984); 39 (1986); 41 (1988)–#
Uu 42 (1989)–#
Yu 16 (1963)–#

G.A.S.B.A.L. (Friends of the University of Michigan G and S Society)
US–?: Friends of the University of Michigan Gilbert and Sullivan Society, ?1969–
[NOT IN BUCOMP1]

Lam 11 (1979), 3–13 (1981/82), 9 [w 12 (1980), 9; 13 (1981/82), 3, 4]; 14 (1982), 1–7; 15 (1983), 1, 3–5; 16 (1984), 1, 3–5; 17 (1985), 1–3

Gaudeamus Information
0533-9235
NL–Amsterdam: Gaudeamus Foundation, ?1967–

AB 1971–83
Bu 1983–# [w 1983, Jan; 1984, Oct; 1985, Oct; 1986, Apr]
Cpl 1975, May/June–#
Cu 1967, Nov/Dec–1978, Mar/Apr
EIR:Driam 1993–#
KE 1975, Mar/Apr; 1981–89*
Lam 1989, Apr
Lu 1994, Jan, July
Mcm 1974, 3, 4, 6; 1975, 1, 2, 4, 5; 1976, 1, 3; 1977–#

Gazeta Musical e de Todas as Artes
P–Lisbon: Academis de Amadores de Musica, 1950–
[NOT IN BUCOMP1]

Lbl 1 (1950)–2 (1951), 22; 8 (1958), 82–12 (1962), 135

Gazeta Muzyczna i Teatralna
Fellinger 1968/520; TNG PL5
PL–Warsaw: J. Ungra, 1865–66
[Included supplementary *Album Muzyczne* during 1865; this is also in **Lbl***]

Lbl 1–26, 1865–66

Gazette Musicale de la Suisse Romande *see* Le Journal Musical: Bulletin International Critique de la Bibliographie Musicale

Gazette Musicale de Paris
Fellinger 1968/117; TNG F21
F–Paris: Gazette Musicale de Paris, 1834–80
[Amalgamated with the *Revue Musicale [1]* in 1835 to form the *Revue et Gazette Musicale de Paris*]

Er 2 (1835)–43 (1876)
Gul (e) 6 (1839)–7 (1840), 1
Lbl 5 (1838)–47 (1880), 53 [w 1841; 1843–48]
Lcm 15 (1848); 19 (1852); 23 (1856); 32 (1865)
Lu 10 (1843); 17 (1850)–18 (1851); 21 (1854)–47 (1880)
Mpl 1 (1834)–2 (1835)
Ob 1 (1834)–46 (1879) [w 6 (1839)–7 (1840)]

Gazette of the College of Violinists
TNG GB263
GB–London, 1914–39
[From 1921 entitled *The Violinist's Gazette*]

AB 1–52, 1914–39
Gm 29– 51, 1928–39
Lbl*
LVp*
Mpl 9–20, 1918–23
Ob 1–52, 1914–39
SA 11–52, 1919–39 [w 25, 33]

Gazzetta Musicale di Milano
Fellinger 1968/192; TNG I18
I–Milan: Ricordi, 1842–48; 1850–62; 1866–1912
[Included a *Biblioteca Illustrata della Gazzetta Musicale di Milano* (Milan, 1886–87). Main title ceased publication with vol. 67 no. 12 (1912); vol. 7 (1848), 12–14 appeared under title *Gazzetta Musicale di Milano ed Eco delle Notizie Politiche*; vol. 7 (1848), 15–22 appeared under title *Gazzetta Musicale di Milano e di Italiana Armonia*; vol. 7 (1848), 23–30 entitled *L'Italiana Armonia e Gazzetta Musicale di Milano*; from vol. 58 (1903)–60 (1905) entitled *Musica e Musicisti, Gazzetta Musicale di Milano*, following merger with that journal; from 61 (1906)–67 (1912) entitled *Ars et Labor, Musica e Musicisti*]

Gul (e) 4 (1845)–7 (1848)
Lbl 31 (1876)–57 (1902)* [+ *Biblioteca Illustrata della Gazzetta Musicale di Milano* (1886–87)]
Lu 58 (1903)–67 (1912)
Ob*

Gazzetta Musicale di Milano e di Italiana
Armonia *see* Gazzetta Musicale di Milano

Gazzetta Musicale di Milano ed Eco delle
Notizie Politiche *see* Gazzetta Musicale di
Milano

Gazzetta Musicale di Napoli
TNG I20
I–Naples, 1852–68
[NOT IN BUCOMP1]

    Gul (e) 4 (1855)–6 (1857)*

The Gem and Musical Herald
Fellinger 1968/955; TNG GB114
GB–London, 1884–85

    Lbl 1 (1884)–2 (1885), 19
    Ob*

Gene Lees Jazzletter
0890–6440
US–Ojai, CA: Gene Lees, 1981–
[NOT IN BUCOMP1]

    Lcml 1987–#

The General Dramatic, Equestrian and
Musical Agency and Sick Fund Association
Almanack
GB–London, 1857–?
[From 1860 entitled *Dramatic, Equestrian and
Musical Agency and Sick Fund Association
Almanack*; from 1862 entitled *Dramatic,
Equestrian and Musical Sick Fund Almanack*;
from 1865 entitled *Dramatic and Musical
Almanack*; from 1867 entitled *Dramatic
Almanack*]

    Lbl*

General Music Journal
8755–5905
US–Oxford, OH: Ohio Music Educators'
Association, 1983–
[NOT IN BUCOMP1]

    BAc 2 (1984), 2; 3 (1985), 1–3; 4 (1986), 2,
    3; 5 (1987), 1–3; 6 (1988)
    Re 2 (1984), 2; 3 (1985), 3–7 (1989)

Generation X
0962–2381
GB–Rotherham: Sight and Sound Music, 1991–
[NOT IN BUCOMP1]

    Lbl*

Generator: the Energy of Dance Music and
Culture
0969–5206
GB–London: Generator, 1993–
[NOT IN BUCOMP1]

    Lbl*

Y Gerddorfa: Cylchgrawn Misol at
Wasanaeth Cerddoriaeth a Barddoniaeth
Cymreig [= The Orchestra: a Monthly
Journal for Welsh Worship, Music and
Poetry]
TNG GB78
GB–Pontypridd: David Davies, 187?–

    AB 1872–81
    Lbl*

German Studies: Section 3: Literature, Music,
Fine Arts
0024–4775
D–Tübingen, 1968–91

    EIR:Dtc 1 (1968)–#
    Lbl*
    Ob*

Gerry and the Pacemakers Monthly
GB–London, 1964–?

    AB 1, 2, 1964
    Cu 1–4, 1964
    Lbl*
    Ob*

Gesangspädagogische Blätter *see* Klavier-
Lehrer

Gesellschaft für Musikforschung:
Mitteilungen
D–Kassel: Gesellschaft für Musikforschung,
1947–48
[Continued as *Die Musikforschung* (q.v.)]

    LAu 1–4, 1947–48

Getting Nowhere Fast
GB–York: K. Alcorn, 1981
[NOT IN BUCOMP1]

    Lbl 1981

Cover of issue 1 of *Gerry and the Pacemakers Monthly*.
Like the musical groups they idolize, fanzines tend to have only a
short life. Much fan material is nowadays published in electronic form on the
World Wide Web, and does not find its way into print.
In 1964 such resources must have seemed like science fiction.

Reproduced by kind permission of the British Library

Gig: the Live Music Newspaper
1048–9916
US–Northridge, CA: Premier Publications,
1987–90
[NOT IN BUCOMP1]

Ob 1989, Apr 12, May 11–1990, Feb 26, Mar
31

Gigue: Revue de Folk
TNG F712
F–Paris: Association de Musique Populaire
Internationale, 1972–75

Lcs 3–8, 1973–75

The Gilbert and Sullivan Journal
TNG GB310; 0016–9951
GB–London: Gilbert and Sullivan Society,
1925–81
[Succeeded by *Gilbert and Sullivan News* (q.v.)]

Bp 6 (1946)–10 (1981), 20
BSdsc*
Cu 1 (1925)–10 (1981), 20*
EIR:Dtc 4 (1934), 2–7 (1956), 11
En*
Lam 10 (1981), 3, 5, 6, 9–20
Lbl*
Lcml 6 (1946), 11–22; 9 (1966)–10 (1981),
20
LVp 9 (1966)
Mpl*
Ob*

Gilbert and Sullivan News
0263–7995
GB–Orpington: Gilbert and Sullivan Society,
1982–
[Previously entitled *The Gilbert and Sullivan
Journal* (q.v.)]

Cu 1, 1982–#
En 1, 1982–#
Lam 1–8, 1982–85
Lbar 3, 1983–#
Lbl*
Ob*

Gitarre + Laute *see* **Gitarre und Laute**

Gitarre und Laute
TNG D1101; 0172–9683
D–Cologne: Gitarre und Laute
Verlagsgesellschaft, 1979–
[NOT IN BUCOMP1; also entitled *Gitarre +
Laute*]

Lcm 5 (1983), 2

Glasgow Orpheus Choir Monthly Record
GB–Glasgow: Glasgow Orpheus Choir, 1912–
51
[Entitled *The Lute* from 1915]

AB 1948, 4
ALb 1944/45, 3, 4
Gm 1912–51
Lam 1924

Gluck-Jahrbuch
Fellinger 1968/2168; TNG D530
D–Leipzig [etc.]: Breitkopf und Härtel, 1913–18

Bu 1 (1913)–4 (1918)
Cu 1 (1913)–4 (1918) [Reprint ed.]
Lbbc 1 (1913)–4 (1918)
Lbl*
Lu 1 (1913)–4 (1918)
Ob 1 (1913)–4 (1918)

Gluck Studien
No ISSN; vol. 1 carried ISBN 3–7618–0929–8
D/GB–Kassel; London: Bärenreiter, 1989–
[NOT IN BUCOMP1]

Cu 1 (1989)–#
Ouf 1 (1989)

The Godowsky Society Newsletter
GB–Edinburgh: The Godowsky Society, 1980–
[NOT IN BUCOMP1]

En 1 (1980)–#
Ep 4 (1984), 2–#

The Golden Years
GB–Cwmbran: F. R. Bristo, 1970–

Cbijs 24, 1972
Gm 29–89, 1973–89
LOnjfa*

The Good CD Guide
GB–Harrow: Gramophone, 1986–93
[NOT IN BUCOMP; succeeded by *The
Gramophone Good CD Guide* (q.v.)]

Cu 1986–93

Good Listening and Record Collector *see* **The
Record Collector; and Easy Listening and
Living with Stereo**

The Good Noise
GB–Plymouth: Patrick Russell, 1960–74
[Ceased publication with no. 266, 1974]

 Cbijs 135–266, 1967–74
 LOnjfa*

Good Songs of All Nations
GB–Glasgow, 1884

 Lbl*

Good Time Jazz and Contemporary Records
see G.T.J. & C.R. News

Goodchilds Jazz Bulletin
GB–Nottingham, 1956–?

 Cbijs 3 (1958), 25

Gottesdienst und Kirchenmusik: Zeitschrift
für Kirchenmusik und Liturgik
TNG D872; 0017–2499
D–Munich: Evangelische Pressverband für
Bayern, 1950–

 BSdsc*

Göttinger Händel-Beiträge
D–Kassel: Bärenreiter, 1984–93 (vols 1–5);
D–Göttingen: Vandenhoeck and Ruprecht,
1994– (vol. 6–)
[NOT IN BUCOMP1. All volumes have
separate ISBNs]

 Bu 1 (1984)–#
 Cu 1 (1984)–#
 Lbl 1 (1984)–#
 Lu 1 (1984)–#
 Ob 1 (1984)–#
 Ouf 1 (1984)–#

Graffiti: Incorporating Hot Hits
GB–Burnham on Crouch: St James Marketing,
1987–
[NOT IN BUCOMP1]

 Lbl*

The Grainger Journal
TNG GB579; 0141–5085
GB–Kenilworth: Percy Grainger Society, 1978–
[From 7 (1985) entitled *The Grainger Society
Journal*]

 ALb 1 (1978)–# [w 2 (1979), 2; 10 (1991), 1]
 DOR 5 (1982)–#
 En 1 (1978)–#

Lbar 5 (1982)–#
Lbl 1 (1978)–#
Lcml 1 (1978)–#
Lcs 1 (1978)–11 (1993), 1
Lki 1 (1978)–7 (1985), 1
Lu 1 (1978), 1, 2
Mcm (1978)–#
MK 1 (1978)–#
Ob*
Ouf 1 (1978)–#*
Yu 1 (1978)–10 (1991), 1

The Grainger Society Journal *see* The
Grainger Journal

The Gramophone
TNG GB302; 0017–310X
GB–Kenton: General Gramophone Publications
Ltd, 1923–
[Later entitled simply *Gramophone*; absorbed
Cassettes and Cartridges (q.v.) in 1977]

 AB 2 (1924/25)–# [w 69 (1991/92), 11]
 ALb 27 (1949/50)–#* [w 57 (1979/80)–61
  (1983/84)]
 Ap 27 (1949/50) [w Oct]; 30 (1952/53)–#
 Au 18 (1940/41), 206; 19 (1941/42), 219,
  225–228; 20 (1942/43), 229–#
 BAc 46 (1968/69), Apr–67 (1989/90) [w 50
  (1972/73), Jan]
 BAR [c (2 years)]
 BEp [c (10 years)]
 BLp 1 (1923/24)–#
 BOL [c (5 years)]
 Bp 1 (1923/24)–#
 BRDp (pon) [c (2 years)]
 BRDp (por) [c]
 BRp 5 (1927/28)–#
 Bs 28 (1950/51)–#*
 BSdsc 20 (1942/43), 239–#*
 BTp 33 (1955/56), 373; 47 (1969/70)–#*
 BTu 46 (1968/69), 547–67 (1989/90), 796
 Bu 25 (1947/48)–#
 BuAME [c (6 months)]
 BuAYp [c (5 years)]
 BuHW [c (2 years)]
 BuMK [c (1 year)]
 BuPR [c (6 months)]
 BYp [c (1 year)]
 Cap 30 (1952/53)–#
 Cat 38 (1960/61)–#*
 CCtc 36 (1958/59)–40 (1962/63); 45
  (1967/68)–#
 CDCp 14 (1936/37), June–#
 CDu 43 (1965/66)–#

Lwwb 40 (1962/63), June–#
LXp 18 (1940/41), 9; 19 (1941/42), 1, 2; 20
  (1942/43), 9; 21 (1943/44), 9–12; 22
  (1944/45)–#
Mcm 47 (1969/70)–#*
MI 36 (1958/59)–#
MK 56 (1978/79)–61 (1983/84)
Mmu (a) [c (3 years)]
Mmu (d) 59 (1981/82)–#
MO 36 (1958/59)–#
MP [c]
Mpl 1 (1923/24)–#
Msuc 65 (1987/88)–#
Mu 37 (1959/60)–#
NHp [c (12 months)]
NO 32 (1954/55), 376–#
NOp 24 (1946/47)–29 (1951/52)*; 31
  (1953/54)–#
NTp 8 (1930/31)–# [w 18 (1940/41)]
Ob 1 (1923/24)–#
OL 68 (1990/91)–#
Op 46 (1968/69)–65 (1987/88), 1–9, 12; 67
  (1989/90)–#
Oub 58 (1980/81)–#
Ouf [c (1 year)]
P [c (2 years)]
PRp 36 (1958/59)–#
R 30 (1952/53)–#
RH [c]
Rp 26 (1948/49)–28 (1950/51); 30
  (1952/53)–#
SA 27 (1949/50), Dec–#
SAu [c (10 years)]
SFp 30 (1952/53)–31 (1953/54); 33
  (1955/56)–#
SFu 36 (1958/59)–#
SHRp 60 (1982/83)–#
SK [c (5 years)]
SLGu 31 (1953/54)–53 (1975/76); 54
  (1976/77), 637–70 (1992/93), 840; 71
  (1993/94), 841#*
SOL 69 (1991/92)–#
SOu 29 (1951/52)–32 (1954/55); 35
  (1957/58)–#
STAp 29 (1951/52)–#
TOd 57 (1979/80), 680–#
Uu 68 (1990/91)–#
WCp [c (6 months)]
WCp (b) [c (2 years)]
WCp (e) [c (3 years)]
WCp (f) [c (5 years)]
WCp (far) [c (1 year)]
WCp (h) [c (1 year)]
WCp (l) [c (1 year)]
WCp (p) 7 (1929/30)–#

WCp (ref) 35 (1957/58)–56 (1978/79);
  59 (1981/82); 63 (1985/86)–#
WCp (s) [c (1 year)]
WF 41 (1963/64)–#
WH 61 (1983/84)– [w 1992, Feb, Mar]#
WOp [c]
WW [c]
Y 32 (1954/55)–43 (1965/66); 44 (1966/67),
  6, 9–12; 45 (1967/68), 1–8, 11; 46
  (1968/69), 1, 8–11; 47 (1969/70)–#
Yu 12 (1934/35)–#

Gramophone and Music Record
Fellinger 1968/2244; TNG GB266
GB–London, 1915–20

  Lbl*

Gramophone Chronicle and Record Review
GB–London, 1928

  Lbl*

Gramophone Classical Catalogue *see* The
Gramophone Long Playing Classical Record
Catalogue

The Gramophone Classical Good CD Guide
see The Gramophone Good CD Guide

**Gramophone Classical New Release
Information Service**
1353–4890
GB–London: Retail Information Data, 1994–
[NOT IN BUCOMP1]

  EIR:Duc 1 (1994)–#
  Lbl 1 (1994)–#
  Lsa*
  Ob *

Gramophone Classical Record Catalogue *see*
The Gramophone Long Playing Classical
Record Catalogue

**Gramophone Compact Disc Digital Audio
Guide and Catalogue** *see* The Gramophone
Long Playing Classical Record Catalogue

The Gramophone Critic *see* The Gramophone
Critic and Society News

The Gramophone Critic and Society News
GB–London, 1928–31
[From 1929 entitled *The Gramophone Critic*]

Lbl*
Lsa 1–12, 1928– 29

The Gramophone Good CD Guide
GB–Harrow: General Gramophone
Publications, 1994–
[NOT IN BUCOMP1; preceded from 1986 to
1993 by *The Good CD Guide* (q.v.); entitled *The
Gramophone Classical Good CD Guide* from
1996 issue]

Cu 1994–#
WW [c]

Gramophone Jazz Good CD Guide
GB–Harrow: Gramophone, 1995–
[NOT IN BUCOMP1]

Cu 1995–#

The Gramophone Long Playing Classical Record Catalogue
TNG GB458
GB–Harrow: General Gramophone
Publications, 1953–
[Entitled the *Gramophone Classical Record
Catalogue* from 1966; from 1975, the
Gramophone Classical Catalogue (ISSN 0309–
4367); from 1983–90, *Gramophone Compact
Disc Digital Audio Guide and Catalogue* (ISSN
0267–2162); from 1990, *The Classical
Catalogue* (ISSN 0961–5237); also known as
the *R.E.D. Classical Catalogue*]

ABDp [c]
BRp 1962–#*
Bs 1989–#*
BSdsc 1977–89
Bu 1984–90
BuAYp [c]
BuCHE [c (1 year)]
BuHW [c (1 year)]
BuMK [c (1 year)]
Cat 1991*; 1993–#
CAu 1988–#
CCtc 1991–#
CFp [c (1 year)]
Cu 1995–#
DU [c (1 year)]
Ea [c]
EIR:Dp 1992, Feb–#
EIR:Dtc 1956–65; 1966, Mar–1974, Dec;
 1975–#

EIR:Duc 1992–#
EIR:MEtc 1979–#
Gul 1991–#
HOp [c]
HUu 1959–#
Je [c]
KE 1969–# [w 1982, Mar]
Lam 1965–#*
Lba 1961–1962; 1965; 1967–1968; 1970–89;
 1990–#
Lbbc [c (1 year)]
Lbl*
Lbx 1985–91, Nov
LCdM [c]
Lcm 1974–85
Lcml 1988–#*
Lcml (c) 1963–73*; 1975–#*
Lcml (m) 1958*; 1959–72; 1973*; 1974–#*
Lgsm*
Lhr [c]
Lis [c (1 year)]
Lk [c]
Lk (nk) [c (1 year)]
Lkc [c]
Lki 1987, Sep–1990, June; [c]
Ll [c (5 years)]
Lro 1994–#
Lsa 1953–70; 1972–#
Lu 1954–# *
Lwwb [c]
Lwwbat [c]
Lwwput [c]
Mcm 1974–#
MK [c (2 years)]
Mmu (a) 1994–#
Mpl 1966–#
Msuc [c]
Mu 1985–#
NO 1964–#
NOp 1958–#* [2nd issue of each year from
 1990]
Ob*
Oub [c (2 years)]
Ouf [c]
R [c]
SA [c (2 years)]
SFu 1970–88; [c]
SLGu 1975–#
TOd 1989–#
Uu [c (2 years)]

Gramophone News
Fellinger 1968/1672; TNG GB198
GB–London, 1903–10
[In 1910, Oct, became *"His Master's Voice"
and Gramophone News* (q.v.)]

   Lbl*

Gramophone Opera Catalogue
GB–Harrow: Gramophone/R.E.D., 1995–
[NOT IN BUCOMP1]

   Cu 1995-#
   Ob 1995-#

Gramophone Popular Catalogue *see* The
Gramophone Popular (Long-Playing Popular)
Record Catalogue

**The Gramophone Popular (Long-Playing
Popular) Record Catalogue**
TNG GB472; 0436–2837
GB–Kenton: General Gramophone Publications,
1954–
[From end 1974 entitled *Gramophone Popular
Catalogue*; from end 1985, *Pop Cat*]

   BSdsc*
   Cpl 1955–75*
   Cu 1959, Sep–1987, Sep
   EIR:Dtc 1963, June–1985, Sep; 1985, Dec–
      1987, Sep
   Lam 1987, June
   Lbl*
   Lcml (m) 1956–61*; 1964–65*; 1966–69;
      1970*; 1971; 1972*; 1973–77; 1978*;
      1979–80; 1981*; 1982–83; 1984*; 1985–87
   Lk [c]
   Lk (b) [c]
   Lk (nk) [c (1 year)]
   Lsa 1954–87 [w 1966, Mar, June, Dec; 1967,
      Mar, Sep, Dec; 1973, Sep, Dec]
   Mpl 1954-#
   Ob*
   Oub 1980–87

The Gramophone Recommended Recordings
GB–London: General Gramophone
Publications, 1966–
[Entitled *Recommended Recordings* (ISSN
0309–0574) from 1991]

   Cu 1967–90*; n.s. 1991-#
   EIR:Dtc 1967, 3–1991, 2
   EIR:Duc 1975–91
   En 1967, 3-#
   Lbl*
   MK 1991
   Ob*

Gramophone Record
GB–Leicester, 1935–44
[NOT IN BUCOMP1]

   Cu 1935–44

**The Gramophone Record: a Monthly Review
of Recorded and Broadcast Music**
TNG GB342
GB–St Austell, 1933–53; 1954–61
[Entitled *The Gramophone Record Review* from
1953; absorbed into *Audio and Record Review*]

   AB n.s. 3–94, 1954–61
   Cu n.s. 3–84, 1954–60
   EIR:Dtc n.s. 3–40, 1954–57, Apr
   Gm 1950, June–1953, Oct
   Lam n.s. 12, 1954; 21, 1955; 27, 34, 1956
   Lbl*
   Lsa 1934, Dec; 1935, Jan–May, Oct–Nov;
      1936, Jan, Feb; 1950, Dec; 1951–52; 1953,
      Jan–Oct; n.s. 1–94, 1953–61
   Lu 37–94, 1956–61
   LVp n.s. 19–48, 1955–57; 1958–60*
   Ob*

The Gramophone Record Review *see* The
Gramophone Record: a Monthly Review of
Recorded and Broadcast Music

**The Gramophone Review of Records,
Machines and Inventions**
GB–Liverpool, 1928–29

   AB 1–18, 1928–29 [w 3]
   Cu 1–18, 1928–29
   Lbl*
   Ob 1–18, 1928–29

Gramophone Shop Inc. Record Supplement
TNG US547
US–New York: The Gramophone Shop, Inc.,
1937–53

   Lsa 1 (1937)–16 (1953)
   Lu 12 (1949)–16 (1953)

**The Gramophone Spoken Word and
Miscellaneous Catalogue**
GB–Harrow: General Gramophone
Publications, 196?–
[NOT IN BUCOMP1]

   EIR:Dtc 1965, Aug–#
   HUu [c]
   Lsa 1964-#
   SOu 1975–87

The Gramophone: Technical Reports
GB–Harrow, 1966–68
[NOT IN BUCOMP1]

Cu 1 (1966)–3 (1968)

Gramophone, Wireless and Talking Machine News *see* Talking Machine News and Journal of Amusements

The Gramophone Yearbook and Diary
TNG GB275
GB–London, 1920

Lbl*

Le Grand Baton: Journal of the Sir Thomas Beecham Society
TNG US743; 0434–3336
US–Cleveland, OH: Sir Thomas Beecham Society, 1964–

DS 1969, May–1978, June
Lsa 1964–#*

Grapevine [1]
GB–South Petherton: English Folk Dance and Song Society (Wessex District), 19?–
[NOT IN BUCOMP1]

Lbl*

The Grapevine [2]
0092–0592
US–Saratoga, CA: L. Ransil, 1972–
[NOT IN BUCOMP1]

LOnjfa*

Grass Seen
0263–3833
GB–London: Grass Seen, 1982–
[NOT IN BUCOMP1]

Lbl*

Gravesaner Blätter: eine Vierteljahresschrift für musikalische, elektroakustische und schallwissenschaftliche Grenzprobleme
TNG D967
CH/D–Gravesano: Experimental Studios; Mainz: Ars Viva Verlag, 1955–66
[Ceased publication with no. 29, 1966; also bore title *Gravesano Review*]

Lam 9, 1957
Lbl*
Lcm 23, 24, 1962

Lcml 8–10, 1957–60
Lsa 5–29, 1956–66
Lu 1–29, 1955–66 [w 4, 6–8, 11–13, 23–26]
Mpl 8–29, 1958–66
Ob*
SA 1–24, 1955–62
SFu 9–26, 1957–65*

Gravesano Review *see* Gravesaner Blätter: eine Vierteljahresschrift für musikalische, elektroakustische und schallwissenschaftliche Grenzprobleme

Greal y Corau [= The Choral Guild]
GB–Denbigh: Thomas Gee, 1861– 63

AB*
Lbl*

Greater London Arts
GB–London, 1985–?

Lcm 1–11, 1985–88 [w 3, 8]

The Gregorian
GB– Enfield [etc.]: The Gregorian Association, ?–

Cu 29, 1979; 41, 1983
Lbl 53, 1989–#
Lcml 39, 1982–#

The Gregorian Quarterly Magazine
Fellinger 1968/791; TNG GB96
GB–London: Gregorian Choral Association, 1879
[Only 4 nos published]

Cu 1–4, 1879
Lbl 1–4, 1879
Ob 1–4, 1879

The Gregorian Review
0434–653X
US–Toledo, OH: Gregorian Institute Press/Gregorian Association of America, 1954–
[NOT IN BUCOMP1]

AB 1 (1954), 5

Gregorianische Rundschau: Monatsschrift für Kirchenmusik und Liturgie *see* Musica Divina: Monatsschrift für Kirchenmusik

Gregoriusblad *see* Sint Gregorius-Blad: Tijdschrift tot Bevordering van Kerkelijke Toonkunst

Gregorius-Blatt: Organ für katholische Kirchenmusik
Fellinger 1968/714; TNG D217
D–Aachen: Internationale Gesellschaft für Erneuerung der Katholischen Kirchenmusik, 1876–1922, 1924–37
[Included a supplement, *Gregoriusbote für katholische Kirchensänger* (q.v.). From 56 (1932)–58 (1934) entitled *Gregorius-Blatt und Gregorius-Bote*; in 1938 became *Die Kirchenmusik: Zeitschrift [...]* (q.v.)]

    Lbl 1 (1877)–61 (1937)

Gregorius-Blatt und Gregorius-Bote *see* Gregorius-Blatt: Organ für katholische Kirchenmusik

Gregoriusbote für katholische Kirchensänger
Fellinger 1968/714; TNG D217
[NOT IN BUCOMP1; published as a supplement to *Gregorius–Blatt: Organ für katholische Kirchenmusik* (q.v.)]

    Lbl 1–53, 1883–1937

Grieg Society of Great Britain Newsletter
GB–London: Grieg Society of Great Britain, 1993–
[NOT IN BUCOMP1]

    Lbar 1, 1993–#

Groove: Liverpool's Premier Music Magazine
1352–6642
GB–Liverpool: Groove Publications, ?1993–
[NOT IN BUCOMP1]

    Lbl 3, 1993–#

Der grosse deutsche Schallplatten Katalog
D–Ludenscheid, ?–?
[NOT IN BUCOMP1]

    Lsa 1964–70 [w 1966, 1968]

G.T.J. and C.R. News [= Good Time Jazz and Contemporary Records]
US–Los Angeles, CA, 1956–61

    Lsa 3 (1958), 2, 3; 4 (1959); 5 (1960), 1, 2; 6 (1961), 1

Guidi Musicali Istituto d'Alta Cultura
I–Milan, 1938–?

    Lbl*

Le Guide du Concert
Fellinger 1968/2015; TNG F413
F–Paris: Legros, 1910–38/39; 1945–
[In 1930 absorbed *Musique* (q.v.); from 1966, 490, entitled *Le Guide du Concert et du Disque*; from 1970, Jan., no. 560 entitled *Le Guide du Concert, du Disque, de la Musique et du Son*; from 1970, Sep., no. 573 entitled *Le Guide musical du Concert, du Disque, de la Musique et du Son*; from 1973, Mar. to 1974, Aug. incorporated *Opéra 61: la Revue de l'Art Lyrique* to form *Le Guide Musical-Opéra*; from 1974, Sep entitled *Le Guide Musical*; also called *Guide du Concert et des Théâtres Lyriques*]

    ALb 1969, 548
    Lcm (p) 1914, Jan 24; 1923, Apr 27; 1946, Oct 25
    Lcml (m) 32 (1952)–34 (1954)*; 35 (1955)–36 (1956); 37 (1957)–38 (1958)*
    Lsa 38 (1958), 164; 39 (1958/59), 208–210, 216–218, 233, 235, 236, 243, 244, 247–250; 1960, 255–258, 261, 262; 1962, 358; 634–658, 1973–75

Le Guide du Concert, du Disque, de la Musique et du Son *see* Le Guide du Concert

Guide du Concert et des Théâtres Lyriques *see* Le Guide du Concert

Le Guide du Concert et du Disque *see* Le Guide du Concert

Le Guide Musical: Revue International de la Musique et des Théâtres [...]
Fellinger 1968/347; TNG B16
B/F–Brussels; Paris: Schott, 1855–1913; 1917
[Ceased publication with vol. 61 (1917/18); from 1894 incorporated *L'Art Musical: Journal de Musique* (q.v.)]

    Bu 52 (1906)–56 (1910)
    En 49 (1903), 48
    Gm 46 (1900)–47 (1901)
    Lbl 7 (1861), 1–43; 20 (1874), 1–52; 32 (1886), 49–35 (1889), 25/26; 40 (1894), 40–53; 43 (1897)–45 (1899), 52; 47 (1901)–57 (1911)
    Ob*

Le Guide Musical du Concert, du Disque, de la Musique et du Son *see* Le Guide du Concert

Le Guide Musical[-Opéra] *see* Le Guide du Concert

Guild for the Promotion of Welsh Music (y Gymdeithas ar Hyrwyddo Cerddoriaeth Cymru): Newsletter
GB–?, ?–?
[NOT IN BUCOMP1]

>AB 1965–69

The Guild Gazette for Musicians of the Church: Official Organ of the Incorporated Guild of Church Musicians
Fellinger 1968/1913; TNG GB232
GB–London: William Reeves [for the Incorporated Guild of Church Musicians], 1908–16

>Lbl 1 (1908)–9 (1916) [w 3 (1910)]

The Guildhall Music Student
TNG GB303
GB–London: Guildhall School of Music, 1924–39; n.s. 1948–?
[From 1935 entitled *The Guildhall Student*]

>Cu 1 (1924)–16 (1939); n.s. 1 (1948)–4 (1951)
>Lam 1 (1948), 1
>Lbl*
>Lgsm 3 (1926)–8 (1931); 11 (1934), 2–16 (1939), 1*
>Ob*

The Guildhall School of Music and Drama Magazine
GB–London: Guildhall School of Music and Drama, 1912–?

>BSdsc*

The Guildhall School of Music and Drama Review
GB–London: Guildhall School of Music and Drama, 1973–

>En 1973–74
>Lam 1973
>Lbl*

The Guildhall Student *see* The Guildhall Music Student

Guitar
GB–Mere, Somerset, 1972–91
[Entitled *Guitar International* from 13 (1984); incorporated into *Classical Guitar* (q.v.) from 1991, Dec.]

>BDp 2 (1974)–20 (1991/92)
>Bs*
>BSdsc*
>Cbijs 2 (1974), 10; 3 (1975), 10, 11
>Cu 9 (1981), 6–17 (1988/89), 11
>EIR:Dp 16 (1987/88), 6–17 (1988/89), 2; 18 (1989/90), 6–19 (1990/91), 9
>EIR:Dtc 9 (1981)–17 (1988/89), 11
>Ep 6 (1977/78), 9–20 (1991/92), 6
>Gm 7 (1979), Aug–20 (1991/92), Jan
>Lbar 11 (1983), 6–18 (1989/90), 12
>Lbl*
>Lcm 1 (1972/73), 6, 11
>Lcml 1 (1972/73), 2–#
>Lcml (m) [c (1 year)]
>Lcml (p) [c 2 issues)]
>Lgu 2 (1974), 8–20 (1991/92), 6
>Lmi 11 (1983)–20 (1991/92), 6
>Lu 1 (1972/73), 9
>Mcm 2 (1973/74)–20 (1991/92)*
>Mpl 1 (1972/73)–20 (1991/92)
>Ob*

Guitar and Lute
TNG US843; 0199–9117
US–Honolulu, Hawaii: Galliard Press, 1974–

>Lcml 1, 1974–#
>Lu 4–11, 1977–79

Guitar and Mandolin *see* Mandolin Notebook

Guitar Heroes
0265–7481
GB–London: Spotlight Publications, 1982–
[Preceded by *Sounds Guitar Heroes*]

>AB 7, 9, 10, 1983
>Cu 7–11, 1983
>Lbl 7, 1983–#*
>Ob*

Guitar International *see* Guitar

Guitar Journal
0960–0841
GB–Leeds: European Guitar Teachers' Association, 1990–
[NOT IN BUCOMP1]

>CHL 3 (1992), 10; 4 (1993), 3–#
>Cu 1 (1990)–#
>EIR:Dtc 1 (1990); 4 (1993)–#
>En 1 (1990); 4 (1993)
>GLp 3 (1992), 10; 4 (1993)–#
>Lbl 1 (1990)–#
>Lcm 6 (1995)–7 (1996)

The Guitar Magazine
0962–2640
GB–London: Northern and Shell, 1990–
[NOT IN BUCOMP1; absorbed *International Musician and Recording World* (q.v.)]

En 1 (1990/92), 2–4
Lbl*
Lgu 1 (1990/92), 9–#
Ob 1 (1990/92)–#

Guitar News
TNG GB436; 0434–9342
GB–Cheltenham: International Classic Guitar Association, 1951–

Cu 17–119, 1954–73
EIR:Dtc 17–117, 1954–72
En 17–119, 1954–73
Lam 20, 21, 1954
Lbl*
Lgsm 51–86, 1960–65; 102–119, 1969–73
Ob*

Guitar Player: the Magazine for Professional and Amateur Guitarists
TNG US773; 0017–5463
US–Saratoga, CA: Guitar Players International, 1967–

BSdsc*
KE 19 (1985)–20 (1986), 3
Lgo 14 (1980), 7– #*
Msuc 24 (1990)–#

The Guitar Review
TNG US594; 0017–5471
US–New York: Society of the Classic Guitar, 1946–
[From 1961, 25, entitled simply *Guitar Review*]

BSdsc*
Lcm 1, 1946; 9, 1949; 13, 1952; 24, 25, 1960–61; 27, 1963; 29, 1966
Lcml 1–6, 1946–48; 13–20, 1952–56; 30, 1967–#
Lu 23–25, 1959–61; 27, 1963
LVp 25–30, 1961–67; 32, 1969–#
Mcm 1–6, 1946–48; 28, 1965; 30, 1967–#
Mpl 1, 1946–#*
Ob*

Guitar Techniques
1352–6383
GB–Ely: Guitar Techniques, 1994–
[NOT IN BUCOMP1]

Cu 1994–#
Lbl*

Guitarist
0953–7023
GB–Cambridge: Music Maker/Guitarist Publications, 1984/5–
[NOT IN BUCOMP1; preceded by *B.M.G.: a Journal devoted to the Banjo, Mandoline and Guitar* (q.v.)]

AB 1 (1984/85), 12–#
CH [c (1 year)]
Cu 3 (1986/87)–#
EIR:Dtc 3 (1986/87)–#
En 3 (1986/87)–4 (1987/88), 1–6, 8–12; 5 (1988/89)–#
Gm 3 (1986/87)–#
IOW 9 (1992), Aug–#
Lbl*
NOp 13 (1997), 8–#
Ob 3 (1986/87)–#

The Gunn Report
GB–Hadleigh, Essex: John and Carole Gunn, ?1967–

Cbijs 35–62, 1972–77
LOnjfa*
Lsa 20, 1970–# [w 23, 24, 28, 29, 31, 33, 36, 37, 44, 105]
Ob*

G. W. Körner's Urania: Musik-Zeitschrift für Alle, welche das Wohl der Kirche besonders zu fördern haben *see* **Urania: ein musikalisches Beiblatt zum Orgelfreunde** [...]

Y Gymdeithas ar Hyrwyddo Cerddoriaeth Cymru *see* **Guild for the Promotion of Welsh Music/y Gymdeithas ar Hyrwyddo Cerddoriaeth Cymru: Newsletter**

Gypsy Explorer: the Marc Bolan and T-Rex Fanzine
0968–6525
GB–Leyland: GEM, 1987–
[NOT IN BUCOMP1]

Lbl 10, 198?–#*

H

Ha'ilono mele [= News of Hawaiian Music]
TNG US855; 0160–8274
US–Honolulu, Hawaii: Hawaiian Music Foundation, 1975–

Lsa 1975–76*

Hallé: a Magazine for the Music Lover
TNG GB388
GB–Manchester: Hallé Concerts Society, 1946–
[Later sub–titled *Journal of the Hallé Concerts Society*; from 1982 entitled *Hallé Magazine*; in 1992 combined with *Hallé News: the Journal of the Hallé Concerts Society* to form *Hallmark*]

> AB 121, 1964; 123, 1967; 126, 1969/70; 1982, July; 1983, Dec
> Cu 1–129, 1946–1972/73; n.s. 4–14, 1975–80
> EIR:Dtc 1–129, 1946–72/73; n.s. 4–14, 1975–80
> En*
> Lam 67, 69, 70, 1954; n.s. 7, 1977
> LAu 13–73, 1948–54 [w 14–17, 20, 22, 26, 35–37, 51–54, 56–72]
> Lcm (p) 1947–52*
> Lcml 1–78, 1946–55*
> LVp 2–55, 1946– 52*
> Mcm 1, 1946–#
> Mpl 1–129, 1946–72.73; n.s. 1–14, 1975–80; 1982–#
> Ob*
> SFp 1–80, 1946–55

Hallé: Journal of the Hallé Concerts Society
see Hallé: a Magazine for the Music Lover

Hallé Magazine *see* Hallé: a Magazine for the Music Lover

Hallé News: the Journal of the Hallé Concerts Society
GB–Manchester: The Hallé Concerts Society, 198?–
[NOT IN BUCOMP1; in 1992 combined with *Hallé: a Magazine for the Music Lover* to form *Hallmark*]

> Cu 3 (1984/85), 2–4 (1986/89), 7
> En 3 (1984/85), 2–4; 4 (1986/89), 1–7
> Lam 4 (1986/89), 2
> Lbl*
> Ob*

Hallé Yearbook
0262–7272
GB–Manchester: The Hallé Society, 1858–
[NOT IN BUCOMP1]

> Lbl*

Hallmark *see* Hallé: a Magazine for the Music Lover; and Hallé News: the Journal of the Hallé Concerts Society

Hamburger Jahrbuch für Musikwissenschaft
TNG D1081
D–Hamburg: K. D. Wagner, 1974–

> Bu 1 (1974)–#
> Cu 1 (1974)–#
> Mu 4 (1980)
> Ob 1 (1974)–#
> Ouf 1 (1974)–11 (1991)

Hampstead Music and Arts
TNG GB411
GB–Hampstead: Hampstead Borough Council, 1948–50

> Lcml 1–5, 1948–50

Handbuch der musikalischen Litteratur, oder Allgemeines systematisch-geordnetes Verzeichniss der bis zum Ende des Jahres 1815 gedruckten Musikalien, auch musikalischen Schriften und Abbildungen mit Anzeige der Verleger und Preise
Fellinger 1968/222; TNG D43
D–Leipzig: Anton Meysel/F. Hoffmeister, 1817–28; 1829–38
[Continued from 1844–1943 as *C. F. Whistling's Handbuch der musikalischen Literatur, oder Allgemeines systematisch-geordnetes Verzeichniss der in Deutschland und in den angrenzenden Ländern gedruckten Musikalien, auch musikalischen Schriften und Abbildungen mit Anzeige der Verleger und Preise* (q.v.)]

> Lbl*
> Ob*
> Ouf [Reprint ed.]

Handel Institute Newsletter
0962–7960
GB–Birmingham: Handel Institute, 1990–
[NOT IN BUCOMP1]

> Cu 1, 1990–#
> EIR:Dtc 1, 1990–#
> Lbl 1, 1990–#
> Lu 1, 1990–#
> Mcm*

Händel-Jahrbuch
TNG D712 (1928–33); TNG D968 (1955–); 0440–0615
D–Leipzig: VEB Deutscher Verlag für Musik [for the Handel–Gesellschaft], 1928–33; 1955–

> AB*
> ALb 1967–73

Bp 1955–57; 1959–63; 1966; 1969–73
BSdsc*
Bu 1928–33; 1955–57; 1974–89
CAu 1981
CDu 1928–33
Cu 1928–33; 1955–#
En 1928–33; 1955–#
Er 1928–33; 1955–#
LAu 1956–88
Lbbc 1928–33; 1955–#
Lbl*
Lcm 1955–68
Lkc 1955; 1957–58; 1960
Lu 1930; 1932–33
Mpl 1933; 1955–#*
Mu 1928–33; 1957–59; 1965; 1971; 1976–93
Ob*
Ouf 1928–33; 1955–#
R 1955–88

Hanes Cerddoriaeth Cymru/Welsh Music History
GB–Cardiff: University of Wales Press, 1996–
[NOT IN BUCOMP1]

BG 1 (1996)–#
BSdsc 1 (1996)–#
Cu 1 (1996)–#
Lbl 1 (1996)–#
Ob 1 (1996)–#

Hang Tough with New Kids on the Block
0959–4590
GB–Iver Heath: Century 22, 1990–
[NOT IN BUCOMP1]

Lbl*

Hans-Pfitzner-Gesellschaft: Mitteilungen
0440–2863
D–Munich, n. F. 1954–

Cu n.F. 1 (1954)–#
Ob*

Harmonia: Rivista Italiana di Musica
I–Rome, 1913–14
[NOT IN BUCOMP1]

Ouf 1 (1913)–2 (1914) [m]

Harmonica-Revue
D–Trossingen: Edition Harmonica–Revue,
?–1952
[NOT IN BUCOMP1; also published in English and French]

Ob*

The Harmonicon: a Journal of Music
Fellinger 1968/60; TNG GB9; Langley, p. 508–515; Langley 1994, pp. 117–18
GB–London: William Pinnock [etc.], 1823–33
[Vols 2–8 published London: Samuel Leigh; vols 9–11 London: Longman, Rees, Brown and Green]

AB 1 (1823)–5 (1827)
ALb 1 (1823)–9 (1831)
Au 1 (1823)–11 (1833) [Reprint ed.]
Bu 1 (1823)–11 (1833)
Cpl 1 (1823)–11 (1833)
Cu 1 (1823)–11 (1833)
DRu 1 (1823)–11 (1833)
EIR:Driam 1 (1823); 6 (1828)–7 (1829)
EIR:Dtc 1 (1823)–11 (1833)
En 1 (1823)–11 (1833)
Ep 1 (1823)–11 (1833)
Er 1 (1823)–11 (1833)
Gm 1 (1823)–11 (1833)
Gul 4 (1826)–11 (1833)
Gul (e) 1 (1823)–11 (1833)
Lam 1 (1823)–8 (1830); 10 (1832), 2
Lbl*
Lcm 1 (1823)–6 (1828); 10 (1832), 2
    [+ complete reprint ed.]
Lcml 1 (1823)–3 (1825); 4 (1826)–9 (1832)*
Lkc 1 (1823)–11 (1833)
Lu 1 (1823)–2 (1824)
Mcm 1 (1823),1, 2; 2 (1824), 1, 2
Mpl 1 (1823)–11 (1833)
Mu 1 (1823)–11 (1833) [Reprint ed.]
NO 1 (1823)–11 (1833)
NWu 1 (1823)–11 (1833)
Ob 1 (1823)–11 (1833)
Ouf 1 (1823)– 11 (1833) [11 (1833) in
    Reprint ed.]
SFu 1 (1823)–11 (1833)

Harmonie: Hi-Fi Conseil
0248–9651
F–?Paris, 1980–
[NOT IN BUCOMP1; previously entitled *Harmonie: Revue Critique de Musique Classique Enregistrée* (q.v.); from 15, 1981 entitled *Harmonie-Opera Hi-Fi Conseil* (ISSN 0751–2295); from 20, 1984, entitled *Harmonie: Panorama Musique: le Journal du Disque Compact* (ISSN 0757–0139)]

ALb 20, 1984, Dec
EIR:Duc 1–37, 1980–83
Lsa 4, 1980; 11–50, 1981–85 [w 43]

Harmonie: Revue Critique de Musique
Classique Enregistrée
TNG F687; 0017–7822
F–Boulogne: Editions Harmonie, ?1964–80
[NOT IN BUCOMP1; from 1981 entitled
Harmonie: Hi–Fi Conseil (q.v.), with new
numbering]

>EIR:Duc 152–156, 1979–80
>Lsa 72–156, 1972–80 [w 78–83, 85–90, 92–
>99, 101–115, 119–152, 154]

Harmonie-Opera Hi-Fi Conseil *see* Harmonie:
Hi-Fi Conseil

Harmonie: Panorama Musique: le Journal du
Disque Compact *see* Harmonie: Hi-Fi Conseil

The Harp [translated title] *see* Delyn: the
Welsh Musical Review

Harp News *see* Harp News of the West

Harp News of the West
TNG US650; 0440–3215
US–Bakersfield, CA: Northern California
Harpists' Association, 1950–66
[From 1950, 2, entitled *Harp News*; from 1967
continued as *American Harp Journal* (q.v.);
ceased publication with vol. 4 no. 4 (1966)]

>Lam 1 (1950/54), 7, 10

Harp of the Sunday School [translated title]
see Telyn yr Ysgol Sabbothol

Harpa
1017– 1142
CH–Dornach: International Harp Centre, 1991–
[NOT IN BUCOMP1]

>EIR:Driam 1991–93

The Harpsichord
TNG INTL25; 0017–792X
US–Denver, CO: International Society of
Harpsichord Builders, 1968–

>Lcml 1 (1968)–8 (1975/76)
>Lgu 7 (1974/75), 4–8 (1975/76), 4
>Lu 3 (1970), 3, 4
>TOd 8 (1975/76), 1–4
>Uu*

Harpsichord and Fortepiano *see* The
Harpsichord Magazine and Early Keyboard
Instrument Review

The Harpsichord Magazine and Early
Keyboard Instrument Review
TNG GB571
GB–Chesham Bois: Edgar Hunt, 1973–87; 1994–
[Entitled *The English Harpsichord Magazine
and Early Keyboard Instrument Review* (ISSN
0306–4395) from 1974, 2–1986, 2; relaunched
1994 as *Harpsichord and Fortepiano* (ISSN
0953–0797), published GB–Hebden Bridge:
Peacock Press, 1994–]

>BDp 1 (1973/77)–3 (1981/84)
>BRp 4 (1986/89), 1–7
>BSdsc 4 (1986/89), 3–7
>Cu 1 (1973/77)–4 (1985/89), 7; 5 (1994)–#
>EIR:Dtc 1 (1973/77)–4 (1985/89), 7
>En*
>Ep 1 (1973/77)–#
>Er 1 (1973/77), 1, 2
>Lam 4 (1986/89), 5–7
>Lbl*
>Lcm 2 (1977/81), 1–7; 5 (1995), 1, 2
>Lcml 1 (1973/77)–#
>Lgsm 1 (1973/77), 8–4 (1985/89), 6*
>Lgu 1 (1973/77)–4 (1985/89), 7
>Lu 1 (1973/77)–#
>Mcm 1 (1973/77), 1–8; 2 (1977/81), 1–8; 3
>(1981/84), 1–3; 4 (1985/89), 3–5
>Mpl 1 (1973/77)–#
>Ob*
>Ouf 4 (1985/89), 3–7
>SFu 1 (1973/77)–3 (1981/84)*
>TOd 1 (1973/77), 2–8; 2 (1977/81), 1, 3, 5, 6,
>8; 3 (1981/84), 1, 3–8; 4 (1985/89), 1, 2,
>4–7
>Uu 3 (1981/84), 4–4 (1985/89), 2
>Yu 1 (1973/77), 1, 5; 2 (1977/81), 8

Hausmusik *see* Collegium Musicum: Blätter
zur Pflege der Haus- und Kammermusik

Havergal Brian Society Newsletter
GB–Potters Bar: The Havergal Brian Society,
1975–

>Cu 33, 1981–#
>En 33, 1981–# [w 66, 73]
>Lbar 41, 1983–#
>Lbl*
>Lcm 22, 1979; 34–36, 38, 1981; 39–58,
>1982–85; 60–72, 1985–87; 74, 1987–#
>Lcml 59, 1985–#
>Lsa 29–62, 1980–85; 65–76, 1987–88; 78,
>80, 1988–#
>Ob*

Das Haydn Jahrbuch *see* The Haydn Yearbook

Haydn Society of Great Britain Journal *see* The Haydn Society of Great Britain Newsletter

The Haydn Society of Great Britain Newsletter
1350–1267
GB–Lancaster [etc.]: Haydn Society of Great Britain, 1979–
[From 12, 1992 entitled *Haydn Society of Great Britain Journal*]

  Cu 1 (1979)–#
  EIR:Dtc 6 (1986)–#
  En 6 (1986)–#
  LAu 1 (1979)–#
  Lbar 1 (1979)–8 (1988); 11 (1991)–#
  Lu 6 (1986)–10 (1990); 12 (1992)–#
  Mcm 2 (1980)–9 (1989)
  Ob*

The Haydn String Quartet Society [Newsletter]
GB–London, 1932–?
[NOT IN BUCOMP1; issued to accompany sound recordings]

  Lsa 1–8, 1932–39

Haydn-Studien
TNG D1048; 0440–5323
D– Munich: Henle, 1965–
[Volumes each span a number of years, and are made up of 4 Hefte, as follows: vol. 1, 1965/67; vol. 2, 1969/70; vol. 3, 1973/74; vol. 4, 1976/80; vol. 5, 1982/85; and vol. 6, 1986/88]

  BG 1 (1965/67), 1, 2; 2 (1969/70)–4 (1976/80); 5 (1982/85), 1–3; 6 (1986/88), 1, 3
  CDu 1 (1965/67)–#
  Cu 1 (1965/67)–#
  Lbbc 1 (1965/67)–#
  Lbl*
  Lcml 1 (1965/67)–#
  Lgo 1 (1965/67)–4 (1976/80), 1
  Lkc 1 (1965/67)–6 (1986/88)*
  Lu 1 (1965/67)–#
  Mcm 5 (1982/85), 3, 4–#
  Mu 4 (1976/80)–#
  Ob 1 (1965/67)–#
  Ouf 1 (1965/67)–#

The Haydn Yearbook/Das Haydn Jahrbuch
TNG US725; 0073–1390
US/A/GB–Bryn Mawr, PA: Theodore Presser; Vienna; London: Universal Edition (vols 1–10, 1962–78); Cardiff: University College Cardiff Press (vol. 11, 1980)–

  AB*
  Bp 1 (1962)–16 (1985)
  BRu 1 (1962)
  BSdsc*
  BTu 9 (1975)
  Bu 1 (1962)–13 (1982); 15 (1984); 17 (1992)
  CDu 1 (1962)–#
  Cpl 1 (1962)–16 (1985)
  Cu 1 (1962)–#
  DRu 1 (1962)–3 (1965)
  EIR:Dtc 1 (1962)–16 (1985)
  EIR:Duc 1 (1962)–16 (1985)
  Er 1 (1962)–14 (1983); 18 (1993)–#
  Gul 1 (1962)–#
  HUu 1 (1962)–#
  LAu 1 (1962)–14 (1983)
  Lbbc 1 (1962)–#
  Lbl*
  Lcm 1 (1962); 3 (1965)–12 (1981); 16 (1985)
  Lu 1 (1962)–#
  Mcm 1 (1962)–#
  Mu 1 (1962)–9 (1975)
  NO 1 (1962)–12 (1981)
  NWu 1 (1962)–16 (1985)
  Ob 1 (1962)–#
  Ouf 1 (1962)–16 (1985)
  R 1 (1962)–13 (1982); 16 (1985)–#
  SA 1 (1962)–16 (1985)
  SFu 1 (1962)–#

Hearsay Magazine: the New Magazine for Self-Recording Bands!
GB–Camberley: Insight Publications, 1992–
[NOT IN BUCOMP1]

  Lbl*
  Ob 1992, May, July

Heartland
0963–1143
GB–Warminster: Heartland, 1989–
[NOT IN BUCOMP1]

  Lbl 3, 1990–#*

Herbert Howells Society Newsletter
GB–Welwyn Garden City: Herbert Howells
Society, 1988–
[NOT IN BUCOMP1]

> **Lbar** 1 (1988)–#

Heterofonia: Revista Musical Bimestral
TNG M16; 0018–1137
ME–Mexico City: Conservatorio Nacional de
Musica, 1968–

> **BSdsc***
> **Lu** 1968–#

HHC
0967–7089
GB–Ely: Popular [for Hip-Hop Connection],
199?–
[NOT IN BUCOMP1]

> **Cu** 94, 1996–#
> **Lbl** 46, 1992–#

Hi Fi
I–Milan, 197?–
[NOT IN BUCOMP1]

> **Lsa** 27–37, 1979

Hi-Fi and Music Review
TNG US692
US–Chicago, IL: Ziff-Davis, 1958–
[From 1958, 11, entitled *HiFi Review*; from
1960, 2, entitled *HiFi/Stereo Review*; from
1968, Nov, entitled *Stereo Review*]

> **EIR:Dp** 50 (1985)–#
> **Lsa** 1 (1958)–48 (1983)*; 54 (1989)–#

Hi-Fi Answers
GB–London: Haymarket Publishing, 1972–
[From May 1990 and entitled *Audiophile with
Hi-fi Answers* (q.v.)]

> **AB***
> **Bp** 7 (1979)–15 (1985); 16 (1986), 2–20
> (1990), 3
> **BSdsc***
> **EIR:Dtc** 1 (1972)–19 (1989), 11
> **En***
> **HOp** 4 (1976), 11–20 (1990), 3
> **Lbl***
> **Lcml (r)** [c (2 years)]
> **MI** 7 (1979)–9 (1981)
> **Ob***
> **WCp** (p) 7 (1983)–#

Hi-Fi Buyer's Guide
GB–London: Spotlight Publications, 1977–78
[NOT IN BUCOMP1; incorporated into *Audio:
the Hi-Fi Magazine for Leisure Listening* (q.v.)
from 1978]

> **EIR:Dtc** 1 (1977)–2 (1978), 3

Hi-Fi Choice
0955–1115
GB–London: Dennis Publishing, 197?–
[NOT IN BUCOMP1]

> **AB** 96–98, 1991; 110, 112, 113, 1992; 116,
> 118, 1993–#
> **BEp** [c (1 year)]
> **BLp** [c]
> **BRp** [c (5 years)]
> **CFp** 1988–#
> **EIR:Dtc** 107, 1992–#
> **Lba** 1990, 3–#
> **Len** [c (3 years)]
> **Lha (f)** 1981–#
> **LXp** 1992, Dec–#
> **Mpl** 1992–#
> **Ob***
> **SFp** 53–89, 1981–90; 95, 1991–#

Hi-Fi for Pleasure *see* Which Compact Disc? and Hi-Fi for Pleasure

Hi-Fi/Musical America *see* Musical America

Hi-Fi Musical Life
TNG HK3
HK–Hong Kong: AVA Promotions, 1962–
[NOT IN BUCOMP1; Chinese title is *Yin-Yueh
Sheng Huo*]

> **ALb** 151, 1976

Hi-Fi Musique: Revue des Disques et de la Haute Fidelité *see* La Revue des Disques

Hi-Fi News
TNG GB465; 0018–1226
GB–Croydon: Link House Publications, 1956–
[Absorbed *Record Review* (q.v.) from 1970, 10,
and entitled *Hi-Fi News and Record Review*
(ISSN 0142–6230); in 1959 incorporated
Record News [2]; also incorporating *The Tape
Recorder* (q.v.)]

> **AB** 4 (1959)–#
> **ALb** 15 (1970)–23 (1978)
> **BAR** [c (2 years)]
> **BLp** 3 (1958)–#

Bp 1 (1956)–#
BRp 1 (1956)–9 (1964); 13 (1968)–#
BSdsc*
BTp [c (1 year)]
BuAYp [c (5 years)]
BuBLE [c (1 year)]
BuBUC [c (3 months)]
BuMK [c (4 years)]
BYp [c (1 year)]
Cap [c (5 years)]
CFp 22 (1977)–#
CH [c (5 years)]
COp [c (10 years)]
Cpl 1 (1956)–#*
DS 33 (1988)–# [w 34 (1989), 8; 35 (1990),
    4; 36 (1991), 3]
DU [c (5 years)]
Ea [c (5 years)]
EIR:Dp 33 (1988)–#
EIR:Dtc 1 (1956)–#
EIR:Duc 21 (1976)–30 (1985), 3
En 1 (1956)–19 (1974); 20 (1975)–21
    (1976)*; 22 (1977)–#
Ep 36 (1991), 4–#
Er 18 (1973), Mar, July; 19 (1974), Feb–Apr
GLp 31 (1986)–#
Gm 15 (1970)–#
HA 32 (1987)–#
HOp 18 (1973), 5–#
Je [c (2 years)]
KC [c]
Lba [c (2 years)]
Lbar 1 (1956); 2 (1957), 2, 4–12; 3 (1958)–
    10 (1965), 6, 10, 11; 11 (1966), 1–3, 9–12
    (1967), 1, 2, 5–7; 13 (1968)–#
Lbk [c (5 years)]
Lbl*
Lbo 29 (1984), 2–12; 30 (1985)–#
Lbx 14 (1969)–37 (1992) [m]
LCdM [c]
Lcml (c) [c (1 year)]
Lcml (g) [c (6 months)]
Lcml (m) 3 (1964)–5 (1966)*; 7 (1967)–8
    (1969); 9 (1970), 68–70; 15 (1970)*; 16
    (1971)–#
Len 6 (1961), 4–#
Lgr (e) [c (1 year)]
Lgsm 35 (1990), Mar–#
Lha (f) [c (5 years)]
Lhg 14 (1969)–#
Lhr [c]
Lis [c (5 years)]
Lk [c (5 years)]
Lk (c) [c (1 year)]
Lmi 37 (1992), Jan –#
Lri 17 (1972)–#

Lsa 1 (1956), 2; 2 (1957)–29 (1984), 6; 30
    (1985)–#
LT [c (1 year)]
Lu 4 (1959), 3–5 (1960), 12
LVp 10 (1965)–#
Lwf [c]
Lwwbat [c]
LXp 12 (1967), Nov–#
Mcm 16 (1971), 12; 17 (1972), 2– 12; 18
    (1973)–#*
MI 17 (1972)–#
MI (h) [c (5 years)]
Msuc [c (5 years)]
NHp [c (1 year)]
Ob*
OL 37 (1992)–#
PRp [c (1 year)]
RH [c]
Rp [c (5 years)]
SHRp 36 (1991)–#
SOL 32 (1987)–#
STAp 15 (1970)–#
TOd 26 (1981)–27 (1982), 3
Uu [c (2 years)]
WCp (a) [c]
WCp (alt) [c]
WCp (b) [c]
WCp (f) [c (3 years)]
WCp (fle) [c (3 years)]
WCp (g) [c (1 year)]
WCp (hi) [c]
WCp (p) 5 (1960)–#
WCp (s) [c (5 years)]
WOp [c]

Hi-Fi News and Record Review see Hi-Fi
News

Hi-Fi News and Record Review Annual see
Audio Annual

HiFi Review see Hi-Fi and Music Review

Hi-Fi Sound
TNG GB532
GB–London, 1967–77
[Succeeded Amateur Tape Recording: the
Magazine of the British Tape Recording Club
(q.v.); incorporated Hi-Fi Sound Annual from
1969; from 1990 entitled High Fidelity [3] (q.v.)]

AB 1 (1967)–10 (1977), June
EIR:Dtc 1 (1967)–10 (1977), 3
En*
Lbl*
Ob*

Hi-Fi Sound Annual *see* Hi-Fi Sound

Hi-Fi-Stereo-Phonie *see* Hi-Fi-Stereo-Praxis

Hi-Fi-Stereo-Praxis
TNG D1030
D–Karlsruhe, 1962–
[From 1963, 5, entitled *H-Fi-Stereo-Phonie*]

   Lsa 4 (1965), Mar–21 (1983)

Hi-Fi/Stereo Review *see* Hi Fi and Music Review

Hi-Fi Today *see* Audio: the Hi-Fi Magazine for Leisure Listening

Hi-Fi Weekly
GB–London, 1976–77

   Cu 1–43, 1976–77
   EIR:Dtc 2– 43, 1976–77
   En*
   Ob*

Hi-Fi Yearbook
TNG GB510
GB–London, 1956–

   Bp 1966; 1967; 1970–76; 1978–81
   En 1956–#
   Gm 1956–67; 1970–#
   Lbl*
   Ob*

Hibernian Minstrel
EIRE–Dublin, 1840
[NOT IN BUCOMP1]

   Lcm 1–22, 24–26, 1840

The Hibernian Musical Review
EIRE–Dublin: Richard Milliken, 1822
[Only one issue published]

   Ob 1 (1822)

High Fidelity [1]
TNG US655; 0018–1455
US–New York; Great Barrington, MA: ABC Consumer Magazines, 1951–89
[From 1958, 12–1959, 3 entitled *High Fidelity and Audiocraft*; from 1965–86 incorporated *Musical America* (q.v.). From 1965, Feb. entitled *High Fidelity/Musical America*; from 1970 entitled *High Fidelity and Musical America*; incorporated into *Stereo Review* from

1989, Sep.; see also *Musical America*, which resumed publication as a separate title from 1987]

   ALb 26 (1976), June–Oct, Dec; 27 (1977), Jan–July, Sep–Dec; 28 (1978); 34 (1984), May–35 (1985), July
   Bp 18 (1968), 3–34 (1984), 1–8, 10–12
   Cpl 5 (1955); 8 (1958), 4; 9 (1959), 4; 10 (1960), 2; 11 (1961), 4, 6; 12 (1962), 3, 6, 12
   HUu 16 (1966)–25 (1975)
   Lam 19 (1969), 9
   Lbl*
   Lsa 1 (1951), 3; 2 (1952)–5 (1955); 6 (1956), 4–12; 7 (1957)–32 (1982), 1–4; 34 (1984), 10–12; 35 (1985), 1–9, 12; 36 (1986), 1–5, 7–9, 11, 12; 37 (1987), 2–4, 7–12; 38 (1988); 39 (1989), 1–6
   Lu 15 (1965)–29 (1979)*
   LVp 15 (1965)–22 (1972); 24 (1974)–25 (1975)
   Mpl 15 (1965)–39 (1989)

High Fidelity [2]
TNG DK93
DK–Copenhagen, 1967–

   Lsa 1973, 12; 1976–80*

High Fidelity [3]
GB–Teddington: Haymarket Publishing, 1990–
[NOT IN BUCOMP1; succeeded *Popular Hi-Fi* (q.v.); *New Hi-Fi Sound*]

   AB 1 (1990), 2–#
   Bp 1 (1990), May–1994
   BRDp (pen) [c]
   BSdsc*
   CDCp [c (2 years)]
   COp [c (5 years)]
   EIR:Dtc 1 (1990)–4 (1993), 1
   En*
   Ep [c (5 years)]
   IOW 4 (1993)
   Lba [c (3 months)]
   Lbl*
   Lbo*
   Lbx* 1 (1990)–3 (1992)
   Lcml (m) [c (1 year)]
   Lcml (r) [c (2 years)]
   Len [c (2 years)]
   Lwwb [c]
   Ob 1 (1990)–#
   PRp [c (1 year)]
   RH [c]
   SFp 1 (1990)–#

High Fidelity and Audiocraft *see* High
Fidelity [1]

High Fidelity/Musical America *see* High
Fidelity [1]

High Fidelity and Musical America *see* High
Fidelity [1]

High Fidelity Monitor
NL–Eindhoven: Philips, 1959–60
[NOT IN BUCOMP1; ceased publication with
vol. 1 no. 6 (1960)]

   Lu 1 (1959/60), 1–6

High Fidelity Record Annual *see* Records in
Review

High Performance
0160–9769
US–Los Angeles, CA: Astro Artz, 1978–
[NOT IN BUCOMP1]

   TOd 3 (1980), 3/4–#

Highly Strung *see* Capital M: Music in the
Capital

Hillandale News: the Official Journal of the
City of London Phonograph and
Gramophone Society
0018–1846
GB–London: City of London Phonograph and
Gramophone Society, 1960–

   BDp 1963–68*
   BSdsc*
   Cu 1, 1960–# [w 17–28]
   Lbl*
   Lcml*
   Lsa 1, 1960–# [w 163, 1988]
   Ob*

The Hillbilly-Folk Record Journal
GB–Bromley, 1954–?

   Cbijs 1 (1954), 3, 4; 2 (1955), 1–4; 3 (1956),
   1, 2

Hindemith-Jahrbuch/Annales Hindemith
TNG D1071; 0172–956X
D–Mainz: Schott, 1971–
[Not published in 1975]

   Cu 1971–#
   DRu 1971
   Lbbc 1971–#
   Lbl*
   Lu 1971–#
   Ob 1971–#
   Ouf 1971–87

Hinrichsen's Music Book *see* Hinrichsen's
Year Book

Hinrichsen's Musical Year Book *see*
Hinrichsen's Year Book

Hinrichsen's Year Book
TNG GB381
GB–London: Hinrichsen Edition, 1944–50;
1952; 1955–56; 1960–61
[From 1945 entitled *Hinrichsen's Musical Year
Book*; vol.11 entitled *Hinrichsen's Music Book*]

   ABc 2 (1945)–7 (1952)
   Ap 1 (1944)
   BLu 1 (1944)–8 (1955); 11 (1961)
   Bp 1 (1944)–11 (1961)
   BRu 1 (1944); 4/5 (1947/48); 7 (1952);
    9 (1956); 11 (1961)
   BSdsc 1 (1944)– 11 (1961)
   BTu 1 (1944)–3 (1946)
   Bu 1 (1944)–11 (1961)
   CDu 7 (1952)–11 (1961
   Cpl 1 (1944)–7 (1952); 10 (1958)–11 (1961)
   Cu 1 (1944)–11 (1961)
   DRu 1 (1944)–6 (1950)
   En 1 (1944)–9 (1956)
   Er 1 (1944)–11 (1961)
   Lam 1 (1944)–7 (1952); 9 (1956)–11 (1961)
   LAu 2 (1945)–11 (1961) [w 8]
   Lbbc 2 (1945)–9 (1956)
   Lbl*
   Lcm 1 (1944)–11 (1961)
   Lk 1 (1944)–11 (1961)
   Lu 1 (1944)–11 (1961)
   Mpl 1 (1944)–11 (1961)
   NO 1 (1944)–9 (1956)
   NTp 1 (1944)–11 (1961)
   Ob 1 (1944)–11 (1961)
   Ouf 1 (1944)–11 (1961)
   R 1 (1944)–11 (1961)
   SA 1 (1944)–11 (1961)
   SFu 1 (1944)–3 (1946); 6 (1950)
   SOu 1 (1944)–2 (1945)
   Yu 1 (1944)–11 (1961)

Hip: the Jazz Record Digest
US–Maclean, VA: E. Steane, 1962–71
[Preceded by *Hip: the Milwaukee Jazz Letter*;
succeeded by *Jazz Digest* (q.v.) in 1972]

   Cbijs 1964, 8; 1967, 4, 5

Hip: the Milwaukee Jazz Letter *see* **Hip: the
Jazz Record Digest**

Hip-Hop Connection *see* **HHC**

"His Master's Voice" and Gramophone News
Fellinger 1968/2018; TNG GB245
GB–London, 1910
[Previously entitled *Gramophone News* (q.v.)]

   Lbl*
   Ob*

Hispania Sacra
0018–215X
E–Madrid: Instituto Enrique Flórez, 1948–

   BSdsc*
   Lbl*
   Ob*
   Ouf 1 (1948)–31 (1978/79)

Historic Brass Society Journal
1045–4616
US–New York: Historic Brass Society, 1989–
[NOT IN BUCOMP1]

   BG 7 (1995)–#
   Cu 1 (1989)–#
   Lam 1 (1989)–#
   Lcm 1 (1989); 4 (1992); 5 (1993)
   Lu 1 (1989)–#
   Ob 1 (1989)–#

Historic Brass Society Newsletter
1045–4594
US–New York: Historic Brass Society, 1989–
[NOT IN BUCOMP1]

   BG 9 (1996)–#
   Cu 4 (1992)–#
   Lam 1 (1989)–#
   Lcm 6 (1994)–#
   Lu 4 (1992)–#
   Ob*

Historic Record and AV Collector Quarterly
see **Historic Record Quarterly**

Historic Record Quarterly
0964–0649
GB–Sheffield: J. R. Wrigley, 1986–
[NOT IN BUCOMP1; from issue 22, 1992,
entitled *Historic Record and AV Collector
Quarterly* (ISSN 1356–8825)]

   Cu 22, 1992–#
   LOnjfa*
   Lsa 1, 1986–#
   Ob 1, 1986–#

**Historical Dance: the Journal of the
Dolmetsch Historical Dance Society** *see*
Dolmetsch Historical Dance Society: Journal

Historical Organ Broadsheets
GB–Folkestone: Historical Organs Information,
1986–
[NOT IN BUCOMP1]

   Bu 1–10, 1986–89
   EIR:Dtc 1–11, 1986–90
   En 1–11, 1986–90
   Lbl 6, 1988–#
   Ob*
   R 1–5, 1986–87

Historical Organ Notes
GB–Folkestone: Historical Organ Notes, 1987–
[NOT IN BUCOMP1]

   Bu 1–9, 1987–90 [w 2]
   EIR:Dtc 1–9, 1987–90
   En 1–9, 1987–90
   Lbl*
   Lu 1, 1987
   Ob*
   R 1, 1987

Historical Organs Information Newsletter
GB–Folkestone: Historical Organs Information,
1986–
[NOT IN BUCOMP1]

   Bu 1–7, 1986–89
   Cu 1–9, 1986–89
   EIR:Dtc 1–9, 1986–89
   Lbl 1, 1986–#
   Ob*

**Historical Organs Information: Publications
Survey**
GB–Folkestone: Historical Organs Information,
1988–
[NOT IN BUCOMP1]

EIR:Dtc 1, 1988
Ob 1, 1988–#

Historical Performance: the Journal of Early Music America
0898–8587
US–New York: Early Music America, 1988–
[NOT IN BUCOMP1. Entitled *Early Music America: the Magazine of Historical Performance* (ISSN 1083–3633) from 1996]

EXu 1 (1988)–#
Lam 5 (1992), 2; 6 (1993)–#
Lu 6 (1993)–#
Ouf 10 (1997)–#

Historical Records
EIRE–Dublin, ?–?
[NOT IN BUCOMP1]

Lsa 1957, Dec; 1958, July

Historisch-kritische Beyträge zur Aufnahme der Musik
TNG D9
D–Berlin: J. Schutzens, 1754–78

Lbl*
Ob 1754–78 [Reprint ed.]

History of Rock
GB–London, 1981–

AB 64–121, 1983–84
EXu 1–120, 1981–84
Lsa 1–120, 1981–84

Hit: the New Music and Lifestyle Magazine
GB–London: IPC Magazines, 1985–
[NOT IN BUCOMP1]

EIR:Dtc 1985, Sep 14–Nov 9
Ob 1985, Sep 14–#

Hits
0958–5877
GB–London: Dennis Oneshots, 198?–
[NOT IN BUCOMP1]

Lbl 5, 1991–#*

Hits Now
0961–7809
GB–London: Dennis Oneshots, 1991–
[NOT IN BUCOMP1]

Lbl*

Hitsville USA
GB–Bexleyheath: Tamla Motown Appreciation Society, 1965–
[NOT IN BUCOMP1; entitled *Rhythm and Soul USA* from 1966]

Cbijs n.s. 1 (1966), 1–3
Cu 1 (1965/66); n.s. 1 (1966)
Lbl*
Ob*

Hochschule für Musik Köln *see* Journal: Hochschule für Musik Köln

Hofmeister's Handbuch der Musikliteratur *see* C. F. Whistling's Handbuch der musikalischen Literatur [...]

Hofmeisters Jahresverzeichnis: Verzeichnis sämtlicher Musikalien, Musikbücher, Zeitschriften, Abbildungen und plastischen Darstellungen, die in Deutschland und in den deutschsprachigen Ländern erschienen sind *see* Kurzes Verzeichnis sämmtlicher in Deutschland und den angrenzenden Ländern gedruckter Musikalien, auch musikalischer Schriften und Abbildungen mit Anzeige der Verleger und Preise

Hogaku [= Japanese Traditional Music]
0886–1862
US–New York: Traditional Japanese Music Society, 1983–
[NOT IN BUCOMP1]

Cu 1 (1983)–3 (1987), 2
Lso 1 (1983)–3 (1987)
Ob 1 (1983)–#

Home and Studio Recording
GB–Ely: Home and Studio Recording, 1984–94
[NOT IN BUCOMP1; combined in 1994, May with *Music Technology: formerly E and MM* (q.v.) to form *The Mix* (q.v.)]

Cat 1989, Sep, Dec; 1990, Feb–1994
EIR:Dtc 1, 1984–2, 1985; 11, 1985–1994
Er 1987, 1, 7, 10–12; 1988, 1, 9
Gam 1987, Oct –1988, June
Lro 1991–94
Lsa 1986–93*
Msuc 1985, Dec–1994
Ob*

Home Keyboard Review *see* Keyboard Review

Home Organist and Keyboard Update *see*
Home Organist and Leisure Music

Home Organist and Leisure Music
0140–7902
GB–London: Cover Publications Ltd, 1977–
[From 1983 entitled *Home Organist and
Keyboard Update* and incorporated into *What
Keyboard?: Portable Keyboards, Organs,
Pianos* (ISSN 0266–030X)]

AB 6, 1983, Mar–Sep
BDp 3 (1980)–6 (1983)
Cu 1 (1977)–6 (1983), 9*; 1 (1983)–#
En*
Lbl*
Ob*

Homeground: the International Kate Bush
Fanzine
GB–Orpington: Homeground, 1982–
[NOT IN BUCOMP1]

Lbl*

Homer, the Slut
GB–London: Homer, the Slut [for Bob Dylan
Fan Club], 198?–
[NOT IN BUCOMP1]

Cu 1990–95
Lbl 3–11, 198?–

Hong Kong Hi-Fi and Music Review
HK–Hong Kong: Hong Kong Media
Corporation, 1976–
[NOT IN BUCOMP1]

Lbl*

Hop [translated title] *see* Taplas

The Horn Call: Journal of the International
Horn Society
TNG US807; 0046–7928
US–Elmhurst, IL [etc.]: International Horn
Society, 1971–
[NOT IN BUCOMP1]

ALb 22 (1991), 1
Bs*
Gam 22 (1991)–#
Lcm 25 (1995), 3; 26 (1996)–#
Mcm 13 (1982/83)–#

The Horn Magazine
GB–Epsom [etc.]: British Horn Society, 1992–
[NOT IN BUCOMP1; no ISSN]

Bs 1 (1992), 1; 2 (1993)–#
Lam 1 (1992), 1
Lcm 1 (1992), 1–3
Ltc 4 (1996), 2–#

Hosanna
0790–3537
EIRE–Dublin: Irish Church Music Association,
1975–
[NOT IN BUCOMP1]

Cu 4 (1982)–5 (1983), 5
EIR:Dtc 5 (1983), 1–5
EIR:Duc 4 (1982)–5 (1983)
EIR:MEtc 1 (1975)–#
Ob*

Hot Buttered Soul
GB–Sheppey, 196?–

Lsa 11, 1972; 16, 17, 1973; 49, 1977

Hot Club de Belgique: Hot Club Magazine *see*
Jazz [2]

Hot Hits [1]
0962–7227
GB–London: Dennis Oneshots, 1991–
[NOT IN BUCOMP1]

Lbl*

Hot Hits [2]
GB–Burnham on Crouch: St James, 1986–?87
[NOT IN BUCOMP1. ?Succeeded from 1987
by *Graffiti* (q.v.)]

Lbl*

Hot Metal
0962–8347
GB–London, 1991–
[NOT IN BUCOMP1]

Lbl*

Hot News and Rhythm Record Review
TNG GB347
GB–London: Hot News, 1935

Lbl*
LOnjfa*

Hot Notes [1]
EIRE–Dublin, 1946–48

  Cbijs 5–13, 1946–48
  EIR:Dtc 12, 13, 1948

Hot Notes [2]
US–New York: New York Jazz Museum, 1969–
?

  Cbijs 6 (1974), 3–12

Hot Press
EIRE–Dublin: Steady Rolling Publishing, 1977–
[NOT IN BUCOMP1]

  AB*
  Cu 12 (1988), 2–#
  EIR:Dp 12 (1988)–#
  EIR:Dtc 1 (1977)–#
  Mpl [c]
  Ob 12 (1988), 2–#

Hot Press Yearbook
EIRE–Dublin, 1982–

  Cu 1982
  EIR:MEtc 1987–88

Hot-Revue: Revue Mensuelle de Jazz-Hot
TNG CH133
CH–Lausanne, 1946–

  Cbijs 1946, 9; 1947, 3

House News: the Magazine of the Royal Opera House
GB–London: Royal Opera House, 1984/85–
[NOT IN BUCOMP1]

  Lcm (p) 1 (1984/85)

The House Organ Magazine
GB–Slough: House Organ Institute, 1944–

  EIR:Dtc 4 (1947), 2–7 (1950), 4
  Lbl*

Hudební Nástroje [= Musical Instruments]
TNG CS209; 0323–1283
CZ–Hradec Kralove: Ceskoslovenske Hudebni Nástroje, Statni Podnik, 1964–90

  BSdsc*
  Ob*

Hudební Revue [= Musical Review]
Fellinger 1968/1914; TNG CS580
CZ–Prague, 1908–20

  LAu 9 (1915), 1–6, 8–10; 10 (1916), 1–10; 11 (1917), 1, 2, 4–10
  Ob*

Hudební Rozhledy [= Music Review]
TNG CS116
CZ–Brno: Pazdirek, 1924–27

  Lbl*
  Ob*

Hudební Rozhledy: Rada B, Hudební Věda
see Hudební Věda

Hudební Rozhledy: Měsíčník pro Hudební Kulturu [= Musical Outlook: Monthly of Musical Culture]
TNG CS176; 0018–6996
CZ–Prague, 1948–

  ALb 46 (1993), 4
  Gul 26 (1973); 29 (1976)–31 (1978); 37 (1984)–#*
  LAu 23 (1970)–27 (1974); 28 (1975), 2–36 (1983)
  Lbl*
  Lcml 22 (1969); 23 (1970)*
  Lu 14 (1961); 23 (1970)–27(1974)
  Mcm 9 (1956), 5
  Ob*

Hudební Věda [= Musicology]
TNG CS204; 0018–7003
CZ–Prague: Panton, 1964–
[Preceded by *Hudební Rozhledy: Rada B, Hudební Věda* (Prague, 1961–62)]

  Cu 1 (1964)–#
  En 6 (1969), 4–#
  LAu 1 (1964) 21 (1984)
  Lbl*
  Lu (RMA) 7 (1970), 2; 9 (1972), 1–4
  Ob*
  Ouf 6 (1969), 4–19 (1982), 3*

Hudobnovedné Štúdie Slowenskej Akadémie Vied [= Musicological Studies of the Slovak Academy of Sciences]
TNG CS190; 0439–8491
SQ–Bratislava: Vydavatel'stvo Slovenskej Akademie Vied, 1953–54; 1955; 1957; 1959–61
[Continued from 1969 as *Musicologica Slovaca* (q.v.)]

  Cu 1 (1955)–5 (1961)
  Lbl*
  Ob*

Hudobny Archív [= Musical Archive]
SQ–Martin: Matica Slovenska, 1974–

Cu 1974–#
Gul 1981–85
Lbl*
Ob*

Hudobny Zivot [= Musical Life]
TNG CS219
SQ–Bratislava, 1969–

BSdsc*
Gul 1980–#
Ob*

Hungarian Choir [translated title] *see* Magyar Kórus

Hungarian Dance News
H–Budapest: Globus Nyomda, 198?–
[NOT IN BUCOMP1]

Gul 1984–#
Lcm 1985, 1, 2; 1986, 1, 2; 1988, 1
Lu 1986, 1, 2; 1988, 1

Hungarian Music [translated title] *see* Magyar Zene

Hungarian Music News
TNG H91; 0441–5973
H–Budapest: Interkoncert Festivalbureau, 1969–83; n.s. 1984–

Cu 1979, 3–4; 1980, 1–4; n.s. 1 (1984)–4 (1987), 2/3
Ep n.s. 2 (1985), 3; 3 (1986)–4 (1987), 3
Gam n.s. 1 (1984); 2 (1985), 1, 2; 3 (1986), 2; 4 (1987), 1–3
Gul n.s. 1 (1984)–4 (1987)
Lam 1977, 3, 4; 1978, 5, 6; 1979, 1; n.s. 3 (1986), 1–4; 4 (1987), 1–3
Lbbc 1973–83; n.s. 1 (1984)–#*
Lcm 1969, 1; 1970, 1–4; 1971, 1, 5, 6; 1972, 1, 2; 1973, 2, 3; 1975, 3; 1976, 1, 6; 1977, 1; 1978, 2, 3; 1980, 3, 4; 1981, 1, 5; 1982, 2–6; 1983, 1; n.s. 1 (1984), 1, 2; 2 (1985), 1–3; 3 (1986); 4 (1987), 1
Lu 3 (1986), 1–4; 4 (1987), 1–3
Mcm 1971, 5, 6; 1972, 1–4; 1973, 2–6; 1974, 1–5
Mu 1 (1984)–4 (1987)
Ouf 1971–76*; 1979–83; n.s. 1 (1984)–#*

Hungarian Music Quarterly
0238–9401
H–Budapest: Editio Musica, 1989–
[NOT IN BUCOMP1]

Bu 1 (1989)–#
Cu 1 (1989)–#
En 1 (1989)–#
Ep 1 (1989)–#
Gam 3 (1992), 2–4
Gsmic [c]
Gul 3 (1992)–#
Lam 1 (1989)–4 (1993), 1; 5 (1994)–#
Lbbc 1 (1989)–#
Lcm 1 (1989)–#
Lsa 1 (1989)–#
Lu 1 (1989), 1, 3, 4; 2 (1990), 1–4
Mu 3 (1992), 3–4 (1993), 2; 5 (1994), 1
Ouf 1 (1989)–#

Hungarian Musical Bibliography [translated title] *see* Magyar Zenemüvek Bibliográfiája

Hungarian Musical Guide
H–Budapest: International Festivalbureau, 1967–84

ALb 22, 1983
Gul 15–22, 1978–83
Lbbc 8–22, 1973–83
Lcm 1–22, 1967–83*
Mcm*

The Hungarian Quarterly *see* The New Hungarian Quarterly

Hungarian Survey
0441–4489
H–Budapest: Corvina, ?1966–68

Lbl*

Hurdy-Gurdy Society Journal
GB–Dorchester: The Hurdy-Gurdy Society, 199?–
[NOT IN BUCOMP1]

Lbl 17, 1994–#
Lcs 18, 1994

Hurdy-Gurdy Society Newsletter
GB–Dorchester: The Hurdy-Gurdy Society, ?–
[NOT IN BUCOMP1]

Lcs 1985–#*

The Hymn: a Journal of Congregational Song
TNG US640; 0018–8271
US–New York [etc.]: Hymn Society of America,
1949–

> BSdsc 30 (1979)–#
> Lbl*
> Lcm 13 (1962)–29 (1978), 3; 30 (1979)–34
> (1983); 35 (1984), 2–43 (1992), 3

Hymn Society of America News Bulletin
US–Springfield, OH, 1946–

> Lbl*

The Hymn Society of Great Britain and
Ireland: Bulletin
TNG GB361; 0018–828X
GB–Oxford: The Hymn Society of Great Britain
and Ireland, 1937–

> BSdsc*
> EIR:Dtc 6 (1965/68)–#
> En 1 (1937)–3 (1955); 4 (1956)*;
> 6 (1965/68)*; 7 (1969)–#
> Lbl*
> Lcm 1 (1937)–#
> Ob*

Hymnologiske Meddelelser [= Hymnology
Reports]
0106–4940
DK–Copenhagen: Salmehistorisk Selskab,
1972–#
[NOT IN BUCOMP1]

> Ob 12 (1983), 3–#

Hymns and Congregational Songs
GB–London: Stainer and Bell, 1988–
[NOT IN BUCOMP1]

> EIR:Dtc 1 (1988)–#

I

IAML see International Association of Music
Libraries, Archives and Documentation
Centres

IAO News see IAO News Supplement

IAO News Supplement
GB–Newcastle [etc.]: Incorporated Association
of Organists, 1985–
[NOT IN BUCOMP1. Entitled IAO News from
no. 14, 1989]

> Cu 1, 1985–#

IASA see International Association of Sound
Archives

IASA Journal see Phonographic Bulletin

Iconographie Musicale
CH–Geneva: Minkoff, 1972–

> BSdsc*
> Lbl*
> Ob 1972–#

ICTM Directory of Interests and Projects see
Directory of Traditional Music

Ifjú Zenebarát: az Országos Filharmónia
Ifjúsagi Folyóirata [= Young Music Lover:
Review of the Junior National Philharmonic
Orchestra]
H–Budapest: Zenemükiado Vállalat, 1962–
[NOT IN BUCOMP1]

> ALb 1 (1962)–3 (1964), Apr

IFPI Bulletin
GB–London: IFPI [International Federation of
the Phonographic Industry], ?1977–

> Lsa 3, 1977

IFPI Journal
GB–London: IFPI [International Federation of
the Phonographic Industry], 1977–

> Lsa 1–15, 1978–82 [w 3, 4, 6, 7, 9]

IFPI Newsletter
GB–London: IFPI [International Federation of
the Phonographic Industry], 1976

> Lsa 1–3, 1976

ILC Quarterly see International Liszt Centre
Quarterly

The Illustrated Ballad Magazine
TNG GB53
GB–London, 1857
[Only one number was published]

> Lbl

The Illustrated Melodist
Fellinger 1968/620; TNG GB73
GB–London, 1870
[Only two numbers were published]

> Lbl 1, 2, 1870

L'Illustration Musicale: Journal de
Composition Musicale
Fellinger 1968/522; TNG F114
F–Paris, 1865–66

    Lbl*

L'Illustration Musicale: Répertoire Moderne
des Compositeurs Contemporains
F–Paris, 1863

    Lbl 1–12, 1863

Illustrirte Theaterzeitung *see* Wiener Theater-
Zeitung

Image
GB–Sunderland: Sunderland Folk Centre, 1968–
[NOT IN BUCOMP1]

    AB 1 (1968), 1

Images Musicales
TNG F588
F–Paris, 1945–48

    Lcml 11–78, 1945–48*

Imago Musicae
0255–8831
D/GB–Kassel; London: Bärenreiter [for the
Répertoire International d'Iconographie
Musicale], 1984–
[NOT IN BUCOMP1]

    BLu 1 (1984)–6 (1989)
    Bu 1 (1984)–#
    Cu 1 (1984)–#
    Er 1 (1984)–5 (1988)
    Gul 1 (1984)–5 (1988)
    Lbbc 1 (1984)–#
    Lbl 1 (1984)–#
    Lgo 1 (1984)–5 (1988)
    LRHBNC 1 (1984)
    Lu 1 (1984)–#
    Ob 1 (1984)–#
    Ouf 1 (1984)–#
    SA 1 (1984)–5 (1988)
    SOu 1 (1984)–#

I.M.I. News
0792–6413
IL–Tel Aviv: Israel Music Institute, 1990–
[NOT IN BUCOMP1]

    ALb 1992, 4–#
    Gsmic [c]

Impetus *see* Impetus: New Music

Impetus: New Music
TNG GB576
GB–London, 1976–
[Entitled *Impetus* from 1978]

    Cbijs 1, 1976–?
    LOnjfa*
    Lsa 1–10, 1976–79 [w 7]
    Lu 1–10, 1977–79 [w 2–4, 7]

Impromptu: a Publication of the Music
Division of the Library of Congress
0737–5190
US–Washington, DC: Library of Congress
Music Division, 1982–85
[NOT IN BUCOMP1; ceased publication with
1985, no. 3]

    Cpl 1 (1982)–3 (1985)
    HUu 1 (1982), 1, 2
    Lam 1 (1982), 1; 3, 1985
    Lu 3 (1985)

In-Choir: Newsletter of the Association of
Irish Choirs
EIRE–Cork: Cumann Naisiunta na
gCor/Association of Irish Choirs, 1985–
[NOT IN BUCOMP1]

    Cu 1 (1985)–#*
    EIR:Dtc 1 (1985)–#
    EIR:MEtc 1 (1985); 2 (1986), 1–3; 3 (1987),
       1–3; 4 (1988), 1; 5 (1989), 1; 1990 (Oct);
       1992 (Dec)–#
    Lbl 1990, Oct–#

In Concert
US–Los Angeles, CA: World Jazz Association,
1975–

    Cbijs 1 (1975), 2, 4, 6; 2 (1976), 1, 2

In the City
0260–0560
GB–London: In the City, 1977–
[NOT IN BUCOMP1]

    Lbl*

In the Groove
US–Camden, NJ: RCA Records, 1946–?47

    Cbijs 1 (1946), 11, 12; 2 (1947), 1

In the Musical World [translated title] *see* V
Mire Muzyki

In Theory Only: Journal of the Michigan
Music Theory Society
TNG US856; 0360–4365
US–Ann Arbor, MI: Michigan Music Theory
Society, 1975–
[From 12 nos 7/8 (1994) published Bowling
Green State University, OH]

BTu 5 (1979)–#
Cu 11 (1989)–#
EXu 1 (1975)–4 (1978), 8 [m]; 4 (1979), 7–#
HUu 12 (1991)–#
LAu 12 (1991)–#
Lcu 12 (1991)–#
Lkc 3 (1977)*–6 (1981/82); 8 (1985/86)–#
LRHBNC 10 (1988), 5–8 –#
NO 3 (1977), 7–8 (1985)
Ouf 1 (1975), 1; 3 (1977), 7–#*
SOu 1 (1975)–3 (1977) [m]; 4 (1979)–#
Uu 11 (1989)–#

In to Jazz
GB–London: Musical New Services, 1974–

Cbijs 1974–#
Lcml 1974, 1, 2
LOnjfa 1974–#
Lsa 1974

In Tune
GB–?: C. Morgan, 1987–
[NOT IN BUCOMP1; entitled *In Tune
International* from no. 26, 1991]

AB 1–13, 1987–89; 15–18, 1989–90; 23–26,
1990–91; 28, 1991–#
Cu 26, 1991–#
EIR:Dtc 1, 1987–#
LOnjfa*
Lsa 1, 1987–# 1, 1987–#

In Tune: the Magazine of the Friends of the
Scottish National Orchestra
TNG GB561
GB–Glasgow: Friends of the Scottish National
Orchestra, 1972–

En 1, 2, 1972; 4, 5, 1973–74
Ob*

In Tune International *see* In Tune

Incorporated Association of Organists:
Quarterly Record *see* National Union of
Organists' Associations: Quarterly Record

Incorporated Association of Organists *see also*
IAO News Supplement

Incorporated Society of Musicians: Handbook
and Register
GB–London, 1898–1983
[NOT IN BUCOMP1; succeeded by
*Incorporated Society of Musicians: Yearbook
and Register of Members* (q.v.)]

BRp 1952–83
Lcm 1937; 1958, 1960–69
Lu 1948–83
Ob*
SA 1906–08

Incorporated Society of Musicians Journal *see*
A Music Journal: Comprising the Report of
the Incorporated Society of Musicians [...]

Incorporated Society of Musicians Monthly
Journal *see* Monthly Journal of the National
Society of Professional Musicians

Incorporated Society of Musicians: Monthly
Report *see* The British Music Society Bulletin

Incorporated Society of Musicians: Monthly
Report *see also* Monthly Journal of the
National Society of Professional Musicians

Incorporated Society of Musicians Periodical
Report *see* Monthly Journal of the National
Society of Professional Musicians

The Incorporated Society of Musicians:
Register of Musicians in Education
0953–5330
GB–London: Incorporated Society of
Musicians, 1986–
[NOT IN BUCOMP1]

Lbl 1986–#
Lu [c]
Ob*
Ouf [c]
SOu 1988–90; 1992–#

**Incorporated Society of Musicians: Register
of Performers and Composers**
0951–6247; 0959–7603
GB–London: Incorporated Society of
Musicians, ?1987–
[NOT IN BUCOMP1; from ?1989 subtitled
Register of Professional Artists]

> **BRp** 1987–89; 1990–#
> **Lbl** 1987–89; 1990–#
> **Lu** [c]
> **Lwwb** [c]
> **WW** [c]

**The Incorporated Society of Musicians:
Register of Professional Artists** *see* The
Incorporated Society of Musicians: Register
of Performers and Composers

**The Incorporated Society of Musicians:
Register of Professional Private Music
Teachers**
0951–6239
GB–London: Incorporated Society of
Musicians, 1987–
[NOT IN BUCOMP1]

> **ABDp** [c]
> **BRp** 1987–#
> **Lbl** 1987–#
> **Lu** [c]
> **Lwwb** [c]
> **Lwwbat** [c]
> **Lwwput** [c]
> **Mpl***
> **Ob***
> **Ouf** [c]
> **WW** [c]

**The Incorporated Society of Musicians:
Report**
TNG GB237
GB–London: Incorporated Society of
Musicians, 1909–29
[NOT IN BUCOMP1]

> **Cpl** 1925–28
> **Lu** 1910–19*
> **Mpl** 1920–27

**The Incorporated Society of Musicians:
Yearbook and Register of Members**
0951–6220
GB–London: Incorporated Society of
Musicians, 1984–
[NOT IN BUCOMP1; preceded 1898–1983 by
the *Incorporated Society of Musicians:
Handbook and Register* (q.v.)]

> **ALb** 1991/92
> **BRp** 1984–#
> **Lam** 1986/87–#
> **Lbbc** [c]
> **Lbl***
> **LU** 1984–
> **Msuc** [c]
> **Ob***
> **WW** [c]

**Incorporated Society of Organ Builders
Journal** *see* **Journal of the Incorporated
Society of Organ Builders**

L'Indépendance Musicale et Dramatique
Fellinger 1968/1045; TNG F210
F–Paris, 1887–88
[19 numbers published in total]

> **Lbl***
> **Ouf** 1 (1887)–2 (1888) [Reprint ed.]

The Independent Catalogue
GB–London, 1993–94
[NOT IN BUCOMP1]

> **CDCp** 5, 8–12, 1993–94
> **Lsa** 1–12, 1993–94

The Independent Label Register
GB–Crewe: A. Tyrrell, 1984–
[NOT IN BUCOMP1]

> **Lbl***

The Independent Theatre Goer
GB–London, 1912

> **Lbl***
> **Ob***

Index to Record and Tape Reviews *see*
Record and Tape Reviews Index

Indian Music Journal
TNG IN10; 0019–5995
IN–New Delhi: Delhi Sangita Samaj, 1964–

> **BSdsc***
> **Er** 3–6, 1965–66
> **Lam** 5, 1966
> **Lbl***
> **Lcml** 4–7, 1965–67
> **Lio** 1, 1964–# [w 17 (1988)]
> **Lso** 1, 2, 1964; 5, 6, 1966; 1967–74; 1984–#
> **Lu** 3–5, 1965–66
> **Lu (RMA)** 4, 1965–#
> **Ob***

Indiana Theory Review
TNG US873; 0271–8022
US–Bloomington, IN: Graduate Theory
Association, Indiana University, 1977–
[NOT IN BUCOMP1]

    NO 1 (1977)–7 (1986), 1
    SOu 11 (1990)–#

Info-RISM
D–Frankfurt-am-Main: RISM Zentralredaktion,
1989–
[NOT IN BUCOMP1]

    Cu 4, 1992–#
    Ouf 1, 1989–#

**Infolk: Music, Song, Dance in and around
Leicestershire**
GB–Leicester, 1982–
[NOT IN BUCOMP1]

    Lbl 1, 1982– #

Information: Fondation Eugène Ysaye *see*
**Fondation Eugène Ysaye: Bulletin
d'Information**

**Informations: International Antonio Vivaldi
Society**
TNG INTL36
DK–Copenhagen [etc.]: International Antonio
Vivaldi Society, 1971–73
[NOT IN BUCOMP1; 1972 issue entitled
*International Antonio Vivaldi Society:
Information*; entitled *Vivaldi Informations* from
vol. 2 (1973)]

    Cu 1 (1971/72)–2 (1973)
    En 1 (1971/72)–2 (1973)
    HUu 1 (1971/72)–2 (1973)
    Lum 1 (1971/72)
    Lcm 1 (1972)–2 (1973)
    Lcml 1 (1971)–2 (1973)
    Lu 1 (1971)–2 (1973)
    NO 1 (1971)–2 (1973)
    R 1 (1971/72)–2 (1973)

Informatsionniy Byuletin *see* **Informatsionniy
Sbornik**

Informatsionniy Muzykalny Byuletin [=
Music Information Bulletin]
TNG BG16
BG–Sofia: Union of Bulgarian Composers, 1969–
[NOT IN BUCOMP1; also published in English
as *Union of Bulgarian Composers: Music News
Bulletin*]

    Lam 1970, 2; 1973, 4, 5; 1987, 1–3; 1988,
    1–4; 1989, 2
    Lu 1987, 2–4

Informatsionniy Sbornik [= **Collection of
Information**]
TNG USSR68
RF–Moscow: USSR Union of Composers,
1946–
[From 1955 entitled *Informatsionniy Byuletin*]

    Cpl 1963, 4; 1964, 1
    KE 1980, 11, 12; 1981, 11, 12; 1982, 1, 5, 6
    Lam 1977, 10; 1978, 1–5; 1981, 11, 12; 1982,
    5, 6; 1985–1986, 2
    Lbbc 1970–76*
    Ouf 1962, 2–1985, 12

Informazioni e Studi Vivaldiani
0393–2915
I–Milan: Ricordi, 1980–

    Au 4 (1983)–#
    BLu 1 (1980)–#
    BRu 7 (1986)–#
    Bu 1 (1980)–#
    CDu 2 (1981)–11 (1990)
    Cu 1 (1980)–#
    EIR:Duc 2 (1981)–#
    En 1 (1980)–#
    Er 1, 1980–#
    EXu 6 (1985)–11 (1990); 13 (1992)–14
    (1993)
    Gam 1 (1980)–#
    Gul 1 (1980)–#
    HUu 1 (1980)–5 (1984)
    Lam 1 (1980)–#
    LAu 1 (1980)–# [w 3 (1982)]
    Lbbc 1 (1980)–#
    Lblᵂ
    Lcm 1 (1980)
    Lcml 1 (1980)–#
    LIp 3 (1982)–5 (1984)
    Lkc 2 (1981)–#
    LRHBNC 2 (1981)–#
    Lu 1 (1980)–#
    LVu 8 (1987)–#
    Mcm 1 (1980)–#
    Mu 1 (1980)–#
    NO 1 (1980); 3 (1982); 5 (1984)–#
    NWu 1 (1980)–4 (1983); 7 (1986)–#
    Ob*
    Ouf 1 (1980)–#
    R 1 (1980)–#
    SFu 1 (1980)–#
    Yu 1 (1980)–#

InHarmoniques
0987–6960
F–Paris: IRCAM, 1986–91
[NOT IN BUCOMP1; ceased publication with nos 8/9, 1991]

Bu 1–4, 1986–88
Lbl 1–8/9, 1986–91

Insight
0959–9509
GB– London: Insight, 1987–
[NOT IN BUCOMP1; also called *Music and Video Insight*]

Lbl 18, 199?–#*

Institute for Advanced Musical Studies Newsletter
GB–London: University of London, King's College, 1993–
[NOT IN BUCOMP1]

Lam 1, 1993–#

Institute for Psychoacoustic and Electronic Music *see* Jaarboek I.P.E.M./I.P.E.M. Yearbook

Institute for Studies in American Music: Newsletter
TNG US811; 0145–8396
US–Brooklyn, NY: Institute for Studies in American Music, 1971–

BSdsc 8 (1979), 2–#
Cpl 8 (1979), 2–#
Cu 1 (1971)–#
KE 1 (1971)–21 (1992)* [w 11 (1981); 13 (1983); 15 (1985); 17 (1988); 20 (1990)]

Institute of Popular Music: Newsletter
GB–Liverpool: University of Liverpool, 1989–
[NOT IN BUCOMP1]

En 1, 1989; 3, 1991
Lam 2, 1991–#*
Lcs 1, 1989–#

Instituto Interamericano de Etnomusicología y Folklore *see* Revista INIDEF

Instituto Interamericano de Investigación Musical: Anuario *see* Anuario/Yearbook

The Instrumentalist
TNG US595; 0020–4331
US–Glen Ellyn, IL [etc.]: The Instrumentalist, 1946–

BLp 23 (1969)–#
Bs 44 (1990), 6–#
BSdsc*
CCtc 42 (1988)–#
EIR:Dp 40 (1986)–#
Lam 3 (1949), 5
Lcml 5 (1951)–6 (1952)*; 21 (1967), 9–#
Mcm 35 (1980/81), 6–#
Msuc 39 (1984/85), Aug–#
Uu 41 (1987)–#

Instrumentenbau Zeitschrift *see* Zeitschrift für Instrumentenbau

Instrumentenbau Zeitschrift, Musik International *see* Musik International

Intégral: the Journal of Applied Musical Thought
1073–6913
US–Rochester, NY: Eastman School of Music, 1987–
[NOT IN BUCOMP1]

EXu 1 (1987)–#
SOu 4 (1990)–#

Intelligenzblatt zur Cäcilia *see* Cäcilia: eine Zeitschrift für die musikalische Welt

Inter-American Institute for Musical Research: Yearbook/Instituto Interamericano de Investigación Musical: Anuario *see* Anuario/Yearbook

Inter-American Music Bulletin
TNG US681; 0020–4978
US–Washington, DC: Department of Cultural Affairs, Pan American Union, 1957–73
[Ceased publication with no. 87, 1973]

BSdsc*
Cpl 1–87, 1957–73*
Lbl*
Lcml 3, 5–14, 1958–59; 16–87, 1960–73
Lkc 1–87, 1957–73
Lu 1–87, 1957–73

Inter-American Music Review
TNG US882; 0195–6655
US–Los Angeles, CA: Inter–American Music
Review, 1978–

    Cu 2 (1979)–#
    Lbl 1 (1978)–#
    Lcml 1 (1978)–#

Interface: Journal of New Music Research
TNG NL125; 0303–3902
NE–Lisse: Swets and Zeitlinger, 1972–
[Preceded 1969–71 by *Electronic Music Reports*
(q.v.) Entitled *Journal of New Music Research*
from 23 (1994)]

    AB*
    BG 24 (1995)–#
    BSdsc*
    Bu 10 (1981)–11 (1982)
    CCtc 9 (1980)–13 (1984)
    Cu 1 (1972)–#
    En 6 (1977)–22 (1993)
    Er 1 (1972)–2 (1973); 20 (1991), 3, 4; 21
      (1992), 2; 22 (1993)–#
    HUu 3 (1974)–4 (1975)
    KE 23 (1994)–#
    Lam 1 (1972)–22 (1993), 4 [w 13 (1984), 4;
      16 (1987), 3]
    Lbl*
    Lcm 1 (1972), 1; 2 (1973), 1; 3 (1974), 1;
      4 (1975), 2; 5 (1976)–10 (1981), 2 [w 8
      (1979), 1]
    Lcml 1 (1972)–#
    Lkc 1 (1972)–16 (1987)
    Lu 1 (1972)–#
    NO 1 (1972)–#
    NWu 2 (1973)–15 (1986)
    Ob*
    SOu 11 (1982)–17 (1988)
    Yu 1 (1972)–23 (1994), 1

Intermezzo: the Magazine of Carnegie Hall
US–New York: Muse Publishing Company, ?–
[NOT IN BUCOMP1]

    ALb 1977, Mar

International ABBA Magazine
0264–4096
GB–Iver Heath: ABBA Magazine, 1981–
[NOT IN BUCOMP1]

    Lbl 5, 198?–#*

The International Alban Berg Society
Newsletter
TNG INTL26
US–Durham, NC [etc.]: International Alban
Berg Society, 1968–

    Cu 1, 1968–#
    Lgo 1, 1968–#
    Mcm 1, 1968–#
    Mu 1–3, 1968–75
    Ouf 1–13, 1968–85

International Antonio Vivaldi Society:
Information *see* Informations: International
Antonio Vivaldi Society

International Association of Music Libraries:
Bulletin d'Information
TNG INTL14
F–Paris: International Association of Music
Libraries, 1952–53
[Succeeded by *Fontes Artis Musicae* (q.v.)]

    Bp 1 (1952)–2 (1953), 1
    BRu 1 (1952)–2 (1953), 1
    Cpl 1 (1952), 2; 2 (1953), 1
    Gul 1 (1952)–2 (1953)
    Lcml 1 (1952)–2 (1953), 1
    Lu 1 (1952)–2 (1953), 1
    Mpl 1 (1952)–2 (1953)

The International Association of Music
Libraries, Archives and Documentation
Centres (UK Branch): Annual Report
GB–London [etc.]: IAML(UK), 1953–
[NOT IN BUCOMP1]

    ALb 1989; 1991
    EIR:MEtc 1986–#
    LAu 1988–#
    Lu 1953–56, 1958, 1962–#
    Ob*
    SOu 1964–92 [w 1968; 1969]

The International Association of Music
Libraries, Archives and Documentation
Centres (UK Branch): Annual Survey of
Music Libraries
0958–4560
GB–London [etc.]: IAML(UK), 1984–
[NOT IN BUCOMP1]

 Au 1984–#
 BRp 1984; 1986–#
 CAu 1985–#
 Lbl 1984–#
 Lwwb 1990–#
 NO 1985; 1990–#
 Ob*
 WW 1988; 1991–#

International Association of Music Libraries,
Archives and Documentation Centres (UK
Branch): Newsletter
0263–9939
GB–IAML(UK), 1982–
[NOT IN BUCOMP1]

 ABc (ILS) 1, 1982–# [w 4, 1983]
 ALb 18– 25, 1990–93 [w 21, 24]
 Au 1, 1982–#
 BLp [c]
 CAu 13, 1987–#
 CDCp 16, 1989–#
 Cu 1, 1982–#
 EIR:Dtc 1–11, 1982–86
 EIR:Metc 25, 1993–#
 Ep 1, 2, 1982; 5–17, 1983–89; 19, 1990–#
 Gam 12, 1987–#
 Gsmic 23, 1992–#
 Gul 6, 1984–#
 Lam 3, 1982; 5, 1983; 6, 1984; 8, 9, 1985;
  16–19, 1989–90; 21, 22, 1991; 27, 1994– #
 LAu 4, 1983–# [w 6]
 Lbl 2, 1982–#
 Lcs 14, 1988–#
 Lgo 21, 1991–#
 Lha (f) [c (5 years)]
 Lu 1–18, 20, 1981–90
 Msuc [c (3 years)]
 Mu 3, 1982–#
 NO 1, 1982–#
 Ob*
 Ouf 1, 1982–# [w 2, 4]
 Rp [c]

International Association of Sound Archives:
Information Bulletin
GB–London: International Association of Sound
Archives, 1990–
[NOT IN BUCOMP1]

 En 1, 2, 1990; 4, 1993–#

International Association of Sound Archives
(Australia) Newsletter
AUS–?, 1979–86; 1986–
[Continued from 1986 as *The Australasian
Sound Archive*, with new numbering system]

 Lsa 1–25, 1979–86

International Association of Sound Archives,
Phonographic Bulletin *see* Phonographic
Bulletin

International Association of Sound Archives,
UK Branch: Newsletter
GB–London: International Association of Sound
Archives, 1980–86
[NOT IN BUCOMP1; succeeded by *B.A.S.C.
News* from 1987 (q.v.)]

 Cu 1–12, 1980–86
 EIR:Dtc 1–12, 1980–86
 Lsa 1–12, 1980– 86

International Chopin Foundation Bulletin
US–Detroit: International Chopin Foundation,
?1959–?

 LAu 3 (1961), Oct, Nov

The International Church Music Review *see*
Rivista Internazionale di Musica Sacra

International Classical Record Collector
GB–Harrow: Gramophone, 1995–
[NOT IN BUCOMP1]

 Cu 1, 1995–#
 Ouf 2 (1997), 9–#

International Council for Traditional Music:
Directory *see* Directory of Traditional Music

International Council for Traditional Music:
Yearbook *see* Yearbook of the International
Folk Music Council

International Council for Traditional Music,
United Kingdom Chapter: Bulletin *see*
International Council for Traditional Music,
United Kingdom Chapter: Newsletter

International Council for Traditional Music, United Kingdom Chapter: Newsletter
GB–London: International Council for Traditional Music, UK Chapter, 1974–
[Continued from 1983 as the *International Council for Traditional Music, United Kingdom Chapter: Bulletin*; entitled *International Folk Music Council UK National Committee: Newsletter* from 1991, with new numbering sequence]

  ALb 2, 1975; 9, 10, 1977; n.s. 25, 1990
  CCtc n.s. 13–22, 1986–89
  Cpl 1, 1974
  Cu 1–32, 1974–82; n.s. 1–27, 1983–90; n.s. 1, 1991–#
  EIR:Dtc 1–31, 1974–82; n.s. 1–27, 1983–90; n.s. 1, 1991–#
  En 1–30, 1974–82*; n.s. 1–27, 1983–90; n.s. 1, 1991–#
  Lbl＊
  Lcs 1–31, 1974–82; n.s. [c]
  Lgo n.s. 9–27, 1985–90; n.s. 1, 1991–#
  Lsa 1–31, 1974–82 [w 3–12, 14, 29, 30]; n.s. 1–27, 1983–90 [w 23]; 1, 1991–#
  LVp ?12–31, 1978–82; n.s. 1–27, 1982–90; n.s. 1, 1991–#
  Ob＊

International Country Music News
0958–756X
GB–Derby: CPS Print and Graphics, 1984–
[NOT IN BUCOMP1]

  Lbl 6 (1989), 6–#＊

International Discography of the New Wave
US–New York, ?1981–

  Cu 1982/83–#

International Federation of the Phonographic Industry *see* IFPI

International Folk Music Council: Bulletin
TNG INTL9; 0020–6768
C–Kingston, Ont. [etc.]: International Folk Music Council, 1948–81; 1982–
[Entitled *Bulletin of the International Folk Music Council* from 1957, 11; succeeded by *Bulletin of the International Council for Traditional Music* (ISSN 0739–1390) from no. 59, 1981]

  AB 1, 1948–#
  BRp [c (2 years)]
  BSdsc＊

Cu 1–33, 1948–68; 60, 1982–; 1–27, 1983–90
EIR:Dtc 1–64, 1948–84
En＊
Lbl＊
Lcs 2, 1949–#
Lgo 81, 1992–#
Lki 61, 1982–#
Lsa 10, 1956; 15, 1959; 17–27, 1960–66; 31, 1967; 35, 36, 1969–70; 39–43, 1971–73; 45, 1974; 46–72, 1975–87; 74, 1988–#
Lso 33 (1968)–#
Lu 29, 1966; 55, 1979; 58, 1981–#
MK 1976–81; 1981–#
Ouf (Howes) 8, 9, 1955; 11, 1957, 20, 21, 1962; 25, 1964; 27–31, 1965–67; 33–44, 1968–74
TOd 1967–73＊

International Folk Music Council UK National Committee: Newsletter *see* **International Council for Traditional Music, United Kingdom Chapter: Newsletter**

International Jazz Archives Journal
1077–9892
US–Pittsburgh, PA: University of Pittsburgh, 1993–
[NOT IN BUCOMP1]

  Ltc 1 (1993), 1 [2 copies]
  Lu 1 (1993), 1

International Journal of Music Education
0225–7614
GB–Reading [etc.]: International Society for Music Education, 1983–
[NOT IN BUCOMP1; superseded the *Australian Journal of Music Education* (q.v.)]

  Cu 9, 1987–#
  EIR:Dtc 9, 1987–#
  En 9, 1987–#
  Lam 1, 1983; 3, 4, 1984; 7, 1986
  Lbl＊
  Lgsm 2, 1983–# [w 7, 8, 11]
  Lie 1, 1983–# [w 2]
  Mcm 1, 1983–#
  MK 1, 1983–#
  Ob＊
  Re 1, 1983–#
  TOd 1, 1983–#

International Journal of Musicology
0941–9535
D–Frankfurt–am-Main: Peter Lang, 1992–
[NOT IN BUCOMP1]

Lbl 1 (1992)–#
Ltc 6 (1997)–#

International Kodály Society Bulletin
0133–8749
H–Budapest: International Kodály Society,
1976–

Bu 1993, 2
Lam 1982, 1, 2; 1983, 1
Lcm 1982

International Liszt Centre Quarterly
TNG INTL38
GB–London: International Liszt Centre for 19th
Century Music, 1972–
[Entitled *Liszt Saeculum* (ISSN 0263–0249)
from no. 23, 1978; also known as *ILC
Quarterly*]

AB 29, 1982
Cpl 4, 5, 1973
Cu 13, 1975–#
EIR:Dtc 13, 1975–26, 1980
En*
Lam 4, 5, 1973
Lbbc 17–28, 1977–81 [w 27]
Lbl 1, 1972–#
Lcm 2, 5, 1973
Lcml 1, 1972–#
Lu 7/8, 1974
Mcm 6, 1974
Ob*

International Military Music Society, United
Kingdom Branch: Newsletter
GB–Manchester: International Military Music
Society, 1988–
[NOT IN BUCOMP1]

Cu 1, 1988–#

International Music and Opera Guide *see*
International Music Guide

International Music Calendar
US–Washington, DC: People–to–People, 1959–
62

Lbl*

International Music Connection
GB–London: British Library National Sound
Archive, 1995–
[NOT IN BUCOMP1; Journal of the
International Music Collection at the National
Sound Archive]

Lsa 1, 1995–#

International Music Education: I.S.M.E.
Yearbook
TNG INTL40; 0172–0597
D–Mainz: Schott [for the International Society
for Music Education], 1973–
[Continued from the *International Music
Educator: Journal of I.S.M.E.* (q.v.)]

BG 1 (1973)–15 (1988)
Bs 3 (1975/76)–11 (1984)*
BSdsc*
CCtc 1 (1973)–15 (1988)
Cu 14 (1987)–#
EIR:Dtc 14 (1987)–15 (1988)
EIR:Duc 1 (1973)–15 (1988)
Lbl*
Lcml 1 (1973)–#
Mcm 1 (1973)–#
Ob*
TOd 15 (1988)

International Music Educator: Journal of
I.S.M.E.
TNG INTL19
S–Stockholm [etc.]: International Society for
Music Education, 1960–72
[Succeeded by *International Music Education:
I.S.M.E. Yearbook* (q.v.)]

BSdsc*
CCtc 1971–72
Lcm 1962–64*; 1968*
Lcml 1968–72*
Re 1960–72

International Music Guide
GB–London: Tantivy Press, 1977–?87
[Continued as *International Music and Opera
Guide*]

BSdsc 1978–84
Cu 1977–84; 1987
EIR:Dtc 1980–84; 1987
Ep 1977–83
Er 1978–81
KE 1977; 1980
Lbl*
Lu 1977–86

Mcm 1977–?
NTp 1980–?
Ob*
Ouf 1977

International Musician
TNG US331; 0020–8051
US–New York: American Federation of
Musicians of the United States and Canada,
1901–

　BSdsc*
　Lam 91 (1993), 10–92 (1993/94), 6, 9–#
　Lcml 42 (1944)–48 (1949)

International Musician: Technology in Music
see **International Musician and Recording
World**

International Musician and Recording World
GB–London: Northern and Shell, 1975–91
[Absorbed into *The Guitar Magazine* (q.v.); also
entitled *International Musician: Technology in
Music* to vol, 17 (1991), 10]

　AB 9 (1983), Apr–17 (1991), Aug
　Cu 1 (1975)–17 (1991), 9*
　EIR:Dp 12 (1986)–18 (1991), 2
　EIR:Dtc 1 (1975)–17 (1991), 9
　En*
　Ep 10 (1984), 2–18 (1991), 2
　Gam 6 (1980), 10, 11; 7 (1981), 1, 5–12; 8
　　(1982)–9 (1983), 1, 4, 6, 11, 12; 10 (1984)–
　　11 (1985), 8
　Lbl*
　Lgo 3 (1977)–17 (1991)*
　Lgu 12 (1986)–18 (1991), 2
　Lsa 5 (1979)–6 (1980)
　Msuc 11 (1985)–17 (1991)
　Ob*

**International Musicological Society:
Communiqué**
CH–Basle [etc.]: International Musicological
Society, 1927–
[NOT IN BUCOMP1]

　ALb 57–58, 61, 1989–92
　LAu 22, 1967; 26, 1968
　Ob 35, 1974–#

International New Wave Discography
US–New York: Omnibus Press, 1980–
[NOT IN BUCOMP1]

　Ob 2 (1982)

International Organ Preservation
US–Selinsgrove, PA: Susquehanna University
[for the International Society for Organ History
and Preservation], 1978–
[NOT IN BUCOMP1]

　Lam (o) 1 (1978), 1–4
　Lcm 1 (1978), 1, 4

International Piano Library Bulletin
0020–8302
US–New York, 1967–?71

　Lsa 1 (1967)–3 (1971), 1

International Piper
0141–7150
GB–Cockenzie: International Piper Ltd, 1978–

　Cu 1 (1978)–4 (1981), 6
　En 1 (1978)–4 (1981)
　Ep 1 (1978)–4 (1981), 6
　Gm 1 (1978)–4 (1981)
　Lbl*
　Ob*

International Record Letter
US–Kirkland, Washington, 1950–52

　Lsa 1950–52

International Repertory of Music Literature
see **RILM Abstracts of Music Literature**

**International Repertory of Musical
Iconography** *see* **RIdIM/RCMI Newsletter:
Répertoire International d'Iconographie
Musicale**

**The International Review of Music Aesthetics
and Sociology**
TNG INTL32; 0047–1208
HR–Zagreb: Muzicka Academija u Zagreby,
1970–
[Entitled *International Review of the Aesthetics
and Sociology of Music* (0351–5796) from
1971]

　AB 1 (1970)–10 (1979)
　Au 6 (1975), 2–20 (1989)
　Bs 15 (1984)–#*
　BSdsc*
　BTu 1 (1970)–13 (1982)
　Bu 18 (1987)–21 (1990)
　Cpl 1 (1970), 1, 2; 3 (1972), 2
　Cu 1 (1970)–#
　EIR:Duc 1 (1970)–#

En 1 (1970)–#
Er 5 (1974)–#
HUu 1 (1970)–5 (1974)
Lam 1 (1970), 1; 3 (1972), 2
Lcml 1 (1970)–#
LRHBNC 1 (1970)–23 (1992)
Lsa 1 (1970)–19 (1988)
Lu 1 (1970)–7 (1976)
Lu (RMA) 1 (1970)–#
LVp 1 (1970), 1
Mcm 3 (1972), 2
MK 11 (1980)–#
NO 1 (1970)–#
NWu 4 (1973)–#
Ob*
Ouf 1 (1970)–# [w 7 (1976), 1; 8 (1977), 2]
R 1 (1971), 2; 3 (1972), 2
SFu 1 (1970); 3 (1972)–11 (1980)
SOu 1 (1970)–8 (1977)
TOd 10 (1979), 1, 2; 15 (1984), 2; 16 (1985),
1, 2; 25 (1994)–27 (1996)
Yu 1 (1970)–#

**International Review of the Aesthetics and
Sociology of Music** *see* **The International
Review of Music Aesthetics and Sociology**

**International Society for Traditional Arts
Research** *see* **ISTAR Newsletter**

International Society of Bassists Magazine *see*
International Society of Bassists: Newsletter

International Society of Bassists: Newsletter
TNG US844; 0885–5633; 0197–7946
US–Cincinnati: University of Cincinnati, 1974–
[Later entitled *International Society of Bassists
Magazine*]

Mcm 2, 1976–#

**International Society of Organbuilders
Yearbook** *see* **I.S.O.**

International Talking Machine Review *see*
The Talking Machine Review

International Theatre
F–Paris, 1903
[Only one vol. published]

Lbl*
Ob*

International Trombone Association Journal
see **ITA**

International Trumpet Guild Journal
0363–2849; 0363–2845
US–Nashville, TN [etc.]: International Trumpet
Guild, 1976–
[Also entitled *I. T. G. Journal*]

Gam 8 (1984), 4; 9 (1985), 2, 3; 10 (1986),
1, 3, 4; 11 (1987)–14 (1990), 2–4; 15
(1991)–#
Lcm 14 (1990)–#
Mcm 1 (1976)–#
Msuc 12 (1988)–#

International Trumpet Guild Newsletter
TNG US859; 0363–2857
US–Nashville, TN [etc.]: International Trumpet
Guild, 1975–

Mcm 1975–#

International Who's Who in Music *see* **Who's
Who in Music**

**Internationale Bruckner-Gesellschaft:
Mitteilungsblatt**
A–Vienna: Internationale Bruckner–
Gesellschaft, 1971–
[NOT IN BUCOMP1]

Ob 1, 1971–#

**Internationale Franz Schubert Institut:
Mitteilungen** *see* **Schubert durch die Brille**

**Internationale Gesellschaft für
Musikwissenschaft: Communiqué** *see*
**International Musicological Society:
Communiqué**

Das internationale Jazz-Podium
TNG A260
A–Vienna, 1952–54; 1955–
[Entitled *Jazz Podium* (ISSN 0021–5686) from
1955]

Cbijs 1958–70*

Into Jazz *see* **In to Jazz**

Intone: Oxford Students' Music Magazine
GB–Oxford: Intone Publications, 1977–
[NOT IN BUCOMP1]

Lbl*

I.P.E.M. Yearbook *see* Jaarboek
I.P.E.M./I.P.E.M. Yearbook

Ireland's Music World
TNG EIRE14
EIRE–Dublin, 1973

    EIR:Dtc 1973, July–Nov

Irish Accordion News
EIRE–Dublin: Irish Accordion Association,
1986–
[NOT IN BUCOMP1]

    EIR:Dtc 1–9, 1986–88*

Irish Bell News
EIRE–Drogheda, 1951–

    EIR:Dtc 1 (1951)–12 (1987)

Irish Composer
EIRE–Dublin: Association of Irish Composers,
1988–
[NOT IN BUCOMP1]

    BLu 1, 1988–#
    EIR:Dtc 1, 1988
    EIR:Duc 1, 1988–#
    EIR:MEtc 1, 1988–#
    Ob*

The Irish Federation of Musicians: Annual
Report
TNG EIRE5
EIRE–Dublin, 1948–
[From 1965 entitled *The Irish Federation of
Musicians: Biennial Report*; from 1969 entitled
*The Irish Federation of Musicians: Four Yearly
Report*]

    EIR:Dtc 1967; 1968/69

The Irish Federation of Musicians: Biennial
Report *see* The Irish Federation of Musicians:
Annual Report

The Irish Federation of Musicians: Four
Yearly Report *see* The Irish Federation of
Musicians: Annual Report

Irish Folk Music Studies/Éigse Cheol Tíre
0332–298X
EIRE–Dublin: Folk Music Society of Ireland,
1972–

    AB 3 (1976/81)–4 (1982/85)
    BG 1 (1972/73)–4 (1982/85)

    BLu 1 (1972/73)–#
    BSdsc*
    Cu 1 (1972/73)–#
    EIR:Dtc 1 (1972/73)–4 (1982/85)
    EIR:Duc 1 (1972/73)–4 (1982/85)
    EIR:MEtc 1 (1972/73)–4 (1982/85)
    En 2 (1974/75)
    Lbl*
    Lcml 1 (1972/73)–#
    Lcs 1 (1972/73)–4 (1982/85)Ob*
    SOu 1 (1972/73)
    Uu 3 (1976/81)

Irish Musical Monthly: a Journal devoted to
the Interests of Music in Church and School
Fellinger 1968/1626; TNG EIRE2
EIRE–Dublin, 1902–03

    Mcm 1902– 03

Irish Performing Arts Yearbook
GB–London: Rhinegold Publishing, 1992–
[NOT IN BUCOMP1]

    Cu 1992–#
    Lbo [c]
    Ob*

Irish Radio and Musical Review *see* Irish
Radio Review

Irish Radio Review
EIRE–Dublin, 1925–29
[From 1926 entitled *Irish Radio and Musical
Review*; from 1927 reverted to *Irish Radio
Review*]

    Lbl*

I.S.A.M. Newsletter *see* Institute for Studies
in American Music: Newsletter

Isbreker: Concertagenda
IS–Iceland: Musiekcentrum, ?–
[NOT IN BUCOMP1]

    Gsmic [c]

I.S.M.E. Yearbook *see* International Music
Education: I.S.M.E. Yearbook

ISMN Newsletter
D–?Berlin: ISMN Office, 1994–
[NOT IN BUCOMP1]

    Lam 1, 1994–#

I.S.O. Information: Zeitschrift für Orgelbau
TNG INTL28; 0579–5613
D–Lauffen/Neckar [etc.]: International Society
of Organbuilders, 1969–90
[Succeeded by *I.S.O. News: the Quarterly
Magazine of the International Society of
Organbuilders* (q.v.)]

BSdsc 9–26, 1973–86
Lam 1, 2, 1969
Lam (o) 1, 2, 1969; 5–7, 1971
Lcml 26, 1986–?90
Lrco 1–32, 1969–90

I.S.O News: the Quarterly Magazine of the International Society of Organbuilders
1017–7515
B–Leuven: International Society of
Organbuilders, 1991–
[NOT IN BUCOMP1; previously entitled *I.S.O.
Information: Zeitschrift für Orgelbau* (q.v.)]

Lrco 1991, 1, 3–#

I.S.O. Yearbook *see* International Society of Organbuilders Yearbook

Israel Music Institute: Bulletin
IL–Tel-Aviv: Israel Music Institute, ?–
[NOT IN BUCOMP1]

Lam 1962, Sum

Israel Music Institute News *see* I.M.I. News

Israel Studies in Musicology
TNG IL17; 0334–2026
IL–Jerusalem: Israel Musicological Society,
1978–

Cu 1 (1978)–#
EIR:Duc 1 (1978)–2 (1980)
Lbl 1 (1978)–#
Lcml 1 (1978)–#
Lgo 1 (1978)–4 (1987)
Lu 1 (1978)–#
Ob*

ISSTIP Journal *see* Journal of the International Society for the Study of Tension in Performance

ISTAR Newsletter
IN–New Delhi: International Society for
Traditional Arts Research, 1984–
[NOT IN BUCOMP1]

Lbl 1, 1984–#

ITA
US–Columbia, SC [etc.]: International
Trombone Association, 1972–
[Entitled *Journal of the International Trombone
Association* (TNG US831) from vol. 3 (1974)–10
(1982); entitled *ITA Journal* from vol. 11 (1983).
The Association makes some material from *ITA*
available via its Internet title *Online Trombone
Journal* (ISSN 1093–0485), at URL http://
www.trombone.org]

Bs 13 (1985), 3–#
Lcm 24 (1996)–#
Mcm 2 (1973)–#

ITA Journal *see* ITA

L'Italia Musicale: Periodico Mensile di Arte
I–Florence: L'Italia Musicale, ?1906–?

Lu 18 (1924), 1–6; 19 (1925), 1

L'Italiana Armonia e Gazzetta Musicale di Milano *see* Gazzetta Musicale di Milano

I.T.G. Journal *see* International Trumpet Guild Journal

Izvestiya na Instituta za Muzika/Bulletin de l'Institut de Musique
TNG BG14
BG–Sofia: Bulgarska Akademiya na Naukite,
1952–

BSdsc*
Ob*
Ouf (Howes) 13, 14, 1969

J

Jaarboek I.P.E.M./I.P.E.M. Yearbook
TNG B155; 0929–8215; 0303–3902
B–Gent: Institute for Psychoacoustic and
Electronic Music, 1967–69
[Succeeded by *Electronic Music Reports* (q.v.)]

AB*
BSdsc*
Cu 1967–69
Lam 1967
Lu 1967–69
Ob*

Jaarboek van het Vlaams Centrum voor Oude Muziek [= Yearbook of the Flemish Centre for Old Music]
B–Peer: VZW Musica, 1985–
[NOT IN BUCOMP1]

    Cu 1 (1985)–3 (1987)

Jacksons Collectors' Magazine
0969–5478
GB–Slough: Jacksons Collectors' Magazine, 1992–
[NOT IN BUCOMP1]

    Lbl 4, 1992/93–#

Jahrbuch alte Musik
0937–1095
D–Wilhelmshaven: Noetzel, 1989–
[NOT IN BUCOMP1]

    Cu 1 (1989)–#

Jahrbuch der deutschen Musik
TNG D798
D–Leipzig: Breitkopf und Härtel, 1943–44

    Lbl*
    Lu 1943

Jahrbuch der Deutschen Musikorganisation
TNG D748
D–Berlin: Max Hesse, 1931

    Lbl 1931

Jahrbuch der Komischen Oper Berlin
0522–9715
D–Berlin: Henschelverlag, 1961–
[NOT IN BUCOMP1]

    LAu 1965
    Lbl†
    Lu 1960/61–1969/70

Jahrbuch der Musikbibliothek Peters
Fellinger 1968/1257; TNG D336
D–Leipzig: C. F. Peters, 1894–1941
[Continued as *Deutsches Jahrbuch der Musikwissenschaft* (q.v.)]

    Cpl 1 (1894)–31 (1924)
    Cu 1(1894)– 47 (1941) [Reprint ed.]
    Er 1 (1894)–47 (1941)
    Lbbc 7 (1900)–46 (1939)*
    Lbl 1 (1894)–47 (1940)
    Lcml 10 (1903); 44 (1937)–45 (1938)
    Lu 1 (1895)–47 (1941) [some vols in reprint ed.]

Ob*
SOu 28 (1921); 31 (1924)–37 (1930); 40 (1933)–42 (1935); 44 (1937); 46 (1939)–47 (1941)

Jahrbuch der Musikwelt/The Yearbook of the Musical World/Annuaire du Monde Musical
TNG D850
D–Bayreuth: J. Steeger, 1950
[Only one issue published]

    Cu 1949
    Er 1949
    LAu 1949
    Lcml 1949
    Lu 1949
    Mpl 1949

Jahrbuch der Tonkunst von Wien und Prag
TNG CS1
A/CZ–Vienna; Prague: Schönfeld, 1796

    Cu 1796
    Ob 1796 [Reprint ed.]

Jahrbuch der Universal Edition
TNG A184
A–Vienna: Universal Edition, 1926–29
[NOT IN BUCOMP1]

    Lu 1926

Jahrbuch des Österreichischen Volksliedwerkes
TNG A261; 1013–056X
A–Vienna: OBV Pädagogischer Verlag, 1952–

    Lbl*

Jahrbuch des Staatlichen Instituts für Musikforschung Preussischer Kulturbesitz
TNG D1061; 0572–6239
D–Kassel: Merseburger, 1968–88; 1992–
[NOT IN BUCOMP1]

    Cu 1981/82–#
    Lu 1983/84; 1985/86; 1987/88; 1993–#

Jahrbuch für Liturgik und Hymnologie
TNG D972; 0075–2681
D–Kassel: J. Stauda, 1955–

    BSdsc*
    Lbbc 6 (1961)–7 (1962)
    Lbl*
    Lu 29 (1985/86)–30 (1986/87)
    Ob*
    Ouf 1 (1955)–33 (1990/91)

Jahrbuch für Musik
Fellinger 1968/195; TNG D94
D–Leipzig: B. Senff, 1843–53

   Lbl*
   Ob*

Jahrbuch für musikalische Volks- und Völkerkunde
TNG D1036; 0075–2703
D–Wiesbaden: Breitkopf und Härtel, 1963–73;
1977–78; 1982–

   Cu 1 (1963)–#
   Lbl*
   Ob*
   Yu 1 (1963)–7 (1973)

Jahrbuch für Opernforschung
0724–8156
D–Frankfurt am Main: Peter Lang, 1985–91
[NOT IN BUCOMP1]

   Cu 1 (1985)–#
   Lu 1 (1985)–#
   Ob 1 (1985)–#
   Ouf 1 (1985)–3 (1991)

Jahrbuch für Volksliedforschung
TNG D714; 0075–2789
D–Berlin: De Gruyter, 1928–
[The journal *Studien zur Volksliedforschung*
(Bern; Frankfurt: Peter Lang, 1940; n. F. 1986–;
ISSN 0930–8636) is issued as a supplement]

   Cu 1 (1928)–#
   Gul 1 (1928)–21 (1976)
   Lbl*
   Lcs 20 (1975)–21 (1976); 27/28 (1982/83)–30
   (1985)
   Lgo 12 (1967); 15 (1970)–19 (1974); 21
   (1976); 23 (1978)–24 (1979)
   Lu 1 (1928)–# *
   Ob*
   Ouf (Howes) 9 (1964); 11 (1966)

Jahrbuch Peters *see* **Deutsches Jahrbuch der Musikwissenschaft**

Jahrbücher des Deutschen National-Vereins für Musik und ihre Wissenschaft
Fellinger 1968/155; TNG D84
D–Karlsruhe: C. T. Groos, 1839–42
[Ceased publication with vol. 4 (1842)]

   Lbl*

Jahrbücher für musikalische Wissenschaft
Fellinger 1968/476; TNG D156
D–Leipzig: Breitkopf und Härtel, 1863–67

   AB*
   Au 1 (1863)–2 (1867) [Reprint ed.]
   Cu 1 (1863)–2 (1867)
   EIR:Dtc 1 (1863)
   EIR:MEtc 1 (1863)–2 (1867)
   Er 1 (1863)–2 (1867)
   Lbl 1 (1863)–2 (1967) [2 copies]
   Lcm 1 (1863)–2 (1867)
   Lu 1 (1863)–2 (1867) [Reprint ed.]
   Ob 1 (1863)–2 (1867) [Reprint ed.]
   Ouf 1 (1863)–2 (1867)
   SA 1 (1863)

Jahresbericht: vorgetragen bei der Plenarversammlung des Dom-Musik-Vereines und Mozarteums zu Salzburg
Fellinger 1968/211; TNG A24
A–Salzburg, 1843–81
[From 1875 entitled *Jahresbericht des Dom-Musik-Vereins*]

   Lbl 1843–49

Jahresbericht der Internationalen Mozart-Gemeinde
Fellinger 1968/1102; TNG A111
A–Salzburg: Internationale Stiftung Mozarteum, 1889–1938
[Reports for 1889–94 are offprints from the *Jahresbericht der Internationalen Stiftung Mozarteum* for 1889–94. Nos 30 (1918)–36 (1924) not published]

   Lbl 1889–1937

Jahresbericht der Internationalen Stiftung Mozarteum
Fellinger 1968/853; TNG A90
A–Salzburg: Internationale Stiftung Mozarteum, 1881–?1926
[NOT IN BUCOMP1]

   Lbl 1881–1926

Jahresbericht der Internationalen Stiftung Mozarteum *see also* **Jahresbericht der Internationalen Mozart-Gemeinde**

Jahresbericht der Staatlichen Akademischen Hochschule für Musik in Berlin
D–Berlin: Hesse, 1918–38
[NOT IN BUCOMP1; preceded by the *Jahresbericht über die mit der Königlichen Akademie der Künste zu Berlin verbundene Hochschule für Musik* (Berlin, 1876–1909); from 1909 to 1918 entitled *Jahresbericht/Königliche Akademische Hochschule für Musik in Berlin*; continued as the *Staatliche Hochschule für Musik in Berlin: Jahresbericht* from 60 (1938/41)]

  Cpl 1925/ 27; 1930/31; 1931/32

Jahresbericht des Dom-Musik-Vereins *see* Jahresbericht: vorgetragen bei der Plenarversammlung des Dom-Musik-Vereines und Mozarteums zu Salzburg

Jahresbericht/Königliche Akademische Hochschule für Musik in Berlin *see* Jahresbericht der Staatlichen Akademischen Hochschule für Musik in Berlin

Jahresbericht über die mit der Königlichen Akademie der Künste zu Berlin verbundene Hochschule für Musik *see* Jahresbericht der Staatlichen Akademischen Hochschule für Musik in Berlin

Jahresverzeichnis der [deutschen] Musikalien und Musikschriften *see* Kurzes Verzeichnis sämmtlicher in Deutschland und den angrenzenden Ländern gedruckter Musikalien, auch musikalischer Schriften und Abbildungen mit Anzeige der Verleger und Preise

JAM: a Journal of Traditional Music
US–Durham, NC [etc.]: Carolina Area Friends of Folk, Bluegrass and Blues, 1980–
[NOT IN BUCOMP1]

  Lcs 1 (1980), 3–2 (1983), 1

Jam UK Live: West Wales Edition
GB–?, 1993–
[NOT IN BUCOMP1]

  AB 1 (1993)

Jamming
GB–London: Jamming, 197?–
[NOT IN BUCOMP1]

  Cu 8–13, 1979–82
  Lbl*
  Lsa 6, 1978; 1984*; 31, 1985

Japanese Traditional Music [translated title]
see Hogaku

Jazz [1]
US–New York: Jazz Magazine, 1942–43
[Ceased publication with vol. 1 no. 10 (1943)]

  Cbijs 1 (1942), 3

Jazz [2]
TNG B121
B–Brussels, 1945–46
[Incorporated into *Hot Club de Belgique: Hot Club Magazine* (29 nos, 1946–48)]

  Cbijs 2, 7, 1945

Jazz [3]
B–Brussels: Hot Club de Belgique, 1956–?

  Cbijs 1, 1956; 2–5, 8–11, 1957; 12, 13, 1958

Jazz [4]
TNG US720; 0196–5727
US–New York: Jazz Press, 1962–71
[Entitled *Jazz and Pop* (ISSN 0021–5627) from vol. 6 no. 8 (Aug 1967)]

  Cbijs*
  Lsa 1 (1962)–5 (1966)

Jazz [5]
CH–Basel: Musik–Verlag, 1982–
[NOT IN BUCOMP1]

  Lsa 1984–85*

Jazz: a Quarterly of American Music
0447–6204
US–Albany, CA [etc.]: Jazz, 1958–60
[Ceased publication with no. 5, 1960]

  Cbijs 1–4, 1958–59
  LOnjfa*

Jazz: Jazz and Modern Music Journal
[translated title] *see* Jazz: List Venovany Jazzu a Moderní Hudbě

Jazz: List Venovany Jazzu a Moderní Hudbě
[= Jazz: Jazz and Modern Music Journal]
TNG CS172
CZ–Prague, 1947–48

  Cbijs 1948, June–Aug

Jazz: Metodiká Publiace Určená Členum
Jazzové Sekce Svazu Hudebnikú ČSR *see*
Jazz Bulletin: Metodiká Publiace Určená
Členum Jazzové Sekce Svazu Hudebnikú
ČSR

Jazz: Miesięcznik Ilustrowany [= Illustrated
Monthly]
TNG PL112
PL–Gdansk, 1956–

Cbijs 1957–70*

Jazz: the Magazine *see* Jazz FM

Jazz and Blues
TNG GB555
GB–Ashford, 1971–73
[Continuation of *Jazz Monthly* (q.v.);
incorporated into *Jazz Journal* (q.v.) as *Jazz
Journal and Jazz and Blues*]

BDp 1 (1971)–3 (1973)*
Cbijs 1 (1971)–3 (1973)
Cu 1 (1971)–3 (1973), 9
EIR:Dtc 1 (1971)–3 (1973), 9
En 1 (1971), 1–3, 5–11; 2 (1972)–3 (1973)
EXu 1 (1972)–3 (1973)
Lbar 1 (1971), 1–6, 8–10; 2 (1972)–3 (1973),
3, 6, 7, 9
Lbbc 1 (1971); 3 (1973), 1–9
Lbl*
Lcml 1 (1971)–3 (1973)
Lcml (m) 1 (1971)–2 (1972); 3 (1973)*
Lkc 1 (1971)–3 (1973)
LOnjfa*
Lsa 1 (1971), Apr–Dec; 2 (1972), Jan–Oct,
Dec; 3 (1973)
LVp 1 (1971)–3 (1973)
Mcm 3 (1973), Sep–Oct
Ob*

Jazz and Pop *see* Jazz [4]

Jazz at Ronnie Scott's
GB–London: Editorial and Publicity Services, ?
[NOT IN BUCOMP1]

LOnjfa*
Lsa 27–59, 1984–89 [w 29, 34, 36, 38, 41–
43, 48, 50, 52,54, 56]

Jazz at the Pizza Express
0967–4187
GB–London: Jazz Express/Peter Boizot, 197?–
[NOT IN BUCOMP1; entitled *Jazz Express*
from vol.29 (Feb 1982); ceased publication
1994; succeeded by *Boz* (London: Peter Boizot,
1994–)]

Lbar 14, 1980; 23–95, 1981–88 [w 27,
1981]; 99–134, 1988–91 [w 104, 123, 126,
131, 132]
Lbl*
Lgo*
LOnjfa*
Lsa 29–35, 1982 [w 33]; 49–114, 1984–90*;
119–149, 1990–93 [w 121, 127, 129, 134]

Jazz Bazaar
D–Neustadt: Hans Ewert, 1969–72

Cbijs 1, 1969; 9, 1971

Jazz Beat
0447-631X
GB–London: Jazzbeat Association, 1964–66
[Succeeded *Jazz News* (q.v.)]

AB 3 (1966), 7–12
Cbijs 1 (1964)–3 (1966)
Cu 1 (1964)–3 (1966)*
Lbl*
LOnjfa*
Ob*
Yu 1 (1964)–2 (1965)

Jazz Bulletin
TNG CH146
CH–Berne, 1952–63
[From 1960 entitled *Jazz Scene*; from 1961
entitled *Swiss Jazz Notes*. Also known as *Jazz-
Bulletin*]

Cbijs 1953, Oct; 81–83, 87–90, 1960; 1965,
Nov

Jazz Bulletin: Metodiká Publiace Určená
Členum Jazzové Sekce Svazu Hudebnikú
ČSR [= Published for the Members of the
Jazz Section of the Musical Union]
CZ–Prague, 1967–?
[Entitled *Jazz: Metodická Publiace Určená
Členum Jazzové Sekce* from 19, 1977]

Cbijs 1967, 1–6; 1968, 1

Jazz Catalogue
0075–3556
GB–London: Jazz Journal, 1960–72

BSdsc*
Cbijs 1960–72
Cu 1964–70
En 1964–70
Lbl*
Lsa 1960–62; 1965–67; 1970–71
NTp 1961–70
Ob*

Jazz CD
GB–Saffron Walden, 1992–
[NOT IN BUCOMP1]

Lsa 1 (1992), 1–3

Jazz Centre Society Newsletter
GB–London, 1968–

Cbijs 1968, Aug; 1970, June, Aug, Oct, Nov;
1974, Mar, Apr, Sep, Oct, Dec; 1975–#
LOnjfa*

Jazz Circle News
GB–Manchester, 1978–

Lcml 1 (1978)–#
LOnjfa*

Jazz Collectors Guide
GB–London, 1949–?

Cbijs 3, 1950

Jazz Column
GB–Letchworth, 1957–67

Cbijs 3, 5, 1957; 7, 1958; 1963–67

Jazz di Ieri di Oggi
I–Florence, 1959–

Cbijs 1959, Feb, Mar

Jazz Digest
0092–0525
US–McLean, VA: E. Steane, 1972–74
[Preceded from 1962–71 by *Hip: the Jazz
Record Digest* (q.v.)]

Cbijs 2 (1973), 2–12; 3 (1974), 1–6

Jazz Down Under: Australia's Jazz Magazine
0155–9680
AUS–Camden, New South Wales, 1974–

Cbijs 11, 1976

Jazz Echo *see* Swinging Newsletter

Jazz Educators Journal
0730–9791
US–Manhattan, KS: International Association of
Jazz Educators, ?1969–
[NOT IN BUCOMP1; sometime entitled *NAJE
Educator*]

Bs 22 (1990), 2–#
BSdsc 13 (1981), 3–#
Lam 19 (1987), 1–22 (1990), 1; 22 (1990),
3–25 (1993), 4; 26 (1994), 2–#
Re 18 (1986), 4; 19 (1987), 4–#

Jazz Express *see* Jazz at the Pizza Express

The Jazz Finder *see* The Jazzfinder

Jazz FM
0959–6593
GB–London: Observer, 1990–
[NOT IN BUCOMP1; entitled *Jazz: the
Magazine* from no. 12, 1992]

CCtc 1994, Sep–#
Cu 1, 1990–# [w 3–10]
EIR:Dtc 1, 1990–#
En*
Lba [c (1 year)]
Lbbc 1, 1990–#
Lbl 7, 1991–#
Lcml 4, 1990–#
Ll [c]
LOnjfa*
Lsa 1, 4, 1990; 5, 7–9, 1991; 11, 14, 1992–#
Ob*
SAu 18, 1993–#
TOd 14–27, 1992–94

Jazz Forum
N–Oslo, 1959–?

Cbijs 2, 1959

Jazz Forum: JF: the Magazine of the European Jazz Federation

TNG PL126
PL/US–Warsaw; New York [etc.]: Jazz Forum, 1967–
[From 8 (1974) entitled *Jazz Forum: the Magazine of the International Jazz Federation* (ISSN 0324–8852); later entitled *Jazz Forum: the Magazine of the International Jazz Federation: International Edition* (ISSN 0021–5635); also published in a Polish edition (ISSN 0324–8801); and in a German edition (ISSN 0324–8852)]

>   **Cbijs** 2–4, 1968–69; 7, 8, 10, 1970; 22, 1973; 33, 36, 1975
>   **Ep** 69–115, 1981–88
>   **Lcml** 1, 1967–#*
>   **Lgo** 78–135, 1982–89 [w 84, 85, 124–131]
>   **LOnjfa***
>   **Lsa** 15–76, 1972–82 [w 17–19, 1972; 30, 1974; 36, 1975; 47, 1977; 51, 54, 55, 1978; 60, 61, 1979; 64, 67, 1980]

Jazz Forum: Quarterly Review of Jazz and Literature

TNG GB389
GB–Fordingbridge, Hants: Delphic Press, 1946–47
[Ceased publication with no. 5, 1947]

>   **Cbijs** 1–5, 1946–47
>   **Lbl***
>   **LOnjfa***

Jazz Forum: the Magazine of the International Jazz Federation [International Edition] *see* Jazz Forum: JF: the Magazine of the European Jazz Federation

Jazz Greats: their Lives, their Music, their Inspiration

1359–9534
GB–London: Marshall Cavendish, 1995
[NOT IN BUCOMP1]

>   **Ltc** 1997–#

Jazz Guide

GB–London: C. Welland, 1964–

>   **Cbijs** 2 (1965), 2–3 (1966), 1
>   **LOnjfa***

Jazz-Hot: Revue Internationale de la Musique de Jazz

TNG F561; 0021–5643
F–Paris: Jazz Diffusion/Hot Club de France, 1935–39; n.s. 1945–91
[From 1945 entitled *Le Bulletin du Hot Club de France* (TNG F590); absorbed *La Revue du Jazz* (q.v.)]

>   **Cbijs** 1960–72*
>   **Lcml** 1987, Oct–#
>   **LOnjfa***

Jazz Illustrated

TNG GB421
GB–London, 1949–50

>   **Cbijs** 1 (1949/50), 1–8
>   **Lbl***
>   **LOnjfa***

Jazz in Kent

GB–Canterbury, 1967– ?

>   **Cbijs** 4–7, 1967–68

Jazz in the Midlands

GB–Birmingham: Jazz Central, 1984–
[NOT IN BUCOMP1]

>   **LOnjfa***

Jazz Index: Bibliographie unselbständiger Jazzliteratur /Bibliography of Jazz Literature in Periodicals

TNG D1094; 0344–5399
D–Frankfurt–am–Main: Rücker, 1977–83
[NOT IN BUCOMP1; ceased publication with vol. 7 (1983)]

>   **BSdsc** 1 (1977)–7 (1983)
>   **Lsa** 1 (1977)–7 (1983)
>   **Ob***

Jazz Information

TNG US549
US–New York: Jazz Information, 1939–41
[Ceased publication with vol. 2 no. 16 (1941)]

>   **Cbijs** 1 (1939/40), 7, 24; 2 (1941), 14, 15

Jazz Journaal

NL–Hilversum, 1964–

>   **Cbijs** 2 (1965), 9, 10; 3 (1966), 1, 2

Jazz Journal
TNG GB412; 0021–5651 [to April 1977]; 0140–2285 (*Jazz Journal International*)
GB–London: Jazz Journal Ltd, 1948–73; 1974–77; London: Billboard, 1977–
[Entitled *Jazz Journal and Jazz and Blues* (ISSN 0307–4439) from vol. 27 (1974), 1–9; from 27 (1974), 11–30 (1977), 4 entitled *Jazz Journal, incorporating Jazz and Blues*; entitled *Jazz Journal International* from vol. 30 (1977), 5; *see also Jazz and Blues*]

AB 25 (1972)–37 (1984); 42 (1989), 3, 7
BDp 25 (1972)–#
BEp [c (1 year)]
BLp 20 (1967)–#
Bp 25 (1972)–#
BRp 27 (1974)–#
BSdsc*
BTp 24 (1971)–26 (1973); 29 (1976)–39 (1986)
BuAYp [c (3 years)]
Cat 33 (1980), 1–7, 9; 34 (1981), 7–10; 35 (1982), 4, 7–12; 36 (1983), 1–8, 10, 12; 37 (1984), 1, 2, 4–12; 38 (1985)–42 (1989); 43 (1990), 1–8, 10–12; 44 (1991), 1–5, 7–12; 45 (1992), 1–7, 9–12; 46 (1993)–#
Cbijs 9 (1956)–30 (1977)
CFp 30 (1977)–#
CH [c (2 years)]
Cu 26 (1973)–#
DDp [c (2 years)]
DOR 43 (1990)–#
DU [c (5 years)]
EIR:Dp 41 (1988)–#
EIR:Dtc 26 (1973)–#
EIR:Duc 29 (1976)–#
EK [c (2 years)]
En 26 (1973)–#
Ep 31 (1978), 6–#
Er 35 (1982)–#
EXu 9 (1956)–#
GLp 46 (1993)–#
Gm 7 (1954)–#
HOp 38 (1985), 9–#
Lam 7 (1954), 8
Lba [c (3 years)]
Lbar 16 (1963)–#
Lbbc 9 (1956); 41 (1988); 43 (1990), 1, 3, 5, 7, 9; 44 (1991), 7, 11; 46 (1993), 10–12
Lbk [c (3 years)]
Lbl*
Lbo 38 (1985)–46 (1993), 1–7, 9–12; 47 (1994)–#
Lbx [c (5 years)]

Lcml 18 (1965)–#
Lcml (c) [c (1 year)]
Lcml (m) 17 (1964)–#
Lcml (p) [c (2 issues)]
Len 21 (1968), 3–#
Lgo 17 (1964)–# [w 26 (1973), 7–30 (1977)]
Lha (f) 3 (1950)–4 (1951); 5 (1952), 1–7, 9–12; 6 (1953), 3, 5–7 (1954); 8 (1955)–#
Lhg 45 (1992)–#
Lhr [c]
Lis [c (2 years)]
Lk [c (6 months)]
Lk (c) [c (1 year)]
Lkc 27 (1974)–29 (1976)
Lki 25 (1972)–37 (1984)*
Ll [c (5 years)]
LOnjfa*
Lsa 10 (1957)–#*
Lsut 25 (1972)–26 (1973); 28 (1975)–#
LT [c (1 year)]
Lth [c (1 year)]
LVp 11 (1958)–16 (1963); 18 (1965)–#
Lwf [c (1 year)]
Lwwput [c]
LXp [c (2 years)]
Mcm 26 (1973), 9–12; 27 (1974)–#
MO 28 (1975)–#
Mpl 25 (1972)–#
Msuc 33 (1980)–#
NOp [c (2 years)]
NTp 13 (1960)–14 (1961); 18 (1965)–# [w 13 (1960, Jan)]
Ob*
Op [c (2 years)]
Oub 35 (1982)–46 (1993)
PRp [c (5 years)]
Rp [c (2 years)]
SHRp 42 (1989)–#
SK [c (5 years)]
SOL 42 (1989)–#
STAp 26 (1973)–#
TOd 34 (1981)–#
Yu 4 (1951)–#

Jazz Journal and Jazz and Blues *see* Jazz Journal

Jazz Journal, incorporating Jazz and Blues *see* Jazz Journal

Jazz Journal International *see* Jazz Journal

Jazz Junction Jive
GB–London: West London Jazz Club, 1943–45

Cbijs 2, 1944

Jazz Magazine [1]
ARG–Buenos Aires, 1945–?

 Cbijs 29–32, 34–36, 1952; 37, 39, 41, 1953;
 53, 57, 1955; 58, 59, 1956; 63, 1957

Jazz Magazine [2]
TNG F649; 0092–0517; 0021–566X
F–Paris: Nouvelles Éditions Musicales
Modernes et Cie, 1954–

 Cbijs 26, 1957; 88, 89, 1962; 1966, Aug;
 1968–69, Jan; 1970, Apr–Aug
 LOnjfa*

Jazz Magazine [3]
GB–Edinburgh: Jazz Magazine, 1984–
[NOT IN BUCOMP1]

 Ep 1 (1983/84), 1, 2

Jazz Magazine *see also* **Jazz Record [1]**

Jazz Monthly
TNG GB459; 0021–5678
GB–St Austell: Jazz Monthly/National Jazz
Federation, 1955–71
[Continued as *Jazz and Blues* (q.v.)]

 AB 7 (1961/62)–12 (1966/67)
 BSdsc*
 Cbijs 1955–71
 Cu 6 (1960/61), 11–16 (1971), 10
 EIR:Dtc 1 (1955/56)–17 (1971), 192
 En 6 (1960/61), 11–12 (1966/67); 13
 (1967/68), 2, 4–16 (1970/71)
 EXu 1 (1955/56)–16 (1970/71)*
 Lbar 1 (1955/56), 6, 8, 10–12; 2 (1956/57),
 3–5, 7–4 (1958/59), 2, 4–12; 5 (1959/60),
 1, 3–9 (1963/64), 4, 6–9, 11, 12; 10
 (1964/65), 2, 4, 6, 10; 11 (1965/66)–16
 (1970/71)
 Lbbc 1 (1955/56), 3–10 (1964/65), 2
 Lcml 17 (1971), 191–2
 Lcml (m) 14 (1968/69), 165–17 (1971), 192
 Lkc 12 (1966/67)*; 13 (1967/68)–16
 (1970/71); 17 (1971)*
 LOnjfa 1 (1955/56)–16 (1970/71)
 Lsa 1 (1955/56)–71 (1971), 192
 LVp 4 (1958/59); 8 (1962)–16 (1970/71)
 Ob*
 Yu 4 (1958/59)–11 (1965/66); 13 (1967/68),
 16

Jazz Music
TNG GB377
GB–London: Jazz Music Magazine, 1942–44;
1945–
[Entitled *Jazz Tempo* from 1945]

 Cbijs*
 EXu n.s. 2 (1946), 2; 3 (1947), 5, 10; 4
 (1949), 2–4
 Lam n.s. 5 (1954), 7
 LOnjfa*

Jazz Music Mirror *see* **Music Mirror [1]**

Jazz News
GB–London: Jazz News, 1956–64
[Entitled *Jazz News and Review* (ISSN 0447–
6263) from vol. 6 no. 44 (1962); absorbed into
Jazz Beat (q.v.) from 1964]

 Cbijs 1956, 11, 12; 1957, 3–7, 12; 1958, 2, 3,
 9–13; 1959, 1, 3–5, 7, 10–13, 15, 16, 19–
 24; 1960, 3, 10, 27, 30, 33–37, 42, 45;
 1961, 4–6, 10, 13–52; 1962, 1–44
 Lbl*
 LOnjfa*
 Yu 1956–63

**Jazz News: Ireland's Jazz and Blues
Magazine**
EIRE–Dublin: Jazznews Publications Ltd, 1986–
[NOT IN BUCOMP1; entitled *Jazz News
International* from vol. 2 (1988), 3]

 Cu 1 (1986)–3 (1989), 5
 EIR:Dp 2 (1988)–3 (1989), 5
 EIR:Dtc 1 (1986)–3 (1989), 5
 EIR:Duc 1 (1986)–3 (1989)
 Lcml 1 (1986), Dec–3 (1989)
 LOnjfa*
 Lsa 2 (1988)–3 (1989)
 Ob*

Jazz News and Review *see* **Jazz News**

Jazz News International *see* **Jazz News:
Ireland's Jazz and Blues Magazine**

Jazz Newsletter *see* **The Jazzologist**

Jazz Notes
US–New York, 1956–?

 Cbijs 1959, Feb, June–Oct

Jazz Notes *see also* **Jazz Notes and Blue
Rhythm**

Jazz Notes and Blue Rhythm
TNG AUS15
AUS–Adelaide, 1941–
[From 1945 entitled *Jazz Notes*]

Cbijs 66–103, 1946–50

Jazz Nu: Maandblad voor Jazz en
Geimproviseerde Muziek [= Jazz Now:
Monthly for Jazz and Improvised Music] *see*
Jazz Press

Jazz-Nytt *see* Jazznytt

Jazz on CD
?GB–London, 1993–
[NOT IN BUCOMP1]

Lsa 1 (1993)–#
SFu 1 (1994), 10–#

Jazz Panorama
F–Paris, 1960–?

Cbijs 1, 2, 1960

Jazz Podium *see* Das internationale Jazz-
Podium

Jazz Press
TNG NL132
NL–Tilburg: Jazz Nu, 1975–
[From 1978 entitled *Jazz Nu: Maandblad voor
Jazz en Geimproviseerde Muziek* (NL–
Hoogland: Uitgeverij Scala; ISSN 0166-7025)]

Cbijs 5, 1975; 25, 27, 1976; 29, 1977
LOnjfa*

Jazz Quiz
GB–London; Ken Williams, 1945–?
[NOT IN BUCOMP1]

LOnjfa*

Jazz Record [1]
TNG GB370
GB–Chilwell, Notts: Jazz Appreciation Society,
1943–51
[From 1946 entitled *Jazz Magazine*]

Cbijs 1 (1943/44); 3 (1946), 1–4; 1951, 1–7
Lbl*
LOnjfa*

Jazz Record [2]
US–New York: Art Hodes and Dale Curran,
1943–47
[Ceased publication with no. 60, 1947]

Cbijs 1943, 1, 3–5, 7, 9, 10, 12, 15; 1944,
Mar–Dec; 1945–47

Jazz Records
GB–St Austell: Jazz Monthly, 1962–65

Cbijs 1962–64; 1965, Feb, June
Ob*

Jazz Register
US–New York, 1963–?

Cbijs 1 (1963), 3

Jazz Report [translated title] *see* Jazz
Sprawozdanie

Jazz Report: the Record Collector's Magazine
TNG US706; 0021–5694
US–Ventura, CA: Paul E. Affeldt, 1955–59; n.s.
1960–63
[Incorporated into *Music Memories: Covering
All Phases of Music Collecting* (q.v.) in 1963,
and became *Music Memories and Jazz Report*]

Cbijs 5 (1959), 3; n.s. 1 (1960/61), 1, 5, 6; 2
(1962), 4

Jazz Reprints
GB–Portsmouth: Jazz Reprints, ?1989–
[NOT IN BUCOMP1]

LOnjfa*

Jazz Research *see* Jazzforschung/Jazz
Research

Jazz Research Papers
US–Manhattan, KS: National Association of
Jazz Educators, 1983–
[NOT IN BUCOMP1]

BSdsc 1983–85

Jazz Review [1]
TNG US699; 0448–925X
US–New York: Jazz Review, 1958–61

LOnjfa*
Lsa 1 (1958)–4 (1961), 1 [w 2 (1959), 2, 8,
12; 3 (1960), 10]

Jazz Review [2]
?NZ–?, 1962–?

    Cbijs 4, 5, 1963

Jazz, Rhythm and Blues/Schweizerische Jazz-Zeitschrift/Revue Suisse de Jazz
TNG CH170
CH–Zurich, 1967–

    Cbijs 1968, Jan, Feb

Jazz Scene
GB–London: EMI Records, 1962–63

    Cbijs 1 (1962), 2–7; 2 (1963), 1–6
    Lbl*
    LOnjfa*
    Yu 1 (1962)

Jazz Scene *see also* **Jazz Bulletin**

The Jazz Session
US–Chicago, IL: Hot Club of Chicago, 1944–46
[Ceased publication with no. 13, 1946]

    Cbijs 6–8, 1945; 11, 1946
    LOnjfa*

Jazz Society
N–Oslo, 1957–?

    Cbijs 4, 1958

Jazz Soundings
GB–Liverpool, 1971–72

    Cbijs 1971–72

Jazz Sprawozdanie [= Jazz Report]
PL–Warsaw, 1965–?

    Cbijs 7, 8, 1967

Jazz Studies
GB–London, 1964–71

    Cbijs 1964–71
    Lsa 1967, Jan–Apr

Jazz Talk International
GB–Coventry: McNall and Chambers, 1991–
[NOT IN BUCOMP1]

    EIR:Dtc 1, 1991
    En 1, 2, 1991

Jazz Tempo *see* **Jazz Music**

Jazz Times [1]
TNG GB511; 0021–5716
GB–Twickenham: British Jazz Society, 1964–

    Cbijs 1 (1964), 3; 2 (1965), 1–3, 5, 7–12; 3
    (1966)–4 (1967), 2, 3, 5, 8–12; 5 (1968)–9
    (1972)
    Lbl*
    LOnjfa*

Jazz Times [2]
0959–8057
GB–Altrincham: A. Garnett, 1986–
[NOT IN BUCOMP1]

    Lbl*
    Mpl 1986, July–1995, Aug

Jazz Today [1]
GB–London: Marquee Club, 1953–?
    Lbl*

Jazz Today [2]
US–New York: Jazz Today, 1956–57

    Cbijs 1956, Oct–Dec; 1957, Mar, Apr, June

Jazz Today [3]
GB–London, 1962–?

    Cbijs 2 (1963), 5, 9, 10; 3 (1963), 2, 3; 1964,
    Jan–May, July–Oct; 1966, Aug

Jazz Up
ARG–Buenos Aires: Ediciones Floryland,
1965–

    Cbijs 3, 1965

Jazz World *see* **Juzz Jazz**

Jazz World *see also* **Swinging Newsletter**

Jazz World Index *see* **Swinging Newsletter**

Jazz Writings
GB–Chilwell, Notts: Jazz Appreciation Society,
1946–?

    Lbl*

Jazzbeat *see* **Jazz Beat**

Jazzbladet [= Jazz Journal]: Officielt Organ for Jysk-Fynsk Jazz Union
DK–Aarhus, 1957–61

    Cbijs 1960, Sep–1961, Jan

Jazz-Bulletin *see* Jazz Bulletin

The Jazzfinder
US–New Orleans: Blackstone, 1948
[Ceased publication 1948, Dec]

Cbijs 1948 [w May]

Jazzforschung/Jazz Research
TNG INTL29; 0075- 3572
A–Graz: Institut für Jazzforschung an der
Hochschule für Musik und Darstellende Kunst,
1969–

Cu 2 (1970)–#
KE 1 (1969)–4 (1972); 10 (1978)
Lbl*
Lcml 1 (1969)–#
Lsa 2 (1970)–#
Ob*
Ouf 1 (1969)–20 (1988)

**Der Jazzfreund: Mitteilungsblatt für
Jazzfreunde in Ost und West**
TNG D998; 0021–5724
D–Menden: IGJ, 1957–

Cbijs 42, 43, 1966; 45–52, 1967–68; 59,
1970; 69, 70, 1973
Cu*

**Jazzline: the Journal of Traditional and
Mainstream Music**
0965–4259
GB–Hull: Pennant, 1992–
[NOT IN BUCOMP1]

Lbl*

Jazzmania
ARG–Buenos Aires, 1959–?

Cbijs 6–8, 1959

Jazznews *see* Jazz News: Ireland's Jazz and
Blues Magazine

Jazznews International *see* Jazz News:
Ireland's Jazz and Blues Magazine

Jazznocracy
0307–2983
GB–?–?

Cbijs 1972–#
EIR:Dtc 1976, 2–5
Lbl 1976, 2–#
Ob*

Jazznytt [=New Jazz]
TNG S103; 0332–7248
S–Stockholm: Svenska Jazzriksforbundet,
1965–67; 1967–?91
[Entitled *Jazznytt från SJR* (ISSN 0047–195X)
from Dec 1967; absorbed into *Orkester
Journalen: Tidskrift for Modern Dansmusik*
(q.v.) in 1991]

BSdsc*
Cbijs 1965, July–Dec; 1966, Mar, Nov; 1967,
Jan, Feb, July, Aug; 1969, 1, 2

Jazznytt från SJR *see* Jazznytt

The Jazzologist
0198–6805
US–Kerrville, TX: New Orleans Jazz Club of
California, 1963–?83; succeeded by *Jazz
Newsletter* from 1984–86]

Cbijs 4 (1966), 2
LOnjfa*

Jazzology
GB–London: American Jazz Society, British
Branch, 194?–?

Cbijs 1945–47
LOnjfa*

Jazzology *see also* CRC Newsletter

Jazzrevy *see* Musikrevue

Jazzspiegel
?D–?, 1966–?

Cbijs 2–6, 1967

JCM: the Journal of Country Music *see*
Journal of Country Music

Jefferson 29 *see* Jefferson Blues Magazine

Jefferson Blues Magazine
0345–5653
S–Taby: Scandinavian Blues Association, 1968–
[Also known as *Jefferson 29* and *Jefferson:
Nordisk Tidskrift för Blues och Folkmusik*]

Cbijs 22–36, 1973–77
Lsa*

**Jefferson: Nordisk Tidskrift för Blues och
Folkmusik** *see* Jefferson Blues Magazine

J.E.M.F. Newsletter
0021–3632
US–Los Angeles: John Edwards Memorial
Foundation, 1965–85
[Entitled *J.E.M.F. Quarterly* (TNG US749) from
vol. 5 (1969); ceased publication with vol. 21
(1985), no. 78]

> **EXu** 7 (1971), 23; 8 (1972), 25–9 (1973), 32;
> 10 (1974), 36; 15 (1979)–21 (1985)Lsa 4
> (1968), 2–21 (1985) [w 5 (1969); 6 (1970),
> 2; 7 (1971), 2, 3; 8 (1972), 4; 11 (1975), 4]

J.E.M.F. Quarterly *see* J.E.M.F. Newsletter

Jewish Music Heritage Trust Newsletter
GB–Harrow, 1993–

> **Lsa** 3, 1993–#

JF *see* Jazz Forum: JF: the Magazine of the
European Jazz Federation

J. G. Winder's Musical Studio and Workshop
GB–London, 1893–96

> **Lbl***

Jimpress
1350–8555
GB–South Wirral: S. Rodham, 1991–
[NOT IN BUCOMP1; Jimi Hendrix fanzine]

> **Lbl***

Jitter Fanzine
0963–7990
GB–Bristol: Jitter Fanzine, ?1990–
[NOT IN BUCOMP1]

> **Lbl** 5, 1991–#

The 'Jo
GB–Bournemouth, 1894–1915
[From 1896 entitled *The Troubadour*]

> **Lbl***
> **Ob***

Jocks
GB–London: Spotlight, 1986–
[NOT IN BUCOMP1; entitled *DJ: Disc Jockey*
(London: Orpheus) from 55, 1991]

> **Cu** 1, 1986–#
> **Lbl***
> **Ob** 1, 1986–#

Johann Adolf Scheibens Critischer Musicus
see Critischer Musicus

Johann-Joseph-Abert-Gesellschaft:
Mitteilungsblatt
D–Stuttgart: Johann–Joseph–Abert–
Gesellschaft, 1986–
[NOT IN BUCOMP1]

> **Lu** 2–8, 1989–91

John Edwards Memorial Foundation
Newsletter *see* J.E.M.F. Newsletter

John Loosemore Centre: Occasional Papers
GB–Buckfastleigh: John Loosemore
Association, 1988–
[NOT IN BUCOMP1]

> **Cu** 1, 1988–#
> **Ouf** 1, 1988–#

The Joint Committee for Church Music in
Ireland: Newsletter
EIRE–Dublin: Joint Committee for Church
Music in Ireland, 1977–
[NOT IN BUCOMP1]

> **AB** 1–12, 1977–81
> **EIR:Dtc** 1, 1977–#

Joseph Williams Musical Gazette
GB–London, 1919

> **Ob** 1 (1919/20), 1–3

Journal: Hochschule für Musik Köln
0936–2940
D–Cologne: Hochschule für Musik, 198?–
[NOT IN BUCOMP1]

> **Lam** 15, 1989; 18, 1990

Journal de Composition Musicale *see* Leçons
de Composition Musicale

Le Journal de Musique
Fellinger 1968/718; TNG F158
F–Paris, 1876–82

> **Lbl***

Journal de Musique Historique, Théoretique et Pratique sur la Musique Ancienne et Moderne
TNG F3
F–Paris, 1770–77
[Entitled *Journal de Musique par une Société d'Amateurs* from 1773]

    Au 1 (1770)–3 (1774/77) [Reprint ed.]
    Cu 1 (1770)–3 (1774/77) [Reprint ed.]
    Er 1 (1770)–3 (1774/77) [Reprint ed.]
    HUu 1 (1770)–3 (1774/7) [Reprint ed.]
    Lgsm 1(1770)–3 (1774/7) [Reprint ed.]
    Ob 1 (1770)–3 (1774/77) [Reprint ed.]

Journal de Musique par une Société d'Amateurs *see* Journal de Musique Historique, Théoretique et Pratique sur la Musique Ancienne et Moderne

Journal der Bayerischen Staatsoper *see* Blätter der Bayerischen Staatsoper

Journal des Maitrises: Revue du Chant Liturgique
F–Paris: J. d'Ortigue, Felix Clement, 1862–63
[NOT IN BUCOMP1]

    Gul (e) 1862–63

Journal Général d'Annonce des Oeuvres de Musique, Gravures, Lithographies etc. publiés en France et à l'Étranger
Fellinger 1968/69; TNG F13
F–Paris, 1825–27

    Lu 1825–27 [Reprint ed.]
    Ob 1825–27 [Reprint ed.]

Journal into Melody
GB–Nottingham: Robert Farnon Society, ?–
[NOT IN BUCOMP1]

    Cu 67, 1982–#

Le Journal Musical: Bulletin International Critique de la Bibliographie Musicale
Fellinger 1968/1352; TNG F271
F–Paris, 1896–1900
[From 1898 incorporated the *Gazette Musicale de la Suisse Romande* (TNG CH14)]

    Ob*

Journal of Band Research
TNG US740; 0021–9207
US–Troy, Alabama [etc.]: Troy State University Press [for the American Bandmasters' Association], 1964–

    Lbl*
    Msuc 22 (1986)–#

Journal of British Music Therapy
0951–5038
GB–London: British Society for Music Therapy/Association of Professional Music Therapists, 1987–
[NOT IN BUCOMP1; entitled *British Journal of Music Therapy* from vol. 10 (1996)]

    EIR:Dp 1 (1987)–7 (1993)
    En 1 (1987)–#
    Lam 1 (1987)–#
    Lbl 1 (1987)–#
    Lcml 1 (1987)–#
    Lcml (m) 1 (1987)–#
    Lcu 1 (1987)–#
    Lgsm 1 (1987)–#
    Lie 1 (1987)–#
    Lki 1 (1987)–#
    Lu 1 (1987)–#
    Mcm 1 (1987)–#
    Mmu (d) 1 (1987)–#
    Mu 1 (1987)–2 (1988), 1
    NOTu 1 (1987)–#
    Ob*
    SFu 1 (1987)–8 (1994)
    TOd 1 (1987)–#
    Yu 1 (1987)–# [w 4 (1990)]

Journal of Country Music
TNG US806; 0092–0517
US–Nashville, TN: Country Music Foundation, Inc., 1970–
[Also known as *JCM*; formerly *Country Music Foundation Newsletter*]

    EXu 8 (1980), 2–#
    Lcs 12 (1987), 1
    Lsa 9 (1983), 3; 10 (1985), 1, 2

Journal of Electroacoustic Music *see* Sonic Arts Network Journal

Journal of Guitar Acoustics
US–Ann Arbor, MI, 1980–
[NOT IN BUCOMP1]

    Lgu 1 (1980)–2 (1983), 3

Journal of Jazz Discography
GB–Newport: C. Evans, 1976–

    Cbijs 1, 1976–
    Lsa 1, 1976–#*

Journal of Jazz Studies: Incorporating Studies in Jazz Discography
TNG US832; 0093–3686
US–New Brunswick, NJ: Rutgers Institute of Jazz Studies, 1973–79
[Continued as *Annual Review of Jazz Studies* (q.v.) from 1982]

    BSdsc*
    Cbijs 1 (1973)–6 (1979)
    CDu 4 (1977), 2; 5 (1978), 1, 2
    Cu 1 (1973)–6 (1979), 1
    EXu 1 (1973)–5 (1978)
    Lcml 1 (1973)–6 (1979)
    Lgo 3 (1976), 2–6 (1979), 1
    Lsa 1 (1973)–6 (1979), 1
    Ob 1 (1973)–6 (1979), 1
    SFu 1 (1973)–3 (1976)
    SLGu 1 (1974), 2–2 (1975), 2; 3 (1976), 2–
      6 (1979), 1

Journal of Jewish Music and Liturgy
0197–0100
US–New York: Cantorial Council of America, 1976–
[NOT IN BUCOMP1]

    Cu 1 (1976)–#*
    Lcu 14 (1991/92)–#

Journal of Music Theory
TNG US683; 0022–2909
US–New Haven, CT: Yale University, 1957–

    AB*
    Au 1 (1957)–32 (1988)
    BAc 26 (1982)–# [w 32 (1988), 2]
    BG 8 (1964); 39 (1995)–#
    BLp 1 (1957)–#
    BLu 1 (1957)–#
    BRu 12 (1968)–# [w 17 (1973), 1]
    BTu 1 (1957)–#
    Bu 1 (1957)–#
    CCtc 27 (1983)–#
    CDu 15 (1971)–#
    Cu 1 (1957)–#
    DRu 1 (1957)–#
    EIR:Dp 31 (1987), 2–#
    EIR:Dtc 35 (1991)–#
    EIR:Duc 21 (1977)–#

    En 1 (1957)–#
    Er 14 (1970)–18 (1974)
    EXu 1 (1957)–10 (1966); 12 (1968)–#
    Gul 1 (1957)–#
    HUu 1 (1957)–20 (1976), 1
    KE 18 (1974)–#
    LAu 1 (1957)–4 (1960); 6 (1962)–10 (1966); 14 (1970)–16 (1972); 18 (1974)–#
    Lbl*
    Lcml 1 (1957)–10 (1966); 12 (1968), 2–#
    LEbc 26 (1982)–#
    Lgo 1 (1957)–# [w 2 (1958); 5 (1961); 8 (1964); 11 (1967), 2]
    Lkc 1 (1957)–#
    Lki 21 (1977)–35 (1991)
    Lmi 22 (1978)–#
    LRHBNC 1 (1957)–3 (1959), 3; 4 (1960); 6 (1962)–11 (1967), 1; 12 (1968); 14 (1970)–16 (1972); 18 (1974)–#
    Lro 22 (1978)–#
    Lu 1 (1957)–#
    LVu 1 (1957)–13 (1969)
    Mcm 22 (1978)–#
    NO 1 (1957)–#
    NWu 13 (1969)–30 (1986)
    Ob 1 (1957)–#
    Ouf 1 (1957)–#
    R 30 (1986)–#
    SFu 13 (1969)–35 (1991)
    SOu 1 (1957)–# [w3 (1959); 30 (1986), 2]
    TOd 19 (1975)–# [w 32 (1988), 2; 33(1989), 1]
    Uu 15 (1971); 16 (1972)*; 17 (1973)–30 (1986); 31 (1987)*; 32 (1988)–#
    Yu 1 (1957)–10 (1966); 21 (1977)–#

Journal of Music Theory Pedagogy
0891–7639
US–Norman, OK: University of Oklahoma School of Music, 1987–
[NOT IN BUCOMP1]

    SOu 5 (1991)–#

Journal of Music Therapy
TNG US741; 0022–2917
US–Silver Spring, MD [etc.]: National Association for Music Therapy, 1964–

    BLp 17 (1980)–#
    BSdsc 4 (1967)–#
    Lgsm 1 (1964), 2–6 (1969); 17 (1980)–20 (1983); 25 (1988)–#*
    Lro 1 (1964)–# [w 7 (1970), 1; 10 (1973), 4; 20 (1983), 3]

Journal of Musick, composed of Italian, French and English Songs, Romances and Duetts, and of Overtures, Rondos, &c, for the Forte Piano
Fellinger 1986, pp. 284–6
US–Baltimore: Mme Le Pelletier, 1810
[NOT IN BUCOMP1. 24 numbers were published, in two parts]

> Mu 1–24, 1810 [m]

Journal of Musicological Research *see* Music and Man

The Journal of Musicology [1]
TNG US552
US–Greenfield, OH: Music Science Press, 1939–?47

> Lam 5 (1947), 1
> Ob 1 (1939), 2, 4; 2 (?1941)–5 (1947), 1

The Journal of Musicology [2]
0277–9269
US–Louisville [etc.]: Imperial Printing Company, 1982–

> BAc 9 (1991)–#
> BG 12 (1994)–#
> BRu 1 (1982), 3–# [w 7 (1989), 3, 4]
> Bs 5 (1987), 3
> BSdsc 1 (1982)–#
> Bu 10 (1992)–#
> CDu 1 (1982), 3, 4; 2 (1983)–3 (1984); 4 (1985/86)–#
> Cu 1 (1982)–#
> DRu 1 (1982)–#
> EIR:Dtc 5 (1987), 4–#
> EIR:Duc 10 (1992)–#
> En 1 (1982)–#
> Er 11 (1993)–#
> EXu 2 (1983), 4–#
> Gul 4 (1985/86)–#
> HUu 10 (1992)–#
> KE 7 (1989)–#
> LAu 1 (1982)–#*
> Lbl 1 (1982)–#
> Lcm 1 (1982)–#
> Lcml 1 (1982)–#
> LEbc 1 (1982), 3–#
> Lgo 1 (1982)–#
> Lgsm 8 (1990)–#
> Lkc 1 (1982)– 3 (1984); 4 (1985/86)*; 5 (1987)–10 (1992); 11 (1993)*; 12 (1994)–#
> LRHBNC 1 (1982)–#
> Lro 1 (1982)–#

> Lu 1 (1982), 3–# [w 3 (1984), 4]
> LVu 3 (1984), 2–#
> Msuc 11 (1993)–#
> Mu 1 (1982), 3–#
> NO 1 (1982)–#
> NWu 4 (1985/86)–#
> Ob 1 (1982)–#
> Oub 13 (1995)–#
> Ouf 1 (1982)–#
> SFu 1 (1982); 4 (1985/86)–#
> SOu 1 (1982)–#
> TOd 5 (1987), 3
> Uu 5 (1987)*; 7 (1989)–#
> Yu 1 (1982)–#

The Journal of Musicology *see also* Ongakugaku: Journal of the Japanese Musicological Society

Journal of New Music Research *see* Interface: Journal of New Music Research

Journal of Performance Practice
US–Purchase, NY: Purchase College Foundation, 1983
[NOT IN BUCOMP1; only one issue published]

> Lcm 1 (1983), 1
> Ob 1 (1983), 1

Journal of Proceedings of the Music Supervisors' National Conference
US–Chapel Hill, NC, 1907–
[From 1931 entitled *Yearbook of Proceedings of the Music Supervisors' National Conference*; from 1934 entitled *Yearbook of Proceedings of the Music Educators' National Conference*]

> NTu 7 (1914)–13 (1920); 15 (1922); 17 (1924)–21 (1928)

Journal of Renaissance and Baroque Music
TNG US590; 1059–8529
US–Cambridge, MA; New Haven, CT: Institute of Renaissance and Baroque Music; American Musicological Society, 1946–
[Entitled *Musica Disciplina* (ISSN 0077–2461) from vol. 2 (1948)]

> AB 2 (1948)–44 (1990)
> Au 12 (1958)–#
> BG 1 (1946)–#
> BLu 1 (1946), 2, 3; 2 (1948)–#
> Bp 1 (1946)–#
> BRu 1 (1946), 2–4; 2 (1948)–#
> BSdsc*

Bu 1 (1946)–#
CDu 16 (1962)–#
Cpl 2 (1948); 4 (1950); 17 (1963)
Cu 1 (1946)–#
DRu 1 (1946)–#
En 1 (1946)
Ep 1 (1946), 1
Er 1 (1946)–#
EXu 1 (1946)–9 (1955); 11 (1957)–#
Gul 1 (1946)–#
HUu 1 (1946), 2–#
Lam 3 (1949), 2–4
LAu 24 (1970)–#
Lbbc 1 (1946)–# [w 4 (1950)]
Lbl*
Lcm 20 (1966); 22 (1968)–23 (1969);
    25 (1971)–#
Lcml 1 (1946)–#
LEbc 1 (1946)–#
Lgo 1 (1946)–#
Lkc 1 (1946)–#
LRHBNC 1 (1946)–5 (1951); 7 (1953)–
    9 (1955); 11 (1957)–#
Lro 28 (1974)–#
Lu 1 (1946)–#
LVp 1 (1946)–26 (1972)
LVu 2 (1948)–#
Mcm 22 (1968)–#
Mu 17 (1963); 19 (1965); 22 (1968);
    24 (1970)–#
NO 1 (1946)–33 (1979); 43 (1989)–#
NWu 21 (1967)–42 (1988)
Ob 1 (1946)–#
Ouf 1 (1946)–#
R 17 (1963)–42 (1988)
SA 6 (1952)–39 (1985)
SFu 1 (1946)–#
SOu 7 (1953)–#

Journal of Research in Music Education
TNG US665; 0022–4294
US– Reston, VA [etc.]: Music Educators'
National Conference, 1953–

BAc 30 (1982),3–34 (1986), 3; 35 (1987), 1,
    2, 4–#
BSdsc 14 (1966)–#
CCtc 23 (1975)–25 (1977)
Cu 1 (1953)–#
EIR:Duc 16 (1968)–39 (1991)
Lcml 16 (1968)–17 (1969); 19 (1971)–
    21 (1973); 23 (1975), 3–#
Lgo 17 (1969)–# [w 27 (1979), 3; 37 (1989),
    4]
Lie 4 (1956)–#*

Lkc 1 (1953)–11 (1963); 15 (1967)*;
    16 (1968)–18 (1970); 19 (1971)*
Lki 1 (1953)–11 (1963); 14 (1966)–#
Lmi 27 (1979)–#
Lu 10 (1962), 1
Mmu (d) 18 (1970)–#
Mu 20 (1972)–31 (1983); 39 (1991)–#
Re 1 (1953)–#
SFu 39 (1991)–#

Journal of Singing see **The Bulletin: the
Official Magazine of the National Association
of Teachers of Singing**

Journal of Synagogue Music
0449–5128
US–New York: Cantors Assembly of America,
1967–
[NOT IN BUCOMP1]

Cu 22 (1992)–#
Lcu 22 (1992)–#

Journal of the Acoustical Society of America
0001–4966
US–Lancaster, PA: American Institute of
Physics [for the Acoustical Society of America],
1929–
[NOT IN BUCOMP1; limited access to
published articles is available at the Journal's
electronic site, at URL http://ojps.aip.org/jasa]

CCtc 55–89, 1974–91

Journal of the American Liszt Society
TNG US874; 0147–4413
US–Louisville, KT: American Liszt Society,
1977–

Cu 1, 1977–#
Lsa 22, 1987–# [w 30, 1991]
Ob*

**Journal of the American Musical Instrument
Society** see **American Musical Instrument
Society: Bulletin**

**Journal of the American Musicological
Society**
TNG US613; 0003–0139
US–Richmond, VA [etc.]: American
Musicological Society, 1948–
[Preceded by the *Bulletin of the American
Musicological Society*]

Au 1 (1948)–#
BAc 34 (1981)–# [w 46 (1993), 2, 3]

BG 11 (1958)–#
BLp 1 (1948)–#
BLu 1 (1948)–#
BRp 15 (1962)–#
BRu 1 (1948)–#
Bs 35 (1982)–#
BTu 25 (1972)–44 (1991)
Bu 1 (1948)–#
CCtc 23 (1970)–#
CDu 1 (1948)–#
Cpl 1 (1948)–#
Cu 1 (1948)–#
DRu 1 (1948)–#
EIR:Dtc 1 (1948)–#
EIR:Duc 17 (1964)–#
En 1 (1948)–#
Er 1 (1948)–#
EXu 1 (1948)–#
Gam 11 (1958)–# [w 15 (1962), 3; 27 (1974), 2]
Gul 1 (1948)–#
HUu 1 (1948)–#
KE 27 (1974)–#
Lam 1 (1948)–20 (1967); 21 (1968), 2–41 (1988), 2; 42 (1989)–46 (1993), 2; 47 (1994)–#
LAu 1 (1948)–#
Lbbc 1 (1948)–#
Lcm 1 (1948)–#
Lcml 1 (1948)–#
Lcu 17 (1964)–35 (1982), 1; 45 (1992)–#
LEbc 1 (1948)–#
Lgo 1 (1948)–#
Lkc 1 (1948)–# [w 6 (1953); 37 (1984)]
Lki 30 (1977)–37 (1984)
Lmi 31 (1978)–#
LRHBNC 1 (1948)–#
Lro 27 (1974)–#
Lu 1 (1948)–#
LVp 1 (1948)–#
LVu 1 (1948)–#
Mcm 2 (1949), 2, 3; 4 (1951), 1; 19 (1966), 1; 28 (1975), 1–3; 29 (1976)–#
MK 23 (1970)–#
Mpl 1 (1948)–#*
Mu 17 (1964)–# [w 23 (1970), 2; 25 (1972), 2]
NO 1 (1948)–#
NWu 1 (1948)–#
Ob 1 (1948)–#
Ouf 1 (1948)–#
R 1 (1948)–#
SA 8 (1955)–46 (1993)
SFu 18 (1965)–#
SOu 15 (1962)–#

TOd 1 (1948)–#
Uu 31 (1978)–#
Yu 27 (1974)–#

Journal of the Arnold Schoenberg Institute
TNG US866; 0146–5856
US–Los Angeles, CA: Arnold Schoenberg Institute, 1976–

ALb 1 (1976)–#
BAc 1 (1976)–2 (1977), 1, 2; 3 (1978), 1, 2, 4–#
CDu 1 (1976), 3; 4 (1979)–#
Cu 1 (1976)–#
EIR:Dtc 10 (1987)–#
En 1 (1976)–#
Er 1 (1976)–14 (1992)
EXu 1 (1976)–#
Lbbc 1 (1976), 1–3
Lcml 1 (1976)–#
Lcu 14 (1992)–#
Lgo 1 (1976)–#
Lkc 1 (1976)–#
Lro 7 (1982)–#
Ltc 1 (1976), 1; 2 (1977/78)–3 (1979), 2; 4 (1980), 1, 2; 5 (1981)–17 (1994), 2
Lu 14 (1992), 1
Mcm 1 (1976)–#
MK 1 (1976)–8 (1983)
NO 1 (1976)–8 (1983)
Ob*
Ouf 1 (1976)–#*
SOu 1 (1976)–#

Journal of the Association for Recorded Sound Collections *see* **Association for Recorded Sound Collections: Journal**

Journal of the Australasian Performing Rights Association *see* **A.P.R.A. Journal**

Journal of the British Association of Symphonic Bands and Wind Ensembles
0268–1676
GB–Croydon: British Association of Symphonic Bands and Wind Ensembles [B.A.S.B.W.E.], 1982–85
[Entitled *Winds: Journal of the British Association of Symphonic Bands and Wind Ensembles* (q.v.) from 1985]

BAc 1 (1982)–4 (1985), 1 [w 3 (1984), 1]
Bs 1 (1982)–4 (1985), 1
Cu 1 (1982)–4 (1985), 1
EIR:Dtc 1 (1982)–4 (1985), 1
En*

Lam 1 (1982)–4 (1985), 1
Lbl*
Lcm 1 (1982)–2 (1983); 3 (1984), 2;
   4 (1985), 1
Lu 1 (1982)
Mcm 1 (1982)–4 (1985)
Msuc 1 (1982)–4 (1985)
Ob*

Journal of the British Music Society *see*
British Music: Journal of the British Music
Society

Journal of the British Sound Recording
Association *see* Sound Recording and
Reproduction

Journal of the Catch Society of America
0008–770X
US–New York: Catch Society, 1969–
[NOT IN BUCOMP1; entitled *Lyric and Song*
(ISSN 0147–1562) from vol. 2 no. 3 (1970)]

   Er 1 (1969), 1

Journal of the Catgut Acoustical Society *see*
The Catgut Acoustical Society Newsletter

Journal of the Central Academy of Music
[translated title] *see* Zhongyang Yin Yue Xue
Yuan Xuebao

Journal of the Cinema Organ Society *see*
Cinema Organ: Journal of the Cinema Organ
Society

The Journal of the Dalcroze Society of Great
Britain and Ireland
TNG GB304
GB–London, 1924–38

   Lbl*
   Ob*

The Journal of the Devon Fellowship of
Music
GB–Devon Fellowship of Music, 19?–
[NOT IN BUCOMP1]

   ALb 8, 1955

Journal of the Dvořák Society of Great
Britain: Newsletter *see* Czech Music: the
Newsletter of the Dvořák Society [of Great
Britain]

The Journal of the English Folk Dance and
Song Society
TNG GB341; 0071–0563
GB–Taunton, London [etc.]: English Folk
Dance and Song Society, 1932–64
[Ceased publication with vol. 9 no. 5 (1964);
continued as *Folk Music Journal* (q.v.);
succeeded *The Journal of the Folk-Song Society*
(q.v.). The volumes are irregularly collated, as
follows: vol. 1 covers 1932–34, in three annual
parts; vol. 2 consists of a single part; vol. 3
covers 1936–39, in four annual parts; vol. 4
covers 1940–45, in 6 annual parts; vol. 5 covers
1946–48, in three annual parts; vol. 6 covers
1949–51, in three annual parts; vol. 7 covers
1952–55, in four annual parts; vol. 8 covers
1956–59, in four annual parts; and vol. 9 covers
1960–64, in five annual parts]

AB*
Au 1 (1932/34)–9 (1960/64)
BRp 1 (1932/34)–9 (1960/64)
BRu 1 (1932/34)–3 (1936/39), 4–4 (1940/45),
   3, 5, 6; 5 (1946/48), 1, 2; 6 (1949/51)–
   9 (1960/64), 5
Cpl 1 (1932/34)–9 (1960/64)*
EIR:Dtc 1 (1932/34)–9 (1960/64)
En 1 (1932/34)–9 (1960/64)
Ep 1 (1932/34)–9 (1960/64)
Gm 1 (1932/34)–9 (1960/64)
Gul 1 (1932/34)–9 (1960/64)
HUu 1 (1932/34)–9 (1960/64)
LAu 8 (1956/59), 1, 2; 9 (1960/64), 1–5
Lbar 1 (1932/34)–9 (1960/64), 5
Lbl*
Lcm 1 (1932/34)–#
Lcs 1 (1932/34)–9 (1960/64)
LEbc 1 (1932/34)–9 (1960/64), 3
Len 1 (1932/34)–9 (1960/64)
Lgo 1 (1932/34)–9 (1960/64)
LIp 6 (1949/51), 3; 7 (1952/55), 2–
   9 (1960/64), 5
Lkc 1 (1932/34)–9 (1960/64)
Lsa 7 (1952/55), 4–9 (1960/64)
Lu 1 (1932/34)–9 (1960/64)
LVp 1 (1932/34)–9 (1960/64)
Mpl 1 (1932/34)–9 (1960/64)
Ob*
Ouf (Howes) 1 (1932/34)–2 (1935);
   3 (1936/39)–5 (1946/48), 2; 6 (1949/51)–
   9 (1960/64), 5
R 1 (1932/34)–9 (1960/64)
TOd 1 (1932/34)–7 (1952/55), 3
WF 1 (1932/34)–9 (1960/64), 5

Journal of the English Folk-Dance Society
TNG GB318
GB–London: Oxford University Press [for the English Folk Dance Society], 1927–31
[NOT IN BUCOMP1; preceded by the *English Folk Dance Society's Journal* (q.v.). The volumes for 1927–31 are therefore designated "2nd series"]

AB*
ALb 1 (1927); 3 (1930)– 4 (1931)
Au 1 (1927)–4 (1931)
BDp 1 (1927)–4 (1931)
Cpl 1 (1927)–3 (1930)
EIR:Dtc 1 (1927)–4 (1931)
En 1 (1927)–4 (1931)
HUu 1 (1927)–4 (1931)
Lam 1 (1927)–2 (1928)
Lbl*
Lcm 1 (1927)–4 (1931)
Lcml 1 (1927)–4 (1931)
Lcs 1 (1927)–4 (1931)
Lu 1 (1927)–4 (1931)
Mpl 1 (1927)–4 (1931)
NTp 1 (1927)–4 (1931)
Ob*
Ouf (Howes) 1 (1927)–4 (1931)
TOd 2 (1928); 4 (1931)

The Journal of the Fine Arts *see* The Message Bird: a Literary and Musical Journal

The Journal of the Fine Arts and Musical World *see* The Message Bird: a Literary and Musical Journal

The Journal of the Folk-Song Society
Fellinger 1968/1484; TNG GB318
GB–London: Folk–Song Society, 1899–31
[Continued as *The Journal of the English Folk Dance and Song Society* (q.v.) from 1932. The collation of volumes is irregular, and is made up of up to five annual parts, as follows: vol. 1 covers 1899–1904, and consists of five annual parts, none of which bears a fascicle number; vol. 2 covers 1905–06, and consists of nos 6 and 7 (1905) and 8 and 9 (1906), vol. 3 covers 1907–09, and consists of 10 and 11 (1907), 12 (1908) and 13 (1909); vol. 4 (1910–13) consists of parts 14 and 15 (1910); 16 (1911); and 17 (1913); vol. 5 (1914/17) is in three parts, 18 (1914); 19 (1915) and 20 (1916); vol. 6 (1918–21) is divided into 21 (1918); 22 (1919); 23 (1920); 24 and 25 (1921); vol. 7 (1922–26) is in five parts, as is vol. 8 (1927/31)]

AB*
ALb 1 (1899/1904)–8 (1927/31), 5
Au 1 (1899/1904)–8 (1927/31)
BDp 1 (1899/1904)–8 (1927/31)
BRp 1 (1899/1904)–8 (1927/31)
BRu 1 (1899/1904)–8 (1927/31)
Bu 1 (1899/1904)–8 (1927/31)
Cpl 1 (1899/1904)–8 (1927/31)
Cu 1 (1899/1904)–8 (1927/31)
EIR:Dtc 1 (1899/1904)–8 (1927/31)
EIR:Duc 1 (1899/1904)–8 (1927/31)
En 1 (1899/1904)–8 (1927/31)
Ep 1 (1899/1904)–8 (1927/31)
Er 1 (1899/1904)–8 (1927/31)
EXu 1 (1899/1904)–3 (1907/09), 2
  [w 1 (1899/1904), 3; 2 (1905/06), 7]
Gm 1 (1899/1904)–8 (1927/31)
Gul 1 (1899/1904)–8 (1927/31)
HUu 1 (1899/1904)–8 (1927/31)
Lam 1 (1899/1904)–8 (1927/31)
Lbar 1 (1899/1904)–8 (1927/31)
Lbl*
Lcm 1 (1899/1904)–8 (1927/31)
Lcml 1 (1899/1904)–8 (1927/31)
Lcs 1 (1899/1904)–8 (1927/31)
LEbc 1 (1899/1904)–8 (1927/31)
Lgo 1 (1899/1904)–8 (1927/31), 5
Lkc 1 (1899/1904)–8 (1927/31)
Lu 1 (1899/1904)–8 (1927/31)
LVp 1 (1899/1904)–8 (1927/31)
Mpl 1 (1899/1904)–8 (1927/31)
Mu 1 (1899/1904)–8 (1927/31)
NO 1 (1899/1904)–8 (1927/31)
NTp 1 (1899/1904)–8 (1927/31)
Ob*
Ouf (Howes) 1 (1899/1904)–6 (1918/21), 25
R 1 (1899/1904)–8 (1927/31)
SA 4 (1910/13), 3

Journal of the Incorporated Society of Musicians *see* Monthly Journal of the National Society of Professional Musicians

Journal of the Incorporated Society of Organ Builders
TNG GB420; ISSN 0073–5744
GB–London [etc.]: Incorporated Society of Organ Builders, 1949–
[NOT IN BUCOMP1]

AB 5 (1984), 2
EIR:Dtc 5 (1984)–#
En 5 (1984/91), 2, 4
Lam*

Lam (o) 1 (1949)–2 (1957), 4; 3 (1958)–4
   (1978), 1
Lbl*
Ob*

Journal of the Indian Musicological Society
see **Sankeet Kala Vihar**

The Journal of the International Double Reed Society
TNG US837; 0092–0827
US–East Lansing, MI [etc.]: International
Double Reed Society, 1973–

Gam 14 (1986)–#
Lam 2 (1974); 6 (1978); 10 (1982)–#
Lcm 11 (1983)–# [w 14 (1986)]
Mcm 5 (1977)–#
Ob*

Journal of the International Folk Music Council
TNG INTL10
GB–Cambridge: Heffer [for the International
Folk Music Council], 1949–68
[Continued from 1969 as *Yearbook of the
International Folk Music Council* (q.v.)]

AB*
ALb 4 (1952)–20 (1968)
BLu 9 (1957)–17 (1965), 1; 18 (1966)–
   20 (1968)
BRu 1 (1949)–16 (1964); 17 (1965), 2
BSdsc*
Cu 1 (1949)–20 (1968)
EIR:Dtc 1 (1949)–20 (1968)
En 1 (1949)–20 (1968)
Ep 1 (1949)–20 (1968)
Lam 1 (1949)–17 (1965), 1; 18 (1966)–
   20 (1968)
Lbl*
Lcm 1 (1949)–20 (1968)
Lcml 1 (1949)–20 (1968)
Lcs 1 (1949)–20 (1968)
Lgo 1 (1949)–20 (1968)
LIp 6 (1954)–8 (1956)
Lsa 1 (1949)–20 (1968) [w 17 (1965)]
Lso 1 (1949)–20 (1968)
Lu 1 (1949)–20 (1968)
LVp 1 (1949)–10 (1958); 12 (1960)–
   20 (1968)
Mpl 1 (1949)–20 (1968)
Ob 1 (1949)–20 (1968)
Ouf (Howes) 1 (1949)–20 (1968)
   [w 17 (1965), 2]
R 1 (1949)–20 (1968)

SFp 1 (1949)–20 (1968)
TOd 2 (1950)–20 (1968)
Yu 1 (1949)–8 (1956); 10 (1958)–20 (1968)

Journal of the International Society for the Study of Tension in Performance
GB–Kingston-upon-Thames: International
Society for the Study of Tension in
Performance, 1983–
[NOT IN BUCOMP1; also known as the *ISSTIP
Journal*]

CCtc 4 (1987)–#
Lgo 1 (1983)–3 (1985)
Lki 1 (1983)–#

Journal of the International Trombone Association *see* **ITA**

Journal of the Irish Folk Song Society
TNG GB203
GB–London: Irish Folk Song Society, 1904–39
[Ceased publication with vol. 29 (1939). Volume
numbering irregular]

AB 1 (1904)–29 (1939)
Au 11 (1912)–24 (1930)
BLu 2 (1905)–29 (1939) [w 17–21]
Cpl 9 (1911); 19 (1922)–22/23 (1927)
Cu 1 (1904)–29 (1939)
EIR:Dtc 1 (1904)–29 (1939)
EIR:Duc 6 (1908)–29 (1939)
EIR:MEtc 1 (1904)–29 (19 39)
En 1 (1904), 1; 2 (1905)–8 (1911); 21
   (1924)–29 (1939)
Er 2 (1905), 1, 2; 12 (1912); 16 (1919)
Gm 1 (1904)–29 (1939)
Lbl*
Lcm 17 (1920)–27 (1936)
Lcml 1 (1904)–29 (1939)
Lcs 1 (1904)–29 (1939)*
LEbc 2 (1905)–10 (1911); 12 (1912)
Lgo 8 (1911)–12 (1912); 17 (1920); 20
   (1923); 22/23 (1927)
Mpl 1 (1904)–29 (1939)
Ob*
Ouf (Howes) 2 (1905), 1/2; 5 (1908)–9
   (1911), June; 10 (1911), Dec–11 (1912),
   June; 12 (1912), Oct; 14 (1914), Apr; 15
   (1915, Mar; 18 (1921), Dec; 19 (1922),
   Dec; 22/23 (1927)–29 (1939)

Journal of the Lute Society of America *see*
The Lute Society of America Inc.: Journal

Journal of the Madras Music Academy
TNG IN4
IN–Madras, 1930–

Cpl 1 (1930), 1
Cu 43 (1972)–#
Lbl*
Lio 1 (1930), 2–9 (1938); 11 (1940)–53
(1982); 55 (1984)–#
Lso 12 (1941)–#
Ob*

Journal of the Music Masters' and Mistresses'
Association
GB–London: Music Masters' and Mistresses'
Association, ?1982–
[Preceded by the *Newsletter of the Music
Masters' and Mistresses' Association*; entitled
*Music Masters' and Mistresses' Association
Journal* from 1994]

AB 1986, Apr–#
Cu 21, 1989–#
EIR:Dtc 21, 1989–#
En 1, 1982–#
Lbl 21, 1989–#
Ob 21, 1989–#

Journal of the Open University Music Society
see Open University Music Society Journal

The Journal of the Organ Club
TNG GB481; TNG GB545; 0306–0357
GB–London: The Organ Club, 1958–
[From 1969 entitled *The Organ Club Journal*]

AB*
BSdsc*
Cu 1965–#
En*
Lam (o) 1958–64; 1966; 1969; 1969–77;
1980, 2, 4
Lbl*
Lrco 1958–#
Ob*

Journal of the Plainsong and Mediaeval
Music Society
TNG GB578; 0143–4918
GB–Englefield Green: The Society, 1978–91
[Ceased publication with no. 13, 1991;
succeeded by *Plainsong and Medieval Music*
(q.v.)]

AB 6 (1983); 8 (1985)
Au 1 (1978)–10 (1987)
BLu 1 (1978)–4 (1981)

Bu 1 (1978)–13 (1991)
CDu 1 (1978)–2 (1979)
Cu 1 (1978)–13 (1991)
EIR:Dtc 1 (1978)–8 (1985)
EIR:Duc 1 (1978)–13 (1991)
Er 1 (1978)–2 (1979)
EXu 1 (1978)–12 (1990)
Gul 1 (1978)–13 (1991)
KE 1 (1992)–#
LAu 1 (1978)–12 (1990)
Lbbc 1 (1978)–2 (1979)
Lbl*
Lcml 1 (1978)–13 (1991)
LEbc 1 (1978)–13 (1991)
Lgo 1 (1978)–13 (1991)
Lkc 1 (1978)–13 (1991) [w 6 (1983)];
1 (1992)–#
LRHBNC 1 (1978)–13 (1991)
Lu 1 (1978)–12 (1990)
Mpl 1 (1978)–13 (1991)
NWu 1 (1978)–2 (1979); 4 (1981)–10 (1987)
Ob*
Ouf 1 (1978)–13 (1991)
R 1 (1978)–12 (1990)
SFu 1 (1978)–2 (1979)

Journal of the Royal Musical Association *see*
Proceedings of the Musical Association

Journal of the Serbian Stage and Musical
Academy [translated title] *see* Zbornik Matice
Srpske za Scenske Umetnosti i Muziku

Journal of the Viola da Gamba Society of
America
TNG US742; 0607–0252
US–Memphis, TN [etc.]: The Viola da Gamba
Society of America, 1964–

Bu 30 (1993)–#
Er 7 (1970); 9 (1972)–#
Lu 1 (1964)–7 (1970); 20 (1983)–#
Mcm 16 (1979)
Ob 1 (1964)–#

Journal of the Violin Society of America
0148–6845
US–Flushing, NY: Queen's College Press for
the Violin Society of America, ?1982–
[NOT IN BUCOMP1]

Lgu 11 (1992), 3–#

Journal of the Welsh Folk-Song Society
[translated title] *see* Cylchgrawn Cymdeithas
Alawon Gwerin Cymru

The Journal of Trinity College
TNG GB98
GB–London: Trinity College of Music, 1880–82
[From 1880, 4, entitled *Education*; from 1881
entitled *Musical Education: a Monthly Review*;
continued as *The Academic Gazette of Trinity
College* (q.v.)]

 Lbl*
 Ob*

Jubilus Review: Church Music Quarterly
GB–Lurgan: Jubilus Trust, 1984–
[NOT IN BUCOMP1]

 EIR:MEtc 1 (1984)–4 (1987)

**Jucunda Laudatio: Rassegna di Musica
Antica**
TNG I262; 0022–5711
I–Venice: Fondazione Cini, 1963–79

 AB 1 (1963); 3 (1965), 1
 BSdsc*
 Cpl 1 (1963)
 LAu 3 (1965), 1
 Ob*

**Jugendmusik: Mitteilungen des Verlages B.
Schott's Söhne, Mainz, für alle die mit der
Jugend musizieren**
D–Mainz: Schott, 1952–78
[50 numbers in all; issued as a supplement to
Musik im Unterricht]

 LAu 1953, 4

The Juilliard Bulletin *see* **Juilliard News
Bulletin**

Juilliard Journal
1064–1580
US–New York: Juilliard School, 1985–
[NOT IN BUCOMP1]

 Lam [c]

Juilliard News Bulletin
TNG US721; 0022–6173
US–New York: Juilliard School of Music,
1962/63–86
[NOT IN BUCOMP1. Preceded 1954–62 by
Juilliard Review; entitled *The Juilliard Bulletin*,
1984–86]

 ALb 6 (1968), 4

Juilliard Review *see* **Juilliard News Bulletin**

Juke Blues: the Blues Magazine
1351–5551
GB–London, 1985–
[NOT IN BUCOMP1]

 EXu 1, 1985–#
 Lbl 28, 1993–#
 LOnjfa*
 Lsa 1–31, 1985–94
 PRp*

Junior Academy News
GB–London: Royal Academy of Music, Junior
Academy, 1987–
[NOT IN BUCOMP1]

 Lam 1–5, 1987–89

Just Jass [*sic*]
GB–Birmingham: J. B. Entertainments, 1962–

 Cbijs 1963, Nov
 Lbl*

Just Jazz
GB–London: P. Davies, 1957–60
[NOT IN BUCOMP1]

 LOnjfa*
 Ob 1 (1957)–2 (1958); 4 (1960)

Juzz Jazz
0960–2801
GB–Stalybridge: Ashton Weekly Newspapers,
1990–
[NOT IN BUCOMP1; entitled *Jazz World*
(ISSN 0962–1873) from 1991]

 Lbl*

K

K Novym Beregam [= Towards New Shores]
TNG USSR44
RF–Moscow, 1923

 Lbl*

Kalender für Musiker und Musikfreunde
Fellinger 1968/993; TNG D280
D–Hannover [etc.], 1885–87
[Numbers 3 and 4, 1887, entitled
Musiktaschenbuch]

 Lbl*

Kansanmusiikki [= Popular Music]
0355–9335
FIN–Kaustinen: Kansanmusiikki–Instituutti,
1975–90; n.s. 1991–
[NOT IN BUCOMP1; entitled *Uusi
Kansanmusiikki* from n.s. (1991–)]

  Lbl 1983, 3–1990, 5; n.s. 1 (1991)–#*

Karg-Elert Society Newsletter
0954–5328
GB–Twickenham: Karg–Elert Society, 1988–
[NOT IN BUCOMP1]

  En 1, 1988–#
  Lbar 1, 1988–#
  Lbl*
  Ob*

**Kemp's International Music and Recording
Industry Yearbook** *see* **Kemp's International
Music Book**

**Kemp's International Music and Recording
Yearbook** *see* **Kemp's International Music
Book**

Kemp's International Music Book
TNG GB513; 0963–8490
GB–London: Kemp's Printing and Publishing
Company, 1965–
[Later titles were *Kemp's International Music
and Recording Industry Yearbook*; *Kemp's
International Music and Recording Yearbook*;
*Kemp's Music and Record Industry Year Book
International* (ISSN 0305–7100); *Kemp's Music
and Record Industry Year Book* (ISSN 0075–
5451); current title is *Showcase International
Music Book*]

  AB*
  BRp 1987–#
  BSdsc*
  EIR:Dtc 1965–#
  Lba [c]
  Lbl*
  Lbo [c]
  LCdM 1993–#
  Lgu [c]
  Lhr [c]
  Lwwput [c]
  Mcm 1973–#
  Msuc [c]
  NTp 1966–#
  Ob*
  SFp [c]
  WW [c]

**Kemp's Music and Record Industry Year
Book [International]** *see* **Kemp's
International Music Book**

**Kenny Ball's Jazzmen Appreciation Society
Newsletter**
GB–London, ?1964–?

  Cbijs 1964; 1965, Feb–Apr

Kerrang!
0262–6624
GB–London: E-Map Metro, 1981–
[Included supplement, *Mega Metal Kerrang!*
(q.v.)]

  AB*
  Cu 1, 1981–#
  Lbl*
  NOp [c]
  Ob*
  STAp [c (1 year)]

Kerrang Kontakzt
0951–1946
GB–London: E-Map Metro, 1987–
[NOT IN BUCOMP1]

  Lbl*

Kerrang! Mega Metal
1353–2189
GB–London: E-Map Metro, 1994–
[NOT IN BUCOMP1]

  Lbl*

Kerrang! Yearbook
GB–London: Omnibus Press, 1986–
[NOT IN BUCOMP1]

  Cu 1986–#
  Lbl*

**Keskidee: a Journal of Black Musical
Traditions**
GB–Rochford: K. Summers, 1986–93
[NOT IN BUCOMP1; ceased publication with
no. 3, 1993]

  Cu 2, 3, 1990–93
  Lbl*
  Ob*

Key [translated title] *see* **Cywair**

The Key Frame
GB–Manchester [etc.]: Fair Organ Preservation
Society, 1964–

Cu 1970–#
EIR:Dtc 1970, Win–#
Lbl*
Lcml 1965–66, 2
Ob*

The Key Note
GB–Maidstone, 1893–95

Lbl*
Ob*

Key Notes: Musical Life in the Netherlands
TNG NL133; 0166–0020
NL–Amsterdam: Donemus, 1975–
[Succeeded *Sonorum Speculum: Mirror of
Musical Life* (q.v.)]

AB 1–22, 1975–85
ALb 21, 1985, 1; 23–26, 1986–92
BLu*
Bp 1–6, 1975–77; 8–25, 1978–88/89
BRu 1, 1975–#
Bs 1–26, 1975–92*
BSdsc*
CCtc 13–21, 1981–85
CFp 2–22, 1975–86
Cpl 1, 1975–#
Cu 1–25, 1975–89
EIR:Dtc 1, 1975–#
EIR:Duc 2, 1975–#
Ep 21, 22, 1985; 24, 1987; 25, 1988/89; 26,
    1992–#
Er ?3–10, 1976–79
Gam 1–11, 1975–80; 13–25, 1981–89
Gul 1, 1975–#
HUu 1, 1975–#
KE 1–4, 1975–76; 6–23, 1977–86; 25,
    1988/89
Lam 6–25, 1977–90 [w 7]; 26 (1992), 1–3
Lbar 8, 1978; 11–14, 1980–81; 16, 1982; 23–
    27, 1986–92
Lbbc 1, 1975–#
Lbl*
Lcm 1, 1975; 4–24, 1976–87; 26, 1992
Lcml 1, 1975–#
Lgo 1–26, 1975–92
Lkc 2, 1975; 3, 1976; 5–23, 1977–86; 25,
    1988; 26, 1992
Lsa 1–23, 1975–86 [w 21]
Lu 1–25, 1975–88
LVp ?1–8, 1975–78

LVu 1–25, 1975–89
Mcm 1–24, 1975–87
Mpl 1–25, 1975–89
Mu 2–26, 1972–92
NO 5, 1977–#
Ob*
Ouf 1–26, 1975–92
R 1, 1975–#*
TOd 1–26, 1975–92
Yu 1–25, 1975–88

**The Key of the Strings: the Journal of the
Society for Instrumental Music** [translated
title] *see* **Allwedd y Tannau: Cylchgrawn
Cymdeithas Cerdd Dant**

The Keyboard
TNG GB539
GB–Tunbridge Wells: Music Industry
Publications, 1969–?73

AB 1–23, 1969–73
Cu 1–23, 1969–73 [w 7]
EIR:Dtc 1–23, 1969–73
En 1–23, 1969–73 [w 7]
Lam 11 (1971)
Lcml (m) 22–24, 1973
Ob*

**The Keyboard: a Popular Monthly Journal
for All interested in the Pianoforte, American
Organ, etc.**
Fellinger 1968/1184; TNG GB148
GB–London, 1892–94
[36 nos in total]

En 1 (1892)–3 (1894)
Gm 1 (1892)–2 (1893)
Lbl 1 (1892)–3 (1894), 36
Lcm (p) 1 (1892)–2 (1893)
Lcml 1 (1892)
Ob 1 (1892)–3 (1894)

Keyboard: Keyboard Magazine *see*
Contemporary Keyboard

Keyboard Cavalcade
GB–Peterborough: Sceptre Promotions, 1987–
[NOT IN BUCOMP1; entitled *Organ and
Keyboard Cavalcade* from 1995]

Cu 1987–#
EIR:Dtc 1987–#
Gm 1988, June–#
Ob*

Keyboard Player *see* Organ Player and
Keyboard Review

Keyboard Review
0962–2675
GB–Ely: Home Keyboard Review, 1991–
[NOT IN BUCOMP1; succeeded *Home
Keyboard Review* (ISSN 0957–6371)]

   BLp [c]
   Lbl 1991, July–#

Keyboards and Music Player
0263–6212
GB–Watford: Doorteam Ltd, 1981–
[NOT IN BUCOMP1]

   Cu 2 (1983), 5–3 (1984), 9
   EIR:Dtc 2 (1983)–3 (1984), 9
   Lbl*
   Ob 2 (1983), 5–#

Keynote
GB–Birmingham, 1956–

   Cbijs 1956, 1–1957, 3
   Lbl*

Keynote: a Magazine for the Arts
TNG US875
US–New York: Radio Station WNCN, 1976–
[NOT IN BUCOMP1]

   ALb 2 (1978), Apr; 3 (1980), Feb

Keynote: the Index of Classical CD Reviews
GB–Eastbourne: Seaford Music Publications, ?–
[NOT IN BUCOMP1]

   Cu 1992–#
   Ob 1992–#

Keynote: the Music Magazine *see* Keynote:
the Progressive Music Quarterly

Keynote: the Progressive Music Quarterly
TNG GB383
GB–London, 1945–47
[From 1947 entitled *Keynote: the Music
Magazine*; in 1945 incorporated *Vox Pop:
Journal of the Workers' Association* (q.v.)]

   Lam 1 (1945), 1, 2
   Lcml 1 (1945)–2 (1947)
   Ob*

Keynotes *see* Keynotes: John Alvey Turner's
Musical Monthly

Keynotes: John Alvey Turner's Musical Monthly
Fellinger 1968/1882; TNG GB227
GB–London, 1907–14, 1925–29
[From 1925 entitled simply *Keynotes* (TNG
GB307)]

   Lbl*

Kieler Beiträge zur Musikwissenschaft
D–Wolfenbüttel; Berlin: Kallmeyer, 1934–
[NOT IN BUCOMP1]

   Cpl 4, 1936

King's Jazz Review: English Traditional Jazz
Jazzitoria
0967– 344X
GB–East Croydon: Ian King, 1989–
[NOT IN BUCOMP1]

   Lbl 4 (1992), 4–#
   LOnjfa*

Kingston Jazz Society Newsletter
GB–Kingston-upon-Thames, 1969–

   Cbijs 48–57, 1973; 60, 63–71, 1974; 72–81,
      1975; 84, 1976

Der Kirchenchor: eine monatliche Zeitschrift
dem Deutsch-Amerikanischen Kirchenchor
gewidmet
Fellinger 1968/1399; TNG US291
US–New York: Lorenz Publishing Company,
1887–1930

   Lbl 19 (1915), 2–21 (1917), 6

Die Kirchenmusik: Zeitschrift des
Allgemeinen Cäcilien-Vereins für
Deutschland, Österreich und die Schweiz
TNG D787
D–Düsseldorf: Schwann, 1938–44
[Succeeded *Musica Divina: Monatsschrift für
Kirchenmusik* (q.v.). Also absorbed *Gregorius-
Blatt: Organ für katholische Kirchenmusik*
(q.v.)]

   BSdsc*
   Lbl*

Kirchenmusikalische Nachrichten
TNG D877; 0939–4761
D–Frankfurt: Amt für Kirchenmusik der
Evangelischen Kirche in Hessen und Nassau,
1950–
[NOT IN BUCOMP1]

   BSdsc 30 (1979)–37 (1986), 3

Kirchenmusikalisches Jahrbuch
Fellinger 1968/1018; TNG D284; 0075–6199
D–Regensburg: Musikwissenschaftliche
Kommission des Allgemeinen Cäcilienvereins
für Deutschland, Österreich und die Schweiz,
1886–1907; 1908–1936/38; 1950–
[Not published between 1912 and 1929;
preceded by *Caecilien-Kalender* (q.v.), 1876–
85]

> AB 1908; 1909; 1930; 1931; 1954–66
> Cpl 1886–1911
> Cu 1950–55; 1957–#
> Ep 1886–88; 1892–1903; 1905–11
> Er 1891–1900
> LAu 1950–54
> Lbl 1886–#
> Lu 1931–32
> Ob 1886–1907; 1930–32; 1935; 1950–#

Der Kirchenmusiker: Mitteilungen der Zentralstelle für evangelische Kirchenmusik
TNG D867; 0023–1819
D–Hamburg: Merseburger, 1950–
[NOT IN BUCOMP1]

> BSdsc*

Kissinger Blätter: Tagesfragen *see* Aufsätze über musikalische Tagesfragen

Klavier-Lehrer
TNG D227
D–Berlin, 1878–1931
[NOT IN BUCOMP1; in 1911 combined with
Gesangspädagogische Blätter (TNG D457) to
form *Musikpädagogische Blätter*]

> Lcm (p) 1878–88

Köhler's Musical Star: a Miscellany of Popular Part-Songs, Glees, Solo &c in the Tonic Sol-Fa Notation
Fellinger 1968/504
GB–Edinburgh: E. Köhler and Son, 1864–1912
[Supplement to *The Musical Star: a Musical
Record and Review* (q.v.)]

> Gul (e) 1885–86
> Lbl*

Köhler's Musical Treasury *see* The Musical Treasury

Kölner Beiträge zur Musikforschung
D–Regensburg, 1938–

> BSdsc*
> Lbl*

Komponist und Musikerzieher *see* Musik-Erziehung

Kompozitory Rossiskoi Federatsiy: Sbornik Statey [= Composers of the Russian Federation: Illustrated Review]
RF–Moscow: Sovetskii Kompozitor, 1981–
[NOT IN BUCOMP1]

> Lbl*

Kontrapunkte: Schriften zur deutschen Musik der Gegenwart, herausgegeben von Heinrich Lindlar
D–Rodenkirchen am Rhein: P. J. Tonger, 1958–

> Lcml 1–3, 1958; 1960–63*

Konzert-Programm-Austausch *see* Concert-Programm-Austausch

Konzertprogramme der Gegenwart
Fellinger 1968/2024; TNG D498
D–Frankfurt-am-Main: Hugo Schlemüller,
1910/11–1920
[Ceased publication with no. 6 (1919/20)]

> Lbl*

Kool Kids
0960–846X
GB–London: Dennis Oneshots, 1990
[NOT IN BUCOMP1]

> Lbl 1, 1990

Körner's Urania *see* Urania: ein musikalisches Beiblatt zum Orgelfreunde

Kritische Briefe über die Tonkunst, mit kleinen Clavierstücken und Singoden begleitet
TNG D10
D–Berlin: F. W. Birnstiel, 1759–64
[Ceased publication with no. 3 (1764), no. 143]

> Lbl 1 (1759)–3 (1764) [2 copies]
> Ob 1 (1759)–2 (1763) [Reprint ed.]

Kultur Chronik
0934–1706; 0724–343X
D–Bonn: Inter Nationes, 1983–
[NOT IN BUCOMP1]

> Lam 3 (1985), 6; 4 (1986), 4, 6; 5 (1987), 1,
> 6; 10 (1992), 2; 11 (1993), 6; 12 (1994), 2
> Lsa*

Kulturbrief
D–Bonn: Inter Nationes, 1971–

> Lbl*
> Ob* [English ed.]

Kunst dem Volk see **Österreichische Kunst**

Kunst und Industrie see **Österreichische Kunst**

Kurt Weill Newsletter
0899–6407
GB–New York: Kurt Weill Foundation for
Music, 1983–
[NOT IN BUCOMP1]

> ALb 1 (1983)–#
> Bu 1 (1983)–#
> Cpl 2 (1984)–#
> HUu 2 (1984)–#
> Lam 4 (1986), 4; 5 (1987), 1
> Lbbc 7 (1989)–#
> Lcm 14 (1996), 2–#
> Lcml 5 (1987), 2–#
> Lgsm 1 (1983)–#
> Lmi 2 (1984)–11 (1993)
> LRHBNC 1 (1983), 2–2 (1984), 2; 4 (1986)–
> 8 (1990), 1; 9 (1991)–#
> Lu 1 (1983), Fall–#
> Mcm 2 (1984)–#
> NO 10 (1992)–#
> Ouf 1 (1983)–#
> R 1 (1983)–8 (1990); 9 (1991), 1

**Kurzes Verzeichnis sämmtlicher in
Deutschland und den angrenzenden Ländern
gedruckter Musikalien, auch musikalischer
Schriften und Abbildungen mit Anzeige der
Verleger und Preise**
Fellinger 1968/304; TNG D123
D–Leipzig: Hofmeister, 1852–59; 2. Reihe
1860–1867; 3. Reihe 1868–70
[From 3. Reihe no. 4 (also numbered 20 in main
series) (1871)–77 (1928) entitled *Verzeichnis
der im Jahre [1871 etc.] im deutschen Reich
und in den Ländern deutschen Sprachgebietes*

*sowie der für den Vertrieb im deutschen Reich
wichtigen, im Auslande erschienen Musikalien,
auch musikalischen Schriften und Abbildungen*;
from 78 (1929)–91 (1942) entitled *Hofmeisters
Jahresverzeichnis: Verzeichnis sämtlicher
Musikalien, Musikbücher, Zeitschriften,
Abbildungen und plastischen Darstellungen, die
in Deutschland und in den deutschsprachigen
Ländern erschienen sind*; from 92 (1943)–117
(1968) entitled *Jahresverzeichnis der deutschen
Musikalien und Musikschriften*. Vol. 93 (1944)
not published. From 118 (1969) entitled
*Jahresverzeichnis der Musikalien und
Musikschriften* (ISSN 0323–3693)]

> CDu 1 (1852)–6 (1857) [Facsim. ed.]
> Lbl*
> Lu 88 (1939)–#
> Ob*

Kurzinformation see **Bulletin: Musikrat der
DDR**

L

La Scala: Rivista dell'Opera
TNG I227
I–Milan: Delfino, 1949–63

> Lcml 1950 [special issue]; 35, 1952
> Lu 1950 [special issue]; 1–161, 1949–63

Lancashire Wakes
GB–Preston: English Folk Dance and Song
Society, Lancashire District, ?–
[NOT IN BUCOMP1]

> Lbl*
> Ob 23, 1983–#*

The Lark
GB–London, 1883–84

> Lbl*

Laserlog: Pop News Sheet
GB–Stamford: Laserlog, ?–
[NOT IN BUCOMP1]

> DU [c]
> Ea [c]
> Lwwb [c]
> Lwwbat [c]
> Lwwput [c]
> NOp [c]
> NTp [c]

Latin American Music Review/Revista de Música Latino Americana
TNG US884; 0163–0350
US–Austin, TX: University of Texas Press, 1980–

Cu 1 (1980)–#
En 1 (1980)–#
Lbl*
Lcml 1 (1980)–#
Lgo 1 (1980)–# [w 4 (1983), 2]
Lsa 1 (1980)–9 (1988), 1; 10 (1989)–#
Lu 1 (1980), 1
Ob*

Laudate: Quarterly Review of the Benedictines of Nashdom see Laudate: the Magazine of the Benedictine Community at Pershore Abbey, Worcestershire

Laudate: the Magazine of the Benedictine Community at Pershore Abbey, Worcestershire
TNG GB298
GB–Burnham: Nashdom Abbey, 1923–53
[From 1930, 39, entitled *Laudate: Quarterly Review of the Benedictines of Nashdom*; ceased publication with vol. 17, 1953]

BSdsc*
Lbl*
Lcml 5 (1927), 17
Ob*

The Laurel Songster
GB–London, 1855

Lbl*

The "Leading Note"
TNG GB324
GB–London: Royal Military School of Music, Kneller Hall, 1928–39
[From 1932, 8, entitled *The Military Musician*]

Lbl*

Leading Notes
GB–London: Robert Simpson Society, ?–
[NOT IN BUCOMP1]

Cu 41, 1996–#

Leading Notes: Journal of the National Early Music Association
0960–6297
GB–Cambridge: National Early Music Association, 1991–
[NOT IN BUCOMP1; preceded by the *National Early Music Association Journal* (q.v.)]

Au 1, 1991–#
Bu 3, 1992–#
CDCp 1, 1991–#
Cu 1, 1991–#
EIR:Dtc 1, 1991–#
Er 1, 1991–#
Gam 6, 1993–#
Lam 1, 1991; 3–7, 1992–94
Lbl*
Lcm 7, 1994–#
Lgu 7, 1994–#
Ltc 10, 1995–#
Lu 1, 1991–#
Mcm*
Ob*
Ouf 1, 1991–#

The League of Composers' Review
TNG US488
US–New York: AMS Press [for the League of Composers], 1924–46
[Entitled *Modern Music: a Quarterly Review* (ISSN 1060–0701) from vol. 3 (1925); ceased publication with vol. 23 no. 4 (1946)]

AB 21 (1944)–23 (1946)*
ALb 1 (1924)–22 (1945)
BSdsc*
Cu 1 (1924)–23 (1946) [Reprint ed.]
Lam 23 (1946), 3
Lbl 3 (1925)–23 (1946)
Lcm 22 (1945), 1
Lcml 1 (1924), 1; 8 (1930)*; 16 (1939)–23 (1946)*
Lu 1 (1924)–23 (1946) [Reprint ed.]
Ob 1 (1924)–23 (1946) [Reprint ed.]

Leçons de Composition Musicale
F–Paris, 1865–66
[From 1865, 3, entitled *Journal de Composition Musicale*]

Lu 1–36, 1865–66

Leeds College of Music Quarterly News
Fellinger 1968/1403; TNG GB172
GB–Leeds, 1897–1902

BDp 1 (1897)–4 (1900)
Lbl 1 (1897)–6 (1902)

Leg Auf
D–Bielefeld, 1959–67

Lsa 1 (1959)–9 (1967)

Leipziger allgemeine musikalische Zeitung
Fellinger 1968/539; TNG D170
D–Leipzig: J. Rieter–Biedermann, 1866–82
[First and second series were entitled
Allgemeine musikalische Zeitung (q.v.)]

Cu 1 (1866)–2 (1867) [Reprint ed.]
Er 1 (1866)–17 (1882)
Lbl 1 (1866)–17 (1882)
NO 1 (1866)–17 (1882) [m]
Ob 1 (1866)–17 (1882) [Reprint ed.]

Leipziger Musik- und Kunst-Zeitung *see*
Parsifal: Halbmonatsschrift

**Leitmotive: Journal of the Wagner Society of
Northern California**
US–198?–?
[NOT IN BUCOMP1]

Lu 5 (1991), 1

**Leonardo: Journal of the International
Society for the Arts, Sciences and Technology**
0024–094X
US–Cambridge, MA: MIT Press, ?1967–
[NOT IN BUCOMP1]

Lcm 27 (1994)–#
Lgu 6 (1973)–21 (1988), 1; 22 (1989)–#

**Leonardo Music Journal: Journal of the
International Society for the Arts, Sciences
and Technology**
0961–1215
GB/US–Oxford: Pergamon; Cambridge, MA:
MIT Press, 1991–
[NOT IN BUCOMP1; later entitled *LMJ*]

Bs 1 (1991)–2 (1992), 1
Cu 1 (1991)–#
EIR:Dtc 1 (1991)–#
EIR:Duc 1 (1991)–#
En 1 (1991)–#
Lbl 1 (1991)–#
Lgu 2 (1992), 1; 3 (1993)–#
MK 1 (1991)–#
Ob*
TOd 1 (1991)–#

Leos Janácek Society Newsletter
CZ–Brno: Czech Music Society, 1985–
[NOT IN BUCOMP1]

Lam 1 (1985)

Less than Zero
GB–Cambridge: E. Witt, ?1985–
[NOT IN BUCOMP1]

Lbl*

Let It Rock
GB–London, 1972–75

Cu 1–35, 1972–75 [w 29]
Lsa 1–35, 1972– 75*
Ob*

Let's Square Dance
0301–8881
GB–Alresford, Hants: British Association of
American Square Dance Clubs, ?1953–
[NOT IN BUCOMP1]

Lcs 28 (1981), 5; 39 (1992), 2, 3, 5–#

**Letopis' Muzikal'noy Literaturi [= Bulletin of
Musical Literature]**
TNG USSR62
RF–Moscow, 1931–
[NOT IN BUCOMP1; entitled *Notnaya Letopis'*
[*Musical Bulletin*] from 1972 no. 1]

Cu 1977–#
En n.s. 1 (1972)–12 (1989)
Ob*

Levende Musik *see* **Dansk Musik Tidsskrift**

Leyland Morris Man
GB–Preston: Leyland Morris Men, ?1967–
[NOT IN BUCOMP1]

Lcs 17 (1984)–20 (1987); 22 (1989)–26
(1993)

Libnotes: Irish Music Librarians' Newsletter
EIRE–?Dublin, 199?–
[NOT IN BUCOMP1]

EIR:Duc 2, 1994–#
Lu 2, 1994–#

**Library Association Audiovisual Group,
Scottish Branch** *see* **AVSCOT Update**

The Library Newspaper and Musical Journal
GB–London, 1806

Lbl*

Library of Congress: Music, Books on Music, and Sound Recordings Catalog
0041–7793 (1953–72); 0092–2838 (1973–89)
US–Totowa, NJ: Rowman and Littlefield [for the Library of Congress], 1953–89
[NOT IN BUCOMP1; entitled *The Music Catalog* (ISSN 1055–5536) from 1990. CD–ROM version, entitled *MUSE*, also includes *RILM Abstracts of Music Literature* (q.v.)]

Ep 1953–#
HUu 1973–# [w 1977]
MK 1968–83
Mpl [CD–ROM version]
Mu [CD–ROM version]
Ob 1953–#
Yu 1983–89; 1990–# [m]

Lidová Tvořivost [= Art and Music]
CZ–Prague, 1953–63
[Entitled *Melodie* (q.v.) from 1963]

Cbijs 1965, 3–5, 7–9; 1966, 8, 9
Lbl*

Liens
0024–2942
MC–Monte Carlo: Editions Cup, 1946–
[Numbering changed after 161; next issue numbered 233]

Lsa 90–258, 1960–68 [w 91, 147, 254]

Life and Worship *see* **Church Music [1]**

Life and Worship *see also* **Music and Liturgy: the Official Organ of the Society of St Gregory**

Life in the Jungle
GB–Corby: Walter Trout Band Fan Club, 1996–
[NOT IN BUCOMP1]

Cu 1, 1996–#

Light Music Magazine
GB–London: Light Music Society, 1957–

Lbl*
Mpl 1957–60

Lilly-Foster Bulletin
TNG US516
US–Indianapolis: J. K. Lilly, 1931–35; 1940–
[From 1931, 3, entitled *Foster Hall Bulletin*]

Cu 8–11, 1933–35
Lbl*
Lu 8–11, 1933–35
Mpl 8–11, 1933–35
Mu 8–11, 1933–35

Lime Lizard
0961–8104
GB–London: Lime Lizard, 1990–
[NOT IN BUCOMP1]

Lbl*

Limited Edition
0959–7255
GB–London: Star Magazine Group, 1989–
[NOT IN BUCOMP1]

Lbl*

Line Out
0962–9378
GB–Reading: Line Out Publishing, 1991–
[NOT IN BUCOMP1]

Lbl*

Ling Nan Yin-Yüeh [= Cantonese Music]
CHN–Beijing, ?1911–

Cu 59, 1970; 70–75, 77, 1980–#

Listen
US–New York: Recorded and Radio Phonograph Research Inc., 1950–

Lbl*
Lcml 1951*
Lsa 1950, Feb–May, July–Oct; 1952, Jan, Feb

Listen Easy
GB–London, 1972–?

Cbijs 1 (1972/73), 3, 4, 9–12; 2 (1973), 1
Ob*

Listen to Norway
0804–3086
N–Oslo: Norwegian Music Information Centre, 1993–
[NOT IN BUCOMP1. Preceded by *Norwegian Music Information Centre Bulletin* (q.v.)]

Bs 1 (1993)–#
Bu 1 (1993)–#
CDu 1 (1993)–#
Ep 1 (1993)–#
Gam 1 (1993)–#
Gsmic [c]
Gul 1 (1993)–#
Lam 2 (1994), 2
Lbar 1 (1993)–#
Lcm 2 (1994), 2, 3; 4 (1996), 1; 5 (1997), 1
Lcs 2 (1994), 2–#
Lsa 1 (1993), 1; 2 (1994)–#
Mu 1 (1993)–#
Ouf 2 (1994)–#
TOd 1 (1993)–#

Listener's Record Guide *see* American Music Lover

Listy Hudební Matice [= Papers of the Hudební Matice]
TNG CS109
CZ–Prague, 1921–38; 1946–48
[Entitled *Tempo* from vol. 7 (1927)]

LAu 7 (1927/28); 14 (1934/35)
Lcml 20 (1948), 8–10

Liszt Saeculum *see* International Liszt Centre Quarterly

Liszt Society Journal
0141–0792
GB–London: The Liszt Society, 1975–

AB 5 (1980)–#
Cu 1 (1975)–#
EIR:Dtc 1 (1975)–#
En 1 (1975); 3 (1978)–#
EXu 7 (1982)–12 (1987)
Lbar 4 (1979)–#
Lbl*
Lcm 17 (1992)–#
Lcml*
Lu 14 (1989)–#
Mcm 17 (1992)–#
Ob*

The Liszt Society Newsletter
TNG GB519
GB–London: Liszt Society, 1965–

Cu 23, 1984–#
EIR:Dtc 23, 1984–#
En 23, 1984–#
Lam 53, 1993

Lbar 14–29, 1982–86 [w 23]; 34, 1988–# [w 42]
Lbl*
Lu 1, 1965; 39, 1990
Mcm*
Ob*

Liszt Studien
D–Munich: Katzbichler, 1977–
[NOT IN BUCOMP1]

Lbbc 1 (1977)–3 (1986)
Lbl 1 (1977)–#
Ob*

Literarisches Jahrbuch: Jahres-Rundschau über die literatischen Erzeugnisse deutscher Zunge auf schöngeistigem, dramatischem und musikdramatischem Gebiet [...]
Fellinger 1968/1630; TNG D425
D–Cologne: Hoursch und Bechstedt, 1902
[Only one vol. published]

Lbl*

The Literary and Musical Review
Fellinger 1968/1979; TNG GB239
GB–London, 1909–14

AB 1, 2, 6, 7, 1909–10
Lbl*
Ob*

Literatur- und Theater-Zeitung
D–Berlin, 1778–84
[Preceded by the *Berlinisches litterarisches Wochenblatt*; succeeded by the *Ephemeriden der Litteratur und des Theaters* (Berlin, 1785–87)]

Er 1 (1778)–4 (1781)
Lbl*

Little Angry in a Very Nice Place *see* A Little Angry in a Very Nice Place

Liturgical Chant Newsletter
0887–3879
US–Newark, DE: University of Delaware, 1985–89
[NOT IN BUCOMP1]

Lam 1 (1985)
LRHBNC 1 (1985)–3 (1988)
Ob*

Liturgisches Jahrbuch
TNG D890; 0024–5100
D–Münster Westfallen: Aschendorffsche
Verlagsbuchhandlung, 1951–
[NOT IN BUCOMP1]

> **Lhey** 3 (1953)–14 (1964) [w 4 (1954)]; 22
> (1972)–#
> **Ob***

**Liturgy: the Official Organ of the Society of St
Gregory** *see* **Music and Liturgy: the Official
Organ of the Society of St Gregory**

**Liverpool Concert and Entertainment
Calendar**
TNG GB219
GB–Liverpool, 1906–51
[From 1908 entitled *The Rushworth and
Dreaper Concert and Entertainment Calendar
and Music Teachers' Directory*; from 1925,
Rushworth and Dreaper Concert Calendar]

> **Lbl***

Liverpool Music Festival
GB–Liverpool, 1827–33

> **Lbl***

**Livewire: the Newsletter of Yehudi Menuhin's
Live Music Now! Scheme**
GB–London: Live Music Now, 1993–
[NOT IN BUCOMP1]

> **Ep** 4, 1994–#
> **TOd** 2, 1993–#

**Living Blues: a Journal of the Black
American Blues Tradition**
0024–5232
US–Chicago, IL: Living Blues Publications,
1970–

> **EXu** 52, 1982–#
> **Gm** 1–11, 1970–72
> **LOnjfa***
> **Lsa** 1–3, 1970; 13, 1973; 17, 1974; 23, 24,
> 1975; 26–28, 1976; 98, 1991; 114, 1994–#

Living Music
TNG GB520
GB–London: Association of Music Instrument
Industries, 1963–73

> **Bs** 25–32, 1970–71
> **Lam** 26, 1970; 32, 1971; 35, 1972; 37, 1973
> **Re** 13–36, 1967–72

> **SOu** 8–34, 1965–72

Living Music [translated title] *see* **Ziva Hudba:
Sborník Prací Hudební Fakulty Akademie
Múzických Umění**

The Living Tradition
1351–4105
GB–Kilmarnock: Inform DATA, 1993–
[NOT IN BUCOMP1]

> **Cu** 6, 1994–#
> **Gsmic** 1, 1993–#
> **Lbbc** 3, 1994–#
> **Lbl***

Llais y Delyn [= Voice of the Harp]
GB–Merthyr Tydfil, 1972

> **AB** 1972, 1

LMJ *see* **Leonardo Music Journal: Journal of
the International Society for the Arts,
Sciences and Technology**

London Academy of Music *see* **The London
Academy of Music: Magazine**

London Academy of Music: Gazette *see* **The
London Academy of Music: Magazine**

The London Academy of Music: Magazine
Fellinger 1968/1773; TNG GB205
GB–London, 1904–35
[Entitled *London Academy of Music: Gazette*
from 1907; from 1911 entitled *London Academy
of Music* (TNG GB249)]

> **AB** 26–81, 1916–35
> **Lbl***
> **Lu** 57–82, 1927–35*
> **Ob***

**The London and Provincial Music Trades
Review**
Fellinger 1968/743; TNG GB89
GB–London: Industrial Journals, 1877–
[Entitled *The Music Trades' Review* from 1916.
See also The Pianomaker; and *The Music-
Trades Diary*]

> **AB** 495–678, 681–1133, 1916–69
> **EIR:Dtc** 774–965, 1939–54
> **Lbl***
> **LVp** 1949–51
> **Ob***

London Association of Organists Newsletter
0309–6955
GB–London: London Association of Organists,
1976–77

    Cu 1–4, 1976–77
    EIR:Dtc 1–4, 1976–77
    Lbl*
    Ob*

London College of Music Annual Register
and Calendar
Fellinger 1968/1136; TNG GB134
GB–London: London College of Music, 1890–99
[NOT IN BUCOMP1]

    Bp 1897–99
    Lbl 1890–99

London College of Music Magazine
GB–London: London College of Music, 1956–

    Cu 1985–#
    EIR:Dtc 1985–90, June
    Lam 1973, Sum; 1975, Sum, Aut; 1979, Spr;
      1980, Aut; 1981, Spr; 1982, Spr, Sum;
      1983, Spr, Sum, Aut; 1984, Spr, Sum; 1985,
      Win; n.s. 1 (1986)–2 (1988), 1; 1990, June
    Lcm 1 (1958), 3; 2 (1959), 3; 3 (1960), 2, 3; 4
      (1961), 1; 1967, Sum; 1975–76; 1978, 2, 3;
      1979–80; 1981, 1; 1983, 1–3; n.s. 1 (1986),
      1, 2
    Ob*

London College of Music Newsletter
GB–London: London College of Music, ?–
[NOT IN BUCOMP1]

    Lam 1988, Apr, Oct; 1989, Apr; 1992, Jan

The London Literary and Musical Observer: a
Journal of Entertaining, Instructive and
General Knowledge
Fellinger 1968/261; TNG GB39
GB–London, 1848

    Cu 1–41, 1848
    Lbl*
    Ob*

The London Mirror *see* The Dramatic and
Musical Circular: an Epitome of Dramatic,
Operatic, and Music Hall Requirements

London Music Diary
GB–London, 1946–?

    Lbl*

London Musical Courier *see* The Musical
Courier

The London Musical Digest *see* The Musical
Digest [2]

London Musical Events
TNG GB390
GB–London, 1946–73
[Entitled *Musical Events: Comprehensive
Musical Guide* from 1960 no. 6; ceased
publication with vol. 27 (1973)]

    ALb 18 (1963), 2
    Cpl 16 (1961), 2–17 (1962), 9
    Cu 7 (1952)–27 (1972), 1*
    En 23 (1968)–26 (1971), 3; 27 (1972), 1
    Lam 2 (1947)–28 (1973)*
    Lbl*
    Lcm (p) 17 (1962), Sep; 20 (1965), June; 24
      (1969), Oct; 26 (1971), Feb; 27 (1972),
      Feb, Apr; 28 (1973), Sep
    Lcml 1 (1946)–20 (1965); 21 (1966)–22
      (1967)*; 23 (1968)–28 (1973)
    Lsa 15 (1960), 16 (1961)*; 18 (1963)–22
      (1967)*
    LVp 4 (1949)–5 (1950); 7 (1952)–8 (1953);
      13 (1958)
    Mcm 28 (1973), 6, 9–11
    Ob*

The London Musical Gazette
GB–London, ?1829

    Lbl 1829, Nov

London Philharmonic Choir Newsletter
GB–London: London Philharmonic Choir,
1962–?
[NOT IN BUCOMP1]

    Lcm 1–6, 1962–63; 8, 1964; 10, 1965

London Philharmonic Post
TNG GB375
GB–London, 1940–55
[From 1947 entitled *Philharmonic Post*; 76 nos
in total]

    Gul 1 (1940)–6 (1952/53)
    Lam 1 (1940), 1–10, 12; 2 (1944/45), 5, 9; 3
      (1946/47), 3, 4, 7, 10, 11; 4 (1948/49), 9,
      10; 5 (1949), 1, 3; 6 (1952/53), 2–12; 7
      (1954), 1, 3, 4
    Lbl*
    Lcm 1 (1940), 1, 2
    Lcml 1 (1940)–3 (1946/47); 4 (1948/49)*; 6
      (1952/53)–7 (1954)*
    Mpl 2 (1941)–7 (1954)

London Sound and Video Archive Newsletter
GB–London: London Sound and Video Archive,
1988–
[NOT IN BUCOMP1]

   EIR:Dtc 1 (1988)–3 (1990), 1

The London Theatre, Concert and Fine Art
Guide *see* London Theatre, Entertainment
and Concert Guide

London Theatre, Entertainment and Concert
Guide
GB–London, 1900–12
[From 1901 entitled *The London Theatre,
Concert and Fine Art Guide*]

   Lbl*

London Theatre Index
GB–Twickenham: London Theatre Record,
1981–91; 1992–
[Entitled *Theatre Index* from 1992; also related
to the *London Theatre Record* (ISSN 0261–
5282)]
[NOT IN BUCOMP1]

   Lgsm ?6 (1986)–#
   Lsa 1 (1981)–4 (1984)

London Theatre Record *see* London Theatre
Index

Long Player
US–New York, ?1952–59

   Lsa 1952–59*

Look-In Pop Annual
GB–London, 1982–

   Cu 1982–#
   Ob*

Lorenz Mizler's neu eröffnete musikalische
Bibliothek, oder gründliche Nachricht nebst
unpartheyischem Urtheil von musikalischen
Schriften und Büchern
TNG D3
D–Leipzig: Lorenz Mizler, 1736–54

   Ob 1736–54 [Reprint ed.]

The Lorgnette *see* The Opera Goer, or Studies
of the Town

The Lorgnette, or Studies of the Town, by an
Opera Goer
Fellinger 1968/279; TNG US26
US–New York, 1850

   Lbl 1850 [2 copies]

Lucrări de Muzicologie [=Proceedings in
Musicology]
TNG R27
RO–Cluj: Conservatorul de Muzica G. Dima,
1965–

   Ob*

Luister: Onafhankelijk Maandblad voor
Grammofoonplatenliefhebbers [= Listening:
an Independent Monthly for Lovers of
Gramophone Records
TNG NL99
NL–Amersfoort, 1952–
[Later issues subtitled *Maandblad voor Muziek,
CD-Besprekingen en Techniek*]

   Lsa 1, 1952; 27–49, 1954–56; 51, 1956;
   55–399, 1957–85; 426, 1988; 429–437,
   1988–89

Lulu: Revista de Teorias y Tecnicas Musicales
ARG–Buenos Aires: Fundacion Musical Da
Camera, 1991–92
[NOT IN BUCOMP1; ceased publication with
vol. 1 no. 4 (1992)]

   Lbl*

The Lute *see* The Lute Society Journal

The Lute *see also* Glasgow Orpheus Choir
Monthly Record

The Lute: a Monthly Journal of Musical News
Fellinger 1968/928; TNG GB107
GB–London: Patey and Willis, 1883–99
[NOT IN BUCOMP1]

   Bu 1–4, 6, 1883–86
   Lbl 1883–99
   Mpl 1883–99*

The Lute: the Journal of the Lute Society
0952–0759
GB–Harrow [etc.]: The Lute Society, 1883–99

   AB 1 (1883),1; 2 (1884), 9; 3 (1885), 5;
   4 (1886), 4; 8 (1890), 89; 10 (1892), 116;
   15 (1897), 180

Cu 1889–92*
Lbl*
Lcm 1 (1883)–3 (1885); n.s. 3 (1892), Mar
Ob*

Lute News: the Lute Society Newsletter
GB–Harrow: The Lute Society, 1986–
[NOT IN BUCOMP1; continued from the *Lute Society Newsletter* (q.v.)]

AB 1, 2, 1986
EIR:Dtc 1, 1986–#
En*
Lbl*
Lcml 1, 1986–#
Ob*
R 1–17, 1986–90

Lute Society Booklets
GB–Richmond: The Lute Society, 1975–
[NOT IN BUCOMP1]

Cu 1 (1975)–#

The Lute Society Journal
TNG GB487; 0460–007X
GB–London: The Lute Society, 1959–
[Entitled *The Lute* (ISSN 0952–0759) from 22 (1982)]

AB 4 (1962)–#
BLu 1 (1959)–#
CCtc 13 (1971)–24 (1984)*
Cpl 1 (1959)–#
Cu 1 (1959)–#
EIR:Dtc 2 (1960)–#
En 4 (1962)–#
Er 1 (1959)–3 (1961); 6 (1964)–8 (1966);
   11 (1969)–#
Gul 32 (1992)–#
Lam 1 (1959)–10 (1968), 14 (1972)–
   16 (1974)
Lbbc 1 (1959)–#
Lbl*
Lcm 23 (1983), 2
Lcm (m) 9 (1967)–#
Lcml 1 (1959)–#
Lkc 1 (1959)–4 (1962); 6 (1964); 8 (1966)–
   9 (1967); 19 (1977)–21 (1981)
Lki 1 (1957)–3 (1961)
LRHBNC 1 (1959)–2 (1960); 11 (1969)–
   12 (1970); 14 (1972)–20 (1978)
Lu 1 (1959)–#
LVu 1 (1959)–3 (1961); 6 (1964)–8 (1966);
   11 (1969)–17 (1975)
Mpl 5 (1963)

NO 18 (1976)–19 (1977)
Ob 1 (1959)–#
Ouf 1 (1959)–#
R 23 (1983)–30 (1990)

Lute Society Newsletter
GB–London: Lute Society, 1974–80
[NOT IN BUCOMP1; superseded by *Lute News: the Lute Society Newsletter* (q.v.)]

Cpl 1974–80*
En*
Lu*

The Lute Society of America Inc.: Journal
TNG US789; 0076–1524
US–Upper Montclair, NJ; Palo Alto, CA [etc.], 1968–

BLu 1 (1968)–#
Bu 1 (1968)–#
Cu 1 (1968)–#
Lcml 9 (1976)–#
Lu 1 (1968)–#
Ob 1 (1968)–#

The Lute Society of America Inc.: Newsletter
TNG US765; 0882–0155
US–Palo Alto, CA [etc.]: The Lute Society of America, 1966–88; Lexington, VA: The Lute Society of America, 1989–
[Entitled *Lute Society of America Quarterly* from 24 (1989)]

BLu 17 (1982)–#
Bu 1 (1966)–15 (1980) [m]; 16 (1981)–#
Cpl 17 (1982)–23 (1988)
Cu 17 (1982)–24 (1989)
Lu 15 (1980), 1–#
Ob*
Ouf 16 (1981)–24 (1989)

Lute Society of America Quarterly *see* The Lute Society of America Inc.: Newsletter

Le Lutrin
TNG CH117
CH–Geneva, 1937–63
[NOT IN BUCOMP1]

Lcm 1 (1943, Dec); 2 (1944), 1, 2

Lyra: the Music Magazine *see* Steinway News

The Lyre: a Musical and Theatrical Register
Fellinger 1968/181; TNG GB25; Langley, p. 598
GB–London: Henry Mitchener, 1841
[Only 22 numbers published, between July and
Dec. 1841]

Lbl*

The Lyre, or the New York Musical Journal
Fellinger 1968/68; TNG US2
US–New York, 1824–25

Cu [m]
Lbl 1824–25 [m]
Mu 1824–25 [m]

Lyric and Song see Journal of the Catch
Society of America

M

MadAminA! A Chronicle of Musical Catalogues
0740–5812
US–Englewood, NJ: Music Associates of
America, 1980–
[NOT IN BUCOMP1]

Ouf 1 (1980)–# [w 1 (1980), 2]

The Maestro [1]
TNG GB32; Langley, p. 619-21
GB-London, 1844
[24 nos in total]

Lbl 4–23, 1844

The Maestro [2]
0541–8771
US–Dumas, TX: Arturo Toscanini Society,
1969–76

Lcm 1 (1969)–2 (1970); 4 (1972)–5 (1973)
Lsa 1 (1969)–3 (1971)

Magazin der Musik
TNG D21
D–Hamburg: Musicalische Niederlage, 1783–
86; n.s. DK–Copenhagen, 1788–89

Cu 1783–86 [Reprint ed.]
Lbl*
Lu 1783–86 [Reprint ed.]
Ob 1783–86 [Reprint ed.]

The Magazine of Music and Journal of the
Musical Reform Association
Fellinger 1968/962; TNG GB115
GB–London: Musical Reform Association,
1884–97

AB 3 (1886), Jan
EIR:Dtc 1 (1884), Christmas
En 1 (1884)–14 (1897)
Ep 1 (1884); 3 (1886)–4 (1887)
Gm 1 (1884)–14 (1897)
Lbl 1 (1884)–14 (1897)
Lcm (p) 2 (1885), 5–3 (1886), 4; 5 (1888)–
   6 (1889); 9 (1892)–11 (1894)
LVp 1 (1884)
Mcm 4 (1887), 37
Mpl 1 (1884)–4 (1887)
Ob*
SA 9 (1892)–12 (1895)

Magazine of Song Hits
GB–London, 1946–?

Lbl*

Magical Music Box
1350–8407
GB–London: Marshall Cavendish, 1993–
[NOT IN BUCOMP1]

Lbl*

Magyar Kórus [= Hungarian Choir]
TNG H69
H–Budapest, 1931–50

Lbl*
Lu (RMA) 13 (1943), 49-16 (1946), 66

Magyar Nemzeti Bibliografia see Magyar
Zenemüvek Bibliográfiája

Magyar Zene [= Hungarian Music]
TNG H88; 0025–0384
H–Budapest: Magyar Zenemuveszek
Szovetsege, 1960–

Lbl*
Ob*
Ouf 8 (1967)–15 (1974), 1

Magyar Zenemüvek Bibliográfiája
[=Hungarian Musical Bibliography]
H–Budapest: Országos Széchényi Könyvtár,
1970–
[Entitled Magyar Nemzeti Bibliografia (ISSN
0133–5782) from vol. 8 no. 3 (1977)]

BSdsc*
Lbl*
Ob*

Mahler Review see Revue Mahler: une Revue
Semestrielle d'Études Mahleriennes

Mahogany Gaspipe
0332–2084
EIRE–Baile Atha Cliath, 1980–
[NOT IN BUCOMP1]

    Lbl*

M.A.I. Monthly Bulletin
TNG EIRE10; 0332–1495
EIRE–Dublin: Music Association of Ireland,
1967–81;1981–84
[Entitled *Counterpoint* (TNG EIRE12) from
1969; succeeded by *Soundpost* (ISSN 0332–
1541) from 1981–84 (new numbering system,
nos 1–23), and by *Music Ireland* (q.v.) from
1985]

    AB 1969, 2–1981, 1
    BLu 1–23, 1981–84
    Cu 1969, Feb–81, Mar*; 1–23, 1981–84
    EIR:Driam 1–23, 1981–84
    EIR:Dtc 1969–81, Mar; 1–23, 1981–84
    EIR:Duc 1969–81
    EIR:MEtc 1–17, 1981–84
    En*
    Lgo 11, 1982; 18–23, 1984–85
    Lu 14, 1983
    Mcm 1973, 9–12; 1974 [w 8]; 1975–76, 2
    Ob*
    Uu 12–23, 1983–84*

M.A.I. News *see* Music Association of Ireland:
Music Diary

Mainstream
?US–Illinois, 1956–

    Cbijs 1956–#
    Lbl*
    LOnjfa*

**Mainzer's Musical Times and Singing
Circular: a Journal of Literature, Criticism
and Intelligence Connected with the Art, and
Advocate of Popular Musical Instruction**
Fellinger 1968/198; TNG GB27; Langley, pp.
599–603
GB–London, 1842–44
[Preceded by *The National Singing Circular*
(TNG GB26) from 1841, Aug–1842, ?June (6
nos); from 1842, Apr–July a musical supplement
appeared under the title *Musical Athenaeum*
(q.v.). Succeeded by *The Musical Times and
Singing Class Circular* (q.v.)]

    Lam 1 (1842)–2 (1843)
    Lbl*
    Lrco 1 (1842)–3 (1844)

Makedonski Folklor/Folklore Macedonien
0542–2108
MA–Skopje: Institut za Folklor, 1968–
[NOT IN BUCOMP1]

    Cpl 1–6, 1968–70
    Lbl*

Making Music [1]
TNG GB391
GB–Hitchin: Rural Schools Music Association,
1946–76
[Succeeded *Rural Music* (q.v.)]

    BSdsc*
    EIR:Dtc 92, 1976
    Lam 1, 1946; 5, 6, 1947; 9–19, 1949–52
       [w 14, 17, 18]; 24, 26, 1954; 36–52,
       1958–63; 64–92, 1967–76
    Lbbc [c]
    Lbl*
    Lcm 1–92, 1946–76
    Lcml 17, 1959*; 59–92, 1965–76
    Lcs 21–23, 1953; 27, 1955; 32, 1956;
       47, 1961; 56, 1965; 60, 1966
    LIp 60–92, 1966–76
    Lu 1–92, 1946–76
    Mcm 78, 79, 1972; 83, 85–92, 1973–76
    Mpl 44–92, 1960–76
    Mu 15–89, 1951–76*
    Ob 92, 1976
    TOd 1–92, 1946–76*

Making Music [2]
0269–2651
GB–London: A. Walker, 1986–
[NOT IN BUCOMP1; rock music magazine]

    CDCp [c (2 years)]
    Cu 1, 1986–#
    En 1, 1986–#
    Gm 1987, May–1993, Feb*
    Lbl*
    Lsa 10, 1987–#
    Ob 1, 1986–#*
    Rp [c (1 year)]

Making Music [3]
GB–Swanley, ?1985–
[NOT IN BUCOMP1]

    Lgu 118, 1996–#

Malayan Dance News
SGP–?, 1947–?

    Lbl*

The Malayan Radio Times
SGP–?, 1935–?

Lbl*

Man and Melody [translated title] *see* Mensch
en Melodie: Algemeen Maandblad
(Nederlandsch Maandblad) voor Muziek

Manamag
?GB: 1986–?
[NOT IN BUCOMP1]

Lam 2, 1986
Lmi 5–11, 1987–90

Manchester Cathedral News
GB–Manchester: Manchester Cathedral, 19?–
[NOT IN BUCOMP1]

Mpl 1966–#

The Manchester Dramatic and Musical Review
GB–Manchester, 1846/47

Lbl 1–16, 1846/47 [w 3]
Mpl 1–43, 1846/47
Mu 1–43, 1846/47

Mandolin Notebook
US–Silver Spring, MD: MIH Publications,
1977–?80
[Entitled *Guitar and Mandolin* from 1979/80, 2]

Lgu 1 (1977)–2 (1979/80), 3

The Mandoline and Guitar
Fellinger 1968/1835; TNG GB223
GB–London, 1906
[In 1907 combined with *The Music Student's
Magazine* (q.v.) to become *The Minstrel: an
Illustrated Monthly Recreation for
Instrumentalists and Singers* (q.v.)]

Lbl*

Many Worlds of Music
?GB–?, 1957–
[NOT IN BUCOMP1]

Lcml 1 (1957)–#

Marching Band News
0141–7169
GB–Beaconsfield, 1978–
[NOT IN BUCOMP1]

Lbl*

Mars Mag: Official Organ of the MARS
Sports Club
GB–London: Royal Academy of Music Sports
Society, 1929–30
[NOT IN BUCOMP1; MARS stood for
"Members Are Real Sports"]

Lam 1 (1929)–2 (1930), 16

The Massenet Journal
GB–London: The Massenet Society, 198?–
[NOT IN BUCOMP1]

AB 6, 1985
EIR:Dtc 6, 1985
Lbar 6–7, 1985–88
Lcm (p) 6–7, 1985–88
Lcml 1992–#
Ob*

Massenet Society Newsletter
GB–London: The Massenet Society, 1974–

EIR:Dtc 4 (1977)
En 4 (1977)
Lbl*
Lcml 1 (1974); 3 (1976)–#
Ob*

Matrix: Jazz Record Research Magazine
TNG GB451; 0025–5971
AUS/GB–1954–59; 1959–75
[In 1959 absorbed *The Discophile: the
Magazine for Record Information* (q.v.)]

Cbijs 1954–55; 10, 13, 14, 1957–60; 32, 33,
1961; 51, 1964; 63, 64, 1966; 72, 73, 1967;
75, 76, 80, 1968; 88, 90, 1970; 91, 94,
1971; 96, 97, 1972; 101, 1973; 1974–75
Lbl*
LOnjfa*
Lsa 23–108, 1959–75

The Matthay News
0360–8484
US–Gettysburg, PA: American Matthay
Association, ?1964–
[NOT IN BUCOMP1]

Lam 21 (1984), 2; 22 (1985), 1; 23 (1986)–24
(1986), 1; 25 (1987)–29 (1992), 2

The Maud Powell Signature
1083–5954
US–Arlington, VA: Maud Powell Foundation,
1995–
[NOT IN BUCOMP1]

Lcm 1 (1995/96), Win

Mayall's Celebrities of the London Stage
GB–London, 1867–68

   Lbl*
   Ob*

Mayday! Magazine
EIRE–Dublin: Trinity College, 1985–
[NOT IN BUCOMP1]

   Ob 1985; 1987

Mayerl School Club Magazine
?GB–Billy Mayerl Club, 1934–?
[NOT IN BUCOMP1]

   Mcm 1, 1934
   Mpl 1934–38

The Mayfair Miscellany and Ladies' Own
Repertoire of Original and Selected
Literature, with which is incorporated "The
Musical Monthly"
Fellinger 1968/524; TNG GB68
GB–London, 1865
[Previously (1864) entitled *The Musical
Monthly and Repertoire of Literature, the
Drama and the Arts* (q.v.); 3 nos only were
published]

   Lbl 1 (1865), 1–3
   Ob 1 (1865), 1

MBI: Music Business International
0961–6365
GB–London: Spotlight Publications, 1991–
[NOT IN BUCOMP1]

   Lbl 1991–#
   Lcml*
   Lsa 1 (1991)–#
   Msuc [c (3 years)]

MBS News Bulletin *see* Musical Box Society
News Bulletin

MD *see* Modern Drummer

MD *see* Muziek en Dans in Onderwijs en
Praktijk

Meddelanden fram Musikvetenskapliga
Institutionen vid Åbo Akademi [= Reports
from the Musicological Institute of the Åbo
Academy]
0781–6529
S–Åbo: Åbo Academy, ?1983–

[NOT IN BUCOMP1. All volumes have
separate ISBNs]

   Lbl*

Mededelingenblad voor Leden en Donateurs
van de Vereniging voor Nederlandse
Muziekgeschiedenis [= Information Bulletin
for Members and Supporters of the Society
for Dutch Music History]
TNG NL108
NL–Lochem: Vereniging voor Nederlandse
Muziekgeschiedenis,? 1961–68
[Ceased publication with no. 26, 1968]

   AB 1–9, 1961–63 [w 7]; 10–12, 1964; 14–26,
   1965–68

Medical Problems of Performing Artists
0885–1158
US–Philadelphia, PA: Hanley and Belfus, 1986–
[NOT IN BUCOMP1]

   CCtc 1 (1986)–#
   Cpl 1 (1986), 1
   Lu 1 (1986), 1

Mega Metal Kerrang!
0268–8468
GB–London: Spotlight Publications, 1986–
[NOT IN BUCOMP1; supplement to *Kerrang!*
(q.v.)]

   Lbl*
   Ob 1, 1986–#

The Meister: the Quarterly Journal of the
London Branch of the Wagner Society
Fellinger 1968/1074; TNG GB126L; Langley
1994, p. 124–25
GB–London: Kegan Paul, Trench, Trübner and
Company [for the Wagner Society], 1888–95
[Ceased publication with vol. 8, no. 32 (1895)]

   ALb 4 (1891), 13
   Cu 1 (1888)–8 (1895)
   EIR:Dtc 1 (1888)–8 (1895)
   En 1 (1888)–8 (1895)
   Ep 2 (1889), 5–6 (1893), 23
   Gm 1 (1888)–5 (1892)
   Lam 1 (1888)–4 (1891)
   Lbl 1 (1888)–8 (1895)
   Lcm 1 (1888)–8 (1895)
   LEbc 1 (1888)–8 (1895)
   Lu 1 (1888)–8 (1895)
   LVp 1 (1888)–8 (1895)
   Mpl 1 (1888)–8 (1895)
   Ob 1(1888)–8(1895)

Das Meisterwerk in der Musik: ein Jahrbuch
TNG D649
D–Munich: Drei Masken Verlag, 1925–26; 1930
Eng. translation GB–Cambridge: Cambridge
University Press, 1994–

    Cu 1 (1925)–2 (1926); 3 (1930)
      [+ Eng. translation]
    Eu [Eng. translation]
    Lu 1 (1925)–2 (1926); 3 (1930)
      [+ Eng. translation]
    Ob 1 (1925)–2 (1926); 3 (1930)
      [+ Eng. translation]
    Ouf [Eng. translation]

Mélanges de Musicologie Critique
F–Paris, 1900–05

    Lbl*

Melodia
RF–Moscow, ?–

    Lsa 1983–#

Melodias: Revista de Musica Liturgica
TNG E95
E–Madrid: V. Predera, 1954–?84

    BSdsc*

Melodie
TNG CS207; 0025–8997
CZ–Prague: Panorama, 1963–?82
[Preceded 1953–63 by *Lidova Tvořivost* (q.v.)]

    Ob 10 (1972)–20 (1982)

Melody *see* New Melody

Melody: a Monthly Magazine for Lovers of
Popular Music *see* The Tuneful Yankee

Melody: a Musical Magazine
GB–London: C. A. Pearson, 1896–98

    Lbl 1 (1896)–3 (1898)

Melody: for the Photoplay, Musician and
Musical Home *see* The Tuneful Yankee

The Melody Maker
TNG GB313; 0025–9012
GB–London: IPC Magazines, 1926–

    AB 1980, Apr 5–#
    BDp 1975–#
    BLp [c]

BSdsc*
CDCp [c (1 year)]
CFp [c (1 year)]
CH [c (3 months)]
CHEp [c (1 year)]
COp [c (1 month)]
DOR 1988, Jan–#
Ea [c (3 months)]
EG [c]
EIR:Dp 1988–92, Nov 7
EIR:Dtc 1978–#
En 1968–#
Ep [c (6 months)]
Er [c]
Gm 1940–#
IOW [c (3 months)]
IP [c]
KC [c]
Lba [c (6 months)]
Lbar [c]
Lbbc 1926–32, Dec 9; 1933–34; 1942;
    1944*; 1945–#
Lbl*
Lbo [c]
Lcml 1988–#
Lcml (c) [c (3 months)]
Lcml (g) [c (3 months]
Lcml (q) [c (6 months)]
LEc [c (1 year)]
Len [c (3 months)]
Lgo [c (6 months)]
Lh [c (1 year)]
Lha (f) [c (6 months)]
Lhg 1993–#
Lhr [c]
Lis [c (1 year)]
Lk [c (3 months)]
Ll [c]
Lmi [c (3 months)]
LOnjfa 1926–81
Lri [c (6 months)]
Lsa 1946–48; 1953–55; 1956–60*; 1961–62;
    1963–65*; 1967; 1968–69*; 1970; 1971–
    74*; 1975; 1976*; 1977–79; 1980*; 1981–
    83; 1984*; 1985–86; 1987*; 1988–#
Lsut [c (6 months)]
LVp [c (3 months)]
Lwf [c (6 months)]
Lwwput [c]
LXp [c (last 2 issues)]
MO [c]
Mpl 1985–#
Msuc 1988–#
NOp [c]
NTp [c (6 months)]

Ob 1928–36; 1968–#
PRp [c (3 months)]
WCp [c (3 months)]
WCp (ald) [c (3 months)]
WCp (f) [c]
WCp (p) [c (6 months)]
WCp (sl) [c]
WCp (y) [c]

Melody Maker File
GB–London, 1974

    Cu 1974
    Ob*

Melody Maker Yearbook and Desk Diary
GB–London: Longacre Press, 1968–

    Bp 1968–71; 1976; 1978–80
    En*
    Ob*

Melody World
GB–London, 1940
[Also entitled *Songwriters Review*]

    Lbl*

Melos *see* Melos: Jahrbuch für zeitgenössische Musik

Melos: Jahrbuch für zeitgenössische Musik
TNG D574; 0025–9020; 0174–7207
D–Berlin; Mainz, 1920–34; 1946–78; 1984–88; 1992–
[From 1934, Nov.–1943, Mar. entitled *Neues Musikblatt*; absorbed into *Musik im Kriege*, Nov. 1943/44–1945/46; from 1946 entitled *Melos*; from 1975 merged with *Neue Zeitschrift für Musik* (q.v.) to become *Melos/NZ: Neue Zeitschrift für Musik* (TNG D1088). From 1979 to 1983 amalgamation continued under *Neue Zeitschrift für Musik*; from 46 (1984) *Melos* continued as a separate journal]

    ALb 14 (1947), Mar, May–June, Aug–Sep, Nov
    Bs 43 (1976)
    BSdsc*
    Bu 41 (1974)–#
    CDu 42 (1975)–45 (1978); 48 (1986), 4–50 (1988)
    Cpl 1 (1920)–7 (1928), 9; 16 (1949), 9–12; 45 (1978), 3
    Cu 46 (1984)–50 (1988)
    EIR:Duc 41 (1974)–45 (1978)
    Er 25 (1958)–45 (1978)

Gul 25 (1958)–42 (1975)
Lam 21 (1954), 3, 6; 27 (1960), 9, 12; 30 (1963), 11; 31 (1964), 2; 34 (1967), 2, 5; 35 (1968), 12; 36 (1969), 1; 37 (1970), 9; 38 (1971), 1, 4
LAu 11 (1932)–35 (1968)*
Lbl 46 (1984)–#
Lcm 7 (1928), 3; 37 (1970)–38 (1971), 1, 2, 4, 9, 10
Lcml 25 (1958)–27 (1960)*; 28 (1961)–50 (1988)
LRHBNC 3 (1977)–4 (1978)
Lsa n.s. 1 (1975)–4 (1978)
Lu 8 (1929), 5/6; 9 (1930), 8/9; 17 (1950), 6; 19 (1952), 12; 20 (1953), 3, 4; 21 (1954)–41 (1974); n.s. 1 (1975)–4 (1978)
LVp 42 (1975)–45 (1978)
LVu 33 (1966)–41 (1974)
Mcm 40 (1973), 5; 41 (1974), 5, 6; 42 (1975), 1, 3–6; 43 (1976)–#
Mu 34 (1967)–45 (1978)
NO 35 (1968)–45 (1978)
NWu 36 (1969)–45 (1978)
Ob*
SA 7 (1928), 10–12
SOu 30 (1963)–45 (1978)

Melos/NZ: Neue Zeitschrift für Musik *see* Melos: Jahrbuch für zeitgenössiche Musik

Memory Lane: Dance Band, Vocal and Jazz Review
0266–8033
GB–Leigh-on-Sea: Memory Lane and Al Bowlly Circle, 1968–

    AB 67, 1985–#
    BLp 66, 1985–#
    Lbar 89, 1991; 93, 1992–#
    Lbbc 1, 1968–#
    LOnjfa*
    Lsa 7, 1975–# [w 77, 1987]
    Mpl 1983–#*

Memory Lane International
GB–Whitley Bay, 1968–?

    Cbijs 1 (1969), 2; 2 (1969/70), 1, 3, 4; 3 (1971/72), 3, 4; 4 (1972), 2–4; 5 (1972/73), 1

Memory Mail
GB–Carshalton, 1971–

    Cbijs 41–44, 1974–75
    Lsa 25–43, 1973–75

Mendelssohn-Studien
0340–8140
D–Berlin: Duncker und Humblot, 1972–

> **Er** 1 (1972)–4 (1979)
> **Lbl***
> **Lu** 1 (1972)–#
> **Ob** 1 (1972)–

Le Ménestrel
Fellinger 1968/106; TNG F18
F–Paris: Heugel, 1833–1914; 1919–40

> **Bu** 72 (1906)–80 (1914)
> **Cu** 26 (1858)–63 (1897) [Reprint ed.]
> **Gul** 68 (1902)–69 (1903)
> **Lbl** 47 (1880)–102 (1940)*
> **Lu** 50 (1884)–70 (1904)
> **Ob** 1 (1833)–6 (1839); 23 (1855); 26 (1858)–
> 102 (1940)

Mens en Melodie *see* **Mensch en Melodie: Algemeen Maandblad (Nederlandsch Maandblad) voor Muziek**

Mensch en Melodie: Algemeen Maandblad (Nederlandsch Maandblad) voor Muziek [= Man and Melody: General Monthly (Dutch Monthly) for Music]
NL–Utrecht: Uitgeverij Het Spectrum, 1946–47; 1948–
[Entitled *Mens en Melodie* (ISSN 0025–9462) from vol. 3 (1948)]

> **LAu** 5 (1950), 5–6
> **Lbl***
> **Lcm** 4 (1949), 1, 2, 4, 6–12; 9 (1954)–11
> (1956), 7 [w 10 (1955), 8; 11 (1956), 3]
> **Lcml** 1 (1946)*; 2 (1947); 3 (1948)*
> **Mcm** 34 (1979)–39 (1984), 2
> **Ob***
> **Ouf (Howes)** 22 (1967), 9–23 (1968), 5/6, 8,
> 9, 12

The Mentor Jazz Directory
0961–3196
GB–London: Mentor, 1990–
[NOT IN BUCOMP1]

> **Lbl***

Le Mercure Musical
Fellinger 1968/1781; TNG F364
F–Paris, 1905–22
[Entitled *Mercure Musical et Bulletin Français de la S.I.M.* from vol. 3 (1907); from 4 (1908)–5 (1909) entitled *Bulletin Français de la S.I.M: ancien Mercure Musical*; from 5 (1909), 11–24 (1922) entitled *Revue Musicale S.I.M.*, except for vols 6 (1910)–7 (1911), which were entitled *S.I.M. Revue Musicale Mensuelle*; combined in 1914 with *Le Courrier Musical, Artistique et Littéraire du Littoral* (q.v.) to form *La Revue Musical S.I.M., et Courrier Musical Réunis*]

> **Bu** 4 (1910)–10 (1914)
> **Cpl** 3 (1907), 5; 5 (1909), 12–10 (1914), 4*
> **Cu** 1 (1905)–10 (1914), 4 [Reprint ed.]
> **Lbl***
> **Lcm** 3 (1907), 10; 7 (1911), 4; 9 (1913)*; 10
> (1914), suppl. 1–5
> **Lu** 6 (1910), Aug–Sep
> **Mpl** 6 (1910)–10 (1914)
> **Ob***

Mercure Musical et Bulletin Français de la S.I.M. *see* **Le Mercure Musical**

Mercurio Musical
TNG AR12
ARG–Buenos Aires, 1931–?57

> **Lcml** 1957, July–Dec

Der Merker: Halbmonatsschrift für Musik, Theater und Literatur *see* **Der Merker: Österreichische Zeitschrift für Musik und Theater**

Der Merker: Österreichische Zeitschrift für Musik und Theater
Fellinger 1968/1981; TNG A162
A–Vienna: Österreichischer Verlag, 1909–22
[From 1915 subtitled *Halbmonatsschrift für Musik, Theater und Literatur*]

> **ALb** 1 (1909)–13 (1922), Jan 15*
> **Cu** 1 (1909)–13 (1922) [Reprint ed.]
> **Er** 1 (1909), 1, 5, 22; 2 (1910), 26, 30; 3
> (1911), 1, 3, 5, 12–16; 4 (1913), 1, 7; 6
> (1915), 1, 3
> **Lbl***
> **Lu** 1 (1909)*; 2 (1910); 3 (1911)–5 (1914)*;
> 6 (1915); 7 (1916)–13 (1922)*

The Message Bird: a Literary and Musical Journal
Fellinger 1968/266; TNG US21
US–New York: M. T. Brockelbank, 1849–60
[From 1851, May, entitled *The Journal of the Fine Arts*; from 1851, June, entitled *The Journal of the Fine Arts and Musical World*; from 1852, Feb, *The Musical World and Journal of the Fine Arts*; from 1852, July, *The Musical World and New York Musical Times*; from 1854, Sep, entitled *Musical World*; from 1856, *New York Musical World*; from 1858, *The Musical World*]

Lbl*

Metal Attack
GB–London, 198?–
[NOT IN BUCOMP1]

Ob 3, 1987–#

Metal CD
0967–442X
GB–London: Northern and Shell, 1992–
[NOT IN BUCOMP1]

Lbl*

Metal Hammer
GB–London, 1987–
[NOT IN BUCOMP1]

Cu 1987, Jan–Sep; 1995, Dec–#
IOW 1993, Aug–#
Ob 1, 1987–#

Metal Hammer Poster Express
0961–4915
GB–London: Rock Team, ?1989–
[NOT IN BUCOMP1]

Lbl*

Metcalf's Musical Express
GB–Wolverhampton, 1885–90

Lbl*

Methodist Church Music Society Bulletin
TNG GB549; 0047–6919
GB–Crewe, 1970–
[Later entitled *Methodist Church Music Society Notes*]

Cu 1, 1970–#
EIR:Dtc 1 (1970)–#
En 1970–84*; 1985–#
Lbl*

Lcm 1–39, 1970–87; 45–47, 1990–91; 49, 1992
Lro 1976–#
Ob*

Methodist Church Music Society Notes *see* **Methodist Church Music Society Bulletin**

Methodist Church Music Society Occasional Papers
GB–?: Methodist Church Music Society, ?–; 1978–
[NOT IN BUCOMP1]

Cu n.s.1, 1978–#

Metronome
Fellinger 1968/996; TNG US196
US–New York: Carl Fischer [etc.], 1885–1961
[Divided into *The Metronome Band Monthly* and *The Metronome Orchestral Monthly* from vols. 30 (1914), 10 to 48 (1932), 1; entitled *Metronome* from vol. 48 (1932), no. 2; entitled *Metronome: Music USA* from vol. 76 (1959), nos 1–10; entitled *Metronome* from vol. 77 (1960), no. 6–78 (1961)]

Cbijs 61 (1945), June; 69 (1953), Mar, June, Aug, Oct–Dec; 71 (1954), Jan, Mar; 74 (1957), Apr–Sep; 75 (1958), Nov; 76 (1959), Jan; 78 (1961), Apr–June, Sep–Nov
LOnjfa*
Lsa 65 (1949)–71 (1954)*; 74 (1957), Oct; 77 (1960), Aug, Dec; 78 (1961), Apr, May, July, Oct, Dec

The Metronome: Mainly about Music
TNG GB305
GB–London, 1924–25

Lbl*

Metronome: Music USA *see* **Metronome**

The Metronome Band Monthly *see* **Metronome**

The Metronome Orchestral Monthly *see* **Metronome**

Metronomische Beiträge
D–Berlin, 1870–90
[NOT IN BUCOMP1; ceased publication with no. 7, 1890]

BSdsc*

Micro Music
0956–0874
GB–Hemel Hempstead: Argus Specialist
Publications, 1989–
[NOT IN BUCOMP1]

EIR:Dtc 1989, June/July
Lbl*

Micrography: Jazz and Blues on Microgroove
NL–Deventer: Golden Age Records, 1968–89
[Ceased publication with no. 78, 1989]

Cbijs 1–3, 1968–69

Microphone
GB–London, 1968–

Cbijs 1972, 6
Lu 1972, 4–7

Microsillon et Haute Fidélité
F–Paris, 1954–?

Lsa 1–10, 1954–55

Microsolco: Rassegna di Musica Incisa
I–Rome, 1952–59
[Incorporated the *Bollettino dell'Associazione Italiana Amici del Disco*]

Lsa 2 (1953), 5, 10; 4 (1955), 5–8; 5 (1956), 8, 9; 6 (1957), 1–5; 7 (1958), 1, 3–8

Microsurco
ARG–Buenos Aires, ?–?

Lsa*

The Midland Musical Journal
GB–Leicester, 1884

Lbl*

The Midland Musician
TNG GB314
GB–Birmingham: Midland Musician, 1926–
[Entitled *British Musician* from 1926, 3; entitled the *British Musician and Musical News* from 1929, 2]

AB 1 (1926)–7 (1932)
Bp 1 (1926)–15 (1938), 12
Bu 1 (1926)–14 (1937)
Cu 1 (1926)–15 (1938)
EIR:Dtc 1 (1926)–15 (1938), 12
Gul 1 (1926)–6 (1931)
Lbar 1 (1926)–13 (1936)
Lbl*

Lcm 3 (1928), 10; 4 (1928)–15 (1938)
Lcm (p) 12 (1935)
LVp 1 (1926)–15 (1938)
Mpl 1 (1926)–15 (1938)
Ob 1 (1926), 1–7; 2 (1926), 8–15 (1938)

Midnite Express
0261–5053
GB–Hull, ?1981–
[NOT IN BUCOMP1]

Lbl*

Mike Oldfield Fan Club Newsletter
GB–Havant: Mike Oldfield Fan Club, 19??
[NOT IN BUCOMP1]

Lbl*

The Military Brass Band Gazette
GB–London, 1887

Lbl*

The Military Musician *see* **The "Leading Note"**

The Military Songster [translated title] *see* **Caniedydd Milwrol**

Miller's Fanclubs
?GB–?
[NOT IN BUCOMP1]

Lcml (r) 1986; 1988
NTp [c (10 years)]

Milo
GB–London: Imperial League of Opera, 1929–?

Er 1929, 2, 3
Lbl*
Lcm (p) 1929, 10–12
Lcml 1929, 1–3

Min Zu Mian Jian Yin Yue [= Chinese National Folk Music]
CHN–?, 1985–
[NOT IN BUCOMP1]

Lso 1985, 1; 1986, 1, 2; 1987–89

The Minim: a Musical Magazine for Everybody
Fellinger 1968/1220; TNG GB154
GB–London: The Minim, 1893–1902

Cpl 4 (1896), 37–5 (1898), 60
Lbl 1 (1893)–9 (1902), 8

Mpl 7 (1900)–9 (1902)
Ob*

Der Minnesänger: musikalische Unterhaltungsblätter
Fellinger 1968/119; TNG D74
D–Mainz: Schott, 1834–38

Ob 3 (1836)

The Minstrel
US–Boston, MA: Boston Folk Club, ?1982–
[NOT IN BUCOMP1]

Lcs 2, 1983

The Minstrel: a Monthly Journal for Poets and Musicians
GB–London, 1892–96; 1899

En 1 (1892)–4 (1895); 5 (1896), 49–58
Lbl*
Ob*

The Minstrel: an Illustrated Monthly Recreation for Instrumentalists and Singers
Fellinger 1968/1885; TNG GB229
GB–London, 1907
[Preceded by *The Mandoline and Guitar* (q.v.) and *The Music Student's Magazine* (q.v.)]

Lbl*

The Minstrel's Offering, or Musical Anthology for 1831
GB–London: Bochsa, 1831

Lbl 1831

Miscellanea Musicologica
I–Rome: Edizioni Torre d'Orfeo, 1986–
[NOT IN BUCOMP1]

BSdsc*

Miscellanea Musicologica: Adelaide Studies in Musicology
TNG AUS19; 0076–9355
AUS–Adelaide: University of Adelaide, 1966–

Au 6 (1972)–#
BRu 1 (1966); 4 (1969)–11 (1980)
BSdsc 1 (1966)–#
Cpl 1 (1966)–#
EIR:Dtc 6 (1972)–#
Ep 1 (1966)
Lbbc 1 (1966)–#
Lbl*

Lcml 1 (1966)–#
Lkc 1 (1966); 4 (1969)–12 (1983); 14 (1985)
Lu (RMA) 1 (1966)–#
Mu 1 (1966)–6 (1972)
Ob 1 (1966)–#
Ouf 1 (1966)–17 (1990)

Miscellanea Musicologica: Český Sborník Hudebně Vědeckých Praci [= Czech Miscellany of Musicological Works]
TNG CS191; 0544–4136
CZ–Prague: Karlova Universita/Charles University, 1956–

BSdsc 29 (1981)–#
Cu 1 (1956)–#
LAu 19 (1966)–20 (1967)
Lbl*
Lcm 30 (1983); 32 (1988)
Lu 18 (1965)–32 (1988)
Mu 25 (1973)–28 (1976); 30 (1983)–32 (1988)
Ob*
Ouf 19 (1966)–32 (1988) [w 24, 27, 28, 31]

Miscellany of the Philosophy Faculty of Brno University: Musicology [translated title] *see* **Sborník Praci Filosofické Fakulty Brneské University, Ser. H: Rada Hudebnevedna**

The Mississippi Rag
0742–4612
US–Minneapolis, MN: Mississippi Rag, 1973–

Cbijs 1 (1973/74), 1
KE 1 (1973/74), 8–4 (1976), 2

Missouri Journal of Research in Music Education
TNG US722; 0085–350X
US–Jefferson City, MO: Missouri State Department of Education, 1962–

BSdsc*
Re 1–5, 1962–88; 27, 1990

Mitteilungen *see* **Collegium Musicum: Blätter zur Pflege der Haus- und Kammermusik**

Mitteilungen *see also* **Mittheilungen**

Mitteilungen der Gesellschaft für Musikforschung *see* **Gesellschaft für Musikforschung: Mitteilungen**

Mitteilungen der Hans Pfitzner Gesellschaft
D–Munich: Hans Pfitzner Gesellschaft, ?–
[NOT IN BUCOMP1; n.F. 1954–]

Cu n.F. 1 (1954)–#

Mitteilungen der Internationalen Gesellschaft für Musikwissenschaft/Bulletin de la Société Internationale de Musicologie
TNG INTL5; 0001–6241
D–Leipzig: Breitkopf und Härtel [for the International Musicological Society], 1928–
[Entitled *Acta Musicologica* from 1929]

AB 35 (1963)–#
Au 1 (1928)–#
BLu 1 (1928)–7 (1935); 27 (1955); 29 (1957); 31 (1959)–#
BRu 1 (1928)–7 (1935); 25 (1953)–#
Bs 42 (1970)–43 (1971)
Bu 4 (1932)–#
CDu 1 (1928)–#
Cpl 1 (1928)–2 (1930); 3 (1931)–#*
Cu 1 (1928)–7 (1935); 20 (1948)–#
DRu 2 (1930)–25 (1953); 37 (1965)–#
EIR:Duc 49 (1977)–#
EIR:MEtc 56 (1984)–#
Er 1 (1928)–7 (1935); 25 (1953); 28 (1956)
EXu 35 (1963)–51 (1979); 54 (1982)–#
Gul 1 (1928)–7 (1935); 29 (1957)–#
HUu 1 (1928)–#
KE 48 (1976)–49 (1977), 1
Lam 23 (1951)–24 (1952); 32 (1960)–42 (1970), 2; 43 (1971), 3, 4
LAu 10 (1938), 3–11 (1939); 20 (1948)–48 (1976); 49 (1977), 2–#
Lbbc 27 (1955)–#
Lbl*
Lcm 4 (1932)–5 (1933); 27 (1955)–#
Lcml 1 (1928)–#
LEbc 22 (1950), 3, 4; 24 (1952)–#
Lgo 44 (1972)–#
Lkc 2 (1930)–#
LRHBNC 35 (1963)–46 (1974); 49 (1977)–#
Lro 47 (1975)–#
Lu 1 (1928)–#
LVp 9 (1937); 11 (1939)–12 (1940); 16 (1944)–17 (1945); 25 (1953)–31 (1959)
LVu 2 (1930)–#
Mcm 46 (1974)–65 (1993)
Mpl 1 (1928)–25 (1953); [+ 2nd copy 2 (1929)–62 (1990)]
Mu 40 (1968)–#
NO 1 (1928)–7 (1935); 25 (1953); 28 (1956)–#

NWu 1 (1928)–14 (1942) [m]; 1 (1928)–7 (1935); 30 (1958)–#
Ob 1 (1928), 1, 3–#
Ouf 1 (1928)–#
R 30 (1958)–62 (1990)
SA 1 (1928)–59 (1987)
SFu 1 (1928)–7 (1935); 27 (1955)–#
SOu 27 (1955)–#
Uu 55 (1983)–57 (1985); 61 (1989)–#

Mitteilungen der Internationalen Stiftung Mozarteum Salzburg
TNG A262; 0541–2331
A–Salzburg: Stiftung Mozarteum, 1952–56; 1962–
[Nos 6 (1957)–10 (1961) not published]

Lbl*
Mcm 31 (1983)–#

Mitteilungen der Karg Elert Gesellschaft
0179–9894
D–Heidelberg: Karg Elert Gesellschaft, 1986–
[NOT IN BUCOMP1]

Lbl*

Mitteilungen der Paul Sacher Stiftung
1015–0536
CH–Basel: Paul Sacher Stiftung, 1988–
[NOT IN BUCOMP1]

ALb 1 (1988)–# [w 4 (1991)]
Cu 1 (1988)–#
Lbbc 3 (1990)–#
Lbl*
Lu 1 (1988)–#
Mcm 3 (1990)–4 (1991); 6 (1993)–#
Ob*
Ouf 1 (1988)–#

Mitteilungen der Schweiz[erischen] Musikforschenden Gesellschaft/Bulletin de la Société Suisse de Musicologie
TNG CH110
CH–Zurich, 1934–36; n.s. 1937–80
[N.s., 1937–80 entitled *Mitteilungsblatt der Schweizerischen Musikforschenden Gesellschaft*]

LAu 39 (1966)–41 (1968)
Lbl*
Lkc 41 (1968)–53 (1980)
Lu 35 (1964)–39 (1966); 41 (1968)–45 (1972)
Lu (RMA) 34 (1963); 36 (1965)–37 (1965); 41 (1968)–45 (1972)

Mitteilungen des Deutschen
Musikalienwirtschafts-Verbandes *see*
Musikhandel

Mitteilungen des Internationales Franz
Schubert Institut *see* Schubert durch die
Brille

Mitteilungsblatt der Gesellschaft für
Bayerische Musikgeschichte
TNG D1045
D–Munich: Gesellschaft für Bayerische
Musikgeschichte, 1964–
[Entitled *Musik in Bayern* from no. 10, 1975]

> **BSdsc***
> **Cu** 5, 1972–#
> **Ob** 26, 29, 1983–#

Mitteilungsblatt der Internationalen
Gesellschaft zur Erforschung und Forderung
der Blasmusik
A–Graz: Internationale Gesellschaft zur
Erforschung und Forderung der Blasmusik,
197?–
[NOT IN BUCOMP1]

> **Lbl** 4, 1978–#*

Mitteilungsblatt der Schweizerischen
Musikforschenden Gesellschaft *see*
Mitteilungen der Schweiz[erischen]
Musikforschenden Gesellschaft

Mitteilungsblatt des Österreichischer
Komponistenbund
TNG A292
A–Vienna, 1968–
[NOT IN BUCOMP1]

> **Lam** 1 (1968), 1

Mittheilungen *see also* Mitteilungen

Mittheilungen der Musikalienhandlung
Breitkopf und Härtel in Leipzig
Fellinger 1968/719
D–Leipzig [etc.], 1876–1940
[197 numbers in total]

> **Lbl** 1–193, 1876–1939 [2 copies]
> **Lcm** 137, 138 (1926); 140–148 (1927–29);
> 192, 193 (1939)
> **Ob***

Mittheilungen der Wiener Akademischen
Mozartgemeinde *see* Wiener Akademische
Mozartgemeinde: Mitteilungen

Mittheilungen des Allgemeinen Deutschen
Musikvereins
Fellinger 1968/1139; TNG D311
D–Leipzig, ?1890–1931
[Entitled *Mitteilungen des Allgemeinen
Deutschen Musikvereins* from 1903, no. 40]

> **Lbl***

Mittheilungen für die Mozart-Gemeinde in
Berlin
Fellinger 1968/1308; TNG D350
D–Berlin: Mozartgemeinde, 1895–1925
[Ceased with vol. 4 (1912/25), no. 43]

> **Cpl** 3 (1911), 10
> **Lbl***

The Mix
1354–4284
GB–Bath: Future Publishing, 1994–
[NOT IN BUCOMP1. Combination of *Music
Technology: formerly E and MM* (q.v.) and
Home and Studio Recording (q.v.)]

> **BAc** 1, 1994–#
> **BLp** [c]
> **Cat** 1, 1994–#
> **Cu** 3, 1997–#
> **EIR:Dtc** 1, 1994–#
> **Lbx** 1, 1994–#
> **Lgo** 1, 1994–#
> **Lgsm** 1, 1994–#
> **Lgu** 1, 1994–#
> **Lki** 1, 1994–#
> **Lro** 1, 1994–#
> **Ltc** 1995–#
> **Ltv** 1, 1994–#
> **Mmu (a)** 1, 1994–#
> **Mmu (d)** 1, 1994–#
> **Mpl** [c]
> **Msuc** 1, 1994–#
> **NTp** [c (5 years)]
> **Ob***
> **Oub** 1, 1994–#
> **SFp** 1, 1994–#
> **WOp** [c]

Mixture
GB–?–?
[NOT IN BUCOMP1]

> **NTp** 1985–87

De Mixtuur: Tijdschrift over het Orgel
[= Organ Journal]
NL–Schagen: De Mixtuur, 1970–
[NOT IN BUCOMP1]

Lam (o) 74–76, 1993

M.L.A. Newsletter *see* Music Library
Association Newsletter

The M.M. Club Magazine
TNG GB354
GB–London: Mainly Music Club, 1935–36
[From 1935, 3 entitled *The M.M. Magazine*]

Lbl*
Lcml 1 (1935), 3

The M.M. Magazine *see* The M.M. Club
Magazine

The Mod *see* Pop Shop

MOD: Music, Opera, Dance and Drama in
Asia, the Pacific and North America
GB–London, ?1996–
[NOT IN BUCOMP1]

Cu 1996–#

Modern Drummer
0194–4533
US–Clifton, NJ: Modern Drummer Publications,
1977–
[NOT IN BUCOMP1; also known as *MD*. See
also *Modern Percussionist*]

En 1977–#*
Mcm*
Msuc 1996–#

Modern Jazz [1]
GB–Wembley, 1955–?

Cbijs 1955, Jan

Modern Jazz [2]
I–Rome, 1962–?

Cbijs 1963, Apr, July; 1964, Jan; 1966, Mar–
July

Modern Music: a Quarterly Review *see* The
League of Composers' Review

The Modern Musician [1]
GB–Salford, 1935

Lbl*

Modern Musician [2]
GB–London, 1966–?

Ob*

Modern Percussionist
8750–7838
US–Cedar Grove, NJ: Modern Drummer
Publications, 1985–87
[NOT IN BUCOMP1; absorbed by *Modern
Drummer* (q.v.)]

En 3 (1987), 3, 4
Lcm 2 (1986), 2–3 (1987)#
Mcm 1 (1984/85)–3 (1987)

Modus
0871–5475
P–Lisbon: Instituto Gregoriano de Lisboa,
1987–
[NOT IN BUCOMP1]

Cu 1 (1987)–#
Ouf 1 (1987)–3 (1989/92)

Mojo
1351–0193
GB–London: Mojo, 1993–
[NOT IN BUCOMP1]

Cu 1, 1993–#
Lbbc 1, 1993–#
Lbl*
Lsa 1,1993; 9, 1994–#

Monatshefte für Musik-Geschichte
Fellinger 1968/609; TNG D188
D–Berlin: Trautwein, 1869–1905

AB 21 (1889)–28 (1896)
Cpl 1 (1869)–37 (1905) [Reprint ed.]
Cu 1 (1869)–37 (1905)
Er 1 (1869)–37 (1905)
HUu 1 (1869)–37 (1905) [Reprint ed.]
Lbl 1 (1869)–37 (1906) [+ Beilage zu den
    Monatsheften 1–24, 1870–1906]
Lu 1 (1869)–37 (1905) [Reprint ed.]
Mpl 1 (1869)–37 (1905)
Ob 1 (1869)–37 (1905) [Reprint ed.]

Monatsschrift für Gottesdienst und kirchliche
Kunst
Fellinger 1968/1355; TNG D358
D–Göttingen: Vandenhoeck und Ruprecht,
1896–1941

Au 29 (1924)–35 (1930)
Lbl*

Monatsschrift für Gottesdienst und kirchliche
Kunst: Beihefte
?D–Göttingen: Vandenhoeck und Ruprecht,
1926–?
[NOT IN BUCOMP1]

    Au 1–7, 1926–30 [w 4]

Monatsschrift für Theater und Musik *see*
Recensionen und allgemeine Bemerkungen
über Theater und Musik

Le Monde de la Musique *see* The World of Music

Le Monde Musicale: Organe de la Facture
Instrumentale et de l'Édition Musicale
Fellinger 1968/1106; TNG F224
F–Paris, 1889–1940
[NOT IN BUCOMP1]

    Mpl 34 (1923)

Il Mondo della Musica
TNG I261
I–Rome, 1963–

    Mcm 20 (1982); 21 (1983), 5, 7, 8

Monographien moderner Musiker: kleine
Essays über Leben und Schaffen
zeitgenössischen Tonsetzer
D–Leipzig, 1906–09

    Lbl*

Monsalvat: Revista Wagneriana y de
Informacion Musical
0210–4083
E–Barcelona, 1973–
[NOT IN BUCOMP1]

    Lam 1973, Sep
    Lsa 29, 1976; 45, 1977; 47–68, 1978–80 [w
    59, 64, 67]

Monster Metal
0964–1440
GB–London: Dennis Oneshots, 1991–
[NOT IN BUCOMP1]

    Lbl*

The Monthly Guide to Recorded Music
GB–London: Sir Thomas Beecham Trust, 1981–
[Cumulated as *The Annual Guide to Recorded
Music* (q.v.)]

CHEp [c (1 year)]
Cu 1(1981)–6 (1985)
Ep 1 (1981)–6 (1985), 6
EXu 5 (1984)–6 (1985), 6
Lcml (m) 1 (1981)–6 (1985), 6
Lsa 5 (1984)–6 (1985)
Mcm 1 (1981)–#
Ob*

Monthly Journal of the Incorporated Society
of Musicians *see* Monthly Journal of the
National Society of Professional Musicians

Monthly Journal of the International Musical
Society *see* Zeitschrift der Internationalen
Musikgesellschaft

Monthly Journal of the National Society of
Professional Musicians
Fellinger 1968/1075; TNG GB125
GB–London: The National Society of
Professional Musicians, 1888–1929
[From 1893 entitled *Monthly Journal of the
Incorporated Society of Musicians*; from 1902,
*Journal of the Incorporated Society of
Musicians*; from 1908/09 entitled *Periodical
Report of the Incorporated Society of
Musicians*; from 1909–29, *Incorporated Society
of Musicians: Monthly Report*. Combined in
1929/30 with *The British Music Society Bulletin*
(q.v.) to form *A Music Journal: Comprising the
Report of the Incorporated Society of Musicians,
and the Bulletin of the British Music Society*
(q.v.)]

    AB 1925–29
    Bu 1 (1888)–18 (1906), 6
    En 1 (1888), 6; 5 (1893), 2; 6 (1894)–13
    (1901); 14 (1902)–19 (1907)
    Lbl*
    Ob*

The Monthly Magazine of Music
Fellinger 1968/62; TNG GB11; Langley, p. 515
GB–London: G. and W. B. Whittaker, 1823
[Only one number published]

    Lbl
    Ob

Monthly Military Companion
EIRE–Dublin: Printed by John Jones, 1801–02
[NOT IN BUCOMP1]

    Cpl 1–6, 1801–02

Monthly Music Broadsheet
TNG GB429
GB–London: HMSO [for the British Council],
1950–66
[Entitled *Music in Britain* from 1955]

ALb 64–73, 1964–66
En 28–73, 1954–66 [w 53]
Er 61–64, 67, 69, 1963–65
Lam 66–73, 1964–66 [w 68, 71]
LAu 66–68, 1964–65
Lbl*
Lcm 54, 1961; 62, 1963; 65–73, 1964–66
Lcm (p) 1955, June
Lu 67–73, 1964–66 [w 71]
Ob*

The Monthly Musical and Literary Magazine
Fellinger 1968/3; TNG GB15; Langley, p. 546
GB–London: James Fraser, 1830
[Only five numbers were published]

Cu 1 (1830), 1–5
Lbl*
Ob 1 (1830), 1–5

The Monthly Musical Record
Fellinger 1968/635; TNG GB75; Langley 1994,
p. 122–23
GB–London: Augener, 1871–1960

AB*
ALb 64 (1934), June; 68 (1938), Oct; 77
(1947), Mar/Apr–78 (1948), Jan, Mar/Apr;
89 (1959), May/June; 90 (1960), Jan/Feb
Au 89 (1959)–90 (1960)
BDp 1 (1871)–40 (1910)
BLu 17 (1940)–90 (1960)*
Bp 42 (1912)*; 52 (1922)*; 56 (1926)–62
(1932)*; 63 (1936 956)
Bu 1 (1871)–40 (1910); 60 (1930); 66
(1943)–84 (1954)
Cpl 34 (1904)–37 (1907); 61 (1931)–87
(1957)*
Cu 1 (1871)–14 (1884); 18 (1888)–90 (1960)
DRu 76 (1946)–90 (1960)
EIR:Dtc 1 (1871)–39 (1909); 55 (1925)–70
(1940); 72 (1942)–90 (1960)
EIR:MEtc 32 (1902)–36 (1906)*
En 1 (1871)–90 (1960)
Ep 1 (1871)–34 (1904); 38 (1908)–40 (1910);
58 (1928)–60 (1930); 65 (1935)–90 (1960)
Er 1 (1871)–56 (1926), Jan, Feb, Apr–Dec;
57 (1927)–59 (1929)11; 60 (1930)–90
(1960)*
EXu 73 (1943), 843–87 (1957), 983

Gm 61 (1931), May–90 (1960), Dec
Gul 1 (1871)–4 (1874)
Gul (e) 1 (1871)–4 (1874)*
HUu 1 (1871)–90 (1960)
Lam 4 (1874); 50 (1920), 598; 69 (1939),
811; 70 (1940), 815, 817–74 (1944), 857;
75 (1945), 867, 868; 76 (1946), 874, 875,
877, 878, 881–77 (1947), 883; 77 (1947),
885, 886, 889–78 (1948), 897, 899, 900,
902; 79 (1949), 904–912; 80 (1950), 914–
922; 81 (1951), 923, 925– 928, 930–89
(1959), 991; 89 (1959), 993–90 (1960)
LAu 77 (1947), 889; 78 (1948), 895, 896; 79
(1949), 908, 910–84 (1954)
Lbl*
Lcm 1 (1871)–29 (1899); 41 (1911), Nov; 43
(1913)–44 (1914); 56 (1926), Jan, Feb; 57
(1927), Apr, June, Aug; 58 (1928), Oct,
Dec; 59 (1929)–62 (1932); 63 (1933), Feb;
64 (1934), July, Aug; 65 (1935), Sep; 67
(1937), Jan, Oct; 68 (1938)–90 (1960)
Lcml 1 (1871)–21 (1891); 23 (1893)–25
(1895); 27 (1897)– 46 (1916); 54 (1924);
56 (1926); 57 (1927)*; 58 (1928)–90
LEu 1 (1871)–41 (1911) [w 11 (1881); 37
(1907)]; 51 (1921)–53 (1923); 90 (1960),
997
Lgsm 51 (1921); 63 (1943)–90 (1960)
Lrco 13 (1883)–16 (1886); 50 (1920), May;
89 (1959), Apr, May; 90 (1960) [w Mar,
Apr, July–Oct]
Ltc 84 (1954), June–85 (1955) [w Feb, June];
86 (1956), Mar, Apr, Sep–Dec; 87 (1957),
Mar–June, Nov, Dec
Lu 1 (1871)–90 (1960)
LVp 1 (1871)–15 (1885); 18 (1888)–22
(1892); 24 (1894)–28 (1898); 30 (1900); 33
(1903)–35 (1905); 85 (1955)–86 (1956)
LVu 65 (1935)–66 (1936)*; 69 (1939)–70
(1940)*; 73 (1943)–74 (1944)*; 76 (1946)–
90 (1960)
Mcm 81 (1951), 926
Mpl 1 (1871)–90 (1960)
NO 52 (1922)–63 (1933); 68 (1938)–69
(1939); 77 (1947)–84 (1954); 86 (1956)–90
(1960)
Ob 1 (1871)–90 (1960)
Ouf 1 (1871)–90 (1960)
R 75 (1945)–90 (1960)
SA 55 (1925), 652
SFu 64 (1934)–87 (1957)*
WOp 34 (1904)–48 (1918)
Yu 74 (1944)–90 (1961)

The Monthly Theatrical Reporter, or Literary Mirror
GB–London: J. Roach, 1814–15

  Lbl*
  Ob*

Moonlight Serenader
GB–New Malden [etc.]: Glenn Miller Society, 1953–

  Cbijs 6 (1958), 6; 7 (1959), 1–3; 11 (1965), 5, 6; 12 (1966), 82; 13 (1967), 89, 90; 15 (1969), 100, 104; 16 (1970)–23 (1977), 105–148
  LOnjfa*

The Moravian Music Foundation Bulletin *see* News Bulletin of the Moravian Music Foundation

Morley College Magazine
GB–London, 1892–

  Lbl*

Morris Dancer
GB–South Croydon: Morris Ring, 1978–
[NOT IN BUCOMP1]

  Lcs 1 (1978)–#

Morris Federation Newsletter
GB–Walthamstow: Morris Federation, ?–
[NOT IN BUCOMP1]

  Lcs 1983, Aut–#*

Morris Matters
GB–Bromley: Morris Matters, 1978–
[NOT IN BUCOMP1]

  Lcs 1 (1978)–#*

Morris Newsletter
GB–Cheadle Hulme: English Folk Dance and Song Society (Manchester District), 1981–
[NOT IN BUCOMP1]

  Lcs 1 (1981), 2

Mosaic: a Quarterly Review of Church Music, Liturgy and the Arts
0545–0705
GB–London: Epworth Press, 1965–67
[NOT IN BUCOMP1]

  AB 1965, Apr–1967, Jan
  Mpl 1965–67

Motorhead Magazine
GB–Poole: Motorhead Appreciation Society, 1980–

  Cu 1–6, 1980–82
  Lbl*

Mousikologia
GR–Athens: Ekdoseis Odysseas, 1985–
[NOT IN BUCOMP1]

  ALb 1 (1985), 2
  Lam 1 (1985), 1, 2

Mousikotropies: Trimeniaia Periodike Ekdose tou Syllogou Phoiteton tou Tmematos Mousikon Spoudon tou Aristoteleiou Panepistemiou Thessalonikes
GR–Thessalonika, 1989–
[NOT IN BUCOMP1]

  Lbl 1989–

Mozart-Jahrbuch
TNG D607 (Munich); TNG D796 (Regensburg); 0077–1805
D–Munich, 1923–29; Regensburg, 1941–43; Salzburg: Drei Masken Verlag, 1950–
[From 1941 entitled *Neues Mozart-Jahrbuch*; from 1950 entitled *Mozart-Jahrbuch des Zentralinstituts für Mozartforschung der Internationalen Stiftung Mozarteum*]

  Bs 1964–66; 1968–75
  CDu 1950–#
  Cpl 1962–63; 1965–66
  Cu 1941–43; 1950–#
  En 1950–#
  Er 1923–29; 1941–43; 1950–1963; 1980–83
  Gul 1950–#
  HUu 1950–1984/85
  LAu 1962–65
  Lbbc 1923–29; 1941–43; 1950–#
  Lbl*
  Lcm 1943; 1950–64
  Lcm (p) 1950–64
  Lkc 1950–#
  Lu 1923–29; 1950–#
  Mcm*
  Mpl 1954–#
  Mu 1980–#
  Ob 1923–29; 1941–43; 1950–#
  Ouf 1923–29; 1950–#
  R 1950–1987/88
  SFu 1962–63; 1973–#

Mozart-Jahrbuch des Zentralinstituts für Mozartforschung der Internationalen Stiftung Mozarteum *see* Mozart-Jahrbuch

Mozarteum Argentino: Anuario
ARG–Buenos Aires: Mozarteum Argentino, 1965; 1968–

   Lu 1965; 1968; 1970

Mozarteums-Mitteilungen
TNG A180
A–Salzburg, 1918–21

   Lbl*

Mozartgemeinde Wien *see* Musik-Erziehung

M.P.A. *see* Music Publishers' Association Catalogue

M.P.M.: Musical Progress and Mail *see* The Musical Mail and Advertiser

M.P.M.: Musical Progress and Mail *see also* Musical Progress

MRIN Register *see* Music Research Information Network: Register [...]

MT: the Music Technology Magazine *see* Music Technology: formerly E and MM

MTI Buyers Guide, Directory and Year Book *see* The Music Trade Directory and Guide

Mudato
NL–Amsterdam; The Hague: Vereeniging tot Bestudeering van de Muziek, de Dans- en Tooneelkunst van Ost- en West-Indie, 1919–22

   Cu 1 (1919)–4 (1922)

Multimedia Information and Technology *see* Audiovisual Librarian

Mundo Musical
TNG AR17
ARG–Buenos Aires, 1938–52

   Lcm 1951, Mar
   Lcml 133–162, 1949–52*

Musashino Ongaku Daigaku Kenkyu Kiyo *see* Bulletin of Musashino Academia Musicae

Musbib: a Music Bibliography
0960–5908
GB–London: Music Press, 1991–?
[NOT IN BUCOMP1]

   Au 1 (1991)–#
   Lbl 2 (1992)–#
   Lgsm 1 (1991)–#

MusDoc: Quarterly Music Documentation Newsletter
0964–5373
GB–London: Music Press, 1992–?
[NOT IN BUCOMP1]

   Au 1, 1992–#
   EXu 1 (1992)–#
   Lbl 1 (1992)–#

MUSE [CD–ROM version of RILM Abstracts of Music Literature, and of the Library of Congress Music Catalog] *see* RILM Abstracts of Music Literature; and Library of Congress: Music, Books on Music, and Sound Recordings Catalog

Music [1]
TNG GB400
GB–London: Decca Record Company, 1947–48

   ALb 1 (1947/48), 3
   Lam 1 (1947/48), 3, 4
   Lbl*
   Lcm 1 (1947/48), 1–4; 2 (1948), 1
   Mpl 1 (1947/48)
   Ob*

Music [2]
GB–London: London Music Club, 1951–52

   Lam 1–3, 1951
   Lcml 3–4, 1951–52

Music [3]
TNG GB437
GB–London: Miles Henslow Publications, 1951–54
[Succeeded by *Music Mirror* [1] (q.v.)]

   Cpl 1 (1951)–3 (1954), 1
   Cu 1 (1951)–3 (1954), 4
   EIR:Dtc 1 (1951)–3 (1954), 1
   En 1 (1951)–3 (1954), 4
   Gm 1 (1951), 8–3 (1954), 1
   Lam 1 (1951)–2 (1953), 10; 3 (1954), 1–3
   Lbl*
   Mpl 1 (1951)–3 (1954)
   Ob*

Music [4]
GB–?Brighton: University of Sussex Music
Federation, 1972–74; n.s. 1979–?
[NOT IN BUCOMP1]

> **BTu** 1–20, 1972–74; n.s. 1 (1979)–3 (1980)

Music *see also* **The Penguin Music Magazine**

Music [translated title] *see* **Sangita**

**Music: a Monthly Journal Devoted to the Art
and Trade, with which is incorporated
Musical Notes**
Fellinger 1968/1310; TNG GB166
GB–London, 1895–1930
[From 1926 entitled *Music, Art and Trade
Journal and Talking Machine Review*; from
1930 incorporated into *The Music Dealer* (q.v.).
Succeeded *Musical Notes* (q.v.)]

> **AB** 7 (1902)–35 (1930)*
> **Lbl***
> **Ob** 23 (1918), 2–35 (1930), 4

**Music: a Monthly Magazine Devoted to the
Art, Science, Technic and Literature of Music**
Fellinger 1968/1166; TNG US236
US–Chicago: W. Mathews, 1891–1902
[NOT IN BUCOMP1]

> **AB** 2 (1892), 1

**Music: a Weekly Newspaper for Musicians
and Amateurs**
Fellinger 1968/820; TNG GB97
GB–London, 1880
[19 nos in total]

> **Lbl***

Music: Boosey and Hawkes
GB–London: Boosey and Hawkes, 1976–82
[Formerly: *Boosey and Hawkes News-Letter*
(q.v.); succeeded by *Quarternotes* [2] (q.v.)]

> **Lbl** 1–14, 1976–82

**Music: Journal of the Schools' Music
Association** *see* **Music: the Official Journal of
the Schools' Music Association**

**Music: Quarterly Devoted to the History and
Theory of Music and to Scientific and Artistic
Criticism** [translated title] *see* **Muzyka:
Kwartalnik Poswieçony Historii i Teorii
Muzyki Oraz Krytyce Naukoweji
Artystycznej**

Music: the A.G.O. Magazine
TNG US776; 0580–2741
US–New York: American Guild of
Organists/Royal Canadian College of Organists,
1967–
[Succeeded *The American Guild of Organists
Quarterly* (q.v.); entitled *Music: the A.G.O. and
R.C.C.O. Magazine* (ISSN 0027– 4208) from
vol. 2 (1968), 10–12 (1978), 12; entitled
*American Organist: the Official Journal of the
American Guild of Organists and the Royal
Canadian College of Organists* from 13 (1979)]

> **ALb** 11 (1977), 11 ; 24 (1990), 1
> **Cpl** 2 (1968), 12–7 (1973), 10*
> **EIR:Duc** 9 (1975)–12 (1978)
> **Gm** 12 (1978)–15 (1981)
> **Lam** 27 (1993), 11, 12; 28 (1994), 1, 2, 4, 7–#
> **Lam (o)** 3 (1969), 12–8 1974), 6, 8–12; 9
> (1975)–10 (1976), 3, 5– 12; 11 (1977)–12
> (1978), 9, 11; 13 (1979)–14 (1980); 18
> (1984), 4, 5; 20 (1986), 12; 21 (1987), 1, 2,
> 5, 6; 22 (1988), 1, 2; 24 (1990)–28 (1994),
> 11
> **Lcml** 25 (1991), 2–#
> **Lrco** 1 (1967)–#
> **Mcm** 15 (1 981), 1–9, 11, 12; 16 (1982), 1–8,
> 10–12; 17 (1983), 11; 18 (1984), 1–3
> **Ob** 19 (1985), 3, 9–#

Music: the A.G.O. and R.C.C.O. Magazine *see*
Music: the A.G.O. Magazine

**Music: the Official Journal of the Schools'
Music Association**
TNG GB527; 0580–2733
GB–London: Newman Neame [for Pergamon
Press], 1966–70
[NOT IN BUCOMP1]

> **AB** 1 (1966)–4 (1970), 2
> **ALb** 1 (1966)–4 (1970)
> **BG** 1 (1966)–3 (1969)
> **BSdsc***
> **Cu** 1 (1966)–4 (1970), 2
> **EIR:Dtc** 1 (1966)–4 (1970), 2
> **EIR:Duc** 1 (1966)–4 (1970)
> **Lam** 1 (1966), 4; 2 (1967)–4 (1970), 2
> **Lbl***
> **Lcm** 1 (1966), 1–4; 2 (1967), 1–4, 6, 7, 11
> **Lcml** 1 (1966)–4 (1970)
> **LIp** 1 (1966)–4 (1970), 2
> **Lkc** 1 (1966)–4 (1970), 2
> **Lki** 1 (1966)–4 (1970)*
> **Lu** 2 (1968), 3

Mcm 1 (1966), 1–4; 2 (1967), 1–4; 3 (1968), 1–6; 4 (1969), 1, 2
Ob*
Re 1 (1966)–4 (1970)
SOu 1 (1966)–4 (1970), 2
TOd 1 (1966), 1; 4 (1970), 2
Yu 3 (1969)–4 (1970)

Music Analysis
0262–5245
GB–Oxford: Blackwell, 1982–

AB 1 (1982)–8 (1989), 2*
Au 1 (1982)–8 (1989)
BAc 1 (1982)–#
BG 1 (1982)–#
BLp 1 (1982)–#
BLu 1 (1982)–#
BRu 13 (1994)–#
Bs 1 (1982)–#*
BSdsc 1 (1982)–#
BTu 1 (1982)–#
Bu 1 (1982)–#
Cat 5 (1986)–#
CCtc 1 (1982)–#
CDu 1 (1982)–#
Cpl 1 (1982)–#
Cu 1 (1982)–#
DRu 1 (1982)–#
EIR:Dtc 1 (1982)–#
En 1 (1982)–#
Er
EXu 1 (1982)–#
Gul 1 (1982)–#
HUu 8 (1989)–#
KE 1 (1982)–#
Lam 1 (1982)–#
LAu 1 (1982)–#
Lbbc 1 (1982)–#
Lbl*
Lcm 1 (1982)–#
Lcml 1 (1982)–#
Lcu 1 (1982)–#
LEbc 1 (1982)–#
Lgo 1 (1982)–#
Lgsm 1 (1982)–#
Lkc 2 (1983)–3 (1984); 5 (1986)–#
Lki 1 (1982)–#
Lmi 5 (1986)–#
LRHBNC 1 (1982)–#
Lro 2 (1983)–#
Ltc 12 (1993)–13 (1994); 15 (1996), 2–#
Lu 1 (1982)–#
LVu 1 (1982)–#

Mcm 1 (1982)–#
MK 6 (1987)–#
Mmu (a) 5 (1986)–#
Msuc 5 (1986)–#
Mu 1 (1982)–#
NO 1 (1982)–#
NWu 1 (1982)–#
Ob 1 (1982)–#
Oub 14 (1995)–#
Ouf 1 (1982)–#
R 1 (1982)–#
SFu 1 (1982)–#
SOu 1 (1982)–#
TOd 1 (1982)–#
Uu 1 (1982)–#
Yu 1 (1982)–#

Music and Automata: from Horology to Mechanical Musical Instruments
0262–8260
GB–London: Arthur W. J. G. Ord-Hume, 1983–
[NOT IN BUCOMP1]

AB 1992–#
BSdsc*
Cu 1 (1983)
Lbar 1 (1983)–2 (1986), 8
Lbl*
Ob*

Music and Communication
TNG I285
I–Florence: Olschki [for the International Music Council], 1970–

BSdsc 1 (1970)–3 (1972)

Music and Copyright see Financial Times Music and Copyright

Music and Dance see Australian Musical News

Music and Drama 1950 see Con Brio: a Scots Music Magazine for the Modern Music Lover

Music and Equipment Mart
0956–6619
GB–Colchester: Aceville, 1987–
[NOT IN BUCOMP1]

Lbl*

Music and Letters
TNG GB280; 0027–4224
GB–London: Oxford University Press, 1920–

AB 1 (1920)–#
ABc 1 (1920)–3 (1922); 8 (1927)–22 (1941); 27 (1946)–#
ALb 8 (1927), 2; 47 (1966), 2; 48 (1967), 1, 3; 49 (1968), 2, 3; 50 (1969), 1, 2; 52 (1971), 4; 53 (1972), 1; 61 (1980)–#
Ap 6 (1925); 14 (1933)–19 (1938)
Au 1 (1920)–#
BAc 1 (1920)–20 (1939); 44 (1963)–47 (1966), 1, 3, 4; 48 (1967)–52 (1971); 54 (1973)–61 (1980); 63 (1982); 65 (1984)–#
BDp 36 (1955)–66 (1985)
BEp [c (5 years)]
BG 7 (1926)–31 (1950); 33 (1952)–#
BLp 1 (1920)–3 (1922); 40 (1959)–#
BLu 1 (1920)–#
Bp 31 (1950)–#
BRp 6 (1925), 3–#
BRu 1 (1920)–#
Bs 1 (1920)–#
BSdsc 1 (1920)–#
BTp 29 (1948)–60 (1979)
BTu 53 (1972)–62 (1981)
Bu 1 (1920)–#
Cat 49 (1968), 1, 2; 50 (1969), 1, 3, 4; 51 (1970), 1, 3, 4; 52 (1971)–53 (1972); 54 (1973), 1, 2, 4; 55 (1974)–68 (1987); 69 (1988), 1–3; 70 (1989)–#
CCtc 6 (1925)–#*
CDCp 70 (1989)–#
CDu 1 (1920)–#
Cpl 1 (1920)–#
Cu 1 (1920)–#
DRu 1 (1920)–#
EIR:Dtc 1 (1920)–#
EIR:Duc 41 (1960)–#
EIR:MEtc 56 (1975)–#
En 1 (1920)–#
Ep 6 (1925)–22 (1941), 3; 23 (1942)–27 (1946), 3; 28 (1947)–#
Er 1 (1920)–#
EXu 31 (1950)–#
Gam 1 (1920)– 14 (1933); 15 (1934), 2, 3; 18 (1937), 2, 4; 19 (1938), 1, 3, 4; 20 (1939)–22 (1941), 3; 23 (1942), 1–3; 24 (1943), 1; 27 (1946), 3, 4; 28 (1947), 1, 3; 30 (1949), 1, 3; 31 (1950), 3; 35 (1954)–37 (1956); 38 (1957), 3; 39 (1958), 4; 40 (1959)–69 (1988), 1, 3, 4; 70 (1989)–#
Gm 1 (1920)–#
Gul 1 (1920)–#

HOp 57 (1976)–#
HUu 1 (1920)–#
KE 32 (1951)–36 (1955); 46 (1965)–#
Lam 1 (1920)–6 (1925), 2 [w 2 (1921), 4]; 7 (1926)–# [w 17 (1936), 3; 24 (1943), 3, 4; 32 (1951), 2]
LAu 16 (1935), 4; 24 (1943), 3–#*
Lbar 1 (1920)–2 (1921); 4 (1923)–#
Lbbc 71 (1990)–#
Lbl*
Lcm 1 (1920)–#
Lcml 1 (1920)–#
Lcml (m) [c (1 year)]
Lcs 1 (1920)–11 (1930)*; 13 (1932), 2; 14 (1933), 1, 3, 4–15 (1934); 18 (1937), 1; 19 (1938), 4; 21 (1940), 3
Lcu 31 (1950)–55 (1974) [m]; 56 (1975)–#
LEbc 1 (1920)–#
LEc 1 (1920)–#
Len 17 (1936)–61 (1980)
Lgo 1 (1920)–#
Lgsm 18 (1937), 2–40 (1959)*; 41 (1960)–#
Lk 27 (1946); 30 (1949); 34 (1953)–#
Lkc 1 (1920)–# [w 58 (1977)]
Lki 1 (1920)–72 (1991)
Lmi 49 (1968)–#
LRHBNC 1 (1920)–#
Lro 45 (1964)–#
Lrscm 14 (1933)–54 (1973), 3
Ltc 10 (1929)–12 (1931), 1, 3, 4; 13 (1932), 2–21 (1940), 1, 4; 22 (1941), 2–24 (1943), 3; 25 (1944); 27 (1946), 1–3; 30 (1949), 4–31 (1950), 1; 32 (1951), 1, 3; 33 (1952), 2, 3; 34 (1953), 3, 4; 35 (1954), 2, 4–36 (1955), 1, 3, 4; 37 (1956)–38 (1957), 1, 3, 4; 39 (1958), 1–3; 40 (1959), 1, 2, 4–42 (1961), 3; 43 (1962), 1–3; 44 (1963)–45 (1964); 46 (1965), 2–49 (1968), 1; 50 (1969)–53 (1972), 3; 54 (1973), 1, 4; 55 (1974), 2–4; 56 (1975), 2; 57 (1976), 4; 58 (1977), 1, 2; 59 (1978)–65 (1984), 3; 66 (1985)–68 (1987), 1, 3, 5; 69 (1988)–73 (1992), 2, 4; 74 (1993), 2, 3; 75 (1994)–76 (1995), 1, 3, 4; 77 (1996), 1, 2, 4–#
Ltv 56 (1975)–61 (1980); 67 (1986)–#
Lu 1 (1920)–#
LVp 1 (1920)–19 (1938); 22 (1941)–43 (1962); 45 (1964)–46 (1965); 49 (1968)–#
LVu 1 (1920), 1; 1 2 (1931), 4; 13 (1932), 1; 17 (1936)–#
Mcm 1 (1920), 1; 3 (1922), 1; 8 (1927), 2; 10 (1929), 4; 11 (1930), 1, 3, 4; 12 (1931)–13 (1932), 3; 14 (1933), 1–3; 15 (1934), 1; 23 (1942), 2; 26 (1945), 4; 31 (1950); 34 (1953)–39 (1958); 41 (1960)–#

MK 51 (1970)–#
Mmu (a) 68 (1987)–#
Mpl 1 (1920)–#
Mu 1 (1920)–#
Msu 8 (1927), 2; 48 (1967), 2–4; 57 (1976)
NO 1 (1920)–#
NOTu 41 (1960)–#
NTp 1 (1920)–6 (1925); 18 (1937)–#
NWu 1 (1920)–37 (1956) [m]; 33 (1952); 35 (1954)–#
Ob 1 (1920)–#
Oub 72 (1991)–#
Ouf 1 (1920)–#
R 1 (1920)–# [w 23 (1942), 3]
SA 7 (1926)–#
SFp 8 (1927)–57 (1976); 59 (1978)–63 (1982); 65 (1984)–66 (1985), 1, 3, 4; 69 (1988) [57 (1976) is [m]]
SFu 1 (1920)–#
SLGu 37 (1956)–# [w 50 (1969), 4]
SOu 1 (1920)–#
STAp 47 (1966)–62 (1981)
TOd 1 (1920)–45 (1964) [m]; 46 (1965)–#
Uu 22 (1941); 26 (1945)–29 (1948); 52 (1971)–61 (1980); 63 (1982); 65 (1984)–#
WCp 63 (1982)–#
WF 49 (1968)–75 (1994)
Yu 1 (1920)–8 (1927); 10 (1929), 2, 4; 12 (1931)–30 (1949); 34 (1953)–#

Music and Life
TNG GB466; 0085–3607
GB–London: Music Group of the Communist Party, 1956–78

AB 13–53, 1961–78
Cu 13–55, 1961–78*
En*
Lbl*
Lcml 25–55, 1964–78*
Ob*

Music and Liturgy: the Official Organ of the Society of St Gregory
TNG GB329; 0305–4438
GB–London: Society of Saint Gregory/Church Music Association, 1929–
[Entitled *Liturgy: the Official Organ of the Society of St Gregory* from 13 (1944), 2–38 (1969); entitled *Life and Worship* (ISSN 0024–5119) from 39 (1970)–43 (1974), and published GB–Tenbury Wells. Entitled *Music and Liturgy* from 1974, with new numbering sequence.]

AB 1 (1929)–12 (1943); 1 (1974), 1; 3 (1977), 3; 9 (1983)–#

BAc 1 (1974)–#
Bp 1 (1974)–#
Bs 2 (1975/76)
BSdsc*
CCtc 1 (1974)–#*
Cu 1 (1929)–43 (1974), 2; 1 (1974)–#
EIR:Dp 12 (1986)–18 (1992)
EIR:Dtc 1 (1929)–43 (1974), 2; 1 (1974)–#
EIR:Duc 1 (1974)–#
EIR:MEtc 1 (1974)–#
En 1 (1974)–#*
Lbl*
Lcml 1 (1974)–#
LEc 1 (1974)–3 (1977), 3; 20 (1994)–#
Mpl 1 (1974)–#
Ob 1 (1929)–43 (1974), 2

Music and Man
TNG GB568; 0306–2082
US/GB–New York; London: Gordon and Breach; 1973–
[Entitled *Journal of Musicological Research* (ISSN 0141–1896) from 3 (1979)]

BSdsc*
Cu 1 (1973)–#
EIR:Dtc 1 (1973)–2 (1976), 1/2; 3 (1979)–12 (1992), 3
Lbbc 9 (1989), 2, 3
Lbl*
Lcm 10 (1990)–11 (1991)
Lcml 1 (1973)–#
Lgo 2 (1976)–#
Lkc 5 (1984)*–#
LRHBNC 11 (1991), 1, 2
Lu 2 (1978), 3/4; 3 (1979)–#
MK 1 (1973)–#
Ob*
SFu 1 (1973)–4 (1983)
TOd 3 (1979), 3/4

Music and Media
NL–Amsterdam: European Music Report, ?1984–
[NOT IN BUCOMP1]

Lbbc [c]

Music and Musicians
TNG GB440; 0027– 4232
GB–London: Hansom Books, 1952–91
[Entitled *Music and Musicians International* (ISSN 0952–2697) from 35 no. 10 (1987)–39 (1990); ceased publication with vol. 39 (1990/91), 3; succeeded by *Music Magazine* [3] (q.v.)]

Len 16 (1967/68), 9–12; 29 (1980/81), 1
Lgo 11 (1962/63); 14 (1965/66)–39 (1990/91), 2 [w 22 (1973/74), 5]
Lgu 32 (1983/84)–39 (1990/91), 2
Lha (f) 22 (1973/74), 5–12; 23 (1974/75)–28 (1979/80), 5, 7–12; 29 (1980/81),1#
LIp 14 (1965/66)–39 (1990/91), 10
Lkc 23 (1974/75)–26 (1977/78)*
Lki 16 (1967/68)–33 (1984/85)
Lmi 28 (1979/80)–39 (1990/91)
LRHBNC 21 (1972/73), Feb–Dec; 22 (1973/74), Jan–Nov; 23 (1974/75), Jan–Apr, June, Aug, Oct–Dec; 24 (1975/76), Feb, Apr, Sep, Nov, Dec; 25 (1976/77), Jan, Mar–Sep, Nov; 26 (1977/78), Jan–Oct, Dec; 27 (1978/79), July; 29 (1980/81), Jan–Mar, May–Sep
Lu 4 (1955/56)–5 (1956/57); 6 (1957/58), 5–12; 7 (1958/59)–13 (1964/65), 4; 14 (1965/66)–29 (1980/81), 1; 30 (1981/82), Sep–38 (1989/90), 3, 5–12; 39 (1990/91)
LVp 1 (1952/53)–7 (1958/59); 9 (1960/61)–15 (1966/67); 17 (1968/69)–39 (1990/91), 10
LVu 18 (1969/70)–25 (1976/77)
Mcm 1 (1952/53), 1; 3 (1954/55), 5–11 (1962/63), 4; 17 (1968/69), 12; 18 (1969/70), 1, 12; 20 (1971/72), 11, 12; 21 (1972/73), 1–6, 9–12; 22 (1973/74), 2–12; 23 (1974/75)–39 (1990/91)*
MI 11 (1962/63)–28 (1979/80)
MK 22 (1973/74)–28 (1979/80)
Mmu (a) 29 (1980/81)–39 (1990/91)
Mpl 1 (1952/53)–38 (1989/90)
Mu 16 (1967/68), 2–28 (1979/80), 4
NTp 13 (1964/65)–29 (1980/81), Sep; 30 (1981/82), Mar–39 (1990/91) [w 1989, Apr]
NWu 13 (1964/65)–15 (1966/67)*; 16 (1967/68)–23 (1974/75); 30 (1981/82)–38 (1989/90)
Ob*
Oub 30 (1981/82)–38 (1989/90)
PRp 13 (1964/65), July– 39 (1990/91), Sep
R 10 (1961/62), 9; 23 (1974/75), 2–7, 10–11; 24 (1975/76), 7, 9–11; 25 (1976/77), 9; 26 (1977/78), 10–12; 27 (1978/79), 2–6; 28 (1979/80), 6; 35 (1986/87), 12
SFu 1 (1952/53)–29 (1980/81)*
SLGu 1 (1952/53)–24 (1975/76), 1
TOd 18 (1969/70)–39 (1990/91)*
Uu 20 (1971/72)–30 (1981/82)*
WCp 30 (1981/82)–35 (1986/87), May, Oct–Dec; 36 (1987/88); 37 (1988/89), 2–12; 38 (1989/90)–39 (1990/91), 1

WF 16 (1967/68), 5–39 (1990/91), 2
Yu 13 (1964/65), 5–29 (1980/81)

Music and Musicians *see also* **Seven Arts**

Music and Musicians International *see* **Music and Musicians**

The "Music and Poetry" "Art and Language" Society: an Instructive Monthly for the English-Speaking World
Fellinger 1968/1634; TNG GB195
GB/US–London; New York, 1902

AB 1902
Lbl*
Ob*

Music and Recordings
TNG US672
US–New York: Oxford University Press, 1955

Cpl 1955
Cu 1955
Lbl*
Ob*

Music and Records: incorporating "Musical Renaissance" *see* **Musical Renaissance: a Monthly Magazine**

Music and Revolution [translated title] *see* **Muzyka i Revolyutsiya**

Music and School
GB–London, 1885

Ob*

Music and the Present [translated title] *see* **Muzyka i Sovremennost**

Music and Theatre [translated title] *see* **Musik og Teater**

Music and Theatre Digest: Union of "Musical Digest" and "Theatre Digest"
TNG GB439
GB–London: Lyford Publications, 1951

Cu 1–3, 1951
Ob 1–3, 1951

Music and Tomorrow's Public
?GB–197?–
[NOT IN BUCOMP1]

   BSdsc 2 (1977)

Music and Video
0144–7114
GB–London, 1980–
[NOT IN BUCOMP1; entitled *Popular Video*
from 1981]

   Cu 1, 1980–#
   EIR:Dtc 1980–81, Mar; 1981–83, Mar
   Lbl*

Music and Video Insight *see* Insight

Music and Video Week Directory
0267–3290
GB–London: Spotlight Publications, 1976–
[From 1981 entitled *Music and Video Week
Yearbook*]

   Cu*
   EIR:Dtc 1979–84; 1987–91 [w 1989]
   Lbl*
   Ob*

Music and Video Week Yearbook *see* Music
and Video Week Directory

Music and Youth
TNG GB287
GB–London: Home Music Study Union, 1921–
34
[Preceded 1915–20 by *Youth and Music* [1]
(q.v.). In 1928 incorporated *Panpipes* (q.v.);
entitled *Music and Youth and Panpipes*, 1928–
29; entitled *The Music Student* from vol. 12 no.
10 (1932)–14 no. 9 (1934). From 1934
succeeded by *The Piano Student* (q.v.)]

   AB 1 (1921)–14 (1934)
   BSdsc*
   Cu 1 (1921)–14 (1934), 9
   Lam 1 (1924), 1; 2 (1922), 6–8; 4 (1924); 7
      (1927), 10, 11; 8 (1928), 5
   Lbl*
   Lcm (p) 1 (1921)–11 (1931)
   Lcml 1 (1921)–7 (1927)
   Mcm 1 (1921)–12 (1932)*
   Mpl 1 (1921)–14 (1934)
   Ob*

Music and Youth and Panpipes *see* Music and
Youth

Music, Art and Trade Journal and Talking
Machine Review *see* Music: a Monthly
Journal Devoted to the Art and Trade, with
which is incorporated Musical Notes

Music Article Guide
TNG US760; 0027–4240
US–Philadelphia, PA: Music Article Guide,
1966–

   EIR:Duc 1 (1966), 4–

Music Association of Ireland Annual Report
EIRE–Dublin: Music Association of Ireland, ?–
[NOT IN BUCOMP1]

   EIR:Dtc 1957; 1968–70; 1972–81
   EIR:MEtc 1976–82
   Ob*

Music Association of Ireland: Music Diary
0332–3811
EIRE–Dublin: Music Association of Ireland, ?–
[NOT IN BUCOMP1; entitled *M.A.I. News*
from 1981]

   AB 1981, May, July–Nov; 1982, July
   EIR:Dtc 1980, May, July, Aug; 1981, Sep–
      1982, July
   EIR:Duc 1981–85, July

The Music Box: an International Magazine of
Mechanical Music: the Journal of the Musical
Box Society of Great Britain
0027–4275
GB–Coventry [etc.]: Musical Box Society of
Great Britain, 1962–

   AB 11 (1983)–#
   BSdsc*
   Cu 10 (1981)–#
   En 10 (1981)–#
   Lcml 2 (1965), 3–3 (1968), 6
   Lgu 10 (1981), 5–16 (1993), 4
   Lsa 13 (1988), 5–8; 14 (1989), 1–3, 5–8;
      15 (1990)–#
   Ob*

The Music Box and British Entertainer
TNG GB319
GB–London, 1927
[4 numbers were published]

   Lbl*

The Music Bulletin *see* The British Music
Society Bulletin

Music Bulletin of the University of Nottingham
GB–Nottingham: University of Nottingham, 1978–?
[NOT IN BUCOMP1]

NO 1–9, 1978–81

Music Business
0269–0292
GB–Colchester: Feedback Publications, ?1986–

Lam 5 (1990), 6 (1991), 1–3, 5, 6, 8; 7 (1992), 4, 6–11; 8 (1993), 1–10
Lgu 2 (1987), 8–#

Music Business Directory
GB–Bushey: Feedback Publications, ?–
[NOT IN BUCOMP1]

Lgu [c]

Music Business International see MBI: Music Business International

Music Business Weekly
TNG GB540
GB–London, 1969–71

En 1969–71*
Lbl*
Lsa 1969, Sep 20–Oct 18, Nov 9–Dec 6, 20; 1970, Jan 3, 17–Mar 28, Sep 19, Oct 31, Dec 12; 1971, Feb 13

Music Canada see Musicanada

The Music Catalog see Library of Congress: Music, Books on Music, and Sound Recordings Catalog

Music Cataloging Bulletin
TNG US802; 0027–4283
US–Ann Arbor, MI: Music Library Association, 1970–

ABc (ILS) 1 (1970)–24 (1993)
Cu 1 (1970)–#
Lbl*

Music Club Magazine
TNG GB556
GB–London: British Broadcasting Corporation, 1970–80 [Also known as B.B.C. Music Club Magazine]

AB*
Cu 1 (1970)–10 (1979), 1

EIR:Dtc 1 (1970)–10 (1979), 3
En 1 (1970)–10 (1979)
Ob*

Music Collector
0959–7166
GB–Cambridge: Music Collector Enterprises, ?1989–
[NOT IN BUCOMP1]

Lbl*

Music Current: the Best Way of Finding Out about Music in Scotland
0954–8122
GB–Glasgow: Scottish Music Information Centre, 1988–
[NOT IN BUCOMP1; superseded Scottish Society of Composers Newsletter (q.v.)]

AB 1, 1988–#
Au 1, 1988–#
EIR:Dtc 1, 1988–#
En 1, 1988–# [w 42]
Ep 1, 1988–#
Er 17, 1990–#
Gam 4, 7, 8, 10, 12, 13, 1989; 15, 1990; 17–41, 1990–93; 43–53, 1993–94; 55, 1994–#
Gm 1, 1988–#
Gsmic 1, 1988–#
Lam 49–51, 1993
Lbl*
Ob*

The Music Dealer
TNG GB320
GB–London, 1927–32
[Incorporated Music: a Monthly Journal Devoted to the Art and Trade, with which is incorporated Musical Notes (q.v.) in 1930]

Lbl*
Ob*

Music Diary see R.T.É. Music Diary

Music Directory Canada
0820–0416
C–Toronto: CM Books, 1983–
[NOT IN BUCOMP1]

BSdsc 1983–84

Music Education Centre Newsletter
GB–Reading: University of Reading, 1981–
[NOT IN BUCOMP1]

Re 1981–85; 1986, Sum–1992, Aut

Music Education Research Papers
TNG GB535; 0077–2399
GB–London, 1968–72

BSdsc*
Cu 1 (1968)–5 (1972)

Music Education Review
0140–6493
GB–London: Chappell, 1977–

BSdsc 1 (1977)–2 (1979)
Cu 1 (1977)–#
EIR:Dtc 1 (1977)–2 (1979)
EIR:Duc 1 (1977)
En 1 (1977)–#
Ob*
Yu 2 (1979)

Music Education Series [translated title] *see*
Řada Hudebné Výchovna

Music Education Yearbook *see* British Music
Education Yearbook

Music Educators' Journal *see* Music
Supervisors' Journal

Music File: the Support Service for Classroom
Music Teachers
0954–0377
GB–Warwick: Mary Glasgow Publications,
1988–
[NOT IN BUCOMP1]

AB 1988–#
Cat (b) 1990–#
Cu 1988–#
EIR:Dtc 1988–#
En 1988–#
Lbl*

Music for All (with which is incorporated
"Radio Music"): a Magazine for Every Home
GB–London: Ascherberg, Hopwood and Crew,
1922–28
[NOT IN BUCOMP1]

EIR:Dtc 48–63, 1925–28
Lbl 1922–28

Music for Socialism
GB–London, 197?–?

Lsa 4–12, 1977–78

Music for the Million
TNG GB330
GB–London, 1929–30

Lbl*

Music Forum
0885–503X
US–New York: Columbia University Press,
1967; 1970; 1973; 1976; 1980; 1987

AB 1 (1967)–4 (1976)
Au 1 (1967)–6 (1987), 1
BSdsc*
Cpl 1 (1967)–#
Cu 1 (1967)–#
DRu 1 (1967)–6 (1987), 1
EIR:Dtc 1 (1967)–2 (1970); 4 (1976)–
6 (1987), 1
Er 1 (1967)–4 (1976)
Gul 1 (1967)–#
HUu 1 (1967)–#
Lbl*
Lgo 1 (1967)–5 (1980)
Lkc 1 (1967)–3 (1973); 5 (1980)–6 (1987), 1
Lu 1 (1967)–#
Mu 1 (1967)–5 (1980)
NO 1 (1967)–5 (1980)
NWu 1 (1967)–4 (1976)
Ob 1 (1967)–#
Ouf 1 (1967)–6 (1987), 1
R 1 (1967)–6 (1987), 1
SFu 1 (1967)–2 (1970)
Yu 1 (1967)–6 (1987), 1

Music from the Empty Quarter
0964–542X
GB–Ilford: The Empty Quarter, 1991–
[NOT IN BUCOMP1]

Lbl*

Music from the Movies
0967–8131
GB–Bridport: Music from the Movies Limited,
?1994–
[NOT IN BUCOMP1]

Lam 13, 1996–#

The Music Hall
Fellinger 1968/1108; TNG GB130
GB–London: W. McWilliam, 1889–112
[Entitled *The Music Hall and Theatre* from vol.
2 (1889), 31; entitled *The Music Hall and
Theatre Review* from vol. 2 (1889), 43]

Lbl*
Lcml (r) 2–4, 1890; 19–23, 1898–1900;
   25–36, 1901–06; 39–41, 1908–09
LEbc 1899–1912

Music Hall *see also* **Music Hall Records**

**Music Hall: le Seul Magazine de la Chanson
et des Variétés**
TNG F660
F–Paris, 1955–60; n.s. 1961–65
[NOT IN BUCOMP1]

Lsa 29–34, 1957; 36–40, 42–46, 1958; 48,
   50–53, 1959; 67, 1961; n.s. 4, 10, 1961

The Music Hall and Theatre *see* **The Music
Hall**

The Music Hall and Theatre Review *see* **The
Music Hall**

The Music Hall Artistes' Association Gazette
Fellinger 1968/1021; TNG GB122
GB–London, 1886–87

Lbl*

**The Music Hall Critic and Programme of
Amusements**
Fellinger 1968/624; TNG GB74
GB–London, 1870

Lbl*

Music Hall Memories
GB–London, 1935–36

En 1935–36
Lbl*

The Music Hall Pictorial and Variety Stage
Fellinger 1968/1729; TNG GB207
GB–London, 1904–05
[3 nos in total]

Lbl*
Ob 1 (1904), 1

Music Hall Records
0143–8867; 0142–6737
GB–Mitcham: Tony Barker, 1978–
[Continued as *Music Hall*]

Cu 1978–#
En*
Lbl*
Lsa 1978–#
Ob*

The Music Halls' Gazette
Fellinger 1968/585; TNG GB72
GB–London, 1868
[36 nos in total]

Lbl*

Music in Action
GB–London, 1968–?

BSdsc*

Music in Britain *see* **Monthly Music
Broadsheet**

Music in Danish Libraries *see* **Musikalier i
Danske Biblioteker**

**Music in Education, incorporating Music in
Schools: a Bi-Monthly Journal** *see* **Music in
Schools**

Music in Germany *see* **There's Music in
Germany**

Music in Middlesex
TNG GB402
GB–London: Middlesex County Music
Committee, 1947–?

Lam 5, 1949
Lbl*
Ob 1–3, 1947–48

Music in Nigeria
1115–9839
GB–London: Commonwealth Music
Association, Nigerian Chapter, 1991–
[NOT IN BUCOMP1]

Lsa 1 (1991/92), 1–3

Music in Poland *see* **La Musique en Pologne**

Music in Schools
TNG GB362; 0027–433X
GB–London: Macmillan, 1937–78
[Entitled *Music in Education, incorporating Music in Schools: a Bi-Monthly Journal* from nos 86/87, 1944]

AB 37 (1973)–41 (1977)
ALb 26 (1962), 299
BAc 12 (1948); 14 (1950)–16 (1952); 18 (1954)–19 (1955), Oct; 21 (1957)– 24 (1960); 26 (1962); 28 (1964), Mar–Dec; 30 (1966)–42 (1978)
BG 31 (1967)–32 (1968); 34 (1970)–42 (1978)
Bp 1 (1937)–41 (1977), 388
BRu 1 (1937)–42 (1978), 390
Bs 17 (1953), Nov/Dec–42 (1978)
BSdsc*
CCtc 31 (1967)–32 (1968); 35 (1971)– 42 (1978)
Cu 33 (1969)–42 (1978)
DOR 38 (1974)–42 (1978)
EIR:Dtc 33 (1969)–42 (1978), 400
EIR:Duc 30 (1966)–42 (1978)
En 1 (1937), 1–10; 33 (1969)–42 (1978)
Ep 6 (1942)–42 (1978)
EXu 39 (1975)–42 (1978)
Gam 29 (1965), 6; 30 (1966)–32 (1968), 3, 5, 6; 33 (1969), 2–6; 34 (1970)–40 (1976), 1, 3–6; 41 (1977)–42 (1978), 1–6, 8, 9, 11, 12
Gm 34 (1970)–42 (1978)
Lam 15 (1951), 178, 179, 188, 189; 18 (1954), 214, 215; 19 (1955), 218, 219–30 (1966), 317; 30 (1966), 319–35 (1971), 347; 35 (1971), 349–36 (1972), 355; 36 (1972), 358, 359; 37 (1973), 361–363; 38 (1974), 365–39 (1975), 375; 40 (1976), 377–379, 381–42 (1978), 400
LAu 25 (1961)–41 (1977)
Lbl*
Lcm 10 (1946)–41 (1977) [w 20 (1956); 24 (1960)]
Lcml 1 (1937); 13 (1949)–42 (1978)
Lcs 21 (1957)–#*
LEc 29 (1965)–42 (1978)
Lgo 18 (1954)–42 (1978)
Lgsm 29 (1965)–34 (1970), Jan/Feb; 35 (1971)–36 (1972); 38 (1974)–42 (1978)
Lie 22 (1958)–42 (1978) [w 41 (1977), 282, 284]
Lki 20 (1956)–42 (1978)*
LRHBNC 36 (1972)–42 (1978)
LVp 19 (1955)–23 (1959); 25 (1961)– 27 (1963); 29 (1965)–42 (1978)

LVu 32 (1968)–38 (1974)
Mcm 1 (1937)–3 (1939); 18 (1954), 204–205; 21 (1957), 240–241, 248–249; 22 (1958), 258–261; 23 (1959), 264–273; 24 (1960)– 41 (1977)
Mmu (d) 32 (1968)–42 (1978)
Mpl 1 (1937)–42 (1978)
Mu 23 (1959)–27 (1963)*
Ob*
SFu 26 (1962)–42 (1978)
SLGu 42 (1978)
SOu 21 (1957)*; 24 (1960)–42 (1978)
TOd 1 (1937)–42 (1978)*
Uu 36 (1972)–41 (1977); 42 (1978)*
Yu 31 (1967)–42 (1978)

Music in Surrey
TNG GB446
GB–Guildford: Surrey County Music Association, ?1945–?

Lcml 26, 1953

Music in Sweden/Musik i Sverige
0348–7296
S–Stockholm: Swedish Music Information Centre, ?1979–

BSdsc 1981–84
Cpl 1979–#
Lam 1980, 1, 2; 1986, Mar, June; 1987, July
Lbar 1983, Sep–1984, Nov; 1985, Sep–1986, June; 1987, July
Lcm 1981, Mar; 1982, June; 1983, Mar, Sep; 1984, Nov; 1986, Mar, June; 1987, June
Lcs 1981, Dec; 1984, Nov; 1985, Sep; 1986, Mar, June; 1987, July
Lsa 1984, Nov; 1986, Mar; 1987, July
Mcm 1979–#

Music in the Curriculum
0144–0926
GB–Southampton: Southern Centre for Music Education, 1979–
[NOT IN BUCOMP1]

Cu 1 (1979)–#
EIR:Dtc 1 (1979)–#
En*
Lbl*
Lie 1 (1979)–#
Mmu (d) 28 (1995)–#
Ob*
Re 1 (1979)–#

Music in the Secondary School Curriculum News Sheet
GB–York: Schools Council, 1973–79

Ob*
Re 2–10, 1974–79

Music in the University of Glasgow
GB–Glasgow: Glasgow University, ?–?
[NOT IN BUCOMP1]

Gul 1954–#

Music in the USSR/Muzyka v SSSR
RF–Moscow: VAAP–Inform, 1981–
[NOT IN BUCOMP1]

Cu 1984, July/Sep
Lbbc 1985–86*
Lcml 1985, Apr–#

Music in Time
IL–Jerusalem: Jerusalem Rubin Academy of Music and Drama, 1983–

BSdsc*
CCtc 1990/91–#
En 1984/85–#
Lam 1983–91; 1993
Lcm 1983–#
Lu 1983–#
Ouf 1984/85; 1986/87; 1993–#
TOd 1988/89; 1992/93

Music in Worship
0141–657X
GB–Worthing [etc.], 1977–88
[Succeeded by *Christian Music* (q.v.)]

CCtc 15–40, 1981–88
Cu 1–41, 1977–88; 1988–93
En 1977–88
Lam 18, 1981
Lbl*
Ob*

The Music Index
TNG US644; 0027–4348
US–Detroit: Information Coordinators, 1949–

AB 6 (1954); 23 (1971)–28 (1976), 11; 33 (1981)–42 (1990)
ABc (ILS) 1 (1949)–34 (1982)
BAc 1 (1949)–# [including monthly issues]
BLp 1 (1949)–36 (1984); 39 (1987)–#
BRp 1 (1949), 12–#
BRu 1 (1949)–#
Bs 1 (1949)–27 (1975)

BSdsc*
CCtc 32 (1980)–#
CDu 1 (1949)–#
Cu 1 (1949)–#
EIR:Dp 39 (1987), May–45 (1993)
EIR:Dtc 23 (1971)–#
EIR:Duc 1 (1949)–#
Er 1 (1949)–# [including CD–ROM 1980–#]
Gm 27 (1975)–38 (1986)
Gul 1 (1949)–21 (1969)
Lam 1 (1949)–#
Lbbc 1 (1949)–# [including CD–ROM 1979–#]
Lcml 1 (1949)–#
LEc 1 (1949)–30 (1978)
Lgo 1 (1949)–#
Lk 18 (1966)–20 (1968)
Lkc 1 (1949)–32 (1980)
Lki 1 (1949)–40 (1988)
Lu 1 (1949)–#
LVp 1 (1949)–8 (1956); 11 (1959)–25 (1973)
Mcm 1 (1949)–#
MK 1 (1949)–#
Mpl 1 (1949)–#
Msuc 1979–# [CD–ROM version]
Mu 1 (1949)–# [+ CD–ROM version]
NO 1 (1949)–6 (1954); 9 (1957); 14 (1962); 16 (1964)–28 (1976)
Ob 1 (1949)–#
Oub 33 (1981)–45 (1993)
Ouf 1 (1949)–#
SFu 1 (1949)–#
SOu 1 (1949)–# [including CD–ROM 1979–#]
TOd 29 (1977)–36 (1984), 12 [monthly issues]

Music Industry
TNG GB514; 0027–4356
GB–London: Tofts and Woolf, 1964–73
[Succeeded by *The Pianomaker* (q.v.)]

AB*
BSdsc*
Cbijs 7, 1965
Lbl*

Music Industry Directory
GB–London, ?–
[NOT IN BUCOMP1]

BSdsc*
EIR:MEtc 1993–#

Music Industry ICC Business Ratio Report
GB– London, ?–
0261–9148
[NOT IN BUCOMP1]

BSdsc 8 (1986)–#

Music Information Bulletin [translated title]
see Informatsionniy Muzykalny Byuletin

Music Ireland
0790–7052
EIRE–Dublin: Amadeus, 1985–91
[NOT IN BUCOMP1; preceded by *M.A.I.
Monthly Bulletin* (q.v.); *Counterpoint*; and
Soundpost]

AB 5 (1990), May–6 (1991), Apr
BLp 1 (1985)–5 (1990)
BLu 1 (1985)–#
Cu 5 (1990), 5–6 (1991), Apr
EIR:Dp 3 (1988)–6 (1991), Apr
EIR:Driam 1 (1985), Feb–6 (1991), Apr
EIR:Dtc 1 (1985)–6 (1991), Apr
EIR:Duc 1 (1985)–6 (1991)
EIR:MEtc 1 (1985)–5 (1990), 3; 5 (1990),
5–6 (1991), Apr
En*
Ob 5 (1990), 5–6 (1991), Apr
Uu 1 (1985)–6 (1991)*

Music Journal *see* Music Publishers' Journal

Music-Journal
TNG GB403
GB–London, 1947–52
[Entitled *Music Survey*, 1949–52]

AB*
ALb 1 (1947), 1–6; 2 (1949), 4; 3 (1950)–
4 (1952), 3
Au 2 (1949)–4 (1952), 3 [Reprint ed.]
Bp 1 (1947)–4 (1952), 3
Btu 2 (1949)–3 (1950)
CDu 2 (1949)–4 (1952)
Cpl 1 (1947)–2 (1949), 3; 3 (1950), 4;
4 (1952), 2
Cu 1 (1947)–4 (1952), 3 [+ Reprint ed.]
EIR:Duc 2 (1949)–4 (1952)
En 1 (1947)–4 (1952)
Er 1 (1947)–4 (1952)
Gm 1 (1947)–4 (1952)
Gul 2 (1949)–4 (1952) [+ Reprint ed.]
HUu 2 (1949)–4 (1952) [Reprint ed.]

KE 2 (1949)–4 (1952) [Reprint ed.]
Lam 1 (1947), 2; 2 (1949), 6; 3 (1950), 4;
4 (1952), 1
LAu 1 (1947), 2–6; 2 (1949)–4 (1952), 3
Lbl*
Lcm 1 (1947), 3–5; 2 (1949), 1, 3, 4;
3 (1950), 4; 4 (1952), 2, 3
Lcml 1 (1947)–3 (1950); 4 (1952)*
LEbc 2 (1949)–4 (1952), 3
Lki 1 (1947)–4 (1952)
Lsa 1 (1948), 3; 2 (1949), 3; 4 (1952), 3
Lu 1 (1947)–4 (1952), 3
LVu 2 (1949)–4 (1952), 3
Mpl 1 (1947)–4 (1952)
Mu 2 (1949)–4 (1952) [Reprint ed.]
NO 2 (1949)–4 (1952)
NWu 2 (1949)–4 (1952) [Reprint ed.]
Ob 1 (1947)–4 (1952)
Ouf 2 (1949)–4 (1952) [Reprint ed.]
SFu 2 (1949)–4 (1952)
Yu 2 (1949)–4 (1952) [Reprint ed.]

A Music Journal: Comprising the Report of
the Incorporated Society of Musicians, and
the Bulletin of the British Music Society
0951–5135
GB–London: Incorporated Society of
Musicians, 1929–39; 1945–
[Previously entitled *Monthly Journal of the
National Society of Professional Musicians*
(q.v.)]

AB*
ALb 27 (1961), 1; 34 (1968), 2; 36 (1970), 1;
43 (1977), 1; 44 (1978), 2–45 (1979), 2;
49 (1983), 1, 4; 51 (1985), 5; 57 (1991),
8–58 (1992), 12
BG 56 (1990), 5–#
BRp [c (2 years)]
Bs 56 (1990)–#*
BSdsc*
Cu 1 (1929)–#
En 1 (1929)–#
Er 21 (1955), 1
Gm 1 (1929)–2 (1931), 10
Lam 9 (1937), 1; 14 (1948), 1; 15 (1949),
1, 2; 16 (1950), 1; 29 (1963), 1; 30 (1964)–
33 (1967), 1; 35 (1969)–56 (1990), 3;
56 (1990), 5– 59 (1993), 3 [w 58 (1992), 2,
5, 7, 8]; 60 (1994), 9– #
Lbl 55 (1989), 4–#
Lcm 10 (1939), 2; 13 (1947), 2; 14 (1948), 2;
15 (1949), 1, 2; 16 (1951), 3; 19 (1953),
2–4; 20 (1954), 1, 2; 21 (1955), 1–3; 22

(1956), 1, 3; 23 (1957), 1–3; 24 (1958), 1,
2; 25 (1959), 1, 2; 26 (1960), 1, 2; 27
(1961), 1; 28 (1962), 2; 29 (1963), 1, 2; 30
(1964), 1, 2; 31 (1965), 1, 2; 32 (1966), 1,
2; 33 (1967)–41 (1975), 1; 42 (1976)–44
(1978), 2, 3; 45 (1979), 1, 3; 46 (1980), 1,
2; 47 (1981), 2, 3; 51 (1986), 2–4, 8–10,
12; 52 (1986)–54 (1988), 2–5, 7
Lcml 1 (1929)–17 (1951)*; 18 (1952)–19
(1953); 20 (1954)– 21 (1955)*; 22 (1956)–
25 (1959); 26 (1960)*; 27 (1961)–37
(1971); 38 (1972)*; 39 (1973)–#
Lki 40 (1974)–48 (1982)
Lu 2 (1930), 8–10; 3 (1931), 1–10; 4 (1932),
1–9; 5 (1933), 1–3; 6 (1934), 1–3; 7 (1935),
1–3; 9 (1937), 1, 2; 10 (1938), 1–3; 42
(1976), 2; 52 (1986), 10
Mcm 34 (1968), 2; 37 (1971), 1–3; 38 (1972),
1–3; 40 (1974), 2; 41 (1975)–#
Mpl 1 (1929)–33 (1967)
Msuc [c (3 years)]
NO 52 (1986), 9–#
NTp [c (2 years)]
Ob*
SA 42 (1976)–46 (1980), 1

Music Lab News
GB–London: Music Lab Hire and Sales, 1987–?
[NOT IN BUCOMP1]

EIR:Dtc 1–4, 1987–89

Music Library Association Newsletter
TNG US796; 0580–289X
US–Ann Arbor, MI: Music Library Association,
1969–
[NOT IN BUCOMP1; also known as *M.L.A.
Newsletter*]

Au 60, 1985–#
Bu 75, 1988–#
Cat 90, 1992–#
Cpl 16, 1974–#
EIR:Dtc 57, 1984–#
Gam 55, 1983–#
Lam 74–89, 1988–91 [w 77, 86]
LVp 71, 1987–#
LVu 56, 57, 1984; 71–75, 1987–88; 84, 1991;
95, 1993
Ob*
Oub 56, 1984–#
Ouf 55, 1983–#

The Music Lover [1]
TNG GB340
GB–London, 1932–34
[In 1933 absorbed *The Musical Mirror and
Fanfare*]

Cu 1 (1932/33), 1–11; 3 (1933/34), 1–39
EIR:Dtc 1 (1932/33)–4 (1934), 1
Gm 1 (1932/33), 1–9; 3 (1933/34), 1–41
Lbl*
Lcm 1 (1932/33), 1, 6, 7, 10, 17, 19, 20, 22,
23, 30
Lcm (p) 1 (1932/33), 33
Mpl 1 (1932/33)
Ob 3 (1933/34), 1–39
Ouf 1 (1932/33), 19

Music Lover [2]
TNG GB404
GB–London, 1947–48

Gm 1 (1947)–2 (1948), 5
Lbl*
Lcml 1 (1947)–2 (1948), 5

Music Lovers' Calendar
US–Boston; New York, 1905–08

Lcml 1 (1905); 3 (1908)

The Music Lover's Diary
Fellinger 1968/2081; TNG GB251
GB–London: Herbert and Daniel, 1911

Lbl*

The Music Lovers' Guide
TNG US521
US–New York, 1933–35
[Succeeded *The Phonograph Monthly Review*
(q.v.); continued as *American Music Lover* (q.v.)]

Lsa 1 (1933), 5–3 (1935), 2

The Music Lover's Portfolio of the World's
Best Music
GB–London, 1921–22

Lam 1921–22
Lcm (p) 1, 3–20, 1921–22
Mcm 1921–22

The Music Magazine [1]
TNG GB505
GB–London: Arts Magazines Ltd, 1963–65

AB*
ALb 2, 3, 1963
Lcm 1–3, 1963; 6, 7, 1964; 27, 1965

Music Magazine [2]
TNG C57; 0705–4009
C–Toronto: Barrett and Colgrass, Inc., 1978–91
[NOT IN BUCOMP1]

ALb 1 (1978), 4
BSdsc 6 (1983)–14 (1991)
CCtc 13 (1990)–14 (1991)
Lam 1 (1978), 1

Music Magazine [3]
0960–6033
GB–London: Orpheus Publishing, 1990–
[NOT IN BUCOMP1; formerly *Music and Musicians International*]

AB 3, 1990
BG 1–4, 1990–91
BSdsc 1–4, 1990–91
BuAYp 3–4, 1990–91
CCtc 1–4, 1990–91
Cu 1, 1990–#
EIR:Dtc 1–4, 1990–91
Lam 1990–91*
Lbar 1–4, 1990–91
Lbl*
LCdM 1–4, 1990–91
Lcml 1–3, 1990–91
Lgo 3–4, 1990–91
Lgsm 1–4, 1990–91
Ob 1–4, 1990–91
TOd 1–4, 1990–91

Music Magazine [translated title] *see* **Yin Yue Zazhi**

The Music Magazine [and Musical Courier] *see* **The Musical and Sewing Machine Gazette**

Music Maker
TNG GB528
GB–London: Longacre Press, 1966–68

AB 1966–68; 1972–73
Cbijs*
Cu 1 (1966)–2 (1968), 6
Ob*

Music Manager and International Promotion
0108–5328
DK–Hvidovre: Music Management International, 1983–
[NOT IN BUCOMP1]

Lbl*

Music Mart and Equipment
0956–6619
GB–?Colchester, 198?–
[NOT IN BUCOMP1]

Lsa 1989–#

Music Master. Several of these titles are also known as "The Official Music Master ...": all such entries have been brought together in this catalogue at **Music Master ...**

Music Master: the World's Greatest Record Catalogue
0308–9347
GB– Hastings: J. Humphries, 1974–
[Continued as *Music Master Albums Catalogue*; also known as *The Official Music Master Albums Record Catalogue*, and the *Music Master Master Catalogue*. Incorporated *Record Prices* (q.v.)]

AB 1978; 1984–#
BEp [c]
BRp 1974; 1976–#
BSdsc*
BuHW 1986–#
BuMK [c (1 year)]
CFp 1986–#
DU [c (1 year)]
Ea [c] [CD–ROM version]
EIR:Duc 1977–83
En*
Gm 1974–#
IP [c] [CD–ROM version]
Lba 1979–#
Lbl*
Lcml 1989–#
Lcml (c) [c (3 years)]
Lcml (m) 1974–#
Lcml (p) [c (3 years)]
Lha [c]
Lhr [c]
Lis [c]
Lk 1976–#
Lk (c) [c]
Lk (nk) [c]
Ll [c (5 years)]
Lsa*
Msuc 1995
NOp [CD–ROM version]
Ob*
SFp 1979–#

Music Master Albums Catalogue *see* Music Master: the World's Greatest Record Catalogue

Music Master CD Catalogue *see* Music Master CD Index

Music Master CD Index
GB–Hastings: J. Humphries, 1986–
[NOT IN BUCOMP1; entitled *Music Master CD Catalogue* from 1989 issue 8]

BuMK [c (1 year)]
EIR:Dtc 1986–#
En*
Lbl*

Music Master Country Music Catalogue
GB–Hastings: Music Master, 1991–
[NOT IN BUCOMP1; also entitled *Official Music Master Country Music Catalogue*]

Cu 1991–#
Lbl 1991–#
Ob 1991–#*

Music Master Films and Shows Catalogue
GB–Hastings: J. Humphries, 1990–

Lbl*
Ob 1990–#

Music Master Folk Music of the British Isles Catalogue
GB–Hastings: Music Master, 1994–
[NOT IN BUCOMP1]

Cu 1994–#

Music Master Heavy Metal
GB–Hastings: J. Humphries, 1990–
[NOT IN BUCOMP1]

Ob 1990–#

Music Master Jazz and Blues Catalogue
GB–London: Music Master, 199?–

Lbl*

Music Master Labels and Distributors Directory *see* Music Master Labels List

Music Master Labels List
1357–3357
GB–Hastings: Music Master, 1981–
[NOT IN BUCOMP1; from 1993 entitled *Music Master Labels and Distributors Directory*]

BSdsc*
Lbl*
Ob 1981–#*

Music Master Master Catalogue *see* Music Master: the World's Greatest Record Catalogue

Music Master Masterfile *see* Music Week Masterfile

Music Master Music on Video Catalogue
0962–354X
GB–Hastings: J. Humphries, 1990–
[NOT IN BUCOMP1]

Lbl 1990–#

Music Master Singles Catalogue
GB–Hastings: J. Humphries, 1990–
[NOT IN BUCOMP1]

Lbl*

Music Master Soul Catalogue
1357–292X
GB–London: Retail Entertainment Data, 1994–

Cu 1994–#
Lbl*

Music Master Spoken Word Catalogue
GB–Hastings: Music Master, 1992–

Cu 1992–93
Lbl*

Music Master Tracks Catalogue *see* Music Master Track Index

Music Master Track Index
0958–4722
GB–Hastings: J. Humphries, 1988–
[NOT IN BUCOMP1; entitled *Music Master Tracks Catalogue* (ISSN 0955–0925) from 1989; later entitled *Tracks Catalogue* (ISSN 1364–7245), and published by Retail Entertainment Data]

EIR:Dtc 1988–#
Lbl*
Lis [c]
Ob*

Music Master Yearbook
GB–Hastings; John Humphries Publishing,
?1984–
[NOT IN BUCOMP1]

  AB 1985–86
  EIR:Dtc 1984–#
  Ob 1984– #

Music Masters' and Mistresses' Association
Journal see Journal of the Music Masters' and
Mistresses' Association

Music Masters' and Mistresses' Association
Newsletter see Journal of the Music Masters'
and Mistresses' Association

Music Matters: News and Views from the
Royal Northern College of Music
GB–Manchester: Royal Northern College of
Music, 1973–

  AB 17–24, 1983/84–90 [w 23, 1988]
  Cpl 16–20, 1983–85
  EIR:Dtc 17, 1983/84–#
  En 17, 1983/84–#
  Lam 15–27, 1982–92 [w 20, 1986]
  Lcm 15–25, 1982–90
  Mcm 1, 1973–#
  Mpl 1976–86
  Ob*
  TOd 17–25, 1983/84–90 [w 20, 1986; 23,
    1988]

Music Memories: Covering All Phases of
Music Collecting
TNG US715
US–Birmingham, AL: Pat Cather, 1961–?
[From 1963, 6, incorporated Jazz Report: the
Record Collector's Magazine, and became
Music Memories and Jazz Report]

  Cbijs 2 (1962), 5; 3 (1962), 6
  LOnjfa*

Music Memories and Jazz Report see Music
Memories: Covering All Phases of Music
Collecting

Music Mirror [1]
TNG GB452
GB–London, 1954–59
[Issues for 1957, 11 and 1958, 1, 3, 5, 7, 9, 11,
13 entitled Jazz Music Mirror; issues for 1957,
12 and 1958, 2, 4, 6, 8, 10, 12 entitled Pop
Music Mirror. Preceded by Music [3] (q.v.)]

  AB 1 (1954)–5 (1958)
  Cbijs 1 (1954), 1–5, 7, 8; 2 (1955), 1–3, 5, 7–
    12; 3 (1956), 1–4, 6–10; 4 (1957), 1–3, 5–
    11; 5 (1958), 1, 3, 5, 7, 9, 11, 13; 6 (1959),
    2, 3
  Cu 1 (1954)–2 (1955), 9; 3 (1956)–5 (1958),
    13
  EIR:Dtc 1 (1954)–4 (1957), 6
  En 1 (1954)–2 (1955), 11; 3 (1956)–5 (1958),
    13
  Lam 1 (1954), 5
  Lbl*
  LOnjfa*
  Ob*

Music Mirror [2]
TNG IN8
IN–Hathras, 1957–59

  Lio 1957, Nov; 1958, Jan–May
  Lso 1957–58

Music Monitor
GB–London, 1995–

  Lsa 1995–#

Music Monograph, Holbourne of Menstrie
Museum, University of Bath
GB–Bath, 1977–
[NOT IN BUCOMP1]

  BSdsc 1 (1977)
  Cu 1 (1977)–#

Music Monthly
GB–London, 1924–25

  AB*
  Lbl*

Music News: Disabled Living Foundation
Music Advisory Service
GB–Dartington: National Music and Disability
Information Service, 1982–?
[NOT IN BUCOMP1]

  Lam 1–10, 1982–89
  Lcml 1–10, 1982–89
  Lcs 6–9, 1987–89
  Lgsm [c (4 issues)]
  Mcm 4–9, 1985–89
  TOd 10, 1989

Music News Bulletin
TNG BG16; 0566–9197
BG–Sofia: Union of Bulgarian Composers,
1970–75; n.s. 1 (1976)–
[English edition of *Informatsionniy Muzykalny
Byuletin* (q.v.)]

Cpl 1970–#
Lbl*
Lcm*
Mcm 1972, 1–10; 1973, 1–9; 1974, 1, 2;
    1975, 6, 7; n.s. 1976–#
Ob*

Music News from Prague
TNG CS210; 0027–4410
CZ–Prague: Czech Music Fund/Český Hudební
Fond, 1964–94
[Ceased publication with 1994, nos 11/12;
succeeded by *Czech Music 95* [*96*, etc.] (q.v.)]

AB 1988, 2–1991, 10*
BSdsc*
Bu 1982–94
Cpl 1964–91*
EIR:Dtc 1973–94
En 1992–94
Lam 1983, 9, 10; 1986, 2, 3–1990; 1991, 5, 6
LAu 1967–73*
Lbar 1988, 9, 10; 1990, 9, 10; 1991, 4–10
Lbbc 1969–94*
Lbl*
Lcm 1964, 2– 9; 1965, 2–10; 1966, 1–10;
    1967, 1–10; 1968, 1–3, 5–10; 1969, 1, 3, 4,
    8–10; 1970, 1–10; 1971, 1–10; 1972, 1–10;
    1973, 1–10; 1974, 1–8; 1975–80; 1981,
    2–10; 1982–84; 1985, 1–7, 9, 10; 1986,
    1–6, 8–10; 1987, 1–4, 5, 6, 9, 10; 1988,
    1–8; 1989–91
Lcm (p) 1981, 4–6, 8–10; 1982, 2/3, 7–9;
    1983, 3–5; 1985, 9/10; 1986, 2/3, 4, 7–10;
    1987, 1–6, 9/10; 1988, 1–6, 9/10; 1989,
    1–7, 9/10; 1990, 1
Lcml 1987–94
Lgu 1975–78
Lkc 1967–78; 1979–91*
Lki 1968–94*
Lsa 1966, 7–10; 1967, 1–7, 9, 10; 1968–70;
    1971, 1–7, 9, 10; 1972–75, 5, 7–10; 1976;
    1977, 2–10; 1978–80; 1981, 2–10; 1982–
    86, 1, 4–#
Lu 1970, 1, 2, 4; 1971–88; 1989, 2–4, 7–10;
    1990–91
Mcm 1974, 8; 1975–94*
NO 1977–94
Ob*

Ouf 1964, 3–1994*
TOd 1982, 10; 1988, 5/6; 1989, 5/6; 1990,
    9/10; 1991, 5/6, 9/10
Yu 1973–91

Music Now: Australian Contemporary Music Quarterly
TNG AUS23
AUS–Sydney: International Society for
Contemporary Music, 1971–72

Cu 1 (1969/71)–2 (1972/74), 1
Lbl*
Ob*

Music of India
TNG IN5
IN–Calcutta: Calcutta Music Association, 1937–
38

Lbl*

Music of the West
TNG US586
US–Los Angeles, CA [etc.]: S. L. Russell,
1945–?61

Lcml 6 (1950), 4

Music of the Year
GB–London, 1897

Lbl*
Ob*

Music of Today *see* Fanfare: a Monthly Magazine [etc.]

Music on the South Bank
GB–London: South Bank Centre, 197?–?
[NOT IN BUCOMP1]

En 1979–85, Mar
Ob 1978*

Music Parade
NL–Hilversum, 1965–

Cu 1–8, 1965–66
Lbl*
Ob 1–6, 1965–66

Music Parade: an Illustrated Miscellany for the Music Lover
TNG GB392
GB–London: Arthur Unwin, 1946–52

    ALb 2 (1952), 6
    EIR:Dtc 2 (1952), 12
    En 1 (1946), 1; 2 (1952), 12
    Lam 1 (1946), 9; 2 (1952), 1
    Lbl*
    Lcm (p) 2 (1952), 7
    Lcml 1 (1946)–2 (1952)*
    Lu 1 (1946), 2–2 (1952), 12
    Mpl*
    Ob 1 (1946)–2 (1952), 12

Music Perception: an Interdisciplinary Journal
0730–7829
US–Berkeley, CA: University of California Press, 1983–

    BG 12 (1995), 3–#
    BRu 7 (1990), 3–8 (1990)
    BSdsc 1 (1983)–#
    Bu 1 (1983)–9 (1991)
    CDu 2 (1985), 4–#
    Cu 1 (1983)–#
    EIR:Dtc 9 (1992), 3–#
    EXu 1 (1983)–#
    KE 7 (1989), 2–#
    LAu 1 (1983)–#
    Lcml 1 (1983)–#
    Lcu 1 (1983)–#
    Lgo 1 (1983)–8 (1990), 2
    Lie 8 (1990)–#
    Lro 2 (1984)–9 (1991)
    Lu 1 (1983), 1
    NO 5 (1987)–#
    NWu 1 (1983)–4 (1986)
    Ob*
    Re 2 (1984)–3 (1985), 3
    SFu 1 (1983)–#
    SOu 1 (1983)–#
    Uu 8 (1990)–#

Music Pictorial
TNG GB484
GB–Birmingham, 1959

    Cu 1–11, 1959
    EIR:Dtc 2–11, 1959
    Lbl*

Music Psychology Index *see* **Music Therapy Index**

Music Publishers' Association Catalogue
GB–London: Music Publishers' Association, ?–
[NOT IN BUCOMP1]

    BRp [c]
    CCtc [c]
    DDp [c: microfiche version]
    Er [c] [m]
    Lbbc [c: CD–ROM version]
    Lwwb [c: microfiche version]
    Lwwbat [c: microfiche version]
    Lwwput [c: microfiche version]
    Msuc [c: microfiche version]
    Mu [c: microfiche version]
    NOp [c: CD–ROM version]
    Ouf [c: microfiche version]
    R [c]

Music Publishers' Association Newsletter
GB–London: Music Publishers' Association, ?–
[NOT IN BUCOMP1]

    Lbbc 485, 1990–#

Music Publishers' Association Printed Music Catalogue *see* **Music Publishers Association Catalogue**

The Music Publishers' Circular and Monthly Trade List
Fellinger 1968/321; TNG GB49
GB–London: M. S. Myers, 1853
[4 nos in total]

    Lbl 1853, 1–4

Music Publishers' Journal
TNG US576
US–New York: Elemo Publishing, 1943–85
[Entitled *Music Journal* (ISSN 0027–4364) from vol. 4 no. 5 (1946); ceased publication with vol. 42 no. 4 (1985)]

    BSdsc*
    Lam 17 (1959), 5
    Lcml 6 (1948), 1; 24 (1966), 1; 26 (1968), 1

The Music Pupil's Monthly Magazine
Fellinger 1968/1587; TNG GB192
GB–Bradford: J. S. Toothill, 1901
[Only one number was published]

    Lbl*

Music Reference Services Quarterly
1058–8167
US–Binghampton, NY: Haworth Press, 1992–
[NOT IN BUCOMP1]

  BSdsc 1 (1992)–#
  Ouf 1 (1992)–#

**Music Research Information Network:
Register of Music Research Students in Great
Britain and Ireland, with Thesis Titles and
General Areas of Study**
0956–263X
GB–Oxford: Music Research Information
Network, 1988–96; London: Royal College of
Music, 1997–
[NOT IN BUCOMP1]

  AB 1989–#
  BG 1989–#
  BTu [c]
  EIR:Duc 1989–#
  Er 1988–#
  KE 1990–#
  LAu 1988–#
  Lbl*
  Lcm 1988–#
  NO 1988–#
  Ob*
  Ouf 1988–#

The Music Review [1]
Fellinger 1968/2131; TNG GB257
GB–London: Riorden Press, 1912–13

  Lbl*
  Lu 1 (1912), 1–4
  Ob*

The Music Review [2]
TNG GB376; 0027–4445
GB–Cambridge: Heffers; Black Bear Press,
1940–

  AB*
  ABc 1 (1940)–47 (1986/87)
  ALb 12 (1951)–48 (1988), 1*
  Au 1 (1940)–#
  BAc 12 (1951)–#
  BDp 17 (1956)–27 (1966); 34 (1973)–42
    (1981)
  BG 2 (1941); 4 (1943)–6 (1945); 8 (1947)–#
  BLu 1 (1940)–#
  Bp 1 (1940)–#
  BRp 1 (1940)–#
  BRu 1 (1940)–# [w 28 (1967), 3; 32 (1971), 4]
  Bs 5 (1944)–#*

  BSdsc 1 (1940)–#
  BTu 33 (1972)–37 (1976)
  Bu 1 (1940)–#
  Cap 1 (1940)–#
  CCtc 1 (1940)–4 (1943); 7 (1946)–9 (1948);
    14 (1953)–27 (1966); 29 (1968)–32 (1971)
  CDCp 1 (1940)–# [w 23 (1962), 1–3]
  CDu 1 (1940)–#
  CFp 38 (1977)–#
  Cpl 1 (1940)–33 (1972)
  Cu 1 (1940)–#
  DRu 1 (1940)–#
  EIR:Dtc 1 (1940)–#
  EIR:Duc 25 (1964)–#
  EIR:MEtc 36 (1975)–#
  En 1 (1940)–#
  Ep 1 (1940)–#
  Er 1 (1940)–#
  EXu 1 (1940)–#
  Gm 1 (1940)–4 (1943); 13 (1952)–#
  Gul 1 (1940)–#
  HUu 1 (1940)–#
  Lam 1 (1940)–4 (1943), 3 [w 1 (1940), 3];
    7 (1946), 3; 8 (1947), 3–9 (1948); 10 (1949),
    2; 11 (1950), 1; 12 (1951); 14 (1953);
    17 (1956)–48 (1987), 1; 49 (1988),
    2–52 (1991), 4
  LAu 1 (1940)–# [w 5 (1944), 1; 6 (1945), 1, 2,
    4]
  Lbar 1 (1940), 4–3 (1942), 1, 3; 4 (1943), 1;
    5 (1944), 1, 3 –11 (1950); 12 (1951), 2, 4;
    15 (1954), 4; 25 (1964), 4; 26 (1965), 4;
    32 (1971), 4; 35 (1974), 4; 38 (1977), 1–3;
    39 (1978), 4
  Lbl*
  LCdM 39 (1978)–#
  Lcm 1 (1940)–#
  Lcml 1 (1940)–#
  Lcu 21 (1960)–35 (1974) [m]; 36 (1975)–51
    (1990)
  LEbc 1 (1940)–43 (1982)
  LEc 1 (1940)–41 (1980)
  Lgo 1 (1940)–#
  Lgsm 1 (1940), 2; 2 (1941), 2, 4; 6 (1945),
    2–4; 7 (1946)–15 (1954), 1; 16 (1955), 1;
    17 (1956), 2; 19 (1958), 1, 2, 4; 20 (1959),
    3, 4; 21 (1960), 2; 25 (1964), 2
  Liu 1 (1940)–#
  Lkc 1 (1940)–17 (1956); 19 (1958)–34 (1973);
    35 (1974)–36 (1975)*; 37 (1976)–#
  Lki 1 (1940)–25 (1964); 38 (1977)–#
  Lmi 21 (1960)–51 (1990), 2
  LRHBNC 1 (1940)–#
  Lsa 27 (1966)–35 (1974)
  Ltv 36 (1975)–52 (1991), 3

LVp 1 (1940)–33 (1972); 35 (1974)–#
LVu 1 (1940)–#
Mcm*
MK 31 (1970)–#
Mpl 1 (1940)–49 (1988)
Mu 1 (1940)–#
NO 1 (1940)–12 (1951); 14 (1953)–45
  (1984)NTp 1 (1940)–47 (1986)
NWu 1 (1940)–15 (1954) [m]; 16 (1955)–27
  (1966); 28 (1967)–29 (1968)*; 30 (1969)–#
Ob*
Op 37 (1976), 1, 2, 4; 38 (1977)–39 (1978);
  40 (1979), 2–4; 41 (1980), 1, 3, 4; 42
  (1981)–48 (1987), 1; 49 (1988)
Oub 46 (1985)–#
Ouf 1 (1940)–#
R 1 (1940)–47 (1986)
SA 1 (1940)–47 (1986)
SFp 27 (1966)–28 (1967); 30 (1969)–47
  (1986), 3; 49 (1988)–#
SFu 1 (1940)–#
SOu 10 (1949)–15 (1954) [m]; 23 (1962)–#
Uu 33 (1972)–47 (1986); 48 (1987)*; 49
  (1988)–#
WF 16 (1955)–38 (1977)
Yu 1 (1940)–4 (1943); 5 (1944), 4 –19 (1958);
  25 (1964)–47 (1986); 49 (1988)–#

Music Review [translated title] see Hudební
Rozhledy

Music Review [translated title] see Musiki
Mecmuasi

Music Review [translated title] see Musikrevy:
Nordisk Tidskrift för Musik och Grammofon

Music Review [translated title] see Muzicka
Revija

Music Review [translated title] see Przeglad
Muzyczny [1] and [2]

Music Scene
TNG GB563
GB–London, 1972–74

  Cu 1972–74
  EIR:Dtc 1972–74
  En 1972–74
  Ob*

Music Scene see also BMI Canada: Newsletter

Music Scholar: an Education Guide for
Young Musicians
GB–London: Rhinegold, ?1996–
[NOT IN BUCOMP1]

  AB 1996–#
  Cu 1996–#
  Lgu 1996, Mar–#

The Music School [translated title] see Ysgol
Gerddorol

Music Search see RILM Abstracts of Music
Literature

Music Seller and Radio Music Trader see The
Music Seller and Small Goods Dealer

The Music Seller and Small Goods Dealer
TNG GB321
GB–London, 1927–36
[Entitled The Music Seller and Wholesale
Publisher from 3 (1929), 5–5 (1932), 8; entitled
Music Seller and Radio Music Trader from 5
(1932), 9–9 (1936), 8. In 1932 incorporated The
Phono-Record (q.v.); in 1936 amalgamated with
The Pianomaker (q.v.)]

  AB 1 (1927)–6 (1933)
  Cu 1 (1927)–9 (1936), 8
  Lbl*
  Ob*

The Music Seller and Wholesale Publisher see
The Music Seller and Small Goods Dealer

The Music Seller Reference Book
TNG GB325
GB–London: Evans Brothers, 1927–36

  EIR:Dtc 1928/29–1932/33
  En 1927–36 [w 1929/30]
  Lbl 1927–36
  Ob*

Music Stand: the CBSO Magazine
GB–Birmingham: City of Birmingham
Symphony Orchestra, 1974–

  ALb 21, 1977
  Lcm (p) 1973–76; 1977, Mar–1979, Sep
  Lki 1974–76
  Mcm 3, 1975
  Re 1–3, 1974–75

Music Star Annual
TNG GB569
GB–London, 1973–

    Cu 1976–77
    EIR:Dtc 1976–77
    Ob*

The Music Student
Fellinger 1968/1494; TNG GB185
GB–London, 1899–1902
[42 nos in total]

    Cu 4–39, 1899–1902
    Lbl 1 (1899), 2–4 (1902), 42
    Ob*

The Music Student: the Magazine of the Home Study Union and of the Music Teachers' Association
Fellinger 1968/1926; TNG GB233
GB–London; Leeds: Home Music Study Union and Music Teachers' Association, 1908–21
[Formerly entitled *The Music Student's Magazine* (q.v.). In Sep. 1921 incorporated *The Musician* [3] (q.v.) and continued as *Music and Youth* (q.v.); supplements entitled *Chamber Music* (1913–16), *Youth and Music* [1] (1915–20). The Music Teachers' Association began its own journal, *The Music Teacher* (q.v.), in 1922]

    AB 3 (1910/11)–14 (1921/22)
    CDu 5 (1912/13)–7 (1914/15)
    Cu 5 (1912/13)–13 (1920)
    En 12 (1919/20)–14 (1921/22)
    Ep 6 (1913/14), 5–12; 7 (1914/15), 1–4
    Gm 6 (1913/14)–9 (1916/17)*
    Gul 9 (1916/17)*
    Lam 3 (1910/11), 5–5 (1912/13), 4
    Lbl*
    Lcm 7 (1914/15), 3, 9; 8 (1915/16), 5;
       10 (1917/18), 5; 12 (1919/20), 5–12;
       13 (1920/21)–14 (1921), 3
    Lcs 11 (1918/19)–12 (1919/20)
    LEbc 1 (1908/09), 1–8; 2 (1909/10), 1–8;
       3 (1910/11)–4 (1911/12), 1–11;
       5 (1912/13), 1; 7 (1914/15), 2; 8 (1915/16),
       8, 10, 11; 9 (1916/17), 1–6; 10 (1917/18),
       3; 11 (1918/19), 2, 3, 6, 12, 13;
       12 (1919/20), 1–4, 6–12; 13 (1920/21)–
       14 (1921), 3
    LEc 2 (1909/10)–14 (1921)
    Lu 4 (1911/12)–9 (1916/17)*; 14 (1921)*
    Mpl 1 (1908/09)–14 (1921)
    Ob*

The Music Student *see also* **Music and Youth**

The Music Student's Magazine
Fellinger 1968/1730; TNG GB208
GB–London, 1904–06
[Combined with *The Mandoline and Guitar* (q.v.) to form in 1907 *The Minstrel: an Illustrated Monthly Recreation for Instrumentalists and Singers* (q.v.); continued as *The Music Student: the Magazine of the Home Study Union and of the Music Teachers' Association* (q.v.)]

    Lbl*

Music Studies [translated title] *see* **Yin Yue Yen-Chiu**

Music Supervisors' Journal
Fellinger 1968/2218; TNG US431; 0027–4321
US–Reston, VA: Music Educators' National Conference, 1914–
[Entitled *Music Educators' Journal* (ISSN 0027–4321) from 1934]

    BAc 70 (1983)–78 (1991); 79 (1992), 1–9;
       80 (1993)–#
    Bs 68 (1981), 1, 8; 70 (1983), 8–75 (1988), 7
    BSdsc 53 (1966), 8–#
    Lam 39 (1952), 3–41 (1954), 4; 45 (1958), 5;
       46 (1959), 3–47 (1960), 4; 48 (1961), 1, 2
    Lcml 63 (1976)–#
    Lgo 62 (1975), 3–# [w 62 (1975), 5, 6; 68
       (1981), 3; 70 (1983), 2, 3]
    Lie 44 (1957), 3–55 (1968), 1; 62 (1975)–#
    Lmi 59 (1972)–#
    Lro 63 (1976)–#
    Msuc 72 (1985), Nov–#
    Re 36 (1949)–38 (1951); 42 (1955);
       45 (1958); 47 (1960)– 59 (1972); 61
       (1974)–62 (1975); 64 (1977)–74 (1987);
       75 (1988)–#*
    TOd 68 (1981)–#
    Uu 61 (1974)–#*

Music Survey *see* **Music-Journal**

Music Talk
GB–London, 197?–

    Lsa 47–99, 1976–77 [w 48–54, 60, 62, 66,
       68–70, 88, 96, 97]; 101–145, 1977–78 [w
       105, 112, 113, 115, 123, 125–127, 130, 135,
       136, 138, 141, 143]

Re 16 (1937)–19 (1940); 29 (1950)–
  33 (1954); 38 (1959)–#*
SFp [c (5 years)]
SFu 31 (1952)–51 (1972)
SOu 38 (1959), 6–49 (1970), 11 [w 48
  (1969), 10]
STAp 44 (1965); 47 (1968)–#
TOd 53 (1974), 10–72 (1993), 2*
Uu 51 (1972)*; 52 (1973); 53 (1974)–56
  (1977)*; 57 (1978)–62 (1983); 63 (1984)*;
  64 (1985)–#
Yu 58 (1979)–72 (1993)

Music Teacher [translated title] see Athraw
Cerddorol

The Music Teacher and Piano Student see
The Music Teacher

The Music Teacher Handbook and Pupils'
Handbook
GB–London, 1932–33
[NOT IN BUCOMP1]

  Ob 1932/33–1933/34

Music Teachers' Yearbook see British Music
Education Yearbook

Music Technology: formerly E and MM
GB–Cambridge: Music Technology, 1986–94
[NOT IN BUCOMP1. Vol. 5 (1990), 7–6
(1992), 8 entitled Music Technology: the World's
Premier Hi-Tech Music Magazine; from 1992,
Aug entitled The Music Technology Magazine
(ISSN 0957–6606); from 1993, Aug, entitled
MT: the Music Technology Magazine.
Succeeded Electronics and Music Maker (q.v.);
succeeded in 1994 by The Mix (q.v.), following
merger with Home and Studio Recording (q.v.).
Vol. 1 no. 1 (1986, Nov)–6 no. 8 (1992, July)
bore volume nos; from 1992, Aug–1993, July
bore no nos at all; 1993, Aug issue designated
issue 82, following which the title bore
successive issue nos until 91 (1994, May)]

  AB 1 (1986/87)–4 (1989/90), Jan
  BAc 1 (1986/87)–4 (1989/90), 3, 5–12;
    5 (1990/91)–91, 1994
  BSdsc 1 (1986/87)–7 (1992/93)
  Cat 1 (1986/87)–91, 1994
  CFp 4 (1989/90)
  EIR:Dtc 1 (1986/87)–3 (1988/89), 3
  Er 1 (1986/87), 1–5; 2 (1987/88), 5, 7
  Gam 1 (1986/87), 1–9; 2 (1987/88), 9–12;
    3 (1988/89)*

Lbl*
Lgo 1 (1986/87)–91, 1994
Lgsm 3 (1988/89), 2–91, 1994
Lgu 1 (1986/87)–91, 1994
Ltv 1 (1986/87); 7 (1992/93)–91, 1994
Ob 1 (1986/87)–91, 1994
Oub 1 (1986/87)–91, 1994
SFp 1 (1986/87); 5 (1990/91)–91, 1994

Music Theory Spectrum: the Journal of the
Society for Music Theory
0195–6167
US–Los Angeles, CA [etc.]: Society for Music
Theory, 1979–

  BG 17 (1995)–#
  BSdsc 1 (1979)–#
  CDu 1 (1979)–#
  Cu 1 (1979)–#
  EIR:Dtc 8 (1986)–#
  EXu 1 (1979)–#
  HUu 14 (1992)–#
  LAu 1 (1979)–#
  Lkc 1 (1979)–#
  LRHBNC 7 (1985)–#
  LVu 2 (1980)–#
  Mu 13 (1991)–#
  NO 1 (1979)–7 (1985)
  Ob*
  Ouf 1 (1979)–#
  R 1 (1979)–10 (1988)
  SOu 1 (1979)–#
  Uu 1 (1979)–#

Music Therapy: the Journal of the American
Association for Music Therapy
0734–7367
US–New York: American Association for Music
Therapy, 1981–
[NOT IN BUCOMP1]

  BSdsc 4 (1984), 1; 5 (1985)–#
  SFu 6 (1986)–11 (1992)

Music Therapy Index: an International
Interdisciplinary Index to the Literature of
the Psychology, Psychophysiology,
Psychophysics and Sociology of Music
0145–6164
US–Phoenix, Arizona [etc.]: Institute for
Therapeutics Research, 1976–
[NOT IN BUCOMP1; later entitled Music
Psychology Index (ISSN 0195–5802)]

  BSdsc*
  Lki 3 (1984)
  Mu*

Music Therapy Perspectives
0734–6875
US–Washington, DC: National Association for
Music Therapy, 1982–
[NOT IN BUCOMP1]

> **BSdsc***

Music Today
HK–Hong Kong: Tom Lee, 1986–
[NOT IN BUCOMP1]

> **Lbl***

**Music Today: Journal of the International
Society for Contemporary Music**
TNG INTL11
GB–London: Dennis Dobson [for the
International Society for Contemporary Music],
1949
[Only one issue published]

> **AB** 1 (1949)
> **BRu** 1 (1949)
> **BSdsc** 1 (1949)
> **BTu** 1 (1949)
> **Cpl** 1 (1949)
> **Cu** 1 (1949)
> **En** 1 (1949)
> **Gm** 1 (1949)
> **HUu** 1 (1949)
> **Lam** 1 (1949)
> **Lbl** 1 (1949)
> **Lcml** 1 (1949)
> **Lu** 1 (1949)
> **Mpl** 1 (1949)
> **Ob** 1 (1949)

The Music Trade
Fellinger 1968/2293; TNG GB271
GB–London, 1917–18

> **Lbl***

The Music Trade Directory *see* **The Music
Trade Directory and Guide**

The Music Trade Directory *see also* **The
British, Colonial and Foreign Trade Directory**

The Music Trade Directory and Guide
TNG GB514; 0077–2453
GB–London: Tofts and Wolff, 1964–
[NOT IN BUCOMP1; entitled *The Music Trade
Directory* from vol. 3 (1968/69); entitled *Music
Trades International Directory* (TNG GB262)
from 1975–78; entitled *MTI Buyers Guide,*

Directory and Year Book (ISSN 0143–2575)
from 1979–81; entitled *Music World Directory*
(ISSN 0265–6094; published London: Turret
Press) from 1981; entitled *The Music World
Directory and Yearbook* from 1983]

> **BSdsc***
> **Lbl***
> **Mu** 1968–81
> **Ob** 1964–

Music Trade ICC Financial Survey
0951–7073
GB–?London, ?1973–
[NOT IN BUCOMP1]

> **BSdsc** 15 (1987)–#

The Music Trades Diary
Fellinger 1968/1541; TNG GB89
GB–London, 1900–
[From 1938 entitled *The Music Trades Review
Reference Book*; issued in connection with *The
London and Provincial Music Trades Review*
(q.v.)]

> **Lbl*** [w 1906, 1907, 1914, 1915, 1919, 1937]

Music Trades International *see* **Music World:
the Definitive Music Trade Magazine**

Music Trades International Directory *see* **The
Music Trade Directory and Guide**

Music Trades International Yearbook
TNG GB262
GB–London: Trade Papers, ?1971–

> **AB** 1985; 1986
> **Mcm** 1974–79
> **Ob***

The Music Trades Pocket Directory
GB–London, 1889–94

> **Ob***

The Music Trades' Record
Fellinger 1968/2082; TNG GB252
GB–Richmond, 1911–12

> **Lbl***

The Music Trades' Review *see* **The London
and Provincial Music Trades Review**

The Music Trades Review Reference Book *see*
The Music Trades Diary

Music Week [1]
0265–1548
GB–London: Spotlight Publications, ?1971–
[NOT IN BUCOMP1; preceded by *Record Retailer and Music Industry News* (q.v.). Subtitles include *For Everyone in the Business of Music*.]

AB*
BEp [c (6 months)]
BLp [c]
BOL [c (6 weeks)]
BRp [c (2 years)]
BSdsc 1988–#
CDCp [c (5 years)]
CFp [c (3 months)]
CH [c (3 months)]
CHEp [c (1 year)]
Cu*
DDp [c]
DS [c (6 months)]
DU [c (3 months)]
EK 1994–#
En*
Ep 1990–#
Gm 1975, Sep–#*
HE [c (6 months)]
IP [c (6 months)]
Lam 1993–#*
Lba [c (1 year)
Lbar [c]
Lbbc 1971–#
Lbk [c (1 year)]
Lbl*
LCdM 1994–#
Lcml 1987. Oct–#
Lcml (m) [c (6 months)]
Lcml (p) [c (6 months)]
LEc [c (1 year)]
Len [c (6 months)]
Lgr (p) [c (6 months)]
Lha (f) [c (2 years)]
Lhg 1991–#
Lhr [c]
LIp [c (1 year)]
Lis [c (1 year)]
Lk [c (3 months)]
Lk (b) [c (3 months)]
Lk (c) [c]
Lk (nk) [c (3 months)]
Lri [c – intermittent]
Lsa 1970–#*
Lsut [c (6 months)]
Lwwb [c]
Lwwbat [c]

Lwwput [c]
LXp [c (2 issues)]
MP [c]
Msuc [c (2 years)]
NHp [c (1 year)]
NOp [c (4 years)]
NTp [c (1 year)]
Ob 1983–
OL [c]
PRp [c (3 months)]
Rp [c]
SFp [c (1 year)]
SHRp [c]
SK [c (1 year)]
WCp (s) [c (1 year)]
WH [c (6 months)]
WOp [c]

Music Week [2]
AUS–Melbourne, 1972–?

Lsa 1 (1972/73), 1–26; 2 (1973/74), 1–11

Music Week Masterfile
0950–6748
GB–London: United Magazines, 1986–
[NOT IN BUCOMP1; entitled *Music Master Masterfile* from 207, 1991; entitled *Music Master* from 216, 1991]

AB 1988–90
Cu 1986, Oct–1990, Nov
EIR:Dtc 1986, Oct–1990, Nov; 1991, 207–#
Lbl*
Lk 1987–#
Lk (c) [c]
Ob*

Music Week's European Trade Commentary
see Europe Etc.: Music Week's European Trade Commentary

Music World
TNG EIRE6
EIRE–Dublin, 1951–52

Lcml 1951, May–Aug

Music World: the Definitive Music Trade Magazine
0263–6956
GB–London: Turret Press, 1979–
[Incorporating *Music Trades International* (ISSN 0305–7178)]

AB 3 (1981), 7–7 (1986), 6
BSdsc*

Cu 3 (1981), 7–7 (1986), 8
En 1 (1979)–#*
Gm 6 (1985), 12–7 (1986), 7
Lbl 3 (1981), 9–#
Lgu 5 (1983), 3–7 (1986), 8
Mcm*
Mpl [c]

Music World and Superstar *see* The Official
Partridge Magazine

Music World Directory [and Yearbook] *see*
The Music Trade Directory and Guide

The Music Yearbook
TNG GB564; 0306–5928
GB–London: Rhinegold, 1972–
[Entitled the *British Music Yearbook* from 1975]

ABc 1975–87; 1992
ABDp [c]
BAc [c]
Bp 1972–#
BRp 1975–#
BRu 1973
BSdsc*
BTu 1972–1975; 1980; 1983; 1985; 1987;
    1989; 1991; 1994–# [purchased every third
    year only]
Bu 1976; 1980; 1983–#
Cat [c]
CDu 1991–#
EIR:Dtc 1972; 1973; 1976–#
En 1972–#
Ep 1972–#
Er 1972–#
Gul 1972–74; 1975–#
HUu 1972; 1977–85
Je [c]
KE 1972–73; 1976; 1977; 1982–92
Lam [c]
LAu 1972–74; 1976; 1980–82; 1984–#
Lba [c]
Lbbc 1972–#; second copy [c]
Lbl*
Lbo [c]
Lcu 1972–90*; 1991–#
Lgo [c]
Lgu [c]
Lhr [c]
Lis [c]
Lk 1972–78; 1980–#
Lri [c – intermittent]
Lu 1975–#
Lwwb [c]

Lwwbat [c]
Lwwput [c]
Mcm 1972–#
Msu 1975; 1977; 1978; 1984; 1985; 1990
Msuc [c]
NO 1972; 1974; 1975–#
NTp 1972–#
Ob*
Ouf [c (2 years)]
R 1972; 1975; 1980–85; 1987; 1988; 1992
SA 1972; 1975–#
SFp [c]
SFu 1972–#
SLGu 1972; 1975–89
SOu 1976; 1980/81; 1984; 1989; [c]
WW [c]
Yu 1972–74

Musica [1]
Fellinger 1968/1635; TNG F335
F–Paris: P. Lafitte, 1902–14
[143 numbers published in 13 vols]

Gm 2 (1903)–13 (1914)
Lbbc 4 (1905)–5 (1906); 8 (1909)–9 (1910)
Lcm (p) 1 (1902), May; 2 (1903), Mar–Sep,
    Nov, Dec; 3 (1904), Jan–Mar, May–Nov;
    5 (1906), Nov; 8 (1909), Feb; 10 (1911),
    Feb, Oct; 13 (1914), Mar
Ob*
SFu 1 (1902)–10 (1911)

Musica [2]
TNG E87
E–Barcelona: Consejo Central de la Musica,
1938

Cpl 1938, 1–4
Ep 1938, 1–5
Lu 1938, 5

Musica [3]
TNG I213
I–Florence, 1942–43

Bu 2 (1943)
Cu 1 (1942)–2 (1943)
LAu 2 (1943)
Lu 1 (1942)–2 (1943)
Ob*

Musica [4]
I–Milan: Edizioni Diapason, 1977–

AB 11, 1979; 23, 1981–#
Lam 11, 1979
Lsa 1, 1977–#

Musica: Archiv für Musikwissenschaft, Geschichte, Aesthetik und Literatur der heiligen und profanen Tonkunst
Fellinger 1968/543; TNG I43
I–Bressanone: A. Weger, 1866–68
[Only two volumes were published]

Lbl 1 (1866)–2 (1868)
Lu 1 (1866)
Ob 1 (1866) [Reprint ed.]

Musica: Boletin
1010-4615
CU–Havana: Casa de las Americas, 196?–?
[NOT IN BUCOMP1]

Lbl 23–28, 30–33, 35–43, 55–70, 79–#
Lu 80, 1980; 94/95–106, 1982–85; 108–112/113, 1988; 115, 1989

Musica: Rassegna della Vita Musicale Italiana
TNG I217
I–Milan, 1945–
[From 1946 entitled *Musica e Dischi: Rassegna Musicale Internazionale*]

Lsa 7 (1951)–21 (1965); 23 (1967)–40 (1984); 45 (1989)–47 (1991); 49 (1993)–#*

Musica: Revista Trimestral de los Conservatorios y de la Seccion de Musicología Contemporánea del Instituto Español de Musicología del CSIC
TNG E94; 0541–4040
E–Madrid: Instituto Español de Musicología del Consejo Superior de Investigaciones Cientificas, 1952–55

Lcml 6, 10, 12–14, 1953–55

Musica: Rivista Internazionale
TNG I219
I–Rome, 1946–

Cpl 2 (1947), 1, 5–8
Lcml 2 (1947)*
Lu 2 (1947), 1, 5, 6

Musica: Zweimonatsschrift
TNG D821; 0027–4518
D/CH–Kassel; Basel: Bärenreiter, 1947–
[Incorporated supplements as follows: *Practica für Haus- und Jugendmusik, Chorwesen und Musikerziehung*; *Musica Schallplatte* (q.v.); and *Phonoprisma*; see also *Collegium Musicum: Blätter zur Pflege der Haus- und Kammermusik*]

ALb 30 (1976), 5
BG 13 (1959)–22 (1968)
Cpl 1 (1947), 1; 7 (1953), 5; 13 (1959), 7, 8; 15 (1961), 2
DRu 13 (1959)–22 (1968)*
En 33 (1979), 4; 34 (1980)–#
Gul 15 (1961)–27 (1973)
Lam 12 (1958), 7/8; 13 (1959), 7/8; 18 (1964), 1–6; 20 (1966), 1–6; 25 (1971), 1, 2, 4–6
LAu 1 (1947), 5, 6; 3 (1949), 5, 7–12; 4 (1950)–22 (1968); 28 (1974), 2–6; 29 (1975)–#
Lbl*
Lcm 13 (1959), 6–11; 14 (1960)–16 (1962), 3, 6; 17 (1963), 1–6
Lcml 1 (1947)–4 (1950); 5 (1951)–6 (1952)*; 7 (1953); 8 (1954)–12 (1958)*; 23 (1969)–#
Lgsm 7 (1953), 2; 28 (1974), 4
Lu 1 (1947), 1–6; 2 (1948), 1, 2, 6; 3 (1949), 1; 4 (1950)–5 (1951); 7 (1953), 5; 9 (1955)–23 (1969); 29 (1975)–#
LVp 8 (1954)–19 (1965)
Ob*
Ouf 7 (1953), 5–30 (1976), 6*
R 12 (1958), 7, 8

Musica Antiqua: Acta Scientifica *see* **Musica Antiqua: Europae Orientalis**

Musica Antiqua: Actuele Informatie over Oude Muziek
0771-7016
B–Peer: Vlaams Centrum voor Oude Muziek, 1983–
[NOT IN BUCOMP1]

Ob 6 (1989)–

Musica Antiqua: Europae Orientalis
0239-9539
PL–Bydgoszcz, 1966–
[From 2 (1969) entitled *Musica Antiqua: Acta Scientifica*]
[NOT IN BUCOMP1]

Lu 6 (1982)–7 (1985)

Musica Asiatica
0140-6078
GB–Cambridge: Cambridge University Press, 1977–

AB 5 (1988)–6 (1991)
BG 1 (1977)–#
BSdsc 2 (1979)–#

Cpl 1 (1977)–#
DRu 1 (1977)–#
Er 1 (1977)–#
Lcml 1 (1977)–#
Lso 1 (1977)–#
Mu 1 (1977)–4 (1984)
NO 1 (1977)–4 (1984)
Ob*
Ouf 1 (1977)–6 (1991)
Yu 1 (1977)–3 (1981)

Musica de Raiz
E–: 1994–?
[NOT IN BUCOMP1]

Lcs 1, 1994–#

Musica Disciplina see Journal of Renaissance and Baroque Music

Musica Divina
D–Regensburg: Regensburger–Institut für Musikforschung, 1950–66

Lbl*

Musica Divina: Monatsschrift für Kirchenmusik
Fellinger 1968/2179; TNG A175
A–Vienna: Universal Edition, 1913–38
[Preceded 1902–13 by Gregorianische Rundschau: Monatsschrift für Kirchenmusik und Liturgie (published A–Graz). Succeeded by Die Kirchenmusik: Zeitschrift des Allgemeinen Cäcilien-Vereins für Deutschland, Österreich und die Schweiz (q.v.)]

EIR:MEtc 1 (1913)–9 (1922)*

Musica d'Oggi: Rassegna di Vita e di Cultura Musicale
TNG I168 (1919–42); TNG I249 (1958–65); 0580–2962 (n.s.)
I–Milan: Ricordi, 1919–42; n.s. 1958–65

Cpl 15 (1933), 8; 17 (1935), 12–22 (1940), 5
Cu 1 (1919)–22 (1940); n.s. 1 (1958)–8 (1965)
Er n.s. 1 (1958), 1, 2, 4, 5, 8–10; 2 (1959), 1, 2, 4, 6–8; 3 (1960), 2, 3
Lam n.s. 2 (1959), 1; 4 (1961), 3, 4
LAu n.s. 2 (1959), 3
Lbl*
Lcm n.s. 3 (1960), 10; 4 (1961), 1, 2; 5 (1962), 4–6; 7 (1964), 4, 6, 10; 8 (1965), 1–4, 6, 8–10
Lcml 5 (1923); 11 (1929); 14 (1932)–19 (1937)*; n.s. 2 (1959)–8 (1965)*

Lsa n.s. 3 (1960)–5 (1962), 3; 6 (1963), 1, 6
Lu 10 (1928)–13 (1931)*; 14 (1932)–15 (1933); 16 (1934)–20 (1937)*; 21 (1939); 22 (1940)–25 (1943)*; n.s. 1 (1958); 2 (1959)*; 3 (1960); 4 (1961)*; 5 (1962)–8 (1965)
Ob 1 (1919)–19 (1937) [w 17 (1935), 1]; n.s. 1 (1958)–3 (1960); 7 (1964)*; 8 (1965)
Ouf (Howes) 17 (1935), 8/9; 18 (1936), 7; 20 (1938), 6, 7

Musica e Dischi see Musica: Rassegna della Vita Musicale Italiana

Musica e Dossier
I–Florence: Giunti Barbera, 1986–
[NOT IN BUCOMP1]

Lu 24, 1988
Ob 59, 1993–#

Musica e Musicisti, Gazzetta Musicale di Milano see Gazzetta Musicale di Milano

Musica Hebraica
TNG ISRAEL2
IL–Jerusalem: S. Levi, 1938
[NOT IN BUCOMP1]

Cpl 1, 2, 1938

Musica Jazz: Rassegna Mensile di Informazione e Critica Musicale
TNG I216; 0027–4542
I–Milan, 1945–80

Cbijs 1952–58; 1964–69*

Musica Judaica: Journal of the American Society for Jewish Music
TNG US857; 0147–7536
US–New York: American Society for Jewish Music, 1976–

BSdsc 3 (1980/81)–#
Cu 1 (1975/76)–#
Lgo 2 (1978)–#

Musica Medii Aevi: Zakład Historii i Teorii Muzyki [= The Department of Music History and Theory]
0077–247X
PL–Kraków: Instytut Sztuki Polskiej Akademii Nauk, 1965–

BSdsc*
Cu 3 (1969)–#
Ob*

Musica/Realtà
I–Milan: Edizioni Unicopli, 1980–
[NOT IN BUCOMP1. Each issue has a separate
ISBN]

Ouf 8 (1987), 22, 24–10 (1989), 30; 11
(1990), 33–12 (1991), 36

Musica Sacra [1]
D–Berlin, 1850–52

Lbl*

Musica Sacra [2]
Fellinger 1968/858; TNG B30
B–Bruges: Desclée de Brouwer [for the Sint-
Gregorius-Vereniging], 1881–1914; 1927–40;
1946–64
[Entitled Musica Sacra "Sancta Sancte" from
1946]

Cpl 35 (1928), 3
Lu 11 (1891)–15 (1895)*

Musica Sacra: A Katolikus Egyhazzenei Élet
[= World of Catholic Sacred Music]
H–Veszprém, 1987–
[NOT IN BUCOMP1]

Ob 1 (1987)–#*

Musica Sacra: Beiträge zur Reform und
Förderung der katholischen Kirchen-Musik
Fellinger 1968/586; TNG D182
D–Regensburg: F. Pustet, 1868–1921; 1925–29
[In 1929 combined with Fliegende Blätter für
katholische Kirchenmusik (q.v.) to form
Cäcilienvereinsorgan/Musica Sacra]

Lu 1893–95*

Musica Sacra: Revue du Chant Liturgique et
de la Musique Religieuse
Fellinger 1968/685; TNG F153
F–Toulouse, 1874–84; 1887–1901

Lu 12 (1890)–16 (1894)*

Musica Sacra: Rivista Bimestrale
Fellinger 1968/745; TNG I243
I–Milan, 1877–
[NOT IN BUCOMP1]

Er 90 (1966), 6
Lu 90 (1966), 6

Musica Sacra: Zeitschrift der Allgemeinen
Cäcilienverbandes für den Ländern der
deutschen Sprache see Fliegende Blätter für
katholische Kirchenmusik

Musica Sacra "Sancta Sancte" see Musica
Sacra [2]

Musica Schallplatte
TNG D1011
D/US–Kassel; New York: Bärenreiter, 1958–67
[From 1962 entitled Phonoprisma: Zeitschrift
für Freunde der Schallplatte und des
Tonbandes; a supplement to Musica:
Zweimonatsschrift (q.v.)]

DRu 2 (1959)–9 (1966)
Gul 5 (1962)
Lsa 1 (1958)–4 (1961), 6; 5 (1962)–10 (1967)
[w 9 (1966)]

Musica Università: Periodico Quindizinale di
Cultura e Informazioni Musicali
TNG I263
I–Rome: Istituzione Universitaria dei Concerti
dell'Università Roma, ?1963–?76
[A further publication, Notiziario Musica, was
issued as a supplement]

Lcm 2 (1964), 3, 5, 12
Lsa 1 (1963), 1, 3; 2 (1964), 2–6, 9–12; 3
(1965), 4, 11; 4 (1966), 1–5; 5 (1967), 1–6;
Notiziario Musica 4 (1966)–14 (1976)*

Musica Viva
D–Munich, 1945–

Lam 1969, 5–1990, 5*
Ouf 1969, 5–1990, 2

Musica Viva: Revue Trimestrielle
TNG B104
B–Brussels [etc.]: Ars Viva, 1933–36

Cpl 1933, 3; 1936, 1
LAu 1936, 1, 2

Musica Viva: Zborník Muzikologických
Stúdii [= Journal of Musicological Studies]
SQ–Bratislava: Opus, 1980–

Cu 1 (1980)–#
Lbl*
Ob*

Musical Accent see Fanfare: a Monthly
Magazine [etc.]

Musical Adviser: Organ of the Łodz Institute
for Folk Music [translated title] see Poradnik
Muzyczny: Organ Ludowego Instytutu
Muzycznego

The Musical Age [1]
Fellinger 1968/1442; TNG GB178
GB–Glasgow; London: Bayley and Ferguson,
1898–99; n.s. 1900–04 [see following entry]

En 1–8, 1898–99
Gm 1–15, 1898–99
Lbl*
Ob 1–8, 1898–99

The Musical Age [2]
Fellinger 1968/1543; TNG GB190
GB–Glasgow; London, 1900–04

Gm 1–60, 1900–04
Lbl*

The Musical Age see also Freund's Weekly

The Musical Age and Journal of Elocution
Fellinger 1968/1141; TNG GB135
GB–Hull, 1890–92
[Wrapper title is Yorkshire Musical Age and
Journal of Elocution]

Lbl 1 (1890), 1
Mpl 3 (1892)

The Musical Amateur: a Monthly Chronicle
of Musical Events
Fellinger 1968/439; TNG GB57
GB–Liverpool, 1861
[Only one published]

Lbl 1 (1861), 1
Ob 1 (1861), 1

Musical America
Fellinger 1968/1443; TNG US299; 0735–777X;
0735–6692
US–New York: ABC Consumer Magazine,
1898–1964; 1987–91
[From 1965–86 incorporated into High Fidelity
[1] (q.v.), and entitled Hi-Fi/Musical America]

BSdsc*
Cpl 59 (1939), 14
Lcm*
Lcml 58 (1938)–62 (1942)*
Lsa 88 (1968)–90 (1970); 94 (1974)–95
    (1975)
Lu 63 (1943)–84 (1964), 10
LVp 76 (1956)–84 (1964)
Mpl 74 (1954)–84 (1964)

Musical America International Directory of
the Performing Arts
0735–7788
US–Hightstown, NJ: K–III Directory
Corporation, ?1980–
[NOT IN BUCOMP1]

BSdsc*
Ob 1989; 1992
Ouf [c]

Musical Analysis
TNG US819; 1830–2545
US–Denton, TX, 1972–74
[Ceased publication with vol. 2 no. 2 (1974);
preceded by Musical Happening (q.v.)]

BSdsc 1 (1972)–2 (1974), 2
Lgo 1 (1972)–2 (1974)
Lkc 1 (1972)–2 (1974)

The Musical and Dramatic Courier see The
Musical and Sewing Machine Gazette

Musical and Dramatic Review see Boosey's
Musical and Dramatic Review

The Musical and Dramatic World
Fellinger 1968/859; TNG GB99
GB– Liverpool, 1881–83; n.s. 1883

Lbl*

The Musical and Sewing Machine Courier see
The Musical and Sewing Machine Gazette

The Musical and Sewing Machine Gazette
Fellinger 1968/823; TNG US153
US–New York: Howard Rockwood, 1880–1962
[From 1880, 4, The Musical and Sewing
Machine Courier; from 1880, 9, The Musical
Machine Courier; from 1880, 41, The Musical and
Dramatic Courier; from 1884, 24, The Musical
Courier; from 1961, Feb, The Musical Courier
and Review of Recorded Music; in Oct. 1961
incorporated The Music Magazine (TNG
US717) to form The Music Magazine and
Musical Courier]

Bu 52 (1906)–71 (1915) [w 69 (1914)]
Lam 143 (1951), 10, 11; 144 (1951), 2–7, 9;
    145 (1952), 1–11; 146 (1952), 1–9; 147
    (1953), 2–11; 148 (1953), 1, 2; 149 (1954),
    4, 6, 7; 150 (1954), 4–8; 151 (1955), 2; 152
    (1955), 4, 5, 7; 153 (1956), 3
Lcm (p)*
Lsa 91 (1925)–96 (1928)*; 102 (1931)

Musical Answers: a Treasury of Informing
and Entertaining Literature for Every Lover
of the Divine Art
Fellinger 1968/1311; TNG GB165
GB–London, 1895–1900

Lbl*
Mpl 1895–99
Ob*

The Musical Antiquary
Fellinger 1968/1985; TNG GB240
GB–Oxford: H. Frowde, Oxford University
Press, 1909–13

AB*
Au 1 (1909/10)–4 (1912/13) [Reprint ed.]
BG 1 (1909/10)–4 (1912/13)
BLu 1 (1909/10)–4 (1912/13)
BSdsc 1 (1909/10)–4 (1912/13)
Bu 1 (1909/10)–4 (1912/13)
CCtc 1 (1909/10)–4 (1912/13)
CDu 1 (1909/10)–3 (1911/12)
Cpl 1 (1909/10)–4 (1912/13)
Cu 1 (1909/10)–4 (1912/13)
DRu 1 (1909/10)–4 (1912/13)
EIR:Dtc 1 (1909/10)–4 (1912/13), Apr
EIR:MEtc 1 (1909/10)–4 (1912/13)*
En 1 (1909/10)–4 (1912/13)
Ep 1 (1909/10)–4 (1912/13)
Er 1 (1909/10)–4 (1912/13)
Gm 1 (1909/10)–4 (1912/13)
Gul 1 (1909/10)–4 (1912/13)
Lam 1 (1909/10)–4 (1912/13)
Lbl*
Lcm 1 (1909/10)–4 (1912/13)
Lcml 1 (1909/10)–4 (1912/13)
Lcs 1 (1909/10)–4 (1912/13)
LEbc 1 (1909/10)–4 (1912/13)
Lgsm 1 (1909/10)–4 (1912/13)
Lkc 1 (1909/10)–4 (1912/13)
Lu 1 (1909/10)–4 (1912/13)
LVu 1 (1909/10)–4 (1912/13)
Mcm 1 (1909/10)–4 (1912/13)
Mpl 1 (1909/10)–4 (1912/13)
Mu 1 (1909/10)–4 (1912/13) [Reprint ed.]
NO 1 (1909/10)–4 (1912/13)
NWu 1 (1909/10)–4 (1912/13)
Ob 1 (1909/10)–4 (1912/13)
Ouf 1 (1909/10)–4 (1912/13)
R 1 (1909/10)–4 (1912/13)
SA 1 (1909/10), 2–4 (1912/13)
SFu 1 (1909/10)–4 (1912/13)
Yu 1 (1909/10)–4 (1912/13) [Reprint ed.]

Musical Archive [translated title] see Hudobny
Archív

The Musical Artists', Lecturers' and
Entertainers' Guide and Entrepreneurs'
Directory
GB–London, 1884–87

Lbl*
Ob*

The Musical Athenaeum: or Nature and Art,
Music and Musicians, in Germany, France,
Italy, England, and other parts of Europe
Fellinger 1968/200; TNG GB29; Langley,
p. 611
GB–London: Simpkin, Marshall and Co. [etc.],
1842
[Only four numbers were published under this
title, which was a musical supplement to
Mainzer's Musical Times and Singing Circular
(q.v.)]

Lbl 1842, 1–4

The Musical Bee: Forming a Monthly Hive, or
Collection of the "Choicest Flowers" of
Melody
GB–London, 1842–50
[NOT IN BUCOMP1]

Lbl*
Lu 1 (1842)–9 (?1850), 4

The Musical Bijou
GB–London, 1872–73

Lbl*

The Musical Bijou: an Album of Music,
Poetry and Prose
Langley, p. 48; Fellinger 1986, p. 910–48
GB–London: Goulding and D'Almaine, 1829–
51
[NOT IN BUCOMP1]

Cpl 1829–30; 1832
Lbl*

Musical Box Annual
GB–London: Amalgamated Press, 1935–36
[NOT IN BUCOMP1]

En 1936
Lbl 1935

The Musical Box Society: International
Bulletin
TNG US684; 1058–7241; 1045–795X
US–Springfield, MA: Musical Box Society,
194?–

> **Cu** 13 (1956), 2–21 (1964), 2*
> **Lsa** 19 (1962)–#*

Musical Box Society News Bulletin
0732–7897
US–St Paul, MN: Musical Box Society, 1974–
[NOT IN BUCOMP1; known also as *MBS News
Bulletin*]

> **Lsa** 1 (1974)–# [w 23–27, 1978–79; 37,
> 1980]

Musical Britain
TNG GB365
GB–London, 1938

> **En** 1, 1938
> **Lbl***
> **Ob***

**Musical Bulletin: a Journal Devoted Entirely
to Music**
Fellinger 1968/799; TNG US137
US–Chicago, IL: Hershey School of Musical
Art, 1879–83

> **Ob***

**The Musical Cabinet: a Monthly Collection of
Vocal and Instrumental Music and Musical
Literature**
US–Boston, MA, 1841–42

> **Cu** [m]
> **Mu** [m]

**Musical Canada: a Monthly Journal of
Musical News, Comment and Gossip, for
Professionals and Amateurs** *see* **The Violin: a
Monthly Journal of Musical News**

Musical Chat
TNG GB328
GB–Leeds, 1929–31

> **Lbl***

**Musical Chat and Northern Counties Musical
Echo**
Fellinger 1968/1731; TNG GB204
GB–Leeds, 1904–05

> **Lbl***
> **Ob***

Musical Chronicle [translated title] *see*
Muzykal'naya Letopis: Stati i Materialy

Musical Composition [translated title] *see* **Yin
Yue Chuang Zuo**

The Musical Courier
Fellinger 1968/1265; TNG GB162
GB–London: Musical Courier, 1894–?1903
[Entitled *London Musical Courier* from 1897,
with new numbering sequence]

> **Lbl***
> **Ob***

**The Musical Courier [and Review of
Recorded Music]** *see* **The Musical and Sewing
Machine Gazette**

Musical Denmark
TNG DK85; 0027–4585
DK–Copenhagen: Danske Selskab, 1952–

> **AB** 1990–#
> **CCtc** 1989–#
> **Cpl** 1954; 1964; 1978–#
> **Cu** 1973–#
> **En** 1969/70–#
> **Ep** 1986; 1988; 1990/91–#
> **Gam** 1985–87; 1989/90–#
> **Gm** 1976/77–#
> **HUu** 1981/82–#
> **KE** 1987
> **Lam** 1966; 1981/82; 1988; 1990; 1992–#
> **Lbar** 1988–#
> **Lbbc** 1989–#*
> **Lbl***
> **Lcm** 1988–#
> **Lsa** 1953–54; 1988–#
> **Lu** 1983; 1987
> **Mpl** 1978–79
> **Mu** 1988–90
> **Ob***
> **Ouf** 1978–#*
> **TOd** 1987; 1991

Musical Denmark Yearbook
DK–Copenhagen: Musical Denmark, 1994–
[NOT IN BUCOMP1]

> **Cu** 1994–#

The Musical Digest [1]
TNG US468
US–New York: Musical Digest, 1920–48
[Ceased publication with vol. 30 (1948/49), 9]

Lcml 29 (1947)–30 (1948)*
Mcm 30 (1948), 1

The Musical Digest [2]
TNG GB401
GB–London: St Kevin's Press, 1947–51
[From 1948, 8, entitled *The London Musical Digest*; in 1951 amalgamated with *Theatre Digest* (q.v.) to form *Music and Theatre Digest: Union of "Musical Digest" and "Theatre Digest"* (q.v.)]

AB 1–15, 1947–50
Cu 2–17, 1947–51
Lam 1, 1947; 10–12, 1950; 17, 1951
Lbl*
Lcm 1–15, 1947–50
Lcm (p) 17, 1951
Lcml 1–13, 1947–50
LVp 1–14, 1947–50 [w 2, 3, 5, 6, 10, 11, 13]
Ob*

The Musical Director
GB–London, 1921–?

Mcm 1922, 3

Musical Directory [Annual and Almanack] *see* Musical Directory, Register and Almanack, and Royal Academy of Music Calendar

Musical Directory, Register and Almanack, and Royal Academy of Music Calendar
Fellinger 1968/322; TNG GB48
GB–London: Rudall, Rose, Carte and Company, 1853–1931
[Entitled *Musical Directory, Register and Almanack* from 1855; from 1870, *Musical Directory, Annual and Almanack*; from 1918, *Musical Directory*]

Bp 1909–31 [w 1920]
BSdsc*
En 1882; 1891–92; 1896–1924; 1926–31
Ep 1916–17; 1919–29; 1931
Gul (e) 1856; 1866
Lbl*
Lcml 1928–29
LEbc 1928–30
Ob*

Musical Education [translated title] *see* Muzykal'noye Obrazovaniye

Musical Education: a Monthly Review *see* The Journal of Trinity College

The Musical Educator
?GB–?London, 1895–96
[NOT IN BUCOMP1]

Lam (o) 1–5, 1895–96

The Musical Era
Fellinger 1968/1785; TNG GB213
GB–London: Musical Reform Association, 1905–10

Lbl*

Musical Europe
TNG GB431
GB–London, 1949–?

Gm 1 (1949/50), 1, 2
Lam 1 (1949/50), 2
Lcml 1 (1949/50), 1

Musical Events: Comprehensive Musical Guide *see* London Musical Events

Musical Events in Czechoslovakia
CZ–Prague, 1975–

Ob*

The Musical Examiner: an Impartial Weekly Record of Music and Musical Events
Fellinger 1968/201; TNG GB30; Langley, p. 614
GB–London: Wessel and Stapleton, 1842–44
[Ceased publication with no. 112, 1844, Dec 21]

AB 1–57, 1842–43
BSdsc 1–112, 1842–44
Cu 1–112, 1842–44 [w 109]
EIR:Dtc 1–112, 1842–44
Gul (e) 1–51, 1842–43
Lbl 1–112, 1842–44
Lcm 5–97, 1842–44 [w 7–13, 16, 22, 55, 58, 61, 73, 75–77, 87, 88, 94–96]
Ob 1–112, 1842–44

The Musical Examiner: Journal of the Galin-
Paris-Chévé School of Music
Fellinger 1968/721; TNG GB87
GB–London, 1876–79; n.s. 1879

En 1–6, 1876–77; 28–30, 1879
Lbl 1, 1876
Ob*

The Musical Exchange Journal and Dramatic
Observer
Fellinger 1968/1266; TNG GB163
GB–London: Simpkin, Marshall, Hamilton,
Kent and Company, 1894–95
[34 nos in total]

Lbl*

Musical Expressions
1353–4637
GB–Dukinfield: Musical Expressions, 1994–
[NOT IN BUCOMP1]

Lbl*

Musical Fare see Fanfare: a Monthly
Magazine [etc.]

The Musical Gazette
Fellinger 1968/1495; TNG GB184
GB–London, 1899–1902

En 1, 1899
Lbl 1–10, 1899–1902
Ob*

The Musical Gazette: an Independent Journal
of Musical Events, and General Advertiser
and Record of Public Amusements
TNG GB52
GB–London: J. Smith, 1856–59

BSdsc 1 (1856)–3 (1858)
Er 1 (1856)–4 (1859), 10
Lbl 1 (1856)–3 (1858), 34
Mpl 1 (1856)

The Musical Gazette and Review: with which
is incorporated "The Penny Melodist"
Fellinger 1968/746; TNG GB91
GB–London: William Reeves, 1877/78
[Only six numbers published]

Lbl 1–6, 1877/78

The Musical Gem, a Companion to the
Musical Bouquet
GB–London, 1858–60

Lbl*

The Musical Gem, a Souvenir for 1830
[–1834]
Langley, pp. 48; Fellinger 1986, pp. 964–72
GB–London: Mori and Lavenu, 1829–33

Lbl*

Musical Georgia
GRG–Tbilisi, 1991–
[NOT IN BUCOMP1]

Cu 1991–#

The Musical Guide
Fellinger 1968/896; TNG GB102
GB–London, 1882
[Only two issues were published]

Lbl 1882, Feb, Mar

Musical Happening
US–Dallas, TX, 1968–?71
[Succeeded by Musical Analysis (q.v.)]

Lkc 1 (1968)–2 (1970), 7

The Musical Herald: a [Weekly] Journal of
Music and Musical Literature
Fellinger 1968/238; TNG GB37
GB–London: G. Biggs, 1846–47

Cpl 1 (1846)–2 (1847)*
Cu 1 (1846)–2 (1847)*
En 1 (1846)–2 (1847)
Ep 1 (1846)–2 (1847)
Er 1 (1846)–2 (1847)*
Lbl 1 (1846)–2 (1847), 52
Lcm (p) 1 (1846), 1–14
Lu 1 (1846)–2 (1847)
Mu 1 (1846)–2 (1847)
Ob*

The Musical Herald see also The Tonic Sol-Fa
Reporter and Magazine of Vocal Music for
the People [2]

Musical Heritage Review Magazine
TNG US877
US–Neptune, NJ, 1977–

Lsa 1 (1977)–3 (1979)*; 13 (1989), 1, 3, 4

The Musical Home Journal
Fellinger 1968/1786; TNG GB214
GB–London: Cassell, 1905–08
[213 numbers in total]

    AB 1905–06
    Ep 1905–07
    Lbl*
    Lcml 1–213, 1905–08

The Musical Instrument Society Newsletter
see Newsletter of the Historical Musical
Society

Musical Instrument Technology
0305–0335
GB–London: Institute of Musical Instrument
Technology, 1969–91; 1994–

    BSdsc*
    Cu 2 (1973)–#
    EIR:Dtc 2 (1973)–#
    En 2 (1973)–#
    Lbl*
    Lgu 1 (1969)–1991
    Mcm 2 (1973), 3–#
    Mpl 1 (1969)–?4 (1981)
    Ob*

Musical Instruments
GB–London, 197?–
[NOT IN BUCOMP1]

    En 1991–#

Musical Instruments [translated title] *see*
Hudební Nástroje

Musical Jottings
Fellinger 1968/722; TNG GB85
GB–London: Moutrie and Son, 1876–81
[43 nos in total]

    En 1 (1876), 1
    Lbl 1–43, 1876–81
    Ob*

The Musical Journal *see* The Nonconformist
Musical Journal

The Musical Journal: a Magazine of
Information on all Subjects Connected with
the Science
Fellinger 1968/167; Langley, p. 593
GB–London: J. Limbird [et al.], 1840
[46 numbers published in all, in two volumes]

    Bp 1 (1840)–2 (1840)
    Lbl 1 (1840), 1–26

The Musical Journal for the Piano-forte in
two Sections, one of Vocal, and one of
Instrumental Music: Selected, and, Arranged
by Benjamin Carr
Fellinger 1986, pp. 115–29
US–Baltimore, MD: Joseph Carr, 1799–1804
[NOT IN BUCOMP1; 5 vols (120 numbers) in
total; also known as *Benjamin Carr Musical
Journal*]

    Lu 1800–03 [Reprint ed.]

The Musical Library Monthly Supplement
Langley, pp. 554–9
GB–London: Charles Knight, 1834–37
[Published in three volumes (28 numbers)
between 1834 and 1836]

    Bu 1 (1834)–3 (1836)
    Cpl 1 (1834), 6–9
    Lbl*
    Ob 1 (1834)–3 (1836)

Musical Life [translated title] *see* **Hudobny
Zivot**

Musical Life [translated title] *see*
Muzykal'naya Zhizn'

Musical Life [translated title] *see* **Ruch
Muzyczny [1]** and **[2]**

Musical Life: Journal of the Music
Performance Research Centre
GB–London: Barbican Centre, Music
Performance Research Centre, 1990–
[NOT IN BUCOMP1]

    ALb 1 (1990)–2 (1991)
    Lbar 1 (1990)–#

The Musical Magazine [1]
Fellinger 1968/124; TNG GB17; Langley,
p. 563
GB–London; F. de Porquet and Cooper, 1835
[Only one volume (12 numbers) published]

Bu 1 (1835)
Cu 1 (1835), 1–11
Lbl 1 (1835), 1–12
Ob*

The Musical Magazine [2]
US–New York: Ezra Collier, 1835–37
[NOT IN BUCOMP1]

Mu 1 (1835)–2 (1837) [m]

The Musical Magazine, containing a Variety
of Favorite Pieces
Fellinger 1968/86
US–Cheshire, CT: Andrew Law, 1792–1801
[NOT IN BUCOMP1. 6 volumes in total]

Mu 1 (1792)–6 (1801) [m]

Musical Magazine, or Monthly Orpheus
Langley, p. 432
GB–London, 1760–61
[20 numbers published in total]

Lbl*

The Musical Magazine, or Repository of
Musical Science, Literature and Intelligence
Fellinger 1968/157; TNG US10
US–Boston, MA, 1839–42

Cu [m]
Mu [m]

The Musical Magazine, Review and Register
GB–London: G. E. Miles, 1809
[NOT IN BUCOMP1]

Gul(e)*

The Musical Mail and Advertiser
TNG GB215
GB–Newmilns (Scotland), 1905–30
[Absorbed by *Musical Progress* (q.v.) to become
M.P.M.: Musical Progress and Mail]

Lbl*

The Musical Mainstream
0364–7501
US–Washington, DC: Library of Congress,
Division for the Blind and Physically
Handicapped, 1977–
[NOT IN BUCOMP1]

Lbl*

Musical Mercury
TNG US527; 0738–0011
US–New York: Edwin F. Kalmus, 1934–49

Bp 1 (1934)–4 (1937), 2
Lbl*
Lu (RMA) 4 (1937), 1
Mpl 1 (1934)–6 (1939)

The Musical Million: a Weekly Periodical
GB–London: European Publishing Company,
1887–96
[110 issues in total]

Lbl*

The Musical Mirror
TNG GB283
GB–London, 1920–33
[Entitled *The Musical Mirror and Fanfare* from
vol. 11 (1931); incorporated *Fanfare: a Musical
Causerie* (q.v.) in 1922; absorbed by *The Music
Lover* [1] (q.v.) in 1933]

AB 3 (1923)–5 (1925)
BSdsc*
Cu 2 (1922)–12 (1932)
EIR:Dtc 8 (1928)–11 (1931), 12
Gm 9 (1929)–12 (1932)
Lbl*
Lcm 1 (1921), 4; 2 (1922)–3 (1923); 6 (1926);
  7 (1927), 9; 8 (1928)
Lcml 10 (1930), 1
Mcm 6 (1926), 7; 8 (1928), 11, 12; 9 (1929),
  1, 2
Mpl 3 (1924)–12 (1932)
Ob*
Ouf 12 (1932), 1–7

The Musical Mirror and Fanfare *see* The
Musical Mirror

Musical Miscellanies
TNG GB2; Langley, pp. 450–53
GB–London: T. Williams, 1784
[Included a supplement, *The Review of New
Musical Publications*]

Lbl 1 (1784), 1–9

The Musical Monthly [and Drawing-Room Miscellany] *see* The Musical Monthly and Repertoire of Literature, the Drama and the Arts

The Musical Monthly and Repertoire of Literature, the Drama and the Arts
Fellinger 1968/503; TNG GB66
GB–London: Adams and Francis, 1864–65
[From 1864, 8, entitled *The Musical Monthly [and Drawing-Room Miscellany]*; then merged with *The Mayfair Miscellany and Ladies' Own Repertoire of Original and Selected Literature, with which is incorporated "The Musical Monthly"* (q.v.); ceased publication with vol. 2 no. 21 (1865)]

BSdsc 1 (1864)–2 (1865), 21
Cu 1 (1864)–2 (1865), 21 [w 2 (1865), 16]
Gul(e)*
Lbl 1 (1864)–2 (1865), 21
Ob*

Musical Monthly, Magazine of New Copyright Music
GB–London: Enoch and Sons, 1873–74

Gul(e) 1873–74
Lbl*

The Musical Museum and Friends *see* Friends of the Musical Museum: Members' Newsletter

Musical News
TNG GB348
GB–London, 1935–38
[Also known as *The Musical News and Dance Band*]

Lbl 1 (1935)–2 (1938), 32

The Musical News: a Weekly Journal of Music
Fellinger 1968/1170
GB–London, 1891–1929
[Amalgamated with *The Tonic Sol-Fa Reporter and Magazine of Vocal Music for the People* [2] (q.v.) in 1921 to form *The Musical News and Herald*, 1921–29]

AB 1 (1891)–68 (1925)
BSdsc 1 (1891)–19 (1900)
Bu 1 (1891)–20 (1901); 30 (1906)–37 (1909); 60 (1921)–62 (1922); 64 (1923); 66 (1924)–67 (1924)
Cu 1 (1891)–59 (1920) [w 12 (1896); 13 (1897); 51 (1916); 55 (1918)–58 (1919); 72 (1927)]

EIR:Dtc 60 (1921)–73 (1928)
En 16 (1898)–29 (1905)
Gm 60 (1921)–73 (1928)
Lam 48 (1915)–50 (1916); 53 (1917)–55 (1918)
Lbl*
Lcm 1 (1891)–54 (1918); 58 (1920)
Lcml 5 (1893)–67 (1924) [w 37 (1909); 51 (1916)]; 72 (1927)*
LEc 6 (1894)–27 (1904); 60 (1921)–71 (1926)
Lrco 1 (1891)–15 (1898); 49 (1915)–54 (1918); 59 (1920)
Lu 58 (1920)–73 (1927) [w 72 (1927)]
LVp 60 (1921)–73 (1928)
Mcm*
Mpl 1 (1891)–73 (1928)
Ob*

The Musical News and Dance Band *see* Musical News

The Musical News and Herald *see* The Musical News: a Weekly Journal of Music

The Musical Newsletter
TNG US812; 0047–8466
US–New York: Musical Newsletter, 1971–77

Lbl*

Musical Notes
Fellinger 1968/1222; TNG GB150
GB–London, 1893–95
[Incorporated into *Music: a Monthly Journal Devoted to the Art and Trade, with which is incorporated Musical Notes* (q.v.)]

Lbl*

Musical Notes: an Annual Critical Record
Fellinger 1968/1022; TNG GB120
GB–London: Robert Cocks, 1887–90

Lbl 1–14, 1887–90
Ob*

The Musical Observer
Fellinger 1968/1171; TNG GB145
GB–London, 1891–96
[From 1896, 61 amalgamated with *The Church Musician: a Monthly Journal of the Church Choir Guild* (q.v.) to form *The Musical Observer and Church Musician* (TNG GB145)]

Lbl*
Mpl 1 (1891)–6 (1896)
Ob*

The Musical Observer: a Monthly Journal of News, Criticism, and Literature, for Professional and Amateur Musicians
Fellinger 1968/2034; TNG GB248
GB–London: R. P. Smith, 1910–13

    AB 3 (1913), 34, 35
    Lbl*

The Musical Observer and Church Musician
see The Church Musician: a Monthly Journal of the Church Choir Guild; and The Musical Observer

Musical Opinion *see* Musical Opinion and Music Trade Review: British, Foreign and Colonial

Musical Opinion and Music Trade Review: British, Foreign and Colonial
Fellinger 1968/747; TNG GB90; Langley 1994, pp. 123–4; 0027 4623
GB–London: Musical Opinion, 1877–
[Entitled *Musical Opinion* [only] from 1964]

    AB*
    ALb 100 (1976), 1192; 116 (1993), 1382
    Au 95 (1971)–96 (1972)*; 98 (1974), 1164–#
    BDp 72 (1948)–77 (1953); 79 (1955)91 (1967); 95 (1971)–114 (1991)
    BG 92 (1968/69)–98 (1974/75); 100 (1976/77)–#
    BLp 1 (1877)–69 (1945) [m]; 70 (1946)–#
    BOL [c (1 year)]
    Bp 1 (1877)–25 (1901); 26 (1902)–51 (1927) [m]; 41 (1917)–102 (1978), 1217; 103 (1979), 1224 –#
    BRu 4 (1880)–80 (1957)*; 84 (1960)– 109 (1986), Nov*
    Bs 62 (1938), Nov–102 (1978), Mar*
    BSdsc*
    BTp 83 (1959)–112 (1989)
    Bu 61 (1937)–87 (1963)
    Cap [c (10 years)]
    CCtc 72 (1948)–74 (1950); 83 (1959)– 93 (1969)
    CDu 82 (1958)–93 (1969); 98 (1974)– 100 (1976)
    CFp 89 (1965)–98 (1974)
    CHEp [c (1 year)]
    Cu 83 (1959)–#
    DS 104 (1980)–109 (1985); 113 (1989)–#
    EIR:Dtc 65 (1941), 769–80 (1956), 955
    EIR:MEtc 98 (1974)–113 (1989)
    En* [part m]
    Ep 50 (1926), 592–600; 51 (1927)–67 (1943);

69 (1945), 819–828; 70 (1946)–72 (1948); 74 (1950)–101 (1977); 102 (1978), 1212–1221, 1223; 103 (1979), 1224–1229, 1231, 1234, 1235; 104 (1980)–105 (1981); 106 (1982), 1260–1267, 1269, 1270; 107 (1983)–#
    Er 41 (1917)*; 42 (1918)–46 (1922), 541, 542; 49 (1925)*; 50 (1926)–54 (1930), 637, 638, 640–648; 55 (1931)–63 (1939), 745–747; 93 (1970), 1111–19; 94 (1971), 1120–22
    EXu 83 (1959)–86 (1962); 91 (1967)– 110 (1986)
    Gam 55 (1931), 9; 62 (1938), 6; 68 (1944), 4–12; 69 (1945)–70 (1946), 3; 71 (1947), 4–12; 72 (1948), 1–3; 82 (1958), 2–12; 83 (1959)–84 (1960), 1, 2, 4–7, 9–12; 85 (1961), 1–6, 8, 9, 11, 12; 86 (1962); 88 (1964), 1–5, 7–12; 89 (1965)–90 (1966), 1, 3–12; 91 (1967)–93 (1969), 11; 94 (1970)– 97 (1973), 1–5, 7–12; 98 (1974), 1–5, 7–12; 99 (1975)–104 (1980), 1–4, 6–10, 12; 105 (1981)–108 (1984); 109 (1985), 1–7, 11, 12; 110 (1986)–112 (1988), 1–3, 5–12; 113 (1989)–115 (1991), 1–5, 7–12; 116 (1992)–#
    Gm 6 (1882)–#*
    HA 111 (1987)–#
    HE 113 (1989), 1352–#
    KE 88 (1964)–108 (1984); 110 (1986), Oct–113 (1989), Mar
    Lam 4 (1880)–12 (1888), Sep; 14 (1890), Feb–18 (1894), June; 42 (1918)*; 43 (1919), 517–519; 44 (1920), 520–88 (1964), 1046; 88 (1964/65), 1048–98 (1974), 1172; 98 (1974), 1174–#
    Lam (o) 30 (1906), 359; 31 (1907), 368– 60 (1936)
    Lbar 7 (1883), Oct–37 (1913); 39 (1915), Oct–73 (1949); 75 (1951), Oct–76 (1952); 78 (1954); 79 (1955), Mar, May–84 (1960); 85 (1961), May, July–87 (1963), Nov; 88 (1964)–98 (1974); 100 (1976)–#
    Lbl*
    Lbo 109 (1985)–112 (1988); 113 (1989), 7–12; 114 (1990)–#
    Lcm 33 (1909)–34 (1910); 36 (1912), 423; 44 (1920), 527, 528; 45 (1921), 533, 536, 538, 539; 46 (1922), 544, 546; 47 (1923), 564; 59 (1935), 706; 60 (1936), 720; 61 (1937), 729; 66 (1942), 769, 775, 779; 67 (1943), 781, 783, 785, 792; 69 (1945), 814; 69 (1945), 827, 828; 70 (1946), 829–840; 71 (1947), 841–852; 72 (1948), 853–863; 73 (1949), 865–876; 74 (1950), 877,

879–888; 75 (1951), 889; 86 (1962), 1021;
87 (1963), 1037, 1039; 88 (1964),
1046–1054, 1056; 89 (1965), 1057–1068;
90 (1966), 1069–1078, 1080; 91 (1967),
1081– 1092; 92 (1968), 1093–1104; 93
(1969), 1105– 1116; 94 (1970), 1117–1128;
95 (1971), 1129–1140; 96 (1972),
1141–1152; 97 (1973), 1153–1163; 98
(1974), 1164–1175; 99 (1975), 1176–1187;
100 (1976), 1188–1199); 101 (1977),
1200–1211; 102 (1978), 1212–1223; 103
(1979), 1224–1233; 104 (1980), 1237; 106
(1980), 1261, 1262, 1265; 107 (1983),
1276, 1281; 108 (1984), 1292; 109 (1985),
1300, 1305–1308; 110 (1986), 1310,
1312–1314; 111 (1987), 1328–1334;
113 (1989), 1347–1350

Lcml 4 (1880)–7 (1883)*; 8 (1884); 9
(1885)–11 (1887)*; 12 (1888)–14 (1890);
15 (1891)*; 16 (1892)–22 (1898);
23 (1899)–24 (1900)*; 25 (1901)–#
Lcml (m) [c (1 year)]
LEc 111 (1987)–#*
Lgsm 98 (1974)*; 99 (1975)*; 108 (1984)–#
Lha 83 (1959)–114 (1990)
Lkc 76 (1952)–102 (1978)
Lrscm 76 (1952)–94 (1970)
Ltc 101 (1977)–116 (1992)*; 117 (1993)–#
Lu 71 (1947), 845–# [w 71 (1947), 853, 854;
72 (1948), 858–864]
LVp 51 (1927); 54 (1930)–64 (1940); 67
(1943)–81 (1957); 84 (1960)–#
Mcm 59 (1935), 702–710; 60 (1936)–61
(1937), 712–718, 722–727; 67 (1943), 795;
72 (1948)–74 (1950), 861–876, 879–888;
78 (1954)–#*
Mpl 1 (1877)–#
Msu 87 (1963), 1035, 1037–93 (1969), 1106,
1108–1124; 94 (1970), 1125, 1127–
101 (1977), 1202
Mu 75 (1951)–77 (1953); 80 (1956)–81
(1957); 83 (1959)
NOp [c (3 years)]
NOTu 94 (1970)–#
NTp 47 (1923)–#
NWu 89 (1965)–101 (1977); 103 (1979)
Ob 6 (1882), Mar; 11 (1887), July–Sep; 12
(1888)–#
Op [c (5 years)]
Ouf 82 (1958)–113 (1989)
PRp 94 (1970), 10–101 (1977), 5#
R 79 (1955), 4–12; 80 (1956), 1–6, 10, 11;
81 (1957), 2–8, 10–12; 82 (1958), 1–7,
9–12; 83 (1959); 84 (1960), 1–5, 7–12;
85 (1961), 1–5, 8–12; 86 (1962); 87 (1963);

88 (1964), 1–6, 8–12; 89 (1965), 1–5;
92 (1968), 2, 4–11; 93 (1969), 1–5, 9–11;
94 (1970), 2–9, 11; 95 (1971), 7–9;
98 (1974), 1, 5, 9, 10; 99 (1975), 2, 4
SA 7 (1883)–11 (1887); 49 (1925)–51 (1927);
69 (1945)–88 (1964) [w 69 (1945), Mar,
June, Aug, Oct; 70 (1946), Oct–Dec;
71 (1947), May]
SFu 91 (1967)–92 (1968)*
SOu 88 (1964), 1047–99 (1975), 1186

Musical Outlook: Monthly of Musical Culture
[translated title] *see* **Hudební Rozhledy:
Měsíčník pro Hudební Kulturu**

The Musical Pearl [translated title] *see* **Perl
Cerddorol**

Musical Pictorial
TNG GB349
GB–London, 1935–36

Lbl*

[The] Musical Pioneer *see* **New York Musical
Pioneer and Choristers' Budget**

Musical Praxis
1354–8182
GB–Edinburgh: Edinburgh University Faculty
of Music, 1994–
[NOT IN BUCOMP1]

Lbl*

Musical Press
Fellinger 1968/232; TNG GB254
GB–London, 1912–13

Lbl*

Musical Progress
Fellinger 1968/1838; TNG GB220
GB–London, 1930–53
[Absorbed *The Musical Mail and Advertiser*
(q.v.) in 1930; entitled *M. P. M.: Musical
Progress and Mail* from 1930, with new
numbering system]

Gm 4 (1933)–22 (1951)
Lbl*
Ob*

Musical Progress and Mail *see* **Musical
Progress**

The Musical Quarterly
Fellinger 1968/2251; TNG US447; 0027–4631
US–New York: Schirmer, 1915–
[Not published 1987–88]

AB 1 (1915)–#
ABc 4 (1918), 1–3; 35 (1949)–76 (1992)
ALb 28 (1942), 1; 35 (1949), 2; 36 (1950),
    4–38 (1952), 3; 46 (1960), 4; 50 (1964), 4;
    51 (1965), 3–55 (1969), 1; 66 (1980),
    3–68 (1982), 2; 69 (1983), 1; 71 (1985), 2;
    73 (1989)–74 (1990), 1; 75 (1991)–#
Au 1 (1915)–80 (1996)
BAc 54 (1968)–#
BDp 1 (1915); 24 (1938); 28 (1942); 30
    (1944)–31 (1945); 34 (1948)–35 (1949);
    39 (1953)–41 (1955); 53 (1967)–56 (1970);
    59 (1973)–67 (1981)
BG 35 (1949)–#
BLu 1 (1915)–#
Bp 1 (1915)–57 (1971), 1; 58 (1972), 2–#
BRp 34 (1948), 2–71 (1985)
BRu 1 (1915)–77 (1993)
Bs 1 (1915)–#
BSdsc 1 (1915)–#
BTu 31 (1945)–37 (1951); 40 (1954)–
    44 (1958); 45 (1959), 2–50 (1964);
    53 (1967)–#
Bu 1 (1915)–#
Cat 60 (1974), 2–72 (1986), 3; 73 (1989)–#
CCtc 31 (1945)–57 (1971); 61 (1975)–#
CDu 1 (1915)–#
COp [c (2 years)]
Cpl 1 (1915)–#
Cu 1 (1915)–#
DRu 1 (1915)–#
EIR:Dp 72 (1986)–#
EIR:Driam 77 (1993)–
EIR:Dtc 1 (1915)–2 (1916); 39 (1953)–
    41 (1955); 58 (1972)–#
EIR:Duc 2 (1916)–7 (1921); 46 (1960)–#
EIR:MEtc 61 (1975)–#
En*
Ep 5 (1919)–7 (1921); 9 (1923), 2–4;
    10 (1924), 1, 3, 4; 12 (1926)–13 (1927), 1,
    2; 14 (1928), 3, 4; 15 (1929), 2, 4; 16
    (1930), 2–4; 17 (1931), 2–4; 18 (1932)–
    26 (1940), 3; 27 (1941), 2–4; 28 (1942)–#
Er 1 (1915)– 69 (1983); 73 (1989)–#
EXu 31 (1945); 34 (1948); 39 (1953)–41
    (1955); 43 (1957); 45 (1959)–47 (1961);
    49 (1963); 51 (1965)–52 (1966); 54 (1968);
    56 (1970); 58 (1972)–66 (1980);
    68 (1982)–#
Gam 1 (1915)–11 (1925); 13 (1927)–22

(1936), 1, 4; 23 (1937),2–24 (1938), 2–4;
    25 (1939)–27 (1941), 3; 28 (1942), 1; 34
    (1948)–36 (1950), 3, 4; 37 (1951), 2; 44
    (1958), 1, 2, 4; 45 (1959)–48 (1962), 1, 2,
    4; 49 (1963)–56 (1970), 1, 2, 4; 57 (1971)–
    72 (1986), 1–3; 73 (1989)–#
Gm 38 (1952)–#
Gul 1 (1915)–#
HUu 1 (1915)–#
KE 39 (1953)–41 (1955); 51 (1965)–#
Lam 13 (1927), 1; 25 (1939), 1, 2; 27 (1941),
    3; 30 (1944), 2–4; 31 (1945), 3; 36 (1950),
    2; 39 (1953)–47 (1961), 2, 4; 48 (1962)–
    50 (1964), 2; 51 (1965)–68 (1982), 2;
    69 (1983), 2, 4–70 (1984), 3; 71 (1985)–
    72 (1986), 3; 74 (1990); 76 (1992)–#
LAu 26 (1940), 1; 37 (1951), 1; 39 (1953), 1;
    40 (1954)–# [part m]
Lbbc 73 (1989), 3–#*
Lbl*
LCdM 63 (1977), 4–#
Lcm 1 (1915)–# [w 30 (1944), 1]
Lcml 1 (1915)–#
Lcu 36 (1950)–61 (1975) [m]; 61 (1975)–#
LEbc 1 (1915), 4; 33 (1947)–39 (1953); 40
    (1954), 2–70 (1984); 72 (1986)–#
LEc 1 (1915)–57 (1971); 58 (1972), 2–4;
    71 (1985), 4–# [w 77 (1993), 2, 4]
Lgo 1 (1915)–25 (1939); 27 (1941)–70
    (1984); 71 (1985), 4–#
Lgsm 27 (1941), 1; 32 (1946), 4–40 (1954),
    3; 41 (1955), 1–3; 46 (1960), 3; 51 (1965),
    2, 3; 52 (1966); 53 (1967)–62 (1976)*
Lkc 1 (1915)–49 (1963); 51 (1965)–67
    (1981)*
Lki 1 (1915)–6 (1920); 75 (1991)
Lmi 54 (1968)–#
LRHBNC 1 (1915)–15 (1929); 17 (1931)–#
Lro 60 (1974)–#
Lsa 54 (1968)–58 (1972); 60 (1974)
Ltv 46 (1960)–#
Lu 1 (1915)–#
LVp 25 (1939); 35 (1949)–53 (1967);
    55 (1969)–59 (1973); 61 (1975)–#
LVu 1 (1915)–#
Mcm 35 (1949), 3; 59 (1973), 4; 60 (1974)–#
MK 56 (1970)–#
Mmu (a) 75 (1991)–#
Mpl 1 (1915)–#
Msu 39 (1953); 50 (1964), 1#
Mu 1 (1915)–12 (1926); 39 (1953)–#
NO 1 (1915)–#
NTp 54 (1968)–72 (1986)
NWu 1 (1915)–50 (1964) [m]; 49 (1963)–#
Ob 1 (1915)–#

Oub 68 (1982)–#
Ouf 1 (1915)–#
R 12 (1926)–#
Re 43 (1957)
SA 1 (1915)–#
SFu 11(1925)–#
SLGu 64 (1978)–#
SOu 32 (1946)–# [w 72 (1986), 4]
TOd 1 (1915)–50 (1964) [m]; 51 (1965)–#
Uu 39 (1953)–54 (1968); 59 (1973)–62
    (1976); 63 (1977)*; 64 (1978)–72 (1986);
    73 (1989)–#
Yu 39 (1953)–#

Musical Record [1]
TNG US524
US–Philadelphia, PA: The Musical Record,
1933–34

Lsa 1 (1933), 4–7

Musical Record [2]
TNG US557
US–New York: Musical Record Company,
1940–41
[NOT IN BUCOMP1]

ALb 2 (1941), 1

The Musical Record *see also* The Chesterian
Musical Record

The Musical Record *see also* Ditson and Co's
Musical Record

The Musical Record and Review *see* Ditson
and Co's Musical Record

Musical Reference Book [translated title] *see*
Muzykal'niy Spravochnik

**The Musical Remembrancer: a Monthly
Guide and Companion to the Church, for the
Clergyman and the Musician**
Fellinger 1968/383; TNG GB54
GB–London: J. H. Jewell, 1857
[4 nos in total]

BSdsc 1–4, 1857
Lbl 1–4, 1857

Musical Renaissance: a Monthly Magazine
TNG GB432
GB–London, 1950–51
[From 1951 incorporated in *Music and Records:
incorporating "Musical Renaissance"* (TNG
GB438)]

Lam [Mengelberg memorial issue]
Lcml [Mengelberg memorial issue]; 1950, 1,
    2
Lsa 1950, 1, 2

The Musical Reporter
TNG US14
US–Boston, MA, 1841

Cu [m]
Mu 1–9, 1841 [m]

Musical Review [translated title] *see* Hudební
Revue

Musical Review [translated title] *see also* Zenei
Szemle

**The Musical Review: a Weekly Musical
Journal**
Fellinger 1968/933; TNG GB108
GB–London: Novello, Ewer and Company,
1883

Bp 1883, 1–26
En 1883, 1–26
Er 1883, 1–26
Gm 1883, 1–26
Lbl 1883, 1–26
Lcm 1883, 1–26
Lu 1883, 1–26
Mpl 1883
Ob*

Musical Review and Choral Advocate *see*
Choral Advocate and Singing-Class Journal

The Musical Review and Musical World *see*
The Choral Advocate and Singing-Class
Journal

Musical Review and Pictorial *see* Fanfare: a
Monthly Magazine [etc.]

**The Musical Review, or Guide to the Musical
World**
Fellinger 1968/480; TNG GB62
GB–London, 1863
[Only one published]

Lbl

The Musical Review, Singapore
TNG MA1
SGP, 1932–?

Lbl*

Musical Salvationist
GB–London: Salvation Army, 1886–
[Continued from 1994 as *Sing to the Lord*]

> **AB***
> **Cu** 1889–1993; 1 (1994)–#
> **EIR:Dtc** 1886–88; 1890–92; 1894–96; 1901;
> 1905–06; 1908; 1911; 1913; 1915; 1917–
> 20; 1923–30; 1932; 1936–37; 1939–42;
> 1944–46; 1949–52; 1955–#
> **En***
> **Lbl***

Musical Six-Six Newsletter
US–Kirksville, MO: Thomas S. Reed, 1972–
[NOT IN BUCOMP1]

> **Lam** 1 (1972), 1

Musical Society: a Magazine of Music and Musical Literature
Fellinger 1968/1023; TNG GB121
GB–London, 1886–87

> **Lbl** 1–17, 1886–87

The Musical Standard: a Newspaper for Musicians, Professional and Amateur
Fellinger 1968/454; TNG GB59; Langley 1994, pp. 120–21
GB–London: Reeves and Turner, 1862–71
[The first of four series, as follows: series 1, 1–14, 1862–71; new series, 1–45, 1871–93; *also* illustrated series, 1 (1894)–38 (1912); new *Lcml* illustrated series, 1 (1913)–38 (1933) (see *from* below)] *1889*

> **Bp** 1 (1862)–13 (1870)
> **BSdsc***
> **Gm** 1 (1862)–2 (1863)
> **Lbl** 1 (1862), Aug 2–14 (1871), Apr 29
> **Lrco** 1 (1862), 1, 6, 12, 13; 2 (1863)–3
> (1864), 48, 50, 51, 54, 56–58, 60–62, 65,
> 67, 68, 70–73; 4 (1865)–7 (1867); 11
> (1869)–14 (1871)
> **Lu** 1 (1862)–14 (1871)
> **Mpl** 1 (1862)–14 (1871)

The Musical Standard: Illustrated Series
Fellinger 1968/1267; TNG GB164
GB–London, 1894–1912
[Included a supplement, *The Violin and String World* (q.v.)]

> **AB***
> **Bp** 1894–1912*
> **Gm** 1894–1912*

> **Lbl** 1894–1912
> **Lcml** 1894–1912
> **Mpl** 1894–1912
> **Ob***

The Musical Standard: New Illustrated Series
Fellinger 1968/2181; TNG GB261
GB–London, 1913–33

> **AB***
> **Bp***
> **Gm** 1 (1913)–42 (1933)
> **Lbl** 1 (1913)–38 (1933)
> **Lcm** 18 (1921); 27 (1926); 30 (1927); 38
> (1933)*
> **Lcml** 1 (1913)–9 (1917); 11 (1918)–17
> (1921); 19 (1922)
> **Mpl** 1 (1913)–42 (1933)

The Musical Standard: New Series
Fellinger 1968/636; TNG GB76
GB–London: Reeves and Turner, 1871–93

> **AB** 6 (1874)–45 (1893)*
> **Bp** 6 (1874)–45 (1893)
> **EIR:Driam** 31 (1886)–41 (1891)
> **Ep** 14 (1878)–15 (1878)
> **Gm** 24 (1883)–45 (1893)
> **Lbl** 1–45, 1871, May 6–45 (1893), Dec 30
> **Lcml** 23 (1883)–45 (1893)
> **Lrco** 1 (1871)–11 (1876); 14 (1878)–17
> (1879); 19 (1880)–44 (1893)
> **Lu***
> **Mpl** 1 (1871)–44 (1893)
> **Ob***

The Musical Star: a Musical Record and Review
Fellinger 1968/504; TNG GB67
GB–Edinburgh, 1864–1912
[Included as supplements *The Musical Treasury* (q.v.); *Köhler's Musical Star* (q.v.)]

> **Ep** 1900–1909*
> **Gul (e)** 1880–82
> **Lbl***
> **Mpl** 1887–95

Musical Studies [translated title] *see* **Zenetudomanyi Dolgozatok**

The Musical Times *see* **The Musical Times and Singing Class Circular**

The Musical Times and Singing Class Circular
Fellinger 1968/223; TNG GB33; Langley 1994,
p. 118; 0958–8434; 0027–4666
GB–London: Novello; Granada, 1844–
[Preceded by *Mainzer's Musical Times and
Singing Circular*; entitled *The Musical Times*
[only] from vol. 45 (1904), no. 731]

AB*
ABc 44 (1903)–45 (1904); 77 (1936); 80
(1939)–81 (1940); 85 (1944); 88 (1947);
92 (1951); 98 (1957); 100 (1959)–#
ALb 91 (1950), 1291, 1293; 92 (1951), 1302;
93 (1952), 1313, 1316; 95 (1954), 1341;
98 (1957), 1377; 100 (1959), 1399–1400;
102 (1961), 1423–1424; 103 (1962), 1428;
104 (1963), 1439–109 (1968), 1505,
1507–1510; 110 (1969), 1516, 1518–115
(1974), 1571, 1573–1582; 116 (1975),
1583–122 (1981), 1663, 1665–1666;
123 (1982), 1667–129 (1988), 1750;
130 (1989); 131 (1990), 1764–1770;
1773–1774; 132 (1991), 1775–79;
1781–86; 133 (1992)–134 (1993), 1807,
1809–1810; 105 (1994), 1812–#
Ap 3 (1849)–7 (1857); 9 (1859)–28 (1887);
[c (3 years)]
Au 1 (1844)–55 (1914); 81 (1940)–#
BAc 108 (1967)–129 (1988); 131 (1990),
1769–1771, 1773, 1774; 1 33(1992),
1787–1789, 1791–1798; 134 (1993)–#
BAR 104 (1963); 118 (1977), 1–4, 6–12;
119 (1978); 129 (1988), 1, 2, 4–10;
130 (1989)–#
BDp 9 (1860/61); 13 (1866)–23 (1882);
25 (1884)–#
BEp [c (5 years)]
BG 25 (1884); 41 (1900)–46 (1905);
47 (1906)*; 48 (1907);49 (1908), 779,
781– 790; 50 (1909)–52 (1911); 54 (1913)–
55 (1914); 62 (1921), 943; 63 (1922), 950;
64 (1923)–79 (1938), 1150; 87 (1946)–
91 (1950), 1283–1289, 1291–1294;
92 (1951)–#
BLBBC 77 (1936), 9–11; 78 (1937), 2, 5–8,
10–12; 79 (1938), 1, 2, 12; 80 (1939), 1–7;
107 (1966), 8–12; 108 (1967), 1–10, 12;
109 (1968)–113 (1972), 5, 7–12; 114
(1973); 115 (1974), 1–9; 117 (1976), 8–10;
118 (1977)–120 (1979), 9, 11, 12; 121
(1980), 1, 3–5, 7, 9–12; 122 (1981)–127
(1986), 5, 7–12; 128 (1987); 129 (1988),
1–7, 9–12; 130 (1989), 1–6, 10–12; 131
(1990), 1, 2, 4–9, 12; 132 (1991)–133
(1992), 9

BLp 1 (1844)–# [m 1 (1844)–17 (1876);
24 (1883)–37 (1896); 56 (1915)–58 (1917)]
BLu 21 (1880)–48 (1907); 53 (1912)–#
Bp 5 (1852)–8 (1858); 26 (1 885); 31 (1890)–
33 (1892); 36 (1895), 7–37 (1896), 6;
39 (1898)–127 (1986), 1–10, 12;
128 (1987)–#
BRp 1 (1844)–33 (1892) [m]; 34 (1893)–#
BRu 1 (1844)–2 (1848); 9 (1860/61); 11
(1864)*; 18 (1877)–55 (1914); 62 (1921);
64 (1923)–132 (1991); 133 (1992)*;
134 (1993)–#
Bs 58 (1917)–#
BSdsc*
BTp 87 (1946)–92 (1951); 95 (1954)–#
BTu 89 (1948), 1260–#*
Bu 1 (1844)–#
BuAYp [c (3 years)]
Cap 91 (1950)–130 (1989), 3–132 (1991), 1,
3, 5–12; 133 (1992)–#
Cat 115 (1974)–# [w 116 (1975), Mar; 118
(1977), Sep; 122 (1981), Apr; 126 (1985),
Sep]
CCtc 88 (1947)–#
CDCp 15 (1872)–50 (1909), 1, 11, 12;
51 (1910)–60 (1919), 8; 62 (1921)–#
CDu 44 (1903)–#
CFp 18 (1877); 41 (1900)–49 (1908);
51 (1910)–52 (1911); 55 (1914)–#
CH [c (5 years)]
CHEp [c (1 year)]
COp [c (2 years)]
Cpl 1 (1844)–#
Cu 1 (1844)–#
DOR 87 (1946)–111 (1970); 114 (1973)–#
DRu 1 (1844)–#
DS 74 (1933)–76 (1935); 81 (1940)–91
(1950); 94 (1953); 107 (1966)–129 (1988);
131 (1990)–#
Ea [c (5 years)]
EIR:Dp 125 (1984)–#
EIR:Driam 21 (1880)–52 (1911)*; 61
(1920)–87 (1946)*; 124 (1983), 5–#
EIR:Dtc 18 (1877)–#
EIR:Duc 105 (1964)–#
EIR:MEtc 32 (1891), 586; 116 (1975)–#
En*
Ep 5 (1852)–#
Er 1 (1844)–10 (1861/62); 16 (1873/74)– 46
(1905); 50 (1909); 52 (1911); 60 (1919);
63 (1922)–#
EXu 91 (1950)–134 (1993)
Gam 24 (1883); 44 (1903)–54 (1913);
56 (1915–74 (1933); 77 (1936)–92 (1951),
1–7, 9, 11, 12; 93 (1952), 1, 2, 4–6, 11, 12;

MO 34 (1893); 36 (1895); 41 (1900); 44
(1903); 49 (1908)– 50 (1909); 52 (1911);
55 (1914); 115 (1974)–#
Mpl 2 (1848)–#
Msu 102 (1961)125 (1984)*
Msuc*
Mu 44 (1903)–50 (1909); 53 (1912); 56
(1915); 58 (1917)–59 (1918); 62 (1921);
64 (1923)–65 (1924); 67 (1926);
69 (1928)–74 (1933); 76 (1935)–#
NHp [c (1 year)]
NO 28 (1887)–33 (1892); 34 (1893)–37
(1896); 43 (1902); 46 (1905)–48 (1907);
71 (1930); 73 (1932)–#
NOp 1 (1844)–68 (1927); 71 (1930)–73
(1932); 75 (1934)–77 (1936); 79 (1938)–
80 (1939); 84 (1943)–#
NOTu 102 (1961)–123 (1982); 126 (1985)–#
NTp 20 (1879)–31 (1890); 36 (1895)–#
NWu 91 (1950)–#
Ob*
Op 113 (1972)–124 (1983); 131 (1990)–#
[w 132 (1991), 3]
Oub 109 (1968)–#
Ouf 15 (1872)–21 (1880); 25 (1884)–
31 (1890); 33 (1892)–34 (1893);
45 (1904)–48 (1907); 75 (1934)–79 (1938);
88 (1947)–#
P [c (2 years)]
PRp 106 (1965)–#
R 16 (1873/74), 1–4; 18 (1877), 5–12;
19 (1878)–#
Re 114 (1973)–130 (1989)
Rp 45 (1904); 47 (1906); 49 (1908)–
59 (1918); 62 (1921)–73 (1932); 76 (1935);
78 (1937)–86 (1945), 7, 9, 11; 92 (1951);
96 (1955)–108 (1967), 9–12; 109 (1968)–#
SA 11 (1864)–134 (1993) [w 59 (1918)]
SAu [c (5 years)]
SFp 27 (1886)–38 (1897); 42 (1901)–46
(1905); 48 (1907)–56 (1915); 71 (1930)–#
SFu 16 (1873/74)–# [w 35 (1894)]
SHRp 130 (1989)–# [w 130 (1989), 10;
131 (1990), 10; 134 (1993), 5]
SLGu 63 (1922), 952–#*
SOu 84 (1943)–# [w 119 (1978), 3;
131 (1990)*; 133 (1992)*]
STAp 107 (1966)–#
TOd 23 (1882), 476; 24 (1883), 485;
28 (1887), 527; 35 (1894)–46 (1905);
56 (1915); 62 (1921)–80 (1939);
81 (1940)–86 (1945)*; 87 (1946)–#
Uu 113 (1972)*; 114 (1973)–122 (1981);
123 (1982)*–#

WCp 127 (1986)–#
WCp (p) 100 (1959)–#
WCp (s) [c (2 years)]
WF 103 (1962); 106 (1965)–#
WOp 16 (1873/74)–#
Y 80 (1939)–91 (1950); 92 (1951), 2–#
Yu 68 (1927)–71 (1930); 72 (1931), 2–12;
73 (1932)–81 (1940); 82 (1941), 6;
83 (1942)–#

**Musical Traditions: Devoted to New
Perspectives on Traditional Music**
0265–5063
GB–Thundersley, Essex: K. Summers, 1983–
[NOT IN BUCOMP1]

AB 1–4, 1983–85
BSdsc 1–4, 1983–85
Cu 1–4, 1983–85; 8, 1990–#
EIR:Dp 8, 1990–#
EIR:Dtc 1, 1983–#
EXu 1–4, 1983–85
Lbl*
Lcs 1, 1983–#
Lsa 3–11, 1987–94 [w 5, 1989]
Ob*

**Musical Transcript: a Weekly Journal of
Music** *see* **The Weekly Musical Transcript**

The Musical Treasury
TNG GB67
GB–Edinburgh, 1864–1912
[Entitled *Köhler's Musical Treasury* from 327,
1900; supplement to *The Musical Star: a
Musical Record and Review* (q.v.)]

Lbl*

Musical Trends [translated title] *see* **Musiikin
Suunta**

Musical Truth
TNG GB279
GB–London, 1920

Lbl*

The Musical Vehicle [translated title] *see*
Cerbyd Cerddorol

The Musical Visitor
TNG US12
US–Boston, MA, 1840–46
[Entitled *Boston Musical Visitor* from 3
(1842/44); entitled *American Journal of Music
and Musical Visitor* from 4 (1844)–5 (1846), 2]

   Cu 1 (1840), 13, 23; 2 (1842), 1–24; 3
     (1842/44); 4 (1844)–5 (1846), 2* [all m]
   Mu 1 (1840)–5 (1846), 2 [m]

The Musical Visitor *see also* The Church's
Musical Visitor

The Musical World [1]
Fellinger 1968/1313
GB–London, 1895–1908

   Lbl*

The Musical World [2]
Fellinger 1968/1732: TNG GB206
GB– London; Manchester, 1904–08
[76 nos in total]

   Lbl*
   Lcml 2–7, 1905–07
   Mpl 1904–08

[The] Musical World *see also* The Message
Bird: a Literary and Musical Journal

The Musical World: a Journal and Record of
Science, Criticism, Literature, and
Intelligence, connected with the Art *see* The
Musical World: a Weekly Record of Musical
Science, Literature and Intelligence

The Musical World: a Magazine of Essays,
Critical and Practical, and Weekly Record of
Musical Science, Literature, and Intelligence
see The Musical World: a Weekly Record of
Musical Science, Literature and Intelligence

The Musical World: a Weekly Record of
Musical Science, Literature and Intelligence
Fellinger 1968/131; TNG GB18; Langley,
p. 573; Langley 1994, pp. 117–18
GB–London: Novello, 1836–91
[Langley notes sub-title from 1839 of *A
Magazine of Essays, Critical and Practical, and
Weekly Record of Musical Science, Literature,
and Intelligence*; from 1841, July, *A Journal and
Record of Science, Criticism, Literature, and
Intelligence, connected with the Art*]

BRp 1–3, 1836; 11, 1841
BSdsc 1–71, 1836–91
Bu 1–49, 1836–71; 52–59, 1873–81; 61,
   1883; 64, 1886, 69, 1889
Cpl 1–7, 1836–37; 21, 1846
Cu 1–33, 35, 42*, 64–70, 1836–90
En 25, 1850
Er 1–16, 1836–41; 34, 1856
Gm 55–71, 1877–91
Gul (e) 1–52, 1836–73
Lam 1–7, 1836–37; 20–29, 1845–51*; 33–36,
   1855–58*
Lbl 1 (1836)–71 (1891), 4 [2nd copy
   1 (1836)–4 (1837)]
Lcm 1–67, 1836–89
Lcml 1–6, 1836–37; 17–19, 1842–44*; 20,
   1845; 21–22, 1846–47*; 23, 1848; 34,
   1856*; 37, 1859*
Lu 1–5, 1837; 7, 1837; 8, 1838; 13, 1841; 17,
   18, 1842–43; 33, 1855; 64–71, 1886–91
LVp 25–29, 1850–51; 31, 1853; 33, 34, 1855,
   1856; 38,1860
Mcm 65–67, 1887–89*
Mpl 1 (1836)–70 (1890)
Ob 1–9, 1836–39; 11–71, 1841–91
Ouf 11, 1841
WOp 17, 1842; 32–38, 1854–60

The Musical World and Journal of the Fine
Arts *see* The Message Bird: a Literary and
Musical Journal

The Musical World and New York Musical
Times *see* The Message Bird: a Literary and
Musical Journal

The Musical Year-Book of the United States
see Boston Musical Year-Book

Musicalbrande
TNG I253
I–Turin, 1959–
[NOT IN BUCOMP1]

   Cpl 4 (1962)

Musicalia
TNG CU2
CU–Havana, 1928–32

   Cpl 1 (1928)–5 (1932)*
   Cu 1 (1928)–5 (1932)*

Musicalia: Rivista Internazionale di Musica
TNG I284
I–Genoa, 1970–

> Lcml 1 (1970), 4; 2 (1971), 1, 2
> Lu 1 (1970)–2 (1971), 2

Musicalische Neu-Jahrs-Gedichte
CH–Zurich, 1685–1777
[Continued as *Neujahrsgeschenk ab dem Musiksaal an die zürcherische Jugend*]

> Lbl*

Musicanada
TNG C40; 0700–4745 (Bilingual edition); 0580–3144 (1967–70); 0700–4745 (1976–88)
C–Toronto: Canadian Music Centre, 1967–70; Ottawa: Canadian Music Council, 1976–88
[Succeeded the *Canadian Music Centre Newsletter* (1964–65)]

> AB 59–62, 1988
> BSdsc*
> Cpl 30, 36, 38, 41, 42, 1976–80
> Lam 1967, June
> Lbbc 30, 33–40, 1976–79
> Lbl*
> Lcm 42, 1980
> Lsa 5–29, 1967–70
> Lu 1967, Jan; 1968, Apr; 59–60, 1988

The Musician [1]
Fellinger 1968/455; TNG GB60
GB–London, 1862
[17 nos in total]

> Lbl*

The Musician [2]
Fellinger 1968/1361; TNG US286
US–New York; Philadelphia, PA: P. Kempf, 1896–1948

> Lbl*
> Lcm (p) 11 (1905), 1; 23 (1918), 4; 34 (1929), 3

The Musician [3]
TNG GB276
GB–London, 1919–21
[Succeeded by *The Music Student: the Magazine of the Home Study Union and of the Music Teachers' Association* (q.v.)]

> Cu 1 (1919)–2 (1921), 18
> Lu 1 (1919)–2 (1921), 24
> Mpl 1 (1919)–2 (1921)
> Ob 1 (1919)–2 (1921), 18

The Musician [4]
GB–London: The Musicians' Union, 1970–

> AB 1975–77*; 1981, Feb
> Lam 1984; 1987, Apr, Sep; 1988, June; 1989, Mar
> Lcm 1978, Dec; 1981, Apr; 1984, Aug
> Mcm 1983, Dec; 1987, Sep
> Mpl 1991–#
> TOd 1988, Mar, June; 1990, June; 1991, Mar

Musician *see also* **Musician Player and Listener**

The Musician [translated title] *see* **Cerddor**

The Musician: a Monthly Publication Devoted to the Educational Interests of Music
TNG GB216
GB–London: Vincent Music Company, 1905, 1906

> Lbl 1 (1905/06), 1–11
> Lcm (p) 1905, Nov–1906, Oct
> Lcml 1 (1905/06), 12

The Musician: a Registered Newspaper Devoted to the Art of Music
Fellinger 1968/1410; TNG GB174
GB–London, 1897
[28 nos in total]

> Lbl*
> Lcm*
> Lcml 1 (1897), 1–28
> LEbc 1 (1897), 1–26, 28
> Mpl 1 (1897), 1–28
> Ob*

The Musician and Concert-Room Reporter
Fellinger 1968/399; TNG GB55
GB–London, 1858
[Only one issue published]

> Lbl

The Musician of the Salvation Army
TNG GB367
GB–London, 1938–86
[Preceded by *The Bandsman and Songster* (q.v.); succeeded from 1986 by *Salvationist* (q.v.)]

> Cu 22 (1959), 14–49 (1986), 10
> EIR:Dtc 22 (1959), 14– 49 (1986), 10
> En 22 (1959)–23 (1960)*
> Lbl*
> Ob*

The Musician of the Welsh [translated title] *see* Cerddor y Cymry

The Musician, Organist and Choirmaster *see* The Church Choirmaster and Organist

Musician Player and Listener
US–New York: BPI Communications, 1976–
[NOT IN BUCOMP1; entitled *Musician* from 1983]

    Lam 171, 1993–#*

The Musician's Chronicle [translated title] *see* Cronicl y Cerddor

Musician's Directory
GB–London, 1932–35
[NOT IN BUCOMP1; absorbed by the *International Who's Who in Music* in 1935]

    Ob 1932

The Musician's Journal
TNG GB201
GB–Liverpool, 1900–14

    Lbl*

The Musicians' Journal *see also* The Musician's Report and Journal

Musicians on Music
0264–6889
GB–London: Toccata Press, 1983–
[NOT IN BUCOMP1]

    BSdsc 1 (1983)–#

The Musicians' Report and Journal
Fellinger 1968/1223; TNG GB151
GB–Manchester: Amalgamated Musicians' Union, 1893–1933
[From 1921 entitled *The Musicians' Journal* (TNG GB289)]

    Gm 109–264, 1904–16; n.s. 1–15, 1929–32
    Lbl*
    Mpl 67–314, 1900–21; 1923–25

Le Musicien Educateur au Canada *see* Canadian Music Educator/Le Musicien Educateur au Canada

Musiciens Oubliés, Musique Retrouvée
F–Paris, 1932–35

    Lbl*

Il Musicista *see* Bollettino dei Musicisti

Musiclub
0966–4459
GB–Kew: Children's Music Club, ?1991–
[NOT IN BUCOMP1]

    Lbl*

Musicología Española
E–Madrid, 1975–
[NOT IN BUCOMP1]

    BSdsc 1 (1975)–#

Musicologia Hungarica
0077–2488
H–Budapest: Országos Széchényi Könyvtar, 1934–41

    Cpl 1–3, 1935–36
    Lbl*

Musicologica Austriaca
TNG D1095
D–Munich: Katzbichler, 1977–

    BSdsc*
    Cu 1 (1977)–#
    Lbl*
    Ob*

Musicologica Lovaniensia
B–Leuven: Catholic University of Leuven, Department of Musicology, 1969–
[NOT IN BUCOMP1]

    BSdsc 1 (1969)

Musicologica Slovaca
TNG CS221; 0581 0558
SQ–Bratislava: Vydavatel'stvo Slovenskej Akadémie Vied, 1969–
[Preceded by *Hudobnovedne Štúdie Slowenskej Akadémie Vied* (q.v.); continued as *Musicologica Slovaca et Europaea* from 17 (1992)]

    BSdsc*
    Cu 4 (1973)–#

Musicologica Slovaca et Europaea *see* Musicologica Slovaca

Musicological Annual *see* Muzikološki Zbornik

Musicological Examiner [translated title] *see* Musicologisch Onderzoëk

Musicological Questions [translated title] *see* Voprosy Muzykoznaniya

Musicological Society of Australia: Newsletter
TNG AUS32; 0155–0543
AUS–Kensington, NSW: Musicological Society of Australia, 1977–
[NOT IN BUCOMP1]

   Ob 1, 1977–#

Musicological Studies of the Slovak Academy of Sciences [translated title] *see* Hudobnovedné Štúdie Slowenskej Akadémie Vied

Musicologisch Onderzoëk [= Musicological Examiner]
IND–Batavia: Koninklijk Bataviaasch Genootschap van Kunsten en Wetenschappen, 1931

   Lbl*

Musicology
TNG US587
US–Middlebury, VT: M. and H. Publications, 1945–49

   Lcml 1 (1946/47), 2, 4

Musicology [translated title] *see* Hudební Věda

Musicology: Journal of the Musicological Society of Australia
TNG AUS18; 0077–250X
AUS–Sydney: Musicological Society of Australia, 1964–68/69; 1974–
[Became *Musicology Australia* (ISSN 0814–5857) from vol. 8 (1985)]

   BSdsc 1 (1964)–#
   Cpl 1 (1964)–3 (1968/69)
   Cu 1 (1964)–#
   EIR:Duc 2 (1965)–#
   En 1 (1964)–#
   Er 1 (1964)–15 (1992)
   HUu 1 (1964)–16 (1993)
   Lcml 9 (1986)–#
   Lu 1 (1964)–5 (1979)
   Ob*

Musicology: Miscellany for Musicology and Music Criticism [translated title] *see* Musikologie: Sbornik pro Hudebni Vĕdu a Kritiku

Musicology Australia *see* Musicology: Journal of the Musicological Society of Australia

Musicology in China [translated title] *see* Zhong Guo Yin Yue Xue

Musicontact: Cleveland County Leisure and Amenities Department Magazine
GB–?Middlesbrough, 197?–?
[NOT IN BUCOMP1]

   MI 3–19, 1971–76

The Musico's Club
US–?: Columbia Gramophone Company, 1920–23

   Cu 1 (1920/21)
   Lu 1 (1920)–3 (1923)

Musicos Españoles
E–Madrid, 1924–?

   Lbl*

Musics: an Impromental Experivisation [sic] Arts Magazine
GB–London: Bread 'n' Roses, 1975–79

   Cu 3–23, 1975–79
   EIR:Dtc 3–23, 1975–79
   En 3–23, 1975–79*
   Er 11, 13–15, 1977
   Lam 1–23, 1975–79
   Lbl*
   Lcml 1–23, 1975–79#
   Lgo 1–23, 1975–79*
   Lsa 3–8, 1975–76; 11–19, 1977–78
   Lu 1–23, 1975–79
   Ob*
   TOd 14, 1977; 16, 1978; 18–23, 1978–79

Musicus
SA–Pretoria: Departement Musiekeksamens, University of South Africa, ?1973–
[NOT IN BUCOMP1]

   BSdsc 10 (1982), 1–2
   Lam 12 (1984), 1

Musicus: Computer Applications in Music Education
0958–0999
GB–Lancaster: CTI [Computers in Teaching Initiative] Centre for Music, 1989–
[NOT IN BUCOMP1]

   AB 1 (1989)–2 (1990), 2

Au 1 (1989)–#
BAc 2 (1990)–#
BRu 2 (1990)–#
EIR:Dtc 1 (1989)–#
En 1 (1989)–#
Er 1 (1989)–#
EXu 1 (1989)–2 (1990)
Gul 1 (1989)–#
KE 1 (1989)–#
LAu 1 (1989)–#
Lbl*
Lcu 2 (1990)–#
LEbc 1 (1989)–#
Lgsm 1 (1989)–#
Lkc 2 (1990)–#
Ltc*
Ltu 2 (1990)–4 (1995)
LVu 1 (1989), 2–#
MK 1 (1989)–#
Msuc 1 (1989)–#
Mu 1 (1989), 2–#
NO 1 (1989)–#
NWu 1 (1989)–2 (1990)
Ob*
Ouf 1 (1989)–#
R 1 (1989); 3 (1993)
SFu 1 (1989)–2 (1990)
SOu 2 (1990)–#
TOd 1 (1989)
Uu 1 (1989)–#

Musicworks
0225–686X
C–Toronto: Music Gallery, 1978–
[NOT IN BUCOMP1]

NO 15–17, 1981; 19, 1982; 31, 1985

Musigraph
TNG GB460
GB–London: Composers and Editors' Lending
Library, 1955–?

Lbl*
Lu 1 (1955)

Musiikin Suunta [= Musical Trends]
0780–0703
FIN–Helsinki: Suomen Etnomusikologinen
Seura, 1979–
[NOT IN BUCOMP1]

Lbl 1987–#
Lsa 1983–88 [w 1984, 1, 2; 1985, 3, 4;
   1988, 4]

Musiikin Tutkimuslaitoksen Julkaisusarja
[= Musical Research Transactions]
FIN–Helsinki: Sibelius Academy, 1989–

Lbl 1989–# [w 2]

Musiikki [= Music]
TNG SF25; 0355–1059
FIN–Helsinki: Suomen Etnomusikologinen
Seura, 1971–

Cu 1971–91
Lbbc 1971, 3, 4

Die Musik [1]
Fellinger 1968/1588; TNG D410
D–Berlin: Max Hesse, 1901–15; 1922–43
[Continued as part of *Musik im Kriege* (q.v.),
1943–45]

BSdsc*
Bu 1 (1901)–13 (1914)
Cpl 21 (1929), 12
Cu 1 (1901)–35 (1943)
DRu 1 (1901)–2 (1902)
En 3 (1903), 5
Ep 27 (1934), 4–12; 28 (1935)–31 (1938);
   32 (1939), 1–7, 9, 10; 33 (1940)–34 (1941),
   1, 3–9, 11, 12; 35 (1942), 3, 4
Er 1 (1901), 1, 2, 4– 19, 22–24; 2 (1902),
   1–18, 20–24; 3 (1903), 12; 5 (1905), 4;
   7 (1907), 13; 9 (1909), 1; 13 (1921)–14
   (1922); 15 (1923), 5; 16 (1923), 1, 3; 17
   (1925), 6, 7; 18 (1926), 6; 20 (1928), 6, 7
Lam 2 (1902/03), 15, 16, 20/21; 3 (1903/04),
   17; 5 (1905/06), 1–2, 7, 19, 23; 17
   (1924/25), 6; 19 (1926/27), 4–21 (1928/29),
   4, 6–22 (1929/30),3; 24 (1931/32), 1
Lbl*
Lcm 1 (1901/02); 2 (1903), 15; 3 (1903/04),
   17; 8 (1908/09), 14, 15, 17, 20, 21, 23, 24;
   10 (1910/11), 2–5, 7, 9, 12–15, 18; 11
   (1911/12)–12 (1912/13); 13 (1913/14), 13–
   19
Lcml 1 (1901)–6 (1907)*; 11 (1911)*; 13
   (1914)*; 15 (1922)–17 (1924)*; 18 (1925)–
   26 (1934); 31 (1939)*
Lu 1 (1901)–2 (1903); 8 (1908)–13 (1914);
   15 (1922); 17 (1924);–29 (1937); 31
   (1938/39)*
Mcm 8 (1908/09), 1
NO 23 (1931), 4; 25 (1933), 7, 10–26 (1934),
   1
Ob*
Ouf 1 (1902)–5 (1906), 4; 8 (1908/09)

Die Musik [2]
D–Berlin: Bard, Marquardt, 1904–28
[Ceased publication with no. 52, 1928]

Lbl*

Musik Aktuell: Analysen, Beispiele,
Kommentare
D–Kassel: Bärenreiter, ?1979–
[NOT IN BUCOMP1]

Ob 3 (?1981)–#

Musik-Almanach: Daten und Fakten zum
Musikleben in Deutschland
0930–8954
D–Kassel; Regensburg: Bärenreiter [for the
Deutscher Musikrat], 1986/87–
[NOT IN BUCOMP1]

Ob 1986/87–#

Musik der Zeit: eine Schriftenreihe zur
zeitgenössischen Musik
D–Bonn: Boosey and Hawkes, 1952–55; n.F.
1958–60

ALb 4, 1953; 7, 1954; 9, 1955
LAu 4, 1953; 11, 1955
Lbl*
Lcml 1, 1952; 3–12, 1953–55

Musik des Ostens: Sammelbände für
historische und vergleichende Forschung
0580–3225
D–Kassel: Bärenreiter [for the Johann–
Gottfried–Herder–Forschungsstelle für
Musikgeschichte], 1962–

BSdsc*
Cu 1 (1962)–#
Lam 1 (1962)–4 (1967)
LAu 1 (1962)
Lu 1 (1962)–#
Ob*

Musik-Erziehung
TNG A239; 0027–4798
A–Vienna: Österreichischer Bundesverlag [for
the Arbeitsgemeinschaft der Musikerzieher
Österreichs], 1947/48–
[NOT IN BUCOMP1; also bore subtitle
Zeitschrift der Musikerzieher Österreichs: Organ
der AGMO; included supplements Komponist
und Musikerzieher; and Mozartgemeinde Wien]

BSdsc*
Lam 3 (1949), 1–3; 4 (1950), 1, 2; 5 (1951),
1–4; 1967 [special issue]
Lcm 1967, Sum

Musik für Alle: Monatshefte zur Pflege
volkstümlicher Musik
Fellinger 1968/1733; TNG D441
D–Berlin, 1904–37

Lbl*
Mcm 1 (1904/05), 7; 2 (1905/06), 18; 3
(1906/07), 25, 26, 29; 4 (1907/08), 7; 5
(1908/09), 4, 10; 6 (1909/10), 65, 71, 72; 7
(1910/11), 73, 77, 80, 82, 83; 8 (1911/12),
89, 90, 93

Musik i Sverige see Music in Sweden

Musik im Kriege
TNG D799
D–Berlin, 1943–45
[Musik im Kriege comprised the following
journals: Allgemeine Musikzeitung; Melos (q.v.);
Die Musik [1] (q.v.)]; Neue Zeitschrift für
Musik; Neues Musikblatt (q.v.)]

Ep 1 (1943), 1–6; 2 (1944), 1–8, 11, 12
Lbl*
Lu 1 (1943)–2 (1944), 8

Musik im Unterricht see Deutsche
Tonkünstler-Zeitung: Fachblatt für Musiker
und Musikerzieher

Musik im Unterricht see also Jugendmusik:
Mitteilungen des Verlages B. Schott's Söhne,
Mainz, für alle die mit der Jugend musizieren

Musik im Unterricht see also Das Musikleben:
Monatszeitschrift

Musik in Bayern see Mitteilungsblatt der
Gesellschaft für Bayerische Musikgeschichte

Musik in der Schule: Zeitschrift für Theorie
und Praxis des Musikunterrichts
TNG D856; 0027–4704
D–Berlin: Volk und Wissen Verlag, 1949–

BSdsc*
Mcm 24 (1973), 9–12; 25 (1974), 1–11;
26 (1975)–34 (1983)

Musik Information
TNG D1067; 0323–438X
D–Berlin: Deutsche Hochschule für Musik
Hanns Eisler, 1970–
[Issue no. 1 dates from 1971; it was preceded by
a preview issue in 1970]

> **BSdsc***
> **Cu** 1970–#

Musik International
0342–1775
D–Siegburg: F. Schmitt, ?1947–90
[NOT IN BUCOMP1; succeeded by
*Instrumentenbau Zeitschrift, Musik
International* (ISSN 0934–3962) in 1990]

> **BSdsc***

Musik-Journal
TNG A293
A–Vienna, 1969–
[NOT IN BUCOMP1]

> **Lam** 1972, 5

Musik Magazin: Tips and Trends
0930–7591
D–Mainz: B. Schott's Söhne, 1987–
[NOT IN BUCOMP1]

> **BSdsc** 1 (1987), 2
> **Lcml** 1 (1987)–#
> **Ob** 1 (1987)–#*

Musik och Ljudteknik [= Music and Sound Engineering]
TNG S98
S–Stockholm, 1959–
[NOT IN BUCOMP1]

> **BSdsc***

Musik og Forskning [= Music and Research]
0903–188X
DK–Copenhagen: Akademisk Forlag, 1975–
[NOT IN BUCOMP1]

> **LRHBNC** 1 (1975)–16 (1991)
> **Ob***

Musik og Teater
0106–3146
DK–Copenhagen: C. Lynge, 1979–89
[NOT IN BUCOMP1; entitled *Teater* (ISSN
0902–1957), 1986–89]

> **Lbl** 1–27, 1979–86

**Musik Psychologie: Jahrbuch der Deutschen
Gesellschaft für Musikpsychologie**
0177–350X
D–Wilhelmshaven: Heinrichshofen [for the
Gesellschaft für Musikpsychologie], 1984–
[NOT IN BUCOMP1]

> **Ob** 1 (1984)–#

**Musik und Bildung: Zeitschrift für Theorie
und Praxis der Musikerziehung**
TNG D1064; 0027–4747
D–Mainz: Schott, 1969–
[See also *Deutsche Tonkünstler-Zeitung:
Fachblatt für Musiker und Musikerzieher*]

> **BSdsc***
> **SOu** 5 (1973), 11 [Mahler issue]

Musik und Gesellschaft
TNG D893; 0027–4755
D–Berlin: Henschelverlag, 1951–90

> **Bs** 32 (1982)–40 (1990)
> **BSdsc***
> **EIR:Dtc** 27 (1977)–40 (1990), 12
> **Lbl***
> **Lcm** 32 (1982), 4, 5
> **Lcml** 32 (1982)–40 (1990)
> **Lu** 16 (1966), 6; 17 (1967)–21 (1971);
> 38 (1988)–40 (1990)
> **Ob** 7 (1957)–34 (1984), 12

**Musik und Gottesdienst: Zeitschrift für
evangelische Kirchenmusik**
TNG CH136; 0027–4763
CH–Zurich: Zwingli-Verlag, 1947–

> **BSdsc***

Musik und Kirche
TNG D727; 0027–4771
D–Kassel: Bärenreiter, 1929–
[Absorbed the *Zeitschrift für evangelische
Kirchenmusik* in 1933]

> **Cpl** 3 (1931), 1; 29 (1959), 2; 30 (1960), 2, 3;
> 31 (1961), 5, 6
> **Lam** 31 (1961), 2
> **Lcml** 17 (1947)*; 18 (1948)–19 (1949); 20
> (1950)–22 (1952)*; 23 (1953); 24 (1954)*
> **Ob***
> **Ouf** 30 (1960), 5–36 (1966), 6

Musik- und Literaturblatt für
Volksschullehrer und Schulfreunde
Fellinger 1968/505; TNG A55
A–Vienna, 1864–73

    Lbl 1 (1864); 4 (1867)–9 (1872)

Musik und Schrifttum
D–Wurzburg: Triltsch, 1942–43

    Lbl*

Musikalienhandel und Vereins-Wahlzettel *see*
Musikhandel und Musikpflege: Mitteilungen
des Vereins der Deutschen Musikalienhändler
zu Leipzig

Musikalier i Danske Biblioteker/Music in
Danish Libraries: Accessionskatalog
DK–Copenhagen: Bibliotekscentralen, 1971–
[NOT IN BUCOMP1]

    Lbl 1973–#

Musikalisch-kritische Bibliothek
TNG D16
D–Gotha: C. W. Ettinger, 1778–79

    Ob 1788–89 [Reprint ed.]

Musikalisch-literarischer Monatsbericht
neuer Musikalien, musikalischer Schriften
und Abbildungen
Fellinger 1968/90; TNG D62
D–Leipzig: Hofmeister, 1829–1942
[From 1943 entitled *Deutsche
Musikbibliographie* (q.v.)]

    Lbl*
    Ob*

Das Musikalische Deutschland des
neunzehnten Jahrhunderts: eine historisch-
biographische, kunstwissenschaftliche
pädagogische Musikzeitschrift
Fellinger 1968/370; TNG D135
D–Berlin, 1856

    Lbl 1856, 1, 2

Musikalische Eilpost: Uebersicht des
Neuesten im Gebiete der Musik
Fellinger 1968/74; TNG D56
D–Weimar: Hoffmann, 1826
[25 numbers in total]

    Lbl*

Musikalische Jugendpost
Fellinger 1968/1024; TNG D286
D–Cologne: P. J. Tonger, 1886–99

    Mp 7 (1892)–12 (1897)

Musikalische Monatsschrift
TNG D27
D–Berlin: Neue Berlinische Musikhandlung,
1791–92; 1793
[Head title of issues 1792, 1 and 2 was
Musikalisches Wochenblatt; head title of 1793
vol. was *Studien für Tonkünstler und
Musikfreunde*]

    Cu 1791–92 [Reprint ed.]
    Er 1791–92; 1793
    Lbl 1791–92; 1793

Musikalische Nachrichten und Anmerkungen
see Wöchentliche Nachrichten und
Anmerkungen die Musik betreffend

Musikalische Neu-Jahrs-Gedichte *see*
Musicalische Neu-Jahrs-Gedichte

Musikalische Real-Zeitung und musikalische
Anthologie für Kenner und Liebhaber
D–Speyer, 1788–90
[NOT IN BUCOMP1]

    Cu 1 (1788)–3 (1790) [Reprint ed.]
    Lbl 1 (1788)–3 (1790) [Reprint ed.]
    Lu 1 (1788)–3 (1790) [Reprint ed.]
    Ob 1 (1788)–3 (1790) [Reprint ed.]

Musikalische Tagesfragen: Zeitschrift für
Musik und Musikfreunde *see* Aufsätze über
musikalische Tagesfragen

Musikalischer Almanach für Deutschland
TNG D19
D–Leipzig: Schwickert, 1782–84; 1789

    Cu 1782–84; 1789 [Reprint ed.]
    Er 1782–84; 1789
    Lbl*
    Lu 1782–84; 1789 [Reprint ed.]
    Ob 1782–84; 1789 [Reprint ed.]

Musikalischer Anzeiger *see* Neue Musik-
Zeitung: illustriertes Familienblatt

Musikalischer Haus-Freund: neuer Kalendar
für das Jahr 1822 [–1824, 1826–31, 1835]
Fellinger 1968/56; TNG D52
D–Mainz: Schott, 1822–31; 1835

> Er 1824; 1826–28
> Lbl 1822–24; 1826–31; 1835

Musikalisches Kunstmagazin
TNG D20
D–Berlin: J. F. Reichardt, 1782; 1791

> Au 1 (1782)–2 (1791) [Reprint ed.]
> Cu 1 (1782)–2 (1791) [Reprint ed.]
> Er 1 (1782)–2 (1791)
> Ob 1 (1782)–2 (1791) [Reprint ed.]
> Ouf 1 (1782)–2 (1791)

Musikalisches Wochenblatt see Musikalische
Monatsschrift

Musikalisches Wochenblatt: Organ für
Musiker und Musikfreunde
Fellinger 1968/625; TNG D193
D–Leipzig: E. W. Fritzsch, 1870–1910
[From 1906, 40, combined with *Neue Zeitschrift
für Musik* (q.v.) to become *Musikalisches
Wochenblatt/Neue Zeitschrift für Musik:
vereinigte musikalische Wochenschriften*; also
included a supplement, *Musikbibliographische
Monatshefte* (1908)]

> Bu 1 (1870)–32 (1901); 37 (1906)–41 (1910)
> Er 1 (1870), 26; 4 (1873), 44–46, 48–52;
> 5 (1874), 1–4; 13 (1882), 27
> Lbl*
> Lcm 1 (1870)–34 (1903)
> Ob*

Musikalisches Wochenblatt/Neue Zeitschrift
für Musik see Musikalisches Wochenblatt:
Organ für Musiker und Musikfreunde

Musik-Almanach für die tchechoslowakische
Republik
TNG CS110
CZ–Prague, 1921
[NOT IN BUCOMP1]

> Ob 1 (1921)

Musikbibliographische Monatshefte see
Musikalisches Wochenblatt: Organ für
Musiker und Musikfreunde

Musikbibliographischer Dienst
TNG D1063; 0580–8421
D–Berlin: Deutscher
Büchereiverband/Deutsches Bibliotheksinstitut,
1970–82

> Lam 1 (1969) [Preview issue]
> Lbl*
> Lu 1 (1969)–5 (1974), 5

Musikbibliothek Aktuell
TNG D1083; 0341–776X
D–Berlin: Deutscher Büchereiverband, 1974–78
[NOT IN BUCOMP1]

> ABc (ILS) 1974–78
> Lcml 1974–78

Musikblatt
0172–8989
D–Göttingen: W. Ulrichs, 1974–
[NOT IN BUCOMP1]

> Lcs 11 (1984), 98; 12 (1985), 102, 104; 14
> (1987), 115; 15 (1988), 123, 127; 19
> (1992), Feb/Mar

Musikblätter des Anbruch
TNG A184
A–Vienna: Universal Edition, 1919–37
[Entitled *Anbruch: Monatsschrift für moderne
Musik* from 1929 to 1937. Absorbed *Pult und
Taktstock: Fachzeitschrift für Dirigenten* (q.v.)
in 1930]

> BSdsc*
> Cpl 2 (1920)–10 (1928)*; 11 (1929)–19
> (1937)*
> Lam 2 (1920)–3 (1921); 6 (1924), 6; 12
> (1930)–13 (1931), 1; 17 (1935), 5
> LAu 6 (1924), Aug, Sep
> Lbl*
> Lcml 2 (1920)–4 (1922)*; 7 (1925)–12
> (1930)*; 17 (1935)*; 19 (1937)*
> Lu 1 (1919)–15 (1933)*
> Mcm 2 (1920), 13–17, 19, 20; 3 (1921), 5
> Ob 1 (1919)–19 (1937) [m]
> SA 5 (1923), 6, 7; 7 (1925), 7–10; 11 (1929)–
> 12 (1930), 6

Musikbuch aus Österreich
Fellinger 1968/1734; TNG A151
A/D–Vienna; Leipzig: C. Fromme, 1904–13

> Lbl*

Musikelektronik: Zeitschrift des
Informationskreises Musikelektronik
0175–9140
D–Münster: IME, 1980–
[NOT IN BUCOMP1]

    BSdsc 5 (1984)–7 (1986), 2

Musikern: Tidning för Civil- och
Militärmusici [= Musicians: a Paper for
Civilian and Military Musicians]
Fellinger 1968/1929; TNG S35; 0027–478X
S–Stockholm: Svenska Musikerforbundet,
1908–
[NOT IN BUCOMP1; from 1910 entitled
Svenska Musikerförbundets Tidning]

    BSdsc*

Musikerreihe
CH–Olten: Otto Walter, 1946–
[NOT IN BUCOMP1]

    BSdsc 5, 1949; 7, 1950; 13, 1953

Der Musikerzieher *see* Deutsche Tonkünstler-
Zeitung: Fachblatt für Musiker und
Musikerzieher

Musikerziehung *see* Musik-Erziehung

Musikethnologische Jahresbibliographie
Europas/Annual Bibliography of European
Ethnomusicology
TNG CS213; 0077–2534
SQ–Bratislava: Slovenske Narodne Muzeum,
1966–75

    Cpl 1 (1966)–7 (1972)
    Lsa 1 (1966)–9 (1974)
    Lu 1 (1966)–8 (1973)
    Ob*

Die Musikforschung
TNG D839; 0027–4801
D–Kassel: Bärenreiter, 1948–
[Previously *Archiv für Musikforschung* (q.v.)
and *Gesellschaft für Musikforschung:
Mitteilungen* (q.v.)]

    AB 1 (1948), 1, 4; 25 (1972)
    Au 29 (1976)–42 (1989)
    BG 12 (1959)–#
    BRu 33 (1980)–46 (1993)
    Bu 7 (1954)–#
    CDu 17 (1964); 19 (1966); 21 (1968);
      24 (1971)–33 (1980); 42 (1989)–#

Cpl 1 (1948)–25 (1972); 26 (1973), 3, 4
Cu 1 (1948)–#
DRu 9 (1956)–11 (1958)
Er 1 (1948)–#
EXu 25 (1972)–40 (1987)
Gul 33 (1980)–#
HUu 19 (1966)–40 (1987)
Lam 14 (1961), 4; 16 (1963)–19 (1966);
    20 (1967), 2, 4–24 (1971), 4; 26 (1973),
    2–28 (1975), 1
LAu 1 (1948)–21 (1968)
Lbbc 4 (1951)–# [w 8 (1955), 1, 2; 9 (1956);
    16 (1963), 2]
Lcm 2 (1949); 5 (1952); 6 (1953), 2; 7
    (1954), 1, 3; 10 (1957), 4; 11 (1958), 2–4;
    12 (1959), 2–4; 13 (1960)–16 (1963);
    25 (1972)–40 (1987)
Lcml 1 (1948)–6 (1953); 7 (1954)*;
    8 (1955)–#
Lkc 1 (1948)–16 (1963); 17 (1964)*;
    18 (1965)–19 (1966); 20 (1967)*;
    21 (1968)–25 (1972); 27 (1974)–#
LRHBNC 41 (1988)–#
Lsa 14 (1961)–19 (1966), 2*
Lu 1 (1948), 2–#
Lu (RMA) 1 (1948)–# [w 11 (1958), 4;
    12 (1959), 1; 13 (1960)–15 (1962), 1]
LVp 3 (1950); 8 (1955)–11 (1958)
LVu 1 (1948)–#
Mcm 4 (1951), 4; 5 (1952), 2–4; 6 (1953), 1;
    11 (1958), 1; 12 (1959), 3; 26 (1973), 3, 4;
    27 (1974)–35 (1982), 1
Mpl 1 (1948)–#
Mu 15 (1962)–# [w 21 (1968), 4]
NO 15 (1962)–#
Ob 1 (1948)–#
Ouf 1 (1948)–45 (1992), 4
R 17 (1964)–27 (1974)
SFu 17 (1964)–30 (1977)
SOu 16 (1963)–34 (1981) [w 26 (1973);
    27 (1974)]

Musikforum: Referate und Informationen des
Deutschen Musikrates *see* Deutscher
Musikrat: Referate und Informationen

Musikforum: Zeitschrift für musikalisches
Volksschaffen *see* Die Volksmusik: Zeitschrift
für das musikalische Laienschaffen

Musikhandel
TNG D855; 0027–481X
D–Wiesbaden: Deutscher Musikverleger-
Verband, 1949–
[Previously *Mitteilungen des Deutschen
Musikalienwirtschafts-Verbandes* (19 numbers,
1946–49)]

  BSdsc*
  Lbl*
  Lsa 10 (1959), 12–14 (1963), 7 [w 11 (1960),
    4–6, 8, 12 (1961), 1, 3–6; 13 (1962), 2, 3, 5,
    6; 14 (1963), 5, 8]

**Musikhandel und Musikpflege: Mitteilungen
des Vereins der Deutschen Musikalienhändler
zu Leipzig**
Fellinger 1968/1444; TNG D378
D–Leipzig: Verlag der Vereins der deutschen
Musikalienhändler, 1898–1944
[From 1900 entitled *Musikhandel und Vereins-
Wahlzettel*; from 1918, *Musikalienhandel und
Vereins-Wahlzettel*]

  ALb 1 (1898)–4 (1902), 52; 13 (1911)–17
    (1915), 20
  Ob*

Musikhandel und Vereins-Wahlzettel *see*
**Musikhandel und Musikpflege: Mitteilungen
des Vereins der Deutschen Musikalienhändler
zu Leipzig**

**Musikhistorisk Arkiv [= Archive of Music
History]**
TNG DK47
DK–Copenhagen: Levin og Munksgaard,
1931–39
[Superseded the *Aarbog for Musik* (q.v.)]

  Cu 1 (1931/39)

Musikhistoriska Museets Skrifter
0081–5675
S–Stockholm, 1964–81
[NOT IN BUCOMP1; ceased with no. 9;
succeeded by *Musikmuseets Skrifter* (q.v.)]

  BSdsc 4 (1972)–8 (1981)

Musiki Mecmuasi [= Music Review]
TNG TUR6
TR–Istanbul, 1948–
[Preceded by *Turk Musiki Dergisi* (q.v.)]

  Cu 17 (1965)–#
  Lsa ?36 (1983), 399

  Lso 18 (1966), 219–223; 19 (1967)–25
    (1972), 278
  Ob 1 (1948)–#*

Musik-Information *see* **Musik Information**

Das Musikinstrument *see* **Das
Musikinstrument und Phono**

Das Musikinstrument und Phono
TNG D901; 0027–4828
D–Frankfurt: E. Bochinsky, 1952–
[Entitled *Das Musikinstrument* from vol. 22
(1973), 7]

  AB 29 (1980), 9
  BSdsc*
  Er 42 (1993), 5–#
  Lam 30 (1981), 11
  Lcml 17 (1968)–#
  Lu 31 (1982), 8
  Mcm 34 (1985), 6
  Ob 1 (1952)–#*

Musikkmagasinet Ballade *see* **Ballade:
Tidsskrift for Ny Musikk**

Musik-Konzepte
TNG D1096
D–Munich: Edition Text und Kritik, 1978–

  Cu 1978–#
  Ob*

Musikktrykk *see* **Norsk Bokfortegnelse:
Musikktrykk**

Das Musikleben: Monatszeitschrift
TNG D832
D–Mainz: Melos Verlag, 1948–55
[Ceased publication with vol. 8 no. 9 (1955);
absorbed into *Neue Zeitschrift für Musik*;
included supplement *Musik im Unterricht*]

  Cpl 2 (1949), 9, 10
  LAu 2 (1949), 4–12; 3 (1950), 1, 2, 4–12;
    4 (1951)–8, (1955), 9
  Lcml 1 (1948); 2 (1949)–3 (1950)*; 4 (1951)

Musikmuseets Skrifter
0282–8952
S–Stockholm: Musikmuseet, ?1985–
[NOT IN BUCOMP1; succeeded
Musikhistoriska Museets Skrifter (q.v.)]

  BSdsc 10 (1985)–14 (1989)

Musikologie: Sbornik pro Hudebni Vĕdu a Kritiku [= Musicology: Miscellany for Musicology and Music Criticism]
TNG CS158
CZ–Prague; Brno: 1938; 1949; 1955; 1958
[2 vols. published in 1955]

  Cpl 1 (1938)
  Lbl*
  Ob 2 (1949)–4 (1955)

Musikpädagogik
0172–8202
D–Mainz: Schott, 1970–
[NOT IN BUCOMP1]

  BSdsc*

Musikpädagogische Blätter *see* **Klavier-Lehrer**

Musikpädagogische Forschung
D–Laaber: Laaber-Verlag [for the Arbeitskreis Musikpädagogische Forschung], 1980–
[NOT IN BUCOMP1]

  Ob 1 (1980)–#

Musikrat der Deutschen Demokratischen Republik: Bulletin *see* **Bulletin: Musikrat der DDR**

Musikrevue
TNG DK87
DK–Copenhagen, 1954–72
[From 1961, 5, entitled *Jazzrevy*; from 1970 entitled *Musikrevue*]

  Cbijs 14 (1967), Mar

Musikrevy: Nordisk Tidskrift för Musik och Grammofon [= Music Review: Northern Journal for Music and the Gramophone]
TNG S92; 0027–4844
S–Stockholm, 1946–?94

  ALb 39 (1984), 7/8
  BSdsc*
  LAu 5 (1950), 1, 7, 8; 6 (1951), 1; 15 (1960), 3
  Lbl*
  Lcml 1951 [Special issue]; 15 (1960), 3; 1967 [Special issue]
  Lsa 32 (1977)–34 (1979), 7 [w 32 (1977), 2]
  Lu 1967 [Special issue]
  Mcm 15 (1960), 3
  Ob*
  SA 15 (1960), 3

Musiktaschenbuch *see* **Kalender für Musiker und Musikfreunde**

Musiktexte: Zeitschrift für neue Musik
0178–8884
D–Cologne: Musiktexte, 1983–
[NOT IN BUCOMP1]

  Lbbc 1, 1983–#
  Lbl*
  Lcm 1, 1983
  Lu 1, 1983–#
  Ouf 1–60, 1983–95

Musiktheorie: Zeitschrift für Musiktheorie
0177–4182
D–Laaber: Laaber-Verlag, 1986–
[NOT IN BUCOMP1; succeeded *Zeitschrift fur Musiktheorie* (q.v.)]

  Cu 1 (1986)–#
  Lbl 1 (1986)–#
  Lkc 1 (1986)–#
  Lu 1 (1986)–#
  Ob 1 (1986)–#
  SOu 4 (1989)–#

Musiktherapeutische Umschau
0172–5505
D–Stuttgart: G. Fischer, ?1979–
[NOT IN BUCOMP1]

  BSdsc*

Der Musikus
TNG D691
D–Berlin: Panorama, 1927
[NOT IN BUCOMP1]

  Lam 1927

Musikvärlden [= Worlds of Music]
TNG S91
S–Stockholm: Bonnier, 1945–49

  Lcml 4 (1948)–5 (1949)*

Musikvertrieb Schallplatten: Neuheiten der Woche
CH– Zurich, 19?–

  Lsa 234–500, 1962–67*

Musikwelt: Monatshefte für Oper und Konzert
TNG D589
D–Hamburg, 1921–31

  Cpl 9 (1929), 4

Musikwissenschaftliche Studien
0931–3095
D–Berlin, 1902–04

Lbl*

Musin' Music Magazine
GB–Cambridge: R. O'Dempsey, 1994–
[NOT IN BUCOMP1]

Lcs 1, 1994–#

Musique
TNG F522
F–Paris: Musique, 1927–30
[Previously (1923–27) *Revue Pleyel* (q.v.); from
1930 incorporated into *Le Guide du Concert*
(q.v.)]

Lcml 1 (1927/28)–3 (1929/30)*

Musique: Adresses Universelles *see* Musique-
Adresses: Annuaire Français de la Facture
Instrumentale, de l'Édition Musicale et des
Industries qui s'y rattachent

La Musique: Gazette Universelle des Artistes
et Amateurs *see* La France Musicale

La Musique, Gazette de la France Musicale
F–Paris: M. and L. Escudier, 1849
[NOT IN BUCOMP1]

Gul (e) 1–52, 1849

Musique-Adresses: Annuaire Français de la
Facture Instrumentale, de l'Édition Musicale
et des Industries qui s'y rattachent
Fellinger 1968/2184; TNG F445
F–Paris, 1913–31
[Entitled *Musique: Adresses Universelles* from
1925]

Lbl*

Musique Ancienne
0182–9653
F–Bourg-la-Reine: CAEL [Centre Animation,
Expression, Loisir], ?197?–
[NOT IN BUCOMP1]

Cpl 18, 19, 1984

Musique Contemporaine: Revue
Internationale
TNG F631; 0464–0640
F–Paris, 1951–52
[6 numbers in total]

Lcml 1951, 1

La Musique des Familles *see* La Musique
Populaire

Musique en Jeu: Revue Trimestrielle
TNG F706; 0767–9742
F–Paris: Seuil, 1970–78
[Ceased publication with no. 33, 1978]

BSdsc*
BTu 1–8, 1970–72; 10, 12, 1973; 15, 1974;
 17, 1975; 25–26, 1976–77; 31, 1978
Bu 2–32, 1971–78*
Cu 1–33, 1970–78
En*
EXu 5–33, 1971–78
Lcml 1–33, 1971–78
Lcu 1–33, 1970–78
Lkc 1–24, 1970–76; 29–33, 1977–78
Mpl 7–33, 1972–78
NO 1–33, 1970–78
NWu 1–33, 1970–78
Ob*

La Musique en l'Année 1862, ou Revue
Annuelle des Théâtres Lyriques et des
Concerts [...]
Fellinger 1968/456; TNG F96
F–Paris, 1863
[Succeeded *L'Année Musicale, ou Revue
Annuelle des Théâtres Lyriques et des Concerts
[...]* (q.v.)]

Lbl*

La Musique en Pologne
0860–9101
PL–Warsaw: Polish Music Council/Conseil
Polonais de la Musique, 1966–81; 1983–
[37 nos in total; succeeded by *Music in Poland*
(TNG PL123; ISSN 0860– 911X) from 1983,
no.38]

BSdsc*
Lbbc*
Lki*
Mpl 5, 1970–#
Ob*
Ouf 1–37, 1966–81; 38 (1983)–43 (1991), 1

Musique et Instruments: Revue du Commerce
et de l'Industrie de la Musique
Fellinger 1968/2086; TNG F42; 0027–4852
F–Paris, 1911–14; 1919–64
[In Sep/Oct 1939 (no. 360) incorporated the
Revue des Machines Parlantes (TNG F469) to
form *Musique et Radio*]

> **Lam** 50 (1960), 595; 53 (1963), 633
> **Lbbc** 62 (1972)–65 (1975)*
> **Lcm** 60 (1970), 2, 4–6; 61 (1971), 1–6; 62
> (1972), 1, 2

Musique et Liturgie *see* La Voix de l'Église

Musique et Radio *see* Musique et Instruments:
Revue du Commerce et de l'Industrie de la
Musique

La Musique Moderne
F–Paris: Aveline, 1926–29

> **Lbl***

Musique-Musicologie
F–Paris: Honoré Champion, 1976–
[NOT IN BUCOMP1]

> **Lbl***

Musique-Musiques: Bulletin d'Information du
Conseil de la Musique de la Communauté
Française de Belgique
0772–3083
B–Brussels: Conseil de la Musique, 1982–90
[Ceased publication with no. 19, 1990]

> **Mcm***

La Musique Populaire
Fellinger 1968/860; TNG F172
F–Paris, 1881–90
[Entitled *La Musique des Familles* from no. 157,
1884]

> **Lcm (p)** 2 (1882/83)

La Musique Populaire: Chorale,
Instrumentale, Religieuse
Fellinger 1968/482; TNG F104
F–Paris: L. Martinet, 1863–70

> **Lbl** 1 (1863)–8 (1870), 8

Musique Suisse sur Disques *see* Schweizer
Musik auf Schallplatten

Musurgia
F–Paris, 1994–
[NOT IN BUCOMP1]

> **Cu** 1 (1994)–#

Muusikalisi Lehekulgi
EW–Talinn: Eesti Raamat, 1979–
[NOT IN BUCOMP1]

> **Lbl** 2 (1979)–#

Muzica: Revista Uniunii Compozitorilor din
Republica Populară Română [= Magazine of
the Composers' Union of the People's
Republic of Rumania]
TNG R24; 0580–3713
RO–Bucharest, 1951–

> **Cu** 12 (1962), 12–14 (1964); 17 (1967)
> **Lbbc** 36 (1986), 10, 1
> **Lbl***
> **Ls** 10 (1960)–#
> **Lu** 13 (1963), 1; 15 (1965); 23 (1973), 6, 7
> [w 13 (1963), 11, 12; 14 (1964)]
> **LVp** 18 (1968), 6–9; 19 (1969)–21(1971);
> 22 (1972), 4, 5, 7
> **NO** 25 (1975), 10–#
> **Ob***

Muzicka Revija [= Music Review]
TNG YU30
HR–Zagreb, 1950–51

> **Cu** 1 (1950)–2 (1951), 1
> **Lcml** 1 (1950), 1

De Muziek
NL–S'Gravenhage, 1938–?

> **Lbl***

De Muziek: Officieel Orgaan van de Federatie
van Nederlandsche Toonkunstenaars-
Vereenigingen [= Official Journal of the
Federation of Dutch Composer
Organisations]
TNG NL74
NL–Amsterdam: Van Seffardt, 1926–33
[Continued as *Caecilia en de Muziek* from
1933/34, following merger with *Caecilia:
Algemeen Muzikaal Tijdschrift van Nederland*
(q.v.)]

> **Lbl***
> **Ob** 1 (1926/27)–7 (1932/33)

Muziek en Dans in Onderwijs en Praktijk
[= Music and Dance in Instruction and
Practice]
TNG NL139
NL–Amsterdam: Stichting Muzisch Tijdschrift,
1977–
[Also known as *MD*]

Mcm 1978, 8–1982, 10

Het Muziekleven in Belgie *see* Belgisch
Muziekleven

De Muziekvereld *see* Orgaan der Federatie
van Nederlandse Toonkunstenaars-
Vereenigingen

Muzika
TNG ETHIOPIA1
ETH–Addis Ababa, 1968–
[NOT IN BUCOMP1]

Lso 1968, 1

Muzikološki Zbornik/Musicological Annual
TNG YU37; 0580–373X
SI–Ljubljana: Department of Musicology, 1965–

Cpl 3 (1967)
Er 1 (1965)–3 (1967)
Lbbc 6 (1970)–#
Lbl*
NO 1 (1965)–#
Ob*
Ouf 1 (1965)–#

Muzsika
TNG H87
H–Budapest, 1958–

ALb 4 (1961), 1
LAu 8 (1965), 9
Mcm 17 (1974), 1, 3–12; 18 (1975), 1–3, 6, 8,
10; 19 (1976), 1–4, 9–12; 20 (1977), 7–12;
21 (1978)–25 (1982); 26 (1983), 3–12; 27
(1984)–28 (1985), 1
Ob*

Muzsika: Képes Havi Zenei Folyóirat
[= Illustrated Monthly Music Review]
TNG H67; 0027–5336
H–Budapest, 1929–30

Cpl 1 (1929), 1
Lbl*
Ob 1 (1929); 2 (1930), 4–5

Muzyka [1]
Fellinger 1968/2036
RF–Moscow, 1910–16
[255 nos in total]

Ob 181–252, 1914–16*

Muzyka [2]
TNG PL48
PL–Warsaw, 1924–38

Cpl 2 (1925), 4, 5–9 (1932), 5, 6*

Muzyka [3]
TNG BG13
BG–Sofia, 1948–49; 1951–

Lbl*
Ouf 1967–91, 2*

Muzyka [4]
PL–Warsaw, 1950–56

Lbl*

Muzyka [5]
LT–Vilnius: Vaga, 1979–
[NOT IN BUCOMP1]

Lbl*

Muzyka: Kwartalnik Poswięcony Historii i
Teorii Muzyki Oraz Krytyce Naukoweji
Artystycznej [= Music: Quarterly Devoted to
the History and Theory of Music and to
Scientific and Artistic Criticism]
TNG PL113; 0027–5344
PL–Warsaw: Panstwowy Instytut Sztuki, 1956–

Lbl*
Lcml 2 (1957), 4, 5
Ouf 4 (1959), 4–31 (1986), 3*

Muzyka: Organ Ministerstva Kul'turi URSR
Spilki Kompozitoriv Ukraine ta Muzichno-
Khorovogo Tovaristva
UKR–Kiev: Muzyczna Ukraina, 1970–
[NOT IN BUCOMP1]

Lbl 1974–#*
Ob 1 (1970)–#

Muzyka: Zhurnal z Pytan' Muzychnoye
Kul'tury [= Journal on Matters of Musical
Culture]
TNG USSR46; 0131–2367
UKR–Kiev: Muzychna Ukraina, 1923–

Ls 1982–#
Ob*

Muzyka i Revolyutsiya [= Music and Revolution]
TNG USSR55
RF–Moscow, 1926–29

    NO 1–43/44, 1926–29 [m]

Muzyka i Sovremennost [= Music and the Present]
0541–4849
RF–Moscow, 1962–

    Ob 3 (1965)–10 (1976)

Muzyka i Zhizn [= Music and Life]
TNG USSR76; 0303–5689
RF–Moscow: Sovetskiy Kompozitor, 1972–
[NOT IN BUCOMP1]

    Lbl*

Muzyka v SSSR *see* Music in the USSR

Muzyka Wspołczesna [= Contemporary Music]
TNG PL89
PL–Warsaw, 1936–39
[NOT IN BUCOMP1]

    Cpl 2 (1937), 4, 5

Muzykal'naya Akademiya *see* Sovetskaya Muzyka

Muzykal'naya Fol'kloristika [= Musical Folklore]
TNG USSR78
RF–Moscow: Sovetskiy Kompozitor, 1973–

    Gul 1973–78

Muzykal'naya Kul'tura Bratskikh Respublik SSSR: Sbornik Statei [= Musical Culture in the Neighbouring Republics: Journal]
UKR–Kiev: Muzyczna Ukraina, 1982–
[NOT IN BUCOMP1]

    Lbl*

Muzykal'naya Letopis: Stati i Materialy [= Musical Chronicle]
TNG USSR42
RF–Petrograd, 1922–1926

    Ob 1922–23; 1926

Muzykal'naya Zhizn' [= Musical Life]
TNG USSR71; 0131–2383
RF–Moscow: Soyuz Kompozitorov SSSR, 1958–

    ALb 1967, 6
    Cu 1969, 1–2, 4; 1963, 11; 1977, 6, 9, 11, 23–24; 1978, 1, 2, 13, 15–24; 1979, 1–7, 12; 1980, 1–3, 5–24; 1982, 14; 1985, 9–23; 1986, 1–3, 9–12
    Lbl*
    Lcml 1961–62*; 1963–64; 1965*; 1966; 1967–69*; 1970; 1971*; 1972; 1973*; 1978–#
    Ls 1986, 21–1988, 14; 1990, 4, 5, 8, 10, 15 [w 1987, 12]
    Lu 1983, 21–24; 1984, 1, 2
    NO 1981–83
    Ob*

Muzykal'niy Sovremennik [= Contemporary Music]
Fellinger 1968/2254; TNG USSR37
RF–Petrograd: A.N. Rimsky-Korsakov, 1915–17

    Lbl*

Muzykal'niy Spravochnik [= Musical Reference Book]
RF–Moscow, 1914

    Lbl*

Muzykal'noye Obrazovaniye [= Musical Education]
TNG USSR56
RF–Moscow: Moscow Conservatoire, 1925; 1927–30

    NO 1 (1925)–5 (1930) [m]

Muzykoznanie [= Musicology]
BG–Sofia: Bulgarska Akademiya na Naukite, Institut za Muzikoznanie, 1977–80
[NOT IN BUCOMP1; ? absorbed into *Bulgarsko Muzykoznanie* (q.v.) in 1980]

    Ob*

My Only Vice: the Journal of the Human Menagerie, the Official Steve Harley and Cockney Rebel Fanzine
0957–4298
GB–Exeter, 1989–
[NOT IN BUCOMP1]

    Lbl*

N

Nachrichten zur Mahler-Forschung *see* News about Mahler Research

NAJE Educator *see* Jazz Educators Journal

NAMA Newsletter *see* New Age Music Association: Newsletter

N.A.O. Review, incorporating Accordion Digest *see* Accordion Digest: a Text-Book of Accordion Knowledge

Nassarre: Revista Aragonesa de Musicologia
0213–7305
E–Zaragoza: Institucion Fernando del Catolico, Sección de Musica Antiqua, 1985–
[NOT IN BUCOMP1]

> CDu 5 (1989)–#

National Association of Percussion Teachers Newsletter
GB–London, 199?–
[NOT IN BUCOMP1]

> Msuc [c (2 years)]

National Association of Teachers of Singing: Journal *see* The Bulletin: the Official Magazine of the National Association of Teachers of Singing

National Centre for the Performing Arts: Quarterly Journal
IN–Bombay, 1972–88

> Lbl*
> TOd 2 (1973), 4; 3 (1974), 1, 2, 4; 4 (1975)

National Council of Music in Wales: Newsletter
TNG GB378
GB–Cardiff: University of Wales, 1942–?

> AB 1 (1942)–5 (1946)
> Lbl*
> Ob 1 (1942)–5 (1946)

National Early Music Association [NEMA] Journal
0951–6573
GB–Cambridge: National Early Music Association, 1984–90
[NOT IN BUCOMP1; succeeded by *Leading Notes: Journal of the National Early Music Association* (q.v.)]

> EIR:Dtc 10–13, 1989–90
> Er 7–10, 1987–89; 12, 13, 1990
> Lam 3, 4, 1985–86; 7, 1987; 9–13, 1988–90
> Lbl*
> Lu 7, 1987; 9–13, 1988–90
> R 9–10, 1988–89; 12, 1990

National Early Music Association [NEMA] News
GB–Cambridge: NEMA, 1989–
[NOT IN BUCOMP1]

> Er 1990–93
> Lam 1989, May, Aug; 1990, Aug, Dec; 1991, Sep; 1992, June–Dec; 1993, Mar, Dec; 1994, Mar–#

National Federation of Gramophone Societies *see* NFGS Bulletin

National Federation of Music Societies: Bulletin
GB–London: National Federation of Music Societies, 1964–73
[?Succeeded by *National Federation of Music Societies: News Bulletin* (q.v.)]

> HUu 2 (1968)–3 (1971)

National Federation of Music Societies: News Bulletin
GB–London: National Federation of Music Societies, 1973–
[NOT IN BUCOMP1]

> Ob 1 (1973)–#*

National Federation of Music Societies: Register of Members and Handbook
GB–London: National Federation of Music Societies, 197?–
[NOT IN BUCOMP1]

> Ob 1976–#

National Federation of Professional Musicians *see* The Bass Drum: the Official Gazette of the N.F.P.M.

National Film and Sound Archive Newsletter (Australia)
0814–6888
AUS–Canberra: Australian National Film and Sound Archive, 1984–
[NOT IN BUCOMP1]

> Lsa 1984–#*

National Folk Australia: Cairns Folk Club
AUS–Cairns: Cairns Folk Club, 1966–71
[NOT IN BUCOMP1]

    Lgo 1966–70

National Music Council: Bulletin
TNG US560; 0027–9749
US–New York: National Music Council, 1940–80
[NOT IN BUCOMP1]

    Lu 27 (1967), 3

National Operatic and Dramatic Association: Yearbook
GB–London: National Operatic and Dramatic Association [N.O.D.A.], 1955–
[NOT IN BUCOMP1]

    Ob 1955–#

National Operatic and Dramatic Association
see also N.O.D.A.

National Orchestral Association Monthly Report
TNG GB264
GB–?London: National Orchestral Association, ? – ?
[NOT IN BUCOMP1]

    Lcm 1913, Nov–1914, Sep; 1915, Feb–1916, Jan, Sep, Nov, Dec

The National Singing Circular *see* Mainzer's Musical Times and Singing Circular

National Society of Professional Musicians Monthly Journal *see* Monthly Journal of the National Society of Professional Musicians

National Union of Organists' Associations: Quarterly Record
Fellinger 1968/2258; TNG GB267; 0048–2161
GB–Stoke-on-Trent: Incorporated Association of Organists, 1913–
[From 1929, *The Quarterly Record of the Incorporated Association of Organists*; from 1966, *The Quarterly Record*; from 1967, Oct, *Organists' Review* (ISSN 0048–2161)]

    AB 56, 1971, 1, 2; 57, 1972, 3; 62, 1978, 1–#
    BDp 54 (1969)–#
    BG 68 (1983), 2–78 (1992), 2
    Bs 57 (1972)–#*
    CCtc 50 (1965)–60 (1975); 68 (1983)

Cpl 47 (1962), 2; 51 (1966), 4 –52 (1967), 2; 55 (1970)– 62 (1977)
Cu 56 (1971)–#
DS 75 (1989)–#
EIR:Dp 74 (1988)–76 (1990), 1
EIR:Dtc 56 (1971), 221–#
EIR:Duc 60 (1975)–76 (1991)
EIR:MEtc 63 (1978)–67 (1982)
En 53 (1968)–#
Gam 57 (1972), 3; 58 (1973)–63 (1978), 3; 64 (1979), 2–4; 65 (1980), 3; 66 (1981), 3, 4; 67 (1982)– 69 (1984), 4; 71 (1986)–75 (1989), 1; 76 (1990)–#
Gm 58 (1973)–#
Gul 60 (1975)–#
Lam 20 (1935), 77–22 (1937), 88; 37 (1952), 145; 42 (1957), 168; 56 (1971), 221; 57 (1972), 228; 58 (1973), 232; 60 (1975), 240; 61 (1976), 241, 243–62 (1977), 247; 63 (1978), 249–64 (1979), 253, 256; 66 (1981), 261–263; 67 (1982), 265–68; 8 (1983), 270, 272; 69/70 (1984/85)–72 (1987), 285, 287, 288; 74 (1988), 289–291; 75 (1989), 293–#
Lam(o) 59 (1974), 233–237; 60 (1975), 240–65 (1980), 263; 67 (1982), 265–268
LAu 73 (1987), 3–74 (1988); 75 (1989), 2
Lbar 53 (1968), 211; 54 (1970), 214–216; 55 (1970), 217, 219–57 (1972), 227, 228; 58 (1973), 230–233; 59 (1974)–#
Lbl*
Lcm 56 (1971)–78 (1992)*
Lcml 53 (1968), 209, 211–213, 215–#
Lgsm 66 (1981)–#
Lrco 1 (1913)–16 (1931); 39 (1954), 4; 41 (1956), 2; 42 (1957), 2; 43 (1958), 3, 4; 44 (1959), 1; 45 (1960), 2, 4; 46 (1961), 1, 2; 47 (1962), 2–4; 48 (1963), 3, 4; 49 (1964), 2–4; 50 (1965), 1, 4; 51 (1966)–54 (1969), 2, 4; 55 (1970)–#
Lu 25 (1970), 217–#
LVp 62 (1977)–#
Mcm 29 (1944)–31 (1946); 32 (1947), 126, 127; 46 (1961), 182; 48 (1963), 192, 193; 49 (1964)–52 (1967)
Mpl 4 (1916)–21 (1936); 58 (1973)–#
NOp [c (5 years)]
Ob*
R 55 (1970), 219; 56 (1971), 221; 57 (1972), 227

National Youth Orchestra News
GB–London: National Youth Orchestra, ?–?
[NOT IN BUCOMP1]

  LOnjfa*

The NATS Bulletin: the Official Magazine of
the National Association of Teachers of
Singing, Inc. *see* The Bulletin: the Official
Magazine of the National Association of
Teachers of Singing

NCS *see* New City Songster

Necrologie des Artistes, Musiciens, Acteurs et
Compositeurs de l'Année 1857
F–Marseilles, 1858

  Lbl*

Nederlandsche Musicalia [= Dutch Music]
Fellinger 1968/1935; TNG NL49
NL–Amsterdam: J. Muller [et al.] [for the
Vereeniging voor Noord–Nederlands
Muziekgeschiedenis], 1908–11

  Lbl*

The Needle: Record Collectors' Guide
US–Jackson Heights, NY: Robert Reynolds,
1944–45

  Cbijs 2 (1945), 1

Needle Time
GB–Swanage: Brian Rust, 1985–90
[NOT IN BUCOMP1; ceased publication with
no. 31, 1990]

  Cu 1–31, 1985–90
  Lbl*
  LOnjfa*
  Lsa 1–31, 1985–90
  Ob*

The Negro Music Journal
TNG US343
US–Washington: Washington Conservatory of
Music, 1902–03
[NOT IN BUCOMP1; ceased publication with
vol. 2, no. 15]

  Lbl 1 (1902)–2 (1903), 15 [Reprint ed.]

Neighbourhood Watch
GB–Mexborough, 1989–
[NOT IN BUCOMP1]

  Lbl*

NEMA Journal *see* National Early Music
Association [NEMA] Journal

NEMA News *see* National Early Music
Association [NEMA] News

NEMA Register of Early Music
TNG GB567; 0307–0816
GB–Cambridge: National Early Music
Association, 1971–91
[NOT IN BUCOMP1; published as supplement
to *Early Music* (q.v.) until 1976, thereafter
separately; from 1993 entitled *The Early Music
Yearbook* (q.v.); sometime entitled *The Register
of Early Music*]

  BRu 1974; 1975
  BSdsc*
  EIR:Dtc 1988–90
  Er 1990–91
  Lam 1988; 1990
  Lbl*
  Mcm 1974–91
  Ob*

Nerve *see* Punk

Neu eröffnete musikalische Bibliothek [...]
see Lorenz Mizler's neu eröffnete
musikalische Bibliothek, oder gründliche
Nachricht nebst unpartheyischem Urtheil von
musikalischen Schriften und Büchern

Neue Bachgesellschaft: Mitteilungsblatt
1015–1877
D–Leipzig: Neue Bachgesellschaft, 1976–
[NOT IN BUCOMP1]

  Ob 7, 1979–#*

Neue Berliner Musikzeitung
Fellinger 1968/252; TNG D108
D–Berlin: Bote und Bock, 1847–96
[Nos 7–38 also carried the head-title *Neue
musikalische Zeitung für Berlin*]

  EXu 1 (1847)–10 (1856) [m]
  Lbl 1 (1847)–50 (1896)
  Mpl 6 (1852)–8 (1854)
  Ob*

Neue Deutsche Rundschau *see* Freie Bühne
für modernes Leben

Neue Leipziger Zeitschrift für Musik *see*
Neue Zeitschrift für Musik

Neue Musik in der Bundesrepublik Deutschland: Dokumentation
TNG D1007; 0548–2879
D–Cologne: Internationale Gesellschaft für Neue Musik, Deutsche Sektion, 1958–

BLu 1 (1957/58)–8 (1964/65)
BRu 2 (1958/59)–6 (1962/63)
Bu 3 (1959/60); 5 (1961/62)–8 (1964/65)
Gam 2 (1958/59)–4 (1960/61)
Lam 1 (1957/58)
LAu 2 (1958/59)–10 (1966/67)*
Lbl*
Lu 1 (1957/58)–12 (1968/69)
Ob*
Ouf 1 (1957/58)–10 (1966/67)

Neue musikalische Zeitung für Berlin *see* Neue Berliner Musikzeitung

Neue Musikzeitschrift: Monatsschrift für Musiker und Musik-Freunde
TNG D809; 0174–982X
D–Munich: Erasmus–Verlag, 1946–50
[NOT IN BUCOMP1]

ALb 1 (1946/47), 7, 8, 10

Neue Musikzeitung
TNG D196; 0028–3290
D–Regensburg: Verband Deutscher Musikschulen, 1952–
[NOT IN BUCOMP1]

Lam 20 (1972), 5

Neue Musik-Zeitung: illustriertes Familienblatt
Fellinger 1968/827; TNG D246
D–Stuttgart: Klett, 1880–1928
[Incorporated the *Musikalischer Anzeiger* from 1882; ceased publication with vol. 49 (1928), 24]

Lbl 37 (1916), 13–49 (1928), 24
Lcm (p) 4 (1883)
Mpl 9 (1888)–18 (1897)
Ob 7 (1886)

Die neue Rundschau *see* Freie Bühne für modernes Leben

Neue Wiener Musik-Zeitung
Fellinger 1968/305; TNG A31
A–Vienna: F. Glöggl, 1852–60

Lbl*

Neue Zeitschrift für Musik
Fellinger 1968/120; TNG D75; 0170–8791; 0028–3509
D–Mainz: B. Schotts Söhne, 1834–1943; 1950–
[Head title in 1834 was *Neue Leipziger Zeitschrift für Musik*; in 1906 combined with the *Musikalisches Wochenblatt: Organ für Musiker und Musikfreunde* (q.v.) to form *Musikalisches Wochenblatt/Neue Zeitschrift für Musik: vereinigte musikalische Wochenschriften*; from 1911 entitled *Neue Zeitschrift für Musik*; from 1920 entitled *Zeitschrift für Musik*; in 1955 absorbed *Das Musikleben: Monatszeitschrift*; from 1955, 10, entitled *Neue Zeitschrift für Musik*; in 1975 merged with *Melos* (q.v.) to become *Melos/NZ: Neue Zeitschrift für Musik* (TNG D1088); from 1979–83 amalgamation continued under the title *Neue Zeitschrift für Musik*; from 1984 new, separate series of *Neue Zeitschrift für Musik* commenced, and from 46 (1984) *Melos* continued as a separate journal; publication suspended in 1943, with the *Zeitschrift für Musik* becoming part of *Musik im Kriege*; included supplement, *Sammlung von Musikstücken alter und neuer Zeit*, 1838–41 (16 nos)]

ALb 153 (1992), 7/8
Bs 145 (1984)–#
BSdsc*
BTu 140 (1979)–146 (1985)
Bu 72 (1905); 78 (1911)–81 (1914)
CDu 127 (1966)–#
Cu 1 (1834)–135 (1974); 148 (1987)–#
EIR:Dtc 123 (1962)–#
EIR:Duc 140 (1979)–152 (1991)
Er 1 (1834)–21 (1854); 44 (1877)–54 (1887); 140 (1979)–147 (1986)
Gul 119 (1958)–132 (1971)
LAu 112 (1951), 5; 114 (1953), 7; 116 (1955)–123 (1962)*
Lbbc 132 (1971)–135 (1974)*; 136 (1975)–# [w 148 (1987)–149 (1988)]
Lbl 140 (1979)–#
Lcm 1 (1834)–16 (1849) [w 2 (1835)]
Lcm (p) 117 (1956), July/Aug; 121 (1960), May
Lcml 91 (1924)*; 112 (1951)–115 (1954); 119 *1958), 11–135 (1974); 140 (1979)–#
Lkc 140 (1979)–148 (1987)*
Lki 132 (1971)–137 (1976)*
LRHBNC 140 (1979)–142 (1981)
Lsa 140 (1979)–153 (1992) [w 147 (1986), 1–3]
Lu 9 (1842)–10 (1843); 127 (1966)–135 (1974); 140 (1979)–#
LVp 1 (1834)–6 (1839); 116 (1955);

119 (1958)–124 (1963); 126 (1965)–
135 (1974)–#
LVu 140 (1979)–#
Mcm 134 (1973), 9, 10, 12; 135 (1974);
140 (1979)–147 (1986); 148 (1987), 1–5,
9–12; 149 (1988); 150 (1989), 1–5;
151 (1990)–154 (1993)
Mpl 12 (1840)–48 (1881); [c]
Mu 140 (1979)–#
NO 140 (1979)–146 (1985)
NWu 140 (1979)–144 (1983)
Ob 1 (1834)–119 (1958); 125 (1964)–#
SOu 140 (1979); 141 (1980), 5–142 (1981)

Neues Beethoven-Jahrbuch
TNG D636
D–Augsburg, 1924–42
[*See also Beethovenjahrbuch*]

Cu 1 (1924)–10 (1942) [Reprint ed.]
Er 1 (1924)–6 (1930)
Lbl 7 (1937)–10 (1942)
Lcm 4 (1930)
Lu 1 (1924)–10 (1942) [Reprint ed.]
Ob 1 (1924)–3 (1927); 6 (1935)
SFu 1 (1924)

Neues Mozart-Jahrbuch *see* Mozart-Jahrbuch

Neues Musikblatt *see* Melos: Jahrbuch für
zeitgenössische Musik

Neues musikwissenschaftliches Jahrbuch *see*
Augsburger Jahrbuch für Musikwissenschaft

**Neujahrsblatt der Allgemeinen Musik-
gesellschaft in Zürich** *see* Neujahrsgeschenk
an die Zürcherische Jugend von der
Allgemeinen Musikgesellschaft in Zürich

**Neujahrsgeschenk ab dem Musiksaal an die
zürcherische Jugend** *see* Musicalische Neu-
Jahrs-Gedichte

**Neujahrsgeschenk an die Zürcherische
Jugend von der Allgemeinen
Musikgesellschaft in Zürich**
Fellinger 1968/30; TNG CH2
CH–Zurich; Füssli, 1813–
[From 1830 entitled *Neujahrstück der
Allgemeinen Musikgesellschaft in Zürich*; from
1838, *Neujahrsstück der Allgemeinen Musik-
gesellschaft in Zürich*; from 1884, *Neujahrsblatt
der Allgemeinen Musikgesellschaft in Zürich*]

Lbl*

**Neujahrs[s]tück der Allgemeinen
Musikgesellschaft in Zürich** *see*
Neujahrsgeschenk an die Zürcherische
Jugend von der Allgemeinen
Musikgesellschaft in Zürich

**Neuland: Ansätze zur Musik der Gegenwart:
Jahrbuch**
0177–4476
D–Cologne: Henck, 1980–85
[NOT IN BUCOMP1]

Lbl*

Never Forever?
0967–2303
GB–[s.l.]: Plasmar, 1987–
[NOT IN BUCOMP1; Kate Bush fanzine]

Lbl*

New: Notes
1350–8989
GB–London: Society for the Promotion of New
Music, ?–
[NOT IN BUCOMP1]

ALb 1990, June, Oct, Dec; 1991, Jan, Mar–
1992, Jan, Mar–Oct, Dec; 1993, Feb, May,
Sep, Nov–#
Bs 1993–# [w 1993, Dec]
Cu 1995–#
Gsmic [c]
Lam [c]
Lbl*
Mu 1996–#

New Age Music Association: Newsletter
?GB, NAMA, 1990–
[NOT IN BUCOMP1]

Cu 1, 1990–#
En 1–3, 1990
Ob 1, 1990–#*

**The New Beat: the World's Brightest Modern
Music Magazine (incorporating Zest)** *see* The
Beat: Official Magazine of the Ted Heath
Club

New Cassettes and Cartridges
GB–St Austell, 1970–?

AB 1976–87
Cu 1970, Apr–1987, Apr
EIR:Dtc 1970, Oct–1987
Lsa 1970–84, Sep*
Mcm 1974–#
Ob*

New City Songster
GB–Beckenham, 1968–
[Later issues entitled *NCS*]

    Cu 13 (1977)–20 (1985)

New Consensus and Review *see* Consensus
and Review [of the Latest Issues of Recorded
and Classical Music]

New Directions
US–New York, 1969
[NOT IN BUCOMP1; also entitled *Novi
Napriamy/New Directions*]

    AB 1 (1969), 1

New Folk Sounds
NL–Utrecht, 1989–
[NOT IN BUCOMP1]

    Lcs 1 (1989), 1, 2

New [*sic*] from the National Youth Jazz
Orchestra
GB–Harrow: National Youth Jazz Orchestra, ?–

    Lsa 1995–#

New Gandy Dancer: the Magazine for
Instrumental Rock Music
0260–3330
GB–Gateshead, 1976–

    Cu 1, 1976–#
    Lbl*
    NTp 1, 1976–#
    Ob*

New Hi-Fi Sound *see* Popular Hi-Fi

The New Hungarian Quarterly
0028–5390
H–Budapest: Lapkiado, 1960–
[Entitled *NHQ: the New Hungarian Quarterly*
from 9 (1968)–33 (1992); *The Hungarian
Quarterly* (Budapest: MTI), 34 (1993)–#]

    Bs 3 (1962)–20 (1979)
    Lbl*
    Lcm 2 (1961), 3; 3 (1962), 6, 8; 6 (1965), 20;
      7 (1966), 24; 8 (1967), 25
    Ob 1 (1960)–#

New Jazz Records
I–Rome, 1953–?

    Cbijs 2 (1955), 6

New Jersey Music and Arts
0028–5854
US–Chatham, NJ: Regina Publications, 1945–?
[NOT IN BUCOMP1]

    ALb 30 (1975), 5

New Lady's Magazine or Polite and
Entertaining Companion for the Fair Sex
GB–London, 1786
[NOT IN BUCOMP1; only one vol. published]

    Cpl 1 (1786)

New Melody
0545–2872
GB–Chard, 1962–
[NOT IN BUCOMP1; also known as *Melody*]

    EIR:Dtc 1 (1962), 4–4 (1968), 15

New Music [1]
GB–London, 1973–77

    AB 3–5, 1974; 9, 10, 1975; 12–16, 1976; 18,
      1971
    SLGu 3–19, 1974–77

New Music [2]
0952–3774
GB–Oxford: Oxford University Press, 1987–89
[NOT IN BUCOMP1]

    AB 1 (1987)–3 (1989)
    ALb 1 (1987)
    BLu 1 (1987)–3 (1989)
    BSdsc 1 (1987)–3 (1989)
    Bu 1 (1987)–3 (1989)
    Cu 1 (1987)–3 (1989)
    En 1 (1987)–3 (1989)
    Gsmic 1 (1987)–3 (1989)
    Lbbc 1 (1987); 3 (1989)
    Lbl*
    Lcml 1 (1987)–3 (1989)
    Lu 1 (1987)–3 (1989)
    Ob*
    Ouf 1 (1987)–3 (1989)
    Yu 1 (1987)–2 (1988)

New Music [translated title] *see* Novaya
Muzyka

New Music: a Quarterly Publishing Modern
Compositions
US–San Francisco, CA: New Music Society of
California, 1927–?35

    Lbl*

New Music from Britain
GB–Oxford: Blackwell's Music Shop, 1973–77
[NOT IN BUCOMP1]

Lbl*

New Music News
0791–5268
EIRE–Dublin: Contemporary Music Centre,
1990–
[NOT IN BUCOMP1]

BG 1993, Sep–#
BLu 1991, Sep–1992, Sep; 1993, Sep–#
Bu 1994, May–#
EIR:Dcmc 1991–#
EIR:Dp 1990–#
EIR:Driam 1991–#
EIR:Dtc 1990–#
EIR:Duc 1991–#
EIR:MEtc 1990–#
En 1991–#
Ep 1992, Sep; 1993, Sep; 1994, Feb–#
Gsmic [c]
Lam 1993, Sep; 1994, Feb–#
Lba [c]
Lbar 1990–#
Lbl*
Lcm 1993–#
Lu 1993, Feb–#
Ob*
Ouf 1993, Sep–#
Rp 1994, Feb–#
TOd 1994, May
Uu 1991–#

New Music Review
1351–1475
GB–London: Arcade Recording Circuit, 1993–
[NOT IN BUCOMP1]

Cu 1 (1993)–#
En 1 (1993)–#
Lbl*

**New Music Review and Church Music
Review** *see* **Church Music Review and
Official Bulletin of the American Guild of
Organists**

**The New Musical and Universal Magazine,
consisting of the most Favourite Songs, Airs
&c, as Performed at all Public Places [...]**
Langley, p. 438
GB–London: R. Snagg [et al.], 1774–76

Gul (e) 1774–75

Lbl*
Ob 1774–76*

New Musical Express
TNG GB442; 0028–6362
GB–London: IPC Magazines, 1952–
[From 1982, Apr 17 entitled *NME: New Musical Express*]

AB 1968; 1982, June–1984, Dec
AR 1983–#
BEp [c]
BLp [c]
BSdsc*
CDCp [c (1 year)]
CH [c (3 months)]
CHEp [c (1 year)]
CW 1992, Nov–#
EIR:Dp 1988–#
EIR:Dtc 1976–#
En*
Gm 1973, June 23–#
IOW [c (3 months)]
KC [c]
Lba [c (3 months)]
Lbbc 1 (1952)–# [part m]
Lbl*
Lbo [c]
LCdM [c]
Lcml 1988–#
Lcml (ch) [c (2 issues)]
Lcml (mv) [c (3 months)]
Lcml (p) [c (3 months)]
Lcml (pim) [c (2 issues)]
Lcml (q) [c (6 months)]
LEc [c (1 year)]
Len [c (3 months)]
Lgr (b) [c]
Lgr (e) [c]
Lgr (w) [c]
Lha (f) [c (1 year)]
Lis [c (1 year)]
Lk [c (3 months)]
Lk (b) [c (3 months)]
Lk (nk) [c]
Ll [c]
LOnjfa 1952–# [m]
Lri [c (6 months)]
Lsa 1971, July 24; 1972, June 3; 1973, Apr
27–May 12, June 16, Nov 10; 1974, Feb
23, June 1; 1975–# [w 1985, Sep 7; 1986,
Nov 29; 1987, Jan 3]
Lth [c (1 year)]
Lwwb [c]
MO [c]

MP [c]
Mpl 1990–#
NHp [c (1 year)]
NOp [c]
NTp [c]
Ob*
PRp [c]
RH [c]
Rp [c (6 months)]
SFp [c]
WCp (f) [c (3 months)]
WCp (fle) [c (3 months)]
WCp (p) [c (6 months)]
WCp (y) [c (1 month)]
WH [c (6 months)]
WOp [c]

The New Musical Magazine: or, Compleat Library of Vocal and Instrumental Music: the Whole accompanied with an [sic] Universal Dictionary of Music
GB–London: Harrison and Company, 1783–86

Lbl*

The New Musical Magazine, Review and Register of Valuable Musical Publications, Ancient and Modern
Fellinger 1968/20; TNG GB3; Langley, p. 476
GB–London: C. Cook, 1809–10
[Entitled *The New Royal Musical Magazine, Review and Register of Valuable Musical Publications, Ancient and Modern* from 1809, Sep]

Lbl 1 (1809), 1–8

New Musical Times: Journal of Cambridge New Music Players
GB–Cambridge, ?1992–
[NOT IN BUCOMP1]

TOd 1, 1992

New Notes *see* **New: Notes**

New Orleans Music
0958–6695
GB–Wheatley, Oxon: Bayou Press, 1989–
[NOT IN BUCOMP1; previously entitled *Footnote: the Magazine for New Orleans Jazz* (q.v.)]

Cbijs 1 (1989)–#*
Cu 1 (1989)–#
EIR:Dtc 1 (1989)–#
En 1 (1989)–#

Lbl*
Lsa 1 (1989)–# [w 2 (1990), 1, 2; 4 (1993), 3]

New Penguin Guide to Compact Discs and Cassettes Yearbook
0959–0757
GB–London: Penguin, 1989–
[NOT IN BUCOMP1]

Lbl*

New Performance
0277–514X
US–San Francisco, CA: Oberlin Dance Collective, 1978–82
[NOT IN BUCOMP1]

Bu 2 (1981/82)

The New Quarterly Musical Review
Fellinger 1968/1227; TNG GB155
GB–London: Robert Cocks, 1893–96

Bp 1 (1893)–3 (1896), Feb
CDu 1 (1893)–3 (1896)
Cu 1 (1893)–3 (1896)
Gm 1 (1893)–3 (1896)
Lbl 1 (1893)–3 (1896)
Lcm 1 (1893)–3 (1896), 12
Lcml 1 (1893); 2 (1894/95), 9
LEbc 1 (1893)–3 (1896)
Lu 1 (1893)–3 (1896)
Mcm 1 (1893), 2; 2 (1894/95), 4–6, 11
Mpl 1 (1893)–3 (1896)
Ob*

The New Record Mirror *see* **Record Mirror**

The New Records [1]
0028–6559
US–Philadelphia, PA, ?1933–77
[From 1930–33 entitled *Disques* (q.v.)]

Lsa 13 (1945), 11–45 (1977) [w 17 (1949), 3; 18 (1950), 2; 39 (1971), 6]

New Records [2]
GB–St Austell, 1954–?87

AB 1954, Oct–1955, Aug, Dec; 1956, Jan–1981, Apr
Cbijs 1955, Apr–Dec; 1956–59; 1970, Jan–Apr
Cpl 291–425, 1976–87
Cu 1–425, 1954–87
En 196, 205, 1968
Lbl*

Lsa 1954–84
Mcm 1974–?87
Ob*

New Release Information Service *see*
Gramophone Classical New Release
Information Service

New Rockpile
GB–?–?
[NOT IN BUCOMP1]

NTp 15, 1973

The New Royal Musical Magazine, Review
and Register of Valuable Musical
Publications, Ancient and Modern *see* The
New Musical Magazine, Review and Register
of Valuable Musical Publications, Ancient
and Modern

New Savoyard
GB–London: Friends of D'Oyly Carte, 1988
[NOT IN BUCOMP1; only one issue published;
superseded by *D'Oyly Carte News: the Journal
of the Friends of D'Oyly Carte* (q.v.)]

Cu 1 (1988), 1
Ob 1 (1988), 1

The New Schwann Record and Tape Guide
see Schwann Long Playing Record Catalog

New Singles
GB–St Austell, 1963–?87

AB 615, 617, 618, 620, 622–1180, 1976–87
Cu 209–234, 1968; 723–1130, 1978–86
Lbl*
Lsa 169–1063, 1967–84 [w 258–261, 270–
273, 279–80, 283, 284, 286, 287, 290–292;
325, 385, 389, 410, 432, 466, 467, 498,
499, 569, 594, 596–600, 603, 607, 886,
935, 1024]
Ob*

New Sixth
GB–London, 1968–89
[NOT IN BUCOMP1; incorporates *Set to Music*
(q.v.)]

Lcml 21 (1988), 3–5

New Songwriters Monthly
EIRE–Limerick: Executive International
Publications, ?–
[NOT IN BUCOMP1]

EIR:Dtc 1971, Aug

New Sound: International Magazine for
Music
0044–555X
SRB–Belgrade: Union of Yugoslav Composers'
Organisations, 1993–
[NOT IN BUCOMP1]

Gsmic [c]

New Sounds, New Styles
0262–5598
GB–Market Harborough: EMAP, 1981–
[NOT IN BUCOMP1]

Lbl*

New Spotlight: Ireland's National Music/
Entertainment Magazine
0028–6834
EIRE–Dublin: Irish Publication Surveys, 1967–
[NOT IN BUCOMP1]

EIR:Dtc 1 (1967), 6–9 (1975), 22

New York Musical Pioneer *see* New York
Musical Pioneer and Choristers' Budget

New York Musical Pioneer and Choristers'
Budget
TNG US33
US–New York: F. J. Huntington, 1855–71
[Entitled *New York Musical Pioneer* from 1859,
Oct.; from 1863, Oct. entitled *The Musical
Pioneer*; from 1865, ?Jan, *Musical Pioneer*]

AB 2 (1856), Oct–1857, Sep

New York Musical Review and Choral
Advocate *see* Choral Advocate and Singing-
Class Journal

New York Musical Review and Gazette *see*
Choral Advocate and Singing-Class Journal

New York Musical World *see* The Message
Bird: a Literary and Musical Journal

New York Rocker
US–Elmhurst, NY: New York Rocker, 1977–
[NOT IN BUCOMP1]

    Lsa 14–55, 1978–82 [w 22, 24, 25, 35]

The New York Weekly Review *see* Choral
Advocate and Singing-Class Journal

The New York Weekly Review of Music,
Literature, Fine Arts and Society *see* Choral
Advocate and Singing-Class Journal

Newnes Home Musical
GB–London: G. Newnes, 1913–14

    AB 1914
    Lbl*

News: the Royal Ballet, the Royal Opera, the
Birmingham Royal Ballet
GB–London: Royal Opera House, 1991–92
[NOT IN BUCOMP1; running title *Royal Opera
House News*]

    Cu 1991–#
    Ob 1991–92

News about Mahler Research/Nachrichten
zur Mahler-Forschung
A–Vienna: International Gustav Mahler Society,
1976–
[NOT IN BUCOMP1]

    ALb 1 (1976)–#
    Lbl 2 (1977)–#

News and Notes
US–Sarasota Music Archive Inc., ?–
[NOT IN BUCOMP1]

    Lu 1993, Oct

News and Views: Friends of Cecil Sharp
House Newsletter
GB–London: English Folk Dance and Song
Society, 1986–

    Lcs 1, 1986–#

News Bulletin of the Moravian Music
Foundation
TNG US688; 0545–0322
US–Winston-Salem, NC: Moravian Music
Foundation, 1957–
[Entitled *Bulletin, Moravian Music Foundation*
from 1964, 2; from 1965, 2 entitled *The
Moravian Music Foundation Bulletin*]

BRu 2 (1958), 2–8 (1964), 2 [w 2 (1958), 3; 5
(1961), 3; 7 (1963), 1]; 9 (1964)–13 (1969)
Cpl 5 (1961), 2–8 (1964), 2*; 9 (1965), 2; 18
(1973), 3–23 (1978)*; 26 (1981), 1
Lcm 16 (1971), 1–22 (1977), 2

News for a New Power Generation
0958–9651
GB–Leeds: New Power Generation, 1989–
[NOT IN BUCOMP1]

    Lbl*

News from the Martinů Society: Society for
Czech Music [translated title] *see* Zprávy
Společnosti Bohuslava Martinů: Česká
Hudební Společnost

News Magazine [of the City of Belfast School
of Music]
GB–Belfast: City of Belfast School of Music,
197?–

    Mcm 9 (1979/80)–#

News of Hawaiian Music [translated title] *see*
Ha'ilono mele

News of Hymnody
0263–2306
GB–Bramcote: Grove Books, 1982–
[NOT IN BUCOMP1]

    En 1, 1982–#
    Ob 1, 1982–#*

Newsflow: a Newspaper for the Members of
the English Folk Dance and Song Society
0143–2400
GB–Cullompton: English Folk Dance and Song
Society, ?1976–
[NOT IN BUCOMP1]

    AB 22, 1979
    Cu 19–33, 1979–81 [w 22, 26, 31]
    Lbl*

Newsletter of the African Music Society *see*
African Music Society Newsletter

Newsletter of the American Handel Society
0888–8701
US–College Park, MD: American Handel
Society, 1986–
[NOT IN BUCOMP1]

    Lu 5 (1990), 3

Newsletter of the Group for Contemporary
Music at Columbia University
TNG US777; 0589–5286
US–New York: Contemporary Music
Newsletter, 1967–77
[entitled *Contemporary Music Newsletter* from
1968, 2; ceased publication with no. 10 (1977),
no. 1/2]

> **HUu** 2 (1968)–10 (1977), 1/2
> **Yu** 2 (1968)–10 (1977), 1/2

Newsletter of the Historical Musical Society
TNG US816
US–Lake Charles [LA] etc. 1971–
[From 1972, 2: *The Musical Instrument Society
Newsletter*; from 1972, 3: *American Musical
Instrument Society Newsletter* (ISSN 0160–
2365)]

> **BG** 24 (1995)–#
> **Cu** 1 (1971)–#
> **Lgu** 9 (1980)–#
> **Lu** 8 (1979)–#
> **Ob** 14 (1985)–#

Newsletter [of the Institute for Studies in
American Music] *see* Institute for Studies in
American Music: Newsletter

Newsletter of the Music Masters' and
Mistresses' Association *see* Journal of the
Music Masters' and Mistresses' Association

Newsletter of the Society for Music Analysis
GB–Newcastle-upon-Tyne [etc.]: Society for
Music Analysis, ?1990–
[NOT IN BUCOMP1]

> **AB***
> **Bu** 4 (1993)–#
> **Cu** 8 (1995)–#

Newsletter of the Traditional Music and Song
Association of Scotland
GB–Aberdeen: The Traditional Music and Song
Association, ?–
[NOT IN BUCOMP1]

> **Gsmic** [c]

The Next Big Thing
GB–Grangemouth: Lindsay Hutton, 1977–
[NOT IN BUCOMP1; rock music periodical]

> **Lsa** 1, 3, 1977

NFGS Bulletin *see* Bulletin of the National
Federation of Gramophone Societies

Ngoma
GAB–Libreville: CICIBA Bulletin Liaison of
the Department of Ethnomusicology, ?–
[NOT IN BUCOMP1. *Ngoma* is a generic name
for an African drum]

> **Lsa** 25, 1989

NHQ: the New Hungarian Quarterly *see* The
New Hungarian Quarterly

Niederrheinische Musik-Zeitung für
Kunstfreunde und Künstler
Fellinger 1968/323; TNG D127
D–Cologne: DuMont–Schauberg'schen
Buchhandlung, 1853–67
[Incorporated the *Rheinische Musik-Zeitung für
Kunstfreunde und Künstler* (q.v.) until 1859]

> **Lbl** 1 (1853)–15 (1867)

Nigerian Music Review
TNG NG3
NGR–Ife-Ife: University of Ife, Department of
Music, 1977–

> **Cpl** 1 (1977)
> **Lbl***
> **Lso** 1 (1977), 1

Nights at the Opera
US–Philadelphia, PA, 1902–24

> **Lbl***

Nineteenth Century Music *see* 19th Century
Music

NME *see* New Musical Express

No. 1!
0266–5328
GB–London: BBC, 1985–92
[NOT IN BUCOMP1; later entitled *Number
One*]

> **AB** 2–65, 1983–92
> **Cu** 1983–92*
> **Ob***

The No. 1 Book
GB–London: IPC Magazines, 1985–
[NOT IN BUCOMP1; continued from 1989 as
Number One Yearbook (ISSN 0955–3401)]

Cu 1985–#
Lbl*
Ob 1986–#*

No. 1 Summer Special
GB–London, 1987–
[NOT IN BUCOMP1]

Ob 1, 1987–#*

Nocomosa *see* Northern School of Music Old
Students' Association Magazine

N.O.D.A. Bulletin
TNG GB350; 0027–6863
GB–London: National Operatic and Dramatic
Association, 1935–
[Also known as *N.O.D.A. News of Amateur
Theatre*; *N.O.D.A. News*]

Ep 30 (1970/71), 2, 3; 31 (1971/72)–
34 (1974/75), 1, 2; 35 (1975/76)–
38 (1978/79), 1; 39 (1980/81), 1, 2;
40 (1981/82)–#
Gm 35 (1975/76)–#
Lbl*
Mcm 33 (1973/74), 1
Ob 36 (1976/77), 3–#

N.O.D.A. News *see* N.O.D.A. Bulletin

N.O.D.A. News of Amateur Theatre *see*
N.O.D.A. Bulletin

N.O.D.A. (Scotland) News
GB–National Operatic and Dramatic
Association (Scotland), 197?–
[NOT IN BUCOMP1]

Gm 6 (1980)–#*

N.O.D.A. Yearbook *see* National Operatic
and Dramatic Association: Yearbook

Noise!
GB–London, 1982–
[NOT IN BUCOMP1; later incorporated into
Record Mirror]

Cu 1–16, 1982

Noise [translated title] *see* Swn

Noise of the Nineties
0968–3887
GB–London: Rock Team, 1993–
[NOT IN BUCOMP1]

Lbl 2 (1993), 1–#*

Nomus News: Information on Music
Cooperation in Denmark, Finland, Iceland,
Norway and Sweden
S–Stockholm: Nämnden for Nordiskt
Musiksamarbete/Committee for Nordic Music
Cooperation, 1970–
[NOT IN BUCOMP1]

Lam 1974, Oct

Nomus Nytt: Information från Nämnderna
för Nordiskt Musiksamarbete *see* Nordic
Sounds

The Nonconformist Musical Journal: a
Monthly Record and Review devoted to the
Interests of Worship Music in the
Nonconformist Churches
Fellinger 1968/1078; TNG GB127
GB–London: 1888–1910
[Entitled *The Musical Journal* from 1906;
amalgamated with *The Choir: a Magazine
Devoted Chiefly to Church Music and
Hymnology* (q.v.) in 1911, and became *The
Choir and Musical Journal*]

AB 1 (1888); 8 (1895), 85
BSdsc 19 (1906)–23 (1910)
Lbl*
LVp 17 (1904)–23 (1910)
Mpl 1 (1888)–10 (1897)
Ob 22 (1909)–23 (1910)

Nordic Sounds
0108–2914
DK–Copenhagen: Secretariat for Nordic
Cultural Cooperation, 1982–
[Preceded by *Nomus Nytt: Information från
Nämnderna för Nordiskt Musiksamarbete* (S–
Stockholm, 1968–80)]

AB 1982, 2
BG 1988, Dec; 1989, 1–3; 1990–91, 2, 4;
1993–94, 1
Bs 1985, 4–#*
Bu 1982, 1; 1985–87, 4; 1988, 2–4; 1989, 3;
1990, 2–3; 1992, 3; 1993, 4–#
CCtc 1988–#
Cpl 1985–#
EIR:Driam 1985–#

Ep1991–#
Gam 1982, 1; 1986, 1, 3, 4; 1987, 1; 1989,
2–4; 1990, 3; 1992, 3; 1993, 3
Gsmic [c]
Lam 1982, 2; 1986, 1–#
Lba [c]
Lbar 1982, 1–#
Lbbc 1982–#*
Lbl*
Lcm 1983, 3; 1985–86, 2, 4; 1987–89, 2, 4;
1990, 1; 1991–# [w 1992, 1]
Lcs 1985, 2–4; 1986–#
Lgo 1983–85
Lgsm 1994–#
Lkc 1985; 1987–92*
LRHBNC 1989, 3; 1991, 1, 2, 4; 1992–#
[w 1993, 3]
Lsa 1982, 1; 1985–# [w 1986, 2]
Lu 1982–#
Mu 1982–83; 1985–91; 1993–#
Ouf 1982, 1–#*
TOd 1988, 2, 4; 1989, 1; 1990, 1, 2; 1991, 2;
1992, 1, 2; 1993–#

Nordisk Musikkultur [= Nordic Music Culture]
TNG DK86
DK–Copenhagen: Gads Forlag/Det Unge
Tonekunstnerselskab, 1952–63
[Combined with *Dansk Musik Tidsskrift* (q.v.) in 1959]

Cu 1 (1952)–12 (1963)
Lcml 1 (1952)–3 (1954)*

Nordisk Musik-Tidende: Maanedsskrift for Musikere og Musikvenner [= Nordic Music News: MonthlyJournal for Musicians and Friends of Music]
Fellinger 1968/831; TNG N4
N–Oslo: C. Warmuth, 1880–96
[NOT IN BUCOMP1; ceased publication with vol. 17]

Lam 4 (1883)–5 (1884), 12

Nordiskt Musikblad *see* **Svensk Musiktidning**

Nordwestdeutscher Rundfunk technische Hausmitteilungen
D–Hamburg, 1949–?

LAu 6 (1954), 1, 2

Norsk Bokfortegnelse: Musikktrykk [= Printed Music]
N–Oslo: Universitetsbiblioteket, 1981–
[NOT IN BUCOMP1; succeeded by *Norsk Musikkfortegnelse: Notetrykk*, 1993– (ISSN 0804–6328)]

Cu 1981/83–#
Lbl*
Ob 1985–#*

Norsk Musikkfortegnelse: Notetrykk *see* **Norsk Bokfortegnelse: Musikktrykk**

Norsk Musikkgranskning: Årbok *see* **Norsk Musikkgranskning: Meddelelser fra Norsk Samfund for Musikkgranskning-Norsk Musikksamlings Venner**

Norsk Musikkgranskning: Meddelelser fra Norsk Samfund for Musikkgranskning-Norsk Musikksamlings Venner [= Norwegian Music Research: Reports from the Norwegian Society for Music Research]
TNG N36
N–Oslo: J. G. Tanum, 1937–71
[Alternative title: *Norsk Musikkgranskning: Årbok*]

Gul 1956–58
Lbl*
Ob*

Norsk Musikktidsschrift [= Norwegian Music Magazine]
TNG N44; 0332–5482
N–Kristiansand: Norske Musikklaereres Landsforbund, 1964–

En 8 (1971)–#
Lbl*
Mcm 4 (1967), 1–3

North East Early Music Forum Newsletter
GB–Durham: Elizabeth Roche, 1982–
[NOT IN BUCOMP1]

Cu 1995–#
En*
Lbl*
LEbc 1–5, 1982–84
NTp 1982, Oct–#
Ob*

North East Early Music Forum Register
GB–Durham: North East Early Music Forum,
198?–
[NOT IN BUCOMP1]

Ob 1983–#*

North West Early Music Forum Newsletter
GB–Manchester: North West Early Music
Forum, 1977–

EIR:Dtc 9 (1985), 1, 2
Lam 5 (1982), 2
Mcm 1 (1977)–#
Mpl 1 (1977)–9 (1985)
Ob*

North West Federation of Folk Clubs News
GB–?Manchester: North West Federation of
Folk Clubs, 1978–
[NOT IN BUCOMP1; later entitled *Folk North
West*]

Lbl*
PRp 1 (1978)–#

The Northern Concert Sphere
TNG GB290
GB–Manchester, 1921–22

Lbl*

Northern Ireland Recorded Music List
GB–Belfast, 1982–

Ob*

Northern Music Scene
GB–?Preston, ?–
[NOT IN BUCOMP1]

PRp 1982

Northern National Society for Jazz Study
GB–Dewsbury, 1943–46

Cbijs 16–23, 1944–46

Northern N.O.D.A. News
GB–?: National Operatic and Dramatic
Association (Northern Region), 198?–
[NOT IN BUCOMP1]

NTp 1982–#

The Northern Recorder
GB–Stockport, 1968–

Mcm 1977–82
Mpl 1977–84

**Northern School of Music Old Students'
Association Magazine**
GB–Manchester, 1937–
[from 1973: *Nocomosa*; from 1974: *Royal
Northern College of Music Old Students'
Association Magazine*]

Mcm 14, 1950; 20, 1956; 29, 1965; 34–35,
1970–71; 37, 1973–#

**Northern Sinfonia Concert Society Annual
Report**
GB–?: Northern Sinfonia Concert Society, 196?–
[NOT IN BUCOMP1]

NTp 1969/70–#

**Northern Sinfonia Orchestra Newsletter and
Press Release**
GB–?: Northern Sinfonia Concert Society,
197?–
[NOT IN BUCOMP1]

NTp 1970–#

Northern Visions
GB–?, 198?–
[NOT IN BUCOMP1]

NTp 1–4, 1982–84

Northumbrian Pipers' Society Magazine
0261–5096
GB–Cramlington: Northumbrian Pipers'
Society, 1980–

Cu 1 (1980)–#
EIR:Dtc 1 (1980)–#
Lbl*
NTp 1 (1980)–#

**Northumbrian Small Pipes Society
Transactions**
GB–?: Northumbrian Small Pipes Society,
189?–?
[NOT IN BUCOMP1]

NTp 1894, 1896–97

**Norwegian Music Information Centre
Bulletin**
0801–1087
N–Oslo: Norwegian Music Information Centre,
1980–93
[NOT IN BUCOMP1. Superseded by *Listen to
Norway* (q.v.)]

Bs 1985; 1987–93
Gam 1986–89; 1991/92–93
Lam 1981; 1986–87

Nostalgia [1]
GB–Newhaven: Street Singer, 1967–
[Incorporated *The Street Singer*]

Cbijs 17, 19, 1970; 21–36, 1971 74
Lsa 17–36, 1970–74 [w 18–20]; n.s. 1–14, 1975–76

Nostalgia [2]
GB–New Barnet: C. Wilson, 1969–
[NOT IN BUCOMP1]

Cu 10 (1979), 38–#
Ob 10 (1979), 38–#

Not Fade Away: the Official Magazine of the Vintage Rock 'n' Roll Appreciation Society
GB–London: Vintage Rock 'n' Roll Appreciation Society, 197?–
[NOT IN BUCOMP1]

Ob 17, 1981–#

Nota Bene *see* **Boosey and Hawkes GmbH: Verlagsnachrichten**

Note d'Archivio per la Storia Musicale
TNG I186
I–Bologna: R. Patron, 1924–43; n.s. Venice: Edizioni Fondazione Levi, 1983–

AB*
Bu 1 (1924)–20 (1943); n.s. 1 (1983)–#
Cu 1 (1924)–20 (1943); n.s. 1 (1983)–5 (1987)
Lbl 1 (1924)–4 (1927), 4; 7 (1930)–16 (1939), 6; n.s. 1 (1983)–5 (1987)
Lcml 9 (1932), 1
Lu 1 (1924)–20 (1943); n.s. 1 (1983)– #
LVu 1 (1924)–4 (1927); 7 (1930)–20 (1943); n.s. 1 (1983)–5 (1987)
NO 1 (1924)–4 (1927); 7 (1930)–20 (1943)
Ob 1 (1924)–4 (1927); 7 (1930)–14 (1937); 15 (1938)*; 16 (1939)–20 (1943); n.s. 1 (1983)–#
Ouf 1 (1924)–20 (1943); n.s. 1 (1983)–#

Notes *see* **Notes for the Members of the Music Library Association**

Notes: Newsletter of the Jerusalem Rubin Academy of Music and Dance
IL–Jerusalem: Rubin Academy, 198?–
[NOT IN BUCOMP1]

Lam 1986, 4

Notes: Quarterly Journal of the Music Library Association *see* **Notes for the Members of the Music Library Association**

Notes: Supplements for Members
TNG US578
US–Ann Arbor, MI [etc.]: Music Library Association, 1947–64
[NOT IN BUCOMP1]

BLu 1–36, 1947–64 [w 22, 23]

Notes for the Members of the Music Library Association
TNG US529 (1st series); TNG US 578 (2nd series); 0027–4380
US–Washington, DC, [etc.]: Music Library Association, 1934–42 (1st series); 1943– (2nd series)
[Entitled *Notes for the Music Library Association* from 7, 1940; *Notes* from 1943; current title is *Notes: Quarterly Journal of the Music Library Association*. No volume was published for 1964/65]

AB 1 (1943/44), 3, 4; 6 (1948/49), 1; 8 (1950/51), 3; 9 (1951/52); 10 (1952/53), 2–4; 12 (1954/55), 2, 3; 13 (1955/56), 1, 3, 4–18 (1960/61), 3; 26 (1969/70)–28 (1971/72), 2, 4; 29 (1972/73)–32 (1975/76), 3
Au 1 (1943/44)–#
BAc 1–15, 1934–42; 1 (1943/44)–30 (1973/74); 35 (1978/79), 1–3; 36 (1979/80), 3, 4; 37 (1980/81)–41 (1984/85), 2
BDp 29 (1972/73)–42 (1985/86)
BG 25 (1968/69)–#
BLp 19 (1961/62)–#
BLu 1 (1943/44)–34 (1977/78), 3
Bp 1–15, 1934–42; 1 (1943/44)–#
BRp 11 (1953/54)–46 (1989/90), 1
BRu 11 (1953/54)–37 (1980/81)
Bs 1 (1943/44)–37 (1980/81), 1*
BTu 28 (1971/72)–42 (1985/86)
Bu 6 (1948/49), 2
Cat 34 (1977/78)–37 (1980/81), 3; 38 (1981/82)–#
CCtc 41 (1984/85)–#
CDu 28 (1971/72)–41 (1984/85)
Cpl 1 (1943/44)–#

Cu 1–15, 1934–42; 1 (1943/44)–#
DRu 1–15, 1934–42; 1 (1943/44)–#
EIR:Dp 37 (1980/81), 3–#
EIR:Dtc 28 (1971/72)–#
EIR:Duc 1 (1943/44)–#
En 23 (1966/67)–#
Ep 18 (1960/61), 2–44 (1987/88)
Er 1 (1943/44)–#
EXu 27 (1970/71)–#
Gam 18 (1960/61)–#
Gm 31 (1974/75)–#
Gul 1 (1943/44)–#
HUu 1–15, 1934–42; 1 (1943/44)–#
KE 18 (1960/61), 3; 30 (1973/74)–41
   (1984/85)
Lam 7 (1949/50)–43 (1986/87), 1, 3, 4; 44
   (1987/88)–49 (1992/93), 2, 4; 50 (1993/94),
   1, 2, 4–#
LAu 6 (1948/49), 4; 9 (1951/52), 4;
   18 (1960/61), 3
Lbar 20 (1962/63), 2–23 (1966/67);
   26 (1969/70)–38 (1981/82), 2
Lbbc 1 (1943/44)–#
Lbl*
Lcm 4 (1946/47)–9 (1951/52); 11 (1953/54)–#
   [w 43 (1986/87), 3, 4]
Lcml 1–15, 1934–43; 1 (1943/44)–#
   [+ supplements 1–36, 1947–64]
LEc 5 (1947/48)–#
Lgo 39 (1982/83)–#
Lgsm 47 (1989/90)–#
Lkc 1 (1943/44)–48 (1991/92), 2
Lki 34 (1977/78)–47 (1990/91)
LRHBNC 29 (1972/73)–#
Lsa 4 (1946/47)–#
Lu 6–14, 1938–42*; 1 (1943/44)–#
LVp 5 (1947/48); 10 (1952/53)–#
LVu 12 (1954/55)–#
LXp 21 (1963/64)–39 (1982/83)
Mcm 32 (1975/76)–#
Mpl 4 (1946/47), 2; 6 (1948/49)–#
Mu 21 (1963/64)–#
NO 1 (1943/44)–#
NWu 6 (1948/49)–27 (1970/71); 29
   (1972/73)–38 (1981/82); 39 (1982/83)*;
   40 (1983/84)–41 (1984/85)
Ob 1 (1943/44)–#
Oub 38 (1981/82)–51 (1994/95)
Ouf 1 (1943/44)–#
R 6 (1948/49), 3; 21 (1963/64)–39 (1982/83),
   2
SFu 22 (1965/66)–31 (1974/75)
SOu 18 (1960/61)–#
Yu 27 (1970/71)–#

Notes for the Music Library Association *see*
Notes for the Members of the Music Library
Association

Notes on Records
GB–London, 1958–
[NOT IN BUCOMP1]

   AB 1–5, 1958; 8, 1961
   Lsa 1957, Dec [unnumbered issue]; 1–8,
   1958–61
   Lu 8, 1961

Notiziario
I–Milan: Edizioni Suvini Zerboni, 1965–

   Cu 1970, Oct– 1984, Nov
   Lam 1971, Jan, Apr, July, Oct; 1972, Apr,
   July, Oct; 1973, Jan, July; 1974, Jan; 1975,
   Jan; 1983, Mar
   Lcm 1965, Sep; 1967, Sep; 1968, June, Oct;
   1970, Jan, Apr, July, Oct; 1971, Jan, Apr;
   1972, Jan; 1975, May; 1983, Mar
   Lu 1983, Mar, Nov
   Mcm 1973–76, Mar

Notiziario Musica *see* Musica Università:
Periodico Quindizinale di Cultura e
Informazioni Musicali

Notizie A.I.B. *see* Associazione Italiana
Biblioteche: Bollettino d'Informazione

Notizie dall'Archivio Sonoro della Musica
Contemporanea
I–Rome: Istituto di Recerca per il Teatro
Musicale, 1987–
[NOT IN BUCOMP1]

   Lbl*

Notizie Teatrali, Bibliografiche e Urbane,
ossia Il Caffé de Petronio, nel quale si parla di
Spettacoli, di Feste, di Musiche, di Poeti, di
Prosatori, di Pittori di Scene, di Maestri di
Cappella, di Attori Cantanti e non Cantanti
[...]
Fellinger 1968/70; TNG I7
I–Bologna, 1825
[53 nos in total]

   Lbl*

Notnaya Letopis' *see* Letopis' Muzikal'noy
Literaturi

Nouvelle Revue Musicale *see* Revue Musicale de Lyon

Nova Giulianiad: Saitenblätter für die Gitarre und Laute
0254–9565
D–Freiburg: Internationale Gitarristische Vereinigung, 1983–
[NOT IN BUCOMP1]

Lam 1983, 1

Novaya Muzyka [= New Music]
TNG USSR58
RF–Leningrad, 1927–28

Lbl*

The Novello Review
0550–2055
GB–London: Novello, ?– 1978
[NOT IN BUCOMP1]

AB 1967–68, Spr; 1970, Spr; 1971–74, Spr; 1975, Spr; 1976–78, Spr

Novi Napriamy/New Directions *see* New Directions

Novi Zvuk *see* Zvuk: Revija za Muziku

Novosti Nauchnoi Literaturi, Bibliograficheskaya Informatsiya: Muzika
RF–Moscow: Biblioteka V.I. Lenina, 1975–
[NOT IN BUCOMP1]

Ob 1977–#

Now!
1353–2308
GB–London: IPC Magazines, 1994–
[NOT IN BUCOMP1]

Lbl*

Now-a-Days
GB–Brighton, 1947

Lbl*

Now Radio
GB: ?, 198?–
[NOT IN BUCOMP1]

Lsa 1987–91*

Nuestra Música: Revista Bimensual editada en México
TNG M12
ME–Mexico City: Ediciones Mexicanas de Musica [for the Consejo Nacional para la Cultura y las Artes], 1946–53

Lcml 1 (1946), 2–6 (1951), 16; 7 (1952), 21–28
Lgo 1 (1946), 3–7 (1952), 28 [w 4–7, 12]
Lu 1 (1946)–8 (1953), 29
Ouf 6 (1951), 21–7 (1952), 28
Ouf (Howes) 1 (1946), 2; 4 (1949), 15

Nuggets
GB–Birmingham, ?1975–
[NOT IN BUCOMP1]

Lsa 3, 4, 6, 7, 1976–77

Number One *see* No. 1!

Number One *see also* Fast Forward

Number One Book *see* The No. 1 Book

Number One Yearbook
0955–3401
GB–London: IPC Magazines, 1988–
[NOT IN BUCOMP1; entitled *No. 1 Book* (q.v.) from 1985–88]

Lbl*

Nuova Rassegna di Studi Musicali
0391–3724
I–Pisa: Giardini, 1977–
[NOT IN BUCOMP1]

Ob 2 (1978), 1, 2

Nuova Rivista Musicale Italiana
TNG I282; 0029–6228
I–Turin: Nuova ERI Edizioni, 1967–
[Superseded *Rivista Musicale Italiana* (q.v.) and *L'Approdo Musicale* (q.v.)]

BG 1 (1967)–#
Bu 1 (1967)–#
CDu 7 (1973), 3–10 (1976)*; 15 (1981), 1; 19 (1985)–25 (1991), 2
Cu 1 (1967)–#
DRu 1 (1967)–6 (1972)
En 1 (1967)–#
Er 3 (1969)–#
Gul 14 (1980)–22 (1988)
HUu 1 (1967)–#

Lam 1 (1967)–3 (1969), 6
LAu 1 (1967)–2 (1968), 3
Lbl*
Lcm 1 (1967)–8 (1974), 2; 11 (1977), 4
Lcml 2 (1968)*; 3 (1969)–#
Lkc 13 (1979)–#
Lu 1 (1967)–#
Mcm 7 (1973), 3, 4; 8 (1974)–10 (1976), 3
NO 4 (1970)–19 (1985)
Ob*
Ouf 1 (1967)–#
SFu 6 (1972)–9 (1975)
SOu 3 (1969)–22 (1988)

Nutida Musik: Tidskrift för vår Tids Musik
[= Today's Music: Journal for Music of Our
Time]
TNG S97; 0029–6597
S–Stockholm: Sveriges Radio, 1957/58–
[subtitle from 1967/68 is *Tidskrift för vår Tids*
Tonkunst]

Lam 1966
Lbl*

Nutida Musik: Tidskrift för vår Tids
Tonkunst *see* Nutida Musik: Tidskrift för vår
Tids Musik

NZ: Neue Zeitschrift für Musik *see* Neue
Zeitschrift für Musik

O

Obbligato: the Newsletter of the Royal
College of Music
GB–London: Royal College of Music, 1994–
[NOT IN BUCOMP1]

Cu 1994–#
Lcm 1994–#

Octave
1355–0225
GB–Kinton: Octave, 1992?–
[NOT IN BUCOMP1; concerns bell-ringing]

Lbl*

Yr Oenig [= The Ewe Lamb]
GB–Swansea; Merthyr Tydfil, 1854–65
[entitled *Telyn-y-Plant* [*The Children's Harp*]
from 1859]

AB 1 (1854/55)–3 (1856); n.s. 1 (1859)–2
(1861)
Lbl*

Off Air
GB–London, 1992–
[NOT IN BUCOMP1]

Lsa 1 (1992)–# [w 7, 1993]

Official Bay City Rollers Magazine
GB–London, 1976–78

Cu 14–43, 1976–78
EIR:Dtc 14–43, 1976–78
En 14–43, 1976–78
Ob 14–43, 1976–78

Official Music Master *see* Music Master

The Official Partridge Magazine
GB–London, 1971–?74
[from 8, 1972 entitled *Superstar*; from 23, 1973
entitled *Music World and Superstar*]

Cu 2–4, 1971–72; 8–29, 1972–74
EIR:Dtc 13–29, 1972–74
Ob 2–4, 8, 1971–#

The Official Radio Luxembourg Book of
Record Stars
GB–London, 1962–66
[NOT IN BUCOMP1]

Ob 1 (1962)–5 (1966)

Oh Play That Thing
US–San Francisco Record Society, 1948–

Cbijs 1 (1948), 2

OHTA News
AUS–?: Organ Historical Trust of Australia,
1977–
[NOT IN BUCOMP1]

Lam (o) 11 (1987), 3

OJ *see* Orkester Journalen: Tidskrift for
Modern Dansmusik

Old Chorister
0141–7622
GB–London: Federation of Old Choristers'
Associations, 1976–
[NOT IN BUCOMP1; continued from vol. 5
(1988) as *Once a Chorister* (ISSN 0954–2841)]

Cu 3 (1977), 2–#
En 4 (1978/87)–#
Lam 4 (1978/87), 7
Lbl*

Lcm 4 (1978/87), 3–10
Ob*

Old Time Music
0048–1653
GB–London: Tony Russell, 1971–89
[Ceased publication with no. 45, 1989]

> **AB***
> **Cu** 1–36, 1971–81
> **EIR:Dtc** 1–36, 1971–81
> **En***
> **EXu** 1–45, 1971–89
> **Lcs** 1–42, 1971–81*
> **Lsa** 1, 1971; 14–39, 1974–84 [w 37]
> **Ob***

The Old Vic and Sadlers Wells Magazine
GB–London: Vic-Wells Association, 1946–
[Formerly *The Old Vic Magazine* (q.v.); later
entitled *Vic-Wells Association: Bulletin*]

> **Lbl***
> **Lcm** 88, 1954; 125–141, 1957–59; 143–201,
> 1959 [w 167, 170–172]; 203, 206, 208,
> 209, 1965

The Old Vic Magazine
GB–London, 1919–30
[Continued as *The Old Vic and Sadlers Wells
Magazine* (q.v.)]

> **Lbl***

**Olympia: Journal der musikalischen
Wettkämpfe**
TNG A255
A–Salzburg: Verlag der Internationalen
Musikfeste, 1950
[Ceased publication with vol. 1 no. 2 (1950)]

> **AB** 1 (1950)
> **Cpl** 1 (1950), 1
> **Lam** 1 (1950), 1
> **Lcml** 1 (1950), 1

L'Omnibus
F–Paris: Boisgard, 1855–62

> **Lbl***

**On the Tracks: the Unauthorized Bob Dylan
Magazine**
US–Grand Junction, CO, 1993–
[NOT IN BUCOMP1]

> **Cu** 1, 1993–#

Once a Chorister *see* **Old Chorister**

One to One
GB–London, 1985–
[NOT IN BUCOMP1]

> **Lsa** 28, 1990; 38, 1992; 41, 1992–#

One, Two, Testing
0265– 7139
GB–London: IPC Magazines, 1982–86
[NOT IN BUCOMP1; original title was
One...two...testing; incorporated *Zigzag* [1]
(q.v.) to become *One, two, testing + Zig Zag*
(q.v.) in 1986, with new numbering]

> **AB** 3, 6, 1984 –35, 1986
> **Cu** 1–36, 1982–86
> **Lbl***

One, Two, Testing + Zig Zag
0950–2440
GB–London: Cover Publications, 1986–
[NOT IN BUCOMP1; previously entitled *One,
two, testing* (q.v.)]

> **Cu** 1–2, 1986
> **Lbl***
> **Ob** 1, 1986–#

**One Two Three Four: a Rock and Roll
Quarterly**
0889–0536
US–Los Angeles, CA: Strong Sounding
Thought Press, 1984–
[NOT IN BUCOMP1]

> **Lgo** 1 (1984)–#
> **Lsa** 2 (1985), 4, 6, 7, 9; 4 (1987); 6 (1988)–9
> (1990)

Ongaku Gaku *see* **Ongakugaku: Journal of
the Japanese Musicological Society**

**Ongakugaku: Journal of the Japanese
Musicological Society**
TNG J37; 0030–2597
J–Tokyo: Japanese Musicological Society, 1954

> **BSdsc***

Online Trombone Journal *see* **ITA**

Onze Lichte Muziek *see* **Dutch Popular Music**

Open University Music Society Journal *see*
Open University Musical Society Journal

Open University Musical Society Journal
0964–7856
GB–Milton Keynes: The Open University,
1985–
[NOT IN BUCOMP1: from end 1993 entitled
Open University Music Society Journal: also
known as *OUMS Journal*]

> **Lbl***
> **MK** 1, 1985–#

Oper: Jahrbuch
0474–2443
D–Hannover: Friedrich, 1966–
[Yearbook published as a companion to the
journal *Opernwelt: Monatshefte für Oper,
Operette, Ballett* (q.v.)]

> **BTu** 1971–73
> **Cpl** 1968, 1972–76
> **LAu** 1974–#

Oper und Konzert: kritische Stimmen
TNG D1039; 0030–3518
D–Munich: Industrie und
Handelswerbung/Hanuschik, 1963–

> **BSdsc***
> **Lcm (p)** 3 (1965), Sep
> **Mcm** 19 (1981), 7–12; 20 (1982)–
> 22 (1984), 1

Opera
TNG GB433; 0030–3526
GB–London: Opera, 1950–
[Absorbed *Ballet* [1] (q.v.) in 1953]

> **AB** 3 (1952)–26 (1975), 2
> **ALb** 1 (1950)–# [w 39 (1988), 4; 43 (1992),
> 4; 45 (1994), 7]
> **BAc** 14 (1963)–39 (1988)
> **BAR** [c (2 years)]
> **BDp** 1 (1950)–#
> **BLp** 1 (1950)–#
> **Bp** 1 (1950)–#
> **BRp** 2 (1951)–#
> **BRu** 1 (1950)–11 (1960), 6
> **Bs** 18 (1967)–#*
> **BSdsc***
> **BTp** 1 (1950)–#
> **BTu** 9 (1958)– # [w 24 (1973), 9; 25 (1974),
> 8; 26 (1975), 2]
> **Bu** 1 (1950), 6; 2 (1951), 1–5, 8, 12; 3 (1952),
> 1, 3– 10, 12; 4 (1953)–7 (1956), 1–8, 10,
> 12; 8 (1957), 2–4, 6–12; 9 (1958)–11
> (1960), 5, 7–10; 12 (1961), 2–5, 9–11;

13 (1962), 1, 11; 15 (1964), 2, 9; 16 (1965),
5, 8; 17 (1966)–#
BuAYp [c (3 years)]
CAu 33 (1982)–34 (1983) [w 3, 5, 6]; 35
(1984)–37 (1986) [w 1, 2]
CCtc 41 (1990)–43 (1992)
CDCp 1 (1950)–#
CDu 5 (1954)–35 (1984); 41 (1990)–#
CFp 28 (1977)–#
CH [c (2 years)]
DOR 33 (1982)–#
DRu 3 (1952)–#
DS 1 (1950)–#
DU [c (5 years)]
Ea [c (1 year)]
EIR:Dp 4 (1953)–#
EIR:Dtc 1 (1950)–#
EIR:Duc 27 (1976)–#
EIR:MEtc 1 (1950)–18 (1967); 19 (1968)*;
1973 Festival issue
En*
Ep 1 (1950)–# [w 29 (1978), 11; 30 (1979), 8]
Er 1 (1950)–#
Gam 2 (1951), 2, 3, 5, 7; 3 (1952), 6, 8–10,
12; 4 (1953), 2–5, 7, 8, 12; 5 (1954), 3–6;
6 (1955), 3–5, 7; 7 (1956), 3–12; 8 (1957),
1–6; 10 (1959), 1–5; 11 (1960), 5, 6, 11;
12 (1961), 1, 2, 4, 8, 9, 11; 13 (1962), 2; 14
(1963), 7, 8, 10; 15 (1964), 2; 16 (1965),
5–8, 10; 17 (1966), 1, 2, 4, 5, 10; 18 (1967),
2, 7, 9, 11, 12; 19 (1968)–24 (1973), 11;
25 (1974)–28 (1977), 1, 3–10, 12; 29
(1978), 1–10; 30 (1979), 8, 11, 12; 31
(1980), 2–6, 9–12; 32 (1981), 1–7, 9, 11,
12; 33 (1982), 1–8, 10–12; 34 (1983), 1–8,
10–12; 35 (1984)–41 (1990), 10; 42 (1991),
1–11; 43 (1992)–#
GLp 41 (1990)–44 (1993), 10
Gm 1 (1950)–#
Gul 25 (1974)–31 (1980)
HA 43 (1992)–#
HE 39 (1988)–#
HOp 15 (1964)–#
HUu 1 (1950), 2–#
KE 1 (1950)–3 (1952), 6; 16 (1965)–35
(1984)
Lam 1 (1950)–#* [+ Festival issues 1960–69,
1971–date]
LAu 15 (1964), 3; 16 (1965), 6; 20 (1969),
10–#
Lbar 1 (1950)–#
Lbbc 8 (1957)–#; second copy 28 (1977), 2–#
Lbl*
Lbo 34 (1983)–#
Lbx 20 (1969)–43 (1992) [m]

LCdM 28 (1977), 4–30 (1979), 1; 31 (1980), 5–#
Lcm 1 (1950)–#
Lcml 1 (1950)–#
Lcml (c) [c (1 year)]
Lcml (m) [c (3 years)]
Lcml (p) [c (2 issues)]
LEc 1 (1950)–#
Len 1 (1950), 2, 4, 6, 8, 9, 11–#
Lgo 14 (1963)–# [w 27 (1976), 7]
Lgsm 1 (1950)–#
Lh [c (10 years)*]
Lha (f) 12 (1961), 6–12; 13 (1962)–16 (1965) [w Festival issue] 18 (1967)–42 (1991)
Lhr [c]
Lk 1 (1950); 9 (1958)–#
Lkc 1 (1950); 3 (1952)–38 (1987)*
Lki 20 (1969)–35 (1984)*
Ll 35 (1984, 2)–39 (1988, 3)
Lmi 25 (1974)–#
LRHBNC 5 (1954)–9 (1958); 11 (1960); 13 (1962); 25 (1974)–29 (1978)
Lsa 1 (1950)–# [w 37 (1986), 2; 38 (1987), 9]
Lsut [c (1 year)]
LT 18 (1967)–#
Ltc 2 (1951), 3; 3 (1952), 9; 7 (1956), 7; 8 (1957), 4, 6; 22 (1971), 11–23 (1972) [w 2, 5]; 24 (1973), 1, 3, 5–10; 25 (1974) [w 5, 6, 8, 11]; 26 (1975)–28 (1977), 6, 8–10, 12; 29 (1978), 1–3, 6–30 (1979) [w 6, 8, 11]; 31 (1980), 1, 2, 5, 6; 33 (1982), 1, 2, 5, 6–10; 34 (1983), 2–4, 6, 10–12; 36 (1985) [w 3, 9, 10]; 37 (1986)–43 (1992), 1, 3–12; 44 (1993), 1–11; 45 (1994) [w 6, 10, 11]; 46 (1995), 1–9, 11, 12; 47 (1996)–# [+ 2nd copy 42 (1991)–46 (1995)]
Ltv 42 (1991), 7–#
Lu 1 (1950)–#
LVp 1 (1950)–3 (1952); 7 (1956)–13 (1962); 15 (1964)–20 (1969); 22 (1971)–#
LVu 1 (1950)–#
Lwwb 13 (1962)–39 (1988) [w 1988, 1]; 40 (1989)–42(1991), 3, 5–12; 43 (1992)–#
LXp [c (1 year)]
Mcm 1 (1950)–#
Mpl 1 (1950)–#
Mu 1 (1950)–33 (1982)*
NHp [c (1 year)]
NO 1 (1950)– #
NOp [c (5 years)]
NOTu 27 (1976)–#
NTp 29 (1978)–#
NWu 16 (1965)*; 17 (1966); 18 (1967)*; 19 (1968)–27 (1976); 28 (1977)*; 29 (1978)–33 (1982)

Ob*
Op [c (3 years)]
Oub 29 (1978)–45 (1994)
Ouf 2 (1951)–43 (1992)
PRp [c (5 years)]
R 1 (1949), 1–4; 2 (1950), 1, 2; 4 (1952), 2, 3, 8, 9; 5 (1954), 1–3; 6 (1955), 12; 7 (1956), 1–7, 10–12; 8 (1957)–20 (1969); 21 (1970), 1–8, 11, 12 [+ festival issue]; 22 (1971); 25 (1974), 5, 9, 10; 28 (1977), 10, 12; 29 (1978); 30 (1979); 31 (1980), 1–11; 32 (1981); 33 (1982); 34 (1983), 1–9
Rp 1 (1950)–14 (1963); 38 (1987), 1–9, 12; 39 (1988)–#
SA 5 (1954), 7–36 (1985), 8*
SFp 24 (1973), 3–#
SFu 17 (1966)–40 (1989)
SHRp 40 (1989)–#
SK [c (5 years)]
STAp 18 (1967)–#
TOd 5 (1954)–8 (1957); 31 (1980)–#
Uu 28 (1977)*; 29 (1978)–#
WCp 23 (1972)–#
WF 1 (1950)–#
Yu 23 (1972)–40 (1989)

L'Opera
1121–4112
I–Milan: Sabino Lenoci, 1987–
[NOT IN BUCOMP1]

Lu 1 (1987), 6

Opera: a Magazine for Music Lovers
TNG GB299
GB–London, 1923–24
[From 1924, 5: *Opera and the Ballet*]

BDp 1 (1923), 1, 2, 4–9, 11, 12; 2 (1924), 1, 2, 4, 6–8
Lam 1 (1923), 1, 8; 2 (1924), 1–3, 5, 7, 8
Lcm (p) 1 (1923), July

Opera: a New Opera Annual
GB–London, ?–?
[NOT IN BUCOMP1]

Lu 1966

Opera-Opera *see* Opera Australia

Opera: Rassegna Internazionale del Teatro Lirico
I–Milan, 1965– ?
[NOT IN BUCOMP1]

Lu 1 (1965)–3 (1967), 3

Opéra: Théâtre Musical, Danse, Disque, Variétés see Opéra 61: la Revue de l'Art Lyrique

Opéra 61: la Revue de l'Art Lyrique
TNG F682
F–Paris, 1961–?77
[From 1973, Mar–1974, Aug incorporated into *Le Guide du Concert* (q.v.) to form *Le Guide Musical-Opéra*; from 98, 1974: *Opera: Théâtre Musical, Danse, Disque, Variétés*; from 1977/78: *Opera International: le Magazine de l'Art Lyrique* (q.v.)]

    Lsa 5 (1965)–11 (1971) [w 8 (1968), 8]; 102–119, 1975–76

Opera and the Ballet see Opera: a Magazine for Music Lovers

Opera Annual
TNG GB453
GB–London; New York, 1954–62

    AB*
    Bp 1954–62
    BSdsc*
    Cu 1954–62
    En 1954–62
    Lam 1958; 1960
    Lbl*
    Lk 1954–62
    Lu 1954–62
    NTp 1954–62
    Ob*
    SFu 1960

Opera Australasia see Opera Australia

Opera Australia
0155–4980
AUS–Sydney, NSW: Pellinor Property, 1974–76; n.s. 1978–
[NOT IN BUCOMP1; superseded by *Opera Australasia* (ISSN 1320–0299) from issue 193 (Jan. 1994); entitled *Opera-Opera* (ISSN 1328–214X) from 1997]

    BSdsc*
    Lcm (p) 1974, Jan, July

Opera, Ballet and Music Hall in the World
GB–London: International Theatre Institute, 1952–55

    Gul 1 (1952)–4 (1955)
    Lbl*

Lcml (r) 1 (1952)–4 (1955)
Ob*

The Opera Box
Fellinger 1968/268; TNG GB42
GB–London: John K. Chapman and Company, 1849–51

    Lbl 1849, Mar 15–1850, Aug 24
    Lu 1850–51

Opera Canada see Opera in Canada

L'Opéra-Comique
TNG F540
F–Paris: Association des Amis de l'Opéra-Comique, 1929–32

    Lbl*

L'Opéra de Paris: Organe Officiel des Théâtres Lyriques Nationaux
TNG F623; 0471–6809
F–Paris, 1950–
[NOT IN BUCOMP1]

    Bp 12 (1956)–26 (1969)
    Lbbc 1984*
    Lcm (p) 1984, Feb–June/July, Sep; 1985, Jan, Mar–June/July

Opera Enthusiast
GB–London, 1984–
[NOT IN BUCOMP1]

    Lbl*
    Lu 1 (1984), Mar
    Ob 1 (1984)–#*

Opera Fanatic
0891–3757
US–Bronx, NY: Bel Canto Society, 1986–
[NOT IN BUCOMP1]

    Lu 1986, Spr

Opera Glass
GB–Glasgow, 1829–?

    Lbl*

The Opera Glass: a Weekly Musical and Theatrical Miscellany
Fellinger 1968/169; TNG GB21
GB–Edinburgh, 1840–41

    En 2 (1841), 10
    Lbl 1–29, 1840

The Opera Goer, or Studies of the Town
Fellinger 1968/306; TNG GB47
GB–London: Thomas Cautley Newby, 1852
[Head title is *The Lorgnette, or Studies of the Town, by an Opera Goer* (q.v.)]

AB*
Lbl 1852

Opera House: the Magazine of the Royal Ballet, the Royal Opera and the Birmingham Royal Ballet
GB–London: Headway, Home and Law [HHL] Publishing Group, 1993–
[NOT IN BUCOMP1]

AB 1 (1993)–#
ALb 1 (1993)–
Bp 1 (1993)–#
CDCp 1 (1993)–#
EIR:Dtc 1 (1993)–#
Ep 1 (1993)–#
Lbar 1 (1993)–#
Lcml 1 (1993)–#
Lgsm 1 (1993)–#
Lu 1 (1993)–#
Ob*

Opera in Canada
TNG C35; 0030–3577
C–Toronto: Canadian Opera Guild, 1960–
[From issue 16, 1963, entitled *Opera Canada*]

ALb 8 (1967), 4; 14 (1973), 4
BSdsc*
BTu 10 (1969), 3–16 (1975), 1
Lbl*
Lu*

Opera International: le Magazine de l'Art Lyrique
TNG F68; 0241–2438
F–Paris: Ytra, 1977–
[NOT IN BUCOMP1; succeeded *Opéra 61: la Revue de l'Art Lyrique* (q.v.)]

BSdsc 5–88, 1978–86
Lcm (p) 1980, Oct; 1981, Jan, June–July/Aug; 1982, Jan–Apr, Nov, Dec; 1983, Jan–Nov
Lsa 1–4, 1977–78
Lu 88, 1986; 102, 1987

Opera International Journal
D–Munich, 1965–?

Lcml 1 (1965), 1–3

Opera Journal
TNG US788; 0030–3585
US–University, Mississippi: National Opera Association, 1968–

BSdsc*
Mcm 6 (1973)–9 (1976), 4

Opera Journal Newsletter
GB–?: ?1978–

Mcm 3 (1980), 4; 4 (1981), 1, 2, 4; 5 (1982), 1, 2, 4; 6 (1983), 2, 4; 7 (1984), 1, 2

Opera Magazine: Devoted to the Higher Forms of Musical Art
TNG US432
US–New York: R. Penfield, 1914–1916

Lcml 3 (1916), 3

Opera News
TNG US542; 0030–3607
US–New York: Metropolitan Opera Guild, 1936/37–

ALb 12 (1947), 21; 31 (1967), 16; 33 (1968),23; 34 (1970), 17; 35 (1970), 1; 39 (1974), 4, 7, 8; 41 (1977), 13; 42 (1978), 7; 44 (1980), 20; 48 (1984), 17; 51 (1986), 2, 3
BSdsc 34 (1969)–#
EIR:Dp 52 (1988)–#
Gm 15 (1950)–22 (1957)*
Lam 12 (1947), 11; 13 (1949), 17–21; 15 (1950), 4, 7–11, 13, 14, 16, 17; 16 (1952), 10, 20; 17 (1953), 14; 26 (1962), 8, 17, 18, 20, 22–24; 27 (1962), 1–8; 27 (1963), 10–19, 21, 23, 24; 28 (1963), 1–11, 13, 15–24; 29 (1964), 2–6, 8–17, 20–23; 30 (1965), 2, 4–7, 9–26; 30 (1966), 1, 3–6, 8, 9, 11, 12, 14, 16, 17, 19–22, 27; 32 (1967), 6–20; 34 (1969), 1–27; 35 (1970),1–9, 12–27
Lbl*
Lcm (p) 45 (1980)–50 (1985)*
Lcml 52 (1987), 5–#
Lsa 17 (1952)–#; 18 (1954); 28 (1963)–30 (1966); 35 (1970)
Lu 35 (1970)–42 (1978)*
LVp 20 (1955)–26 (1962)
Mcm 46 (1981)–49 (1984)*
Ob*

Opera North
0306–8099
GB–Newcastle-upon-Tyne, 1974–79

AB*
BDp 2–20, 1974–79
Cu 1–20, 1974–79
En*
Mcm 17–20, 1978–79
NTp 1–20, 1974–79
Ob*

Opera Now
0958–501X
GB–London: Opera Now Enterprises Ltd,
1989–
[NOT IN BUCOMP1]

AB 1989–#
ALb 1989, Apr–1990, Oct, Dec; 1991, Jan,
   Mar–#
BLBBC 1989, 5, 6, 11; 1990, 2; 1992, 10, 12;
   1993, 3, 5, 10, 12; 1994–#
BLp 1990–#
BRp [c (2 years)]
BSdsc*
BuHW [c (3 years)]
CDCp [c (2 years)]
EIR:Dtc 1989–#
En*
Ep 1989–#
Gam 1990–#*
Gm 1990, May–#
HE 1991, Feb–#
Je [c (2 years)]
Lam 1989– [w 1994, Apr]–#
Lbbc 1989–#
Lbl*
Lcm 1989–90*; 1991–#
Lcm (p) 1989, June, July, Sep–Dec,
   Christmas extra; 1990, Jan
Lcml 1989–#
LEc 1989–#
Lgsm 1990–# [w 1991, Feb]
Lha (f) [c (5 years)]
Lk (c) [c (1 year)]
Lro 1989–91
Lsa 1989, Aug–#
Lsut [c (1 year)]
Ltc 1991–# [w 1996, Feb, Sep, Oct]
Lu 1989–#
Mcm 1991, Oct–#
Msuc 1990–#
NOp [c (5 years)]
NTp 1989, Apr–#
Ob*

Op [c (2 years)]
PRp 1992–#
RH [c]
STAp 1990, Apr–#

The Opera Quarterly
0736–0053
US/GB–Chapel Hill, NC; London: University of
North Carolina Press, 1983–

ALb 1 (1983)–#
BSdsc 1 (1983)–#
En 5 (1987/88)–#
Lam 8 (1991), 1
Lbbc 1 (1983)–#
Lcml 1 (1983)–#
Lgo 1 (1983)–4 (1986)
Lu 2 (1984), 3; 9 (1992)–#
LVu 2 (1984)–#
Ob*
Uu 6 (1988/89)–#

Opéra Soixante et Un see Opéra 61: la Revue
de l'Art Lyrique

The Operatic Association Gazette
GB–London, 1930–?

Lbl*

Das Opernglas
0935–6398
D–Hamburg: Opernglas, 1980–
[NOT IN BUCOMP1]

Lu 8 (1987), 9

Opernwelt: die internationale
Opernzeitschrift see Opernwelt: Monatshefte
für Oper, Operette, Ballett

Opernwelt: Monatshefte für Oper, Operette,
Ballett
TNG D1019; 0030–3690; later 0474–2443
D–Seelze: Erhard Friedrich Verlag, 1960–
[Also bore subtitle Die internationale
Opernzeitschrift. Oper: Jahrbuch (q.v.) is
published as an annual companion]

ALb 17 (1976), 1–12; 18 (1977), 4, 6–10; 19
   (1978), 1–8, 10–12
BTu 10 (1969), 7–12; 11 (1970)–15 (1974)
Bu 7 (1966)–10 (1969), July
EIR:Dtc 11 (1970)–#
LAu 6 (1965), 12; 15 (1974)–#
Lbl*
Lcml 6 (1965)–9 (1968)

Lu 5 (1964), 7; 6 (1965), 5–8; 12 (1971)–17
(1976); 28 (1987), 9; 33 (1992)–#
Ouf 1 (1960)–13 (1972), 9*

Opry Yearbook
GB–Walderslade, 1969

Cu 1969

Opus [1]
GB–Tring, 1942–43

Lbl*

Opus [2]
EIRE–Dublin, 1957–?

EIR:Dtc 1958, 1

Opus [3]
GB–Nottingham, 1966–

Lbl*
NO 2, 3, 1967

Opus [4]
1066–2138
US–Chatsworth, CA: ABC Consumer
Magazines, 1990–?96
[NOT IN BUCOMP1; succeeded *Schwann Long
Playing Record Catalogue* (q.v.), and *Schwann
Compact Disc Catalog* (q.v.). Entitled *Schwann
Opus* from 4 (1992/93). Published by Valley
Record Distributors, Danbury, CT from ?1998.]

BRp 1 (1990)–#
CAu ?1 (1990)–#
Lsa 2 (1991), 3–#
Mp 1 (1990)–#
Mu 1 (1990), 2–#

**Opus: Revista de la Musicoteca del Banco
Central del Ecuador**
ECU–Quito: Banco Central del Ecuador, 1986–
[NOT IN BUCOMP1]

Lu 18–37, 1987–89 [w 24, 28, 36]

**Opus Musicum: Hudební Měsíčnik [= Musical
Monthly]**
TNG CS222; 0231–7362
CZ–Brno: Státní Filharmonie Brno, 1969–

Ob*

Orbis Musicae: Studies in Musicology
TNG IL15; 0303–3937
IL–Tel Aviv: Department of Musicology, Tel
Aviv University, 1971–

AB 1 (1971)–10 (1990/91)
BSdsc 1 (1971)–#
Cu 1 (1971)–#
En 1 (1971)–#
Lbl*
Lu 1 (1971)–9 (1987)
Ob*

Orbit
GB–Leicester, 1973–

Cbijs 1973–#

**Das Orchester: Organ der Deutschen
Orchestervereinigung**
TNG D927; 0030–4468
D–Mainz: Schott, 1953–
[Alternative sub-title: *Zeitschrift für deutsche
Orchesterkultur und Rundfunk-Chorwesen*]

Bs 24 (1976)–#*
BSdsc*
CCtc 24 (1976)–36 (1988)
EIR:Dtc 19 (1971)–#
Gam [c]
Lam 18 (1970), 6–#
LAu 27 (1979)–30 (1982)
Lbl 21 (1973)–# [w 26 (1978), 8]
Lcm [c (3 issues)]
Lcml 7 (1959)*; 10 (1962)*; 13 (1965)*; 14
(1966)–18 (1970); 19 (1971)*; 20 (1972)–#
Lgsm 39 (1991)–#
Ltc [c]
Lu 23 (1975), 4–6; 31 (1983), 7, 8; 40
(1992)–#
Mcm 22 (1974), 1–6, 9–12; 23 (1975), 5–12;
24 (1976)–28 (1980), 2, 6, 8–12; 29
(1981)–#
Mpl [c]

**Das Orchester: Zeitschrift für deutsche
Orchesterkultur und Rundfunk-Chorwesen**
see Das Orchester: Organ der Deutschen
Orchestervereinigung

**The Orchestra: a Monthly Journal for Welsh
Worship, Music and Poetry** [translated title]
see Gerddorfa: Cylchgrawn Misol at
Wasanaeth Cerddoriaeth a Barddoniaeth
Cymreig

The Orchestra: a Monthly Review, Musical, Dramatic and Literary *see* The Orchestra: a Weekly Review of Music and the Drama

The Orchestra: a Weekly Review: Musical, Dramatic, and Literary *see* The Orchestra: a Weekly Review of Music and the Drama

The Orchestra: a Weekly Review of Music and the Drama
Fellinger 1968/484; TNG GB63; TNG GB81 (n.s.); Langley 1994, pp. 121–22
GB–London: Cramer, Beale and Wood, 1863–74, n.s.1874–87
[From 11, 1868, entitled *The Orchestra: a Weekly Review: Musical, Dramatic, and Literary*; became *The Orchestra: a Monthly Review, Musical, Dramatic and Literary* from 1875]

   BSdsc*
   Bu 1 (1863)–11 (1868/69); 13 (1869/70)–22 (1874)
   EIR:Dtc 1 (1863)–14 (1870); n.s. 1 (1874)–5 (1879)
   En 1 (1863)–22 (1874)*; n.s. 1 (1874)–12 (1886)
   Gul (e) 1 (1863)–22 (1874)
   Lbl 1 (1863)–22 (1874); n.s. 1–230, 1875–87
   LVp 11 (1868)–22 (1874); n.s. 1 (1874)–10 (1884)
   Mu 1 (1863)–18 (1872)
   Ob*

Orchestra Canada/Orchestres Canada
0380–1799
C–Toronto: Ontario Federation of Symphony Orchestras and Association of Canadian Orchestras, 1973–
[NOT IN BUCOMP1]

   Lbbc 16 (1989), 7; 17 (1990), 4, 5

Orchestra World
GB–London, 1980–

   EIR:Dtc 1980–82, Apr/May
   En*
   Lam 1980, Mar, May
   Lu 1980, Feb
   Mcm 1980–82, Apr/May

The Orchestral Association Gazette
Fellinger 1968/1229; TNG GB156
GB–London, 1893–1910
[Entitled *The Orchestral Gazette* from 88, 1901]

   Lbl*

   Lcm 1–87, 1893–1900
   Ob*

Orchestral Association Monthly Report
TNG GB246
GB–?London: Orchestral Association, 1910–13
[NOT IN BUCOMP1]

   Lcm 1910, Oct–1913, Sep

The Orchestral Gazette *see* The Orchestral Association Gazette

The Orchestral Times and Bandsman *see* The British Bandsman: a Monthly Magazine for Bandmasters and Members of Military and Brass Bands

The Orchestral Times and Military Band Record
Fellinger 1968/1595; TNG GB193
GB–London: Orchestral Times, 1901–06

   Cu 1 (1901)–6 (1906)
   Lbl*
   Mpl 1 (1901)
   Ob*

Orchestres Canada *see* Orchestra Canada/ Orchestres Canada

Orff Echo: Quarterly Publication of the American Orff-Schulwerk Association
0095–2613
US–Cleveland Heights: The American Orff-Schulwerk Association, ?1969–
[NOT IN BUCOMP1]

   TOd 26 (1994), 3

Orff-Institut an der Akademie "Mozarteum" Salzburg: Jahrbuch
TNG D1033; 0174–9056
D–Mainz: Orff-Institut, 1962–69

   Lcm 3 (1964/68)

Orff Schulwerk Informationen
TNG A291
A– Salzburg, 1964–
[NOT IN BUCOMP1]

   Lam 27, 1981; 33, 34, 1984; 36–47, 1985–91
   Lcm 14, 1974; 20–36, 1977–85 [w 27, 34]; 39, 1987–# [w 43, 46, 49–51]; plus Symposium 1980; 1985
   TOd 36, 1985; 42–44, 1988–90; 47, 1991

Orff Times
GB–London: Orff Society, 1980–

    Cu 1 (1979/80), 3–#
    En 1 (1979/80), 3; 2 (1980/81)–#
    Lbar 1 (1979/80)–#
    Ob*

Orgaan der Federatie van Nederlandse Toonkunstenaars-Vereenigingen [= Journal of the Federation of Dutch Composer Organisations]
TNG NL82; 0923–7941
NL– Amsterdam, 1933–43
[NOT IN BUCOMP1; entitled *Die Muziekvereld* from 1936; *De Wereld der Muziek, Jaargang* 3 no. 2 (1936)–9 no. 11 (1943); Aug/Sep 1934 issues not numbered; 1 *Jaargang* starts at October 1934]

    Ob 1934–43*

The Organ: a Quarterly Review for its Makers, its Players, and its Lovers
TNG GB291; 0030–4883
GB–London: Musical Opinion, 1921–

    AB 1 (1921)–65 (1985), 258
    Au 17 (1937), 65–46 (1966), 182
    BDp 1 (1921)–73 (1993)
    BLp 1 (1921)–#
    Bp 1 (1921)–62 (1982); 63 (1983)–65 (1985)*; 66 (1986)–#
    BRp 1 (1921)–#
    BRu 5 (1925)–50 (1970); 56 (1976), 224; 57 (1977)–60 (1980) [w 24 (1944); 40 (1960); 46 (1968)–48 (1970)]
    Bs 1 (1921); 9 (1929)–56 (1976), Apr
    BSdsc*
    Bu 32 (1952); 34 (1954)–#
    CDu 27 (1947)–48 (1968)*
    CFp 1 (1921)–56 (1976); 63 (1983)–65 (1985); 69 (1989)–#
    Cu 1 (1921)–#
    DS 1 (1921)–6 (1926); 7 (1927), 25–27; 8 (1928), 32; 9 (1929), 33, 35; 10 (1930)–18 (1938); 19 (1939), 73, 74; 22 (1942), 85, 87, 88; 23 (1943)–35 (1955); 46 (1966)–49 (1969); 50 (1970), 197, 199, 200; 51 (1971)–62 (1982); 63 (1983), 247–149; 64 (1984)–65 (1985); 66 (1986), 259, 261, 262; 67 (1987); 68 (1988), 268–270; 69 (1989), 271–#
    EIR:Dp 67 (1987)–73 (1993), Jan
    EIR:Dtc 1 (1921)–#

    En 1 (1921)–65 (1985); 67 (1987), 263, 265, 266; 68 (1988)–#
    Ep 1 (1921)–#
    Er 5 (1925)–23 (1943); 25 (1945)–31 (1951); 43 (1963)–#
    Gam 22 (1942)–30 (1950); 32 (1952)–38 (1958)
    Gm 1 (1921)–#
    Gul 1 (1921)–#
    HOp 61 (1981), 242–#
    KE*
    Lam 1 (1921)–64 (1984), 253; 65 (1985), 256, 258–67 (1987), 266; 68 (1988), 268, 270; 69 (1989), 271–#
    LAu 61 (1981), 240; 62 (1982), 246
    Lbar 1 (1921)–15 (1935); 16 (1936), 62; 17 (1937), 67; 18 (1938), 69, 72; 19 (1939); 20 (1940), 78–80; 23 (1943), 89, 91, 92; 24 (1944)–26 (1946); 27 (1947), 106–108; 28 (1948)–#
    Lbl*
    Lcm 1 (1921)–56 (1976); 58 (1978)–#
    Lcml 1 (1921)–20 (1940); 21 (1941)*; 24 (1944)*; 25 (1945), 97–#
    Lcml (m) [c (2 years)]
    LEc 1 (1921)–14 (1934), 55, 56; 56 (1976), 221–223; 73 (1993)–#
    Lrco 1 (1921)–#
    Ltc 75 (1995)–#
    Lu 1 (1921)–#
    LVp 1 (1921)– #
    LVu 2 (1922); 4 (1924)–9 (1929)
    LXp [c (5 years)]
    Mcm 1 (1921)–5 (1925); 19 (1939), 73; 23 (1943), 92; 26 (1946), 104; 31 (1951)–32 (1952), 122–127; 34 (1954), 133; 39 (1959)– 43 (1963); 47 (1967), 185, 187; 48 (1968)–#
    Mpl 1 (1921)–#
    Mu 27 (1947/48)–30 (1950); 45 (1965)–61 (1981)
    NOp 31 (1951)–38 (1958), 149, 151, 152; 39 (1959)–49 (1969); 60 (1980), 237–#
    NTp 1 (1921)–66 (1986)
    Ob 1 (1921)–#
    Op [c (2 years)]
    R 1 (1921)–55 (1975); 56 (1976), 222, 223; 57 (1977), 225
    SFp 1 (1921)–58 (1978); 59 (1979), 2–64 (1984), 1; 65 (1985)–66 (1986), 3; 67 (1987), 1, 3, 4; 69 (1989)
    SFu 18 (1938)–#
    SLGu*
    SOu 1 (1921)–60 (1980), Apr [w 56 (1976), 223–224; 57 (1977), 225–227]

Organ and Keyboard Cavalcade *see* **Keyboard Cavalcade**

Organ Club Annual Bulletin
GB–London: The Organ Club, 1979–

  Cu 1979–#
  En 1979; 1981; 1983–#
  Ob*

The Organ Club Journal *see* **The Journal of the Organ Club**

Organ Handbook
0882–2085
US–Virginia: Organ Historical Society, ?1956–
[NOT IN BUCOMP1]

  Lam (o) 1986–92; 1994

Organ Historical Society Annual Convention Reports
0148–3099
US–Wilmington, OH: Organ Historical Society, 1955–82
[NOT IN BUCOMP1]

  Lam (o) 19 (1974)–20 (1975); 23 (1978)

Organ Historical Trust of Australia News *see* **OHTA News**

Organ Institute Bulletin
TNG US659
US–Andover, MA: The Organ Institute, 1951–64
[Entitled *Organ Institute Quarterly* from 1951, 2]

  Lam 3 (1953), 3
  Lam (o) 2 (1952)–11 (1961), 2
  Mcm 3 (1953), 3; 4 (1954), 1
  Yu 1 (1951)–11 (1961)

Organ Institute Quarterly *see* **Organ Institute Bulletin**

Organ News
NZ–Christchurch: New Zealand Association of Organists, ?–
[NOT IN BUCOMP1]

  Lam 30 (1994), 2

Organ Player and Keyboard Review
0144–8331
GB–Watford: Trade Papers Ltd, 1980–85;
London: Bookrose Ltd, 1985–
[Entitled *Keyboard Player* (ISSN 0263–3836) from 1985, 12]

  AB 7 (1986), 4–#
  CH [c (1 year)]
  Cu 1 (1980), 7–#
  EIR:Dtc 1 (1980)–#
  En*
  GLp 14 (1993)–#
  Gm 7 (1986)–#
  IOW 13 (1992), July–#
  Lbl*
  NHp [c (1 year)]
  NOp [c (2 years)]
  Ob*
  RP [c (1 year)]
  SA 2 (1981), 11–3 (1982), 5

The Organ Voice
AUS–Carseldine, Queensland: Organ Society of Queensland, ?–
[NOT IN BUCOMP1]

  Lam (o) 19 (1992), 4, 5

The Organ Yearbook: a Journal for the Players and Historians of Keyboard Instruments
TNG NL124; 0078–6098
NL–Amsterdam: Frits Knuf, 1970–93
[Ceased with vol. 23 (1993)]

  Au 1 (1970)–19 (1988)
  BRu 1 (1970)–23 (1993)
  Bs 9 (1978)–18 (1987) [w 16 (1985)]
  Bu 1 (1970)–5 (1974); 7 (1976)–9 (1978); 12 (1981)
  CCtc 1 (1970)–23 (1993)
  CDu 1 (1970)–23 (1993)
  Cpl 1 (1970)–23 (1993)
  Cu 1 (1970)–23 (1993)
  DRu 1 (1970)–16 (1985)
  EIR:Duc 1 (1970)–22 (?1991)
  EIR:MEtc 7 (1976)–23 (1993)
  Ep 1 (1970)–23 (1993)
  Er 1 (1970)–#
  Gul 1 (1970)–23 (1993)
  HUu 1 (1970)–16 (1985)
  KE 1 (1970)–12 (1981)
  Lam 1 (1970)–23 (1993)
  Lbbc 1 (1970)–23 (1993)
  Lbl*

Lcml 1 (1970)–23 (1993)
Lgsm 4 (1973)–9 (1978)
Lkc 1 (1970)–23 (1993) [w 11 (1980)]
Lrco 1 (1970)–18 (1987)
Lro 14 (1984)–23 (1993)
Lu 1 (1970)–23 (1993)
Mcm 1 (1970)–23 (1993)
Mpl 1 (1970)–23 (1993)
Mu 1 (1970)–23 (1993)
NO 1 (1970)–10 (1979)
NWu 1 (1970)–13 (1982)
Ob 1 (1970)–23 (1993)
Ouf 1 (1970)–21 (1990)
SA 1 (1970)–16 (1985)
SFu 1 (1970)–10 (1979) [w 5 (1974);
  8 (1977)]
SOu 1 (1970)–11 (1980)
Uu 1 (1970)–23 (1993)
Yu 1 (1970)–23 (1993)

The Organbuilder
0264–4746
GB–Oxford: Positif Press, 1983–
[NOT IN BUCOMP1]

Cu 1 (1983)
EIR:Dtc 1 (1983)
Lam 4 (1986), May; 5 (1987)–7 (1989)
Lrco 1 (1983)–11 (1993)
Mpl 1 (1983)–#
Ob*

Organised Sound: an International Journal of
Music Technology
1355–7718
GB–Cambridge: Cambridge University Press,
1996–
[NOT IN BUCOMP1]

BG 1 (1996)–#
Cu 1 (1996)–#
Oub 1 (1996)–#
TOd 1 (1996), 1
Yu 1 (1996)–#

Der Organist: Monatschrift für Orgelspiel,
kirchliche wie instruktive Instrumental- und
Gesangmusik, musikalische Theorie [...]
Fellinger 1968/832; TNG D241
D–Berlin: Wolf Peiser, 1880

Lbl 1–12, 1880

The Organist see The Organist and
Choirmaster

The Organist: a Monthly Musical Journal and
Review
GB–London: J. W. Brewster, 1866
[NOT IN BUCOMP1; succeeded by The Church
Choirmaster and Organist (q.v.)]

Bp 1–9, 1866

Organist: Newsletter of the Royal College of
Organists
0964–9832
GB–London: Royal College of Organists, 1990–
[NOT IN BUCOMP1]

Bu 1 (1990)–#*
Cu 1 (1990)–#
EIR:Dtc 1 (1990)–#
En 1 (1990)–#
Lam 1 (1990), 1; 2 (1992), 4
Lbl*
Ob 1 (1990)–#*

The Organist and Choirmaster
Fellinger 1968/1230; TNG GB157
GB–London, 1893–1920
[Succeeded by The Sackbut: a Musical Review
(q.v.). Numbers 321–324 entitled The Organist]

AB 17 (1909), 196; 18 (1911), 214; 20
  (1913)–27 (1919)
Bu 1 (1893)–6 (1898) [w 2 (1894), 22]
CDu 13 (1905)–24 (1916)
Cpl 1 (1893)–2 (1894)
Cu 28 (1920)
EIR:Dtc 1 (1893)–3 (1895), 36
En 1 (1893)–3 (1895)
Lam (o) 1 (1893)–6 (1898)
Lbl 1–320, 1893–1919*; 321–324, 1920,
  Jan–Apr
Lcm 1 (1893)–24 (1916)
Lcml 5 (1897)– 10 (1902); 25 (1917)
Lrco 1 (1893)–18 (1910)
LVp 1 (1893)–5 (1897); 10 (1902)–28 (1920)
Mpl 1 (1893)– 27 (1919)
Ob*

Organists' Benevolent League: Annual Report
GB–London, 1911–19
[NOT IN BUCOMP1]

Ob 2–5, 7–10, 1911–19

Organists' Review see National Union of
Organists' Associations: Quarterly Record

L'Organo: Rivista di Cultura Organaria e
Organistica
TNG I256; 0474–6376
I–Brescia [etc.], 1960–

HUu 7 (1969)–20 (1982)
Lbl*
Lu 1 (1960), 2–#
NO 9 (1971)–15 (1977)
Ob*
Ouf 9 (1971)–26 (1989), 2

Die Orgel: Centralblatt für Kirchenmusiker
und Freunde Kirchlicher Tonkunst see Die
Orgel: Monatsschrift für Orgelmusik und
Kirchgesang

Die Orgel: Monatsschrift für Orgelmusik und
Kirchgesang
Fellinger 1968/1112; TNG D302
D–Leipzig: Klinner, 1889–97; 1909–14
[Later subtitled *Centralblatt für Kirchenmusiker
und Freunde kirchlicher Tonkunst*]

Lbl 1 (1890)–8 (1897)

Orgel: Tidskrift för Svensk Orgelkonst
TNG S101
S–Årset: S. Nygren, 1962–
[NOT IN BUCOMP1]

Er 2 (1963), 3, 4
Lu 2 (1963), 3, 4

Orgel-Monographien
D–Mainz: P. Smets, 1932–34

Lbl*

Orgel-Studien
D–Hamburg: K. D. Wagner, 1977–
[NOT IN BUCOMP1]

Ob 1 (1977)–#

Die Orgelbau-Zeitung [...]
Fellinger 1968/802; TNG D235
D–Berlin, 1879–84
[Entitled *Die Orgel- und Pianobau-Zeitung*
from 1882]

Lbl 1 (1879)–3 (1881); 4 (1882)–6 (1884)

Der Orgelspiegel: Informationsbrief der
Gesellschaft der Orgelfreunde
D–Esslingen, 1963–
[NOT IN BUCOMP1]

Yu 8–58, 1966–92 [w 30, 40, 55, 56]

Die Orgel- und Pianobau-Zeitung see Die
Orgelbau-Zeitung

De Orgelvriend [= Friend of the Organ]
NL–Baarn: De Orgelvriend, ?1959–
[NOT IN BUCOMP1]

Lam (o) 20 (1978), 2–6, 9–12; 24 (1982),
3–12; 25 (1983), 1, 4–12; 26 (1984), 1; 31
(1989), 4–7/8; 32 (1990), 1–3, 12; 33
(1991), 1, 4–12; 34 (1992), 107, 9–12; 35
(1993), 1–7, 9–12; 36 (1994)–37 (1995), 3

Orglet: Medlemsskrift for Det Danske
Orgelselskab
TNG DK95
DK–Copenhagen: Danske Orgelselskab, 1971–
[NOT IN BUCOMP1]

Lam (o) 1976, 2; 1980, 1; 1990, 1

L'Orgue see also Cahiers et Mémoires de
l'Orgue

L'Orgue: Bulletin de Liaison de la Fédération
Francophone des Amis de l'Orgue
F–Lyons: Fédération Francophone, ?–
[NOT IN BUCOMP1]

Lam (o) 16, 17, 1994

L'Orgue: Bulletin Trimestriel see Bulletin
Trimestriel des Amis de l'Orgue

L'Orgue: Histoire – Technique – Esthethique –
Musique
0030–5170
F–Paris: Association des Amis de l'Orgue,
1928–
[NOT IN BUCOMP1]

Lam (o) 218, 219, 1991; 221–228, 1993–94
Mpl 1990–#

Orgues Méridionales
TNG F729; 0181–4958
F–Toulouse: Association Orgues Méridionales,
1978–
[NOT IN BUCOMP1]

Lu 1980, 9–12

[From 1991 entitled *OJ*; incorporated *Jazznytt från SJR* from 1991]

Cbijs 1964, Nov

Orlando di Lasso: Registratur für die Geschichte der Musik in Bayern
Fellinger 1968/590; TNG I49
I–Bressanone: A. Wegers Buchhandlung, 1868
[Only one published]

Lbl*

Orpheus: musikalisches Album *see* **Orpheus: musikalisches Taschenbuch**

Orpheus: musikalisches Taschenbuch
Fellinger 1968/170; TNG A20
A–Vienna: F. Riedl's Witwe und Sohn, 1840–42
[Entitled *Orpheus: musikalisches Album* in 1842]

Lbl 1 (1840)–2 (1841); 3 (1842)
Ob 3 (1842)

Osmonds' World
GB–London, 1973–77

Cu 27–48, 1976–77
EIR:Dtc 27–48, 1976–77
En 27–48, 1976–77
Lbl*
Ob*

Osmonds' World Year Book
GB–London, 1977–78
[NOT IN BUCOMP1]

Cu 1977–78

Österreichisch-ungarische Cantoren-Zeitung *see* **Oesterreichisch-ungarische Cantoren-Zeitung**

Österreichisch-Ungarische Kunst-Chronik *see* **Österreichische Kunst-Chronik**

Österreichische Gesellschaft für Musik: Beiträge *see* **Beiträge [der] Osterreichische Gesellschaft für Musik**

Österreichische Kunst
A–Vienna, 1929–
[From 1938: *Kunst und Industrie*; from 1939: *Kunst dem Volk*]

Lcm (p) 3 (1932), Mar/Apr

Österreichische Kunst-Chronik[: illustrierte Zeitschrift für Kunst, Kunstgewerbe, Musik und Literatur]
Fellinger 1968/751; TNG A77
A–Vienna, 1877–94
[From 1879 entitled *Österreichisch-Ungarische Kunst-Chronik*; from 1883 bore subtitle *Illustrierte Zeitschrift für Kunst, Kunstgewerbe, Musik und Literatur*; from 1891 entitled *Allgemeine Kunst-Chronik*]

Lbl*

Österreichische Bibliographie *see* **Österreichische Musikbibliographie**

Österreichische Musikbibliographie
TNG A249
A–Vienna: Österreichische Nationalbibliothek, 1949–53
[Continued as Group 13a of the *Österreichische Bibliographie*]

Lbl*
Ob 1949–53

Österreichische Musikzeitschrift
TNG A233; 0029–9316
A–Vienna: H. Bauer [et al.], 1946–
[Absorbed *Phono: internationale Schallplatten Zeitschrift* (q.v.)]

ALb 31 (1976)–34 (1979), 3
Bs 35 (1980), 9–#
Bu 1 (1946), 1, 2, 4–8
CDu 31 (1976)–39 (1984); 49 (1994), 3–#
Cu 22 (1967)–#
Er 21 (1966), 10; 22 (1967), 12; 23 (1968), 3, 12; 24 (1969), 2; 25 (1970), 1, 4; 38 (1983), 1, 3–12; 39 (1984), 1–11; 40 (1985), 1–6, 9–12; 41 (1986)–42 (1987), 1, 4–9, 12; 43 (1988), 1–9, 12; 44 (1989), 1, 3, 4, 6–12; 45 (1990)– #
Gam 38 (1983), 1–3, 6–9, 12; 39 (1984), 2–4, 6, 9–12; 40 (1985), 1–5, 9, 11, 12; 41 (1986), 1, 2, 5, 7–12; 42 (1987), 1, 4–6, 9; 43 (1988), 4, 5, 9–12; 44 (1989), 3, 4, 6, 9– 11; 45 (1990), 1, 5, 9, 10, 12; 46 (1991), 7, 8
Lam 6 (1951), 10; 7 (1952), 1–6; 9 (1954), 5; 11 (1956) [Mozart issue]; 15 (1960) [Mahler issue]; 17 (1962),12; 18 (1963), 6; 19 (1964)–25 (1970), 5; 25 (1970), 7–26 (1971), 1, 4, 12 [+ special numbers for 1964 and 1966]
LAu 2 (1947)–40 (1985)*

Lbl*
Lbbc 30 (1975)–37 (1982)*
Lcm 18 (1963)–28 (1973)*; 35 (1980), 9;
  38 (1983)–#*
Lcml 3 (1948)–4 (1949); 5 (1950)–11
  (1956)*; 16 (1961)*; 17 (1962)–18 (1963);
  19 (1964)*; 23 (1968)–#
Lsa 16 (1961), 2– 12; 17 (1962)–18 (1963),
  4; 22 (1967)–23 (1968), 5
Lu 3 (1948)–4 (1949); 9 (1954); 18 (1963)–
  #*
Mcm 22 (1967), 12; 23 (1968), 3, 12; 24
  (1969), 2, 11, 12; 25 (1970), 1, 12; 26
  (1971), 4, 12; 28 (1973)*; 29 (1974), 1;
  31 (1976), 10–12; 33 (1978), 1–3, 9, 10;
  34 (1979), 1–10; 35 (1980), 1, 9, 12;
  36 (1981), 1, 10, 11; 37 (1982), 2–#
Mu 35 (1980)–45 (1990)
NO 30 (1975), 11; 33 (1978)–40 (1985);
  46 (1991)–#
Ob*
Ouf 10 (1955)–21 (1966); 23 (1968)–29
  (1974); 31 (1976); 41 (1986), 11, 12;
  42 (1987)–44 (1989), 1, 9; 47 (1992),
  4 + supplement

Österreichischer Courier *see* **Wiener Theater-
Zeitung**

Österreichischer Musikrat: Mitteilungen
TNG AA288
A–Vienna: Österreichischer Musikrat, 1964–

  Cpl 1964–#
  Gam 1983, 2; 1984; 1986–87
  Lam 1965, 1–5; 1967, 1; 1968, 2; 1969, 1–
    1972, 2; 1973, 2; 1975, 1, 2; 1978–1981, 1
    [+ 1979 special issue]; 1983, 1; 1984,
    1–1988, 2
  Lcm 1964, 3; 1965–69, 1; 1970–73, 1; 1977,
    1; 1978, 1, 2; 1979, 1, 2; 1980, 1; 1981, 1;
    1983, 1, 2; 1986–88; 1990, 1, 2, 6–10, 12
  Mcm 1978–88, 2

Ostinato: a Magazine of Jazz Related Poetry
0955–6958
GB–London: Completely Improvised
Productions, 1989–
[NOT IN BUCOMP1]

  Lbl*

**Ostinato: Lettre d'Information Trimestrielle
du CDMC**
0989–5353
F–Neuilly-sur-Seine: Centre de Documentation
de la Musique Contemporaine, ?1988–
[NOT IN BUCOMP1]

  Gsmic [c]

Ostpreussische Musik
TNG D786
D–Königsberg, 1937–39

  Lbl*

OUMS Journal *see* **Open University Musical
Society Journal**

Out Now
GB–?, 197?–
[NOT IN BUCOMP1]

  NTp 1976–79

Out of Print
GB–Bexhill-on-Sea: Out of Print, 1979–
[NOT IN BUCOMP1; rock music journal]

  Lbl*

Outlet: Record Review
GB–Ilford: Outlet Magazines, 1978–
[NOT IN BUCOMP1]

  Lbl*

**Outlet Magazines: the Cassette Tape
Explosion Revealed and Reviewed**
GB–Ilford: Outlet Magazines, 198?–
[NOT IN BUCOMP1]

  Ob 25, 1982–#

**Ovation: the Magazine for Classical Music
Lovers**
0196–433X
US–New York: Ovation Magazine Associates,
1979–89
[NOT IN BUCOMP1; ceased publication with
vol. 10 no. 8 (1989)]

  ALb 6 (1985), 6, 11

Overtones
0887–6800
US–Philadelphia, PA: Curtis Institute of Music,
1929–33; 1938–39; 1986–

  Cu 1 (1929), 2–3 (1932)
  Ob*

The Overture: a Monthly Musical Journal for
Students and Friends of the Royal Academy
of Music
Fellinger 1968/1144; TNG GB136
GB–London: F. Corder, 1890–94
[Entitled *The Overture: Monthly Musical
Journal written by Musicians for Musicians*
during 1894]

Bp 1 (1890)–4 (1894), 9
Lam 1 (1890)–4 (1894), 9
Lbl 1 (1890)–4 (1894), 9
Lcm 1 (1890)–4 (1894), 9
Mpl 2 (1891)–4 (1894)
Ob*

The Overture: Monthly Musical Journal
written by Musicians for Musicians *see* The
Overture: a Monthly Musical Journal for
Students and Friends of the Royal Academy
of Music

Oxford and Cambridge Music Club: Report
GB–?London, 1901–?
[NOT IN BUCOMP1]

Ob 1901–03; 1905–07

Oyez
GB–Cambridge: A. Kenton, 1966–67

Cu 1 (1966/67), 1–4
Lcs 1 (1966/67), 5

P

Pacific Radio News *see* Audio

Pacific Review of Ethnomusicology
US–Los Angeles, CA: University of California
at Los Angeles Ethnomusicology Students'
Association, 1984–
[NOT IN BUCOMP1]

Lcm 4 (1987)

Paganini: Periodico Artistico Musicale
I–Genoa, 1887–92

Lcm 1 (1887)–5 (1892)

Pagine: Polsko-Włoskie Materiały Muzyczne
[= Pages: Polish-Italian Music Materials]
0137–3935
PL–Kraków: Polskie Wydawnictwo Muzyczne;
Warsaw: Polskie Centrum Muzyczne, 1972–80
[NOT IN BUCOMP1]

Cu 3 (1979)–4 (1980)

Paint It Red
0964–3184
GB–Newcastle-upon-Tyne: Paint It Red, 1987–
[NOT IN BUCOMP1]

Lbl*

Palace Peeper
US–New York: Gilbert and Sullivan Society of
New York, 1937–
[NOT IN BUCOMP1]

SFu 47 (1985), 10

The Palais Dancing News
GB–London, 1920–24
[From 1920, 5: *The Dancing World*]

Lbl*

Pan: Journal of the British Flute Society
GB–London: British Flute Society, 1983–
[NOT IN BUCOMP1]

Bs 6 (1988), 2–#*
Cu 6 (1988), 2–#
EIR:Dtc 6 (1988)–#
Gam 12 (1994)–#
Lam 8 (1990), 2–#
Lbl 9 (1991), 4–#
Lcm 14 (1996), 4–#
Lcml 5 (1987)–#
Mcm 11 (1993), 3–#
TOd 2 (1984), 2– 4; 3 (1985)

Pan: Rassegna di Lettere, Arte e Musica
TNG I209
I–Milan, 1933–35

Lbl*

Pan Pipes of Sigma Alpha Iota
0031–0611
US–Menasha, WI: ?G. Banta, 1907–80; 1981–
[From vol. 73 (1981) entitled *Pan Pipes: Sigma
Alpha Iota Quarterly* (ISSN 0889–7581)]

Lcml 41 (1949), 2

Pan Pipes: Sigma Alpha Iota Quarterly *see*
Pan Pipes of Sigma Alpha Iota

Panorama de la Musique et des Instruments
TNG F702; 0336–2574
F–Paris: Panorama de la Musique, 1974–80
[NOT IN BUCOMP1; preceded from 1969 to
1973 by *Panorama Instrumental*; ceased
publication with no. 36, 1980]

Lam 20, 1977
Lcm (p) 1977, Nov, Dec

Panorama Instrumental *see* **Panorama de la
Musique et des Instruments**

Panpipes
TNG GB300
GB–London, 1923–28; incorporated into *Music
and Youth* (q.v.)]

AB*
Lam 1 (1923); 3 (1925), 12
Lbl*
Mcm 1 (1923), 1; 4 (1926), 3

Papers of the American Musicological Society
TNG US543
US–New York: American Musicological
Society, 1936–41
[NOT IN BUCOMP1]

BRu 1936; 1940
Cpl 1936–41
Lkc 1939–41
LRHBNC 1936–41
Ob*
Ouf 1937–41

Papers of the Hudební Matice [translated title]
see **Listy Hudební Matice**

Parade
GB–London, 1925

Lbl*

Paris Qui Chante
F–Paris, 1903–10
[NOT IN BUCOMP1]

Cu 1 (1903)–3 (1905); 7 (1909)–8 (1910)*

The Parish Choir, or, Church Music Book
GB–London: Society for Promoting Church
Music, 1846–51

Cpl 1846–51*
En 1846–51
Lbl*
LVp 1846–51

Mpl 1847–51
Ob 1846–51

**The Parlour Review and Journal of Music,
Literature and the Fine Arts**
TNG US8
US–Philadelphia, PA, 1838
[Also produced in a French edition as *Revue des
Salons: Journal de Musique, de Littérature, et
des Beaux Arts*]

Cu [m] [English and French editions]

Paroles et Musique
0247–0357
F–Paris: Editions de l'Araucaria, 1980–
[NOT IN BUCOMP1]

Mu n.s. 3, 1988–#

Parsifal: Halbmonatsschrift
Fellinger 1968/971; TNG A97
A–Vienna: J. H. Holzwarth, 1884–85
[NOT IN BUCOMP1. Succeeded 1886–88 by
the *Leipziger Musik- und Kunst-Zeitung*]

Lbl 1/2 (1884/85)

**Parsifal: Leipziger Musik-, Theater- und
Kunst-Zeitung**
Fellinger 1968/972; TNG A97
A/D–Vienna; Leipzig: E. Schloemp, 1884–88

Lbl*

**The Parthenon: a Magazine of Art and
Literature**
Langley, p. 522
GB–London: Alexander Black, Young and
Young, 1825–26
[16 nos in total]

Lbl*
Ob*

Pastoral Music
TNG US868; 0363–6569
US–Washington: National Association of
Pastoral Musicians, 1976–
[Previously *Catholic Music Educators' Bulletin*
(TNG US611)]

BSdsc*

Pastoral Music Newsletter
GB–Bristol, 1987–88
[NOT IN BUCOMP1]

Au 1987, Feb/Mar–1988, June/July
Cu 1987, Feb/Mar–1988, June/July
EIR:Dtc 1987–88, June/July
Lcs 1987, Feb/Mar; 1988*
SFu 1987, Oct/Nov

Pelham Pop Annual
GB–London, 1970

Cu 1970
Ob 1970

**Pelog: a Newsletter for Players,
Ethnomusicologists and Lovers of Gamelan**
GB–Cambridge: Cambridge Gamelan Society,
198?–
[NOT IN BUCOMP1]

Cu 4, 1987–#

Pendyrus Male Choir
GB–?Pendyrus: Pendyrus Male Choir, 1969
[NOT IN BUCOMP1; only 1 issue published]

AB 1 (1969)

The Penguin Music Magazine
TNG GB396
GB–Harmondsworth: Penguin Books, 1946–52
[Entitled *Music* (TNG GB430) from 1950–52]

ABc 1–9, 1946–49; 1950–52
ALb 1–9, 1946–49
BLu 1–7, 1946–48
Bp 1–9, 1946–49
BRp 5, 1948; 7–9, 1949
BRu 1–9, 1946–49
BSdsc*
BTu 1–9, 1946–49; 1952
Cpl 1, 1946; 3–7, 1947–48
Cu 1–9, 1946–49; 1950–52
DRu 1–3, 1946–47; 5, 1948
EIR:Dtc 1–9, 1946–49
En 1–9, 1946–49; 1950–52
Ep 1–9, 1946–49; 1950–52
Gm 1–9, 1946–49
Gul 1–9, 1946–49; 1950–52
HUu 1–9, 1946–49
Lam 1–9, 1946–49; 1950–52
LAu 1950–52
Lbl*
Lcm 1–9, 1946–49
Lcml 1–9, 1946–49

Lsa 1–9, 1946–49
Lu 1–9, 1946–49; 1950–52
LVp 1–9, 1946–49
Mcm 1–9, 1946–49; 1950–52
Mmu 1–9, 1946–49
Mpl 1–9, 1946–49; 1950–52
NWu 1–9, 1946–49
Ob*
Ouf 1–9, 1946–49 [w 4, 5, 7, 8]
SA 1, 1946; 1950–52
SOu 1–9, 1946–49

The Penniman News
GB–Leicester: Official Little Richard Club,
19??–

Lsa 45, 47, 1973

People's Music [translated title] *see* **Ren Min
Yin Yue**

Percussion
GB–London, 1934–36

Lbl*

**Percussion News: the Newsletter of the
Percussive Arts Society**
US–Columbus, OH: Percussive Arts Society,
1982–
[NOT IN BUCOMP1]

Lam 1992, Mar, May, Nov; 1993, Jan, May,
July, Sep, Nov; 1994, May–#
Mcm*
Msuc 1992, July–#

Percussionist
TNG US734
US–Knoxville, TN [etc.]: Percussive Arts
Society, 1963–82
[Ceased publication with volume 19 no. 3
(1982). From 18 (1981) entitled
*Percussionist/Percussive Notes Research
Edition. See also Percussive Notes* below]

Cu 17 (1980), 2–19 (1982), 3
En 1 (1963)–17 (1980)*
Lam 4 (1967), 2; 6 (1969), 1; 8 (1971), 4;
9 (1972), 4; 10 (1973)–12 (1975), 3; 13
(1976), 1–3
LRHBNC 17 (1980), 3
Mcm 11 (1974)–#
Mpl 7 (1970)–19 (1982)

Percussionist/Percussive Notes Research
Edition *see* Percussionist

**Percussive Notes: the Official Journal of the
Percussive Arts Society**
TNG US723; 0553–6502
US–Indianapolis: Indianapolis Percussion
Ensemble; Knoxville, TN [etc.]: Percussive Arts
Society, 1963–
[*Percussive Notes* was originally a publication
of the Indianapolis Percussion Ensemble,
beginning with vol. 1 no. 1 in 1963, Feb. From 6
(1967), 1, it was incorporated by the Percussive
Arts Society. From 21 (1983), 3, the title
became *Percussionist/Percussive Notes
Research Edition*, succeeding *Percussionist*
(q.v.); this latter title ceased in 1987, with
volume 25. Since 1987 *Percussive Notes* has
continued under its original title]

BRp [c (2 years)]
Cu 18 (1980), 3–23 (1985), 5
En*
Gam 32 (1994), 3–#
Lam 11 (1973)–14 (1976), 3; 18 (1980); 19
  (1981), 2–24 (1986), 2; 24 (1986), 4–26
  (1988), 5; 27 (1989), 3–31 (1993), 1; 31
  (1993), 3–#
Lcm 26 (1988), 5; 27 (1989), 1, 3, 5; 28
  (1990)–#
Mcm 12 (1974), 2, 3; 14 (1976)–#
Mpl 8 (1970)– 23 (1985)
Msuc 23 (1985), 3–25 (1987), 5; 27 (1989)–#

Percussive Notes Research Edition *see*
Percussionist; *see also* **Percussive Notes**

Percy Grainger Society Newsletter
GB–Aylesbury: Percy Grainger Society, 198?–
[NOT IN BUCOMP1]

Lcs 1986, Feb, Aug; 1988, Jan

Percy Whitlock Trust Newsletter
GB–Staplehurst, Tonbridge: Percy Whitlock
Trust, ?1988–
[NOT IN BUCOMP1]

Lam 1988, Oct; 1992, Oct
Lbar 1988, Apr–#

Perfectly Frank
GB–London: Sinatra Music Society, 1969–73
[NOT IN BUCOMP1]

LOnjfa*

The Performance
0955–8012
GB–London: National Centre for Orchestral
Studies, 1987–
[NOT IN BUCOMP1]

Lam 2 (1988), 2
Lbl*

**Performance: an International Quarterly
Review of Records and Music**
0260–3861
GB–Monmouth: Nimbus Records, 1980–
[NOT IN BUCOMP1]

Lbl*
Lcml 1–8, 1980/81–82
Lsa 1–4, 1980/81
Lu 1–8, 1980/81–82
Mpl*
Ob*
TOd 1–4, 1980/81

**Performance: an International Review of the
Arts**
0144–5901
GB–London: Brevet Publishing, 1979–92
[NOT IN BUCOMP1; from issue 30, 1984,
entitled *Performance: the Review of Live Art*
(London: Performance Magazine, 1984–92)]

Lu 1–66, 1979–92
TOd 1–66, 1979–92

Performance: the Review of Live Art *see*
**Performance: an International Review of the
Arts**

Performance Practice Review
1044–1638
US–Claremont, CA: Claremont Graduate
School, 1988–
[NOT IN BUCOMP1: ?to cease in 1997]

BAc 3 (1990),2 –#
Bu 3 (1990)–#
CCtc 1 (1988)–#
CDu 1 (1988)–#
Cu 1 (1988)–#
Er 1 (1988)–#
EXu 5 (1992)–#
Lam 3 (1990); 5 (1992), 1, 2; 6 (1993)–#
LAu 1 (1990)–#
Lbbc 1 (1988)–#
Lcm 3 (1990), 2; 4 (1991)–#
Lcml 1 (1988)–#
LEbc 5 (1992)–#

Lgo 6 (1993)–#
Lgsm 3 (1990), 2–#
Lro 2 (1989)–#
Ltc 9 (1996)–#
Lu 1 (1988)–#
Mcm 1 (1988), 1, 2; 3 (1990), 2
MK 3 (1990)–#
NWu 1 (1988)–#
Ob 1 (1988)–#
Oub 8 (1995)–#
Ouf 1 (1988)–#
SOu 1 (1988)–#
TOd 3 (1990), 2
Uu 4 (1991)–#
Yu 1 (1988)–#

Performance Research
1352–8165
GB–London: Routledge, 1996–
[NOT IN BUCOMP1]

Ltc 1997–#

Performing Arts: the Theatre and Music Magazine
0031–5222
US–Los Angeles, CA: Performing Arts Network, 1967–
[NOT IN BUCOMP1]

ALb 26 (1992), 4

Performing Arts Journal
0735–8393
US–New York: Johns Hopkins University Press, 1976–
[NOT IN BUCOMP1]

Lgsm 1994–#

Performing Right *see* **Performing Right Gazette**

Performing Right Bulletin *see* **Performing Right Gazette**

Performing Right Gazette
TNG GB296; 0309–0019 (1976–)
GB–London: Performing Right Society, 1922–76; 1976–
[Cover title *P.R. Gazette*; from 1939–45 entitled *Performing Right Society Emergency Bulletin*; from 1945 entitled *Performing Right Society Bulletin*; from 1948, Apr entitled *Performing*

Right Bulletin; from 1954, Oct–1976 entitled *Performing Right*; from 1976–87, *Performing Right News*; from 1988, *PRS News*]

AB 1–6, 1922–39; n.s. 26–63, 65, 1955–75
ALb 38–40, 1963–64; 42, 1965; 44, 1966; 48, 49, 1967–68; 52, 1969; 59, 60, 1973; 65, 1975; n.s. 30–32, 1990–91
BAc 32, 1990–#
CCtc n.s. 30, 1990–#
CDu [c]
Cpl 1968–76*; n.s. 1, 1976–#
Cu 1–6, 1922–39; n.s. 1–65, 1939–76 [w 13, 1948]; n.s. 1, 1976–#
EIR:Dtc 1–6, 1922–39; n.s. 2, 1940–#
En*
Er 49–55, 1968–71; 62, 1974; 65, 1976
Gsmic [c]
HUu 6, 1939, 3
Lam n.s. 23–33, 1986–91; 36, 1993; 39, 1994–#
LAu 44, 1966; n.s. 27, 1988–#
Lbl*
Lcm 6, 1939, 2; n.s. 31–65, 1959–76; n.s. 24–27, 1987; 29–32, 1989–90
Lcml 53, 1970–#
Lha (f) [c (10 years)]
Lkc 52–65, 1969–76; n.s. 1, 1976–#*
LRHBNC n.s. 30, 1990; 32, 1990–#
Lsa 1–66, 1939–76 [w 12–14, 16, 17, 32, 36, 46, 64]; n.s. 1 (1976)–# [w 3, 4, 7, 10–12, 27]
Mcm 1979, Feb
Msuc [c (2 years)]
NO n.s. 1970–76*
Ob*
Oub [c (5 years)]
SFu [c]
TOd 27, 1988; 29, 1989; 35, 1992; 36, 38, 1993; 40, 1994–#

Performing Right News *see* **Performing Right Gazette**

Performing Right Society Bulletin *see* **Performing Right Gazette**

Performing Right Society Emergency Bulletin *see* **Performing Right Gazette**

Performing Right Society Yearbook *see* **Performing Right Year Book**

Performing Right Society Members' Handbook
0964–9875
GB–London: Performing Right Society, 1991
[NOT IN BUCOMP1]

> BRu 1991
> Cu 1991–#
> Lbl 1991–#

Performing Right Year Book
0309–0884
GB–London: Performing Right Society, 1977–
[Also bore title *Performing Right Society
Yearbook*. Entitled *PRS Yearbook* from 1990]

> ALb 1977/78; 1981; 1985/86; 1988/89;
>   1989/90; 1991/92
> BAc [c]
> BRu 1990/91; 1992/93
> CDu 1988/89
> Er 1977/78; 1982; 1985/86; 1987/88;
>   1989/90–#
> KE 1977/78; 1979; 1983/84; 1986/87–#
> Lam 1985/86; 1987/88–1989/90; 1991/92–#
> LAu 1981; 1984/85–#
> Lbbc 1980–#
> Lbl*
> Lcm [c]
> Lgo 1986/87–#
> Lkc 1977–79; 1981–86; 1988–#
> Lu 1977/78–#
> Mcm 1985/86–#
> NTp 1991/92–#
> Ob*
> SA 1977/78–#
> SFu [c]
> Uu 1977/78; 1979–#

Periodica Musica: Newsletter of the Répertoire International de la Presse Musicale du XIXe Siècle
0822–7594
C–Vancouver, BC: Centre for Studies in
Nineteenth-Century Music, 1983–95
[Ceased publication with nos 10/11 (1995)]

> Bu 1 (1983)–?10/11 (1995)
> Cu 1 (1983)–?10/11 (1995)
> Lbl*
> Lcm 1 (1983)–9 (1991)
> Lcml 1 (1983)–?10/11 (1995)
> Lgo 1 (1983)–7 (1989)
> Lu 1 (1983)–?10/11 (1995)
> Ob*
> Ouf 1 (1983)–9 (1991)

Periodical Report of the Incorporated Society of Musicians *see* Monthly Journal of the National Society of Professional Musicians

Y Perl Cerddorol [= The Musical Pearl]
GB–Merthyr Tydfil, 1880

> AB 1880

Perspectives
US–New York, 1952–

> EIR:Dtc 1–16, 1952–56
> Lam 1–6, 1952; 10, 1955
> Lbl*
> Lgo 1–16, 1952–56

Perspectives of New Music
TNG US724; 0031–6016
US–Princeton, NJ: Princeton University Press
[for the Fromm Music Foundation], 1962–

> AB*
> Au 1 (1962/63)–#
> BAc 21 (1982/83)–#
> BG 1 (1962/63)–20 (1981/82); 22
>   (1983/84)–#
> BLu 1 (1962/63)–#
> BRu 18 (1979/80)–#
> Bs 2 (1963/64)–#*
> BSdsc*
> BTu 1 (1962/63)–#
> Bu 1 (1962/63)–#
> Cat 13 (1974/75), 1, 2; 20 (1981/82),1, 2;
>   32 (1993)–#
> CCtc 1 (1962/63)–7 (1968/69);
>   12 (1973/74)–#
> CDu 9 (1970/71)–#
> Cpl 2 (1963/64)–10 (1971/72)
> Cu 1 (1962/63)–#
> DRu 1 (1962/63)–25 (1987); 31 (1993)–#
> EIR:Dtc 11 (1972/73), 2–23 (1984/85), 1
> EIR:Duc 13 (1974/75)–21 (1982/83)
> En 1 (1962/63)–#
> Er 11 (1972/73)–#
> EXu 1 (1962/63)–#
> Gm 1 (1962/63)–#
> Gul 1 (1962/63)–#
> HUu 16 (1977/78)–25 (1987); 30 (1992)–#
> KE 1 (1962/63)–3 (1964/65) [w 1 (1962/63),
>   2]; 12 (1973/74)–#
> Lam 1 (1962/63)–#
> LAu 11 (1972/73)–#
> LCdM 11 (1972/73)–#
> Lcm 1 (1962/63)–#
> Lcml 1 (1962/63)–#

Lcu 1 (1962/63)–#
LEbc 1 (1962/63)–20 (1981/82), 1/2
LEc 1 (1962/63)–# [w 30 (1992), 2]
Lgo 1 (1962/63)–#
Lgsm 14 (1975/76)–#
Lkc 1 (1962/63)–#
Lki 1 (1962/63)–#
Lmi 15 (1976/77)–#
LRHBNC 2 (1963/64)–4 (1965/66);
    6 (1967/68)–#
Lro 32 (1994)–#
Ltv 11 (1972/73)–20 (1981/82)
Lu 1 (1962/63)–#
LVp 1 (1962)–6 (1968); 9 (1970)–#
LVu 3 (1965), 2–#
Mcm 11 (1972/73)–#
Mpl 1 (1962/63)–#
Msuc 26 (1988)–#
Mu 1 (1962/63)–#
NO 1 (1962/63)–23 (1984/85); 26 (1988)–#
NWu 1 (1962/63)*; 2 (1963/64)–#
Ob 1 (1962/63)–#
Oub 33 (1995)–#
Ouf 1 (1962/63)–#
R 2 (1963/64)–20 (1981/82)
SFu 1 (1962/63)–#
SLGu 14 (1975/76)–#
SOu 1 (1962)–#
TOd 2 (1963/64); 4 (1965/66); 6 (1967/68),
    1; 7 (1968/69), 2; 9 (1970/71), 2; 10
    (1971/72), 1; 11 (1972/73), 2; 12
    (1973/74)–18 (1979/80); 20 (1981/82)–27
    (1989), 1; 29 (1991), 2 –31 (1993), 2, 4
Uu 17 (1978/79)–#
Yu 1 (1962/63)–#

Peter Warlock Society Newsletter
TNG GB530; 0266–366X
GB–London: Peter Warlock Society, 1966–

    ALb 31–36, 1983–86
    Cu 1, 1966; 21, 1977–#
    DOR 30, 1983–#
    EIR:Dtc ?22, 1978–#
    En*
    Gam 49, 1992–#
    Lbar 1, 1966–#
    Lcm 36, 1986–#
    Lcml 4, 1970–#
    Ltc 58, 1996–#
    Mcm*
    Ob*

Philharmonia Club Magazine see **Con Brio**
[2]

Philharmonia Orchestra
GB–London, 1980–
[NOT IN BUCOMP1]

    Cu 1980–#

Philharmonic Post see **London Philharmonic Post**

The Philharmonicon: a Periodical of Pianoforte and Vocal Music
Langley, p. 552
GB–London: William Sherwood and Company
[etc.], 1833
[Only 4 nos published]

    Lbl*

Philharmonische Blätter
TNG D1040
D–Berlin: Berlin Philharmonic Orchestra,
1963/64–
[NOT IN BUCOMP1]

    ALb 5 (1974/75)

Philips Music Herald: a Quarterly about Music and Records Published by N.V. Philips' Phonographische Industrie
TNG NL103; 0031–790X
NL–Baarn: Philips, 1955–70

    En 1955–70
    Lcm*
    Lcml 1962–63*; 1964; 1965–70*
    Lsa 1957–70*

Philomusica News
GB–?, 199?–
[NOT IN BUCOMP1]

    AB 1993–#

Philosophy of Music Education Review
1063–5734
US–Bloomington, IN: School of Music, Indiana
University, 1993–
[NOT IN BUCOMP1]

    Re 1 (1993)–#

Phono: internationale Schallplatten-Zeitschrift
TNG A275
A–Vienna, 1954–66
[Supplement to Österreichische Musikzeitschrift
(q.v.)]

    Lsa 1 (1954)–12 (1966) [w 1 (1954), 2; 7
    (1961), 2–6; 8 (1962), 4, 5]

The Phono-Record
TNG GB258
GB–London, 1912–32
[Incorporated into *The Music Seller and Small Goods Trader*]

   Cu 1928–30*
   Lbl*

The Phono Trader and Recorder
GB–London, 1904–13

   Lbl*

The Phonogram: a Monthly Journal devoted to the Science of Sound and the Recording of Speech
GB–London, 1893

   Lsa 1 (1893), 1, 2

The Phonograph Monthly Review
TNG US497
US–Boston, MA: Phonograph Publishing Company, 1927–32
[From 1933 entitled *The Music Lovers' Guide* (q.v.)]

   Lsa 1 (1927), 8–6 (1932), 4*

Phonograph Record Magazine
US–Hollywood, CA: Phonograph Record Ltd, ?196–
[NOT IN BUCOMP1; includes *Soul and Jazz Record* from April 1974]

   Lsa 1972, Nov–1977, Apr*

Phonographic Bulletin
TNG INTL34; 0253–004X
GB–Milton Keynes: Open University [for the International Association of Sound Archives], 1971–92
[Ceased publication with no. 61, 1992; succeeded by the *IASA Journal* (AUS–Canberra: International Association of Sound Archives, 1 (1993)–; ISSN 1021–562X)

   AB 1–17, 1971–77; 19–37, 1977–83; 46, 1986
   En 1–61, 1971–92
   Lsa*

Phonographic Monthly
GB–Croydon, ?–1936
[NOT IN BUCOMP1]

   Ob 32 (1928)–40 (1936), 5

Phonoprisma *see* Musica Schallplatte

Phonothèque Nationale Bulletin
F–Paris: Phonothèque Nationale, ?–

   Lsa 1963–74

Pianissimo: the Blackheath Magazine *see* Pianissimo: the Blackheath Musical Paper

Pianissimo: the Blackheath Musical Paper
Fellinger 1968/1174; TNG GB139
GB–London, 1891–93
[Subtitled *The Blackheath Magazine* from 16, 1893; 20 nos in total]

   Lbl*

The Pianist: the Official Magazine of the International Piano Teachers' Association
TNG US607
US–Erie, PA: International Piano Teachers' Association, 1947–
[NOT IN BUCOMP1]

   Lam 5 (1951), 2

The Pianista, or, Promenade Concert Magazine
GB–London: Sherwood, Gange and Templeman, 1941–?42
[NOT IN BUCOMP1]

   Lam 1 (1941)–2 (1942), 18

Le Pianiste: Journal Spécial pour le Piano, les Théâtres Lyriques et les Concerts
Fellinger 1968/108; TNG F19
F–Paris; Meudon: J. Delacour [printer], 1833–35

   Cu 1 (1833)–2 (1835) [Reprint ed.]
   Ob 1 (1833)–2 (1835), 24

Piano Accordion
TNG GB359
GB–London, 1936–37

   Lbl*

Piano and Keyboard: the Bimonthly Piano Quarterly *see* Piano Quarterly Newsletter

Piano Jahrbuch
0173–8607
D–Recklinghausen: Piano-Verlag, 1979–
[NOT IN BUCOMP1]

> Lbl*
> Lu*

Piano Journal
0267–7253
GB–London: European Piano Teachers'
Association, 1980–

> BLp [c]
> Bs 1 (1980)–15 (1994), 45 [w 24–27]
> Cu 1 (1980)–#
> EIR:Dp 9 (1988)–15 (1994)
> EIR:Dtc 1 (1980)–#
> En 1 (1980)–#
> Ep 1 (1980)–#
> Er 1 (1980)–13 (1992)
> EXu 1 (1980)–9 (1988)
> Gam 1 (1980), 1, 3; 2 (1981), 4, 6; 3 (1982),
>   8; 4 (1983), 11, 12; 5 (1984), 13; 6 (1985)–
>   #
> Gm 7 (1986)–#
> Lam 1 (1980), 1, 3; 2 (1981), 4–#
> Lbar 1 (1980)–#
> Lbl*
> Lcm 4 (1983), 11
> Lcml 1 (1980)–#
> Lgo 1 (1980)–7 (1986)
> Lgsm 1 (1980)–#
> Lu 1 (1980)–#
> Mcm 1 (1980)–#
> Ob*
> TOd 3 (1982), 8–#
> Uu [c (2 years)]

Piano Journal *see also* **The Pianoforte
Dealers' Guide**

The Piano Lover
TNG GB356
GB–London: Blüthner, 1935

> Lbl*
> Lcml 1 (1935), 3
> Mcm 1 (1935), 4

Piano, Organ and Music Trades Journal *see*
The Pianoforte Dealers' Guide

Piano Quarterly *see* **Piano Quarterly
Newsletter**

Piano Quarterly Newsletter
TNG US663; 0735–7125
US–New York: Piano Teachers Information
Service, 1952–
[Entitled *The Piano Quarterly* (Wilmington, VT:
Piano Quarterly, Inc.), 1958–92; from no. 160,
1993, *Piano and Keyboard: the Bimonthly
Piano Quarterly* (San Anselmo, CA: String
Letter Press, 1993– ; ISSN 0031–9554)]

> Lcml 1–67, 1952–60
> Lgo 158, 1992–#
> Lgsm 25, 1977–#*
> Lu 58–85, 1967–74 [w 67, 1969]
> Uu 160, 1993–#

The Piano Student
TNG GB287
GB–London, 1921–37
[Incorporated into *The Music Teacher* (q.v.). *See
also Music and Youth*]

> AB 14 (1934)–17 (1937), 4
> Bs 15 (1935)–17 (1937), Nov
> Cu n.s. 1 (1934)–4 (1937), 2
> Lbl*
> Lcm (p) 14 (1934), Oct –15 (1935), Dec
> Lu n.s. 1 (1934), 2–7
> Mpl 14 (1934)–17 (1937)
> Ob 14 (1934), 10–17 (1937), 12

Piano Teachers' Repertoire
GB–Thames Ditton, 197?–
[NOT IN BUCOMP1]

> Cu 6 (1982), 2–8 (1984), 3
> EIR:Dtc 6 (1982)–8 (1984), 3

Piano Teachers' Yearbook
GB–London, 1947–

> Lbl*
> Mcm 1947
> Ob*

Piano Technician's Journal
US–Seattle, WA, 1958–

> Lgu 18 (1975), 12–#

Piano Tuner's Quarterly
TNG GB454; 0048–4105
GB–London: Royal National Institute for the
Blind, 1954–

> Lbl*
> Lgu 25 (1979), 3–40 (1994), 4 [non–braille];
>   33 (1986), Oct–39 (1993), July [braille]

Piano World and Music Trades International
see The Pianomaker

Piano World and Music Trades Review *see*
The Pianomaker

Il Pianoforte: Rivista Mensile della Fabbrica
Italiana Pianoforte (F.I.P.)
TNG I169
I–Turin, 1920–27
[Succeeded by *La Rassegna Musicale* (q.v.)]

Cpl 1 (1920)–8 (1927)*
Lcml 4 (1923), 1
Ob 1 (1920)–4 (1923); 6 (1925)–7 (1926)

The Pianoforte Dealers' Guide
Fellinger 1968/902; TNG GB103
GB–London, 1882–1914
[From 1882, 7, entitled *Piano, Organ and Music
Trades Journal*; from 1901, 231, entitled *Piano
Journal*; from 1904, 267, entitled *British and
Colonial Piano Journal*]

Lbl 1–6, 1882

The Piano-Forte Magazine: or, Compleat and
Elegant Library of Ancient and Modern
Musick
Langley, p. 21; Fellinger 1986, p. 86–104
GB–London: James Harrison, 1797–1802
[NOT IN BUCOMP1]

AB 1–9, 1797–99
Lbl*
Lu 1–13, 1797–1800 [w 6, 11, 12]

The Pianoforte Teacher
TNG GB355
GB–London, 1935–40

En 1 (1935)–2 (1936)
Gam 1 (1935), 6, 8–10; 2 (1936), 4, 5; 3
(1937), 1, 6; 4 (1938), 9, 11, 12; 5 (1939),
3, 4
Lbl*
Lcml 1 (1935), 10–2 (1936), 7, 8, 10
Ob 1 (1935)–3 (1937), 8

Pianola Journal
0952–6323
GB–West Wickham: Pianola Institute, 1987–
[NOT IN BUCOMP1]

AB 1 (1987)–#
Cu 1 (1987)–#
EIR:Dtc 1 (1987)–#

En 1 (1987)–#
Lbl*
Lcml 1 (1987)–#
Lsa 1 (1987)–#

The Pianomaker
Fellinger 1968/2188; TNG GB262
GB–London: Sinclair's Publications, 1913–81
[Amalgamated with the *Music Seller and Small
Goods Dealer* (q.v.) in 1936. Later entitled *The
Pianomaker, Music and Radio Retailer*; from
1969 entitled *Piano World and Music Trades
International*; in 1971 incorporated *The London
and Provincial Music Trades Review* (q.v.) to
become *Piano World and Music Trades Review*;
in 1973 incorporated *Music Industry* (q.v.) to
become *Music Trades International* (ISSN
0305–7178); from 1981 incorporated in *Music
World: the Definitive Music Trade Magazine*
(q.v.)]

AB 61 (1973)–69 (1981)
Bp 59 (1971)–60 (1972), 707
Cpl 60 (1972)–69 (1981)*
Cu 23 (1935)–69 (1981)
EIR:Dtc 30 (1942), 344–43 (1955), 502
En 61 (1973)–69 (1981)
Lam 42 (1954), 495
Lbl*
Lcml 1 (1913)–40 (1952)
Len 57 (1969)–68 (1980), 10
Lsa 58 (1970), 680–60 (1972), 708 [w 692,
697, 701, 702]
LVp 59 (1971)–61 (1973); 63 (1975)–65
(1977); 67 (1979)–69 (1981)
Mcm 60 (1972)–69 (1981)*
Ob*

The Pianomaker, Music and Radio Retailer
see The Pianomaker

The Piano-Player Review: a Monthly Musical
Journal for Users of Piano-Player [and all
Music Lovers]
Fellinger 1968/2144; TNG GB259
GB–Birmingham, 1912–14

Lbl*
Lcm (p) 2 (1913), Sep
Ob 21, 22, 1914

The Pibroch [1]
GB–Glasgow, 1888

En*
Lbl*

The Pibroch [2]
GB–Glasgow: Highland Light Infantry, 1895–1900

En 1 (1895)–4 (1898)

Piccolo Bollettino di Informazioni e Notizie: Associazioni dei Musicologi Italiani, Sezione Italiana della Società Internazionale di Musica
Fellinger 1968/225; TNG I162
I–Parma: Alfonso Zerlini, 1914–19

Lbl*

Pick Up: Mensile di Dischi e Musica
GB–London, ?1946–?

Lsa 1946–47 [m]

Pickin' the Blues
GB–East Calder: M. S. and F. A. Harris, 1982–84

Cu 1–25, 1982–84
Lbl*
Lsa 20–25, 1983–84
Ob 1–25, 1982–84

Pickings: Issued for Banjo-, Mandoline- and Guitar-Enthusiasts
TNG GB343
GB–London, 1934–57

Lbl*

Pickup: the Record Collector's Guide
GB–Birmingham, 1946–47

Cbijs 1 (1946)–2 (1947)
LOnjfa*
Lsa 1 (1946), 1, 3–5, 7– 11; 2 (1947), 2, 3

Pieces of Jazz
GB–Canterbury: Pete Webb, 1968–71

Cbijs 1968–71

Pierre Key's International Music Year Book
see Pierre Key's Music Year Book

Pierre Key's Music Year Book
TNG US491
US–New York: Pierre Key, 1926–38
[NOT IN BUCOMP1; also entitled *Pierre Key's International Music Year Book*]

Er 1926/27

Piob Mhor: a Quarterly Journal for Pipers
TNG GB393
GB–London, 1946–57

Cu 1 (1946/47), 1, 2
EIR:Dtc 1 (1946), 1
En 1 (1946/47), 1, 2
Lbl*
Ob*

Piobaire [= Piper]
EIRE–Dublin: Na Piobairi Uilleann, n.s. 1978–
[NOT IN BUCOMP1]

EIR:Dtc n.s. 1 (1978)

The Pipe Band see The Piping, Drumming and Highland Dancing Journal

Piping and Dancing: a Monthly Journal
TNG GB351
GB–Ardrossan, 1935–41

En 5 (1939/40), 2–5, 7–6 (1940/41), 5
Gm 1 (1935)–6 (1940/41)
Lbl*
Ob*

The Piping, Drumming and Highland Dancing Journal
TNG GB416
GB–Edinburgh: Scottish Pipe Band Association, 1948–
[From 1950, 3: *The Pipe Band*]

BLp [c]
Cu 1 (1948)–#
EIR:Dtc 1 (1948)–#
En*
Ep 1 (1948)–2 (1949)
Gm 90, 1964; 105, 107, 1966–#
Lbl*
Ob*

The Piping Times
TNG GB417
GB–Glasgow: Pipers' Guild and League of
Young Scots College of Piping, 1948–

> AB*
> Cu 1 (1948), 2–#
> EIR:Dtc 1 (1948), 2–9 (1957), 6
> En 1 (1948), 2–#
> Ep 37 (1985)–#
> Er 3 (1951), 12
> Gm 1 (1948), 2–#
> Gsmic 12 (1960), 8–12; 13 (1961)–33
> (1981), 5
> Lbl*
> Ob*

Piping World
TNG GB541
GB–Glasgow, 1969–

> Lam 1 (1969), 1
> Lbl*
> Ob*

**Pitman's Musical Monthly: Original and
Popular Vocal and Instrumental Music**
Fellinger 1968/936; TNG GB106
GB–London: F. Pitman, 1883–93

> Gm 1 (1883)–4 (1887)
> Lbl 1 (1883)–10 (1893), 120
> Mpl 1 (183)–10 (1893)

PL Yearbook of Jazz
GB–London: Editions Poetry London, 1946
[NOT IN BUCOMP1]

> Cu 1946

Plade Parade [= Disc Parade]
DK–Copenhagen, 1962–?

> Lsa 1 (1962), 1, 4; 3 (1963), 1

Plainsong and Medieval Music
0961–1371
GB–Cambridge: Cambridge University Press,
1992–
[NOT IN BUCOMP1; succeeded *Journal of the
Plainsong and Mediaeval Music Society* (q.v.)]

> AB 1 (1992), 2–#
> BAc 1 (1992)–#
> BLu 1 (1992)–#
> Cu 1 (1992)–#
> EIR:Dtc 1 (1992)–#
> En 1 (1992)–#

> EXu 1 (1992)–#
> Gul 1 (1992)–#
> KE 1 (1992)–#
> LAu 1 (1992)–#
> Lbl*
> LEbc 2 (1993)–#
> Lkc 1 (1992)–#
> Mu 1 (1992)–#
> Ob 1 (1992)–#
> Ouf 1 (1992)–#
> Yu 2 (1993)–#

Plateau
0032–1354
NL–Amersfoort, 1961–?

> Lsa 1965–71*

Platenieuws [= Disc News]
NL–?, 195?–

> Lsa 13 (1962/63)–16 (1966)*

Platenwereld [= Disc World]
TNG NL111; 0015–6159
NL–Amersfoort, 1963–

> Lsa 7, 1964; 14–20, 1965; 24, 27, 1966;
> 32–34, 36–41, 1967; 43–57, 1968–69

Playback
US–New York, 1949–50

> Cbijs 1949–50, Mar

**Playback: Bulletin of the National Sound
Archive**
0952–2360
GB–London: British Library National Sound
Archive, 1992–
[NOT IN BUCOMP1]

> ALb 1, 1992; 6, 1993–#
> Ep 1, 1992; 6, 1993–#
> Gul 1995–#
> Lam [c]
> LAu 1, 1992–#
> Lsa 1, 1992–#
> Ob*
> TOd 6, 7, 1993–94

Player Piano Group Bulletin
0140–7589
GB–Ruislip: Player Piano Group, 1959–
[NOT IN BUCOMP1]

> Lu 61, 1976

Plays and Players *see* Seven Arts

PM *see* Przeglad Muzyczny [2]

PMRU *see* Popular Musicology Quarterly

The Podium
US–Chicago, 1976–

  Lsa 1 (1976), 1

Point du Jazz
TNG B161; 0776–216X
B–Brussels: Sweet and Hot, 1969–?

  Cbijs 1973, 9

Polish Music/Polnische Musik
TNG PL124; 0032–2946
PL–Warsaw: Ars Polona Foreign Trade
Krakowskie Przedmiescie; Agencja Autorska,
1966–92
[Ceased publication with vol. 27 no. 4 (1992)]

  BSdsc*
  Bu 1 (1966)–13 (1978)
  Lam 3 (1968), 8–4 (1969), 15; 6 (1971), 20–7
    (1972), 24; 8 (1973), 29; 10 (1975), 37–12
    (1977), 47
  Lbbc 8 (1973)–9 (1974)
  Lcm 20 (1985), 3, 4
  Lkc 3 (1968)–13 (1978); 15 (1980)–16
    (1981), 2
  Mcm 7 (1972)–11 (1976)*

Polish Musicological Studies
TNG PL130
PL–Krakow: Polskie Wydawnictwo Muzyczne,
1977–

  Cu 1 (1977)–#
  Ob*
  Ouf 1 (1977)–2 (1986)

Political Song News
GB–London, 1987–
[NOT IN BUCOMP1]

  Lcs 1–12, 1987–92 [w 6]

Polnische Musik *see* Polish Music/Polnische
Musik

**Polyhymnia: eine musikalische Monatsschrift
für das Piano-Forte**
Fellinger 1986, p. 763–812
D–Meissen: Christian Ehregott Klinkicht,
1825–32; n.s. 1832–39

  Lbl*

Polyphonie: Revue Musicale Trimestrielle
TNG F604; 0996–2956
F–Paris: Editions Richard–Masse, 1947–56

  AB 3, 4, 6, 1949
  Cpl 5–10, 1949–54
  Lam 10, 1954
  Lbl*
  Lcml 1–10, 1947–54
  LEbc 1–10, 1947–54
  Lu 1–12, 1947–56
  Mpl 1–?8, 1947–50
  Ob*

Polyphony *see* Electronic Musician

POMPI: Popular Music Periodicals Index
0951–1318
GB–London: British Library National Sound
Archive, 1984–91
[NOT IN BUCOMP1]

  BEp 1989
  BRp 1988–89
  BSdsc*
  CCtc 1984–89
  Cu 1988–91
  EIR:Dtc 1984–89
  Gm 1984–89
  Lbl 1, 1984–89
  Lgo 1984
  MK 1988–91
  NOp 1984–91
  Ob 1984–89

Pop Cat *see* The Gramophone Popular (Long-
Playing Popular) Record Catalogue

Pop Express
0962–2489
GB–London, ?1990–
[NOT IN BUCOMP1]

  Lbl*

Pop in 3-D
0956–8921
GB–London: Star Tracker Publications, 1989–
[NOT IN BUCOMP1]

Lbl*

Pop Music Mirror *see* Music Mirror [1]

Pop Pics
GB–London: George Newnes, ?1963–
[NOT IN BUCOMP1]

AB 3– 26, 1963–65

Pop Pix
GB–London, 1981–
[NOT IN BUCOMP1]

Cu 1–13, 1981–82
Ob*

Pop Puzzler
GB–London, 1986
[NOT IN BUCOMP1]

Cu 1–10, 1986

Pop Records
GB–London, 1956–?

Lbl*
Ob 1 (1956), 1–10

Pop Shop
GB–Heanor, 1964–
[From 1965, 7 entitled *Pop Shop and Teen Beat*;
in 1966 incorporated *Pop Weekly* (q.v.); later
incorporated *The Mod*]

AB 36, 1966
Cu 1965, May–1966, Feb
Lbl*
Ob*

Pop Shop and Teen Beat *see* Pop Shop

Pop Shop International *see* Pop Weekly

Pop Singles
GB–London, 1967–79

AB 1–44, 1967–78
Cu 1–44, 1967–78; n.s. 1 (1978)–2 (1979)
EIR:Dtc 12–44, 1969–78; n.s. 2 (1979)
En*
Lbl*
Lsa 1–44, 1967–77 [w 14–23, 1970–72]
Ob*

Pop-Up
GB–London, 1973–?

Lbl*

Pop Weekly
GB–London, 1962–66
[In 1966 incorporated into *Pop Shop* (q.v.) and
subsequently entitled *Pop Shop International*]

AB 4 (1966), Mar, May, June, July
Cu 1 (1962)–4 (1966), 25
Lbl*
Ob*

Popshop *see* Rage

Popster
I–Rome, 1972–75

Cu 1– 34, 1972–75
Ob*

Popswop
GB–London: Spotlight Publications, 1973–
[From 1974 entitled *Record and Popswop
Mirror*; from 1975 entitled *Record Mirror with
Popswop*]

AB 1983–91
Cu 32– 103, 1973–74
Ob*

Popular Hi-Fi
0309–5355
GB–Teddington: Haymarket Publishing, 1971–
76, 1977–
[Entitled *What Hi-Fi?* (ISSN 0309–3336) from
1976; relaunched as *Popular Hi-Fi*, with new
numbering sequence, from 1 (1977); from 1983
entitled *New Hi-Fi Sound*, with new numbering
sequence; entitled *What CD?* and *Digital Audio*
from 1987; entitled *High Fidelity* [3] from 1990,
with new numbering sequence (q.v.). Succeeded
Audiophile with Hi-Fi Answers (q.v.); also
entitled *Popular Hi-Fi and Sound* sometime
during its existence]

AB*
BLp*
BSdsc*
EIR:Dtc 1976; 1 (1977)–7 (1983), 10;
1 (1983)–7 (1990), 3
En*
Gm 1 (1977)–2 (1978)
Lbl*
Lbo*

Lbx* [m]
Lsa 6 (1988), 8–7 (1989), 1
Ob*
SFp 2 (1978)–7 (1983), 10; 1 (1983)–7
  (1990), 3

Popular Hi-Fi and Sound see **Popular Hi-Fi**

Popular Music
0261–1430
GB–Cambridge: Cambridge University Press,
1981–

  AB 1 (1981)–#
  BAc 6 (1987)–#
  BG 1 (1981)–10 (1991); 13 (1994)–#
  Bs 1 (1981)–#
  BSdsc 1 (1981)–#
  BTu 1 (1981)–#
  Bu 1 (1981)–#
  CCtc 7 (1988)–#
  Cu 1 (1981)–#
  DRu 1 (1981)
  EIR:Dtc 6 (1987)–#
  En 1 (1981)–#
  Er 1 (1981)–#
  EXu 1 (1981)–#
  Gm 6 (1987)–#
  KE 1 (1981)–3 (1983); 10 (1991)–#
  Lbbc 1 (1981)–#
  Lbl*
  Lcs 1 (1981)–#
  Lcm 1 (1981)–#
  Lcml 1 (1981)–#
  Lcu 11 (1992)–#
  Lgo 1 (1981)–#
  Lgsm 1 (1981)–#
  Lgu 11 (1992)–#
  Lie 1 (1981)–4 (1984)
  Lki 6 (1987)–#
  Lro 3 (1983)–#
  Lsa 1 (1981)–#
  Lso 10 (1991), 2, 3
  Ltc 14 (1995)–#
  Ltv 1 (1981)–#
  MK 1 (1981)–#
  Mmu 1 (1981)–#
  Mmu (a) 1 (1981)–#
  Mpl 6 (1987)–#
  Msuc 6 (1987)–#
  NWu 1 (1981)–#
  Ob 1 (1981)–#
  Oub 13 (1994)–#
  Ouf 11 (1992)–#
  Re 1 (1981)–#

SFu 1 (1981)–#
SLGu 1 (1981)–7 (1988)
SOu 1 (1981)–#
TOd 6 (1987)–#
Yu 1 (1981)–12 (1993)

**Popular Music: an Annotated Index of
American Popular Songs**
0886–442X
US–Detroit, MI: Gale Research Company,
?1974–
[NOT IN BUCOMP1]

  AB 9 (1986)–15 (1992)
  BSdsc*
  Lsa 7 (1984)–?

Popular Music and Dancing Weekly
GB–London: Amalgamated Press, 1934–35

  AB 1–44, 1934–35
  Cbijs 1, 1934; 37, 1935
  Lbl*
  Ob*

Popular Music and Film Song Weekly
GB–London, 1937–38

  AB 1–20, 1937–38
  Cbijs 2, 1937
  Ob 1–20, 1937–38

Popular Music and Society
TNG US817; 0300–7766
US–Bowling Green, OH: Bowling Green State
University, 1971–

  BSdsc*
  BTu 2 (1973), 3
  KE 9 (1983), 2–#
  Lbl*
  Lsa 1 (1971), 3; 4 (1974), 1–4
  Mmu 12 (1988)–#
  Yu 1 (1971)–#*

Popular Music Periodicals Index
0095–4101
US–Metuchen, NJ: Scarecrow Press, 1973–?76

  BSdsc*
  Cpl 1974; 1976
  Cu 1973–76
  KE 1974–76
  Ob*

Popular Music Periodicals Index see also
POMPI

Popular Musicology Quarterly
1357–0951
GB–Salford: University College Salford Centre
for Media, Performance and Communications,
Popular Music Research Unit, 1994–
[NOT IN BUCOMP1; also known as *PMRU
Quarterly*]

   Msuc 1, 1994–#

Popular Radio [1]
US–New York: Popular Radio, 1922–28

   Lbl*

Popular Radio [2]
S–Stockholm, ?–?
[NOT IN BUCOMP1]

   BSdsc*

Popular Video *see* Music and Video

Poradnik Muzyczny: Organ Ludowego
Instytutu Muzycznego [= Musical Adviser:
Organ of the Łodz Institute for Folk Music]
TNG PL103; 0551–5351
PL–Łodz: Łodz Institute for Folk Music,
1947–89

   BSdsc*
   Lu 15 (1961)–17 (1963)

Poradnik Muzyczny *see also* Przeglad
Muzyczny [2]

Posterpop Chart Club
0264–4533
GB–Iver: Century Merchandising, 1983–

   Lbl*

Pour la Musique
B–Brussels: Association pour l'Information
Musicale, 1969–

   Lcml 13, 1970–# [w 17, 1970]

P.R. Gazette *see* Performing Right Gazette

Prachya Pratibha *see* Pracya Pratibha/
Prachya Pratibha: Journal of Prachya
Niketan, a Division of the Birla Institute of
Art and Music

Practica für Haus- und Jugendmusik,
Chorwesen und Musikerziehung *see* Musica:
Zweimonatsschrift

Practical Hi-Fi [and Audio] *see* Hi-Fi Today

Pracya Pratibha/Prachya Pratibha: Journal of
Prachya Niketan, a Division of the Birla
Institute of Art and Music
IN–Bhopal: Prachya Niketan, Birla Institute of
Art and Music, 1973–
[NOT IN BUCOMP1]

   Lbl*

Prague Museum Bedřicha Smetany: Sborník
[= Journal]
CZ–Prague: The Bedřich Smetana Museum,
1959–

   Ob*

Praxis: Studi e Testi sull'Interpretazione della
Musica
I–Rovereto: Accademia Roveretana di Musica
Antica, 1983–
[NOT IN BUCOMP1]

   Lbl*

The Precentor
Fellinger 1968/1600; TNG GB194
GB–London: Iliffe, Sons and Sturmey, 1901–06

   Lbl*
   Ob 1 (1901)

Prelude
TNG GB476
GB–London: Ibbs and Tillett, 1958–66

   Lam 1–11, 1958; 13, 15–27, 1959; 30–37,
     1961
   Lcml 2, 1958; 16, 1959; 37, 1961

Prelude, Fugue and Riffs: News for the
Friends of Leonard Bernstein
1070–2652
US–New York: Jalni, 199?–
[NOT IN BUCOMP1]

   EXu 1991, Aut–1994, Wint

Première: the Only Magazine to have Music
instead of Words
0269–7769
GB–London: Dickinson, 1986–87
[NOT IN BUCOMP1]

   Cu 1–4, 1986–87
   Lam 1, 2, 1986
   Lcm 1–4, 1986–87

Lcml 1–4, 1986–87
Lgo 1–4, 1986–87
Ob 1–4, 1986–87

The Presbyterian Psalmodist: a Monthly Magazine Designed to Aid in the Presbyterian Service of Praise
Fellinger 1968/641; TNG GB77
GB–Edinburgh, 1871–72
[Succeeded by *The Psalmodist* (q.v.) in 1873]

Gul (e) 1–10, 12, 1871–72

Preview [of Welsh National Opera]
GB–Cardiff: Welsh National Opera, 1982–

Cu 1, 1982–#
EIR:Dtc 1–6, 1982–83

Pribaltiskiy Muzykovedcheskiy Sbornik
LT–Vilnius: Soyuz Kompozitorov Litovskoi SSSR, 1982–
[NOT IN BUCOMP1]

Lbl*

Přírustky Hudebnin v Československých Knihovnách [= Musical Acquisitions in Czechoslovak Libraries]
0552 1246
CZ–Brno: Univ. Knihovna v Brne, 1955–
[Later entitled *Přírustky Hudebnin v Českých a Slovenských Knihovnách*]

Bu 32 (1986)–#
Lbl*
Ob*

Přírustky Hudebnin v Českých a Slovenských Knihovnách *see* **Přírustky Hudebnin v Československých Knihovnách**

Příspěvky k Dějinám České Hudby [= Contributions to the History of Czech Music]
CZ–Prague, 1971–

Ob*

Private Affair
0143–9006
GB–Tewkesbury, 1979–
[NOT IN BUCOMP1; rock music journal]

Lbl*

Pro Musica
TNG YU36; 0555–2117
HR–Belgrade: Udruženje Muzickih Umetnika Srbije, 1964–

BSdsc*
Ob*

Pro Musica: Blätter für Musik von Volk zu Volk
TNG D937; 0552–1475
D–Wolfenbüttel: Möseler [for the Internationaler Arbeitkreis für Jugend- und Volksmusik Pro Musica, Landesgruppe Deutschland], 1953–66
[NOT IN BUCOMP1]

Gul 1957–61
Lbl*

Pro Sound News
0269–4735
GB–Croydon: Pro Sound, 1986–
[NOT IN BUCOMP1; later entitled *Pro Sound News Europe*; incorporated *Studio Week/Studio* (q.v.)]

CCtc 6 (1991), May–#
EIR:Dtc 2 (1987), 3–7; 4 (1989), 8–#
Lcml 6 (1991), Aug–#
Lsa 5 (1990), 10–# [w 9 (1994), 8]
Ob 2 (1987)–#

Pro Sound News Europe *see* **Pro Sound News**

Probe: SOCAN's Monthly Newsletter
1180–3746
C–Ontario: Society of Composers, Authors and Music Publishers of Canada, 1990–
[NOT IN BUCOMP1]

Er 1, 1990–#
Lbbc 1, 1990–#*

Proceedings in Musicology [translated title] *see* **Lucrari de Muzikologie**

Proceedings of the International Computer Music Conference
GB–?: Computer Music Association, 1977–
[NOT IN BUCOMP1]

Yu 1983–92

Proceedings of the Musical Association

Fellinger 1968/688; TNG GB80; Langley 1994, p. 123

GB–London: Musical [later Royal Musical] Association, 1874/75–

[From vol. 71 (1944/45) entitled *Proceedings of the Royal Musical Association* (ISSN 0080–4452); from 112 (1986/87) entitled *Journal of the Royal Musical Association* (ISSN 0269–0403)]

AB*
ABc 5 (1878/79)–9 (1882/83); 14 (1887/88); 16 (1889/90)–21 (1894/95); 26 (1899/1900)–47 (1920/21); 52 (1925/26)–117 (1992)
ALb 81 (1954/55); 86 (1959/60)–97 (1970/71); 99 (1972/73); 101 (1974/75)–109 (1982/83); 112 (1987)–#
Au 1 (1874/75)–#
BAc 105 (1978/79); 108 (1981/82)–112 (1987)
BG 77 (1950/51)–82 (1955/56); 84 (1957/58)–91 (1964/65); 96 (1969/70)–# [w 112 (1987), 2]
BLu 1 (1874/75)–#
Bp 1 (1874/75)–# [w 102 (1975/76); 104 (1977/78)]
BRp 1 (1874/75)–#
BRu 1 (1874/75)–#
Bs 90 (1963/64)–100 (1973/74); 106 (1979/80); 110 (1983/84)–111 (1984/85)
BSdsc*
BTu 94 (1967/68)–115 (1990)
Bu 1 (1874/75)–95 (1968/69); 112 (1987)–#
CCtc 76 (1949/50)–#
CDu 1 (1874/75)–#
Cpl 1 (1874/75)–#
Cu 1 (1874/75)–#
DRu 1 (1874/75)–#
EIR:Dtc 1 (1874/75)–#
EIR:Duc 75 (1948/49)–#
EIR:MEtc 1 (1874/75)–36 (1909/10); 112 (1987)–#
En 1 (1874/75)–#
Ep 4 (1877/78)–12 (1885/86); 22 (1895/96); 30 (1903/04)–43 (1916/17); 48 (1921/22)–49 (1922/23); 72 (1945/46)–76 (1949/50); 78 (1951/52)–99 (1972/73); 101 (1974/75)–#
Er 1 (1874/75)–#
EXu 1 (1874/75)–#
Gam 1 (1874/75)–#
Gm 27 (1900/01); 34 (1907/08)–49 (1922/23); 51 (1924/25); 60 (1933/34)–#
Gul 1 (1874/75)–#
HUu 1 (1874/75)–#

KE 112 (1987)–#
Lam 1 (1874/75)–76 (1949/50); 80 (1953/54)–#
LAu 33 (1906/07)– #
Lbar 1 (1874/75)–114 (1989)
Lbbc 75 (1948/49)–# [w 106 (1979/80)]
Lbl*
Lcm 1 (1874/75)–#
Lcml 1 (1874/75)–#
Lcs 31 (1904/05); 48 (1921/22)–50 (1923/24); 53 (1926/27); 56 (1929/30); 61 (1934/35); 77 (1950/51); 80 (1953/54)
LEbc 1 (1874/75)–#
Lgo 91 (1964/65)–#
Lgsm 59 (1932/33)– #
Lkc 3 (1876/77)–75 (1948/49); 77 (1950/51)–93 (1966/67); 95 (1968/69)–96 (1969/70); 99 (1972/73)–#
Lki 53 (1926/27)–#
Lmi 101 (1974/75)–116 (1991)
LRHBNC 5 (1878/79)–6 (1879/80); 8 (1881/82)–10 (1883/84);14 (1887/88); 19 (1892/93)–21 (1894/95); 24 (1897/98); 26 (1899/1900)–28 (1901/02); 31 (1904/05)–49 (1922/23); 51 (1924/25)– 61 (1934/35); 67 (1940/41)–70 (1943/44); 72 (1945/46)–#
Lrscm 28 (1901/02)–104 (1977/78)
Lsa 83 (1956/57)–96 (1969/70) [w 84 (1957/58)]
Ltc 1 (1874/75)–15 (1888/89); 42 (1915/16)–98 (1971/72); 112 (1987)–#
Lu 26 (1899/1900)–#
Lu (RMA) 1 (1874/75)–#
LVp 1 (1874/75)–14 (1887/88); 50 (1923/24)–51 (1924/25); 53 (1926/27)–63 (1936/37); 65 (1938/39); 67 (1940/41)– 69 (1942/43); 71 (1944/45)–98 (1971/72); 100 (1973/74)–#
LVu 3 (1876/77); 5 (1878/79)–13 (1886/87); 26 (1899/1900)–27 (1900/01); 32 (1905/06); 39 (1912/13); 43 (1916/17); 48 (1921/22); 90 (1963/64)–#
Mcm 7 (1880/81)–8 (1881/82); 11 (1884/85)–12 (1885/86); 19 (1892/93); 22 (1895/96)–23 (1896/97); 29 (1902/03); 31 (1904/05); 33 (1906/07)–34 (1907/08); 36 (1909/10); 38 (1911/12); 40 (1913/14); 43 (1916/17)–44 (1917/18); 46 (1919/20); 48 (1921/22); 50 (1923/24); 52 (1925/26); 56 (1929/30); 64 (1937/38); 74 (1947/48); 95 (1968/69)–#
MK 95 (1968/69)–#
Mpl 1 (1874/75)–#
Msuc 118 (1993)–#
Mu 1 (1874/75)–#

NO 51 (1924/25); 53 (1926/27)–#
NTp 12 (1885/86); 21 (1894/95)–36 (1909/10)
NWu 63 (1936/37)–#
Ob 1 (1874/75)–#
Oub 120 (1995)–#
Ouf 1 (1874/75)–#
R 24 (1897/98)–#
SA 4 (1877/78)–#
SFu 1 (1874/75)–#
SLGu 100 (1973/74)–115 (1990), 1
SOu 1 (1874/75)–#
TOd 76 (1949/50); 78 (1951/52); 83
  (1956/57)–86 (1959/60); 88 (1961/62); 91
  (1964/65)–110 (1983/84); 112 (1987), 2–#
Uu 75 (1948/49)–95 (1968/69); 98
  (1971/72)–#
Yu 19 (1892/93)–30 (1903/04) [w 24
  (1897/98); 27 (1900/01)]; 81 (1954/55); 85
  (1958/59)–#

Proceedings of the Royal Musical Association
see Proceedings of the Musical Association

The Professional
GB–Holland–on–Sea, 1974

  Cbijs 1974
  LOnjfa*

Professional Composer [Newsletter]
GB–London: Association of Professional
Composers, ?–
[NOT IN BUCOMP1]

  Gsmic [c]

Progress Reports in Ethnomusicology
US–Baltimore, MD, 1983–
[NOT IN BUCOMP1]

  Lsa 1 (1983)–# [w 1 (1983), 2–4]

Promoting Church Music
TNG GB503; 0033–1122
GB–Croydon: Royal School of Church Music,
1963–
[Entitled *Church Music Quarterly* (ISSN 0307–
6334) from vol. 9 (1977), 57. Incorporated
R.S.C.M. News and *Treble Clef* from 1970, Apr]

  AB 1 (1963)–#
  Au 26 (1994), 124–#
  BG 16 (1984), 87, 88; 17 (1985), 89, 91, 92;
    18 (1986); 20 (1988), 102–104; 23 (1991);
    24 (1992), 117, 118
  Bp 3 (1971), 34; 4 (1972), 37, 39–8 (1976),
    56

BSdsc*
CCtc 15 (1983)–#
CH [c (5 years)]
Cu 1 (1963)–#
EIR:Dtc 1 (1963)–#
En 1 (1963)–#
Lam 15 (1983), 83; 16 (1984), 87; 18 (1986),
  94–96; 19 (1987), 99, 100; 20
  (1988), 101–#
LAu 8 (1976)–#*
Lbl*
Lcm 6 (1974), 47–7 (1975), 51; 8 (1976), 53;
  9 (1977), 57–28 (1996), 137
Lcml 1 (1963)–#
Lkc 1 (1963)–18 (1986)
Lrscm 1 (1963)–8 (1976)
Ltc 25 (1993)–26 (1994)*; 28 (1996)–#
Lu 8 (1976), 56; 9 (1977)
LVp 2 (1970)–#
Mcm 5 (1973)–8 (1976); 15 (1983), 84–16
  (1984), 87
NOp [c (5 years)]
Ob*
SFu 11 (1979)–12 (1980); 15 (1983)–17
  (1985)*

The Prompter
GB–Glasgow, 1893

  Lbl*

Propaganda: U2 World Service Magazine
0964–9859
EIRE/GB–Dublin; Wellingborough, 1984–
[NOT IN BUCOMP1; U2 fanzine]

  Lbl*

La Prora, Rassegna Mensile della
Corporazione delle Nuove Musiche
I–?, 1924
[NOT IN BUCOMP1]

  Bu 1924*
  Cpl 1924, Feb, Apr, May/June

The Proscenium: an Amateur Dramatic and
Musical Review
Fellinger 1968/1449; TNG GB179
GB–Manchester, 1898/99
[Only one was published]

  Lbl 1898/99
  Ob*

PRS News *see* Performing Right Gazette

PRS Yearbook *see* Performing Right Year Book

Przeglad Muzyczny [1] [= Music Review]
Fellinger 1968/753; TNG PL7
PL–Lwow, 1877

    Lbl*

Przeglad Muzyczny [2] [= Music Review]
0866–9945; 0867–0234
GB–London, 1962–
[Previously entitled *Poradnik Muzyczny*; also known as *PM*]

    Lcml 1962*

The Psalmodist: a Monthly Magazine designed to Promote Improvement in the Service of Praise
Fellinger 1968/671; TNG GB79
GB–Paisley, 1873–74
[Succeeded *The Presbyterian Psalmodist* (q.v.)]

    Gul (e) 1873, Sep–Nov
    Lbl 1873, Jan–1874, Apr
    Ob 1873–74, Mar

Psalmodist and Magazine of Sacred Music
GB–Edinburgh: Johnstone and Hunter, 1856

    Lbl 1–5, 1856
    Mpl 1–5, 1856
    Ob 1–5, 1856

Psalterium: Rivista Internazionale di Musica Sacra
0033–2550
I–Rome: Edizioni Musicali Casimiri, 1963–

    Lbl*

Psychology of Music
TNG GB570; 0305–7356
GB–Manchester: University of Manchester [for the Society for Research in the Psychology of Music and Music Education], 1973–

    AB 1 (1973)–#
    BAc 12 (1984)–16 (1988)
    BSdsc 1 (1973)–#
    Cat 10 (1982)–#
    CAu 2 (1974)*; 8 (1980)–13 (1985)
    CCtc 1 (1973)–5 (1977)
    Cu 1 (1973)–#
    EIR:Dp 14 (1986)–#

    EIR:Dtc 1 (1973)–#
    EIR:Duc 1 (1973)–19 (1991)
    En 1 (1973)–#
    EXu 1 (1973)–22 (1994), 1
    KE 1 (1973)–8 (1980); 1982 special issue
    LAu 1 (1973)–2 (1974)
    Lbl*
    Lcu 1 (1973)–#
    Lgo 1 (1973)–#
    Lie 1 (1973)–9 (1981), 1; 10 (1982)–11 (1983), 1; 12 (1984)–#
    Lkc 1 (1973)–15 (1987)
    Lki 1 (1973)–#
    Lmi 1 (1973)–17 (1989)
    Lro 1 (1973)–#
    Ltc 24 (1996)–#
    Lu 1 (1973), 1; 2 (1974), 1; 3 (1975), 2; 4 (1976), 1; 5 (1977), 1
    LVu 1 (1973)–3 (1975)
    Mmu (a) 1 (1973), 2; 2 (1974)–#
    Mu 1 (1973)–11 (1983); 24 (1996)–#
    NOTu 1 (1973)–#
    Ob*
    Oub 10 (1982)–23 (1995)
    Re 1 (1973)–#
    SFu 1 (1973)–#
    SOu 14 (1986), 2–# [w 19 (1991), 2; 20 (1992), 2]
    TOd 1 (1973)–#*
    Yu 1 (1973)–#

Psychomusicology: a Journal of Research in Music Cognition
0275–3987
US–Nacogdoches, TX: Stephen F. Austin State University, 1981–
[NOT IN BUCOMP1]

    Lcu 1 (1981)–#
    Lro 1 (1981)–#
    Mu 1 (1981)–7 (1988)
    SFu 1 (1981)–#

Publikationen der Internationalen Musikgesellschaft: Beihefte
D–Leipzig, 1901–03; n. F. 1905–14

    Bu 1–10 [w 8], 1901–03; n. F. 1, 2 (1905)
    Ob 1901–03; n.F. 1905–11

Publikationen der Sammlungen der Gesellschaft der Musikfreunde in Wien
D–Munich: Emil Katzbichler, 1976–

    Lbl*

Publikationen des Instituts für Österreichische Musikdokumentation
D–Tutzing: Hans Schneider, 1974–

    Lbl*

Pult und Taktstock: Fachzeitschrift für Dirigenten
TNG A195
A/D–Vienna; Leipzig: Universal Edition, 1924–30
[Absorbed into *Musikblätter des Anbruch* (q.v.)]

    Cpl 4 (1927)–7 (1930), 2
    LAu 1927, Mar, Apr
    Ob 1 (1924)–7 (1930) [m]

Punk
US–New York: Trans–High Corp., 1977–93
[NOT IN BUCOMP1; later entitled *Nerve*; from 1988 to 1993 incorporated *Reflex*]

    Lsa 1 (1976/77), 3, 11

Punk Lives
GB–London, ?1982–
[NOT IN BUCOMP1]

    Cu 1–11, 1982
    Ob 1, 1982–#

Punk's Not Dead!
GB–London, 1981–
[NOT IN BUCOMP1]

    Ob 1, 1981–#

Q

Q: the Modern Guide to Music and More
0955–4955
GB–London: Emap Metro, 1986–
[NOT IN BUCOMP1]

    AB 1986–#
    ABDp [c]
    BAR [c (2 years)]
    BDp 1987–#
    BEp [c (1 year)]
    BRp [c (2 years)]
    BTp [c (1 year)]
    BYp [c (1 year)]
    CCtc 28–75, 1989–92
    CDCp 43, 1990–# [w 48, 53, 69, 81, 93, 94]
    CH [c (1 year)]
    COp [c (4 months)]

Cu 1986–#
CW 1992, Nov–#
DS [c (2 years)]
DU [c (5 years)]
Ea [c (1 year)]
EIR:Dp 1994, Feb–# [w 1994, Oct]
EK [c (2 years)]
Ep 1991–#
Gm 1988, July; 1989, Oct–#
HA 1992, June–#
IOW 1992, Oct–#
KC [c]
Lbar 64, 1992–#
Lbbc 1986–#
Lbk 1991, Dec–#
Lbl*
Lcml (p) [c (2 issues)]
LEc 1987–#
Lgr (w) [c (6 months)]
Lgu [c (3 years)]
Lha (f) [c (2 years)]
Lis [c (2 years)]
Lk [c (1 year)]
Lk (b) [c (6 months)]
Lk (c) [c (1 year)]
Lk (nk) [c]
Ll [c]
Lri 1987, Sep–#
Lsa 1987*; 1988–#
Lsut [c (2 years)]
LT [c (1 year)]
LVp [c (10 years)]
Lwf [c (6 months)]
Lwwb [c]
Lwwput [c (1 year)]
LXp [c (6 months)]
MP [c]
Mpl [c]
Msuc 1991–#
NHp [c (1 year)]
NOp [c]
NTp 1986, Oct–#
Ob*
OL 1992–#
Op [c (1 year)]
P [c (2 years)]
PRp [c (1 year)]
Rp [c (1 year)]
SFp 1991–#
SHRp 76, 1993–#
SK [c (1 year)]
SOL 1991–#
STAp 1991, Aug–#
WCp (far) [c (1 year)]

Quad Magazine
GB–London: Quad Electronics Limited, 1985
[NOT IN BUCOMP1]

   Cu 1 (1985), 1

Quaderni dell'Accademia Chigiana
I–Siena: Accademia Chigiana, 1942–60; 1988–
[NOT IN BUCOMP1]

   Ob 2–12, 14–41, 1942–60

Quaderni dell'Istituto di Studi Verdiani
TNG I265; 0506–6360
I–Venice: Nuova Editoriale, 1963–

   EIR:MEtc 1 (1963)–4 (1971)
   Lu 1 (1963)–#
   Ob*

Quaderni della Civica Scuola di Musica [di Milano]
I–Milan: Comune di Milano, Ripartizione Educazione, 1980–
[NOT IN BUCOMP1]

   Ob 9 (1989), 17

Quaderni della Rassegna Musicale
TNG I272
I–Turin, 1964–72
[Previously entitled *La Rassegna Musicale* (q.v.)]

   BSdsc*
   DRu 1 (1964)–5 (1972)
   Er 1 (1964)–5 (1972)
   Lbl*
   Ob 1 (1964)–5 (1972)
   Ouf 1 (1964)–5 (1972)

Quaderni della Rivista Italiana di Musicologia
TNG I279; 0394–4395
I–Florence: Olschki, 1966–

   LAu 1966
   Lu 1966–#
   Ob 1966–#

Quaderni Pucciniani
I–?Lucca: Istituto di Studi Pucciniani, 1982–
[NOT IN BUCOMP1]

   Ob 1982–#

Quaderni Zandonaiani
I–Padua: Zanibon, 1987–
[NOT IN BUCOMP1]

   Cu 1 (1987)–2 (1989)

Quadrivium: Rivista di Filologia e Musicologia Medievale
TNG I245; 0392–1530; 0481–1194
I–Bologna: University of Bologna, 1956–
[From 1970, subtitled *Studi di Filologia e Musicologia*]

   AB 1 (1956)
   Lbl*
   Lu 1 (1956)–#
   NO 1 (1956)–17 (1976)
   Ob*

Quadrivium: Studi di Filologia e Musicologia
see Quadrivium: Rivista di Filologia e Musicologia Medievale

The Quarterly
1046–9133; 1066–0437
US–Greeley, CO: School of Music, University of North Colorado, 1990–
[NOT IN BUCOMP1; later entitled *The Quarterly Journal of Music Teaching and Learning*]

   Lie 1 (1990)–
   Re 4 (1993), 4–#

Quarterly Check-List of Musicology
TNG US703; 0033–541X
US–East Northrop, NY [etc.]: American Bibliographic Service, 1959–77
[Ceased publication with vol. 19 (1977)]

   ABc (ILS) 1 (1959)– 19 (1977), 2
   BRu 1 (1959)–10 (1968)
   BSdsc*

Quarterly Journal of Music Teaching and Learning *see* The Quarterly

Quarterly Journal of the Library of Congress
0041–7939; 0090–0095
US–Washington, DC: Library of Congress, 1943–
[NOT IN BUCOMP1]

   Lbbc 35 (1978), 3; 37 (1980), 3, 4; 40 (1983), 1, 2#

Quarterly Magazine of the International Musical Society *see* Sammelbände der Internationalen Musikgesellschaft

The Quarterly Musical Magazine and Review
Fellinger 1968/44; TNG GB6; Langley, p. 489; Langley 1994, pp. 115–16
GB–London: Baldwin, Cradock and Joy, 1818–28 [40 nos in 10 vols]

BSdsc*
Bu 1 (1818)–10 (1828)
Cpl 1 (1818)–6 (1824)
Cu 1 (1818)–9 (1827)
EIR:Dtc 1 (1818)–9 (1827)
Er 1 (1818)–10 (1828)
Gul (e) 1 (1818)–10 (1828)
Lam [The holdings of this title assigned to **Lam** in Langley 1994 are no longer there]
Lbl*
Lcm 1 (1818)–10 (1828)
Lu 1 (1818)–9 (1827)
Mpl 1 (1818)–10 (1828)
Ob 1 (1818)–10 (1828)
Ouf 1 (1818)–10 (1828)
SA 1 (1818)–10 (1827)*

Quarterly Musical Register
Fellinger 1968/28; TNG GB4; Langley, p. 479
GB–London: ? A. Coleman, 1812
[Only two nos published]

Cpl 1, 2, 1812
Mpl 1, 2, 1812

Quarterly Musical Review
Fellinger 1968/1000; TNG GB118
GB–Manchester, 1885–88

BRp 1 (1885)–4 (1888)
BRu 1 (1886)–4 (1888)
BSdsc 1 (1885)–4 (1888)
Bu 1 (1885)–4 (1888)
Cu 1 (1885)–4 (1888)
DRu 1 (1885)–4 (1888)
EIR:Dtc 1 (1885)–4 (1888)
En 1 (1885)–4 (1888)
Ep 1 (1885)–4 (1888)
Er 1 (1885)
Gm 1 (1885)–4 (1888)
Lbl 1 (1885)–4 (1888)
Lu 1 (1885)–4 (1888)
LVp 1 (1886)–4 (1888)
Mcm 1 (1885)–4 (1888)

Mpl 1 (1885)–4 (1888)
Ob 1 (1885)–4 (1888)
SA 1 (1885)–4 (1888)

The Quarterly Record [of the Incorporated Association of Organists] *see* National Union of Organists' Associations: Quarterly Record

Quarternotes [1]
GB–Milton Keynes, 1974–

Cbijs 1974–#

Quarternotes [2]
GB–London: Boosey and Hawkes, ?1983–
[NOT IN BUCOMP1; succeeded *Music: Boosey and Hawkes* (q.v.)]

ALb 1983, Oct; 1984, Jan; 1985, Jan/Feb, Oct; 1986, May, Nov; 1987, Feb; 1989, Sep; 1990, Jan, Oct–1991, Oct; 1992, June, Oct; 1993, June, Oct; 1994, June–#
Cu 1996–#

Quarternotes: the Cleo Laine–John Dankworth Newsletter
GB–Wavendon, 1977–
[NOT IN BUCOMP1]

Cu 1977–#

The Quarto: an Artistic, Literary and Musical Quarterly
Fellinger 1968/1371; TNG GB169
GB–London: J. S. Virtue, 1896–98

En 1 (1896)–3 (1898)
Gm 1 (1896)–4 (1898)
Lbl 1 (1896)–4 (1898)
Ob*

The Quaver: a Monthly Advocate of Popular Musical Education
Fellinger 1968/726: TNG GB88
GB–London: F. Pitman, 1876–85

Lbl 1 (1876)–2 (1885)

Der Querschnitt
D–Berlin, 1921–36
[NOT IN BUCOMP1]

Cpl 10 (1930), 4

Les Questions Liturgiques
0774–5532
B–Louvain: Abbaye de Mont César, 1910–
[From 1915 entitled *Questions Liturgiques et Paroissiales* (ISSN 0779–2050); reverted to original title in 1971 (ISSN 0774–5524)]

> **Lhey** 1956–# [w 1960–64]
> **Ob***

Questions Liturgiques et Paroissiales *see* **Les Questions Liturgiques**

Questions on Music Theory and Aesthetics
[translated title] *see* **Voprosy Teory i Estetiki Muzyki**

R

R. and B. Collector
US–Northridge, CA, 1970–

> **Lsa***

R. and B. Monthly
GB–Kenley, Surrey, 196?–

> **Cbijs** 18, 19, 21–23, 1965
> **Lsa** 21, 22, 1965; 1970*

Rachmaninoff Society Journal
GB–South Woodham Ferrers: Rachmaninoff Society, 1990–92
[NOT IN BUCOMP1. Only three published]

> **Ouf** 1 (1990)–3 (1992)

Rachmaninoff Society Newsletter
GB–South Woodham Ferrers; Rotherfield, East Sussex [etc.]: The Rachmaninoff Society, 1990–
[NOT IN BUCOMP1]

> **Lbar** 1, 1990–#
> **Ouf** 1, 1990–#

Řada Hudebné Výchovna [= Music Education Series]
CZ–Prague: Prague University, 1966–
[From 1972 entitled *Sborník Katedry Hudební Vychový*]

> **Ob***

Radio and Music
0956–8263
GB–London: EMAP, 1991–
[NOT IN BUCOMP1]

> **Lbl***

Radio and Music Directory
0959–9878
GB–Croydon: EMAP, 1991–
[NOT IN BUCOMP1]

> **Lbl***

Radio Directory
0263–1318
GB–Brixworth: Hamilton House, ?–
[NOT IN BUCOMP1]

> **Lbbc** 1983–85
> **Lsa** 1983; 1985–86*
> **Ob***

Radio Guide *see* **Tune-In, to the Music of Television, Radio and Records**

Radio Industry Directory
GB–Croydon: EMAP Vision, 1991–
[NOT IN BUCOMP1]

> **Lbl** 1991–92–#

Radio Merchant *see* **Radio Music Merchant**

Radio Month
GB–London: Needletime Music, 1979–
[NOT IN BUCOMP1]

> **Lbl***

Radio Music *see* **Music for All (with which is incorporated "Radio Music"): a Magazine for Every Home**

Radio Music Merchant
TNG US363
US–New York: Federated Business Publications, 1932–34
[NOT IN BUCOMP1; entitled *Radio Merchant*, 1932–34]

> **Lbl** 1930, Aug–1934, Oct [m]

Radio One Story of Pop
GB–London, 1973–?76
[From 1975 entitled *Story of Pop*]

    EIR:Dtc 1–53, 1973–76
    Lbbc 1–26, 1973

Radio Quarterly
GB–London, 1953–?

    EIR:Dtc 1 (1953), 1, 2

Radio Review
EIRE–Dublin, 1945–?

    EIR:Dtc 8 (1953), 391

Radio 3 Magazine *see* **3: the Radio Three Magazine**

Radio Times
0033–8060
GB–London: British Broadcasting Corporation, 1923–

    AB*
    BRp 1923–# (all except past six months are [m])
    Bs [c (3 months)]
    Bu [c (6 months)]
    Cat [c (6 months)]
    CDu [c (6 months)]
    EIR:Dtc 73 (1941), 944–#; [2nd copy] 88 (1945), 1139–# [Northern Ireland ed.]
    En*
    Ep [c (6 months)] [Scottish ed.]; 1980–# [m] [London ed.]
    Er [c]
    Gam [c]
    Lam [c]
    Lbbc 1923–#
    Lbl*
    Lgsm*
    Lsa 1939–# [w 1958, Sep–1959, Jan 3; 1972, Dec–1973, Jan 5; 1983, Mar 26–Apr 22; 1986, Sep 20, 26]
    Ltc [c]
    LXp [c (1 year)]
    Mcm 1975–#
    Mu [c (1 year)]
    Ob 1923–#
    STAp 1992, Aug–#

Rage
GB–London: Maxwell Consumer Magazines, 1991–
[NOT IN BUCOMP1; incorporates *Popshop*]

    Ob 1, 1991–#

The Ragtimer
0033–8672
C–Weston, Ontario: Rag Society, 1967–
[NOT IN BUCOMP1]

    Cu 1967–80

The Rakeway Brass Band Yearbook
GB–Hollington, 1987–
[NOT IN BUCOMP1]

    Ob 1987–#

R.A.M. *see* **Royal Academy of Music**

Rampages
GB–London: Royal Academy of Music, Students' Union, 1977–?80
[NOT IN BUCOMP1]

    Lam 1, 1977; 9,11, 1978; 16, 17, 1979; 23, 1980

R.A.M.S.U. News
GB–London: Royal Academy of Music, Students' Union, 1994–
[NOT IN BUCOMP1]

    Lam 2, 1994–#

Rare Record Price Guide
GB–London, 1992–
[NOT IN BUCOMP1; at head of title: *Record Collector*; running title *Record Collector Price Guide*]

    Lbl 1992–#
    Ob 1993–#

Rassegna Gregoriana per gli Studi Liturgici e pel Canto Sacro
Fellinger 1968/1645; TNG I112
I–Rome: Desclée Lefebvre [for the Società di San Giovanni Evangelista], 1902–14
[Ceased publication with vol. 13 (1914), 3]

    Cpl 4 (1905), 11, 12
    Lbl*
    Lu 1 (1902), 5, 7–10
    LVp 1 (1902)–6 (1907)
    Ob*

La Rassegna Musicale
TNG I197
I–Turin: Fedetto, 1928–43; 1947–62
[Ceased publication with vol. 32 (1962); continued as *Quaderni della Rassegna Musicale* (q.v.).
Preceded by *Il Pianoforte: Rivista Mensile della Fabbrica Italiana Pianoforte (F.I.P.)* (q.v.)]

> **Bu** 1 (1928), 2, 4; 4 (1931), 5, 6; 7 (1934), 1; 21 (1951), 2; 23 (1953), 4; 24 (1954), 1–3; 25 (1955), 1; 26 (1956)–28 (1958); 30 (1960)
> **Cpl** 1 (1928)–13 (1940), 4
> **Er** 24 (1954)–25 (1955), 1
> **LAu** 8 (1935), 1; 24 (1954), 4; 28 (1958), 3; 31 (1961), 3, 4
> **Lbl***
> **Lcm** 20 (1950)–23 (1953)
> **Lcml** 1 (1928)–6 (1933)*; 12 (1939); 17 (1947)–24 (1954); 25 (1955)–28 (1858)*; 30 (1960)–32 (1962), 1
> **Lu** 1 (1928), 1, 3, 8–9; 4 (1931), 2, 6; 5 (1932), 4; 6 (1933), 1–3; 7 (1934), 1; 8 (1935), 4; 9 (1936), 3, 9–10; 10 (1937), 2; 11 (1938), 1, 3, 4, 7–12; 15 (1942); 17 (1947)–18 (1948); 29 (1959)–32 (1962)
> **Lu (RMA)** 4 (1931), 5; 6 (1933), 5, 6; 8 (1935), 1; 19 (1949)–25 (1955), 1; 26 (1956)–27 (1957); 28 (1958), 3, 4
> **Ouf** 17 (1947)–32 (1962), 4

Rassegna Musicale delle Edizione Curci
TNG I225; 0033–9806
I–Milan: Edizioni Curci, 1948–
[Later entitled *Rassegna Musicale Curci: Quadrimestrale: Periodico di Cultura e Attualità Musicali*]

> **Cu** 31 (1978), 3–#
> **Mcm** 26 (1973), 3; 27 (1974), 1, 2; 28 (1975), 1–3; 29 (1976), 1; 30 (1977)–42 (1989), 2
> **Ouf** 50 (1997), 2–#

Rassegna Veneta di Studi Musicali
I–Padua: CLEUP, 1985–
[NOT IN BUCOMP1]

> **Bu** 5 (1989)–6 (1990)
> **Cu** 1 (1985)–#
> **DRu** 2 (1986)–3 (1987)
> **Lbl** 2 (1986)–#
> **Lcml** 2 (1986)–3 (1987)
> **Ob***
> **Ouf** 2 (1986)–3 (1987)

Rave [1]
GB–?, 1964–70

> **AB***
> **Ob***

Rave [2]
0959–6151
GB–London: L.P. Publications, 1989–
[NOT IN BUCOMP1]

> **Lbl***

Rave [3]
0964–1254
GB–London: Dennis Oneshots, 1991–
[NOT IN BUCOMP1]

> **Lbl***

Rave On
0960–5916
GB–London: Dennis Oneshots, 1990
[NOT IN BUCOMP1]

> **Lbl***

Raw: Rock Action Worldwide
GB–London, 1988–?
[NOT IN BUCOMP1]

> **Cu** 1, 7–112, 1988–92
> **Ob** 3–112, 1988–92

Razzmatazz Annual
GB–London: IPC Magazines, 1985–
[NOT IN BUCOMP1]

> **Cu** 1985–#
> **Lbl***

RCD: Rock Compact Disc Magazine
0965–190X
GB–London: Northern and Shell, 1992–
[NOT IN BUCOMP1]

> **Lbl***

The R.C.M. Magazine: a Journal for Past and Present Students and Friends of the Royal College of Music, and Official Organ of the R.C.M. Union
Fellinger 1968/1747; TNG GB209; 0033–684X
GB–London: Royal College of Music, 1904–

> **ALb** 18 (1921), 2–# [w 81 (1984), 2; 96 (1988), 3; 88 (1991)–89 (1992), 1]
> **Bu** 78 (1981), 2; 80 (1983)– #
> **Cpl** 79 (1982)–#

Cu 16 (1919), 3–#*
EIR:Dtc 16 (1919)–#
En*
Er 26 (1929), 1, 2
Lam 1 (1904)–18 (1921), 1, 3; 19 (1922)–62
(1966), 3; 64 (1967), 2–66 (1969), 1, 3; 67
(1970)–86 (1989), 1; 87 (1990), 1–3; 88
(1991), 2, 3; 89 (1992), 2 [+ Jubilee
number of 1933; 1982 Centenary Appeal
brochure]
Lbar 1 (1904)–64 (1967)
Lbl*
Lcm 1 (1904)–#
Lcml 15 (1919)–16 (1920)*; 18 (1921)–20
(1924); 22 (1925)–27 (1930)*;30 (1933)*;
36 (1939)–37 (1940)*; 43 (1946)*; 47
(1950)*; 53 (1956)–57 (1960)*; 59 (1962)*
Lu 45 (1948)–56 (1959); 62 (1965), 3; 63
(1966)–64 (1967); 68 (1971)–86 (1989), 1,
2; 87 (1990)
Mcm 72 (1975), 2; 73 (1976), 3; 74 (1977)–
76 (1979), 1; 77 (1980)–#
Ob*
TOd 87 (1990), 3

R.C.O. Journal
GB–London: Royal College of Organists, 1993–
[NOT IN BUCOMP1]

Bu 1993–#
Lam (o) 1994, 2
Lcm 1993–#
Mcm*

Recensionen und allgemeine Bemerkungen über Theater und Musik
Fellinger 1968/326; TNG A3
A–Vienna: J. F. Gress, 1853–55
[Continued as *Monatsschrift für Theater und Musik*]

Lbl 1–7, 1853–55 [2 copies]

Recerca Musicologica
0211–6391
E–Barcelona: Institut Universitari de
Documentacio i Investigacio Musicologica
[IUDIM], 1981–
[NOT IN BUCOMP1]

CDu 8 (1988)–#
Cu 1 (1981)–#
Lbl*

Recercare: Rivista per lo Studio e la Pratica della Musica Antica
1120–5741
I–Lucca: Libreria Musicale Italiana, 1989–
[NOT IN BUCOMP1; preceded 1971–88 by *Il Flauto Dolce: Rivista per lo Studio e la Pratica della Musica Antica* (q.v.)]

Bu 2 (1990)–#
Cu 1 (1989)–#
Lbl 1 (1989)–#
Ob 1 (1989)–#
Ouf 1 (1989)–#

Recherches sur la Musique Française Classique
TNG F677; 0080–0139
F–Paris: A. and J. Picard, 1960–

BRu 25 (1987)
BSdsc 1 (1960)–#
Cpl 2 (1961/62)
Cu 1 (1960)–#
EIR:Duc 20 (1981); 23 (1985)–#
Er 1 (1960)–#
Gul 1 (1960)–#
HUu 1 (1960)–#
Lbbc 1 (1960)–16 (1976)
Lcml 1 (1960)–#
Lgo 1 (1960)–#
Lkc 1 (1960)–10 (1970)
Lu 1 (1960)–#
Mcm 17 (1977)–#
NO 1 (1960)–10 (1970)
Ob 1 (1960)–#
Ouf 1 (1960)–#
SOu 1 (1960)–2 (1961/62); 8 (1968)–20
(1981)

Recommended Recordings *see* The
Gramophone Recommended Recordings

Record Advertiser
GB–Solihull, 1970–74

Lsa 1 (1970)–3 (1973)

Record and Popswop Mirror *see* Popswop

Record and Show Mirror *see* Record Mirror

Record and Sound Retailing *see* Record
Retailing

Record and Tape Reviews Index
0097–8256
US–Metchuen, NJ: Scarecrow Press, 1971–?
[From 1975 entitled *Index to Record and Tape Reviews*]

   BSdsc*

Record and Tape Service Catalogue
GB–Craigavon, Northern Ireland: Southern Education Library Board, 1977–78
[NOT IN BUCOMP1. A supplement, in three parts, was issued between Winter 1976/77 and Jan/Mar 1977]

   EIR:Dtc 1977–78, Dec

Record Bargains Collector
GB–London, 1971–

   Lsa 1971, June–1972, Jan

Record Business
GB–London, 1978–83

   Cu 1 (1978)–6 (1983)*
   Lsa 1 (1978)–4 (1981)

The Record Buyer
GB–London, 1969–70
[Continued as *The Record Collector* (q.v.); during 1970 entitled *Record Buyer and Tape Review*]

   AB*
   Cu 1 (1969)–2 (1970), 1–6, 8, 9
   EIR:Dtc 1 (1969)–2 (1970), 9
   En 1 (1969)–2 (1970)
   Lbl*
   Ob*

Record Buyer and Tape Review *see* **The Record Buyer**

Record Changer
TNG US571
US–New York: Hadlock Publications, 1942–57
[Ceased publication with vol. 15 no. 2 (1957)]

   Cbijs ?4 (1945), Feb, Apr, June; 5 (1947), May; 8 (1949), June–Sep, Dec; 9 (1950), Apr; ?13 (1954), May
   LOnjfa*
   Lsa 5 (1947), 12; 6 (1947), 3; 8 (1949), 10; 9 (1950), 3, 4, 10

The Record Collector
0261–250X
GB–London: Diamond Publishing Group, 1970–
[Succeeded *The Record Buyer* (q.v.); entitled *Record Collector for Good Listening* from June–Aug 1972; *Good Listening and Record Collector*, Sep 1972–June 1973; then absorbed into *Easy Listening and Living with Stereo* (q.v.). Also bore title *The Record Collector: for all Serious Collectors of Rare Records, CDs, Videos, Pop Memorabilia, etc.* from around 1980]

   CDCp [c (3 years)]
   Cu 1972, June–Aug; 1980–#
   EIR:Dtc 1972, Jan–July; 1980–#
   En 7, 1980–#
   Gm 53, 1984–#
   Lbbc*
   Lbl*
   LEc [c (5 years)]
   Lsa 1980, Mar–# [w 1987, May]
   Lsut [c (1 year)]
   NHp [c (1 year)]
   NOp 125, 1990–#
   NTp 1989, June–#
   Ob*
   STAp 180, 1994–#

Record Collector *see also* **Rare Record Price Guide**

The Record Collector *see also* **Record Collectors' Bulletin: a Magazine for Collectors of Recorded Vocal Art**

Record Collecter [translated title] *see also* **Skivsamlaren**

The Record Collector: for all Serious Collectors of Rare Records, CDs, Videos, Pop Memorabilia, etc. *see* **The Record Collector**

Record Collector for Good Listening *see* **The Record Collector**

Record Collector Price Guide *see* **Rare Record Price Guide**

Record Collectors' Bulletin: a Magazine for Collectors of Recorded Vocal Art
TNG GB396; 0034–1568
GB–Ipswich: J. Dennis, 1946–
[Entitled *The Record Collector* from 1947]

AB 18 (1969)–#*
BLp 9 (1954)–#
Cu 19 (1970)–33 (1988)
EIR:Dtc 11 (1957); 19 (1970)–34 (1989), 1/2
En*
Lbl*
Lsa 1 (1946)–# [w 16 (1967), 5, 6; 17 (1968), 1, 2]
SFp 24 (1975)–33 (1988), 6/7

Record Collectors' Journal
0099–0817
US–Covina, CA: Markell Publishing Company, 1975–

Cbijs 1 (1975), 1, 2

Record Exchanger
US–Anaheim, CA, 1969–?75
[NOT IN BUCOMP1]

Lsa 1 (1969)–4 (1975), 4

Record Information
0268–3881
GB–Chessington: Record Information Services, 1983–
[NOT IN BUCOMP1]

EIR:Dtc 6, 1986
Lbl 4, 1985–#
Lsa 1, 1983
Ob 6, 1986–#

Record Mail: a Monthly Review and Details of the latest "Popular" Records issued by E.M.I Records Ltd
GB–London: EMI, 1958–66

Lbl*
Lsa 1 (1958)–9 (1966)

Record Mirror
TNG GB455; 0144–5804
GB–London: Spotlight Publications, 1954–
[From 1959 entitled *Record and Show Mirror*; from 1985–90 entitled *RM: the New Record Mirror* (ISSN 0956–0823); later reverted to *The Record Mirror.* Incorporated *Noise!* (q.v.)]

Cu 1985, Sep 21–1990, Feb 10, May 5–#
Lam 41, 1955
Lbl*

Record Mirror [translated title] *see* **Skiv Spegeln**

Record Mirror with Popswop *see* **Popswop**

Record News [1]
TNG GB422
GB–Brighton: Southdown Box Company, 1949–61

Cu 1 (1949)–2 (1951), 9; n.s. 1 (1956)–5 (1961)
Lbl*

Record News [2]
TNG GB447
GB–London, 1953–59
[Entitled *Record News and Stereo Disc* from 6 (1958), Aug; *Record News* from 1959, Apr; incorporated into *Hi-Fi News* (q.v.)]

Bp 1 (1953)–7 (1959), 4
Cpl 1 (1953)–7 (1959), 4
Cu 1 (1953)–7 (1959), 4
EIR:Dtc 1 (1953)–3 (1955), 12
En 1 (1953)–6 (1958)
Lam 2 (1954), 8, 9; 3 (1955), 4, 5; 4 (1956), 5
Lbl*
Lsa 2 (1954)– 6 (1958) [w 5 (1957)]
Lu 2 (1954)–7 (1959) [w 2 (1954), 4]
Mpl 2 (1954)–7 (1959)
Ob*

Record News [3]
C–Toronto, 1956–61

Lsa 1 (1956)–5 (1961)

Record News and Stereo Disc *see* **Record News [2]**

The Record of the Musical Union
Fellinger 1968/234; TNG GB34; Langley, p. 628–32; Langley 1994, pp. 118–19
GB–London: Cramer, Beale and Company, 1845–80
[Entitled *Record of the Musical Union*, 1845–47 (seasons 1–3); *Record of the Fourth [Fifth] Season of the Musical Union*, 1848–49; *The Sixth [-Thirteenth] Annual Record of the Musical Union*, 1850–57; *Fourteenth [-Thirty-sixth] Annual Record of the Musical Union*, 1858–80. Some issues have subtitles; subtitles vary]

Cu 1 (1845)–23 (1867)
Ep 3 (1847)–25 (1869)
Lbl 1 (1845)–36 (1880) [+ 2nd copy of 1845, 1848, 1858]
Lcm (p)*

Record Prices
GB–London, 1976–?
[Later incorporated into *Music Master: the World's Greatest Record Catalogue* (q.v.)]

Ob*

Record Research: the Magazine of Record Statistics and Information
0034–1592; 0481–0829
US–Brooklyn, NY, 1955–

Cbijs 1, 4–9, 1955–56; 31, 1960; 42, 1962; 54, 55, 1963; 58, 64, 1964; 112, 1971; 131, 1975
LOnjfa*
Lsa 26, 1960–# [w 111, 142, 182, 193, 194, 199, 200, 205, 206]

Record Retailer and Music Industry News
0265–1548
GB–London: Spotlight Publications, 1959–71
[Succeeded by *Music Week* [1] (q.v.)]

Cu*
Lbl*
Lsa 1959–70*
Ob*

Record Retailing
US–New York: Lincoln Publications, 1933–62
[Entitled *Record and Sound Retailing* from vol. 24 (1956)]

Lsa 17 (1951), 1; 21 (1953), 6; 22 (1954), 1; 23 (1955), 1, 3, 4, 6; 24 (1956)–39 (1962)*

Record Review
TNG GB495
GB–London: Hanover Press; Croydon: Link House Publications, 1961–70
[entitled *Audio and Record Review* from 1964–66; entitled *Audio Record Review* from 5 (1966), 6–1969; ; from 1970 entitled *Record Review*; absorbed by *Hi-Fi News* (q.v.) from 1970, Oct]

AB 1 (1961)–9 (1969); 10 (1970), 2–9
ALb 8 (1967), Dec; 10 (1970), 1–9
Bp 3 (1963), 10–12; 4 (1964), 5, 6, 9–12; 5 (1965), 1–3, 5–11; 6 (1966)–10 (1970), 9
BSdsc*
Cu 1 (1961)–10 (1970)
En 1 (1961)–10 (1970), 9
Er 4 (1964); 8 (1968), 1
Gm 3 (1963), 5–9 (1969), 12
Lam 9 (1969), 9
LAu 8 (1968), 3

Lbl*
Lcm 1 (1961), 6, 7, 9–11; 2 (1962), 5, 9, 11; 3 (1963), 1, 3
Lcml (m) 4 (1964)–6 (1966)*; 7 (1967)–10 (1970)*
Lsa 1 (1961)–9 (1969)
Lu 1 (1961), 6–8
LVp 2 (1962)–9 (1969)
Mcm 7 (1967), 9; 8 (1968), 3, 6–9, 11
Mpl 1 (1961)–10 (1970)
Ob*
WF 4 (1964), 7–10 (1970), 9

The Record Review *see also* **Fenton's Letter: a Monthly Review of New Records**

Record Times: featuring the Latest Classical Recordings of E.M.I. His Master's Voice, Capitol, Columbia, Parlophone, Mercury
TNG GB478
GB–London: EMI Records, 1958–67
[Incorporated into *Records and Recording* (q.v.)]

Lbl*
Lsa 1 (1958)–9 (1966)

Record World
TNG US593; 0034–1622
US–New York: Record World, 1942–
[NOT IN BUCOMP1]

Lsa 31 (1975)–33 (1977)*

The Record Year [1]
GB–London, 1952–53

Ob 1 (1952)–2 (1953)
SA 1 (1952)–2 (1953)

The Record Year [2]
GB–London: Duckworth, 1979–

Cpl 1 (1979)–2 (1981)
Ob*

Recorded Folk Music: a Review of British and Foreign Folk Music Recordings
TNG GB477; 0484–1476
GB–London: Colletts, 1958–59

AB*
Bp 1 (1958)–2 (1959)
BSdsc*
Cu 1 (1958)–2 (1959)
EIR:Dtc 1 (1958)–2 (1959), Dec
En 1 (1958)–2 (1959)

Ep 1 (1958)–2 (1959)
Lbl*
Lcs 1 (1958)–2 (1959)
Lsa 1 (1958)–2 (1959)
LVp 1 (1958)–2 (1959)
Mpl 1 (1958)–2 (1959)
Ob*

Recorded Sound: Journal of the British Institute of Recorded Sound
TNG GB494; 0034–1630
GB–London: British Institute of Recorded Sound [National Sound Archive], 1961–84
[Previously entitled *British Institute of Recorded Sound: Bulletin* (q.v.)]

AB 1–77, 1961–80; 85, 86, 1984
ALb 10–11, 1963; 29–32, 1968; 35, 1969; 45, 46, 1972; 66, 77, 1977; 74, 75, 1979; 79, 1981; 81–85, 1982–84
BAc 1–86, 1961–84
BDp 1–86, 1961–84
BLu 1–64, 1961–76
Bp 1–86, 1961–84
BRp 1–12, 1961–84
BSdsc*
BTp 1–54, 1961–74
Btu 1–64, 1961–76
DRu 1–44, 1961–71
EIR:Dtc 1–86, 1961–84
EIR:Duc 37–86, 1970–84
En 1–86, 1961–84
Ep 1–86, 1961–84
EXu 79–86, 1981–84
Gm 1–86, 1961–84
HUu 1–60, 1961–75
Lam 80, 1981
Lbar 1–86, 1961–84
Lbbc 1–46, 1961–72 [w 32]
Lbl*
Lcm 2–86, 1961–84
Lcml 1–86, 1961–84
Lcml (m) 5–54, 1961/62–73; 1974*
Lcs 8–86, 1962–84*
Lgo 61–86, 1976–84
LIp 1–85, 1961–84
Lk 1–86, 1961–84
Lkc 3, 5, 6, 1961; 12–26, 1963–67; 28–86, 1967–84 [w 32, 1968]
Lki 53–85, 1974–83
Lsa 1–86, 1961–84
Lu 1–86, 1961–84
LVp 1–52, 1961–73
LVu 17–86, 1965–84
Mcm 42,43, 1971; 57–83, 1975–83; 85, 86, 1984

MK 35–86, 1969–84
Mpl 1–86, 1961–84
NO 1–77, 1961–80
NWu 41–84, 1971–83
Ob*
Oub 81–86, 1982–83
Ouf 1–86, 1961–84
R 1–72, 1961–78
SFp 20–76, 1965–79; 81–86, 1982–84
SFu 1, 1961; 14–80, 1964–81
TOd 2–86, 1961–84
Yu 41–44, 1971–72; 49–60, 1973–75

Recorder and Music *see* The Recorder and Music Magazine

The Recorder and Music Magazine
TNG GB506; 0961–3242
GB–London: Schott [for the Society of Recorder Players], 1963–
[Entitled *Recorder and Music* (ISSN 0306–4409), 1969, 7–1989; from vol. 10 (1990) entitled *Recorder Magazine* (ISSN 0961–3544). Preceded 1937–63 by *The Recorder News [...]* (q.v.)]

AB 1 (1963/65)–5 (1975/77), 3; 9 (1987/89), 5, 7
ALb 1 (1964/65), 4, 9; 3 (1969/71), 3, 6, 10–12; 6 (1978/80), 9, 10; 7 (1981/83), 1, 2, 4–6, 8, 9, 11–12; 8 (1984/86), 1, 2
BDp 4 (1972/74)– 7 (1981/83)*
BLp 6 (1978/80)–#
Bp 4 (1972/74)–7 (1981/83), 4, 6–12; 8 (1984/86)–#
BRp 1 (1963/65)–#
Bs 14 (1994)–#
BSdsc 7 (1981/83)–#
CCtc 4 (1972/74)–7 (1981/83)*; 8 (1984/86)–#
Cu 1 (1963/65)–#
EIR:Dp 9 (1987/89), 5–#
EIR:Dtc 1 (1963/65)–9 (1987/89), 12; 10 (1990)–#
En*
Ep 1 (1963/65)–5 (1975/77); 6 (1978/80), 1–4, 6–12; 7 (1981/83)–#
Er 1 (1963/65), 11; 2 (1966/68), 1; 3 (1969/71), 10; 7 (1981/83)–#
Gm 1 (1963/65)–#
Lam 7 (1981/83), 6–10; 12 (1992), 2
LAu 4 (1972/74), 5–6 (1978/80), 4
Lbl*
Lcm 1 (1963/65), 1, 11; 2 (1966/68), 1, 8; 7 (1981/83), 6–8, 10, 11

Recorder Magazine *see* **The Recorder and Music Magazine**

The Recorder News: the Journal of the Society of Recorder Players
TNG GB364
GB–New Malden: The Society of Recorder Players, 1937–63
[Incorporated into *The Recorder and Music Magazine* (q.v.) in 1963]

Recording Engineer/Producer
0034–1673
US–Hollywood, CA, ?1970–90
[NOT IN BUCOMP1; ceased publication with vol. 21 no. 6 (1990)]

Recording Industry Index
0276–6078
US–Cherry Hill, NJ: National Association of Recording Musicians, 1977–
[NOT IN BUCOMP1]

Recording Musician
0966–484X
GB–St Ives, Cambridgeshire: SOS, 1992–93
[NOT IN BUCOMP1; incorporated into *Sound on Sound* (q.v.) in May 1993]

Recording Rights Journal
0557–7020
GB–London: Mechanical Copyright Protection Society, 1965–

Recordings
GB–Edinburgh, 1966–

Recordings News
GB–?, 1983–?
[NOT IN BUCOMP1]

Records
GB–London, 1926–28

Records and Recording
TNG GB468; 0034–169X
GB–London: Hansom Books, 1957–82
[In Feb. 1967 incorporated *Record Times* (q.v.) to become *Records and Recording and Record Times*; from Apr. 1968 reverted to *Records and Recording*]

Cu 1 (1957/58)–23 (1979/80), 12
DOR 10 (1966/67)–12 (1968/69); 14 (1970/71)–23 (1979/80)
EIR:Dtc 25 (1981/82)–26 (1982/83), 298
EIR:Duc 19 (1975/76)–#
En*
Ep 15 (1971/72)–26 (1982/83), 289–298
Gm 10 (1966/67)–23 (1979/80), 8
KE 11 (1967/68), 12–18 (1974/75), 4*
Lam 10 (1966/67), 9; 11 (1967/68), 2; 12 (1968/69), 1, 5; 14 (1970/71), 3–16 (1972/73), 4; 16 (1972/73), 6–22 (1978/79), 10
Lbar 1 (1957/58)–23 (1979/80), 11; 25 (1981/82), June, July
Lbl*
Lcm 1 (1957/58), 1; 2 (1958/59), 9; 4 (1960/61), 8; 5 (1961/62), 5– 11; 6 (1962/63), 2, 10–12; 7 (1963/64), 1; 8 (1964/65), 7, 9, 10; 9 (1965/66), 6
Lcml (m) 10 (1966/67)*; 11 (1967/68)–23 (1979/80), Aug; 24 (1980/81), 290–25 (1981/82), 298
LEc 13 (1969/70), 4–6, 8–25 (1981/82)
Len 8 (1964/65), 8–23 (1979/80), 11
Lgo 21 (1977/78), 233–25 (1981/82), 298
LIp 10 (1966/67), Feb–24 (1980/81), Aug
Lki 21 (1977/78)–23 (1979/80)
Lsa 1 (1957/58)–23 (1979/80), 11; 25 (1981/82)*
Lu 7 (1963/64), 12
LVp 2 (1958/59)–3 (1959/60); 5 (1961/62)– 25 (1981/82), July
Mcm 14 (1970/71), 5, 7, 9, 10, 12; 15 (1971/72), 1–3, 5–8, 10; 16 (1972/73), 2, 3, 12; 17 (1973/74)–24 (1980/81), Aug
MK 17 (1973/74)–23 (1979/80)
Mpl 14 (1970/71)–26 (1982/83)
NTp 8 (1964/65)–25 (1981/82), Aug*
Ob 21 (1977/78)–#*
SFp 13 (1969/70), 4–26 (1982/83), 298
SFu 9 (1965/66)–18 (1974/75)
WF 13 (1969/70), 4–23 (1979/80), 11
WOp 13 (1969/70)–23 (1979/80), Aug

Records and Recording *see also* **Seven Arts**

Records and Recording and Record Times
see **Records and Recording**

Records and Tapes [ICC] Keynote Report
0266–1845
GB–?London, 1982–
[NOT IN BUCOMP1; later entitled *Records and Tapes Keynote Report*]

BSdsc 5 (1986)–#

Records in Review
US–Philadelphia, 1957–81
[Preceded by *High Fidelity Record Annual*]

Cu 1 (1957)–26 (1981)

Records International
US–Los Angeles, CA, 1975–

Lsa 1 (1975)–# [w 151, 152, 156–158, 167, 170–172]

Records Magazine
GB–London: Decca Record Company, 1958–66

ALb 3 (1960), 8
Lbl*
Lsa 2 (1959/60)–9 (1966)

Records of the Month
0034–1746
GB–London: Trade Papers, 1936–72

Cu 306–431, 1962–72*
Lam 218, 1954
Lsa 318–431, 1963–72

Red and Green Songs
GB–London, 1988–
[NOT IN BUCOMP1]

Lcs 1–3, 1988–89

Red Bank Special
GB–Southgate, West Sussex: Count Basie Society, 1981–
[NOT IN BUCOMP1]

LOnjfa*

R.E.D. Classical Catalogue *see* **The Gramophone Long Playing Classical Record Catalogue**

R.E.D. Soundtracks Catalogue
GB–London: Retail Entertainment Data, 1995–
[NOT IN BUCOMP1]

Cu 1995–#

Reeves' Musical Almanac
GB–London, 1894

Ob*

Reeves' Musical Directory, with Calendar: an Alphabetical List of Professors of Music, Organists, &c., and the Music Trades
Fellinger 1968/803; TNG GB92
GB–London: Reeves, 1879–1902

Bp 1898–1903
Gm 1888
Lbl 1879–1902
Ob*

Referate Informationen, Deutscher Musikrat
see Deutscher Musikrat: Referate und Informationen

Reflex *see* Punk

Reggae Report
1065–3023
US–Miami, FL: Standard Yard Music, 198?–
[NOT IN BUCOMP1]

LEc [c (5 years)]

The Register of Early Music *see* NEMA Register of Early Music

Register of Music Research Students in Great Britain and the Republic of Ireland *see* Music Research Information Network: Register

Die Reihe
TNG US691; 0080–0775 [English language ed.]; 0486–3267 [German language ed.]
US/A–Bryn Mawr, PA, 1958–68 [English language ed.]; Vienna: Universal Edition, 1955–62 [German language ed.]

Bp*
BRp 1 (1958); 3 (1959)–8 (1968) [English ed.]
Bu 1–8, 1958–68 [English ed.]
CAu 1 (1955)–8 (1962) [English ed.]
CDu 1 (1958)–8 (1968) [English ed.]
Cpl 1 (1958)–7 (1965) [English ed.]
Cu 1 (1958)–8 (1968) [English ed.]
DRu 1 (1958)–7 (1965) [w 4] [English ed.]
EIR:Dtc 1 (1958)–8 (1968) [English ed.]
En 1 (1958)–7 (1965) [English ed.]
EXu 1 (1958)–7 (1965) [English ed.]
Gam 1 (1958)–3 (1959); 5 (1961)–8 (1968) [English ed.]
Gul 1 (1958)–8 (1968) [English ed.]
HUu 1 (1958)–8 (1968) [English ed.]
KE 1 (1955)–8 (1962) [German ed.] [Reprint ed.]

Lam 1 (1958)–8 (1968) [English ed.]
Lam 2 (1955) [German ed.]
LAu 1 (1955)–8 (1962) [German ed.]; 1 (1958)–8 (1968) [English ed.]
Lbbc 2 (1959)–7 (1965) [English ed.]
Lbl*
Lcm 1 (1958)–8 (1968) [English ed.]
Lcml 1 (1955)–3 (1957) [German ed.]
Lcml 1 (1958)–8 (1968) [English ed.]
LEbc 1 (1958)–8 (1968) [English ed.]
Lgo 1 (1958)–8 (1968) [English ed.]
Lkc 1 (1958)–8 (1968) [w 2, 4] [English ed.]
LRHBNC 1 (1958)–8 (1968) [English ed.]
Lu 1 (1958)–8 (1968) [English ed.]
LVp 1 (1958)–5 (1961) [English ed.]
LVu 4 (1960); 6 (1964)–8 (1968) [English ed.]
Mcm 1 (1958)–8 (1968) [English ed.]
Mpl 1 (1958)–8 (1968)* [English ed.]
Mu 1 (1958)–8 (1968) [English ed.] [2 copies]
Mu 5 (1959)–8 (1962) [German ed.]
NO 1 (1955); 3 (1957)–8 (1962) [German ed.]
NWu 1 (1958)–8 (1968) [English ed.]
Ob 1 (1958)–8 (1968) [English ed.]
Ouf 1 (1958)–8 (1968) [English ed.]
R 1 (1958)–8 (1968) [English ed.]
SFp 2 (1955)–8 (1962) [German ed.]
SFu 1 (1958)–8 (1968) [English ed.]
SLGu 1 (1958)–8 (1968) [English ed.]
SOu 1 (1958)–8 (1968) [English ed.]
Uu 1 (1958); 3 (1959)–8 (1968)* [English ed.]

Ren Min Yin Yue [= People's Music]
TNG CHI3; 0447–6573
CHN–Beijing: Zhongguo Wenlian Chuban Gongsi, 1950–
[NOT IN BUCOMP1]

Cu 108 (1962)–#
Lso 1961, 1–6, 9–12; 1962–65, 6; 1966, 1, 2; 1976, 1–5; 1977, 1–6; 1978, 1–6; 1979–81; 1982, 2–#
Ob (ICS) 107 (1962), 2; 108 (1962), 3; 117 (1963), 1; 120 (1963), 1, 4–148 (1966), 2; n.s. 3 (1976), 3–#

Renaissance de l'Orgue
TNG F700; 0034–4303
F–Paris: Bärenreiter, 1968–70; 1971–
[Continued from 1971 as *Connaissance de l'Orgue* (TNG F707)]

Cu 1–8, 1968–70; 1 (1971)–#

Repercussion: International Gospel Music
Magazine
0954–9099
GB–London: P.R.R. Enterprises, 1988–
[NOT IN BUCOMP1]

Lbl*

Repercussions
US–Emeryville, CA, 1992–
[NOT IN BUCOMP1]

Cu 1, 1992–#

Répertoire International de la Littérature
Musicale *see* RILM Abstracts of Music
Literature

Repertorium der musikalischen Journalistik
und Literatur
Fellinger 1968/284; TNG D116
D–Dillingen, 1850

Lbl 1 (1850), 1, 2

Replay
0965–7088
GB–Stansted, 1992–
[NOT IN BUCOMP1]

Lbl*

Report of the Musical Antiquarian Society:
Annual General Meeting
Fellinger 1968/188; TNG GB24
GB–London, 1841–46

Lbl 1842

ReR Records Quarterly Magazine
0954–8807
GB–London: November Books, 1986–
[NOT IN BUCOMP1]

Lbl*
Lsa 1 (1986)–3 (1989), 1
Lu*

Rescue Trust Music Arts Briefing
EIRE–Dublin: Rescue Trust, 1993–
[NOT IN BUCOMP1]

EIR:Dtc 1 (1993)–#

Research Studies in Music Education
1321–103X
AUS–Toowoomba: University of Southern
Queensland Press and the Faculty of Arts,
University of Southern Queensland, 1993–
[NOT IN BUCOMP1]

Ltc 1997–#

Resonance
1352–772X
GB–London: London Musicians' Collective,
1992–
[NOT IN BUCOMP1]

Lbl*
Lsa 2 (1994)–#

Resound: a Quarterly of the Archives of
Traditional Music
0749–2472
US–Bloomington, IN: Indiana University
Archives of Traditional Music, 1982–

Lsa 1 (1982)–# [w 1 (1982), 2; 6 (1987), 1]

Reverberations
GB–Ashton-under-Lyme: Handbell Ringers of
Great Britain, 1967–

Cu 1, 1967–#
Ob*

Review of London Recitals
GB–London, ?1971–
[NOT IN BUCOMP1]

Cu 1980–#
EIR:Dtc 1980–83, Dec
Lcm (p) 1976, Dec; 1978, May; 1980, Feb,
Oct
Lu 1971, 1, 2
Ob 1980–#*

The Review of New Musical Publications *see*
Musical Miscellanies

Review of Popular Music
GB–Exeter: International Association for the
Study of Popular Music, 1982–
[NOT IN BUCOMP1]

EIR:Dtc 1–3, 1982–83
Lbl*

Review of Psychology in Music
GB–London, 1963–?

Re 1 (1963)–2 (1965)

Revista Brasileira de Música
TNG BR16; 0486–6398
BR–Rio de Janeiro: Instituto Nacional de
Música da Universidade do Rio de
Janeiro/Brazil National School of Music, 1934–
44; 1981–

Lbl*
Lu 1 (1934)-6 (1939); 8 (1942)

**Revista Brasileira de Música: Orgaõ Oficial
do Conselho Federal da Ordem dos Musicos
do Brasil**
TNG BR27
BR–Rio de Janeiro: Conselho Federal da Ordem
dos Músicos do Brasil, 1962–63

Lu 1 (1962), 1–3

Revista Colombiana de Investigacion Musical
CO–Bogota: Seccion de Musicologia, Facultad
de Artes, Universidad Nacional de Colombia,
1985–
[NOT IN BUCOMP1]

Lu 1 (1985), 1

Revista de Acustica
0210–3680
E–Madrid: Sociedad Española de Acustica,
1970–

Lu 2 (1971), 1, 2

Revista de Estudios Musicales
TNG AR26
ARG–Mendoza: Universidad Nacional de Cuyo,
1949–54

Cpl 1 (1949), 2, 3–2 (1950/51), 4
Lam 1 (1949)–2 (1950/51), 6
Lbl*
Lcml 1 (1949), 1; 2 (1950/51), 3–3 (1954), 7
Lu (RMA) 2 (1951), 5, 6; 3 (1954), 7
Mcm 1 (1949), 2; 2 (1950/51), 4–6; 3 (1954),
7
Ouf (Howes) 1 (1949), 1, 2; 2 (1950/51),
4–5/6

Revista de Etnografie si Folclor *see* **Revista de
Folclor**

Revista de Folclor [= Folklore Journal]
TNG R26; 1015–4779
RO–Bucharest: Institutul de Folclor, 1956–
[From vol. 9 (1964) entitled *Revista de
Etnografie si Folclor* (ISSN 0034–8198)]

Lbl*
Lcs 21 (1976), 1; 29 (1984)–38 (1993), 4
Lsa 5 (1960)–34 (1989) [w 6 (1961), 3, 4;
9 (1964), 1; 14 (1969), 6; 26 (1981), 1]]

Revista de Folklore
0211–1810
E–Valladolid: Obra Social y Cultural de Caja
España, ?–
[NOT IN BUCOMP1]

Lcs 41, 1984–#

La Revista de Música [1]
TNG AR10
ARG–Buenos Aires, 1927–30
[Ceased publication with no. 11, 1930]

Cpl 1 (1927), 1
Lcml 1 (1927)–3 (1929)*

Revista de Música [2]
TNG CU11; 0556–6207
CU–Havana: Departamento de Música,
Biblioteca Nacional, 1960–61

Lam 1 (1960)–2 (1961), 4
Ob*

Revista de Música Latino Americana *see*
Latin American Music Review

Revista de Musicologia
TNG E103; 0210–1459
E–Madrid: Sociedad Española de Musicologia;
1978–

CDu 12 (1989), 1–2B; 13 (1990), 1–3; 14
(1991), 1, 2
Cu 1 (1978)–#
Lu 1 (1978)–3 (1980); 6 (1983)–12 (1989), 2;
13 (1990)–#
Ob*

**Revista del Conservatorio: Organo del
Conservatorio Nacional de Musica**
TNG M15; 0034–7833
ME–Mexico City, 1962–
[NOT IN BUCOMP1]

Lam 4–15, 1963–67

Revista del S.O.D.R.E.
URG–Montevideo: SODRE [= Servicio Oficial
de Difusion Radio Electrica], 1955–58; 1966–

    Lcml 1957, 5

Revista INIDEF
VNZ–Caracas: Instituto Nacional de Cultura y
Bellas Artes, 1975–
[NOT IN BUCOMP1; INIDEF = Instituto
Interamericano de Etnomusicología y Folklore]

    BLu 1 (1975)–4 (1980)

Revista Literaria Musical
TNG E88
E–Madrid, 1943–51

    Lcml 7 (1949), 44–9 (1951), 56*

Revista Musical [1]
Fellinger 1968/1940; TNG E56
E–Bilbao, 1909–13
[NOT IN BUCOMP1; succeeded in 1914 by the
Revista Musical Hispano-Americana (Fellinger
1968/2228)]

    Cpl 1 (1909)–5 (1913)

Revista Musical [2]
TNG CL3; 0035–0192; 0716–2790
CHL–Santiago de Chile: Universidad de Chile,
1945–
[Entitled *Revista Musical Chilena* from 1946]

    BSdsc*
    Cu 7 (1952), 42–#*
    Er 21 (1967)
    Lam 8 (1954), 47–9 (1955), 49; 11 (19576),
        52, 54–24 (1970), 110; 24 (1970), 112–36
        (1982), 157
    Lcm 16 (1962), 79–24 (1970), 110; 25
        (1971), 112–37 (1983), 159; 38 (1984),
        161–42 (1988), 170
    Lcml 3 (1947)–21 (1967)*
    Lsa 19 (1965)–# [w 25 (1971)]
    Lu 6 (1950)–13 (1959); 20 (1966), 98; 23
        (1969); 24 (1970); 110, 112; 25 (1971)–#
    Mpl 11 (1957)–38 (1984)
    Ob*
    Ouf (Howes) 8 (1952), 43; 16 (1962), 79; 18
        (1964), 90; 19 (1965), 93, 94; 20 (1966),
        95, 98; 21 (1967), 102; 22 (1968), 103–23
        (1969), 106

Revista Musical [3]
0103–5525
BR–Saõ Paolo: Universidad de Saõ Paolo, 1990–
[NOT IN BUCOMP1]

    BSdsc 1 (1990)–#
    Lu 1 (1990), 1, 2

**Revista Musical Catalana: Bulletí del "Orfeó
Català"**
Fellinger 1968/1744; TNG E50
E–Barcelona: Orfeó Català, 1904–36; 1984–
[From issue 73, 1990 entitled *Catalunya Musica*]

    BSdsc*
    CDu 1989–95
    Ob*

Revista Musical Chilena *see* **Revista Musical
[2]**

Revista Musical Hispano-Americana *see*
Revista Musical [1]

Revista Venezolana de Folklore
0035–0575
VNZ–Caracas: Ministerio de Educacion
Musical, 1947–75

    Lbl*
    Lsa n.s. 1 (1968)–6 (1975)

**Revue Belge de Musicologie/Belgisch
Tijdschrift voor Muziekwetenschap**
TNG B126; 0771–6788
B–Brussels: Société Belge de Musicologie,
1946–

    AB*
    Bu 4 (1950)–12 (1958); 31 (1977)–33 (1979)
    CDu 18 (1964)–35 (1981)
    Cu 1 (1946)–#
    Er 1 (1946)–#
    Gul 34 (1980)–#
    HUu 18 (1964)–#
    Lbl*
    Lcml 1 (1946)*; 2 (1947)–5 (1951); 19
        (1965)–#
    Lkc 1 (1946)–25 (1971); 28 (1974)–44
        (1990); 46 (1992)–#
    Lu 1 (1946)–#
    LVu 8 (1954)–#
    Mu 43 (1989)
    Ob 1 (1946)–#
    Ouf 1 (1946)–#
    SOu 45 (1991)–#

La Revue Blanche
F–Paris: Revue Blanche, 1891–1903

Lbl*

Revue d'Art Dramatique
Fellinger 1968/1029; TNG F204
F–Paris, 1886–96; n.s. 1897–1909
[Entitled *Revue d'Art Dramatique et Musical: Organe International du Théâtre et de la Musique*, 1897–1909]

Lbl 1–140, 1886–96; n.s. 1–24, 1897–1909

Revue d'Art Dramatique et Musical: Organe International du Théâtre et de la Musique *see* Revue d'Art Dramatique

Revue de la Musique Religieuse, Populaire et Classique
Fellinger 1968/235; TNG F45
F–Paris: Blanchet, 1845–48; 1854

Lbl 1 (1845)–4 (1854)
Lu 1 (1845)–3 (1848)*
Ob 1 (1845)–3 (1848); 4 (1854)

Revue de Musicologie *see* Bulletin de la Société Française de Musicologie

Revue de Musique Ancienne et Moderne
TNG F79
F–Rennes, 1856
[NOT IN BUCOMP1; included a supplementary *Bulletin de la Revue Ancienne et Moderne*]

Ouf [Reprint ed.; including *Bulletin*]

Revue de Musique Religieuse et de Chant Grégorien
TNG F264
Fellinger 1968/1322
F–Marseilles, 1895–1900
[Entitled *Revue du Chant Grégorien et de Musique Religieuse*, 1898–99]

Lu 9–25, 1896–97*

La Revue des Disques
TNG B137
B–Brussels: Editions Dereume, 1950–
[Entitled *La Revue des Disques et de la Haute Fidelité* from 1964; from 1980, 281–284 entitled *Hi-Fi Musique: Revue des Disques et de la Haute Fidelité*]

BSdsc*
Lsa 32–280, 1955–80

La Revue des Disques et de la Haute Fidelité
see La Revue des Disques

Revue des Machines Parlantes *see* Musique et Instruments: Revue du Commerce et de l'Industrie de la Musique

Revue des Salons: Journal de Musique, de Littérature, et des Beaux Arts *see* The Parlour Review and Journal of Music, Literature and the Fine Arts

Revue d'Histoire et de Critique Musicales: Publication Mensuelle principalement consacrée à la Musique Française Ancienne et Moderne
Fellinger 1968/1604; TNG F320
F–Paris: H. Welter, 1901–12
[Entitled *La Revue Musicale* from vol. 2 no. 10 (1902) to vol. 12 no. 1 (1912); absorbed into *Revue Musicale S.I.M.* in 1912]

Bu 6 (1906)–10 (1910)
Cu 1 (1901)–12 (1912), 1 [Reprint ed.]
Lu (RMA) 1 (1901), 8
Ob 1 (1901)–2 (1902)

Revue du Chant Grégorien
Fellinger 1968/1193; TNG F239
CH–Grenoble: Baratier et Dardelet, 1892–1914; 1919–40

Cpl 1 (1892)–4 (1896), 8*
Lbl 23 (1919)–26/27 (1923)
Lu 1 (1892)–20 (1912) [w 2 (1893), 1; 20 (1912), 6]
LVp 1 (1892)–15 (1907)
Ob*

Revue du Chant Grégorien et de Musique Religieuse *see* Revue de Musique Religieuse et de Chant Grégorien

La Revue du Jazz
F–Paris: Revue du Jazz, 1949–?
[Combined with *Bulletin du Hot Club de France* (TNG F619)]

Cbijs 1949, 1, 2; 1952, 1

Revue du Monde Musical, Dramatique et Littéraire *see* Revue du Monde Musical et Dramatique

Revue du Monde Musical et Dramatique
Fellinger 1968/777; TNG F163
F–Paris, 1878–84
[Later entitled *Revue du Monde Musical, Dramatique et Littéraire*]

>Ob 1 (1878)–2 (1879), 26

Revue et Gazette Musicale de Paris *see*
Gazette Musicale de Paris

Revue et Gazette Musicale de Paris *see also*
Revue Musicale [1]

Revue Française de Musique *see* Revue
Musicale de Lyon

Revue Grégorienne: Études de Chant Sacre et
de Liturgie
Fellinger 1968/2092; TNG F423
F–Solesmes, 1911–39; 1946–64

>AB*
>Lu 6 (1921), 3–5; 11 (1926)–17 (1932)*
>Ob*
>Ouf 8 (1923), 2–42 (1964), 3

La Revue Indépendante des Théâtres et des
Concerts
Fellinger 1968/1052; TNG F209
F–Paris, 1887–88

>Lbl*

La Revue Internationale de Musique
TNG F579
F/B–Paris; Brussels, 1938–40; 1950–52
[Included supplement, *La Vie Musicale: Bulletin Mensuel d'Information de la Revue Internationale de Musique* (q.v.)]

>Cu 1–13, 1938–52
>EIR:MEtc 8–13, 1950–52
>Lam 12, 13, 1952
>Lbl*
>Lcm 1, 1938; 10, 1951
>Lcml 1, 2, 1938–40
>LEbc 8–13, 1950–52
>Lu 11, 1951
>Mpl 1, 1938
>Ob 1–11, 1938–52
>Ouf 11–13, 1951–52

Revue Internationale de Musique: Bi-
Mensuelle et Illustrée, absolument Éclectique
et Indépendante
Fellinger 1968/1451; TNG F296
F–Paris: P. Dupont, 1898–99
[Ceased publication with vol. 2 (1899), 22]

>Lbl*
>Lcm 1 (1898)
>Lu 1 (1898)–2 (1899), 22
>Ob*

Revue Internationale de Musique Française
0244-2957
CH–Geneva: Slatkine [for the Société
Internationale de Musique Française], 1980–89;
1994–

>Cu 1 (1980)–10 (1989)
>Lcml 1 (1980)–#
>Lkc 7 (1986)–10 (1989)
>Lu 1 (1980)
>Ob 1 (1980)–#

Revue Internationale de Musique Sacrée *see*
Rivista Internazionale di Musica Sacra

Revue Liturgique et Musicale *see* La Voix de
l'Église

Revue Mahler: une Revue Semestrielle
d'Études Mahleriennes/Mahler Review
F–Paris: Bibliothèque Gustav Mahler, 1987–
[NOT IN BUCOMP1]

>ALb 1, 1987
>Lbl*

Revue Musicale [1]
Fellinger 1968/80; TNG F14
F–Paris: F.-J. Fétis, 1827–35
[Amalgamated with the *Gazette Musicale de Paris* (q.v.) in 1835, to form the *Revue et Gazette Musicale de Paris*]

>Er 1827–35
>Lcml*
>Lu 6–10, 1830–31
>Ob 1827–35

La Revue Musicale [2]
Fellinger 1968/1452; TNG F285
F–Avignon, 1898–1900

>Cu 1–86, 1898–1900

La Revue Musicale [3]
TNG F475; 0035–3736; 0768–1593
F–Paris: Editions Richard–Masse, 1920–40;
1946–48; 1952–90
[Issues from 1952 also called *Les Carnets
Critiques*; ceased publication with no. 424,
1990]

   BG 208–274/275, 1948–71 [w 224]
   BLu 1 (1920/21), 1, 2, 12; 2 (1921/22), 3–12;
   3 (1922/23), 1, 3–12; 4 (1923/24), 1–10,
   12; 5 (1924/25), 2, 12; 6 (1925/26), 2–12; 7
   (1926/27)–208, 1948
   BRu 1 (1920/21)–10 (1928/29) [w 10
   (1928/29), 2]; 220–387, 1953–86; 400/401,
   1987
   BSdsc*
   Bu 1 (1920/21), 1, 2; 2 (1921/22), 3–10; 3
   (1922/23), 1; 4 (1923/24), 4; 5 (1924/25), 2,
   3; 117–118, 1931; 125, 1932; 156,159, 161,
   1935; 166, 1936; 172, 174, 176, 178, 1937;
   187, 1938; 191, 1939; 196, 1940; 198–268,
   1946–70*; 298–385, 1975–85; 400, 401,
   1986; 405–407, 1987
   CCtc 288–327, 1972–80
   CDu 226, 1955; 268–307, 1970–77
   Cpl 1 (1920/21)–5 (1924/25), 10; 22 (1947)–
   25 (1949)
   Cu 1 (1920/21)–424, 1991
   EIR:Duc 2 (1921/22)–6 (1925/26)
   Ep 1935–39*
   Er 1 (1920/21)–#
   EXu 203–337, 1946–80
   HUu 1 (1920/21)–357, 1982
   Lam 210–219, 1952–53
   LAu 3 (1923/24), Mar; 6 (1925/26), Dec,
   May; 125, 127, 1932; 210, 212, 1952
   Lbl*
   Lcm*
   Lcml 1 (1920/21)–#
   Lu 1 (1920/21)–#
   LVp 4 (1923/24)–20 (1939); 223–224, 1953–
   54; 226–31, 1955–56; 233–52, 1956–63;
   255–67, 1962–68
   LVu 4 (1923/24), 3, 5; 5 (1924/25), 2
   Mcm 2 (1921/22); 5 (1924/25), Apr; 5, 10
   (1928/29); 200, 1946
   Mpl 1 (1920/21)–#
   NO 1 (1920/21)–23 (1948)
   Ob*
   Ouf *Numéros spéciales* only*
   R 210, 212, 1952; 233, 1956; 258–305, 1964–
   77
   SA 1 (1920/21)–16 (1935); 272–273, 1971
   SFu 2 (1921/22), 11; 204–307, 1947–77
   SOu 244, 1959

Revue Musicale *see also* Revue d'Historie et
de Critique Musicales

La Revue Musicale de France
TNG F599
F–Paris: S. Berthoumieux, 1946–47
[NOT IN BUCOMP1]

   Lam 8, 1947

Revue Musicale de Lyon
Fellinger 1968/1685; TNG F351
F–Lyon: Waltener, 1903–29
[Entitled *Revue Française de Musique*, 1912–
14; from 1920 entitled *Nouvelle Revue
Musicale*]

   Cu 1 (1903)–12 (1914); 18 (1920)–23 (1925);
   25 (1927)–26 (1929), 4 [Reprint ed.]
   Ob*

Revue Musicale du Suisse Romande [...] *see*
Feuilles Musicales: Revue Musicale Romande
et Courrier Suisse du Disque

Revue Musicale S.I.M. *see* Le Mercure
Musical

Revue Musicale S.I.M. *see also* Revue
d'Histoire et de Critique Musicales

La Revue Musicale S.I.M. [et Courrier
Musical Réunis] *see* Le Courrier Musical,
Artistique et Littéraire du Littoral

Revue Musicale Suisse: Feuillets Suisses de
Pédagogie Musicale *see* Schweizerische
Musikzeitung und Sängerblatt: Organ des
eidgenossischen Sängervereins

Revue Musical Suisse: Organe Officiel de
l'Association des Musiciens Suisses (AMS) et
de la SVISA, Société Suisse des Auteurs et
Éditeurs *see* Schweizerische Musikzeitung
und Sängerblatt: Organ des eidgenossischen
Sängervereins

Revue Pleyel
TNG F502
F–Paris, 1923–27
[NOT IN BUCOMP1; succeeded by *Musique*
(q.v.)]

   Cpl 42, 44, 46, 48, 1927

Revue Pratique de Liturgie et de Musique
Sacrée *see* La Voix de l'Église

Revue Roumaine d'Histoire de l'Art: Série
Théâtre, Musique, Cinéma
0556–8080
RO–Bucharest: Academie de la République
Socialiste de Roumanie, 1964–
[French edition of *Studii si Cercetări de Istoria
Artei* (q.v.)]

> Lbbc 7 (1970)–11 (1974); 14 (1977)–15
> (1978)
> Lbl*
> Ob*

Revue Suisse du Jazz *see* Jazz, Rhythm and
Blues

Revue Wagnérienne
Fellinger 1968/1002; TNG F199
F–Paris, 1885–88

> Au 1 (1885)–3 (1888) [Reprint ed.]
> Cu 1 (1885)–3 (1888) [Reprint ed.]
> DRu 1 (1885)–3 (1888)
> EIR:Duc 1 (1885)–3 (1888)
> Er 1 (1885)–3 (1888)
> HUu 1 (1885)–3 (1888) [Reprint ed.]
> Lbl 1 (1885)–3 (1887)
> Lu 1 (1885)–3 (1888), 12
> Ob 1 (1885)–3 (1888) [Reprint ed.]
> SLGu 1 (1885)–3 (1888)
> SOu 1 (1885)–3 (1888)

Rhech: Cylchgrawn Pop: Bawb
GB–?, 198?–
[NOT IN BUCOMP1]

> AB 1984, 1

Rheinische Musik-Zeitung für Kunstfreunde
und Künstler
Fellinger 1968/286; TNG D117
D–Cologne, 1850–59
[NOT IN BUCOMP1; absorbed into the
*Niederrheinische Muzik-Zeitung für
Kunstfreunde und Künstler* (q.v.)]

> Mpl 1853

Rhythm: a Magazine for All Interested in
Modern Music
GB–London, ?1928–
[NOT IN BUCOMP1]

Mcm 3 (1930), 31; 4 (1931), 43, 44, 48;
5 (1932), 53

Rhythm: Art, Music, Literature Quarterly
Fellinger 1968/2095; TNG GB250
GB–London: St Catherine Press, 1911–13

> BSdsc*
> En 1 (1911)–2 (1912), 5
> Gm 1 (1911)–3 (1913)*
> Lbl*
> Ob*

Rhythm: Issued Monthly in the Interest of
Drummers and Banjoists
TNG GB316
GB–London, 1926–39

> Cbijs 7 (1933), 73; 9 (1935), Dec; 11 (1938),
> 126, 131, 134, 135; 12 (1939), 136–140,
> 143, 144
> Lbl*
> LOnjfa*
> Ob 9 (1935), Dec–10 (1936), May

Rhythm and Blues
US–New York, 1961–?

> Cbijs 1964, Jan, Apr, July; 1965, Jan

Rhythm and Blues Collector *see* R. and B.
Collector

Rhythm and Blues Panorama
B–Brussels, 1960–?

> Cbijs 12, 1961; 36, 38, 39, 1965; 41, 42, 44,
> 45, 1966

Rhythm and Soul USA *see* Hitsville USA

Rhythm Rag
GB–Edgware, ?1976–

> Cbijs 1976
> Cu 33–49, 1986–93
> En*
> LOnjfa*

Rhythmen: Jahrbuch Freie Akademie der
Künste in Hamburg
D–Hamburg: Freie Akademie der Künste, ?–
[NOT IN BUCOMP1]

> ALb 1962

Der Rhythmus: ein Jahrbuch
Fellinger 1968/2096; TNG D505
D–Jena: Eugen Diederichs/Bildungsanstalt
Jacques–Dalcroze, 1911–13
[NOT IN BUCOMP1]

   Er 1 (1911)

Ricerche Musicali
TNG I290
I–Milan, 1977–82
[NOT IN BUCOMP1; ceased publication with
vol. 6 (1982)]

   Lbl*

Richard Strauss Blätter
TNG INTL35; 0720–9827 (n.F.)
A–Vienna: International Richard Strauss
Gesellschaft, 1971–72; n.F. D–Tutzing:
Schneider, 1979–

   Cu n.F. 1 (1979)–#
   Lu 1, 1971; n.F. 1 (1979)–#
   Ob 9–12, 1972; n. F. 1 (1979)–#
   Ouf 9–12, 1977–78; n.F. 1–18, 1979–87

Richard Strauss Jahrbuch
TNG D958; 0556–9834
D–Bonn: Boosey and Hawkes, 1954–60

   Cu 1954; 1959/60
   LAu 1954
   Lu 1954; 1959/60
   Ob 1954; 1959/60

**Richard Wagner Blätter: Zeitschrift des
Aktionskreises für das Werk Richard
Wagners**
TNG D1097
D–Tutzing: Schneider, 1977–89
[NOT IN BUCOMP1; ceased publication with
vol. 13, 1989]

   Cu 7 (1983)–?13, 1989

Richard Wagner-Jahrbuch [1]
Fellinger 1968/1030; TNG D287
D–Stuttgart: Joseph Kürschner, 1886

   Lbl 1 (1886)
   Lu 1 (1886)

Richard Wagner-Jahrbuch [2]
Fellinger 1968/1846; TNG D463
D–Leipzig; Berlin, 1906–08; 1912–13

   Lbl 1 (1906)–5 (1913) [+ 2nd copy of 1
   (1906)–4 (1912)]

   Lcm 2 (1907)–3 (1908)
   Lu 2 (1907)–3 (1908); 5 (1913)

**Ricordi Musicali Fiorentini: Raccolta per gli
Amatori di Musica, Riproduzione di
Programmi**
Fellinger 1968/1947; TNG I128
I–Florence: Brizzi e Niccolai, 1906–13

   Lbl*

Ricordiana: a Quarterly Review
TNG GB456
GB–London, 1954–55; 1956–67

   AB 11 (1966), Oct
   BLu 1 (1956)–12 (1967), 1
   Bu 1 (1956)–12 (1967)
   Cpl 1 (1956)–12 (1967), 2
   Cu 4 (1959), 1, 4–12 (1967), 2
   Er 1 (1954)–12 (1967), 1, 2
   HUu 8 (1963), 3–12 (1967), 2
   Lam 1 (1956), 2–2 (1957), 4; 3 (1958), 2–9
   (1964), 1, 3; 10 (1965), 1–4; 11 (1966), 3;
   12 (1967), 2
   Lbbc*
   Lbl*
   Lcm 1 (1956), 1–3; 2 (1957)–4 (1959), 1, 2,
   4; 7 (1962), 2, 4; 8 (1963)–12 (1967), 2
   Lcml 1 (1956)*; 2 (1957)–12 (1967), 2
   LIp 3 (1958), Oct–12 (1967), Apr
   Lu 2 (1957)–6 (1961); 7 (1962), 1, 3, 4; 8
   (1963)–12 (1967), 2
   LVp 8 (1963)–11 (1966)
   NO 6 (1961), 3; 10 (1965), 3–11 (1966), 4; 12
   (1967), 2
   Ob*
   R 6 (1961), 3; 7 (1962); 9 (1964), 2, 4; 10
   (1965), 3, 4; 11 (1966), 2, 4; 12 (1967), 1
   SOu 8 (1963)–12 (1967), 2
   TOd 8 (1963), 3–12 (1967), 1*

**Ricordiana: Rivista Musicale della Casa
Ricordi**
TNG I231; 0483–0377
I–Milan: Ricordi, 1951–54; 1955–57
[Later subtitled *Rivista Mensile di Vita
Musicale*. New series, *Ricordiana: Rivista
Mensile di Vita Musicale, Nuova Serie*, began
1955 and ceased publication in 1957]

   Cpl n.s. 1 (1955), 1–5
   Er n.s. 1 (1955), 6–10; 2 (1956), 1–5, 7–10; 3
   (1957)
   Lam n.s. 1 (1955), 4–9; 2 (1956), 1, 4, 10
   Lcm n.s. 1 (1955), 2–4

Lcml 2 (1952)–4 (1954)*; n.s. 1 (1955)–3
(1957)*
Ob n.s. 1 (1955), 2–3 (1957), 10

Ricordiana: Rivista Mensile di Vita Musicale
[Nuova Serie] *see* **Ricordiana: Rivista**
Musicale della Casa Ricordi

Ride: the Network!
1350–5971
GB–Oxford: Ride: the Network!, 1991–
[NOT IN BUCOMP1]

Lbl*
Ob 6, 199?–#

RIdIM/RCMI Inventory of Music
Iconography
0889–6607
US–New York: Research Center for Music
Iconography, 1986–
[NOT IN BUCOMP1]

Bu 1 (1986)–#
Lu 1 (1986)–# [w 4–6]
Ob*

RIdIM/RCMI Newsletter: Répertoire
International d'Iconographie Musicale/
International Repertory of Musical
Iconography
TNG INTL41; 0360–8727
US–New York: Research Center for Music
Iconography, 1975–

ALb 17 (1992), 2
Bu 1 (1975)–#
Cu 6 (1981), 2–#
En 12 (1987)–#
Lu 1 (1975)–#
R 16 (1991)–#
Yu 1 (1975)–#

RILM Abstracts of Music Literature:
Répertoire International de la Littérature
Musicale/International Repertory of Music
Literature
TNG INTL23; 0033–6955
US–New York: RILM/International
Musicological Society/International Association
of Music Libraries/American Council of
Learned Societies, 1967–
[Also available in CD–ROM version on MUSE,
which further includes the *Library of Congress:*
Music, Books on Music, and Sound Recordings
Catalog (q.v.)]

AB 1 (1967)–24 (1990)
BAc 1 (1967)–17 (1983), 1
BLp 1 (1967)–#
Bp 1 (1967)–12 (1978)
BRp 1 (1967)–#
BRu 1 (1967)–#
Bs 10 (1976), 4–11 (1977), 1
BSdsc 1 (1967)–#
BTu 1 (1967)–18 (1984)
Bu 1 (1967)–#
CDu 1 (1967)–#
Cpl 1 (1967)–#
Cu 1 (1967)–#
EIR:Dtc 5 (1971)–#
EIR:Duc 1 (1967)–#
EIR:MEtc 10 (1976)–17 (1983), 1
En 1 (1967)–#
Er 1 (1967)–#
Gam 1 (1967)–22 (1988)
Gm 1 (1967)–16 (1982)
Gul 1 (1967)–#
HUu 1 (1967)–15 (1981)
KE 10 (1976), 4–#
Lam 1 (1967)–#
LAu 1 (1967)–#
Lbbc 1 (1967)–#
Lbl*
Lcml 1 (1967)–#
Lcu 1 (1967)–#
LEbc 1 (1967)–#
Lgo 1 (1967)–#
Lk 1 (1967)–#
Lkc 1 (1967)–5 (1971); 6 (1972)*; 7 (1973)–
15 (1981); 16 (1982)*; 17 (1983)–#
Lki 1 (1967)–# [+ CD–ROM version]
LRHBNC 1 (1967)–#
Lsa 1 (1967)–#
Lu 1 (1967)–#
LVp 1 (1967)–#
LVu 1 (1967)–#
Mcm 1 (1967)–#
MK 1 (1967)–#
Mpl 1 (1967)–# [+ CD–ROM version]
Msuc 13 (1979)–#
Mu 1 (1967)–18 (1984) [+ CD–ROM
version]
NO 1 (1967)–#
Ob 1 (1967)–#
Oub 11 (1977)–#
Ouf 1 (1967)–#
R 1 (1967)–#
SFu 1 (1967)–10 (1976)
SOu 1 (1967)–#
Uu 1 (1967)–#
Yu 1 (1967)–#

RIMF *see* Revue Internationale de Musique Française

Rimington's Review: a Magazine Devoted Principally to Recorded Music
GB–London, 1934–?

ALb 9 (1942), 1
Cu 1 (1934)–11 (1949) [w 10]
Lsa 1 (1934)–11 (1949)

The Ringing World
0035–5453
GB–Guildford, 1911–

Bu ?79 (1983), 3741–#
Cu 1 (1911)–#
EIR:Dtc 36 (1941), 1598–53 (1957), 2400
En 35 (1940)–#
Lbl*
Ob*

Ripped and Torn?
GB–?, ?1976–
[NOT IN BUCOMP1]

Lsa 2–11, 1977

Ritmo: Revista Musical Ilustrada
TNG E77; 0035–5658
E–Madrid, 1929–36, 1940–

Lcml 1961, 318; 1966, 367, 368
Lsa 1944–51*; 1972–75*

Rivista Internazionale di Musica Sacra/The International Church Music Review/Revue Internationale de Musique Sacrée
0394–6282
I–Milan: Nuove Edizioni Duomo, 1980–

Cu 1 (1980)–#
EIR:Duc 1 (1980)–5 (1984)
HUu 1 (1980), 4; 3 (1982)–8 (1987)
Lam 1 (1980), 1, 4
Lbbc 1 (1980), 1, 4; 11 (1990), 3
Lbl 1 (1980)–11 (1990)
Lu 1 (1980), 4
Ob*

Rivista Italiana di Musicologia
TNG I280; 0035–6867
I– Florence: Olschki [for the Società Italiana di Musicologia], 1966–

Bu 1 (1966), 1; 8 (1973)–#
CDu 3 (1968), 2; 6 (1971)–#

Cu 1 (1966)–#
DRu 7 (1972)–#
En 1 (1966)–#
Gul 15 (1980)–#
LAu 1 (1966)–#
Lbl*
Lkc 1 (1966)–#
LRHBNC 13 (1978)–#
Lu 1 (1966)–#
Mu 15 (1980)–#
NO 1 (1966), 2; 3 (1968)–16 (1981)
Ob 1 (1966)–#
Ouf 1 (1966)–#
SOu 26 (1991)–#

Rivista Liturgica
0035–6956
I–Padua, 1914–

Lhey 56 (1969)–#

Rivista Musicale Italiana
Fellinger 1968/1277; TNG I84
I–Milan: Fratelli Bocca, 1894–1932; 1936–43; 1946–55
[Continued as *L'Approdo Musicale* (q.v.) and *Nuova Rivista Musicale Italiana* (q.v.)]

BRu 54 (1952)–57 (1955), 2 [w 54 (1952), 2, 3]
Bu 7 (1900)–8 (1901)*; 9 (1902); 10 (1903)*; 12 (1905)–22 (1915); 24 (1917)–25 (1918); 28 (1921)*; 29 (1922); 30 (1923)*; 31 (1924); 33 (1926)–36 (1929); 37 (1930)–38 (1931)*; 39 (1932); 45 (1941)–50 (1948); 55 (1953)*; 57 (1955)*
CDu 1 (1894)–57 (1955) [part m]
Cpl 1 (1894), 1, 3, 4; 8 (1901), 2
Cu 1 (1894)–57 (1955), 2
DRu 1 (1894)–40 (1936); 44 (1940); 53 (1951)–55 (1953)
Er 6 (1899), 2; 55 (1953), 4; 56 (1954), 1–3
Lam 48 (1946), 1
Lbl 1 (1894)–57 (1955), 2
Lcm 1 (1894)–5 (1898); 48 (1946), 2; 52 (1950), 1–3; 53 (1951), 3, 4; 54 (1952)
Lcml 38 (1931)–40 (1936); 42 (1938); 43 (1939)*; 50 (1948)–51 (1949)*; 52 (1950)–55 (1953); 56 (1954)*
Lu 1 (1894)–57 (1955)
LVp 51 (1949)–55 (1953)
LVu 1 (1894)–57 (1955), 2
Mpl 1 (1894)–16 (1909)
Ob*
Ouf 1 (1894)–57 (1955)

Rivista Nazionale di Musica
TMG I170
I–Rome, 1920–43
[NOT IN BUCOMP1]

 Cu 1 (1920)–24 (1943)*

RM: the New Record Mirror *see* Record
Mirror

R.M.A. Newsletter *see* Royal Musical
Association Newsletter

R.M.A. Research Chronicle
TNG GB496; 0080–4460
GB–London [etc.]: Royal Musical Association,
1961–

 AB 1 (1961)–#
 ABc 1 (1961)–25 (1992)
 ALb 2 (1964)–17 (1981); 19 (1983)
 Au 1 (1961)–#
 BG 1 (1961)–#
 BLu 1 (1961)–13 (1977)
 BRp 1 (1961)–#
 BRu 1 (1961)–#
 BSdsc 1 (1961)–#
 Bs 1 (1961)–#*
 Bu 1 (1961)–#
 Cat 1 (1961)–#
 CCtc 1 (1961)–#
 CDu 1 (1961)–#
 Cpl 1 (1961)–#
 DRu 1 (1961)–22 (1989)
 EIR:Dtc 1 (1961)–#
 EIR:Duc 1 (1961)–#
 En 1 (1961)–#
 Er 1 (1961)–#
 EXu 1 (1961)–#
 Gam 1 (1961)–#
 Gm 1 (1961)–12 (1974); 14 (1978)–16 (1980)
 Gul 1 (1961)–14 (1978); 16 (1980)–#
 HUu 1 (1961)–#
 KE 1 (1961)–#
 Lam 1 (1961)–19 (1983); 21 (1988)–#
 LAu 1 (1961)–#
 Lbbc 2 (1962); 4 (1964)–# [w 6 (1966)]
 Lbl*
 Lcm 1 (1961)–28 (1995)
 Lcml 1 (1961)–#
 LEbc 1 (1961)–#
 Lgo 1 (1961)–#
 Lkc 2 (1962)–# [w 21 (1988)]
 Lki 1 (1961)–#

 LRHBNC 1 (1961)–#
 Lu 1 (1961)–#
 LVp 1 (1961)–#
 Mcm 1 (1961)–#
 MK 1 (1961)–#
 Mpl 1 (1961)–#
 Msuc 25 (1992)–#
 Mu 1 (1961)–#
 NO 1 (1961)–#
 NWu 1 (1961)–#
 Ob 1 (1961)–#
 Ouf 1 (1961)–#
 R 1 (1961)–#
 SA 1 (1961)–#
 SFu 1 (1961)–#
 SLGu 13 (1977)–21 (1988)
 SOu 1 (1961)–#
 TOd 1 (1961)–17 (1981)
 Uu 1 (1961)–#
 Yu 1 (1961)–#

Rock Album
0265–0371
GB–London, 1983–

 Cu 1 (1983)–#
 Lbl*
 Ob*

Rock and Folk: Pop Music, Rhythm'n'Blues,
Jazz, Chanson
TNG F694; 0048–8445
F–Paris: Editions Larivière, 1966–

 Cbijs 4–9, 1967; 18, 23, 1968; 24, 25, 27, 32–
  35, 1969; 36–46, 1970; 48–59, 1971; 60–
  67, 69, 70, 1972; 73, 76, 80, 81, 83, 1973
 Lsa*

Rock Compact Disc Magazine *see* RCD:
Rock Compact Disc Magazine

Rock Hard
0962–175X
GB–London: Dennis Oneshots, 1991–
[NOT IN BUCOMP1]

 Lbl*

Rock News (France)
F–?:, 197?–
[NOT IN BUCOMP1]

 Lsa 2, 4, 6, 7, Rolling Stones Special, 1976

Rock 'n' Reel
0964–3257
GB–Cleator Moor, Cumbria: S. McGhee, 1989–
[NOT IN BUCOMP1]

Lbl*
Lcs 1, 1989–#

Rock On! *see* **Supersonic**

Rock On! Annual
GB–London, 1979/80

Cu 1980
Ob*

Rock Power
0962–7065
GB–London: Maxwell Specialist Magazines,
1991–92
[NOT IN BUCOMP1]

Cu*
Lbl*
Ob 1–13, 1991–92

Rock Scene
0090–3353
US–Bethany, CT [etc.], 1973–

Lsa*

Rock Video International
GB–Heanor: HRC Editorial Services, 1985–?86
[NOT IN BUCOMP1]

AB 1986
Cu 1–4, 1985–86
EIR:Dtc 1–4, 1985–86
Ob*

Rock World
0965–9471
GB–London: Rock Team Publishing and
Productions, 1992–
[NOT IN BUCOMP1]

Lbl*

Rock Year Book
0275–9187
GB/US–London: Virgin Books; New York:
Delilah Grove Press, 1981–87
[Continued as *Schweppes Rock Yearbook*]

AB 1985–87
Cu 1981–#
Lbl*
Ob*

Rocket 88
GB–Glasgow, 1986–87
[NOT IN BUCOMP1]

Ob 7–15, 1986–87*

Rocznik Chopinowski [= Chopin Yearbook]
TNG PL114; 0570–1562
PL–Warsaw: Polskie Wydawnictwo Muzyczne,
1956–78
[Also entitled *Annales Chopin* (ISSN 0208–
5992) from 1958]

Cu 1 (1956)–11 (1978)
Lam 2 (1957); 5 (1960)
Lbl*
Lcm (p) 3 (1958)
Ob*

R.O.H. News
GB–London: Royal Opera House, ?1991–
[NOT IN BUCOMP1]

EIR:Dtc 1991, Sep/Oct–#
En 1991, Sep–#

**Roll of the Union of Graduates in Music [...]
and Calendar**
Fellinger 1968/1236; TNG GB152
GB–London: Music News Office, 1893–1963

Bp 1910–14
Gul 1895–1908; 1912–15; 1928–39
Lbl*
Lcm 1893/94; 1897; 1900; 1909; 1913; 1920;
    1939; 1961/62; 1963
Lu 1926–63*
Ob*

Rolling Stone
TNG US778; 0035–791X
US–New York: Straight Arrow, 1967–

BLp [c]
BSdsc 404, 1983–1992
CDCp [c (1 year)]
EIR:Dp 480–550, 1986–89
EIR:Dtc 178–218, 1975–76
EXu 1–282, 1967–78; 387, 1983–# [m]
Gm 1982, Jan–June; 1985–#
Lbbc 1969–#
Lbl*
Lcml 519, 1988–#
Lgo 489/90, 1986–#*
Lsa 2–116, 1967–72 [w 8, 24, 26, 28–41, 46,
    57, 76, 82, 84, 88, 105, 114]; 129–229,

1973–76*; 259– 408, 1978–83*; 421,
1984–#*
Mpl 1968–#*
Msuc 1993, July–#
NOTu 1992–#
Ob 95–218, 1971–76
Rp [c]

Rolling Stone Review
GB–Poole, 1985–
[NOT IN BUCOMP1]

BSdsc*
Cu 1, 1985–#*
Ob 1, 1985–#

Rolling Stones Book
GB–London, 1964–66

Cu 1–29, 1964–66ᴸ
Lbl*
Ob 1–29, 1964–66

Ronald Stevenson Society Newsletter
GB–Edinburgh: Ronald Stevenson Society,
1994–
[NOT IN BUCOMP1]

Ep 1, 1994–#

Rondo: die Zeitschrift der internationalen Verständigung
TNG A233
A–Vienna, 1953–
[NOT IN BUCOMP1]

LAu 1 (1953)

Rostrum
GB–Cambridge, 1971–

EIR:Dtc 1 (1971), 1
Ob*

The Rotunda: a Journal of Artistic Organ-Building and Musical Progress
TNG GB311
GB–London: Henry Willis and Son, 1925–34

AB*
Bs 1930, Sep; 1933, Mar–Apr, Sep
Cu 1 (1925/27), 3–5 (1934), 3
EIR:Dtc 1 (1925/27), 3–5 (1934), 3
En 1 (1925/27)–5 (1934)
Gm 1 (1925/27)–5 (1934)
Lam 1 (1925/27)–4 (1931/33)

Lam (o) 1925–32
Lbl*
Lcm 1 (1927)–5 (1934), 2
Lrco 1 (1925/27)–4 (1931/33); 5 (1934), 1–3
LVp 1 (1925/27)–5 (1934), 2
Mpl 1 (1925/27)–5 (1934)
Ob*
SOu 1 (1925/27)–5 (1934)
Yu 1 (1925/27)–5 (1934)

The Royal Academy of Music Academic Yearbook
GB–London, 1989–
[NOT IN BUCOMP1]

Lam 1989/90–1991/92

Royal Academy of Music Bulletin
GB–London: Royal Academy of Music,
1968–73
[NOT IN BUCOMP1]

Lam 1–10, 1968–73

Royal Academy of Music Club Magazine
TNG GB187
GB–London: The Royal Academy of Music,
1900– 94
[Entitled the *Royal Academy of Music
Magazine: Incorporating the Official Record of
the RAM Club* from issue 107, 1937]

ALb 197, 1969; 200, 1971; 202, 1972; 238,
1985
Cu 199, 1970–#
EIR:Dtc 199, 1970–#
En 205, 1972–#
Lam 1, 1900–# [w 245, 1989; 251, 1992]
Lbl*
Lcm 91, 1931; 112, 1938; 185–207, 1963–75;
211, 212, 1976; 217, 1978; 224, 1980; 230–
235, 1982–84; 237–240, 1985–86
Lcm (p) 193, 1967; 206, 207, 1974–75
LEbc 61–117, 1924–40*
Lu 150–183, 1951–62; 190–229, 1966–82;
231–243, 1983–87 [w 234, 235]
Mcm 230–244, 1982–87 [w 234]
Ob*

The Royal Academy of Music Magazine: Incorporating the Official Record of the RAM Club *see* Royal Academy of Music Club Magazine

Royal Academy of Music News
GB–London: Royal Academy of Music, 1986–
89
[NOT IN BUCOMP1; entitled *Royal Academy
of Music Newsletter* (q.v.) from Sep 1989, with
various numbering sequences]

   Lam 1986–89 [w 1988, Jan–1989, Apr]

Royal Academy of Music Newsletter
GB–London: Royal Academy of Music, 1989–
[NOT IN BUCOMP1]

   Cu 1992–94; 1996–#
   Lam 1989–91, Apr; 1992–93*; 1994, Apr–#
   Lcm (p) 1992, Sep; 1993, Sep

**Royal Academy of Music Students' Union
News** *see* **R.A.M.S.U. News**

The Royal Academy Student
GB–London: Royal Academy of Music, 1936
[NOT IN BUCOMP1; only two issues were
published]

   Lam 1936, Mar, Dec

Royal Albert Hall
GB–London, 197?–
[NOT IN BUCOMP1]

   Lcm (p) 1974/75–1978; 1983

Royal Canadian College of Organists *see*
Music: the A.G.O. Magazine

Royal College of Music: Annual Review
GB–London: Royal College of Music, ?–
[NOT IN BUCOMP1]

   Cu 1995–#

Royal College of Music: Report of the Council
GB–London: Royal College of Music, 1913–
[NOT IN BUCOMP1]

   Ob*

Royal College of Music News
GB–London: Royal College of Music, 1985–
[NOT IN BUCOMP1]

   Lbl*

Royal College of Music *see also* **The R.C.M.
Magazine**

**The Royal College of Organists: Calendar and
Annual Report** *see* **The College of Organists:
Prospectus and [1st-] Annual Report**

**Royal College of Organists: [29th etc.] Annual
Report** *see* **The College of Organists:
Prospectus and [1st-] Annual Report**

Royal College of Organists: Year Book
0080–4320
GB–London: Royal College of Organists, 1964–
1993
[NOT IN BUCOMP1; formerly entitled *The
College of Organists: Prospectus and [1st-]
Annual Report* (q.v.)]

   BRp 1964–93
   EIR:Dp 1987–92
   Lam 1964–92
   Lcm 1965–93
   Lu*
   Ob*

Royal College of Organists *see also* **R.C.O.
Journal**

The Royal Military Musical Journal
GB–London: J. J. Ewer, 1854
[NOT IN BUCOMP1; 8 nos in total]

   Lbl 1–8, 1854

Royal Musical Association Newsletter
GB–London [etc.]: Royal Musical Association,
198?–97; 1998–
[NOT IN BUCOMP1; relaunched 1997, Sep as
RMA Newsletter; 1997, Sep issue numbered 0.
Vol. 1 no. 1 issued 1998, Mar]

   Au 1985, Sep–#
   EIR:Dtc 1987–#
   Lbl 1986–#
   Ouf*

**Royal Northern College of Music Old
Students' Association Magazine** *see* **Northern
School of Music Old Students' Association
Magazine**

Royal Opera House Annual Report
TNG GB469
GB–London: Royal Opera House, 1957–
[NOT IN BUCOMP1]

    Lcm (p) 1957/58; 1961/62–1979/80; 1981/82
    Lcml (r) 1957/58 [w 1975/76, 1986/87]
    Lkc 1965; 1968–81
    NTp 1958/59–1982/83; 1985/86–#
    Ob*

Royal Opera House News *see* News: the
Royal Ballet, the Royal Opera, the
Birmingham Royal Ballet

Royal Opera House News *see also* R.O.H.
News

The Royal Opera Yearbook
GB–London: Royal Opera House, 1979–

    EIR:Dtc 1979/80–1980/81
    Lcm (p) 1979/80–1980/81

Royal Philharmonic Orchestra Yearbook and
Music-Lover's Guide
GB–London: Royal Philharmonic Orchestra,
1983–
[NOT IN BUCOMP1]

    Ob 1983–#*

Royal School of Church Music Annual
Report
TNG GB331
GB–Croydon: Royal School of Church Music,
1929–
[NOT IN BUCOMP1]

    AB 1988–91
    Cu 1994–#
    Ob 1963–#*

Royal School of Church Music News
TNG GB504
GB–Croydon: Royal School of Church Music,
1963–70
[At some time entitled *R.S.C.M. News and
Treble Clef*; incorporated into *Promoting Church
Music* (q.v.)]

    AB 16–28, 1966–69
    Cu 1–29, 1963–70
    EIR:Dtc 1–29, 1963–70
    Lbl*

    Lcml 1–29, 1963–70
    Ob*
    Ouf 2–29, 1962–70

Royal Scottish Country Dance Society:
Bulletin
GB–Edinburgh: The Scottish Country Dance
Society, 1924–
[NOT IN BUCOMP1]

    En 34, 1956; 58, 1980–#

RPM Weekly
GB–London: Music Industry Research
Organisation, 1991–
[NOT IN BUCOMP1]

    Cu 1 (1991)–#*
    EIR:Dtc 1 (1991)–#

R.S.A.M.D.
GB–Glasgow: Royal Scottish Academy of
Music and Drama, ?–
[NOT IN BUCOMP1]

    En

R.S.C.M. News [and Treble Clef] *see* Royal
School of Church Music News

R.S.V.P.: Record Sales Various Prices: the
Record Collector's Journal
GB–London, 1965–?74

    Cbijs 49–76, 1969–74
    LOnjfa*
    Lsa 6–57, 1965–74

R.T.É Guide
1821–6231
EIRE–Dublin: Radio Telefís Éireann, 1963–

    EIR:Dtc 5 (1968), 10; 7 (1970)–#

R.T.É. Music Diary
EIRE–Dublin: Radio Telefís Éireann, 197?–
[Entitled *Music Diary* from 1977]

    EIR:Dtc 1973–76, Oct/Nov; 1977–83,
    Jan/Mar

Ruch Muzyczny [1] [= Musical Life]
TNG PL101
PL–Krakow: Polskie Wydawnictwo Muzyczne,
1945–49
[Ceased publication with vol. 5, no. 16 (1949)]

    Lbl*

Ruch Muzyczny [2] [= Musical Life]
TNG PL116; 0035–9610
PL–Warsaw: Wydawnictwa Artystycne i
Filmowe; Biblioteka Narodowa, 1957–

ALb 21 (1977), 8, 9
Lbl*
Lcml 1 (1957)*; 6 (1962)–7 (1963)*; 8
(1964)–12 (1968); 13 (1969)*; 14 (1970)–
15 (1971); 16 (1972)–17 (1973)*; 18
(1974)–#
Lu 6 (1962), 33; 7 (1963), 2–24; 8 (1964), 1–
13, 15–24; 10 (1966), 1–20
Ob*

**Rumble: the Magazine for Collectors of
Instrumental Records**
GB–Mansfield: SMG Publications, 197?–
[NOT IN BUCOMP1]

Lsa 4 (1984)–5 (1985)

Rural Music
TNG GB363
GB–Hitchin: Federation of Rural Music
Schools, 1937–40
[Continued as *Making Music [1]* (q.v.)]

Ep 1 (1937/38)–2 (1938/39); 3 (1939/40), 1,
2; 4 (1940/41), 1
Lbl*
Lu 1 (1937/38)–4 (1940/41), 1

Rural Music Schools Association: Bulletin
GB–Hitchin: The Rural Music Schools
Association, 1972–77

Lbl*
Mcm 14, 15, 1977
Re 14, 15, 1977

**The Rushworth and Dreaper Concert and
Entertainment Calendar and Music Teachers'
Directory** *see* Liverpool Concert and
Entertainment Calendar

Rushworth and Dreaper Concert Calendar
see Liverpool Concert and Entertainment
Calendar

Russian Musical Journal [translated title] *see*
Russkaya Muzykal'naya Gazeta

**Russkaya Muzykal'naya Gazeta [= Russian
Musical Journal]**
Fellinger 1968/1278; TNG USSR19
RF–St Petersburg, 1894–1917

Lbl*

**Russkaya Muzïkal'naya Literatura
[= Russian Musical Literature]**
RF–Leningrad: Muzyka, Leningradskoe
Otdelenie, 1974–
[NOT IN BUCOMP1]

Lbl*

Rythme
TNG ET6
EG–Alexandria: Conservatoire de Musique
d'Alexandrie W. Axisa, 1951–?

LAu 5, 1954

Rytmi
TNG SF18
FIN–Helsinki: Suomen Jazzliitto, 1949–

Cbijs 1964, 11

S

Sabin's Radio Free Jazz USA
0093–0490
US–Washington, DC: Sabin's Discount
Records, 1961–?

Cbijs 13 (1973), 10; 14 (1974), 1, 2, 7, 8, 10;
15 (1975), 1–6

The Sackbut: a Musical Review
TNG GB284
GB–London, 1920/21–1933/34
[Succeeded *The Organist and Choirmaster*
(q.v.); ceased publication with vol. 14, no. 7
(1934)]

AB*
ALp 2 (1921/22), 4, 6–9
Bp 1 (1920/21), 1, 5, 6, 8; 2 (1921/22), 7; 3
(1922/23)–14 (1934), 7
Bu 5 (1924/25); 8 (1927/28)
Cu 1 (1920/21)–14 (1934), 7*
En 1 (1920/21)–14 (1934)
Ep 6 (1925/26), 9–12; 7 (1926/27)–12
(1931/32), 3
Gm 1 (1920/21), 1
Lam 13 (1932/33), 1

Lbl*
Lcm 1 (1920/21), 2–9; 2 (1921/22), 1
Lcml 1 (1920/21)–13 (1932/33)
Lu 2 (1921/22); 4 (1923/24)–11 (1930/31)*
Mpl 1 (1920/21)–14 (1934)
Ob 1 (1920/21)–14 (1934), 7

The Sacred Melodist
GB–London, 1885–?94

AB 1 (1885)–2 (1886)
Mpl 1885–94

The Sacred Musician: a Sacred Music Magazine
TNG US522
US–South Pasadena, CA: Harkness Music Company, 1932–

Lbl*

Sadler's Wells Opera Annual Report
GB–London: Sadler's Wells Opera, 197?–
[NOT IN BUCOMP1]

Lcm (p) 1972/73; 1973/74

Sadler's Wells Opera Magazine
GB–London: Sadler's Wells Opera Club, 1965–70

ALb 4, 1966
EIR:Dtc 1–10, 1965–68
Lbl*
Lcm (p) n.s. 2 (1969/70), 3
Lcml n.s. 2 (1969/70), 1–4
Mpl n.s, 2 (1969/70)
Ob*

Il Saggiatore Musicale
I–Florence, 1994–
[NOT IN BUCOMP1]

Cu 1 (1994)–#
Ouf 4 (1997)–#
RHBNC 1 (1994)–#

Sagittarius: Beiträge zur Erforschung und Praxis alter und neuer Kirchenmusik
0080–5408
D–Kassel [etc.]: Bärenreiter [for the International Heinrich-Schütz-Gesellschaft], 1966–73

Ob 1 (1966)–4 (1973)
Ouf 1 (1966)–4 (1973)

Sailor's Delight see Blues and Rhythm: the Gospel Truth

Saint Cecilia Magazine: a Journal Devoted to Music
Fellinger 1968/905; TNG GB101
GB–Edinburgh, 1882–85
[NOT IN BUCOMP1]

Gm 1 (1882)–3 (1884)
Lbl 1 (1882)–3 (1884), 27
Mpl 1 (1882)–2 (1883)
Ob 1 (1882)–2 (1883)

St Gregorius-Blad: Tijdschrift tot Bevordering van kerkelijke Toonkunst see Sint Gregorius-Blad: Tijdschrift tot Bevordering van Kerkelijke Toonkunst

La Saison Musicale, par une Réunion d'Écrivains Spéciaux
Fellinger 1968/548; TNG F117
F–Paris: A. Faure, 1866
[Only one issue was published]

Lbl 1866
Lu 1866

Salisbury Diocesan Guild of Ringers: Annual Report
GB–Salisbury, 1996–
[NOT IN BUCOMP1]

Cu 1996–#

The Salvation Army Brass Band Journal: General Series
GB–?London, ?–
[NOT IN BUCOMP1]

AB 1988, Apr–1991, July*

The Salvationist
GB–St Alban's, 1986–
[NOT IN BUCOMP1; formerly entitled *Musician of the Salvation Army* (q.v.)]

Cu 1 (1986)–#
En 1 (1986)–#
Lbl*
Ob*

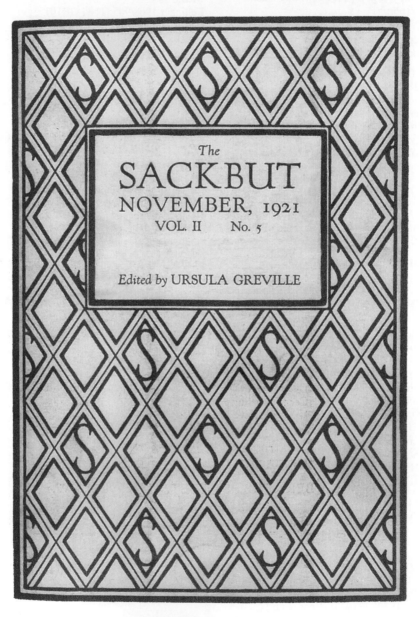

Cover of the November 1921 issue of *The Sackbut*,
edited for a time by Philip Heseltine (Peter Warlock)

Reproduced by kind permission of the British Library

Samfundet til Udgivelse af Dansk Musik: Bulletin
0109–8438
DK–Copenhagen: Samfundet til Udgivelse af Dansk Musik/Society for Publishing Danish Music, 19??–
[NOT IN BUCOMP1]

 Lbl 1981, Aut–#
 Lu 1989–90

Sammelbände der Internationalen Musikgesellschaft
Fellinger 1968/1505; TNG INTL2
D–Leipzig: Breitkopf und Härtel, 1899–1914
[From 1903 bore wrapper title *Quarterly Magazine of the International Musical Society*]

 AB 2 (1900/01)–15 (1913/14)
 ALb 15 (1913/14)
 Au 1 (1899/1900)–15 (1913/14) [Reprint ed.]
 BLu 1 (1899/1900)–15 (1913/14)
 Bu 1 (1899/1900)–15 (1913/14), 3
 Cpl 1 (1899/1900)–15 (1913/14)
 Cu 1 (1899/1900)–15 (1913/14)
 EIR:Dtc 1 (1899/1900)–10 (1908/09)
 Er 1 (1899/1900)–15 (1913/14)
 Gul 1 (1899/1900)–15 (1913/14)
 HUu 1 (1899/1900)–15 (1913/14) [Reprint ed.]
 Lbl*
 Lcm 1 (1899/1900)–15 (1913/14)
 Lcml 1 (1899/1900)–15 (1913/14)
 LEbc 1 (1899/1900)–7 (1905/06); 8 (1906/07), 2; 11 (1909/10)–14 (1912/13)
 Lkc 2 (1900/01)–3 (1901/02); 6 (1904/05); 12 (1910/11)–15 (1913/14)*
 Lu 1 (1899/1900)–7 (1905/06); 12 (1910/11)–15 (1913/14)*
 Lu (RMA) 1 (1899/1900)–15 (1913/14)
 LVu 1 (1899/1900)–15 (1913/14)
 Mpl 1 (1899/1900)–15 (1913/14)
 Ob 1 (1899/1900)–15 (1913/14)
 Ouf 1 (1899/1900)–15 (1913/14)
 R 1 (1899/1900)–12 (1910/11), 3; 13 (1911/12)–15 (1913/14)

Sammelbände für vergleichende Musikwissenschaft
D–Munich, 1922–23

 Cu 1–4, 1922–23 [w 3] [Reprint ed.]

Sammler
A–Vienna: A. Strauss, 1809–?34
[NOT IN BUCOMP1]

 Lu 9/10 (1817/18), 78

Sammlung musikalischer Vorträge
D–Leipzig: Breitkopf und Härtel, 1879–84; 1898
[Ceased publication with no. 63, 1898]

 Er 1 (1879)–6 (1884)
 Lbl*

Sammlung musikwissenschaftlicher Abhandlungen
F–Strasbourg, 1930–39

 Lbl*

Sammlung musikwissenschaftlicher Einzeldarstellungen
D–Leipzig, 1922–35

 Lbl 1–17, 1922–25

Sammlung von Musikstücken alter und neuer Zeit *see* **Neue Zeitschrift für Musik**

San Francisco Opera *see* **San Francisco Opera Magazine**

San Francisco Opera Magazine
US–San Francisco, 1923–
[NOT IN BUCOMP1; later entitled *San Francisco Opera* (ISSN 0892–7189)]

 ALb 1978

Sancta Cecilia *see* **Santa Cecilia**

Sandy Bell's Broadsheet: Scotland's only National Folk Magazine
GB–Edinburgh, 1973–85
[NOT IN BUCOMP1]

 Ep 1 (1973)–4 (1985)*

Sangeet Natak: Journal on the Performing Arts
TNG IN11; 0036–4339
IN–New Delhi: Sangeet Natak Akademi, 1965–

 TOd 83, 1987; 87, 88, 1988; 95, 97, 98, 1990; 99–107, 1991–93

Sängerblatt *see* **Schweizerische Musikzeitung und Sängerblatt: Organ des eidgenossischen Sängervereins**

Sangita [= Music]
IN–Hathras, 1935–
[NOT IN BUCOMP1]

Lso 21 (1955), 6; 22 (1956)–32 (1966), Mar,
May–Dec; 33 (1967)–52 (1986); 57
(1992)–#

Sankeet Kala Vihar [= Journal of the Indian
Musicological Society]
TNG IN13; 0036–4320; 0251–012X
IN–Bombay: Indian Musicological Society,
1970–

ALb 8 (1977), 2, 3; 9 (1978)–11 (1980), 2; 12
(1981), 2–13 (1982), 1; 14 (1983), 1
Cu 4 (1973)–#
En 2 (1971)–#
Lbl*
Lio 1 (1970); 2 (1971)–#
Lsa 5 (1974)–14 (1983), 1
Lso 2 (1971)–#
Ob*

Santa Cecilia
TNG I235
I–Rome: Accademia Nazionale di Santa Cecilia,
1952–
[Also known as *Sancta Cecilia*]

Lam 5 (1956), 5
Lcml 4 (1955)–5 (1956)*

Sant'Andrea Dischi Microsolco
I–Milan, 1954–?72
[NOT IN BUCOMP1]

Lsa 1 (1954)–19 (1972)*

S.A.T.I.P.S. Music Broadsheet
GB–?: Society of Assistants
Teaching in Preparatory Schools, ?–
[NOT IN BUCOMP1]

Re 41–49, 1979–82

Saturday Musical Review: a Record of Music
and the Drama, with which is incorporated
"The Choir"
Fellinger 1968/807; TNG GB93
GB–London, 1879
[42 nos in total; *see also The Choir*]

Bp 1 (1879), 1–42
Lbl 1 (1879), 1–42

The Savoyard
GB–London: D'Oyly Carte Opera Trust, 1962–

BLp 5 (1966)–21 (1982)
Gm 1 (1962)–21 (1982)*
Lam 11 (1972), 3–12 (1973), 2; 13 (1974)–21
(1982), 2
Lcml 1 (1962)–14 (1975), 2
Mpl 4 (1965)–13 (1974)*
Ob*

Saxophone Journal
0276–4768
US–Medfield, MA: Dorn Publications, ?–
[NOT IN BUCOMP1]

CCtc 15 (1991), 5–#
Lsa 11 (1986), 2

Sborník Janáčkovy Akademie Múzických
Umění [= Almanac of the Janáček Academy
of Musical Art]
TNG CS199
CZ–Brno: Janáčova Akademie Múzických
Umění, 1959–
[NOT IN BUCOMP1]

Cpl 3 (1961)–4 (1963)
Er 3 (1961)–4 (1963)
Ob 6 (1972)–#

Sbornik Katedry Hudební Vychový *see* Řada
Hudebné Výchovna

Sborník Praci Filosofické Fakulty Brneské
University, Ser. H: Rada Hudebnevedna [=
Miscellany of the Philosophy Faculty of Brno
University: Musicology]
TNG CS214; 0324–6213; 0524–7233
CZ–Brno: University of Brno, Philosophy
Faculty, 1966–

Ob*

Scala, La: Rivista dell'Opera *see* La Scala:
Rivista dell'Opera

Scene in Southampton
GB–Southampton: Southampton City Council,
1975–78
[NOT IN BUCOMP1; formerly (1964–75)
entitled *Southampton's Programme of Events*]

SOu 1–15, 1975–78

Das Schallarchiv: Informationsblatt der Arbeitsgemeinschaft Österreichischer Schallarchive
TNG A299
A–Vienna: Arbeitsgemeinschaft Österreichischer Schallarchive, 1977–
[From 23, 1988 entitled *Das audiovisuelle Archiv*]

En*
Lsa 1977–#*

Die Schallplatte: Musik aus aller Welt
TNG D947
D–Hamburg: Teldec Schallplattengesellschaft, 1954–59

Lsa 1954, 1, 11; 1955, 2, 9–12; 1956, 1, 3–6, 9–12; 1957; 1958, 1–3, 5, 7, 9, 10; 1959, 1–6

Das Schallplatten ABC: eine deutsche Discographie
D–?, ?1963–?
[NOT IN BUCOMP1]

Lsa 1–11, 1963 [w 4–6, 8, 10]

Scherzo: Revue d'Information sur la Musique et les Musiciens
TNG F710
F–Paris: Vie Musicale, 1971–77
[Entitled *Scherzo Guide Musical* from no. 46, 1975]

Mcm 1973, Nov; 1977

Scherzo Guide Musical *see* Scherzo: Revue d'Information sur la Musique et les Musiciens

The School Music Review: a Monthly Periodical
Fellinger 1968/1196; TNG GB149
GB–London: Novello, 1892–1930
[Ceased publication with no. 456, 1930]

AB*
Cu 1 (1892/93)–38 (1929/30)*
Ep 1 (1892/93)–17 (1908/09); 32 (1923/24)–39 (1930/31)*
Lbl 1 (1892)–38 (1929/30), 456
Lcml 31 (1922/23); 35 (1926/27)*; 38 (1929/30)
LEu 1 (1892/93)–35 (1926/27) [w 29 (1920/21), 9; 35 (1926/27), 2]

Mpl 1 (1892/93)–39 (1930/31)
Ob 1 (1892/93)–39 (1930/31)
Re 35 (1926/27)–38 (1929/30)
TOd 29 (1920/21), 341–39 (1930/31), 452*

Schools Music Association: Annual Report
GB–?: Schools Music Association, ?–
[NOT IN BUCOMP1]

Lie 1985/86–#

Schools Music Association News Bulletin
GB–?: Schools Music Association, 1952–

Lam 102, 1986
Lie 96, 1984; 103, 1987–#

Schubert durch die Brille
D–Tutzing: Hans Schneider [for the Schubert Institute], 1990–
[NOT IN BUCOMP1; published under the series title *Internationale Franz Schubert Institut: Mitteilungen*: first issue was no. 4, nos 1–3 of the series having already been used for other, non serial, items. Each issue has a separate ISBN]

Cpl 8, 1992–#
Ouf 6–12, 1991–94

Schubert Institute (UK) Newsletter
GB–London: Schubert Institute, 1991–
[NOT IN BUCOMP1]

ALb 1, 1991–#
Cpl 1, 1991–#
Ouf 2–9, 1992–94

The Schubertians: Gentleman Singing Pupils of the University of California, Santa Barbara
US–Santa Barbara, CA: University of California, ?–
[NOT IN BUCOMP1]

ALb 1964–89

Schumann Studien
0863–2340
D–Zwickau/Cologne: Rat der Stadt Zwickau, Abteilung Kultur, 1988–
[NOT IN BUCOMP1]

Cu 1 (1988)–#
Lbl*

Schütz-Jahrbuch
D–Kassel: Bärenreiter, 1979/80–

ALb 1982/83
Cu 1979–#
Lbl 1979–#
Lu 1979–87
Mu 1979
Ob 1979–#
Ouf 1979–90
SFu 1979–87

Schwann-1, Record and Tape Guide *see* Schwann Long Playing Record Catalog

Schwann-1, Records, Tapes *see* Schwann Long Playing Record Catalog

Schwann-2, Record and Tape Guide *see* Spectrum

Schwann-2, Records and Tapes *see* Spectrum

Schwann CD *see* Schwann Compact Disc Catalog

Schwann Compact Disc Catalog
0893–0430
US–Boston, MA: Schwann, 1986–90
[NOT IN BUCOMP1; from vol. 4 (1989) entitled *Schwann CD* (ISSN 1042– 5047); ceased publication 1990; absorbed from 1990 into *Opus* [4] (q.v.)]

CAu 1986, July–?4 (1989), 12
Lsa 1 (1986), 3–4 (1989), 12 [w 1 (1986), 4; 3 (1988), 11]

Schwann Long Playing Record Catalog
US–Boston, MA: Schwann, 1949–90
[From vol. 23 (1971), 2–12 entitled *Schwann Record and Tape Guide* (ISSN 0036–715X); from Nov. 1970 to Jan. 1971 entitled *Schwann Stereo Record Guide*; from vol. 24 (1972) to 26 no. 4 (1974) entitled *Schwann-1, Record and Tape Guide* (ISSN 0160–1571); from vol. 26 no. 5 (1974) to 29 no. 6 (1977) entitled *Schwann-1, Records, Tapes* (ISSN 0098–356X); from vol. 29 no. 7 (1977) to 35 (1983) entitled *Schwann-1, Record and Tape Guide*; from vol. 35 no. 12 (1983) to 38 no. 5 (1986) entitled *The New*

Schwann Record and Tape Guide (ISSN 0742–7239); from vol. 38 no. 6 (1986) to 42 no. 1 (1990) entitled *Schwann/Super Schwann* (ISSN 0893–0449); then absorbed into *Opus* [4] (q.v.)]

CAu 22 (1970), 1, 7; 1972–86, June
Lbl*
Lsa 4 (1952)–38 (1986), 4 [w 36 (1984), 2]
Lu 20 (1968), 9–26 (1974), 3*
Mp 36 (1984)–42 (1990), 1
Mu 27 (1975)–42 (1990)*

Schwann Opus *see* Opus [4]

Schwann Record and Tape Guide *see* Schwann Long Playing Record Catalog

Schwann Spectrum *see* Spectrum

Schwann Stereo Record Guide *see* Schwann Long Playing Record Catalog

Schwann/Super Schwann *see* Schwann Long Playing Record Catalog

Schweizer Beiträge zur Musikwissenschaft
CH–Bern: Paul Haupt, 1972–80
[NOT IN BUCOMP1]

Lu 1, 1972
Mu 4, 1980
Ouf 3, 4, 1980

Schweizer Jahrbuch für Musikwissenschaft
CH–Bern: Paul Haupt [for the Schweizerische Musikforschende Gesellschaft], 1981–
[*See also* the *Schweizerisches Jahrbuch für Musikwissenschaft*]

Cu 1981–#
Lu 1991–#
Mu 1981–#
Ob*
Ouf 1981–82

Schweizer Musik auf Schallplatten/Musique Suisse sur Disques/Swiss Music on Records
CH–Zurich: Schweizerisches Musik–Archiv, 1976–
[NOT IN BUCOMP1]

Lbl*

Schweizer Musikpädagogische Blätter/
Feuillets Suisses de Pédagogie Musicale
TNG CH53
CH–Zurich: Schweizerischer Musikpädogischer
Verband, 1912–47, 1949–?60
[NOT IN BUCOMP1; from 1960 incorporated
into *Schweizerische Musikzeitung und
Sängerblatt: Organ des eidgenossischen
Sängervereins* (q.v.)]

    Lam 72 (1984), 1

Schweizerische Jazz-Zeitschrift *see* Jazz,
Rhythm and Blues

Schweizerische Musikzeitung: offizielles
Organ des Schweizerischen
Tonkünstlervereins und der "SUISA",
Schweizerische Gesellschaft der Urheber und
Verleger/Revue Musicale Suisse: Organe
Officiel de l'Association des Musiciens Suisses
(AMS) et de la SUISA, Société Suisse des
Auteurs et Éditeurs *see* Schweizerische
Musikzeitung und Sängerblatt: Organ des
eidgenossischen Sängervereins

Schweizerische Musikzeitung und
Sängerblatt: Organ des eidgenossischen
Sängervereins
Fellinger 1968/442; TNG CH4; 0036–7710
CH–Zurich: Hug [for the Gesellschaft
Schweizerische Musikzeitung], 1861–1983
[Entitled *Schweizerische Musikzeitung:
offizielles Organ des Schweizerischen
Tonkünstlervereins und der "SUISA",
Schweizerische Gesellschaft der Urheber und
Verleger/Revue Musicale Suisse: Organe
Officiel de l'Association des Musiciens Suisses
(AMS) et de la SUISA, Société Suisse des
Auteurs et Éditeurs* from 77 (1937)–99 (1959);
entitled *Schweizerische Musikzeitung, Schweizer
musikpädagogische Blätter/Revue Musicale
Suisse: Feuillets Suisses de Pédagogie Musicale*
from 100 (1962)–123 (1983). Succeeded by
*Dissonanz/Dissonance: die neue schweizerische
Musikzeitschrift* (q.v.)]

    BSdsc*
    Bu 114 (1974)–123 (1983)
    Cpl 74 (1934), 14/15, 16/17
    Cu 69 (1929)–123 (1983)
    EIR:Duc 121 (1981)–123 (1983)
    Er 103 (1963)–123 (1983)
    Gul 113 (1973)–123 (1983)
    Lam 111 (1971), 4; 113 (1973), 4–123
      (1983), 6

LAu 74 (1934)–96 (1956)*
Lbl*
Lcm 123 (1983), 4–6
Lcml 78 (1938)*; 83 (1943)–84 (1944)*; 86
  (1946)–90 (1950)*;91 (1951)–94 (1954);
  108 (1968)–123 (1983)
Lki 119 (1979)–123 (1983)
Lu 76 (1936), 14/15; 90 (1950), 10; 101
  (1961), 6; 104 (1964)–123 (1983)
LVu 113 (1973)–123 (1983), 6
Mu 113 (1973)–123 (1983)
Ob*
Ouf 100 (1960)–123 (1983), 6*
SFu 113 (1973)–123 (1983)

Schweizerisches Archiv für Volkskunde
0036–794X
CH–Basel: Schweizerisches Archiv für
Volkskunde; Zurich: Emil Cotti, 1897–
[NOT IN BUCOMP1]

    Lcs 80 (1984), 3–#*

Schweizerisches Jahrbuch für
Musikwissenschaft
TNG CH80
CH–Basel: Heinrich Majer, 1924–38
[From 1933 has parallel title *Annuaire de la
Nouvelle Société Suisse de Musique*; continued
as the *Schweizer Jahrbuch für
Musikwissenschaft* (q.v.)]

    AB 1 (1924)–5 (1931)
    Cu 1 (1924)–7 (1938) [Reprint ed.]
    Lbl*
    Lcml 1 (1924)
    Ob*
    Ouf 1 (1924)–7 (1938)

Schweppes Rock Yearbook *see* Rock Year
Book

S.C.I. Journal of Music Scores *see* A.S.U.C.
Journal of Music Scores

S.C.O. News
GB–Edinburgh: Scottish Chamber Orchestra,
1995–#
[NOT IN BUCOMP1]

    Ep 1, 1995–#

Score
TNG IN6
IN–Bombay, 1952–
[NOT IN BUCOMP1]

    Lam 6 (1957), 7

The Score *see* The Score: a Music Magazine

The Score: a Music Magazine
TNG GB427
GB–London: International Music Association, 1949–61
[Entitled *The Score and I.M.A. Magazine* from 1954, 10; *The Score* from 1957, 22]

ALb 17, 1956; 28, 1961
Au 25–28, 1959–61
Bp 1–28, 1949–61
BRp 1–28, 1949–61
BTp 1–28, 1949–61*
Bu 1–27, 1949–60
CDu 11–27, 1955–60
Cpl 1–28, 1949–61
Cu 1–28, 1949–61
DRu 1–28, 1949–61
EIR:Dtc 1–28, 1949–61
En 1–28, 1949–61
Ep 1– 28, 1949–61
Er 1–28, 1949–61
EXu 1–28, 1949–61
Gam 24–26, 1958–60; 28, 1961
Gm 1–28, 1949–61
HUu 1–28, 1949–61
Lam 1, 1949; 3–5, 1950–51; 7–27, 1952–60
LAu 1–6, 1949–52
Lbar 1–5, 1949–51; 19, 21, 1957 –28, 1961
Lbbc 1–11, 1949–55; 14–27, 1956–60
Lbl*
Lcm 1–28, 1949–61
Lcm (p) 1–28, 1949–61*
Lcml 1–28, 1949–61
LEbc 1–28, 1949–61
Lgo 1–28, 1949–61
Ltv 1–27, 1949–60 [w 2–4, 6, 9, 12, 13, 18]
Lu 1–28, 1949–61
LVp 1–28, 1949–61
LVu 15,1956
Mcm 26–28, 1960–61
Mpl 1–28, 1949–61
Mu 1–28, 1949–61 [Reprint ed.]
Ob 1–28, 1949–61
Ouf 1–28, 1949–61
R 1–28, 1949–61
SFu 1–28, 1949–61
SOu 1–28, 1949–61
TOd 11, 1955
Yu 1–28, 1949–61

The Score and I.M.A. Magazine *see* The Score: a Music Magazine

Scottish Arts Council Bulletin
0144–2821
GB–Edinburgh: Scottish Arts Council, 1980–82
[NOT IN BUCOMP1]

Gam 6–10, 1981; 12–14, 1982

Scottish Ballet Magazine
GB–Glasgow: Friends of Scottish Ballet, 1978–
[NOT IN BUCOMP1]

EIR:Dtc 1 (1978)–12 (1991)

Scottish Central Committee on Music: Newsletter
GB–Aberdeen (nos 1–4); Dundee (nos 5–7): Consultative Committee on the Curriculum, 1980–
[NOT IN BUCOMP1]

Gam 1–7, 1980–85
Lbl 5, ?1984–#*

Scottish Chamber Orchestra Year-Book
0144–722X
GB–Edinburgh: Scottish Chamber Orchestra, 1979–

Lbl*
SA 1985/86

Scottish Chamber Orchestra *see also* S.C.O. News

Scottish Country Dance Society Bulletin
GB–Edinburgh: The Scottish Country Dance Society, 193?–
[NOT IN BUCOMP1]

Lcs 3–7, 1933–35 [w 6]; 64 (1986)–68 (1990)

Scottish Country Dancing Euronews
GB–?Edinburgh, ?–
[NOT IN BUCOMP1]

En 116, 1991–#

Scottish Country Music Express
0263–2527
GB–Glasgow, 1982
[NOT IN BUCOMP1]

Cu 1982, Jan–Sep
Lbl*

Scottish Dance Archives
GB–Liverpool: Clowes and Donald, ?–
[NOT IN BUCOMP1]

    EIR:Dtc 1972, Sep–1982, Sep

The Scottish Dancing Journal
GB– Glasgow, 1933–?

    Lbl*

Scottish Folk Arts Directory
GB–Edinburgh: Scottish Folk Arts Group, ?–
[NOT IN BUCOMP1; later entitled *Scottish Folk Directory*]

    Ep 1980; 1982–85; 1988; 1990; 1992/93
    Ob 1985–#

Scottish Folk Directory *see* Scottish Folk Arts Directory

Scottish Folk Gazette: Diary and News of the Scottish Folk Scene
GB–Kilmarnock: Inform, 1994–
[NOT IN BUCOMP1]

    Cu 1994
    Ob 1994–

Scottish Folk Notes
GB–Glasgow: Glasgow Folk Centre, 1969–
[NOT IN BUCOMP1; entitled *Folk Notes* from no. 2, 1970]

    EIR:Dtc 1, 2, 1969–70
    Ob 1, 1969–#

Scottish Jazz Network Programme
GB–?: Scottish Jazz Network, ?–
[NOT IN BUCOMP1]

    En*

Scottish Music and Drama *see* Con Brio: a Scots Music Magazine for the Modern Music Lover

The Scottish Music Guide
GB–Glasgow: Music in Scotland Trust, ?–
[NOT IN BUCOMP1]

    Ep 1994

Scottish Music Hall and Variety *see* Sir Harry Lauder Society Newsletter, incorporating Scottish Music Hall and Variety

Scottish Music Handbook
GB–Glasgow, 1995–
[NOT IN BUCOMP1]

    Au 1995–#
    Cu 1995–#

Scottish Music Press
GB–Perth, 1974–?

    En 11–18, 1975

Scottish Musical Magazine
TNG GB272
GB–Edinburgh, 1919–31

    Au 7 (1925/26), 59 (1927/28), 9
    Cu 9 (1927/28)–12 (1930/31), 3
    EIR:Dtc 9 (1927/28)–12 (1930/31), 3
    En 9 (1927/28)–12 (1930/31), 3
    Ep 4 (1922/23), 5–12; 5 (1923/24)–9
       (1927/28); 10 (1928/29), 1–5; 11
       (1929/30)–12 (1930/31), 3
    Er 1 (1919/20)–9 (1927/28), 9
    Gm 7 (1925/26)–12 (1930/31)
    Gul 1 (1919/20)–12 (1930/31)
    Lbl*
    Mpl 1 (1919/20)–12 (1930/31)
    Ob*

The Scottish Musical Monthly
TNG GB158
GB–Glasgow, 1893–96

    Ap 1 (1893)–3 (1896)
    En 1 (1893)–3 (1896)
    Ep 1 (1893)–3 (1896)
    Gm 1 (1893)–3 (1896)
    Lbl*
    Mpl 1 (1893)– **2** (1895)

Scottish Musical Review
GB–Glasgow, 1894–97

    Gm 1894, Oct 1–1897, June 4*

Scottish National Orchestra Scene *see* SNO Scene

Scottish National Orchestra Yearbook
GB–Glasgow: Scottish National Orchestra, ?–

    Cu 1973/74–1976/77

Scottish Opera Magazine
TNG GB550
GB–Glasgow: Scottish Opera, 1966–?74
[Succeeded by *Scottish Opera News [2]* (q.v.)]

En*
Ep 1966–73
Gul 1966–74*
Lam 1968, Spr, Aut, Win; 1969, Spr, Aut;
 1970, Aut; 1971, Aut; 1972, Aut
LAu 1968, Aut
Lcm 1966, Spr, Aut, Win; 1967, Spr, Win;
 1968 [w Sum]; 1969, Spr, Win; 1970
 [w Sum]; 1971, Spr, Aut; 1972, Aut
Lcm (p) 1967, Aut, Wint; 1968, Spr, Aut;
 1969, Aut; 1972, Spr, Aut; 1973, Spr, Aut
 [+ Special Edition "The case for the
 Theatre Royal"]

Scottish Opera News [1]
TNG GB515
GB–Glasgow, 1964–69

En 1964, 1, 3

Scottish Opera News [2]
TNG GB577; 0309–7323
GB–Glasgow: Scottish Opera, 1976–8?
[Superseded *Scottish Opera Magazine* (q.v.)]

EIR:Dtc 1–25, 1976–78
En 1, 1976–#
Ep 1–113, 1976–88*
Gm 1976, Oct–1986, May
Gul 1976–87
Lam 11, 1977; 72, 1982; 88–89, 1984
NTp*
Ob*

Scottish Opera Yearbook
GB–Glasgow: Scottish Opera, 1975–

ALb 1986/87
Cu 1984/85–#
Gul 1975–1987/88
Ob*
SA 1984/85
SLGu 1975–76

The Scottish Organist: the Annual Journal of the Scottish Federation of Organists
GB–Aberdeen: Scottish Federation of Organists,
1985–
[NOT IN BUCOMP1]

Ep 1 (1985)–2 (1986)
Lam (o) 1 (1985)–6 (1993)

The Scottish Philharmonic Club Newsletter
GB–?: Scottish Philharmonic Club, ?–
[NOT IN BUCOMP1]

Ep 1979–87

Scottish Pipe Band Monthly
GB–South Queensferry: Dal Riada, ?1988–
[NOT IN BUCOMP1]

Cu 8–15, 1988–89
EIR:Dtc 2–15, 1988–89

Scottish School Music
GB–Edinburgh, 1946–?

Gm 2–9, 1946–50

Scottish Society of Composers Newsletter
0261–3018
GB–Glasgow: Scottish Music Archive, 1980–88
[From 1981 entitled *Stretto* (ISSN 0263–5763);
succeeded from 1988 by *Music Current: the
Best Way of Finding Out about Music in
Scotland* (q.v.)]

Au 2 (1982), 4–7 (1988), 4
Cu 1 (1980)–7 (1988), 4
EIR:Dtc 1 (1980)–7 (1988)*
En 1 (1980)–7 (1988)
Ep 1980–88
Er 1 (1980), 2–7 (1988)
Gam 1 (1980), 1–6; 2 (1982), 1, 3, 4; 3
 (1983)–4 (1984), 2, 3; 5 (1985)–6 (1986),
 1, 4; 7 (1987), 2
Gsmic 1 (1980)–7 (1988)
Gul 4 (1984)–7 (1988)
Lam 1 (1980)*; 2 (1982), 3, 4; 4 (1984), 3–7
 (1988), 1, 3
Lbbc 4 (1984)–7 (1988)*
Lbl*
Lcm 1 (1980)–7 (1988)*
Lcml 1 (1980)–#
Lsa 2 (1982)–7 (1988)*
Mcm 5 (1985), 1, 3; 6 (1986), 3; 7 (1988), 1
Ob*
SA 2 (1982), 2; 3 (1983), 3; 7 (1988), 4

Scream: Pop Journal [translated title] *see*
Sgrech: Cylchgrawn Pop

Second Line
TNG US624; 0037–0576
US–New Orleans: New Orleans Jazz Club,
1950–

    Cbijs 4 (1953), 1, 2, 4, 7, 8; 5 (1954), 11, 12;
    6 (1955), 1, 2, 7–10; 7 (1956), 1, 2; 8
    (1957), 1–8, 11,12; 13 (1963), Sep–Oct
    LOnjfa*
    Lsa 2 (1951)–19 (1968)*

Select
0959–8367
GB–London: Emap Metro, 1990–
[NOT IN BUCOMP1]

    Lbbc 1, 1990–#
    Lsa 1–8, 1990–91 [w 3, 7]
    Ob*

**Selected Reports [of the University of
California Institute of Ethnomusicology]**
TNG US764; 0361–6622
US–Los Angeles, CA: University of California
Institute of Ethnomusicology, 1966–
[Entitled *Selected Reports in Ethnomusicology*
from 2 (1974)]

    BLu 1 (1966/70); 2 (1974)–#
    Cpl 1 (1966/70), 1–3; 2 (1974)–#
    Cu 1 (1966/70)–#
    DRu 2 (1974)–3 (1978)
    Lgo 1 (1968), 2– #
    Lsa 10 (1994)–#
    Lu 1 (1966/70), 1–3; 2 (1974)–#
    Ob*
    Ouf 1 (1966/70)–8 (1990)
    Yu 1 (1966/70)–#

S.E.M. Newsletter
TNG US779; 0036–1291
US–Ann Arbor, MI: Society for
Ethnomusicology, 1967–
[Entitled *Society for Ethnomusicology
Newsletter* from 1981]

    BLu 7 (1973)–#
    CDu 5 (1971)–18 (1984)
    Cu 15 (1981), 1
    EIR:Dtc 19 (1985)–#
    EXu 18 (1984), 2–#
    Gam 23 (1989); 24 (1990), 1, 2, 4; 25
    (1991)–26 (1992), 1, 2, 4; 27 (1993)–#

Lcu 9 (1975)–#
Lgo [c]
Lki 11 (1977), 4– #
LRHBNC 12 (1978)–#
Lsa 1 (1967)–#*
Lu 2 (1968), 4–#
Mu 22 (1988)–#*
NO 11 (1977), 1; 15 (1981)–24 (1990)
Ob*
Ouf 4 (1970)–26 (1992), 4*
SLGu 14 (1980)–#
TOd 15 (1981)–#*

**Serial: Newsletter of the Friends of the Arnold
Schoenberg Institute/USC School of Music**
1045–3482
US–Los Angeles: Arnold Schoenberg Institute,
University of Southern California, 1987–
[NOT IN BUCOMP1]

    ALb 1 (1987), 3; 2 (1988), 1

Servicio Oficial de Difusion Radio Electrica
see Revista del S.O.D.R.E.

Set to Music
GB–London: Eye to Eye Publications, 1976–?88
[Later absorbed into *New Sixth* (q.v.)]

    ALb 4 (1979/80), 1
    BDp 3 (1978)–11 (1987)
    Bs 6 (1981/82), 4–10 (1985/86), 1*
    CCtc 2 (1977/78)–12 (1987/88)
    Cpl 3 (1978), 1; 4 (1979/80), 2; 7 (1982/83),
    4; 8 (1983/84), 1–5; 9 (1984/85), 1
    Cu 5 (1980/81), 3–12 (1987/88), 1
    EIR:Dtc 4 (1979/80)–12 (1987/88)
    Ep 4 (1979/80), 1, 3–8; 5 (1980/81)–6
    (1981/82), 6; 7 (1982/83), 1–5; 8 (1983/84),
    1–5; 9 (1984/85), 1–4; 10 (1985/86), 1–4;
    11 (1986/87), 1–4; 12 (1987/88)
    Er 2 (1977/78), 2–12 (1987/88)
    Gam 3 (1978/79), 4; 4 (1979/80), 1, 4
    Lam 2 (1977/78), 3; 10 (1985/86), 3
    Lcml 2 (1977/78)*; 3 (1978/79); 4
    (1979/80)*; 5 (1980/81)–12 (1987/88), 5
    Lcs 4 (1979/80)– 5 (1980/81)
    Mcm 4 (1979/80), 6–8; 5 (1980/81)–6
    (1981/82), 6; 7 (1982/83), 1–5; 8 (1983/84),
    2–5; 9 (1984/85), 1, 2, 4; 10 (1985/86), 2–
    4; 11 (1986/87), 1–5; 12 (1987/88), 1, 2
    Ob*

Seven Arts
0037–2986
GB–London: Hansom Books, 1958–
[NOT IN BUCOMP1; monthly cumulation of
Art and Artists; *Books and Bookmen*; *Dance and
Dancers*; *Film and Filming*; *Music and
Musicians*; *Plays and Players*; and *Records and
Recording*]

> **Gam** 4 (1960/61), 3–10, 12; 5 (1961/62), 5–7,
> 9–11; 1962, Sep, Oct; 1963, Jan, Apr–June

Seventy Eight RPM *see* **78 RPM**

**Sgrech: Cylchgrawn Pop [= Scream: Pop
Journal]**
GB–Caernarvon: Sgrech, 1978–85
[Ceased publication with no. 40, 1985]

> **AB***
> **Lbl***

**Sheet Music: the Magazine of the
International Sheet Music Industry**
GB–Ashford: Plus PR Ltd [for the International
Sheet Music Industry], 1994–
[NOT IN BUCOMP1]

> **ALb** 2, 1994
> **Cu** 1, 1994–#
> **TOd** 1, 1994–#

Sheffield University Jazz Club Magazine
GB–Sheffield: Sheffield University Jazz Club,
1966–?

> **Cbijs** 1–4, 1966–67

Sheng Hsueh Hsueh Pao *see* **Acta Acustica**

Shindig *see* **B.B.C. Folk Club Magazine**

Shire Folk
GB–Bicester: J. Eastmond, S. Rose, 197?–
[NOT IN BUCOMP1]

> **Bu-AYp** 1978–87
> **Lbl***

Shout *see* **Soul Music**

Show Times *see* **A.I.M.S. Bulletin**

Showcase International Music Book *see*
Kemp's International Music Book

**Sibelius-Akatemian Julkaisuja [= Proceedings
of the Sibelius Academy]**
0359–2308
FIN–Helsinki: Sibelius Academy, 1982–
[NOT IN BUCOMP1]

> **Lbl***

**Sibelius-Akatemian Koulutusjulkaisusarja [=
Proceedings in Education of the Sibelius
Academy]**
FIN–Helsinki: Sibelius Academy, 1982–
[NOT IN BUCOMP1]

> **Lbl***

The Sibelius Society
GB–Hayes: Gramophone Company [for the
Sibelius Society], 1932–?
[NOT IN BUCOMP1]

> **Lcm** 2, 1933
> **Lsa** 1–6, 1932–?

**Sic: Sibelius-Akatemian Vuosikirja [=
Yearbook of the Sibelius Academy]**
0781–0423
FIN–Helsinki: Sibelius Academy/Sibelius-
Akatemia, 1983–
[NOT IN BUCOMP1]

> **Lbl** 1983–90

**Sightline: Journal of Theatre Technology and
Design**
0265–9808
GB–London: Association of British Theatre
Technicians, 1967–
[NOT IN BUCOMP1]

> **Lgsm** 20 (1986)–26 (1992), 1*

Signale für die musikalische Welt
Fellinger 1968/213; TNG D98
D–Leipzig: Bartholf Senff, 1843–1941
[Ceased publication with vol. 99 (1941)]

> **Er** 28 (1870)*; 31 (1873)–35 (1877)*
> **Lbl*** [w 5 (1847); 7 (1849)–9 (1851); 11
> (1853); 15 (1857)]
> **Lcm** 1 (1843)–12 (1854); 15 (1857)–16
> (1858); 18 (1860)–21 (1863); 28 (1870); 35
> (1877)–37 (1879); 66 (1908)
> **Mpl** 10 (1852)–12 (1854)
> **Ob** 2 (1844); 3 (1845), 10–13 (1855); 15
> (1857); 19 (1861), 21 (1863)–23 (1865); 26
> (1868)–42 (1884); 62 (1904)–68 (1910); 70
> (1912)

Silences
F–Paris: Editions de la Différence/Silences,
1985–
[NOT IN BUCOMP1]

> Cu 1 (1985)–#

S.I.M. Revue Musicale Mensuelle *see* Le
Mercure Musical

Simrock Jahrbuch
D–Berlin: Simrock, 1928–30

> Lbl*
> Lu 1 (1928)–2 (1929)

Sinfonye: the Journal of the Hurdy-Gurdy
Society
GB–Hemel Hempstead [etc.]: Hurdy-Gurdy
Society, 1982-
[NOT IN BUCOMP1]

> Cu 7 (1993)–#
> Lcs 1 (1982)–7 (1993)
> Ob 7 (1993)–#*

Sing
TNG GB457
GB–London: Eric Winter, 1954–74
[From 1961, Sep. entitled *Sing: Britain's Folk
Song Magazine*]

> Cu 1 (1954)–9 (1966), 1
> Lbl*
> Lcs 1–65, 1954–74

Sing: Britain's Folk Song Magazine *see* Sing

Sing Out!: the Folk Song Magazine
TNG US651; 0037–5624
US–New York: Sing-Out Corporation, 1950–

> BDp*
> EIR:Dp 31 (1985)–#
> En*
> Lbl*
> Lcml 14 (1964)*; 16 (1966)–17 (1967)*
> Lcs 1 (1950)–#*
> Lsa 1 (1950)–28 (1980)*
> Ob*
> Ouf (Howes) 6 (1956/57), 4; 7 (1957), 1, 2; 8
> (1958), 1; 16 (1966), 4

Sing to the Lord *see* Musical Salvationist

Singabout: the Quarterly Magazine of the
Bush Music Club
0037–5632
AUS–Wooloomooloo: Bush Music Club,
1956–?67

> Lcs 1 (1956), 3, 4; 2 (1957/58)–6 (1966), 1
> Lgo 1 (1956)–5 (1965)
> Lsa 2 (1957/58), 2; 4 (1960/61), 1, 2

The Singer
0969–9686
GB–London: Rhinegold Publishing, 1993–
[NOT IN BUCOMP1; supplied free with
Classical Music (q.v.)]

> ALb 1 (1993), May–#
> Bs 1 (1993)–#
> Bu 1 (1993), Oct–#
> Cat 1 (1993)–#
> CDCp 1 (1993), May–#
> Cu 1 (1993)–#
> DOR 2 (1994)–#
> EIR:Dp 1 (1993)–#*
> EIR:Driam 1 (1993)–#
> EIR:Dtc 1 (1993), May–#
> En 1 (1993)–#
> Ep 1 (1993)–#
> Gsmic 1 (1993)–#
> HE 1 (1993), May–#
> Lam 1 (1993), July, Aug, Oct, Dec;
>   2 (1994), 3–#
> Lbar 1 (1993)–#
> Lbl*
> Lbo 1 (1993), May–#
> Lcm 1 (1993)–#
> Lgo 1 (1993), May, July–#
> Lgsm 1 (1993)–#
> Lsa 1 (1993)–#
> Ltc 1 (1993)–#*
> Lu 1 (1993)–#
> Mcm 1 (1993), May–#
> Mu 1 (1993)–#
> Ob*
> TOd 1 (1993)–2 (1994), 3

Singing
GB–?London, 1981–
[NOT IN BUCOMP1]

> CCtc 5–10, 1983–86
> Lgsm 1, 1981–#

Sint Gregorius-Blad: Tijdschrift tot
Bevordering van Kerkelijke Toonkunst
= Journal for the Promotion of Church
Music]
Fellinger 1968/729; TNG NL23; 0017–4122
NL–Haarlem: Nederlandsche St Gregorius-
Vereeniging, 1876–1941; 1946–
[NOT IN BUCOMP1; from 1959 entitled
Gregoriusblad]

   Lbl 37 (1912)–44 (1919)

Sir Arthur Sullivan Society Magazine *see* Sir
Arthur Sullivan Society Newsletter

Sir Arthur Sullivan Society Newsletter
0261–6610
GB–Royston: Sir Arthur Sullivan Society,
1977–
[Entitled *Sir Arthur Sullivan Society Magazine*
from no. 9, 1980]

   Cu 7, 1980–#
   EIR:Dtc 1, 1977–#
   En*
   Lam 8–14, 1980–83; 16–31, 1983–90; 34,
     1991–#
   Lbar 8, 1980–#
   Lbl*
   Lcml 8, 1980–#
   Ob*
   SFu 1–23, 1977–86*

Sir Harry Lauder Society Newsletter,
incorporating Scottish Music Hall and Variety
GB–Edinburgh: Sir Harry Lauder Society,
1979–
[NOT IN BUCOMP1]

   Ep 1, 1979–#

Sir Thomas Beecham Society Bulletin *see* The
Sir Thomas Beecham Society News-Letter

The Sir Thomas Beecham Society News-
Letter
TNG GB524
GB–London; Westcliff-on-Sea: Sir Thomas
Beecham Society, 1965–87
[Ceased publication with no. 128, 1987;
originally entitled *Supplementary Newsletter,
Sir Thomas Beecham Society*; and *Sir Thomas
Beecham Society Bulletin*]

   Cu 4–128, 1967–87
   EIR:Dtc 4–128, 1967–87
   En*

   Lbar 1–128, 1965–87
   Lcml 60–62, 64, 66, 1976/77; 69–128, 1978–
     87
   Lsa*
   Ob 4–128, 1967–87*

Siren: the Credible Alternative
0963–1194
GB–Birmingham: Pegasus, ?1991–
[NOT IN BUCOMP1; rock music periodical]

   Lbl*

Skiv Spegeln (Klassica) [= Record Mirror
(Classical)]
S–Stockholm, ?1957–

   Lsa 2 (1958)–5 (1962)*; 13 (1970)–14
     (1971), 2

Skivsamlaren [= Record Collector]
S–Goteborg, 19??–
[NOT IN BUCOMP1]

   Cu 11, 12, 15, 1981–#

Sky
0955–6915:
GB–London, 1987–
[NOT IN BUCOMP1]

   Lcml (q) [c]
   Lk [c]
   Ob 1, 1987–#*

Slovak Music
TNG CS224; 0862–0407
SQ–Bratislava: Information Centre of the
Slovak Music Fund, 1969–?90; n.s. 1991–

   ALb n.s. 1 (1991)–2 (1992)
   BSdsc*
   Lbar 1989, 2–1990, 3/4; n.s. 1 (1991)*
   Lbbc 1970–81*; 1982–90; n.s. 1 (1991)–2
     (1992)
   Lcm*
   Lcm (p) 1982, 4; 1983, 1; 1985, 2/3–1989, 4
   Lkc 1969–84*
   Lki 1979–89*
   Lsa 1978–80*; 1984–89*
   Ouf 1971, 3–1990 [w 1986, 1; 1987]; n.s. 1
     (1991)–2 (1992) 1]

Slovak Music: Journal of the Union of Slovak
Composers [translated title] *see* **Slovenská
Hudba: Časopis Zväzu Slovenských
Skladateľov**

Slovenská Hudba: Časopis Zväzu
Slovenských Skladatel'ov [= Slovak Music:
Journal of the Union of Slovak Composers]
TNG CS192; 0037–6965
SQ–Bratislava, 1957–71
[Ceased publication with vol. 15, 1971]

Lbl*
Ob*
Ouf 3 (1959), 9–15 (1971), 7

Slovenská Narodna Bibliografia, Registracny
Rad. Serie H: Hudobniny [Music]
SQ–Martin: Matica Slovenska, 1981–

Ob 1981–#

Slow Air
GB–Belfast: Arts Council of Northern Ireland,
1976–

BLu 1 (1976), 1–3
EIR:Dtc 1 (1976), 1, 2
Ob*

Smash Hits
0260–3004
GB–Peterborough: Emap Publications, 1978–

AB 10 (1988), 21
CH [c]
Cu 1 (1978)–#
En 1 (1978)–#
Lbbc 14 (1992), Apr–#
Lcml [c (6 months)]
Lcml (cg) [c]
Lcml (m) [c (1 month)]
Lcml (pim) [c (2 issues)]
Lcml (q) [c (3 months)]
Lcml (sjw) [c]
Len [c]
Lgr [c]
Lha (f) [c (1 year)]
Lis [c]
Lk [c]
Lk (b) [c]
Lk (c) [c]
Lk (nk) [c]
Ll [c]
Lsa 1986–#
Lwf [c]
Lwwb [c]
Ob*
PRp [c (3 months)]
RH [c]

WCp [c]
WCp (a) [c]
WCp (b) [c]
WCp (cf) [c]
WCp (e) [c]
WCp (far) [c]
WCp (fle) [c]
WCp (g) [c]
WCp (l) [c (3 months)]
WCp (lp) [c]
WCp (p) [c]
WCp (pet) [c]
WCp (r) [c]
WCp (se) [c]
WCp (t) [c (3 months)]
WCp (w) [c]
WH [c]
WOp [c]

Smash Hits Yearbook
GB–London, 1985–
[NOT IN BUCOMP1]

Cu 1985–

Smetana: Hudební List [= Musical Leaf]
Fellinger 1968/2047; TNG CS88
CZ–Prague: series 1, 1911–35; series 2, 1936–
[NOT IN BUCOMP1]

Ob series 2, 1 (1936)–2 (1938)

Sniffin' Glue
GB–Deptford, 1976–?77
[NOT IN BUCOMP1]

Lsa*

SNO Scene
0140–9379
GB–Glasgow: Scottish National Orchestra,
1977–

Cu 3–62, 1977–91*
EIR:Dtc 3–62, 1977–91
En*
Lbl*
Ob*

Social Dance and Ceilidh
GB–London: English Folk Dance and Song
Society, 1993–
[NOT IN BUCOMP1]

Lcs 1, 1993–#

Sociedad Folklorica de Mexico: Anuario
TNG M4
ME–Mexico City: Sociedad Folklorica de
Mexico, 1942–

    Lu 1 (1942)–7 (1951)*

Sociedad Uruguaya pro Opera: Revista
URG–?: Sociedad Uruguaya pro Opera, ?1986–
[NOT IN BUCOMP1]

    Lu 4 (1989), 5–8; 5 (1990), 5

**Société des Amis de la Phonothèque
Nationale: Bulletin**
F–Paris, 1961–74

    Lsa 1, 1961; 2–4, 1962

Société d'Études Mozartiennes: Bulletin
TNG F546
F–Paris: Librairie "Au Pont d'Europe", 1930–32

    Cu 1930–32
    Lu 1930–32

**Société Française de Musicologie: Rapports et
Communications** *see* Bulletin de la Société
Française de Musicologie

Society for Ethnomusicology Newsletter *see*
S.E.M. Newsletter

Society for Folk Life Studies Newsletter
GB–Leeds: Society for Folk Life Studies, 1985–
[NOT IN BUCOMP1]

    Lcs 1 (1985)–#

**Society of Assistants Teaching in Preparatory
Schools** *see* S.A.T.I.P.S. Music Broadsheet

Society of St Gregory: Annual Report
GB–?: Society of St Gregory, ?–
[NOT IN BUCOMP1]

    Cu 1996–#

SOKOJ Letter *see* Bilten, SOKOJ

Solent Waves
GB–?Southampton: English Folk Dance and
Song Society, South Hampshire District, 1977–
[NOT IN BUCOMP1]

    SOu 1, 1977–#

Y Solffaydd [= Tonic Sol-Fa]
Fellinger 1968/1175; TNG GB146
GB–Pontardulais, 1891–92

    AB 2–8, 13, 14, 1891–92
    BG 1 (1891)– 2 (1892)
    Lbl 1–12, 1891

Solid and Raunchy
GB–Hitchin, 1973–74

    Cbijs 13, 1974

**Somerset Music Maker: Journal of the
Somerset Fellowship of Music and the
Somerset Associations of Organists and
Choirmasters**
GB–Taunton, ?–?

    Y 17, 1951–#

Son
F–Paris, 197?–
[NOT IN BUCOMP1]

    Lsa 79–111, 1977–80

**Sonda: Problema y Panorama de la Música
Contemporanea**
TNG E99; 0584–1135
E–Madrid: Juventudes Musicales, 1967–

    HUu 1 (1967)–6 (1973)
    Lam 6 (1973), May 6
    Lcm 4 (1968)

Song [1]
GB–London, 1895

    Lbl*

Song [2]
D–Erlangen: R. Geleker, ?1985–
[NOT IN BUCOMP1]

    Lcs 2 (1986)

Song [translated title] *see* Énekszó

Song and Music Bulletin [translated title] *see*
Věstník Pěvecky a Hudební

**Song and Speech: a Monthly Journal of
Practical Information for Singers, Speakers,
Preachers and Teachers**
Fellinger 1968/1176; TNG GB140
GB–London, 1891–92

    Lbl 1 (1891)–2 (1892)
    Mpl 1 (1891)–2 (1892)

Song Bulletin [translated title] *see* **Věstník Pěvecky**

Song, Dance and Screen Monthly
GB–London, 1931

> **Lbl***

Song Hit Guild Folio
US–New York, 1936–?

> **Lbl***

The Song Service Reporter: a Journal chiefly devoted to Sunday School Music
Fellinger 1968/1147; TNG GB137
GB–Leeds, 1890–?

> **Lbl***

Songs from the Ship and Castle
GB–Bristol, 1929–?

> **EIR:Dtc** 5 (1934); 8 (1937)–9 (1938)
> **Lbl***

Songsmith
GB–Walsall; Crewe, 1977–79

> **Cu** 1–7, 1977–79
> **EIR:Dtc** 1–7, 1977–79
> **En***
> **Lcs** 1–7, 1977–79

The Songster's Jewel
GB–London, 1823

> **Lbl***

The Songwriter [1]
GB–London, 1937

> **Lbl***

Songwriter [2]
EIRE–Limerick: International Songwriters Association, 1967–
[Also known as *The Songwriter: ISA Magazine*]
[NOT IN BUCOMP1]

> **Cu** 85, 1983–#
> **EIR:Dtc** 1980–#
> **En***
> **Lbl***

The Songwriter: ISA Magazine *see* **Songwriter [2]**

Songwriters Review *see* **Melody World**

Songwriting and Composing
GB–Penzance: Society of International Songwriters and Composers, ?–
[NOT IN BUCOMP1]

> **Lcs** 1987, 2–1988, 3

Sonic Arts Network Journal
1355–7726
GB–London: Sonic Arts Network, 1989–
[NOT IN BUCOMP1; from no. 6, 1992, entitled *Journal of Electroacoustic Music*]

> **Lgu** 5, 1991–#
> **TOd** 27–33, 1993–94

The Sonneck Society Bulletin *see* **The Sonneck Society Newsletter**

The Sonneck Society Newsletter
0196–7967
US–Boulder, CO [etc.]: The Sonneck Society, 1975–
[NOT IN BUCOMP1; from vol. 13 (1987), entitled *The Sonneck Society Bulletin*]

> **Bu** 9 (1983)–#

Sonorum Speculum: Mirror of Musical Life
TNG NL106; 0038–1438
NL–Amsterdam: Donemus Foundation, 1958–74
[Succeeded by *Key Notes: Musical Life in the Netherlands* (q.v.)]

> **AB***
> **BG** 1–15, 1958–63; 41, 1969
> **BLu** 2–57, 1958–74*
> **Bp** 12, 1962; 14–57, 1963–74
> **BRu** 3–57, 1959–74 [w 8, 36, 41]
> **Bs** 23–48, 1965–71; 52–57, 1973–74
> **BSdsc***
> **Bu** 4–57 [w 9, 15, 34], 1960–74
> **Cpl** 1–57, 1958–74
> **Cu** 1–57, 1958–74
> **EIR:Dtc** 45–57, 1970–74
> **EIR:Duc** 2–57, 1958–74
> **En** 1–57, 1958–74
> **Ep** 1–13, 1958–62
> **Er** 1–57, 1958–74
> **Gam** 2–15, 1958–63; 17–22, 1963–65; 24–28, 1965–66; 30, 31, 33, 1967; 35–37, 1968; 39–49, 1969–72; 52–57, 1973–74
> **Gul** 1–57, 1958–74
> **HUu** 1–57, 1958–74

Lam 1–57, 1958–74 [w 19, 1964]
LAu 33, 1967
Lbbc 2–57, 1958–74 [w 25, 31, 35, 37]
Lbl*
Lcm 2–5, 1958–60; 8–51, 1961–72; 53–56, 1973–74
Lcml 1–49, 1958–71; 52–57, 1972–74
LEbc 8, 10–57, 1961–74
Lgo 44–57, 1970–74
Lkc 1–57, 1958–74 [w 55, 1974]
Lsa 1–57, 1958–74 [w 18–21, 37, 55]
Lu 2–57, 1958–74 [w 4, 20]
LVp 2–57, 1958–74
LVu 2–57, 1958–75
Mcm 49–57, 1971–74
Mpl 1–57, 1958–74
Mu 20–57, 1964–74
Ob*
Ouf 3–57, 1959–74
R 18–57, 1964–74
SFu 3–57, 1959–74*
TOd 20, 1964; 52–54, 1973; 56, 57, 1974

Sonus: Materiali per la Musica Contemporanea
1121–5380
I–Potenza: Sonus, 1989–
[NOT IN BUCOMP1]

Lbl 1 (1989)–#

Soul and Jazz Record see **Phonograph Record Magazine**

Soul Bag: le Magazine du Blues et de la Soul
0398–9089
F–Paris, 1968–
[NOT IN BUCOMP1]

Lsa 1–23, 1968–73 [w 11, 1970]

Soul Cargo
0140–7422
GB–Newcastle-under-Lyme, 1977–79

Cu 1–12, 1977–79
En 1–12, 1977–79
Lbl*
Ob*

Soul CD
0966–5471
GB–London: Sequel Records, 199?–
[NOT IN BUCOMP1]

Lbl*

Soul Music
GB–Chislehurst, 1967–?77
[From 1968 entitled Shout (ISSN 0583–1296)]

Cu 8–110, 1968–76
Lsa 34–112, 1968–77
Ob*

Soul Sounds see **Soul Sounds and Stars**

Soul Sounds and Stars
US–New York, ?–1976
[NOT IN BUCOMP1; later entitled Soul Sounds]

LOnjfa*

Soul Underground
0958–5729
GB–London: Soul Underground Ltd, 1987–
[NOT IN BUCOMP1]

Lbl*

Sound
GB–London, 1946–?

Cbijs 1946, Jan, Feb, Apr, Dec; 1947, Mar; 1949, Jan

Sound: Music Review [translated title] see **Zvuk: Revija za Muziku**

Sound: the Monthly Music Magazine
AUS–Sydney, 1967–68

Lsa 1–9, 1967/68 [m]

Sound and Communications
0038–1845
US–Port Washington, NY [etc.]: Sound and Communications, ?1955–
[NOT IN BUCOMP1]

NOTu 1982–#

Sound and Picture Tape Recording Magazine see **Tape Recording and Reproduction Magazine**

Sound and Vision see **Tape Recording and Reproduction Magazine**

The Sound Box: Official Monthly
TNG GB277
GB–Liverpool, 1919–20

Lbl*

Sound Engineer and Producer
0957–9508
GB–London, 1984–
[NOT IN BUCOMP1]

Lsa 1984–90*

Sound International
0144–6037
GB–Croydon: Link House Publications, 1978–81
[From 1980 incorporated with *Beat Instrumental, Songwriting and Recording*; itself later incorporated into *Studio Sound* (q.v.)]

Cu 1–40, 1978–81
En 1–40, 1978–81*
Lbl*
Ob*

Sound 'n Vision
EIRE–Dublin, ?1983–
[NOT IN BUCOMP1]

EIR:Dtc 1983, 1–3

Sound on Sound: Europe's No. 1 Hi-Tech Music Recording Magazine
0951–6816
GB–St Ives, Cambridgeshire: Sound on Sound, 1986–
[NOT IN BUCOMP1; incorporated *Recording Musician* (q.v.) in May 1993]

AB 1 (1985)–#
Cu 1 (1985)–#
EIR:Dtc 1 (1985)–#
Lam 8 (1993), 3–#
Lbar 8 (1993), 3–#
Lgsm 6 (1991)–#
Lki [c (5 years)
Lmi 5 (1990)–#
Lro 9 (1994)–#
Lsa 1 (1985), 2, 9–#
Mmu (d) 8 (1993), 9–#
Msuc [c (5 years)]
Ob*
Oub 6 (1991), 7–#
TOd 7 (1992), 6–#

Sound Recording and Reproduction
GB–London: British Sound Recording Association, 1945–62
[From vol. 6 (1959) entitled *Journal of the British Sound Recording Association*]

AB 7 (1962)
BSdsc*
Cu 3 (1948)–7 (1962), 2*
EIR:Dtc 3 (1948), 2–7 (1962), 2
En 3 (1948)–7 (1962)
Lbl*
Ob*

Sound Recordings Group Newsletter
GB–London [etc.]: Library Association Audiovisual Group, 1969–72
[From 1972, 7 entitled *Audiovisual Group Bulletin*; from 1973 absorbed by *Audiovisual Librarian* (q.v.)]

EIR:Dtc 7, 1972
Mcm 1969–72
Ob*

Sound Scrutiny *see* Cassette Scrutiny

Sound Verdict
GB–Camden: Camden Libraries and Arts Department, 1969–81

EIR:Duc 8 (1976)–13 (1981)
Lkc 1 (1969)–6 (1974)
Mpl 1 (1969)–12 (1980)
Ob*

Sound Waves: Journal of the Edinburgh Competition Festival Association
GB–Edinburgh: Edinburgh Competition Festival Association, 1987–
[NOT IN BUCOMP1]

Ep 1–5, 1987–89

Sounding Board: Newsletter of the Dartington Institute of Traditional Arts and Centre for Asian Music
GB–Totnes: Dartington College of Arts, ?1970–?
[NOT IN BUCOMP1]

TOd 1970

Sounding Brass and the Conductor
TNG GB558; 0308–5554
GB–London: Novello, 1972–82
[Ceased with vol. 10 no. 3 (1982); incorporated into *Brass International*; *see also The Conductor: the Quarterly Journal of the National Association of Brass Band Conductors*]

    AB 1 (1972)–7 (1978), 1; 10 (1982), 2, 3
    BDp 1 (1972)–9 (1980)
    CCtc 2 (1973)–10 (1982)
    Cu 1 (1972)–9 (1980)
    EIR:Dtc 1 (1972)–9 (1980), 4; 10 (1982), 1–3
    En*
    Lam 1 (1972)–9 (1980) [w 5 (1976), 1]; 10 (1982), 1, 3
    Lcml 2 (1973); 3 (1974)*; 4 (1975)–10 (1982), 3
    Mcm 3 (1974)–10 (1982), 1
    Mpl 1 (1972)–9 (1980)
    Ob*

Soundings
TNG US823; 0049–1373
US–Santa Fe, CA [etc.]: Peter Garland, 1970–

    Cu 1–16, 1970–90
    HUu 1–13, 1970–85
    LCdM 3–9, 1972–75
    Lu 5–16, 1973–90
    NWu 7–10, 1973–76
    Yu 1–13, 1970–85 [w 12]

Soundings *see also* **Aldeburgh Soundings: the Newsletter of the Friends of the Aldeburgh Foundation**

Soundings: a Musical Journal
TNG GB551; 0081–2080
GB–Cardiff: University College, Cardiff, 1970–85
[Ceased publication with no. 13, 1985]

    AB*
    ALb 1, 1970; 3–4, 1973–74; 10, 1983; 12, 1984
    Au 1–13, 1970–85
    BG 1–13, 1970–85
    BLu 1–13, 1970–85
    Bp 1–13, 1970–85
    Bs 7–12, 1978–84*
    Bu 1–13, 1970–85
    CDu 1–13, 1970–86
    Cu 1–13, 1970–85

    EIR:Dtc 1–13, 1970–85
    EIR:Duc 1–11, 1970–84
    En 1–13, 1970–85
    Er 1–11, 1970–84
    EXu 1–13, 1970–85
    Gam 1–13, 1970–85
    Gul 1–13, 1970–85
    Lbbc 1–13, 1970–85 [w 5, 1975]
    Lbl*
    Lcm 1–13, 1970–85
    Lcml 1–13, 1970–85
    LEc 1–13, 1970–85
    Lgo 1–13, 1970–85
    Lkc 1, 1970; 3–13, 1973–85
    Lki 1–11, 1970–84
    LRHBNC 1–13, 1970–85
    Lu 1–13, 1970–85
    LVp 1–5, 1970–75
    LVu 1–13, 1970–85
    Mpl 1–13, 1970–85
    Mu 1–13, 1970–85 [w 7, 1978]
    NO 1–13, 1970–85
    NWu 1–13, 1970–85
    Ob*
    Ouf 1–13, 1970–85R 1–13, 1970–85
    SA 1–13, 1970–85
    SFu 1–13, 1970–85

Soundmaker *see* **Electronic Soundmaker and Computer Music**

Soundpost *see* **M.A.I. Monthly Bulletin**

Sounds
TNG GB552; 0144–5774
GB–London: Spotlight Publications, 1970–92

    EIR:Dtc 1970–88, Feb 27
    En*
    Gm 1974–83
    Lsa 1971, Mar–1991 [w 1974, Dec–1984, Mar]
    Ob*

Sounds Alternative: Free Radio Campaign, Ireland
EIRE–Dublin: Free Radio Campaign, 1977–81
[NOT IN BUCOMP1]

    EIR:Dtc 1–14, 1977–81

Sounds and Fury
0584–1690
US–Utica, NY: Castell [etc.], 1965–

    Cbijs 1 (1965), 4; 2 (1966), 1, 2

Sounds Australian: Journal of Australian
Music *see* Australia Music Centre: Quarterly
Newsletter

Sounds Fan Library
GB–London: Spotlight, 1982–83
[NOT IN BUCOMP1; heavy metal magazine]

　Lbl*

Sounds Guitar Heroes *see* Guitar Heroes

Sounds Vintage: the Leading Magazine for
the Vintage Sound Enthusiast
0268–5329
GB–Barnehurst: Sounds Vintage, 1979–
[NOT IN BUCOMP1]

　Lbl*
　Lsa 1 (1979)–6 (1985)

Soundtrack
GB–Ashstead, 1950–51
[NOT IN BUCOMP1]

　Ob 1950–51*

Soundwaves
0963–6846
GB–London: Dennis Oneshots, 1991–
[NOT IN BUCOMP1; Guns 'n' Roses fanzine]

　Lbl*

Source: Music of the Avant Garde
TNG US780
US–Davis, CA: Composer/Performer Edition,
1967–74

　Bu*
　Lbl*
　Lcml 10, 11, 1972–73
　Lgo 4–11, 1968–74 [w 8]
　Lkc 1–6, 1967–69; 8–11, 1971/72
　Lu 1–11, 1967–74
　NO 7–11, 1970–74
　Ob 1–11, 1967–74

South African Journal of Musicology/Suid-
Afrikaanse Tydskrif vir Musiekwetenskap
0258–509X
SA–Pretoria: Musicological Society of South
Africa, 1981–
[NOT IN BUCOMP1]

　Cpl 1 (1981); 3 (1983)
　Lbl 1 (1981)–#
　Lu 1 (1981)–#
　Ob 1 (1981)–#*

The South African Music Teacher/Die Suid-
Afrikaanse Musiekonderwyser
TNG SA2; 0038–2493
SA–Cape Town: South African Society of Music
Teachers, 1931–

　Lam 33, 1947
　Lbl*

The South African Musical Review
TNG SA3
SA–Cape Town, 1938

　Lbl*

The South Wales Musical Review: a Monthly
Record and Review
Fellinger 1968/1421; TNG GB1751
GB–Cardiff, 1897

　AB*
　Lbl 1–8, 1897

South West Early Music Forum Journal
GB–?: South West Early Music Forum, 198?–
[NOT IN BUCOMP1]

　TOd 2–4, 1981–82

Southampton's Programme of Events *see*
Scene in Southampton

Southern Arts: Bulletin *see* Southern Arts:
Diary and Review

Southern Arts: Diary and Review
GB–Winchester, 1970–91
[Entitled *Southern Arts: Bulletin* from 1983;
entitled *The Arts Business*, 1990–91 (ISSN
0960–3859)]

　Lbl*
　SOu 1970, Feb–1979; 22–36, 1983–86

Southern Cross
0966–5064
GB–Crewe: P. Scott, 1991
[NOT IN BUCOMP1; Black Sabbath magazine]

　Lbl*

Southern Rag

GB–Farnham, 1979–
[Entitled *Folk Roots* from vol. 6 no. 4 (June 1985)]

BLp [c]
BRp [c (2 years)]
Bs 14 (1992/93)–#*
BTp [c (1 year)]
BYp [c (1 year)]
CDCp [c (2 years)]
CH [c (2 years)]
COp [c (2 years)]
Cu 1 (1979/80)–#
DOR 7 (1985/86)–#
DS [c (2 years)]
EIR:Dp 10 (1988/89)–#
En 7 (1985/86)–#
Gm 7 (1985/86)–#
HA 14 (1992/93)–#
HE 14 (1992/93)–#
IOW 14 (1992/93)– #
Lba [c (1 year)]
Lbar 7 (1985/86)–#
Lbk 10 (1988/89)– #
Lbl 7 (1985/86)–#
Lbo 16 (1994/95)–#
Lcml (p) [c (2 issues)]
Lcs 1 (1979/80)–#
LEc 10 (1988/89)–#
Len [c (1 year)]
Lgsm 12 (1990/91)–#
Lh [c (2 years)]
Lha (f) 10 (1988/89)–# [w 1989, May]
Ll [c]
Lmi 8 (1986/87), 31–#
Lsa 2 (1980/81); 4 (1982/83)–#*
Lsut [c (2 years)]
Ltv 15 (1993/94), 6–#
LVp 11 (1989/90)–#
Lwwb 13 (1991/92), 96–107; 14 (1992/93), 109, 13–#; [c] (2nd copy)
Mpl 9 (1987/88)–#
Msuc 11 (1990)–#
NOp [c (2 years)]
Ob*
Rp 11 (1989/90), 7–#
SFp [c]
SHRp 14 (1992/93)–# [w 15 (1993/94), 4]
SOL 14 (1992/93), 117–126; 15 (1993/94)–#
TOd 9 (1987/88), 51–##
WCp [c]
WF 10 (1988/89), 7–#
WW [c]

Southwestern Musician

TNG US531; 0038–4895
US–San Antonio, TX:Texas Music Teachers Association, 1934–54
[In Sep. 1954 absorbed *Texas Music Educator* (TNG US533) to become *Southwestern Musician/Texas Music Educator* (ISSN 0162–380X)]

Lam 15 (1948), 8
Lcml 18 (1951/52)*

Southwestern Musician/Texas Music Educator *see* Southwestern Musician

Sovetskaya Muzyka: Notnoe Prilozhenie k Zhurnalu "Sovetskaya Muzyka" [= Musical Appendix to the Journal "Soviet Music"]

RF–Moscow, 1952–
[NOT IN BUCOMP1. A musical supplement to *Sovetskaya Muzyka* (q.v.)]

Lbl*
LVu 1957–58

Sovetskaya Muzyka [= Soviet Music]

TNG USSR66; 0131–6818
RF–Moscow: Soyuz Kompozitorov, 1933–43, 1946–
[Included a musical supplement, *Sovetskaya Muzyka: Notnoe Prilozhenie k Zhurnalu "Sovetksaya Muzyka"* (q.v.). From 1993 became a quarterly, under the title *Muzykal'naya Akademiya* (ISSN 0490–1061)]

ALb 1973, 7
Bu 1988–91
Cpl 1940, 1–7, 10, 12; 1941, 1–5; 1943, 1; 1946, 2/3, 10–12Cu 1935–46*; 1977–91*
Ep 1937, 4, 7, 10–12; 1938, 2–12; 1939, 2, 5; 1940, 1, 2
Gul 1936–43; 1946–74*
KE 1979, 1, 2, 4–7; 1980, 3–12
Lam 1948, 2; 1950, 7; 1964, 2; 1970, 1, 2; 1971, 8, 9
Lbl*
Lcm 1965, 9
Lcml 1959*; 1960–64; 1965*; 1966; 1967–68*; 1969–72; 1973*; 1978–#
LEbc 1951–53, 3; 1954–91
Lu 1974, 2, 8; 1975, 3, 6
LVu 1933, 1, 3, 5, 6; 1934–1935; 1936, 2, 4, 6–12; 1937–39, 5, 8–12; 1940, 1, 2; 1957–

74; 1975, 1–8, 11, 12; 1976–78; 1979, 1–5, 7–12; 1980–86
Mcm 1976, 6–1982, 5
NO 1976, 3–1982
Ob 1959–#*
Ouf 1962–71*; 1984–86*; 1991, 6

Soviet Long Playing Records
RF–Moscow, 19?–
[NOT IN BUCOMP; later entitled *Soviet Records*]

Lsa 1961–88*

Soviet Music Chronicle
TNG USSR67
RF–Moscow: USSR Society for Cultural Relations with Foreign Countries, 1939–?

Lcm 1945, Sep, Oct

Soviet Records *see* **Soviet Long Playing Records**

Sovremennaya Muzyka [= Contemporary Music]
TNG USSR50
RF–Moscow, 1924–29
[Ceased publication with no. 32, 1929]

Lbl*

Spanish Train
0955–8519
GB–Exeter: Spanish Train Productions, 1987–
[NOT IN BUCOMP1; Chris de Burgh fanzine]

Lbl*

Speaker
GB–Stockport: Stockport Music and Gramophone Club, 195?–
[NOT IN BUCOMP1]

Mpl 1956–59

Spectra
US–New York, 1974–

Lam 2 (1975), 2, 4; 3 (1976), 2–4; 4 (1977), 1, 3, 4; 5 (1978), 1, 3, 4; 6 (1979)–10 (1983)

Spectrum
0099–0167
US–Santa Fe, NM: Schwann, 1990–?96; Danbury, CT: Valley Record Distributors, ?1998–
[NOT IN BUCOMP1; formerly entitled *Schwann-2, Record and Tape Guide* (ISSN 0271–5783), and *Schwann-2, Records and Tapes*; from 1990–91 entitled *Spectrum* (ISSN 1047–2371); from 1991 entitled *Schwann Spectrum* (ISSN 1065–9161)]

BRp 1 (1990)–#
Lsa 4 (1993), 3–#

Spectrum: the Arts Newsletter of Lewes District Council
GB–Lewes: Lewes District Council, ?–
[NOT IN BUCOMP1]

LT [c]

Spelmannen [= Folk Musician]
0348–5420
S–Hudiksvall: Sveriges Spelmans Riksforbund, 1978–
[NOT IN BUCOMP1]

Lbl 1983–#*

Spin: the Folksong Magazine
0038–7533
GB–Wallasey: B. Davis, 1961–73

Cu 1 (1961)–9 (1973), 4*
Lcs 1 (1961)–9 (1973)
Ob*

Spinners Newsletter
GB–Wallasey: B. Davis Associates, ?–
[NOT IN BUCOMP1]

Lcs 1985, Sum

Spins and Needles
US–Boston, MA, 1955–?

Lsa 1 (1955), 5, 7–13; 2 (1956), 1

Spiral Scratch: the Record Collector's Monthly Magazine
0954–7290
GB–Cambridge: Spiral Scratch, 1988–
[NOT IN BUCOMP1]

Lbl*

Spohr Journal
GB–Etchingham: Spohr Society, 1970–

EIR:Dtc 6 (1979)
Lam 6 (1979)
Lbar 9 (1982)–11 (1984); 15 (1988); 18 (1991)–#
Lbl*
Lcm 1 (1970), 1, 2
Lcml 1 (1970), 1–3
Lsa 1 (1970), 1, 2
Mcm 6 (1979)–9 (1982)
Ob 6 (1979)–9 (1982); 11 (1984)–#

Spohr Society of Great Britain Newsletter
GB–Etchingham: Spohr Society of Great Britain, 197?–

Cu 24, 1978–
EIR:Dtc 24, 1978–#
En*
Lbar 36–38, 1982; 40–48, 1983–85; 57–64, 1987–89; 68–78, 1990–93
Mcm 31–37, 1981–82; 39, 1983

The Sprat: Newsletter of the Alan Rawsthorne Society
GB–Rotherham: Alan Rawsthorne Society, 199?–
[NOT IN BUCOMP1]

ALb 1993, Oct–#

Squawk
GB–London: English Folk Dance and Song Society, 1993–
[NOT IN BUCOMP1]

Lcs 1, 1993–#

St Cecilia Magazine *see* **Saint Cecilia Magazine**

St Gregorius-Blad: Tijdschrift tot Bevordering van Kerkelijke Toonkunst *see* **Sint Gregorius-Blad: Tijdschrift tot Bevordering van Kerkelijke Toonkunst**

Staatliche Hochschule für Musik in Berlin: Jahresbericht *see* **Jahresbericht der Staatlichen Akademischen Hochschule für Musik in Berlin**

The Stage
0038–9099
GB–London: 1880–
[Later entitled *Stage and Television Today*]

AB*
CH [c (3 months)]
En*
Lbl*
Lgsm*
Ltu [c]
NOTu 1991–
Ob*

Stage and Television Today *see* **The Stage**

The Stage Yearbook
GB–London, 1908–28; 1949–

Lbl*
Ob*

Stagebill
US–New York: B. and B. Enterprises, Inc. [for the Lincoln Center for the Performing Arts, New York], 1973–
[NOT IN BUCOMP1]

ALb 2 (1974), 2, 3; 4 (1976), 4; 5 (1977), 7, 8; 6 (1978), 1; 7 (1980), 2, 7

Star File Annual
GB–Feltham: Hamlyn, ?1977–?

Cu 2 (1978)

Star Gossip Monthly
0956–4349
GB–London: Voice Communications, 1988–?
[NOT IN BUCOMP1]

Lbl*

Starblitz
GB–London, 1984–
[NOT IN BUCOMP1]

Cu 1, 1984–#
Ob 2, 1984–#*

Starfile
0965–6499
GB–London: IPC Marketforce, 1992–
[NOT IN BUCOMP1]

Lbl*

Starlight
EIRE–Dublin, 197?–
[NOT IN BUCOMP1]

 EIR:Dtc 14–25, 1976–79

Starzone: the Official Magazine of David Bowie
GB–Watford, 1982–
[NOT IN BUCOMP1]

 Cu 3–17, 1982–87
 Lbl*
 Ob 13, 1984–#*

Stave: the Paper for Students of Music
GB–London: Royal College of Music Students Association, 1966–
[NOT IN BUCOMP1]

 EIR:Dtc 1966
 Ob 1966–#*

Stave News
GB–London: Crescendo, 1984–
[NOT IN BUCOMP1; jazz journal]

 Lbl*

Steinway News
US–Long Island, NY: Steinway, 1935–
[NOT IN BUCOMP1; from 1994 entitled *Lyra: the Music Magazine*]

 Lcm (p) 1982, Spr

Steirischer Tonkünstlerbund: Mitteilungen
A–Graz: Steirischer Tonkünstlerverband, 196?–

 LAu 33–38, 1967–68

Stephen Sondheim Society Newsletter
1352–6340
GB–London: Stephen Sondheim Society, 1993–
[NOT IN BUCOMP1]

 Lbl*

Stereo
US–Great Barrington, MA, 1960–81
[NOT IN BUCOMP1]

 Cpl 1961–65

Stereo: Hi-Fi und Musikmagazin
0340–0778
D–Munich, 1974–

 Lsa 35, 44, 50, 51, 1977; 1978, 1–5, 7–12; 1979, 2, 3, 5, 6, 8; 1980, 4–6, 9–#

Stereo: the Magazine
GB–Poole, 1983–
[NOT IN BUCOMP1]

 Ob 1983–

Stereo Guide
0319–2592
C–Toronto, ?1972–
[NOT IN BUCOMP1; entitled *Stereo-Video Guide* (ISSN 0833–9570) from 1986]

 Lsa 3 (1974), Win–9 (1980)*

Stereo Record Guide
GB–Blackpool: Long Playing Record Library, 1960–73

 Mcm 1960–?73
 Ob*

Stereo Review *see* **Hi-Fi and Music Review**

Stereo Review *see also* **High Fidelity [1]**

Stereo Sound and Music Magazine
GB–London: Print and Press Service, 1959–
[NOT IN BUCOMP1]

 EIR:Dtc 1 (1959/60)*
 Ob 1 (1959/60)–#

Stereoplay
1122–1747
I–Rome, 1972–

 Lsa 58–64, 1978–79

Stereotype: a Birmingham Fanzine
0260–9398
GB–Birmingham, 1981–
[NOT IN BUCOMP1]

 Lbl*

Stereo-Video Guide *see* **Stereo Guide**

Stimmen: Monatsblätter für Musik
TNG D826
D–Berlin: Internationale Gesellschaft für Neue Musik, Sektion Deutschland, 1947–49
[Ceased publication with no. 19, 1949]

 LAu 5, 15, 16, 19, 1948–49

Stop, Open and Reed
US–New York: Skinner Organ Company,
1922–39
[NOT IN BUCOMP1]

   Lam (o) 5 (1929), 1

Story of Pop *see* Radio One Story of Pop

Storyville
0039–2030
GB–Chigwell: Storyville Publications, 1965–95
[Ceased publication with no.162, 1995]

   Cu 25–30, 1969–70; 81–162, 1979–95
   LOnjfa 1–162, 1965–95
   Lsa 1–162, 1965–95
   Ob*
   Ouf 1–162, 1965–95

**The Strad: a Monthly Journal for
Professionals and Amateurs of all Stringed
Instruments Played with the Bow**
Fellinger 1968/1148; TNG GB138; Langley
1994, p. 125; 0039–2049
GB–London: Lavender and Co., 1890/91–

   AB 23 (1912/13)–#
   ALb 62 (1951/52), July
   BDp 84 (1973/74)–101 (1990)
   BLp 70 (1959/60)–#
   Bp 70 (1959/60)–99 (1988), 1–4, 6–#
   BRp 70 (1959/60)–#
   Bs 39 (1928/29)– #
   BSdsc*
   Cat 85 (1974/75), 1009–#
   CCtc 78 (1967/68)– 82 (1971/72)*; 84
      (1973/74)–103 (1992)*
   CDu 87 (1976/77)–88 (1977/78)
   CFp 100 (1989)–#
   Cu 1 (1890/91)–#
   DS 84 (1973/74)–#
   EIR:Dp 90 (1979/80), 1077–#
   EIR:Driam 36 (1925/26)–78 (1967/68)*; 83
      (1972/73)–101 (1990)*; 106 (1995)–#
   EIR:Dtc 67 (1956/57), 800–#
   EIR:Duc 74 (1963/64), 103–#
   En*
   Ep 3 (1892/93)–11 (1900/01); 13 (1902/03),
      145–147, 149–156; 14 (1903/04)–25
      (1914/15); 26 (1915/16), 301–309, 311,
      312; 27 (1916/17)–55 (1944/45); 56
      (1945/46), 661–666, 668–672; 57 (1946–
      47)–#
   Er 1 (1890/91)–36 (1925/26)*
   Gam 69 (1958/59), 7–12; 70 (1959/60)–71

(1960/61), 1–4, 6, 7, 9–12; 72 (1961/62)–
74 (1963/64), 1–10, 12; 75 (1964/65), 1, 3–
8, 10–12; 76 (1965/66), 1, 2, 4–12; 77
(1966/67), 1–6, 8–12; 78 (1967/68)–85
(1974/75), 1–7, 9, 11, 12; 86 (1975/76); 87
(1976/77), 1–11; 88 (1977/78)–91
(1980/81), 2, 3, 6–12; 92 (1981/82), 1–9,
11, 12; 93 (1982/83), 1–3, 5–12; 94
(1983/84), 1–4, 6, 7, 9–12; 95 (1984/85),
1–4, 6–8, 12; 96 (1985/86), 1–9, 11, 12; 97
(1986/87), 1–4, 6–8, 10– 12; 98 (1987/88)–
100 (1989), 1–7, 10–12; 101 (1990)– #
   Gm 18 (1907/08), 205–216; 20 (1909/10),
      229–24 (1913/14), 288; 33 (1922/23),
      385– #
   HE 102 (1991), 1209–#
   HUu 66 (1955/56)–88 (1977/78)
   KE 73 (1962/63), 866, 867; 74 (1963/64),
      887–103 (1992), 1220*
   Lam 53 (1942/43)–#*
   Lbar 76 (1965/66), 909–77 (1966/67), 923;
      78 (1967/68), 925–79 (1968/69), 944; 87
      (1976/77), 1040–90 (1979/80), 1080; 92
      (1981/82), 1093, 1101, 1102; 98 (1987/88),
      1161; 101 (1990)–102 (1991), 1212–1214;
      (1991), 1219; 103 (1992), 1222–#
   Lbl*
   Lcm 1 (1890/91)–22 (1911/12); 50
      (1939/40)*; 56 (1945/46)–66 (1955/56)*;
      70 (1959/60)–72 (1961/62)*; 77 (1966/67)–
      80 (1969/70)*; 82 (1971/72)*; 84
      (1973/74)–#
   Lcml 1 (1890/91)–6 (1895/96); 10
      (1899/1900); 15 (1904/05)–26 (1915/16);
      29 (1918/19)–33 (1922/23); 36 (1925/26)–
      45 (1934/35); 46 (1935/36)– 47 (1936/37)*;
      49 (1938/39)*; 56 (1945/46)*; 60
      (1949/50)*; 61 (1950/51)–#
   Lcml (m) [c (1 year)]
   LEc 74 (1963/64)–103 (1992), 1227, 1229–
      1232; 105 (1994)–#
   Len 76 (1965/66)–97 (1986/87), 8
   Lgo 77 (1966/67)–101 (1990) [w 97
      (1986/87), 1157; 98 (1987/88), 1163, 1165]
   Lgsm 91 (1980/81)–#
   Lkc 95 (1984/85)–96 (1985/86)*
   Lki 80 (1969/70)–102 (1991)*
   Lsut [c (1 year)]
   Ltv 100 (1989)–#
   Lu 17 (1906/07)–66 (1955/56)*; 67
      (1956/57)–#
   LVp 61 (1950/51)–#
   LVu 75 (1964/65)–#
   Mcm 36 (1925/26)–#*
   Mpl 1 (1890/91)–#

Mu 78 (1967/68)–81 (1970/71)
NO 75 (1964/65), 855; 76 (1965/66), 901–90 (1979/80), 1065
NOp [c (5 years)]
NWu 77 (1966/67), 921–89 (1978/79), 1064
Ob*
Oub 106 (1995)–#
Ouf 16 (1905/06), 188–49 (1938/39), 582*
PRp [c]
R 77 (1966/67), 921, 923; 78 (1967/68), 925; 79 (1968/69), 942, 945–947; 80 (1969/70), 949, 950, 952–954, 956–960; 81 (1970/71)–86 (1975/76); 87 (1976/77), 1033–1043; 88 (1977/78), 1055
Rp 105 (1994), 3–#
SFp 86 (1975/76)–101 (1990), Jan–June, Aug–Oct
SFu 78 (1967/68)–98 (1987/88)*
TOd 1 (1890/91); 49 (1938/39), 581; 89 (1978/79), 1060–#
Uu 83 (1972/73)–#*
Yu 63 (1952/53)–#

The Strad International Yearbook
GB–London: Orpheus, 1992–
[NOT IN BUCOMP1]

Lbl*

Straight No Chaser
0958–8124
GB–London: Paul Bradshaw, 1988–
[NOT IN BUCOMP1]

Bs 8, 1990–#
LOnjfa*
Lsa 1–10, 1988–90; 18, 1992–#

The Strand Musical Magazine
Fellinger 1968/1327; TNG GB168 (1st series); TNG GB180 (2nd series)
GB–London: Newnes, 1895–97; n.s. 1898–99

BSdsc*
Cpl 1–6, 1895–97
Cu 1–6, 1895–97; n.s. 1 (1898)–2 (1898), 5
EIR:Driam 1–6, 1895–97
EIR:Dtc 1–6, 1895–97; n.s. 1 (1898)
En 1–6, 1895–97; n.s. 2 (1898), 1–5
Ep 1–6, 1895–97
Er 1–3, 5, 1895–97
Gm 1–6, 1895–97; n.s. 1 (1898)–2 (1898)
Lam 1, 1895
Lbl*
Lcm (p) 1–6, 1895–97
Lcml 1–6, 1895–97; n.s. 1 (1898), 1–3

Lu 1–6, 1895–97
LVp 2, 1895
Mcm 1–3, 1895–96
Mmu 1–6, 1895–97 [w 5]
Mpl 1–6, 1895–97
R 1–6, 1895–97*
SOu 1–4, 1895–96

Strange Things are Happening
0953–5527
GB–St Albans, 1988–
[NOT IN BUCOMP1]

Cu 1 (1988), 1–7
Lbl*
Lsa 1 (1988)–#

Strangled: a Bi-Monthly Enthuzine
0266–1675
GB–Shepperton: Stranglers [musical group] Information Service, 1977–
[NOT IN BUCOMP1]

Cu 17–26, 1984–87
Lbl 16, 1983–#*
Ob 1980–#*

Street Life
GB–London, 1975–
[NOT IN BUCOMP1]

AB 1, 5, 7, 10–12, 14, 16, 17, 1975–76
Lsa 4–17, 1975–76

Street Singer
GB–Eton: Eton College, 1930

EIR:Dtc 1930, Founders Day
Lbl*
Ob 1930 [no more published]

The Street Singer see also Nostalgia [1]

Streets Full of People: the Jonathan King Fanzine
GB–Rochdale: R. Lysons, 1990–
[NOT IN BUCOMP1]

Lbl*

Stretto
GB–London: Mills Music, 1957–?
[NOT IN BUCOMP1]

AB 1957, 1

Stretto see also Scottish Society of Composers Newsletter

Strict Tempo
GB–?: Victor Sylvester Society, ?–
[NOT IN BUCOMP1]

LOnjfa*

String Talk
US–?: American String Teachers' Association,
1959–
[NOT IN BUCOMP1]

Cpl 2 (1960), 2; 3 (1961), 1, 2

Strings: the Fiddler's Magazine
Fellinger 1968/1280; TNG GB160
GB–London, 1894–98

Lbl 1–7, 1894; 21, 1895
Ob 1 (1894)–4 (1898)

Strings: the Magazine for Players and Makers of Bowed Instruments
0888–3106
US–San Anselmo, CA, 1986–
[NOT IN BUCOMP1]

Mcm 41, 1994–#

The Stroller
GB–London, 1905–06

Lbl*
Ob*

Studi di Musica Veneta
0394–4417
I–Milan: Universal Edition (vol. 1, 1968);
Florence: Olschki [for the Fondazione Giorgio
Cini], (vol. 2, 1973, onwards)
[NOT IN BUCOMP1; new series entitled *Studi
di Musica Veneta: Opera e Libretto* from 1990]

Cpl 4 (1988)
Cu n.s. 1 (1990)–#

Studi di Musica Veneta: Opera e Libretto *see* Studi di Musica Veneta

Studi Donizettiani
I–Bergamo: Centro di Studi Donizettiani, 1962–

Cu 1 (1962)–#
Lu 1 (1962)–#

Studi Gregoriani
I–Cremona: Associazione Internazionale per gli
Studi di Canto Gregoriano, 1985–
[NOT IN BUCOMP1]

Bu 1 (1985)–2 (1986)
Cu 1 (1985)–#
Er 1 (1985)–3 (1987)
Ob 1 (1985)–2 (1986)

Studi Musicali
TNG I288; 0391–7789
I–Florence: Olschki [for the Accademia
Nazionale di Santa Cecilia], 1972–

Bu 1 (1972)–#
Cu 1 (1972)–#
DRu 1 (1972)–2 (1973)
Er 1 (1972)–2 (1973); 9 (1980)–#
Gul 8 (1979)–#
LAu 1 (1972)–#
Lbl*
Lkc 4 (1975)–#
LRHBNC 17 (1988)–#
Lu 1 (1972)–#
NO 1 (1972)–11 (1982)
Ob 1 (1972)–#
Ouf 1 (1972)–#
SOu 20 (1991)–#

Studi Pergolesiani
I–?: Scandicci, 1986–
[NOT IN BUCOMP1]

Cu 1 (1986)–#

Studi Verdiani
0393–2532
I–Parma: Istituto di Studi Verdiani, 1982–

Cpl 5 (1988)–6 (1990)
Cu 1 (1982)–#
Lu 1 (1982)–#
Ob*
Ouf 1 (1982)–#

Studia Instrumentorum Musicae Popularis
S–Stockholm: Musikhistoriska Museet, 1969–
[NOT IN BUCOMP1]

Er 2 (1972); 4 (1976)–8 (1985)

Studia Liturgica
0039–3207
NL–Rotterdam: Liturgical Ecumenical Centre
Trust, 1962–
[NOT IN BUCOMP1]

    Lhey 1 (1962)–3 (1964); 8 (1969)–#

Studia Musica
FIN–Helsinki: Sibelius Academy/Sibelius-
Akatemia, 1990–
[NOT IN BUCOMP1]

    Lbl 1990–#

Studia Musicologica Academiae Scientiarum Hungaricae
TNG H89; 0039–3266
H–Budapest: Academia Scientiarum
Hungaricae/Hungarian Academy of Sciences,
1961–

    AB 7, 1965
    Bp 1–23, 1961–81; 29, 1987
    Bs 26, 1985–#
    Bu 23, 1981
    Cu 1, 1961–#
    En 1, 1961–#
    Er 1, 1961; 7, 1965
    EXu 7, 1965; 9–18, 1967–76
    Lam 1–6, 1961–64
    LAu 1, 1961
    Lcm 7, 1965
    Lgo 1–19, 1961–77 [w 2, 4, 17, 18]
    Lu 1, 1961–#
    LVp 1–15, 1961–73
    Mcm 14–17, 1972–75; 19, 1977
    Ob*
    Ouf (Howes) 7, 1965 [2 copies]

**Studia Musicologica Norvegica: Norsk
Årsskrift for Musikforskning [= Norwegian
Yearbook for Music Research]**
TNG N45; 0332–5024
N–Oslo: Universitetsforlaget, 1968; 1976–

    Cu 1 (1968)–#
    Lbl*
    Mu 1 (1968)
    Ob 1 (1968); 8 (1976)–#

Studia Musicologica Upsaliensia
0081–6744
S–Stockholm: Uppsala University, ?–?; n.s.
1965–
[NOT IN BUCOMP1]

    Mu*

Studia Muzykologiczne [= Musicological Studies]
TNG PL109
PL–Kraków: Polskie Wydawnictwo Muzyczne,
1953–54; 1956

    BSdsc*
    Ob*

Studien für Tonkünstler und Musikfreunde
see **Musikalische Monatsschrift**

Studien zur Musik Afrikas
D–Hohenschlaftlarn: Renner, 1980–
[NOT IN BUCOMP1]

    Lbl*

Studien zur Musikgeschichte
D–Leipzig, 1913–14

    Lbl*

**Studien zur Musikgeschichte des 19.
Jahrhunderts**
0081–7341
D–Regensburg: Gustav Bosse, 1965–89
[NOT IN BUCOMP1; ceased publication with
no. 60, 1989]

    NO 1, 3–9, 1965–67; 11–19, 1968–70; 21–31,
        1971–73; 33–44, 1973–74; 46–60, 1975–89
    Ouf 1–60, 1965–89

**Studien zur Musikwissenschaft: Beihefte der
Denkmäler der Tonkunst in Österreich**
Fellinger 1968/2196; TNG D536; 0081–3222
D–Leipzig [etc.]: Breitkopf und Härtel, 1913–
16; 1918–34; 1955–

    Cpl 1 (1913)
    Cu 1 (1913)–#
    Er 22 (1955)LAu 22 (1955); 25 (1961)–26
        (1964)
    Lbl*
    Lcm 1 (1913)
    Lu 1 (1913)–#
    LVu 1 (1913)–21 (1934)
    Mpl 22 (1955)
    Mu 31 (1980)–39 (1988)
    Ob*
    Ouf 1 (1913)–39 (1988)

Studien zur Volksliedforschung *see* **Jahrbuch
für Volksliedforschung**

393

Studies in Eastern Chant
0585–6663
GB–London: Oxford University Press, 1966–
[NOT IN BUCOMP1]

BLu 1 (1966)–3 (1973)
BRu 1 (1966)–3 (1973)
DRu 4 (1979)
HUu 1 (1966)–3 (1973)
Lu 1 (1966)–#
Ob*
Ouf 1 (1966)–5 (1990)
SFu 1 (1966)–3 (1973)

Studies in Ethnomusicology
0081–7902
US–New York: Folkways Records, 1961–65

Lbl*
Lu 1 (1961)–2 (1965)
Ob*

Studies in Indian Music
IN–Poona, 1889
[NOT IN BUCOMP1]

Lbl 1 (1889), 2
Lio 1 (1889), 2

Studies in Jazz Discography *see* Journal of Jazz Studies: Incorporating Studies in Jazz Discography

Studies in Jazz Research *see* Beiträge zur Jazzforschung/Studies in Jazz Research

Studies in Music [1]
TNG AUS20; 0081–8267
AUS–Nedlands: University of Western Australia, 1967–92
[Ceased publication with vol. 26 (1992)]

ABc 1 (1967)–21 (1987)
ALb 16 (1982)
BG 1 (1967)–26 (1992)
Bu 1 (1967)–26 (1992)
CDu 2 (1968)
Cu 1 (1967)–26 (1992)
En 1 (1967)–26 (1992)
Er 1 (1967)–26 (1992)
EXu 1 (1967)–25 (1991)
Gam 1 (1967)–23 (1984); 25 (1991)–26 (1992)
Gul 1 (1967)–26 (1992)

HUu 1 (1967)–26 (1992)
Lam 1 (1967)–7 (1973)Lbl*
Lcm 3 (1969)–4 (1970); 6 (1972)–7 (1973)
Lcml 1 (1967)–7 (1973)
Lgo 9 (1975)–24 (1990)
Lkc 1 (1967)–2 (1968); 4 (1970)–10 (1976); 12 (1978)–26 (1992)
Lu 1 (1967)–26 (1992)
Lu (RMA) 1 (1967)–26 (1992)
LVu 1 (1967)–8 (1974)
Mcm 7 (1973)–9 (1975)
Mpl 1 (1967)–26 (1992)
Mu 6 (1972)–26 (1992)
NO 2 (1968); 4 (1970)–7 (1973)
Ob*
Ouf 1 (1967)–26 (1992)
SFu 1 (1967)–24 (1990)

Studies in Music [2]
TNG C55; 0703–3052
C–London, Ontario: University of Western Ontario, 1976–

BSdsc 1 (1976)–#
Bu 7 (1982)–12 (1987)
CDu 7 (1982)–11 (1986)
Cu 1 (1976)–#
DRu 7 (1982)–12 (1987)
EIR:Dtc 1 (1976)–#
En 1 (1976)–12 (1987)
Gul 7 (1982)–#
Lbl*
Lcm 1 (1976)–12 (1987); 15 (1990)
Lcml 1 (1976)–#
LEbc 1 (1976)–3 (1978); 5 (1980)–6 (1981); 8 (1983)–10 (1985)
Lu 1 (1976)–#
Mu 3 (1978)–10 (1985); 12 (1987)
Ob*

Studies in Oriental Music [translated title] *see* Toyo Ongaku Kenkyu

Studies in the History of Music
0743–9822
US–New York: Broude Brothers, 1983–
[NOT IN BUCOMP1]

AB 1 (1983)–#
Er 1 (1983)–#
Lu 1 (1983)–#
Ob 1 (1983)–#

Studies in the Psychology of Music
0090–2888
US–Iowa City, IA: University of Iowa Press,
1932–37

    BSdsc*
    Cu 1932–37
    Gul 1932–37
    Lu 1932–37

Studies on Music [translated title] see Yin Yue
Lun Cong

Studii de Muzicologie
TNG R28; 0491–3418
RO–Bucharest: Editura Muzicala a Uniunii
Compozitorilor din RSR, 1965–

    Cu 6 (1970)–#
    Ob*

Studii si Cercetări de Istoria Artei
[= Rumanian Review of Art History]
TNG R25; 0039–3983
RO–Bucharest: Editura Academiei Republicii
Socialiste România, 1954–
[Also published in French as Revue Roumaine
d'Histoire de l'Art (q.v.)]

    Lbl*
    Ob*

Studio Sound
0144–5944
GB–Croydon: Link House Publications, 1959–
[NOT IN BUCOMP1; entitled Studio Sound and
Broadcast Engineering from 1973. Incorporated
Sound International from 1981]

    Cat 15 (1973), 10; 19 (1977), 1, 3, 5, 12; 21
      (1979); 22 (1980), 2–8; 23 (1981), 4–12; 24
      (1982)–25 (1983), 2, 5–8, 10–12; 26
      (1984)–27 (1985), 1, 3–5, 8–10, 12; 28
      (1986)–30 (1988); 31 (1989), 2–6; 32
      (1990), 5–12; 33 (1991)–#
    Lki [c (5 years)]
    Lsa 12 (1970), 5–#*
    NOTu 24 (1982)–#
    Oub [c (2 years)]

Studio Sound and Broadcast Engineering see
Studio Sound

Studio Sound's Pro-Audio Directory see
Studio Sound's Pro-Audio Yearbook

Studio Sound's Pro-Audio Yearbook
0260–8537
GB–Croydon: Link House Publications, 1982–
[NOT IN BUCOMP1; later entitled Studio
Sound's Pro-Audio Directory]

    Ob 1982–#

Studio Week/Studio
0953–8976
GB–London: Studio Week, ?1988–?91
[NOT IN BUCOMP1; at some time subtitled
The Studio Magazine read by the Record
Industry; incorporated into Pro Sound News
(q.v.)]

    Cu 1988, Feb–1991, July*
    Lbl 1986–91*
    Lcml 1987, Nov–1991, July
    Lsa 1986, Apr–1991

Studio Week: the Studio Magazine read by
the Record Industry see Studio Week/Studio

Submerge
0969–6180
GB–London, 1989–
[NOT IN BUCOMP1]

    Lbl*

Subsidia Musica Veneta
I–Bologna: Forni, 1980–
[NOT IN BUCOMP1]

    Cu 1 (1980)–#

Die Suid-Afrikaanse Musiekonderwyser see
The South African Music Teacher

Suid-Afrikaanse Tydskrif vir
Musiekwetenskap see South African Journal
of Musicology

The Sunbeam: a [Weekly] Journal devoted to
Polite Literature and Music
Fellinger 1968/149; TNG GB19; Langley,
p. 585
GB–London: George Berger, 1838, Feb–1839,
Dec
[100 nos published in 2 vols]

    Cu 1 (1838)–2 (1839)
    Gm 1 (1838)–2 (1839)
    Lbl*
    Ob*

Sunday School and Choir Music *see* The
Choir Musician: a Journal for Choirs and
Sunday Schools

Super Schwann *see* Schwann Long Playing
Record Catalog

Supersonic
GB–London: IPC Magazines, 1976–78
[Continued as *Rock On!* (ISSN 0141–7177)]

Cu 1976, Mar–1978, Apr
Lbl*

Supersonic Annual
GB–London, 1977–79
[NOT IN BUCOMP1]

Cu 1977–79
Ob 1977–79

Superstar *see* The Official Partridge
Magazine

Superstars' Official David Cassidy Magazine
GB–London, 1972–75
[From 1975 entitled *David Cassidy Magazine*]

Cu 1–33, 1972–75
En 1–43, 1972–75
Ob 1–43, 1972–75

Supplementary Newsletter, Sir Thomas
Beecham Society *see* The Sir Thomas
Beecham Society News-Letter

The Surrey Musical Journal
Fellinger 1968/1003; TNG GB119
GB–London, 1885–86

Lbl 1–4, 1885–86

Sussex Jazz Society Newsletter
GB–Brighton, 1967–?

Cbijs 1969, June, Aug, Oct–Dec; 1970, Jan–
May, Aug–Dec; 1971, Apr–June, Sep, Oct

Sussex Pie
GB–Brighton: English Folk Dance and Song
Society, Sussex District, 1994–
[NOT IN BUCOMP1]

Lcs 1, 1994–#

Svensk Musik [= Swedish Music]
0283–2526
S–Stockholm: Swedish Music Information
Centre, 1986–
[NOT IN BUCOMP1]

Cu 1986–#
Gsmic [c]
Lam 1992, 3, 4; 1993, 1
Lbbc 1990–#
Lsa 1994–#
Ouf 1990–#

Svensk Musikförteckning [= Swedish Music
Catalogue]
0347–8289
S–Stockholm: Svenska
Musikhandlareföreningen, 1916–

Cu 1986–#
Lbl*
Ob*

**Svensk Musikkatalog: Uppslagsbok för
Svenska Musikhandeln** [= Swedish Music
Catalogue: Reference Book for the Swedish
Music Trade]
0283–4650
S–Stockholm: Svenska
Musikhandlareföreningen, ?1978–
[NOT IN BUCOMP1. Preceded 1899–1977 by
the *Uppslagsbok för Svenska Musikhandeln*]

Ob 1976/80–#

Svensk Musiktidning [= Swedish Music
Magazine]
Fellinger 1968/870; TNG S17
S–Stockholm, 1881–1913
[From 1892 entitled *Nordiskt Musikblad*]

Lbl*

Svensk Tidskrift för Musikforskning [=
Swedish Journal of Musicology]
TNG S46; 0081–9816
S–Stockholm: Svenska Samfundet för
Musikforskning, 1919–

ALb 69 (1987)
Cu 1 (1919)–#
En 51 (1969)–#
Lbl*
Lcml 31 (1949); 33 (1951)
Lu 39 (1957)–#
Ob*

Svenska Musikerförbundets Tidning [Swedish Musicians' Alliance] *see* Musikern: Tidning för Civil- och Militärmusici

Swelingh: Jaarboekje aan de Toonkunst in Nederland gewijd [= Yearbook for Dutch Music]
Fellinger 1968/413; TNG NL16
NL–Amsterdam: Gebroeders Binger, 1859–60

    Lbl 1859–63

Swing 51
GB–Sutton: Swing 51, 1979–
[NOT IN BUCOMP1]

    Lbl*
    Lsa 7–9, ?1983–89
    Ob 1, 1979–#

Swing Music: a Monthly Magazine for Rhythm Clubs
TNG GB352
GB–London: Leonard Hibbs, 1935–36

    Cbijs 1 (1935/36), 1, 2, 4–10; 2 (1936/37), 1–3
    Lbl*

The Swing Shop "Mag-list"
GB–?, 1952–55

    Cbijs 1–7, 1952–55

Swinging Newsletter
US–New York: International Jazz Federation, ?–
[From no. 39, 1979–45, 1981 entitled *Jazz Echo* (ISSN 0277–5980); from 46, 1981–58, 1984 entitled *Jazz World Index* (ISSN 0886–1927); from 59, 1984 entitled *Jazz World* (ISSN 0749–4564)]

    Cbijs 12, 13, 18, 19, 1975; 33, 1977

Swiss Jazz Notes *see* Jazz Bulletin

Swiss Music on Records *see* Schweizer Musik auf Schallplatten

Sŵn [= Noise]
GB–Cardiff, 1972–?

    AB 1972–74

Syd Lawrence Appreciation Society Newsletter
GB–?London: Syd Lawrence Appreciation Society, ?–
[NOT IN BUCOMP1]

    LOnjfa*

The Sydney Organ Journal
TNG AUS25; 0817–2285
AUS–Sydney: Organ Society of Sydney, 1970–
[NOT IN BUCOMP1]

    Lam (o) 21 (1990)–23 (1992), 2, 4; 24 (1993)–25 (1994), 4

Symphonia: Algemeen Nederlands Muziektijdschrift *see* Symphonia: Tijdschrift gewijd aan Instrumentale Muziek

Symphonia: Tesori Musicali della Radio Svizzera Italiana
I–Bologna: Radio Svizzera Italiana, ?1990–
[NOT IN BUCOMP1]

    Lsa 1991–#*

Symphonia: Tijdschrift gewijd aan Instrumentale Muziek [= Journal of Instrumental Music]
TNG NL72
NL–Hilversum, 1923–60
[From 1948 entitled *Symphonia: Algemeen Nederlands Muziektijdschrift*; ceased publication with vol. 37 (1960)]

    Lu (RMA) 25 (1948), 6–35 (1958), 6*

Symphony
TNG GB395
GB–London: H. Liversedge, 1946–?
[NOT IN BUCOMP1]

    Lam 1966, Nov–1967, July, Sep–Dec; 1968, Jan–July, Sep–Dec; 1969, Jan–1972, Sep; 1973, Jan–Mar,May–June, Aug–Sep

Systematische Musikwissenschaft
SQ–Bratislava, 1993–
[NOT IN BUCOMP1]

    Cu 1 (1993)–#

Systematische Übersicht über die Neuigkeiten des Deutsche Musikalienhandels für Lehrer und Freunde der Musik
Fellinger 1968/731; TNG D222
D–Wolfenbüttel: Julius Zwissler, 1876

Lbl 1 (1876)

T

Les Tablettes de Polymnie: Journal consacré à Tous qui intéressent l'Art Musical
Fellinger 1968/22; TNG F10
F–Paris: Imprimérie de Dondey–Dupré, 1810–11

Cu 1810–11 [Reprint ed.]
Ob 1810–11 [Reprint ed.]

Tagebuch see Aus unserem Tagebuch

Tagesfragen see Aufsätze über musikalische Tagesfragen

Tagesfragen: Kissinger Blätter: Organ für Musiker, Musikfreunde und Freunde der Wahrheit see Aufsätze über musikalische Tagesfragen

Take Cover
GB–London: Southern Rag, 1990–
[NOT IN BUCOMP1]

Lcs 1 (1990), 1

Talkback
GB–Heathfield, 199?–
[NOT IN BUCOMP1]

Lsa 1992, June, Sep, Oct; 1993, May–#*

Talking Blues
GB–London: Record Information Services, 1976–79
[Ceased publication with no. 10, 1979]

Cbijs 1–10, 1976–79
Cu 1–10, 1976–79
EIR:Dtc 1–10, 1976–79
En 1–10, 1976–79
Lsa 1–10, 1976–79
Ob*

Talking Machine and Wireless Trade News see Talking Machine News and Journal of Amusements

Talking Machine News and Journal of Amusements
TNG GB231
GB–London, 1908–31
[Entitled Gramophone, Wireless and Talking Machine News from 1923; bore various other variant titles, including Talking Machine and Wireless Trade News at some time]

AB 16 (1924)–23 (1931)
BSdsc 4 (1911/12); 7 (1914/15)–10 (1917/18)
Lbl*
Ob*

The Talking Machine Review
TNG GB548; 0039–9191
GB–Bournemouth: E. Bayly, 1969–
[From 77, 1990 entitled International Talking Machine Review]

AB 1, 1969–#
Cu 1, 1969–#
EIR:Dtc 1, 1969–#
Lbar 1–26, 1969–74; 28, 1974; 33, 1975; 38, 40, 1976–49b, 1977; 51–69, 1978–84
Lsa 1–31, 1969–74; 33, 1975–# [w 74, 1988]
Ob*

Talking Machine World
TNG US363
US–New York: Federal Business Publications, 1905–32
[NOT IN BUCOMP1; entitled Talking Machine World and Radio-Music Merchant, 1929–32]

Lbl*

Talking Machine World and Radio-Music Merchant see Talking Machine World

Tallis's Dramatic Magazine and General Theatrical and Musical Review
GB–London: John Tallis, 1850–53

Lbl*
Ob 1850, Nov–1851, June

Tanz aktuell see Ballett International

Tanzen
0724–1062
D– Cologne: Ballet International, 1983–
[NOT IN BUCOMP1; entitled Tanzen Heute from 1988; reverted to Tanzen in 1989]

Lcs 4 (1986)–10 (1992), 3*

Tanzen Heute *see* Tanzen

Tape *see* Tape Recording and Reproduction Magazine

Tape Music Parade
TNG GB542
GB–Salisbury, 1970–

   Cu 1 (1970), 3–6
   EIR:Dtc*
   En 1 (1970), 3–6
   Ob 1 (1970), 1–6

The Tape Recorder
TNG GB489
GB–London, 1959–?70
[NOT IN BUCOMP1; incorporated into *Hi-Fi News* (q.v.)]

   Lsa 1 (1959/60), 1, 2; 7 (1965/66), 5–12; 8
   (1966/67), 1–3, 5; 11 (1969/70), 1–9, 11, 12
   Ob 1 (1959/60), 2–12 (1970/71), 1

Tape Recording and Hi-Fi Magazine *see* Tape Recording and Reproduction Magazine

Tape Recording and Reproduction Magazine
0039–9558
GB–London: Anglia Newspapers, 1957–
[Later entitled *Sound and Vision* (ISSN 0126–6127); *Tape Recording and Hi-Fi Magazine* (1958–60); *Tape Recording Magazine* (1961–?70); *Sound and Picture Tape Recording Magazine* (1971–73); (incorporating *Tape Recording and Stereo Sound Magazine*); from 1973 entitled *Tape*]
[NOT IN BUCOMP1]

   BSdsc*
   Lsa 2 (1958)–15 (1971), 3 [w 11 (1967), 6,
   9]; 1973, Dec–1975, Jan [w 1974, Mar]
   Ob 1 (1957)–17 (1973), 9

Tape Recording and Stereo Sound Magazine *see* Tape Recording and Reproduction Magazine

Tape Recording Magazine *see* Tape Recording and Reproduction Magazine

Tape Recording Yearbook
GB–London: Tape Recording Fortnightly, 1959–69
[NOT IN BUCOMP1]

   Ob 1958/59–69

Tape Teacher: a Magazine of Audio Visual Teaching
0306–7858
GB–Bracknell: 3M, 1971–?
[NOT IN BUCOMP1]

   Lsa 1–19, 1971–77*

Taplas [= Hop]: a Folk Music Magazine for Wales
GB–Cardiff, 1982–

   AB*
   CDCp 1–4, 1982–83; 8, 1984; 15, 1985; 33,
   35, 36, 1989; 38–42, 1990; 47, 48, 50,
   1992–#
   EIR:Dp 23, 1987–#
   EIR:Dtc 6–10, 1983–84
   Lcs 1, 1982; 6, 1983; 8, 11, 1984; 12, 14,
   1985–#
   Ob*

Taschenbuch für den Kirchenmusiker
0082–187X
D–Regensburg: Friedrich Pustet Verlag, 1958–
[From 1975 entitled *Taschenbuch für Liturgie und Kirchenmusik*]

   BSdsc 1979–84

Taschenbüch für deutsche Sänger [...]
Fellinger 1968/509; TNGA56
A–Vienna: Hoffmann und Ludwig, 1864

   Lbl 1 (1864)

Taschenbuch für Liturgie und Kirchenmusik *see* Taschenbuch für den Kirchenmusiker

T.C.M. Bulletin: a Journal published by Trinity College of Music, London
GB–London: Trinity College of Music, ?–
[NOT IN BUCOMP1]

   Lbl*
   Ob 43, 1985–#

T.C.M. Magazine
TNG GB338
GB–London: Trinity College of Music, 1931–
[From issue 53, 1990 entitled *The Trinity Magazine*]

EIR:Dtc n.s. 43, 1985–#
Lam n.s. 8–55, 1968–91; 58, 59, 1992
Lbl*
Ob 1–14, 1931–35

Teaching Music
1069–7446
US–Reston, VA: Music Educators' National Conference, 1993–
[NOT IN BUCOMP1]

BAc 1 (1993)–#
Lie 1 (1993)–#
Msuc 1 (1993)–#
Re 1 (1993)– #
TOd 1 (1993)–#
Uu 1 (1993)–#

Teater *see* Musik og Teater

Ted Heath Music Appreciation Society Newsletter
GB–?: Ted Heath Music Appreciation Society, ?–[NOT IN BUCOMP1]

LOnjfa*

Tele Tunes: Television, Film and Show Music on CD, Record, Cassette and Video
GB–Morecambe, 1979–
[NOT IN BUCOMP1]

ABDP 1993
BRp 1979–#
BuAYp 1985–#
CH [c (5 years)]
DDp 1987/88–#
En*
Ep 1988/89–#
Gm 1980; 1985–#
Lbbc 1979– #
Lis 1988/89; 1990; 1992
Lsa 1984–#
Lwwb [c]
Lwwbat [c]
Lwwput [c]
NOp 1984–#
NTp 1984–#
Ob*
SFp 1975; 1979; 1984; 1988; 1992–#

Telyn-y-Plant [= The Children's Harp] *see* Oenig

Telyn yr Ysgol Sabbothol [= Harp of the Sunday School]
GB–Denbigh, 1864–66

BG 1864–65

Tempo *see also* Listy Hudební Matice

Tempo: a Magazine for Music Lovers and Those Who Want to Know More about Music
TNG US532
US–New York: The Music Education League, 1934–35

Lbl*

Tempo: a Quarterly Review of Modern Music
see Tempo: the Boosey and Hawkes News-Letter (Quarterly)

Tempo: the Boosey and Hawkes News-Letter (Quarterly)
TNG GB371; 0040–2982
GB/US–London: Boosey and Hawkes, 1939–46; n.s. 1946–; American ed. New York: Boosey and Hawkes, 1940–44
[From 1946 entitled *Tempo: a Quarterly Review of Modern Music*]

AB 57, 1961–#
ALb 1–15, 1939–46 [UK ed.]; n.s. 1–29, 1946–53; 32–36, 1954–55; 38, 39, 1955–56; 41– 106, 1956–73; 108, 109, 1974; 113–57, 1975–86; 159, 1986–#; 1 (1940)–2 (1942), 3; 3 (1944), 1 [American ed.]
Au 26, 1952–#
BAc n.s. 28–169, 1953–89; 172, 1990–#
BG n.s. 41–107, 1956–73 [w 45]; 112, 1975–#
BLBBC n.s. 65, 1963; 70, 1964; 87–146, 1968–83*
BLp 1–15, 1939–46 [UK ed.]; n.s. 1, 1946–#
BRp n.s. 80, 1967–#
BRu n.s. 128–139, 1979–81
Bs n.s. 1, 1946–#
BSdsc*
BTp n.s. 87–146, 1968–83*
Btu 1–15, 1939–46 [UK ed.]; n.s. 4–62, 1947–62 [w 41, 43]; 98–139, 1972–81
Bu n.s. 1, 1946–#
CCtc n.s. 11, 13, 14, 23, 1949–52; 70, 1965–#
CDu n.s. 75, 1965–#

Cpl n.s. 1–71, 1946–64; 180, 1992–#
Cu 1–15, 1939–46; n.s. 1, 1946–#
DRu 1–15, 1939–46 [UK ed.]; n.s. 1, 1946–#
EIR:Dp n.s. 156–189, 1986–89
EIR:Dtc n.s. 84, 1968–#
EIR:Duc 1–7, 1939–44 [UK ed.]; n.s. 69, 1964–#
En 6–15, 1944–46 [UK ed.]; n.s. 1–175, 1946–90; 177–180, 1991–92; 182, 1992–#
Ep n.s. 28, 1953–#
Er 1–15, 1939–46 [UK ed.]; n.s. 1–25, 1946–52; 40, 1956–#; 1–3, 1940–44 [American ed.]
EXu n.s. 14, 1950–#
Gam n.s. 106, 1974–#
Gm n.s. 108, 1974–#
Gsmic n.s. 168–171, 1988–89
Gul 1–15, 1939–46 [UK ed.]; n.s. 1, 1946–#
HUu n.s. 1, 1946–#
Ke n.s. 107, 1973–#
Lam 1, 2, 6, 7, 15, 1939–46 [UK ed.]; n.s. 1, 1946, 4–7, 1947–48; 13, 14, 1949; 26, 1953; 32, 1954; 36, 38, 1955; 40, 1956; 44, 45, 1957; 47, 1958; 53–56, 1960; 59–75, 1961–65; 78–84, 1966–68; 87–93, 1969–70; 95–98, 1971–72; 100–176, 1972–91; 178–181, 1991–92; 183, 1993–#
LAu 1–15, 1939–46 [UK ed.]; n.s. 1, 1946–#; 1 (1940)–3 (1944), 1 [American ed.]
Lbar n.s. 7–38, 1948–55; 41, 42, 1956; 44, 45, 1957; 47, 1958; 53/54–78, 1960–66; 80–136, 1967–81; 138, 1981–#
Lbbc n.s. 95, 1970–# [w 97, 121]
Lbl*
LCdM n.s. 74, 1965–#
Lcm 7–10, 13, 1944/45 [UK ed.]; n.s. 11, 12, 1949; 15–18, 1950/51; 20–54, 1951–60 [w 23, 28]; 59–187, 1961–93
Lcml 1–15, 1939–46 [UK ed.]; n.s. 1, 1946–#; 1 (1940)–3 (1944) [American ed.]
Lcml (m) [c (1 year)]
Lcu n.s. 112–39, 1975–81
LEbc n.s. 99, 1972–#
LEc n.s. 4, 1947–#
Lgo n.s. 1, 1946–#
Lgsm n.s. 8, 1948; 11–14, 1949; 53–56, 1960; 59, 60, 1961; 88, 89, 1969; 108, 1974–#
Lk n.s. 160, 1986–#
Lkc n.s. 83–105, 1967–73 [w94, 1970; 104, 1973]; 108–127, 1973–79; 129–139, 1979–82; 141–# [w 168, 1981]
Lki 1–15, 1939–46 [UK ed.]; n.s. 1, 1946–#
Lmi n.s. 107, 1973–#
LRHBNC n.s. 5–60, 1947–62; 8, 1969–#
Lro n.s. 104, 1973–#

Lsa 7, 1944 [UK ed.]; n.s. 1 (1946); 5–8, 1947–48; 14, 1949; 19, 20, 1951; 37, 1955; 45, 1957; 57, 1961; 65, 1963; 69, 1964; 74, 1965; 76, 1966–#
Ltc 194, 1995–#
Ltv n.s. 157, 1986–#
Lu 1–15, 1939–46 [w 2] [UK ed.]; n.s. 1, 1946–#; 1 (1940), 1, 4; 2 (1942), 2 [US edition]
LVp n.s. 36–40, 1955–56; 88, 89, 1969
LVu n.s. 75, 1966–#
Mcm n.s. 13, 1949; 31, 34, 1954; 36, 1955–#*
Mmu (a) 18, 1947–#*
Mpl n.s. 1, 1946–#
Msuc n.s. 168–83, 1989–93
Mu n.s. 1, 1946–#; 1 (1940)–3 (1944) [US edition]
NO n.s. 26, 1952; 72–77, 1965–66; 79–130, 1970–79; 136, 1981–#
NOp [c (5 years starting 1994)]
NTp n.s. 68–169, 1964–89
NWu 1–15, 1939–46 [UK ed.]; n.s. 1, 1946–#
Ob*
Oub n.s. 140, 1982–#
Ouf n.s. 6, 1947–#*
R n.s. 68, 1964–#
SFu n.s. 76, 1966–#
SHRp n.s. 168, 1989–#
SOu n.s. 4–5, 7, 9, 10, 12–19, 1947–51; 48, 1958; 60, 1962–#
TOd n.s. 60, 1962; 64, 1963; 68–70, 1964; 101, 1972; 112, 1975–#
Uu n.s. 100, 1972–#
Yu 71, 1974; 74, 1967; 79, 1972–#*

Tempo Booklet
GB–London: Boosey and Hawkes, 1978–
[NOT IN BUCOMP1]

Cu 1, 1978–

Tempo e Musica: Rassegna Musicale di Propaganda Ricordi
TNG I250
I–Milan: Ricordi, 1958–60

Cpl 4, 5, 7, 1958–60
Lam 2– 6, 1958–59
Lcml 1–7, 1958–60

The Ten Years Flexi-Disc see The 10 Years Flexi-Disc

Terrorizer: Extreme Music Magazine
1350–6978
GB–Camborne: Terrorizer, 1993–
[NOT IN BUCOMP1]

   Lbl*

Tesoro Sacro Musical: Revista Mensual de Musica Sagrada
Fellinger 1968/2300; TNG E68; 0563–1858
E–Madrid: Tesoro Sacro Musical, 1917–78
[Ceased publication with vol. 61 no. 4 (1978); also included a *Supplemento Polifónico*, containing music]

   Cu 51 (1968)–61 (1978)
   En*
   EXu 54 (1971), 1, 3, 4–61 (1978)
   HUu 55 (1972)–61 (1978)
   Lam 53 (1970), 611; 56 (1973), 626
   Lbbc 53 (1970)–57 (1974)*
   Lcm 53 (1970); 56 (1973)
   Lu 53 (1970), 611; 56 (1973), 625
   Ob*

Tetlow's Vintage Record Guide
GB–Millbrook, Southampton: F. Tetlow, 196?–
[NOT IN BUCOMP1]

   LOnjfa*

Texas Music Educator *see* **Southwestern Musician**

Theater-Zeitung *see* **Wiener Theater-Zeitung**

The Theatre
GB–London: Wyman and Sons, 1878–97

   Lbl*
   Ob*

Theatre Design and Technology
0040–5477
US–Pittsburgh, PA [etc.]: United States Institute for Theater Technology, 1965–
[NOT IN BUCOMP1]

   Lgsm 23 (1987)–#

Theatre Digest
TNG GB424
GB–London: Theatre Digest, 1949–51
[From 1951 entitled *Music and Theatre Digest: Union of "Musical Digest" and "Theatre Digest"* (q.v.)]

   Lbl*

Theatre Index *see* **London Theatre Index**

The Theatre, Music-Hall and Cinema Blue Book
GB–London, 1917–?

   Lbl*

Theatre Notebook
0040–5523
GB–London: Society for Theatre Research, 1945–
[NOT IN BUCOMP1]

   Lgsm 31 (1977)–#
   Lu 1 (1945)–#
   Ob 1 (1945)–#

Theatre Organ Review
TNG GB405; 0040–5558
GB–Leeds, 1947–
[NOT IN BUCOMP1]

   Lam (o) 5 (1951), 17–10 (1956), 40
   Mpl 16 (1962)–26 (1972)

Theatre Research International
0307–8833
GB–London: Oxford University Press, 1975–
[NOT IN BUCOMP1]

   Lgsm*
   Lu 1 (1975)–#
   Ob 1 (1975)–#

The Theatrical and Concert Companion
Fellinger 1968/174; TNG GB22; Langley, p. 590
GB–London: Joseph Onwhyn [etc], 1838–40
[Langley notes that title varies, e. g. *The Concert Companion and Musical Journal*; *The Concert Companion*; *Concert and Theatrical Companion and Record of Music and the Drama*; *The Concert Companion and Record of Music and the Drama*, etc. 65 nos in total]

   Lbl 1838–40

Theatrical and Music Hall Life
Fellinger 1968/1460; TNG GB177
GB–London, 1898

   Lbl*

The Theatrical and Musical Guide: Containing Complete Programmes of all the Principal London Theatres […]
Fellinger 1968/978; TNG GB116
GB–London, 1884–86

   Lbl*

Theatrical and Musical Review: an
Independent Journal of Criticism
Fellinger 1968/592; TNG GB71
GB–London: Holloway and Company, 1868–69

Lbl 1 (1868), 1–7

The Theatrical Manager
GB–London, 1928–31

Lbl*

The Theatrical Observer
EIRE–Dublin: J. Nolan, 1821

EIR:Dtc 1 (1821), Jan 19–4 (1821), July 6
Lbl*
Ob*

Theme
US–New York, 1954–?

Cbijs 4 (1957), 1, 2

Theoria: Historical Aspects of Music Theory
US–Denton, TX: North Texas State University,
1985–
[NOT IN BUCOMP1]

Cu 1 (1985)–#
EXu 5 (1990)–#
Ouf 1 (1985)–#

Theory and Practice
0741–6156
US–Cincinatti, OH: Music Theory Society of
New York State, 1975–
[NOT IN BUCOMP1]

Cu 13 (1988)–#
Lgo 8 (1983)–#
Lkc 1 (1975)*; 2 (1976)–7 (1982); 9 (1984)
NO 1 (1975)–10 (1985); 13 (1988)
Ouf 3 (1978), 2–#*

There's Music in Germany
0495–4610
D–Bonn: Inter Nationes, 1954/55–
[In 1959 and from 1977 entitled *Music in
Germany*; German edition entitled *Deutsches
Musikleben* (TNG D946)]

BSdsc 1987–#
Cpl 1958–#
Cu 1972; 1974–76
Lbl*
Lcm 1956; 1963–69
Mu 1982–89; 1992; 1996–#

Thirty Three and a Third *see* 33 1/3

This Stuff'll Kill Ya!
GB–Grangemouth: L. Hutton, 1986–
[NOT IN BUCOMP1]

Ob 1 (1986)–#*

Thrash 'n' Burn
0963–7265
GB–Stevenage: Force 10, 1991–
[NOT IN BUCOMP1]

Lbl*

Three: the Radio 3 Magazine *see* 3: the Radio
3 Magazine

Tibia: Magazin für Freunde alter und neuer
Bläsermusik
TNG D1092; 0176–6511
D–Celle: Moeck, 1976–

Cu 1 (1976)–#
Ob*

Tijdschrift der Vereeniging voor
Nederlansche Muziekgeschiedenis *see*
Tijdschrift der Vereeniging voor Noord-
Nederlands Muziekgeschiedenis

Tijdschrift der Vereeniging voor Noord-
Nederlands Muziekgeschiedenis
Fellinger 1968/906; TNG NL26; 0042–3874
NL–Amsterdam: Vereeniging voor Nederlands
Muziekgeschiedenis, 1882–
[Previously (1869–?81) entitled *Bouwsteenen:
Jaarboek der Vereeniging voor Noord-
Nederlandsche Muziekgeschiedenis* (q.v.); from
1909 to 1946 entitled *Tijdschrift der Vereniging
voor Nederlandsche Muziekgeschiedenis* (ISSN
0921–3260); from 1948 entitled *Tijdschrift voor
Muziekwetenschap*; from 1960 to 1994 entitled
*Tijdschrift van de Vereniging voor Nederlandse
Muziekgeschiedenis* (ISSN 0042–3874); from
1995 entitled *Tijdschrift van de Koninklijke
Vereniging voor Nederlandse
Muziekgeschiedenis* (ISSN 1353–7079)]

AB 9 (1909/14), 2, 4; 10 (1915/22), 1–3; 11
(1923/25), 3, 4; 12 (1926/28)–34 (1984), 1
ALb 20 (1966), 3–28 (1978), 2
BG 44 (1994)–#
Bu 32 (1982), 1, 2
Cu 1 (1882/85)–#
Gul 30 (1980)–#
Lam 32 (1982), 1/2

LAu 17 (1955), 3, 4–19 (1963), 2
Lbbc 1 (1882/85)–#
Lbl*
Lcm 1 (1882/85)–2 (1885/87); 5 (1895/97);
32 (1982), 1, 2
Lcml 17 (1955), 2; 20 (1967)–21 (1969/70)*;
22 (1972)–#
Lkc 17 (1955), 2–4; 18 (1959)–#
LRHBNC 19 (1963)–22 (1972); 24 (1974)–
26 (1976); 41 (1991)–#
Lu 1 (1882/85)–9 (19109/14); 11 (1923/25)–
14 (1932/35); 19 (1963)–26 (1976); 29
(1979)–#
Mu 30 (1980)–#
Ob 1 (1882/85)–#
Ouf 42 (1992)–#
R 1 (1882/85)–8 (1907/08)
SOu 41 (1991)–#

Tijdschrift van de Koninklijke Vereniging
voor Nederlandse Muziekgeschiedenis *see*
Tijdschrift der Vereeniging voor Noord-
Nederlands Muziekgeschiedenis

Tijdschrift van de Vereeniging voor
Nederlandse Muziekgeschiedenis *see*
Tijdschrift der Vereeniging voor Noord-
Nederlands Muziekgeschiedenis

Tijdschrift voor Muziekwetenschap *see*
Tijdschrift der Vereeniging voor Noord-
Nederlands Muziekgeschiedenis

Time Out
0049–3910
GB–London, 1968–
[NOT IN BUCOMP1]

Lbbc [c]
Lgsm*
Lsa 167, 1973; 255–577, 1975–81*

Tinkle [translated title] *see* Tonc

Tippett in Focus
1057–2074
GB–London: Schott Publishers, 198?–
[NOT IN BUCOMP1]

Cu 19, 1991–#
Lbar 18, 1990; 20, 1992–#
Lbl 23, 1993–#
Ob*

To the Fore!: International Percy Grainger
Society News
US–Humble, TX: International Percy Grainger
Society, 1992–
[NOT IN BUCOMP1]

ALb 1 (1992)–3 (1994), 1 [w 2 (1993), 2]
Lcs 1 (1992), 1

Toccata: the Magazine of the Leopold
Stokowski Society
GB–Godalming [etc.]: The Leopold Stokowski
Society, 1978–

AB 1985–86
Cu 1985–87; 1993–#
EIR:Dtc 1985–88
Lam 1993, Spr
Lbar 1982, Aut–#
Lp 1983–#*
Ob*

Tocher: Tales, Songs, Traditions
0049–397X
GB–Edinburgh: Edinburgh University School of
Scottish Studies, 1971–

EIR:Dtc 1, 1971–#
Gam 1–12, 1971–73; 14–18, 1974–75; 20–
31, 1975–79; 34, 1980; 39, 1985–#
Gm 1, 1971–#
Gsmic 1, 1971–#*
Lcs 1, 1971–# [w 46]
Lsa 1–34, 1971–80 [w 33, 1980]
Mpl 1, 1971–?24, 1976
Ob*

Today's Liturgy
1080–2452
US–Portland, OR: Oregon Catholic Press,
?1979–
[NOT IN BUCOMP1]

CCtc 11 (1989), 3–#

Tonc [= Tinkle]
GB–Chwilog, 1963–?

AB*

Tonhalle: musikalische Familien-Zeitung *see*
Die Tonhalle: Organ für Musikfreunde

Die Tonhalle: Organ für Musikfreunde
Fellinger 1968/593; TNG D178
D–Leipzig: A.H. Payne, 1868–73
[Entitled *Tonhalle: musikalische Familien-Zeitung* from 1872]

  Ob*

Tonic
0260-7425
GB–London: Robert Simpson Society, 1980–

  AB 1 (1980)–3 (1987/89), 1
  Cu 1 (1980)–3 (1987/89), 3
  Lbar 1 (1980)–#
  Lbl*
  Lcml 1 (1980)–#
  LRHBNC 1 (1980)–4 (1992)
  Lsa 1 (1980), 1–3
  Ob*

Tonic Sol-Fa [translated title] *see* **Solffaydd**

The Tonic Sol-Fa College Record *see* **The Tonic Sol-Fa Record**

Tonic Solfa Journal
GB–London, 1894–?

  AB 1–5, 1894
  Gul (e) 1–4, 1894

Tonic Sol-Fa Musician [translated title] *see* **Cerddor y Tonic Sol-Ffa**

The Tonic Sol-Fa Record
Fellinger 1968/1756; TNG GB211
GB–London: Tonic Sol-Fa College, 1904–06
[Also called *The Tonic Sol-Fa College Record*]

  AB*
  Lbl*

The Tonic Sol-Fa Reporter and Magazine of Vocal Music for the People [1]
Fellinger 1968/296; TNG GB44
GB–London: Tonic Sol-Fa Advocate, 1851
[Only two numbers published. Edited by John Curwen, and succeeded by an identical title (see below)]

  En 1, 1851
  Gm 1, 1851
  Lbl*
  Ob 1, 2, 1851

The Tonic Sol-Fa Reporter and Magazine of Vocal Music for the People [2]
Fellinger 1968/328; TNG GB50; Langley 1994, pp. 119–20
GB–London: Tonic Sol-Fa Advocate, 1853–1920
[Entitled *The Musical Herald and Tonic Sol-Fa Reporter*, 1889–90; *The Musical Herald* from 1891 (no. 514)–1920 (no. 873). Combined with *The Musical News: a Weekly Journal of Music* (q.v.) in 1921 to form *The Musical News and Herald*]

  AB*
  Au 1896/97–1914/15
  Bp 4, 1855
  Cu 1880; 1882; 1887–88
  EIR:Dtc*
  EIR:Duc 1912–15
  En 1–47, 1853–56 [w 30, 32–34, 36–38, 41–45]; 106, 107, 1861
  Ep 1889–1910
  Gm 1853–88; 1891–1920
  Gul (e) 1 (1853)–16 (1874)* [+ letterpress portions*, and some musical supplements]
  Lbl 1853–1920
  Lcm 1920, Dec 1
  Lcml 490–873, 1899–1920
  LEc 1912–20
  Lu 559–848, 1894–1918
  LVp 1881–82; 1885–88; 1898–1920
  Mcm 646–717, 1902–07
  MO 1892, 1893; 1895; 1897, 1898; 1900, 1901
  Mpl 1853–88; 1899–1920
  Ob*
  SFu 538–549, 1893; 562–597, 1895–1897

Die Tonkunst: Organ des Verbandes der Deutschen Tonkünstler-Vereine *see* Die Tonkunst: Wochenschrift für den Fortschritt in der Musik

Die Tonkunst: Wochenschrift für den Fortschritt in der Musik
Fellinger 1968/734; TNG D216
D–Berlin: G. Stilke, 1876–86
[Subtitle from 1880: *Organ des Verbandes der Deutschen Tonkünstler-Vereine*]

  Lbl 1–16, 1876–86

Der Tonwille: Flugblätter zum Zeugnis unwandelbarer Gesetze der Tonkunst einer neuen Jugend dargebracht
TNG A185
A–Vienna: Der Tonwille, 1921–24

    Cpl 1921–24
    Cu 1921–24
    Lbl*
    Ob 1921–24 [Reprint ed.]
    SOu 1–6, 1921–23

Top
GB–London: Tower Records, 1987–
[NOT IN BUCOMP1]

    Cu 1992– #
    Lsa 1987, July
    Ob 1992, May–#

Top Pop Scene *see* **Top Pop Stars**

Top Pop Stars
GB–London, 1962–?
[From 1972 entitled *Top Pop Scene*]

    Cu 1962–78
    Lbl*
    Ob*

Top Twenty
GB–London, 1965–?

    Cu 1965–67
    Lbl*
    Ob*

Total Guitar
1355–5049
GB–Bath: Future Publishing, 1994–
[NOT IN BUCOMP1]

    BSdsc*
    Msuc 1996–#

Towards New Shores [translated title] *see*
K Novym Beregam

Tower Hamlets Music News
GB–London, ?–
[NOT IN BUCOMP1]

    Lam 1980, Dec

Tōyō Ongaku Kenkyū [= Studies in Oriental Music]
TNG J22; 0039–3851
J–Tokyo: Toyo Ongaku Gakkai, 1937–42; 1951–

    Lso 33 (1970)–37 (1974); 41 (1976)–45 (1980); 47 (1981); 49 (1984)–#

Tōyō Ongaku Sensho: the Series of Research in Asian Music
J–Tokyo: Society for Research in Asian Music, 1980–
[NOT IN BUCOMP1]

    Ob 1 (1980)–#

The Tracker: Journal of the Organ Historical Society
TNG US678; 0041–0330
US–Richmond, VA [etc.]: Organ Historical Society, 1957–
[NOT IN BUCOMP1]

    Lam (o) 1 (1957)–5 (1961), 2, 4; 6 (1962)–22 (1978), 3; 24 (1980), 1–3; 35 (1991)–38 (1994)
    Lrco 22 (1978), 3, 4; 23 (1979), 1–4; 25 (1981), 2; 28 (1984), 1–3

Tracks Catalogue *see* **Music Master Track Index**

Trade Winds: Stern's World Music Review
GB–London: Priory Press, ?1988–
[NOT IN BUCOMP1]

    Lsa 1, 1988–#*

Tradition
GB–London: University College London Union Folk-Song Society, 1966–67

    AB*
    Cu 1966
    Ob*

Tradition: Newsletter of the Southern Folk Music Federation
GB–Southampton: Southern Folk Music Federation, 1965–?
[NOT IN BUCOMP1]

    SOu 1–4, 1965

Traditional Dance
0263–9033
GB–Crewe: Crewe and Alsager College of
Higher Education, 1982–
[NOT IN BUCOMP1]

EIR:Dtc 1 (1982)–4 (1986)
Lbl*

Traditional Music
0306–7440
GB–London: Alan Ward, 1975–?78

BSdsc*
Cu 1–10, 1975–78
EIR:Dtc 1–10, 1975–78
EIR:Duc 2–10, 1976–78
En*
Lcs 1–10, 1975–78
Lsa 1–10, 1975–78
Ob*
Ouf (Howes) 2–4, 1975–76

Trash!
0960–491X
GB–London: Dennis Oneshots, 1990–
[NOT IN BUCOMP1]

Lbl*

Treoir
TNG EIRE11; 0790–004X
EIRE–Dublin: Comhaltas Ceoltóiri Éireann,
1969–

BLp 6 (1974)–#
BLu 1 (1969), 8, 9; 2 (1970), 3, 5; 3 (1971)–#
Cu 6 (1974)–#
EIR:Dp 20 (1988)–#
EIR:Dtc 2 (1970), 3–#
EIR:Duc 1 (1969)–#
EIR:MEtc 2 (1970)–#*
En 6 (1974), 4; 7 (1975)–#
Lcs 12 (1980)–#*
Ob*

Tribschener Blätter
TNG CH157
CH–Lucerne: Schweizerische Gesellschaft
Richard-Wagner-Museum, 1956–

Lbl*

**La Tribune de l'Orgue: Revue Suisse
Romande**
TNG CH138; 1013–6835
CH–Lausanne [etc.], 1948–

[NOT IN BUCOMP1; in 1957 absorbed the
*Bulletin de l'Association des Organistes et
Maîtres de Chapelle Protestants Romands*]

Lam (o) 7 (1955), 2–8 (1956), 1, 2, 5; 9
(1957), 1–5; 10 (1958)–13 (1961), 1, 3–5;
14 (1962)–27 (1975), 1, 3, 4; 28 (1976)–29
(1977), 1; 30 (1978), 1–4

**La Tribune de Saint-Gervais: Bulletin
Mensuel de la Schola Cantorum**
Fellinger 1968/1328; TNG F261
F–Paris: Schola Cantorum, 1895–1929
[Subtitled *Revue Musicologique de la Schola
Cantorum* from 1908; *Revue Musicologique de
l'Art Religieux, publiée sous les Auspices de la
Schola Cantorum* from 1919/20; ceased
publication with vol. 26 (1929)]

Lu 1 (1895)–14 (1908)*
Ob*

**La Tribune de Saint-Gervais: Revue
Musicologique de la Schola Cantorum** *see* La
Tribune de Saint-Gervais: Bulletin Mensuel
de la Schola Cantorum

**La Tribune de Saint-Gervais: Revue
Musicologique de l'Art Religieux, publiée sous
les Auspices de la Schola Cantorum** *see* La
Tribune de Saint Gervais: Bulletin Mensuel de
la Schola Cantorum

Trick
0140–7929
GB–London: Wishcastle Ltd, 1977
[NOT IN BUCOMP1; punk rock magazine]

Lbl*

The Trinity Magazine *see* T.C.M. Magazine

**Tritsch-Tratsch: the Magazine of the Johann
Strauss Society of Great Britain**
TNG GB531; 0300–3086
GB–Bridgwater, 1966–

AB 1–60, 1966–90
Cu 1, 1966–#
EIR:Dtc 1, 1966–#
En 1, 1966–# [w 44]
Lbar 44–47, 1982–84; 51, 1986–#
Lbl*
Ob*
Ouf 59, 1990–#

The Trombonist: Journal of the British
Trombone Society
GB–London: British Trombone Society, 1987–
[NOT IN BUCOMP1]

CCtc 1987–#
Cu 1991–#
En*
Gam 1988, Sum, Aut; 1989, Spr–Aut; 1990,
    Sum, Aut; 1991, Spr, Sum; 1992, Sum, Aut;
    1993, Spr–Aut–#
Lbl 1991–
Lcm 1989, Aut; 1990, Spr, Aut; 1991–#
Lcml 1986, Sum–#
Ltc 1995, Sum–#
Mcm 1987, Spr–#
Msuc 1991–#
Ob*

Troubadour
GB–London, 1976–
[Entitled *Troubadour Bimonthly Newsletter*
from 1984]

Lcs 4 (1980)–7 (1984), 2*; n.s. 1 (1984), 6;
    2 (1985), 3, 5
Ob*

The Troubadour *see* The 'Jo

Troubadour Bimonthly Newsletter *see*
Troubadour

The Trumpeter
GB–Bedford: National School Band
Association, 1954–

Bp 47, 1971–# [w 83, 99]
Re 25–28, 1964–65; 31–86, 1966–84;
    88–106, 1985–92

Tuba Journal: for Euphonium and Tuba
0363–4787
US–Denton, TX [etc.]: Tubists Universal
Brotherhood Association, ?1973–
[NOT IN BUCOMP1]

Bs 21 (1993)–#
Gam 19 (1991)–#
Mcm 13 (1986), 3–#

Tune In
NL–Groes: C. Morgan, 1988–
[NOT IN BUCOMP1]

Ob 1 (1988)–#

Tune-In, incorporating Radio Guide *see*
Tune-In, to the Music of Television, Radio
and Records

Tune-In, to the Music of Television, Radio
and Records
GB–London: TV Times, 1977–
[NOT IN BUCOMP1; from Spring 1978
entitled *Tune-In, incorporating Radio Guide*]

Ob 1977–#

Tune Times
GB–London, 1933–35

Cbijs 2 (1934), 2
Lbbc 1 (1933)–2 (1935), 9
Lbl*

The Tuneful Yankee
Fellinger 1968/2301; TNG US458
US– Boston, MA: Walter Jacobs, 1917–30
[From vol. 2 (1918) entitled *Melody: a Monthly
Magazine for Lovers of Popular Music*; from 9
(1925) entitled *Melody: for the Photoplay,
Musician and Musical Home*]

Lbl*

Turk Musiki Dergisi
TNG TUR5
TR–?Istanbul, 1947–49
[Succeeded by *Musiki Mecmuasi* (q.v.)]

Cu 1–12, 1947–49

Turkish Musical Quarterly
US–Catonsville, MD: University of Maryland,
Center for Turkish Music, 1988–
[NOT IN BUCOMP1]

Cu 1 (1988)–
Lso 4 (1991), 4–5 (1992), 1

TVNM *see* Tijdschrift der Vereeniging voor
Noord-Nederlands Muziekgeschiedenis

Twangsville: the Duane Eddy Circle
Newsletter
US–Zephyr Cove, Nevada, ?–

Lsa 28, 1982–#

Twentieth Century Music
GB–London, 1952–?

Cpl 1 (1952), 3
Lam 1 (1952), 3

Twenty Five Years the King *see* **25 Years the King, 1956–81**

Twenty Four over Seven *see* **24–7**

Twist: Rock Skrift
DK–Aarhus, 1980–?

Lsa 1, 1980

U

UKCMET Newsletter/UK Council for Music Education Newsletter *see* United Kingdom Council for Music Education and Training (UKCMET) Newsletter

UK Council for Music Education Newsletter *see* United Kingdom Council for Music Education and Training (UKCMET) Newsletter

UK Mix
GB–London, 1986–
[NOT IN BUCOMP1]

Ob 1, 1986–#*

Ultra Postermag
GB–London, 1986–
[NOT IN BUCOMP1]

Ob 1 (1986)–#

Underground
0951–502X
GB–London: Spotlight, 1987–
[NOT IN BUCOMP1; rock music magazine]

Lbl*
Lsa 2–15, 1987–88
Ob 1987, Apr–#

Undertow
0953–9786
GB–Hanley: Undertow, 1988–
[NOT IN BUCOMP1]

Lbl*

Unhinged
0958–9112
GB–Calne, 1988–
[NOT IN BUCOMP1]

Lbl*

Union Musicologique: Bulletin *see* Bulletin de la Société "Union Musicologique"

Union of Bulgarian Composers: Music News Bulletin *see* Informatsionniy Muzikalny Byuletin; and Music News Bulletin

Union of Graduates in Music: Calendar *see* Roll of the Union of Graduates in Music [...] and Calendar

Union of Yugoslav Composers Organisations Bulletin *see* Bilten, SOKOJ

United Kingdom Council for Music Education and Training (UKCMET) Newsletter
GB–?: United Kingdom Council for Music Education and Training, 198?–
[NOT IN BUCOMP1]

Lam 1986, Win–1987, Win
TOd 1982/83–1987*

United Kingdom Harpists' Association Magazine *see* United Kingdom Harpists' Association Newsletter

United Kingdom Harpists' Association Newsletter
GB–London: United Kingdom Harpists' Association, 1965–
[Later (?1966) entitled *United Kingdom Harpists' Association Magazine*]

EIR:Dtc 76, 1985–#
En 78, 1985–
Lam 70–96, 1983–91
Ltc 112, 1995–#Ob 76, 1985–#

United Kingdom Sibelius Society Newsletter
GB–London: United Kingdom Sibelius Society, 1984–
[NOT IN BUCOMP1]

ALb 28, 1993–#
Lbar 1–21, 1984–91

Universal Jazz
GB–Reading, 1946–?

Cbijs 1 (1946), 1, 2, 4–7

Unknown Public
GB– Reading: Unknown Public/Guardian Newspapers, ?1994–
[NOT IN BUCOMP1; issued as a CD or cassette, with printed notes on contemporary music]

TOd 1994, 1, 3, 4–#

Uppslagsbok för Svenska Musikhandeln *see* Svensk Musikkatalog: Uppslagsbok för Svenska Musikhandeln

Urania: ein musikalisches Beiblatt zum Orgelfreunde [...]
Fellinger 1968/225; TNG D103
D–Erfurt; Leipzig: G.W. Körner [etc.], 1844–1911
[NOT IN BUCOMP1; from vol. 3 (1846) bore subtitle *Eine musikalische Zeitschrift zur Belehrung und Unterhaltung für Deutschlands Organisten [...]*; from 29 (1872) entitled *G. W. Körner's Urania: Musik-Zeitschrift für Alle, welche das Wohl der Kirche besonders zu fördern haben*. From 33 (1876) entitled *Urania: Musik-Zeitschrift für Orgelbau und Orgelspiel [...]*; from 46 (1889) subtitled *Musik-Zeitschrift für Orgelbau, Orgel-und Harmoniumspiel*. 68 vols in all]

   Lam (o) 3 (1846)–11 (1854); 15 (1858); 17 (1860); 43 (1886)– 47 (1890)

Urania: eine musikalische Zeitschrift zur Belehrung und Unterhaltung für Deutschlands Organisten [...] *see* Urania: ein musikalisches Beiblatt zum Orgelfreunde [...]

Urania: Musik-Zeitschrift für Orgelbau und Orgelspiel [...] *see* Urania: ein musikalisches Beiblatt zum Orgelfreunde [...]

Urania: Musik-Zeitschrift für Orgelbau, Orgel- und Harmoniumspiel *see* Urania: ein musikalisches Beiblatt zum Orgelfreunde [...]

USSR Union of Composers Information Bulletin
RF–?Moscow: Union of Composers, ?–
[NOT IN BUCOMP1]

   ALb 1973*
   Gul 1983–86
   Lsa 1975–82*

Uusi Kansanmusiikki *see* Kansanmusiikki

V

V Mire Muzyki [= In the Musical World]
RF–Moscow: Sovetskiy Kompozitor, 1970–
[NOT IN BUCOMP1]

   Gul 1981, 1984

Variety, Music, Stage and Film News
GB–London, 1931–33

   Lbl*

Variety, Stage and Music Hall Pictorial
GB–London, 1905

   Lbl*

Vaughan Williams Memorial Library Newsletter
GB–London: Vaughan Williams Memorial Library, 1987–
[NOT IN BUCOMP1]

   Lcs 1, 1987–#

VdGSA Journal *see* Journal of the Viola da Gamba Society of America

VdGSA News
TNG US735; 0506–306X
US–New York: Viola da Gamba Society of America, 1963–

   Bu 30 (1993), 2–#

Verdi: Bollettino Quadrimestrale dell'Istituto di Studi Verdiani *see* Bollettino dell'Istituto di Studi Verdiani

Verdi Newsletter *see* A.I.V.S. Newsletter

Vereeniging voor Muziekgeschiedenis Antwerpen: Jaarboek *see* Vlaamsch Jaarboek voor Muziekgeschiedenis

Veröffentlichungen des Instituts für Neue Musik und Musikerziehung Darmstadt
D–Darmstadt: Institut für Neue Musik und Musikerziehung, 1965–
[NOT IN BUCOMP1]

   Lu 1 (1965)–#
   Mu*

Verzeichnis der im Jahre [1871 etc.] im deutschen Reich und in den Ländern deutschen Sprachgebietes sowie der für den Vertrieb im deutschen Reich wichtigen, im Auslande erschienen Musikalien, auch musikalischen Schriften und Abbildungen *see* Kurzes Verzeichnis sämmtlicher in Deutschland und den angrenzenden Ländern gedruckter Musikalien, auch musikalischer Schriften und Abbildungen mit Anzeige der Verleger und Preise

Věstník Jednoty Zpěvákých Spolků
Ceskoslovanských [= Bulletin of the Union of
Czechoslovak Choral Societies]
Fellinger 1968/1375; TNG CS65
CZ–Prague, 1896–1948
[From 1903 entitled *Věstník Pěvecky* [*Song
Bulletin*]; from 1907 entitled *Věstnik Pěvecky a
Hudebni* [*Song and Music Bulletin*]

Ob*

Věstník Pěvecky *see* Vestník Jednoty
Zpěvákých Spolků Ceskoslovanských

Věstník Pěvecky a Hudebni *see* Věstník
Jednoty Zpěvákých Spolků
Ceskoslovanských

Victorian Organ Journal
AUS–Melbourne: Society of Organists
(Victoria) Incorporated, 1972/73–
[NOT IN BUCOMP1]

Lam (o) 1986, June; 1987, Oct; 1988, Apr;
1989, Oct–Dec; 1990, Oct; 1991–93; 1994,
Feb, Apr, June, Aug, Dec

Vic-Wells Association: Bulletin *see* The Old
Vic and Sadlers Wells Magazine

Video Home Entertainment
0950–2347
GB–London: Video Business Publications,
1981–
[NOT IN BUCOMP1]

SFp [c]

Vie Musicale
0042–5591
C–Quebec: Ministère des Affaires Culturelles,
1965–71
[Ceased publication with no. 19, 1971]

BSdsc*
Lcm 18, 1970

**La Vie Musicale: Bulletin Mensuel
d'Information de la Revue Internationale de
Musique**
TNG B135
B–Mettet: Palate Corneille, 1950–53

[Published as a supplement to *La Revue
Internationale de Musique* (q.v.)]

Lbl*

La Vie Musicale Belge *see* Bulletin
d'Information de la Vie Musicale Belge

Vierteljahrsschrift für Musikwissenschaft
Fellinger 1968/1005; TNG D282
D–Leipzig: Breitkopf und Härtel, 1885–94

AB*
Au 1 (1885)–10 (1894)
Cpl 1 (1885)–10 (1894)
Cu 1 (1885)–10 (1894) [Reprint ed.]
EIR:Dtc 1 (1885), 1
Er 1 (1885)–4 (1888); 6 (1890)–10 (1894)
Gul 1 (1885)–10 (1894)
Lbl 1 (185)–10 (1895) [2 copies]
Lcml 1 (1885)–4 (1888)
Lu 1 (1885)–10 (1894) [Reprint ed.]
Mpl 1 (1885)–10 (1894)
Ob 1 (1885)–10 (1894)
Ouf 1 (1885)–10 (1894)

Village Voice
0042–6180
US–New York: Village Voice, 1955–
[NOT IN BUCOMP1]

Msuc 1993, June–#

Viltis: a Folklore Magazine
0042–6253
US–Denver, CO: Beliajus, 1942–

Lcs 25 (1967), 2–#*
Ouf (Howes) 23 (1965), 6; 25 (1967), 4, 6

Vintage Jazz Mart
0042–6369
GB–London: T. H. Benwell, 1953–
[Entitled *VJM's Jazz and Blues Mart* from 94,
1994]

Cbijs 1954–62
Cu 1970–#
En*
LOnjfa*
Lsa 55–58, 1958; 60–78, 1959–60; 1963–75*
Ob*

Vintage Light Music: for the Enthusiast of Light Music on 78 r.p.m. Records
0307–5524
GB–West Wickham: Vintage Light Music Society, 1975–
[Preceded by *Commodore: for the Enthusiast of Light Music on 78s* (q.v.)]

    BDp 1975–#
    Cu 1975–#
    EIR:Dtc 1975, Win–#
    En 1975–# [w 45]
    Lsa 1975–# [w 51, 1987]
    Ob*

Vintage Record Mart
GB–Rayleigh, 1970–

    Cbijs 1972*; 1973–77
    Lsa 12 (1982), 4

Vintage Sound Waves
GB–?, 198?–
[NOT IN BUCOMP1]

    NTp 1, 2, 1980

Die Viola: Jahrbuch der Internationalen Viola-Forschungsgesellschaft/The Viola: Yearbook of the International Viola Council
0172–9098
D–Kassel: Bärenreiter [for the International Viola Research Society], 1979–

    Ob 1979–#

The Viola: Yearbook of the International Viola Council *see* **Die Viola: Jahrbuch der Internationalen Viola-Forschungsgesellschaft**

Viola da Gamba Society: Bulletin
TNG GB428
GB–London: Viola da Gamba Society, 1948–68
[Ceased publication with no. 28, 1968; succeeded by *Chelys: the Journal of the Viola da Gamba Society* (q.v.)]

    Cpl 20, 22–28, 1963–68
    Cu 24–27, 1965–67
    Lam 16–28, 1 961–68
    Lbbc 17–28, 1962–68 [w 25, 27]
    Lbl*
    Lcml 13–28, 1959–68
    Lkc 5–28, 1952–68*
    Lu 26–28, 1967–68
    Ob*

Viola da Gamba Society: Newsletter
TNG GB547
GB–London: Viola da Gamba Society, 1969–
[NOT IN BUCOMP1]

    Cpl 1, 1969–#*
    Ob 4, 1970/71; 7, ?1972–#

Viola da Gamba Society of America: Journal *see* **Journal of the Viola da Gamba Society of America**

Viola da Gamba Society of America News *see* **VdGSA News**

Viola Research Society (British Branch) Newsletter
GB–Harlow, 1976–

    Lam 1–28, 1976–86 [w 6–13, 15, 16]

The Violexchange
0892–5437
US–Ann Arbor, MI: LFS Publications, 1986–
[NOT IN BUCOMP1]

    Mcm 1 (1986)–3 (1988)

The Violin: a Monthly Journal of Musical News
Fellinger 1968/1858; TNG C11
C–Toronto, 1905–20; n.s. 1920–33
[From 1907 entitled *Musical Canada: a Monthly Journal of Musical News, Comment and Gossip, for Professionals and Amateurs*]

    Lbl*

The Violin: Monthly Magazine for all Lovers of the Instruments [sic]
Fellinger 1968/1117; TNG GB131
GB–London, 1889–94

    Cu 1 (1889)–3 (1891)
    En 1 (1890)–5 (1894)
    Gm 2 (1890), 1–5
    Lbl*
    Ob 1 (1889)

El Violín: Periodiquin con Dibujitos
Fellinger 1968/465; TNG M1
ME–Mexico City, 1862

    Lbl*

The Violin and String World
Fellinger 1968/1267
GB–London, 1908–13
[Ceased publication with no. 61, 1913]
[Supplement to *The Musical Standard: Illustrated Series* (q.v.)]

   Lbl 1908–13
   Mpl 1909–13

Violin Makers Journal
C–Vancouver: Violin Makers Association of British Columbia, 1957–64
[NOT IN BUCOMP1]

   Mp 1963–64

The Violin Soloist
GB–London: F. Pitman, 1886–94
[92 nos in total]

   Lbl*

The Violin Times: a Monthly Journal for Professional and Amateur Violinists and Quartet Players
Fellinger 1968/1241; TNG GB159
GB–London, 1893–1907

   Bp 1 (1893)–14 (1907), Nov
   En 1 (1893)–12 (1905)
   Lbl 1 (1893)–14 (1907), 169
   Ob*

The Violinist *see* The Cremona: with which is incorporated "The Violinist", a Record of the String World

The Violinist's Gazette *see* Gazette of the College of Violinists

Violins and Violinists
TNG US548
US–Evanston, IL: E. N. Doring, 1938–60
[Entitled *Violins and Violinists Magazine* (ISSN 0748-8645), 1942–60]

   LVp 18 (1957)–21 (1960)

Violins and Violinists Magazine *see* Violins and Violinists

Virtuoso
GB–London: Brysson Ling, 1981–
[NOT IN BUCOMP1]

   EIR:Dtc 1, 1981

Vivacity [translated title] *see* Asbri

Vivaldi Informations *see* Informations: International Antonio Vivaldi Society

Vivaldiana
0507–6331; TNG INTL30
B–Brussels: Centre International de Documentation Antonio Vivaldi, 1969–?

   Lbl*
   Lkc (1969), 1
   Lu 1 (1969)
   Ob*

VJM'S Jazz and Blues Mart *see* Vintage Jazz Mart

Vlaamsch Jaarboek voor Muziekgeschiedenis
[= Flemish Yearbook of Music History]
TNG B114
B–Antwerp: Vereeniging voor Muziekgeschiedenis, 1939–42; 1959
[Vol. 5 (1959) entitled *Vereeniging voor Muziekgeschiedenis Antwerpen: Jaarboek*]

   AB 1 (1939); 1959
   Cu 1959
   Lcml 1 (1939)–4 (1942)
   Lkc 1 (1939)–4 (1942)
   Ob*

Vocal Art
GB–London, 1946–

   Lsa 20 (1972), Dec–23 (1975), Feb

Vocal Lines
GB–Sevenoaks: Novello, 1983–88

   Cu 1–12, 1983–88
   EIR:Dtc 1–12, 1983–88
   Lbl*
   Ob*

The Vocalist
Fellinger 1968/1652; TNG GB196
GB–London: The Vocalist Company, 1902–05
[45 nos in total]

   Cu 1–12, 1902–03 [w 3]
   En 1–9, 1902–03
   Lbl*
   Lcm 10, 1903
   Lcm (p) 1, 1902
   Ob*

The Voice [1]
0263–8169
GB–London: The Gramophone Company, 1917–

 Lsa 17 (1933), 10–12; 18 (1934), 8; 19
 (1935), 9; 30 (1948), 2; 31 (1949), 2; 33
 (1951), 1, 4

The Voice [2]
IN–Calcutta, 1958–

 Lsa 6 (1963/65), 1–12; n.s. 1 (1966)–2
 (1967)*

Voice *see also* **Werner's Magazine**

Voice: Journal of the British Voice Association
0966–789X
GB–London: Whurr Publishers, 1992–
[NOT IN BUCOMP1]

 EIR:Dtc 1 (1992), 2–#

Voice: [Newsletter of] the Friends of Scottish Opera
GB–Glasgow: Friends of Scottish Opera, 1989–
[NOT IN BUCOMP1]

 Ep 1–4, 1989–90; 6, 7, 1990

Voice and Verse
TNG GB312
GB–London: British Federation of Music Competition Festivals, 1925–26

 En 1925–26
 Lbl*
 Lcml 1925–26
 Ob*

Voice of Buddha
GB–London, ?1981–
[NOT IN BUCOMP1; punk rock magazine]

 Lbl*
 Ob 1, 1981–#*

Voice of the Harp [translated title] *see* **Llais y Delyn**

La Voix de l'Église
Fellinger 1968/2281; TNG F458
F–Lille: Société Saint-Augustin; Paris: Desclée de Brouwer, 1916/17–39
[NOT IN BUCOMP1; from 1920 entitled *Revue Pratique de Liturgie et de Musique Sacrée*; from 1928, July entitled *Revue Liturgique et Musicale*; from 1937, July entitled *Musique et Liturgie*]

 Cpl 16 (1932)–22 (1939)

Voknoviny [?= Vocal News]
GB–London: Palach Press, 1987–
[NOT IN BUCOMP1]

 Ob 1, 1987–#*

Volksdans
0929–7235
NL–Utrecht, 1969–
[NOT IN BUCOMP1]

 Lcs 1984–#*

Volkskunst: Fachausgabe *see* **Die Volksmusik: Zeitschrift für das musikalische Laienschaffen**

Volkslied, Volkstanz, Volksmusik: Zeitschrift für deren Kenntnis und Pflege
A–Vienna: Österreichische Gesellschaft für Volkslied- und Volkstanzpflege, ?1899–
[NOT IN BUCOMP1]

 Ouf (Howes) 48 (1947), 1/2; 49 (1948), 1/2, 3/4

Die Volksmusik: Zeitschrift für das musikalische Laienschaffen
TNG D984; 0042–8558
D–Leipzig: Deutscher Verlag für Musik, 1956–
[Vols 1–11 also entitled *Volkskunst: Fachausgabe*; entitled *Musikforum: Zeitschrift für musikalisches Volksschaffen* from vol. 16 (1971) (ISBN 0323–5106)]

 Cu 19, 1974–#
 Lam 68–71, 1988–90; 74, 1991–#
 Lcm 69–71, 1988–90; 73–75, 1990–91; 78, 1993

Volksmusik in Bayern
0177–445X
D–Munich: Bayerischer Landesverein für
Heimatpflege, 1984–
[NOT IN BUCOMP1]

   BSdsc 3 (1986), 3; 4 (1987), 2–11 (1994), 2

Volkstanz
D–Leipzig: Teubner, 1925–
[NOT IN BUCOMP1]

   Lcs 1983, 2–#

Der Vollklang
D–Hamburg, 1949–?

   Lsa 1953, 3–6

**The Volunteer Choir: a Monthly Magazine
devoted to the Interests of Untrained Choirs**
US–Dayton, NY: Lorenz Publishing Company,
?1913–

   Lbl*

**Voprosy Muzykoznaniya [= Musicological
Questions]**
TNG USSR70
RF–Moscow, 1953–60

   Cpl 2 (1956)
   Cu 1 (1953), 1, 2; 2 (1956)–3 (1960)
   Lbl*
   Lu 1 (1954)–3 (1960)
   Ob*

**Voprosy Teory i Estetiki Muzyki [= Questions
on Music Theory and Aesthetics]**
RF–Leningrad, 1962–68

   Lbl*

Vox [1]
GB–London, 1929–30

   Lbl*
   Lcm 1 (1929/30), 1–14
   Lsa 1 (1929/30), 1–14
   Ob 1 (1929/30), 1–14

Vox [2]
0960–300X
GB–London: Reed International, 1990–
[NOT IN BUCOMP1]

   BRp [c (2 years)]
   Cu 1, 8, 9, 1990–91; 42, 1994–#

   EIR:Dtc 1, 1990–#
   Lbbc 1, 1990–#
   Lri [c (2 years)]
   Lsa 1, 1990–#
   Lwwbat [c]
   Msuc 1992–#
   Ob 1–13, 1990–91
   PRp [c]

Vox Pop: Journal of the Workers' Association
TNG GB382
GB–London, 1944–45
[Incorporated into *Keynote: the Progressive
Music Quarterly* (q.v.)]

   Lbl*

VSA Journal *see* **Journal of the Violin Society
of America**

W

Wagner *see* **The Wagner Society Newsletter**

Wagner News *see* **The Wagner Society
Newsletter**

Wagner: the Magazine of the Wagner Society
see **The Wagner Society Newsletter**

The Wagner Society Newsletter
GB–London, 1965–80; n.s. 1980–
[From 1971, Nov. entitled *Wagner: the
Magazine of the Wagner Society*; from 1980,
June divided into *Wagner* and *Wagner News* (the
latter beginning with a new numbering
sequence) (ISSN 0261–3468)]

   Cu 71, 1978–#; n.s. 1, 1980–#
   EIR:Dtc 71, 1978–#
   En 71–84, 1978–80; n.s. 1 (1980)–#
   Gm 32, 1984–#
   Lbar 4 (1983)–#; 22–67, 1983–89; 75,
      1990–# [w 81, 1990]
   Lbl*
   Lcm 32–84, 1974–80 [w 65, 69]; 1 (1980), 1;
      2 (1981)–5 (1984), 3; 6 (1985)–7 (1986), 1,
      3; 8 (1987), 1, 2; 9 (1983), 3
   Lcm (p) 7 (1986), 4
   Lcml*
   LRHBNC 4 (1983), 3 –10 (1989), 4; 11
      (1990), 3–#
   Lsa*
   Lu 15, 1982–# [w 18, 47, 48]
   Ob 1 (1980)–# [+ Wagner News 1 (1980)–#]
   Ouf 3 (1982)–8 (1987), 4

Wagner Society Review
TNG GB525
GB–London, 1965

Lcml 1965, Jan
Lu 1965, Jan

Wake Up! Punk Fanzine
GB–?, 198?–
[NOT IN BUCOMP1]

Ob 4, 1984–#*

Walcker
GB–?, 195?–
[NOT IN BUCOMP1]

Lam (o) 17–31, 1957–63
Yu 1–41, 1949–70 [w 16–19, 23–27, 30, 37]

Washington Opera Magazine
0196–3236
US–Washington, DC: Washington Opera Guild,
1974–
[NOT IN BUCOMP1]

ALb 10 (1982/83), 2

Watch This: the Official Publication of the
Vindicators
GB–Grangemouth, 1986–
[NOT IN BUCOMP1]

Lbl*
Ob 4, 1986–#*

Wavelength: New Orleans Music Magazine
0741–2460
US–New Orleans, LA: 1980–
[NOT IN BUCOMP1]

EXu 45 (1984)–#
LOnjfa*

Weekend Country Music Extra
GB–London, 1982–
[NOT IN BUCOMP1]

Ob 2, 1982–#

The Weekly Musical Review
Fellinger 1968/1695; TNG GB202
GB–London, 1903

Lbl*

The Weekly Musical Transcript
Fellinger 1968/330; TNG GB51
GB–London: Henry Crozier, 1853–54
[Entitled *Musical Transcript: a Weekly Journal
of Music [...]* from 1853, 7]

Lbl*

The Weekly Pianist
GB–London, 1863
[17 nos in total]

Lbl*

The Weekly Theatrical Reporter and Music
Hall Review
GB–London, 1867–68

Lbl 1–14, 1867–68

Der Weihergarten: Hausmitteilungen des
Hauses B. Schott's Söhne, Mainz *see* Der
Weihergarten: Verlagsblatt des Hauses B.
Schott's Söhne, Mainz

Der Weihergarten: Verlagsblatt des Hauses B.
Schott's Söhne, Mainz
TNG D746
D–Mainz: B. Schott's Söhne, 1931–39
[Later issues entitled *Der Weihergarten:
Hausmitteilungen des Hauses B. Schott's Söhne,
Mainz*]

Lcml 1931*; 1937*

Well Red
0960–2577
GB–London: Red Wedge, 1986–
[NOT IN BUCOMP1]

Lbl*

Welsh Folk Dance Society Newsletter
[translated title] *see* Cymdeithas Ddawns
Werin Cymru: Cylchlythyr

Welsh Folk Song Society: Annual Reports
GB–?: Welsh Folk Song Society, ?–
[NOT IN BUCOMP1]

Bp 1909–66/67; 1970/71–1972/73; 1974/75

Welsh Hymn Society Bulletin [translated title]
see Bwletin Cymdeithas Emynau Cymru

Welsh Music/Cerddoriaeth Cymru
TNG GB490; 0043–244X
GB–Swansea: Guild for the Promotion of Welsh Music, 1959–

> **AB***
> **ABc** 1 (1959/63), 7, 8; 2 (1964/67), 6–8; 3 (1968/71), 2– 10; 4 (1972/74), 1–3, 6, 9, 10; 5 (1975/76)–7 (1982/85), 1, 2, 5–10; 8 (1986/88)–#
> **ABc (ILS)** 3 (1969)–6 (1982)
> **ALb** 6 (1980/81), 6; 7 (1984), 7
> **Au** 5 (1976)–7 (1982)
> **BG** 1 (1959)–#
> **BSdsc** 6 (1981)–#
> **CDCp** 1 (1959)–#
> **CDu** 2 (1963/65)– #*
> **Cu** 1 (1959), 2–#*
> **EIR:Dtc** 2 (1966), 10–#
> **En***
> **LAu** 1 (1959/61), 7, 9, 10; 2 (1962/66), 5, 6, 8–10
> **Lbl***
> **Mcm** 3 (1967/71), 1, 2; 6 (1980/82), 5; 7 (1983/84), 5
> **MO** 1963–#
> **Ob***
> **RH** 5 (1976/79)–#*

Welsh Music History *see* **Hanes Cerddoriaeth Cymru/Welsh Music History**

The Welsh Musician [translated title] *see* **Cerddor Cymreig**

Welsh National Opera News
0260–8138
GB–Cardiff: Welsh National Opera, 1978–83

> **AB** 3–23, 1978–83 [w 13, 15]
> **Cu** 1–23, 1978–83
> **En** 1–23, 1978–83
> **Lbl***
> **Ob***

Welsh National Opera Preview *see* **Preview [of Welsh National Opera]**

Die Welt der Musik *see* **The World of Music: Quarterly Journal of the International Institute for Comparative Music Studies and Documentation, Berlin, in Association with the International Music Council, UNESCO**

De Wereld der Muziek *see* **Orgaan der Federatie van Nederlandse Toonkunstenaars-Vereenigingen**

Wereldmuziek [= World Music]
NL–Amsterdam, 1989–

> **Lsa** 1, 1989

Werner's Magazine
Fellinger 1968/808; TNG US144
US–New York: Edgar S. Werner, 1879–1902
[NOT IN BUCOMP1; from 1879 entitled *Voice*; from 11 (1889), *Werner's Voice Magazine*; from 1893, *Werner's Magazine*]

> **Gm** 16 (1894)–17 (1895)

Werner's Voice Magazine *see* **Werner's Magazine**

Wesley Society Gazette
0309–0442
GB–West Bridgford: Wesley Society of Great Britain, 1976–

> **EIR:Dtc** 1 (1976), 2 –2 (1978), 2
> **Lbl***
> **NO** 1 (1976)–2 (1978), 2
> **Ob***
> **SFu** 1 (1976)–2 (1978)

West Gallery: the Newsletter of the West Gallery Music Association
0960–4227
GB–Wolverhampton: West Gallery Music Association, 1990–
[NOT IN BUCOMP1; sacred music magazine]

> **Lbl***

The Westminster and Covent Garden Journal *see* **The Covent Garden Journal [1]**

WH-News: Information from the Wilhelm Hansen Group of Music Publishers
DK–Copenhagen: Wilhelm Hansen, 197?–
[NOT IN BUCOMP1]

> **Lcm** 1981, 3; 1983, 1; 1984, 1; 1985, 2; 1986, 1; 1987, 1

What CD? and Digital Audio *see* **Popular Hi-Fi**

What Hi-Fi? *see* **Popular Hi-Fi**

What Karaoke and Music Maker
0964–8828
GB–London: WV Publications, 1991–
[NOT IN BUCOMP1]

Lbl 1 (1991)–#

What Keyboard?: Portable Keyboards, Organs, Pianos *see* Home Organist and Leisure Music

What Satellite *see* What Video

What Video
0956–2354
GB–London, 1980–
[NOT IN BUCOMP1; *What Satellite* and *CD Video Magazine* are issued together with this publication; from 1994 entitled *What Video and What Home Cinema* (ISSN 1352–6162)

Lhg 1992–#
Ob*

What Video and What Home Cinema *see* What Video

What's Afoot: Magazine of the Devon District of the English Folk Dance and Song Society
GB–?: English Folk Dance and Song Society (Devon District), 198?–
[NOT IN BUCOMP1]

TOd 15, 1985; 23, 1987

Where's Eric!
0969–9171
GB–Maidenhead, 1992–
[NOT IN BUCOMP1; Eric Clapton fanzine]

Lbl*

Which CD: Systems, News, Music, Reviews *see* Which Compact Disc? and Hi-Fi for Pleasure

Which Compact Disc? and Hi-Fi for Pleasure
0267–0925
GB–London: Greater London House, 1984–
[NOT IN BUCOMP1; from vol. 5 (1989), 8 entitled *Which CD: Systems, News, Music, Reviews*; absorbed *Hi-Fi Today*]

AB 1986, 11 –1990, Aug
Bp 1 (1984)–6 (1990), 6
BSdsc*
CFp 1 (1984)

Cu 1 (1984)–6 (1990), 6
EIR:Dp 1 (1985)–6 (1990), Aug
EIR:Dtc 1 (1985)–6 (1990), 6
Lbar 1 (1985)–6 (1990), 5
Lbl*
Ob*

Whiskey, Women, and …
0091–7664
US–Haverhill, MA, 1971–

Cbijs 1–3, 1972

White Book
0265–8224
GB–Staines, 1984–
[NOT IN BUCOMP1]

BRp 1990–#
Msuc [c]

White Noise
GB–London: White Noise Club, ?1986–
[NOT IN BUCOMP1; rock music magazine]

Lbl*
Ob 3, 1987–#*

White Stuff
GB–London, 1977–
[NOT IN BUCOMP1]

Lsa 1, 5, 7, 1977

Who Put the Bomp?
0039–7873
US–Burbank, CA, ?1957–
[NOT IN BUCOMP1; also known as *Bomp!*]

Lsa 2 (1958), 2; 6–21, 1971–79*

Who's Who in Music [and Musician's International Directory]
0083–9647
US/GB: New York: Hafner; Cambridge, UK: Melrose Press, 1918–
[NOT IN BUCOMP1; absorbed the *Musician's Directory* (q.v.) in 1935; later entitled *Who's Who in Music and Musician's International Directory*; *International Who's Who in Music*]

AB 1985–#
Ap 1935; 1949/50; 1962; 1969; 1972; 1975; 1977; 1980; 1985; 1988; 1990/91–#
BRu 1st ed. (1935); 3rd ed. (1949/50); 4th ed. (1962); 5th ed. (1969)

Ep 1975–#
HUu 1937; 1962
Lba 1935; 1949/50; 1962; 1969; 1972–#
Lk 1918, 1935, 1937, 1950, 1962, 1969, 1972, 1975, 1977–#
Lk (c) 1935, 1950–#
Lu 5th ed. (1969); 6th ed. (1972); 1975–#
Ob*
SA 1st ed. (1935); 3rd ed. (1949/50); 4th ed. (1962); 6th ed. (1972); 1977
SOu 1972; 1975–1980

Who's Who in Opera
US–New York: Arno Press, 1976–
[NOT IN BUCOMP1]

    SA 1976

Wiener Akademische Mozartgcmeinde: Arbeits- und Kulturbericht
A–Vienna, 1943–44

    Lbl*

Wiener Akademische Mozartgemeinde: Mitteilungen
A–Vienna, 1930–43
[From 1940 entitled *Wiener Figaro*]

    Lbl*

Wiener allgemeine musikalische Zeitung
Fellinger 1968/31
A–Vienna: Tendler, 1813
[NOT IN BUCOMP1]

    Cu 1–52, 1813 [Reprint ed.]
    Er 1 (1813) [Reprint ed.]
    Lbl 1–52, 1813 [+ Reprint ed.]
    Ob 1 (1813) [Reprint ed.]
    Ouf 1 (1813) [Reprint ed.]

Wiener allgemeine musikalische Zeitung *see also* **Allgemeine musikalische Zeitung mit besonderer Rücksicht auf den Österreichischen Kaiserstaat**

Wiener allgemeine Musik-Zeitung *see* **Allgemeine Wiener Musik-Zeitung**

Wiener allgemeine Theaterzeitung [Theater-Zeitung] *see* **Wiener Theater-Zeitung**

Wiener allgemeine Zeitung *see* **Wiener Theater-Zeitung**

Wiener Conversationsblatt *see* **Wiener Theater-Zeitung**

Wiener Figaro *see* **Wiener Akademische Mozartgemeinde: Mitteilungen**

Wiener Theater-Zeitung
Fellinger 1968/17; TNG A6
A–Vienna, 1806–08; 1811–60
[From 1807 entitled *Zeitung für Theater, Musik und Poesie*; from 1811 entitled *Theater-Zeitung*; from 1817 entitled *Wiener allgemeine Theaterzeitung*; from 1823 entitled *Allgemeine Theaterzeitung und Unterhaltungsblatt für Freunde der Kunst, Literatur, und des geselligen Lebens*; from 1831 entitled *Allgemeine Theaterzeitung und Originalblatt für Kunst, Literatur, Musik, Mode und geselliges Leben*; from 1845 entitled *Illustrirte Theaterzeitung*; from 1846 entitled *Allgemeine Theaterzeitung*; from 1848 entitled *Österreichischer Courier*; from 1850 entitled *Wiener allgemeine Theaterzeitung*; from 1851 entitled *Wiener allgemeine Zeitung*; from 1853 entitled *Wiener allgemeine Theater-Zeitung*; from 1855 entitled *Wiener Conversationsblatt*; from 1856 entitled *Wiener Theaterzeitung*]

    Lbl*

Wiener Waldhorn Verein *see* **W.W.V. Blatter**

William Morris Musical Society Bulletin
GB–London: Workers' Musical Association, 1941–?

    Lgo 1, 1941

Williams's Musical Annual and Australian Sketch Book [for 1858]
Fellinger 1968/402; TNG AUS1
AUS–Melbourne: W. H. Williams, 1858
[Only one issue was published]

    Lbl

WIM Bulletin *see* **Women in Music Newsletter**

Window on Music
GB–London: Junior Missionary Association of the Methodist Church, ?–
[NOT IN BUCOMP1]

    AB 1977, Sum

Winds: Journal of the British Association of
Symphonic Bands and Wind Ensembles
0269-2015
GB–Baldock, 1985–
[NOT IN BUCOMP1]

Bs 1 (1985)–#
CCtc 1 (1986)–#
Cu 1 (1985)–#
EIR:Dcmc 8 (1993)–#
EIR:Dtc 1 (1985)–#
Gam 3 (1988)–#
Gm 1 (1985)–#
Lam 1 (1985)–#
LCdM 1 (1985)–#
Lcm 1 (1986), 3–#
Lcml 2 (1983); 3 (1984)–4 (1985), 1; n.s. 1
    (1985)–#
LEc 5 (1990)–6 (1991), 1–3; 7 (1992), 1, 2, 4;
    9 (1994)–#
Lgsm n.s. 2 (1987)–#
Ltc 7 (1992)–8 (193)*; 9 (1994)–#
Mcm 1 (1985)–#
Msuc 1 (1985)–#
Ob*
Y 3 (1988, Sum)–#

Winter Gardens Society Magazine
GB–Bournemouth, 1951–56

DS 1–25, 1951–56
Lbl*

Wir teilen mit: Hausmitteilungen des
Musikverlages *see* Der Aufstieg

The Wire: Adventures in Modern Music *see*
The Wire: Jazz, Improvised Music, and …

The Wire: Jazz, Improvised Music, and …
0952–0686
GB–London: Namara Group, 1982–
[Various subtitles include *The Shape of Music
Magazines to Come* and *Adventures in Modern
Music*]

Bs 79, 1990–#
BTp [c (1 year)]
BYp [c (1 year)]
CDCp [c (5 years)]
CCtc 118/119, 1994–#
Cu 11, 1985–#
DS [c (2 years)]
Ep 28, 1986–#
EXu 1, 1982; 3, 1983–#

Lam 44–51, 1987–88; 54–57, 1988; 60–62,
    65, 66, 68, 1989; 70–77, 1990; 79–101,
    1990–92; 103–111, 1992–93; 113, 115,
    1993–#
Lbar 1, 1982–#*
Lbl*
LCdM 11, 1985–#
Lcml 1, 1982; 3, 1983; 6, 1984–#
LEc [c (5 years)]
Len [c (1 year)]
Lgo 1, 1982–#
Lgsm 77, 1990–#
Lh [c (2 years)]
Lha (f) [c (2 years)]
Lis [c (2 years)]
Lk [c (6 months)]
Lmi 23, 1986–#
LOnjfa 1, 1982–#
Lsa 1, 1982–# [w 31, 1986]
Lsut [c (2 years)]
Ltc 151, 1996–#
Lwf [c (6 months)]
Lwwb [c]
Lwwbat 8–10, 1984; 12, 1985–#
Lwwput [c]
LXp [c (1 year)]
MK 33, 1986–#
Mpl 1, 1982–#
Msuc 21, 1985–#
NOTu 84, 1991–#
Ob*
Oub 120, 1994–#
Ouf 13, 1985–#
R 38, 39, 1987
SHRp 1997–# (5 year file)
TOd 1, 1982–#

The Wire: the Shape of Music Magazines to
Come *see* The Wire: Jazz, Improvised Music,
and …

Wireless and Gramophone Trades Yearbook
and Diary
GB– London, 1925–?

En 1932–33; 1935

Wöchentliche Nachrichten und
Anmerkungen die Musik betreffend
TNG D12
D–Leipzig, 1766–1770
[Entitled *Musikalische Nachrichten und
Anmerkungen* from 1770]

Au 1 (1766)–4 (1770) [Reprint ed.]
Cu 1 (1766)–4 (1770) [Reprint ed.]

Er 1–13, 1766–70
Lu 1766–1770 [Reprint ed.]
Ob 1766–70 [Reprint ed.]

Women in Music Bulletin *see* **Women in Music Newsletter**

Women in Music Newsletter
GB–Battersea: Women in Music, ?1988–93;
1994–
[NOT IN BUCOMP1; entitled *Women in Music [WIM] Bulletin* from 1994, with new numbering system]

BAc 15 (1991)–23 (1993); 1 (1994)–#
EIR:Dtc 1991, May–#
En*
Gsmic [c]
Lbbc 1992, May–1993, Sep; 1 (1994)–#
Lcml 12, 1991; 16, 1991–#
Ob 15–23, 1991–93 [w 18]
Ouf 16, 1991–#
TOd 5–23, 1989–93*

Woodwind/Brass and Percussion *see* **Woodwind World**

Woodwind Quarterly
1070–2512
US–Colville, West Virginia, 1993–
[NOT IN BUCOMP1]

Lgu 1, 1993–#

Woodwind World
TNG US689; 0512–199X
US–Bedford Hills, NY: Woodwind World,
1957–
[Entitled *Woodwind World Brass and Percussion* from vol. 14 (1975) (ISSN 0098–4574); from vol. 20 no. 4 (1981)–24 (1985) entitled *Woodwind/Brass and Percussion*]

Cpl 3 (1960), Sep 15
Lam 12 (1973), 2–5; 13 (1974), 2–5; 14
 (1975), 1, 2, 4, 5; 15 (1976), 1–6; 16
 (1977)–20 (1981), 7
Lcml*
Lu 10 (1971), 1; 12 (1973), 1–5; 13 (1974),
 1–5; 14 (1975), 1–5
Mcm 11 (1972, 4, 5; 12 (1973), 1–5; 13
 (1974), 1–3, 5–#
Uu 11 (1972)–24 (1985)*

Woodwind World Brass and Percussion *see* **Woodwind World**

The Word: Your Monthly Music Guide to Sussex
0964–6361
GB–Sheffield Park Gardens, 1991–
[NOT IN BUCOMP1]

Lbl*

World Music [translated title] *see* **Wereldmusik**

Words: Soul, Pop, Rock
GB–London, ?1978–?

Ob

Words and Music [1]
TNG GB326
GB–London: British Song Society, 1928–30

AB 1930, 1–6
Lbl*

Words and Music [2]
0950–9097
GB–Tadworth: Goodall and Goodall, 1986–
[NOT IN BUCOMP1]

Lbl*

Words and Music [3]
1195–8316
C–Toronto: Society of Composers, Authors and Music Publishers of Canada, 1994–
[NOT IN BUCOMP1; formerly entitled *Canadian Composer/Le Compositeur Canadien* (q.v.)]

Cu 1 (1994)–#

Words and Music: Original and Selected
GB–London: George Ingram, 1887

Lbl*

Words for Music: a Journal for Composers and Lyric Writers
Fellinger 1968/2001; TNG GB242
GB–London: D. M. Amiss, 1909–10

Lbl*

Workers' Music Association Bulletin
GB–?: Workers' Music Association, 19?–
[NOT IN BUCOMP1]

Lcs 1958, Dec; 1984, Nov, Dec; 1985, May;
 1986, Jan; 1987, July, Oct, Dec; 1988, Feb,
 May

World Beat: the Global Music, Travel and
Lifestyle Magazine
0960–7498
GB–London: Maxwell Specialist Magazines,
1990–
[NOT IN BUCOMP1]

Lbl*

The World Harp Congress Newsletter
US–Marina del Rey, CA, ?1984–
[NOT IN BUCOMP1; entitled *World Harp
Congress Review* from 1986]

Lam 1984, 2; 1985, 4

World Harp Congress Review *see* The World
Harp Congress Newsletter

World Music
A–Vienna, 1949–52

Bp 1 (1949)–2 (1952)
Ep 1 (1949)–2 (1952)
Gm 1 (1949)–2 (1952)
Lam 1 (1949)–2 (1952)
Lcml 1 (1949)–2 (1952)
Lu 1 (1949)– 2 (1952)
Ob 1 (1949)

World Music Magazine
GB–Cheltenham, 1993–94
[NOT IN BUCOMP1]

Lsa 1–4, 1993/94

The World of Church Music *see* English
Church Music: a Quarterly Record of the Art

The World of Music: Quarterly Journal of the
International Institute for Comparative
Music Studies and Documentation, Berlin, in
Association with the International Music
Council, UNESCO
TNG INTL18; 0043–8774
CH/D–Basel: Bärenreiter [for the International
World Music Council]; Wilhelmshaven:
Noetzel; Mainz: Schott, 1957–
[Also entitled *Die Welt der Musik/Le Monde de
la Musique* from 1967]

BLu 9 (1967), 2, 3; 10 (1968), 1; 11 (1969),
1, 3; 13 (1971), 1, 2; 14 (1972), 1
BRp 9 (1967)–#
BSdsc 1 (1957)–9 (1967), 1; 14 (1972)–#
Bu 1 (1957)–5 (1963)
CCtc 14 (1972)–19 (1977)

Cu 1 (1957)–12 (1970), 1; 17 (1975), 1
EIR:Driam 85–149, 1986–91
EIR:Dtc 14 (1972)–26 (1984), 3
EIR:Duc 6 (1964)–21 (1976)
En*
Er 1 (1957)–#*
EXu 13 (1971)–29 (1987)
Gam 9 (1967)–12 (1970), 2–4; 13 (1971)–#
Gul 1 (1957)–9 (1967)*
Lam 1957, 1–6; 1 (1959), 1, 4; 2 (1960), 1–5
(1963), 3, 5; 6 (1964), 6; 9 (1967)–29
(1987); 30 (1988), 2, 3; 31 (1989), 2, 3; 32
(1990)–35 (1993), 2; 36 (1994)–#
Lbbc 13 (1971)–19 (1977); 20 (1978)–22
(1980)*
Lbl*
Lcu 17 (1975)–23 (1982); 34 (1992)–#
Lgo 21 (1979)–#
Lgsm 19 (1977)–#
Lkc 8 (1966)–23 (1981)
Lki 18 (1986), 3–26 (1984); 35 (1993)–#
Lsa 31 (1989)–#
Lso 1978, 1; 1983, 1, 3; 1984, 2; 1985, 1;
1986, 1
Lu 1 (1959), 1, 4–3 (1961), 6; 9 (1967)–#
Lu (RMA) 2 (1957)–3 (1958)
Mcm 15 (1973), 3; 16 (1974), 1–4; 18 (1976),
1; 20 (1977), 3, 4
Mpl 2 (1959)–#
NTp 9 (1967)–28 (1986), 3
Ob*
R 1 (1957)–6 (1959); 1 (1959)–4 (1962); 5
(1963), 1–5, 7; 6 (1964)–11 (1969)
TOd 19 (1977)–#*
Yu 19 (197)–26 (1984); 27 (1985), 2, 3

The World of Opera
0160–8673
US–New York: M. Dekker, 1978–80

BSdsc 1978–80
EXu 1–6, 1978–79
Lcml 1–6, 1978–79

Worldbeat: an International Journal of
Popular Music
C–Ottawa: International Association for the
Study of Popular Music, 1991–
[NOT IN BUCOMP1]

Lsa 1991, Mar–Sep

Worlds of Music [translated title] *see*
Musikvärlden

Worship: Concerned with the Issues of
Liturgical Revival
0043–941X
US–Collegeville, MN: Liturgical Press, 1926–
[NOT IN BUCOMP1]

Lhey 26 (1951)–34 (1960); 44 (1970)–#

Worship Together see Deo: Today's Music
and Worship

W. S. Gilbert Society Journal
0953–3281
GB–Dagenham: W. S. Gilbert Society, 1985–
[NOT IN BUCOMP1]

EIR:Dtc 1 (1985), 1–4
Lam 1, 2, 1985; 4, 5, 1986
Lbl*
Ob 1 (1985)–#

W.W.V. Blätter
A–Vienna: Wiener Waldhorn Verein, 1988–
[NOT IN BUCOMP1]

Gam 6–10, 1989–91; 12, 1991–#

Y

Yamaha Education Supplement see Yes

YCAT Artist File
GB–London: Young Concert Artists Trust,
1987–
[NOT IN BUCOMP1]

Cu 1991–93
Ob 1987–#

The Year in American Music
TNG US598
US–New York: Allen, Towne and Heath,
1947–48
[NOT IN BUCOMP1]

Ob*

Yearbook for Inter-American Musical
Research see Anuario/Yearbook

Yearbook for Traditional Music see Yearbook
of the International Folk Music Council

Yearbook of Jazz
GB–London: Citizen Press, 1946
[NOT IN BUCOMP1]

Ob 1946

Yearbook of Music
GB–London, 1897

Lbl*
Ob*

Yearbook of Proceedings of the Music
Educators' National Conference see Journal
of Proceedings of the Music Supervisors'
National Conference

Yearbook of Proceedings of the Music
Supervisors' National Conference see Journal
of Proceedings of the Music Supervisors'
National Conference

Yearbook of the Flemish Centre for Old
Music [translated title] see Jaarboek van het
Vlaams Centrum voor Oude Muziek

Yearbook of the International Folk Music
Council
TNG INTL31; 0316–6082
US/GB–Urbana; London: University of Illinois
Press, 1969–
[Previously Journal of the International Folk
Music Council (q.v.); from vol. 13 (1981)
entitled the Yearbook for Traditional Music
(ISSN 0740–1558). Also sometime entitled
International Council for Traditional Music:
Yearbook]

ALb 1969–71; 1973–77
BRp 1969–#
BRu 1969–79
Bs 1971–86
BSdsc*
BTu 1969
Cu 1 (1969)–#
DRu 2 (1971)–#
Ep 1969–70
Gul 1974–#
KE 1969; 1970
Lbl*
Lcm 1969–1979
Lcml 1982–#
Lcs 1969–81; 1984–#
Lcu 1985; 1991; 1992
Lgo 1969–79; 1992–#
Lsa 1969–# [w 1983]
Lso 1969–#
Lu 1969–#
LVp 1969–71; 1973–74
MK 1976–#
Mpl 1969–#
Ob*

Ouf 1969–91
Ouf (Howes) 1973; 1975
R 1969–76
SOu 1991–#
TOd 1969; 1971; 1987–88; 1991–93
Yu 1969–76

The Yearbook of the Musical World *see*
Jahrbuch der Musikwelt

Yearbook of the Society of British Composers
GB–London, 1906–12

Ep 1912
Lbl*
Ob 1907/08; 1912

The Year's Music
Fellinger 1968/1377; TNG GB170
GB–London: J. S. Virtue, 1896–99

BSdsc*
Cu 1896–98
En 1896–99
Ep 1896; 1898–99
⇒ Lbl 1896–99
Mpl 1896–99
Ob*

The Year's Work in Music
TNG GB408
GB–London: Longmans [for the British
Council], 1948–51

BLu 1 (1947/48)–4 (1950/51)
Bp 1 (1947/48)–4 (1950/51)
BRu 3 (1949/50)–4 (1950/51)
BSdsc 1 (1947/48)–4 (1950/51)
BTu 1 (1947/48)–4 (1950/51)
Cpl 1 (1947/48)–4 (1950/51)
Cu 1 (1947/48)–4 (1950/51)
HUu 1 (1947/48)–4 (1950/51)
KE 1 (1947/48)–4 (1950/51)
LAu 2 (1948/49)–4 (1950/51)
Lbl*
Lcml 1 (1947/48)–4 (1950/51)
Lu 1 (1947/48)–4 (1950/51)
Ob*

Yehudi Menuhin School Newsletter
GB–Stoke D'Abernon: Yehudi Menuhin School,
198?–
[NOT IN BUCOMP1]

Lam 1987, Mar

Yes [Yamaha Education Supplement]
GB–?London: Yamaha, 198?–
[NOT IN BUCOMP1]

Lam 13, 1992; 18, 1994
Msuc [c (3 years)]
Oub (w) 13, 1992–#

"Yes" Music Circle
0962–7332
GB–Reigate: "Yes" Music Circle, 1991–
[NOT IN BUCOMP1]

Lbl*

Yin Yue Lun Cong [= Collected Studies on
Music]
CHN–Beijing: Yinyue Chubanshe, 1978–?
[NOT IN BUCOMP1]

Lso 2 (1979)–4 (1981)
Ob (ICS) 1 (1978)–4 (1981)

Yin-Yueh Sheng Huo [translated title] *see* Hi-
Fi Musical Life

Yin Yue Yen-Chiu [= Music Studies]
TNG CHI6; 0512–7939
CHN–Beijing, 1958–

Cu 1–3, 1958; 7– 12, 1959; 19, 1980–#
Ob (ICS) 20, 1981–#

Yin Yue Yi Shu [= The Art of Music]
1000–4270
CHN–Shanghai: Shanghai Yinyue Xueyuan,
1979–
[NOT IN BUCOMP1]

Lso 1979, 1
Ob (ICS)1979, 1

York Minster Old Choir Boys' Magazine
Fellinger 1968/1949; TNG GB234
GB–York, 1908

Lbl*
Ob 1 (1907)

Yorkshire Musical Age and Journal of
Elocution *see* The Musical Age and Journal of
Elocution

The Yorkshire Musical Record: a Monthly
Record and Review devoted to the Interests of
Music and Musicians
Fellinger 1968/1513; TNG GB186
GB–Leeds, 1899–1900

Lbl*
Ob 1 (1899), 1

The Yorkshire Musician
Fellinger 1968/1033; TNG GB123
GB–Stanningley, 1886–89

Lbl 1 (1886)–4 (1889), 41

The Yorkshire Orchestra
Fellinger 1968/572; TNG GB70
GB–Leeds: Buckton and Masser, 1867–68

Lbl*

Yorkshire Songs
GB–Bradford, 1860

Lbl*

Young Concert Artists Trust see YCAT Artist
File

The Young Musician
TNG GB345
GB–London, 1934–?

AB 6 (1940), 4–10, 12; 7 (1941), 2–8 (1942),
    1–9, 12; 9 (1942)–11 (1944), 2
EIR:Dtc 6 (1940), 8–7 (1941), 10
Lam 21 (1954), 2
Lbl*
Ob 4 (1938)–9 (1943), 12

The Young Musician and the School
Orchestra: the Organ of the National Union
of School Orchestras
Fellinger 1968/2002; TNG GB241
GB–London: National Union of School
Orchestras, 1909–28

Lbl*

Your Record Choosing
GB–Kirby Muxloe, 1956–?

Cpl 57, 61, 62, 64, 65, 70, 1965–67
Lbl*
Lsa*

Youth and Music [1]
Fellinger 1968/1926; TNG GB233
GB–London: Home Music Study Union,
1915–20
[Published as a supplement to The Music
Student: the Magazine of the Home Study Union
and of the Music Teachers' Association;
continued under title Music and Youth (q.v.)
from 1921)]

AB 1 (1915)–3 (1917)
Lbl*
Lcml 1 (1915)–2 (1916)*; 4 (1919)*
Mcm 6 (1920), 4–6
Mpl 1 (1915)–6 (1920)

Youth and Music [2]
GB–London: Sir Robert Mayer Concerts, ?–
[NOT IN BUCOMP1]

Lbl 1978–85*
Mcm 1973–85*

Youth and Music News
TNG GB492
GB–London, 1960–?66

ALb 12, 1966
Lam 3, 1963

Yr Ysgol Gerddorol [= The Music School]
GB–Llanelli, 1878–80

AB*

Yuval
0084–439X
IL–Jerusalem: The Hebrew University, 1968–

Ob*

Z

Zbornik Matice Srpske za Scenske Umetnosti
i Muziku [= Journal of the Serbian Stage and
Musical Academy]
0352–9738
SRB–Novi Sad, 1987–
[NOT IN BUCOMP1]

Cu 1 (1987)–#

Zeitschrift der Internationalen Musikgesellschaft

Fellinger 1968/1514; TNG INTL3
D–Leipzig: Breitkopf und Härtel, 1899–1914
[From 1903 wrapper title is *Monthly Journal of the International Musical Society*]

BLu 1 (1899/1900)–15 (1913/14)
Bu 1 (1899/1900)–15 (1913/14), 9
CDu 1 (1899/1900)–15 (1913/14)
Cpl 1 (1899/1900)–15 (1913/14), 9
Cu 1 (1899/1900)–15 (1913/14), 9
EIR:Dtc 1 (1899/1900)–10 (1908/09)
Ep 1 (1899/1900)–15 (1913/14)
Er 1 (1899/1900)–15 (1913/14)
Gul 1 (1899/1900)–15 (1913/14)
HUu 1 (1899/1900)–15 (1913/14)
Lbl 1 (1899/1900)–15 (1913/14) [2 copies]
Lcml 1 (1899/1900)–15 (1913/14)
LEbc 2 (1900/01), 2–5; 3 (1901/02); 5
  (1903/04), 9; 7 (1905/06), 10, 12
Lu 2 (1900/01)–3 (1901/02); 12 (1910/11)–15
  (1913/14)*
Lu (RMA) 1 (1899/1900)–15 (1913/14)
LVu 1 (1899/1900)–15 (1913/14), 9
Mpl 1 (1899/1900)–15 (1913/14)
Ob 1 (1899/1900)–15 (1913/14)
Ouf 1 (1899/1900)–15 (1913/14)
R 1 (1899/1900)–15 (1913/14)

Zeitschrift der Musikerzieher Österreichs: Organ der AGMO *see* Musik-Erziehung

Zeitschrift für Deutschlands Musik-Vereine und Dilettanten

Fellinger 1968/189: TNG D92
D–Karlsruhe: C. F. Müller, 1841–?45
[Only 1 vol. published]

Lbl*

Zeitschrift für evangelische Kirchenmusik *see* Musik und Kirche

Zeitschrift für Hausmusik *see* Collegium Musicum: Blätter zur Pflege der Haus- und Kammermusik

Zeitschrift für Instrumentenbau

Fellinger 1968/840; TNG D249
D–Leipzig: Paul de Wit, 1880–1943
[Continued publication from 1946–56 under title

Instrumentenbau-Zeitschrift (TNG D806); n.s. 1956–. Bore several subtitles, including *Central-Organ für die Interessen der Fabrikation von Musikinstrumenten und des Handels, für ausübende Künstler und Musikfreunde*; and *Offizielles Organ der Berufsgenossenschaft der Musikinstrumenten-Industrie*]

BSdsc*
Er 11 (1891), 24
Lbl*

Zeitschrift für Instrumentenkunde

0372–8420
D–Berlin: Springer Verlag, 1881–1967
[NOT IN BUCOMP1]

BSdsc*

Zeitschrift für katholische Kirchenmusik

Fellinger 1968/594; TNG A61
D–Gmunden: Habert, 1868–86
[NOT IN BUCOMP1]

EIR:MEtc 1 (1868)–15 (1886)

Zeitschrift für Kirchenmusik: CVO: Cäcilien-Vereins-Organ *see* Fliegende Blätter für katholische Kirchenmusik

Zeitschrift für Musik *see* Neue Zeitschrift für Musik

Zeitschrift für Musikpädogogik

TNG D1093; 0341–2830
D–Regensburg: Erhard Friedrich Verlag, 1976–

BSdsc*
Cpl 3 (1978), 6
Lam 3 (1978), 6
Lbl*

Zeitschrift für Musiktheorie

TNG D1068; 0342–3395
D–Herrenberg: Döring, 1970–78
[Superseded by *Musiktheorie: Zeitschrift für Musiktheorie* (q.v.)]

BSdsc*
Lbl*
Lu 1 (1970)–9 (1978)
Ob*

Zeitschrift für Musikwissenschaft
TNG D556
D–Leipzig: Breitkopf und Härtel, 1918–35
[Succeeded 1936–43 by *Archiv für Musikforschung* (q.v.)]

AB*
Cpl 1 (1918)–17 (1935)
Cu 1 (1918)–17 (1935)
Er 1 (1918)–17 (1935)
Lbl*
Lcml 1 (1918)–17 (1935)
LVu 1 (1918)–17 (1935)
Mpl 1 (1918)–17 (1935)
NO 1 (1918å)–17 (1935)
Ob*
Ouf 1 (1918)–17 (1935)

Zeitschrift für Orgel-, Clavier- und Flügelbau sowie für die Anfertigung der Geigen, Bratschen, Cello's und Bässe, der dazu gehörigen Saiten und Bogen, ingleichen sämmtlicher [sic] Blas- und anderer musikalischen Instrumente
Fellinger 1968/226; TNG D104
D–Weimar: B. Voigt, 1844–55

Lbl*

Zeitschrift für vergleichende Musikwissenschaft
TNG D766
D–Berlin: Max Hesses Verlag, 1933–35

ALb 1 (1933), 2, 4; 2 (1934),1, 4; 3 (1935), 1, 2
Cpl 1 (1933)–3 (1935)*
Cu 1 (1933)–3 (1935) [Reprint ed.]
Lbl*
Lu 1 (1933)–3 (1935)

Zeitschriftendienst Musik
TNG D1055; 0044–3824
D–Berlin: Deutscher Bibliotheksverband, 1966–
[NOT IN BUCOMP1]

Ouf 25 (1990)–#

Zeitung für Theater, Musik und Poesie *see* Wiener Theater-Zeitung

Zenei Szemle [= Musical Review]
Fellinger 1968/2302; TNG H59
H–Budapest: Szabolcsi, 1917–29; n.s. 1947–49
[NOT IN BUCOMP1]

Cpl 11 (1927), 3/4–9/10; 12 (1928), 5/6; 13 (1929), 1–3/4

Zenetudomanyi Dolgozatok [= Musical Studies]
0139–0732
H–Budapest, 1979–

Cu 1979–#
Ob*

Zest *see* The Beat: Official Magazine of the Ted Heath Club

ZFMP *see* Zeitschrift für Musikpädogogik

Zhong Guo Yin Yue [= Chinese Music]
CHN–Beijing: Zhongguo Wenyi Lianhe Chuban Gongsi, ?1986–
[NOT IN BUCOMP1]

Lso 1 (1986); 4 (1990)
Ob (ICS)*

Zhong Guo Yin Yue Xue [= Musicology in China]
CHN–Beijing: Wenhua Meishu Chubanshe, 1985–
[NOT IN BUCOMP1]

Lso 1985, 1; 1987, 1, 4; 1988, 1, 3, 4; 1989, 1–4; 1990, 2, 3; 1991, 2–#

Zhongyang Yin Yue Xue Yuan Xuebao [= Journal of the Central Academy of Music]
1001–9871
CHN–Beijing, ?1977–

Cu 6 (1982)–#
Ob (ICS) 6 (1982)–#

Zigzag [1]
GB–London: Zigzag, 1968–?81
[Later incorporated in *One, Two, Testing* (q.v.)]

Cu 17–72, 1970–77
Lsa 6–96, 1969–79 [w 7, 8, 10]; 116, 1981
Ob*

Zigzag [2]
0959–7913
GB–London: Emap, 1990–
[NOT IN BUCOMP1]

Lbl*

The Zither World
Fellinger 1968/1379; TNG GB171
GB– London, 1896
[Only one issue was published]

Lbl 1896, June 3

Ziva Hudba: Sborník Prací Hudební Fakulty Akademie Múzických Umění [= Living Music: Almanac of the Music Faculty of the Academy of Musical Art]
TNG CS200
CZ–Prague, 1959–86
[NOT IN BUCOMP1]

Ob 1965; 1968; 1973; 1976; 1980; 1983; 1986

Zoot
0958–0867
GB– Glasgow: Zoot, 198?–
[NOT IN BUCOMP1; reggae magazine]

Lbl*

Zprava: Journal of the Dvořák Society of Great Britain see Czech Music: the Newsletter of the Dvořák Society

Zprávy Společnosti Bohuslava Martinů: Česká Hudební Společnost [= News from the Martinů Society: Society for Czech Music]
CZ– Prague, 1977–
[NOT IN BUCOMP1]

Ob 1 (1977)–#

Zvuk: Jugoslovenska Muzička Revija see Zvuk: Revija za Muziku

Zvuk: Revija za Muziku [= Sound: Music Review]
TNG YU26; 0044–555X
YU– Belgrade: Savez Kompozitora Jugoslavije; 1932–36; n.s. Sarajevo, 1955–
[Entitled Zvuk: Jugoslovenska Muzička Revija from 1955; new series 1 (1989)– entitled Novi Zvuk]

Cpl 77/78, 1967; 1979, 1
Lbbc 1973, 4; 1974, 2
Lbl*
Ob*

Addenda

The following titles came in too late for inclusion in the main sequence.

Bayreuther Taschenkalendar: mit Ansicht und Plan des Bayreuther Festspielhauses
Fellinger 1968/981; TNG D275
D–Munich: Allgemeiner Richard-Wagner-Verein; Berlin: Bote und Bock, 1885–94

   LEu 5 (1889)–10 (1894)

Cahiers Franz Schubert
1168–9501
F–Paris: Université de Paris, ?1992–
[NOT IN BUCOMP1]

   Ouf 10, 1997–#

Dracht
GB–Wales: Pwyllgor Golygyddol Dracht, 1985–
[NOT IN BUCOMP1; pop music periodical]

   AB*

International Opera Collector
1361-925X
GB–Harrow: Gramophone Publications, 1996–
[NOT IN BUCOMP1; also known as *IOC*]

   Ouf 1 (1997), 4–#

International Piano Quarterly
GB-London: Gramophone Publications, 1997–
[NOT IN BUCOMP1]

   Ltv 1 (1997)-#

Letys
GB–Wales: Esyllt Williams, 1994–
[NOT IN BUCOMP1]

   AB*

Macher
GB–Wales: Dave Jones, 1988–
[NOT IN BUCOMP1; pop music journal]

   AB*

Musical Performance
1049-8869
NL–Amsterdam [etc.]: Harwood Academic Publishers, 1996–

[NOT IN BUCOMP1]

   Lbar 1 (1996)-#

Musik und Ästhetik
D–Stuttgart: Klett-Cotta, 1997–
[NOT IN BUCOMP1; issues have separate ISBNs]

   Ouf 2 (1998), 5-#

Muziek en Wetenschap [=Music and Musicology]
0925–725X
NL–Utrecht: Stichting Muziek en Wetenschap Nederland, 1991–
[NOT IN BUCOMP1. Subtitle varies: from 2 (1992), subtitled *Dutch Quarterly for Musicology*; from 4 (1994), 1/2 subtitled *Dutch Journal for Musicology*]

   Ouf 1 (1991), 2-#

Nightshift: Oxford's Music Magazine
GB–Oxford: Nightshift, 1995–
[NOT IN BUCOMP1; rock music periodical]

   AB*

Oesterreichisch-ungarische Cantoren-Zeitung: Central Organ für die Interessen der Cantoren und Cultusbeamten
Fellinger 1968/864; TNG A91
A–Vienna, 1881–98
[NOT IN BUCOMP1]

   Ouf 11 (1891)-18 (1898) [m]

Yin Yue Chuang Zuo [=Musical Composition]
CHN–Beijing, ?–
[NOT IN BUCOMP1]

   Ob(ICS) 63 (1962), 3–104 (1966), 2

Yin Yue Zazhi [= Music Magazine]
CHN–Shanghai, ?1946–
[NOT IN BUCOMP1]

   Ob(ICS) 1, 2, 1946

Addenda